THE PAPERS OF
THOMAS JEFFERSON

THE PAPERS OF
Thomas Jefferson

Volume 21
Index, Volumes 1–20

CHARLES T. CULLEN, EDITOR

R. R. CROUT AND EUGENE R. SHERIDAN,

ASSOCIATE EDITORS

RUTH W. LESTER, ASSISTANT EDITOR

PRINCETON, NEW JERSEY

PRINCETON UNIVERSITY PRESS

1983

Copyright © 1983 by Princeton University Press
Published by Princeton University Press, 41 William Street,
Princeton, New Jersey
IN THE UNITED KINGDOM
Princeton University Press, Guildford, Surrey

All Rights Reserved
L.C. Card 50-7486
ISBN 0-691-04687-5

This book has been composed in Linotron Monticello

Clothbound editions of Princeton University Press books
are printed on acid-free paper, and binding materials
are chosen for strength and durability

Printed in the United States of America by
Princeton University Press, Princeton, New Jersey

DEDICATED TO THE MEMORY OF

ADOLPH S. OCHS

PUBLISHER OF THE NEW YORK TIMES

1896-1935

WHO BY THE EXAMPLE OF A RESPONSIBLE

PRESS ENLARGED AND FORTIFIED

THE JEFFERSONIAN CONCEPT

OF A FREE PRESS

ACKNOWLEDGMENTS

As INDICATED in the first volume, this edition was made possible by a grant of $200,000 from the New York Times Company to Princeton University. Since this initial subvention, its continuance has been assured by additional contributions from the New York Times Company; by grants of the Ford Foundation, the Andrew W. Mellon Foundation, the J. Howard Pew Freedom Trust; and by other benefactions from the Charlotte Palmer Phillips Foundation, Time Inc., the Dyson Foundation, and from such loyal supporters of the enterprise as James Russell Wiggins and David K. E. Bruce. In common with other editions of historical documents, The Papers of Thomas Jefferson is a beneficiary of the good offices of the National Historical Publications and Records Commission, tendered in many useful forms through its officers and dedicated staff. For these and other indispensable aids generously given by librarians, archivists, scholars, and collectors of manuscripts, the Editors record their sincere gratitude.

INTRODUCTION

THE FIRST VOLUME in this series announced that outside indexers would prepare "temporary indexes" from time to time, each covering several volumes of the edition. The "permanent index" was to be a corrected, cumulated version of these. The most important point in this announcement was that the Editors themselves did not intend to prepare any indexes until all the volumes in this enterprise had appeared. Moreover, it was hoped that users of the periodic indexes would notify the Editors of errors and supply missing information. The result promised a better final index while allowing the Editors to focus their efforts on publishing the all-important documents. The plan did not work.

Julian Boyd readily admitted that his decision to forgo single-volume indexes was his greatest error in designing the series. His confidence in the public's willingness and ability to notify the editorial office of errors and omissions proved to be unfounded. Although readers faithfully reported occasional errors in the documents, very few if any ever pointed out flaws in the indexes. One might have expected a specialist on the Continental Congress to have noted that the index entry for "Speaker of Congress" was in error, since Congress had no such position, and one would have hoped that the reader would have written the Editors about it. It is possible, of course, that users did not read the request for corrections in the foreword to the first index. It is also likely that the temporary indexes have been used very little.

The greatest problem seems to be the physical design of the indexes. Because they were meant to be temporary, they were soft-bound, printed in a typewriter typeface, and were often less than one-fourth the thickness of the regular volumes. Consequently, on many library shelves the indexes were lost or easily misplaced. More importantly, if one happened to be off the shelf for any reason, no guide was available for the six volumes it covered. By the time the first index appeared, ten volumes of the *Papers* were in print. Considering the handicaps inherent in the original indexing design, it is an indication of the attraction and fundamental importance of Thomas Jefferson, as well as a tribute to the impressive editorial ability of Julian Boyd and his associates, that the first twenty volumes in this series have been so widely used.

A change of editors after this milestone presented the opportunity to correct an old error and to immerse a new staff in the previously edited materials in preparation for editing the remaining documents.

This volume represents the successful completion of that goal and is the first of the periodic "permanent" indexes now expected to appear after each decimal volume of the *Papers*. In addition, each single volume of the *Papers* will henceforth contain an index prepared by the Editors.

I

The decision to prepare a comprehensive cumulative index for twenty volumes of Jefferson's papers might not have been made had there been no foundation on which to build. The need to assemble a staff to carry on the editorial work begun by Julian Boyd and to meet the financial crisis caused by drastically reduced federal support for the project left little time to devote to the preparation of index cards covering the 13,650 pages published thus far. As promised in the first temporary index, dozens of cartons of 3 x 5 cards were dutifully preserved in the editorial office, taking up needed space and gathering dust. To have set about merging those cards and then checking them against the volumes to make necessary corrections, additions, and improvements would have taken several years. Fortunately, the relatively recent recognition by computer scientists that their machines are adaptable to words as well as numbers suggested a method that has great appeal to the new Editor of Jefferson's papers. The preparation of programs that could sort the thousands of entries already identified in the temporary indexes would lessen the time required to make a new index sufficiently to justify its undertaking.

The plan finally adopted required learning what had already been indexed on each page in each volume, adding names and subjects missed, and correcting erroneous entries. The Editors had the temporary indexes read by a Kurzweil Optical Scanner and then ran the index through DEINDEX, a special program that produced a separate record for every entry from every page—the equivalent of more than 100,000 index cards. These records were arranged in volume and page order and served as the foundation of this volume. The Editors next spent several months comparing each printed page with the index entries listed for that page, stopping when the indexer had entered "Prentis, Mr." to determine which Mr. Prentis was intended, whether the subject indexed was actually what the writer had referred to, and adding entries the first indexers had missed. The Editors also prepared original indexes for volumes 19 and 20, which were published after the compilation of the third temporary index in 1973.

After this review, the separate files were merged in the Princeton University Computer using CINDEX, a series of programs prepared for *The Papers of Henry Laurens* at the University of South Carolina. The resulting twenty-volume cumulative index appeared in a matter of minutes and comprised 3,000 manuscript pages. The Editors spent the next several months editing the copy; subentries from early and late volumes that now appeared to be related were combined, and entries that seemed inappropriate were removed. Then CUMTYPE, the last program in the CINDEX package, automatically inserted typesetting codes. The result, after a full year's effort, is a comprehensive guide to the vast amount of material spread over the first twenty volumes.

II

Main entries in this index appear in alphabetical order, but the subentries follow a different arrangement. References to letters to or from Thomas Jefferson always come first. All other subentries appear in sequential volume and page order, except for references collected under the general heading "mentioned," which always follow other subentries. Subentries for "correspondence with" an individual refer to letters between the person named as the main entry and the individual identified in the subentry; the letters involved may be printed, quoted, or simply cited in documents or notes. The Editors have attempted to identify fully those individuals who appeared in the temporary indexes by last name only. In a few instances, a main entry contains so many subentries that it has proven expedient to categorize them under a few general subentries. Such subentries appear in alphabetical order, with their sub-subentries listed in sequential order.

The Editors have made no systematic attempt to prepare new subject entries in this index. As revision of the three temporary indexes progressed, it became apparent that coverage of some subjects was uneven. The second index contained references to "farm implements," but neither the first nor the third indexer included references to these. Similarly, the first indexer collected references to Indian languages under "Indians: vocabulary"; the second listed no references to language under "Indians" but added a main entry specifically for "Indian languages"; the third indexer used a main entry for "languages: Indian." These obvious differences have been corrected, but the Editors did not attempt to review volumes 1 through 6 and 13 through 20 for "farm implements" when they discovered that subject in the index for volumes 7 through 12. In some cases unevenly covered subjects were deleted from the final index unless they seemed sufficiently important to be of use. Readers are cautioned, however, that such subject references are incomplete. One cannot look at the entry for "speech, freedom of: TJ comments on, 16: 45," for example, and assume that the topic appears in the twenty volumes only once. The Editors retained this reference because of its potential use to someone interested in the topic; they did not attempt to locate other references, although there is little question that others exist somewhere in the volumes printed thus far.

Many single entry and some multiple entry subject categories included in the old indexes were deleted completely. Such an entry as "sick: removal to safety in case of Va. invasion, 3: 240" was removed because the subject is covered adequately in other entries, and the Editors considered it inappropriate for a main entry in any case. An entry under "geography: Martha asked to trace TJ's journey on map" seemed misleading; it is covered under another, more appropriate subject and was therefore omitted. Some misleading subentries were modified for clarity: under Jefferson, Journeys, "Havre: looks for dog and sees suicide," "peas: come with strawberries," and "generals: Congress orders one sent to Canada" were among those that required rewording. The three individuals who compiled the temporary indexes employed a literal approach to the documents, perhaps because they were not historians. Eighteenth-century letters often contain metaphors that must be recognized for accurate indexing. The old reference to "military school: proposed by Va. delegate to Congress" proved to be such a case. The writer was in fact referring to Boston at the outbreak of the Revolution as a good place for young men to be schooled in military skills. The Editors hope they have recognized and corrected all such occurrences.

It is the Editors' premise that no single index can serve everyone who will want to consult *The Papers of Thomas Jefferson* as long as this edition survives on the shelves. The changing interests of readers, especially historians and the many other professionals who make use of this edition, suggest that sometime in the future another index will be required. As Julian Boyd wrote in the introduction to the first index, we hope that anyone who discovers errors herein will relay them to the Jefferson Office so that they may be noted and used later by anyone who might want to assemble a revision to this and other indexes in the series. The computer files for each volume will remain in storage for such an eventuality.

III

The Editors have been assisted in this undertaking by several persons to whom it is a pleasure to express thanks. Michael K. Donegan devised the computer program that first broke up the temporary indexes into card images that could then be sorted into page order records. His willingness to prepare this first program and his encouragement of the Editor's interest in using computers for this task are largely responsible for bringing this volume into being. David R. Chesnutt designed and Jean W. Mustain wrote the series of programs called CINDEX that enabled the Editors to obtain new and revised single-volume indexes that were subsequently merged into one index. We are greatly indebted to them for sharing those programs and hope that our experience with them has been of some benefit in perfecting CINDEX.

The staff of the Princeton University Computer Center, especially Hannah Kaufman, Howard Strauss, Victor Bearg, and Gary Burns, provided expert assistance with various computer programs, making them work as the Editors needed them to and writing modifications when they were required.

In the editorial office, the Editors have benefited from the work of E. Wayne Carp, the fellow in advanced historical editing assigned to this project by the National Historical Publications and Records Commission. Mr. Carp worked on the index for volume 20 and assisted in the copyediting of the final manuscript, and we thank him for his many contributions.

Finally, we appreciate the moral support offered by many people as we tired of the task of editing index entries. They reinforced our belief in the fundamental importance of this volume to users of *The Papers of Thomas Jefferson*, a conviction that has sustained us for the past year. Our delight in seeing it in print will be well understood by anyone who has tried to use this edition without a cumulative, consistent index and by anyone who has ever had a hand in preparing one.

Volume 21
Index, Volumes 1–20

ADAMS, JOHN (*cont.*)

2, 458-9, 539, 581-2; **14**: 410-1, 599; **20**: 305-8; quoted on TJ, **1**: 304n, 676; French opinion of, **3**: 220; praised by Mazzei, **3**: 460; **7**: 122; elected to American Philosophical Society, **4**: 545n; Monroe introduced to, **6**: 126; characterized by TJ, **6**: 241; **8**: 548; **11**: 94-5; letters from cited, **6**: 265, 275, 354; **8**: 209, 268n, 369; **9**: 47, 230, 250, 325, 650; **10**: 95, 134, 208, 405, 431; **12**: 220, 543; **18**: 313n, 378n-80n; letters from quoted, **7**: 227n, 382n; **9**: 48n; **12**: 123, 548n; **14**: 191-2, 194; aid solicited for Mazzei, **7**: 556n; **8**: 538, 677-8; English attitude toward, **8**: 241; friendship with Dr. Price, **8**: 258, 668; queried as to insurance on Houdon, **8**: 283; orders wine, **8**: 368; **9**: 25, 54; wax bust of proposed by Patience Wright, **8**: 380; illness of, **8**: 653; letters to cited, **9**: 169, 365, 376; **11**: 134; **12**: 72, 146, 173, 508, 509, 510; **14**: 514; **16**: 61n, 283n; **18**: 379n, 380n, 415n, 517n; visits English gardens with TJ, **9**: 374n-5n; **13**: 35n; concerned about injury to TJ's wrist, **10**: 417-8; portrait of by Mather Brown, **10**: 479; **12**: xxxvii, 514 (illus.), 597, 647; **13**: 178, 199, 281n; **14**: 365n; portrait of desired by TJ, **10**: 518, 620; **11**: 169, 531, 573; **12**: 484, 517, 558, 622, 630; wishes to have *Notes on Virginia* published in England, **10**: 545; Maury introduced to, **10**: 588, 628; **11**: 371; influence on Mass. politics, **11**: 411n; studies Italian, **11**: 575; Dal Verme introduced to, **12**: 43n; connection with Agence générale de Correspondance, **12**: 317, 333, 344-5; **13**: 112, 116; recommends Parker, **12**: 322; books sent to, **12**: 530-1, 554; unpopularity of in U.S., **12**: 602; **14**: 17-8; Mme de Corny's anger at, **12**: 668; Gordon's use of information from, **13**: 365n; reception on return to Mass., **13**: 402-3, 436, 437n, 454, 471, 474, 512n; criticism of, **14**: 17-8; **18**: 33; **20**: 279-80, 287, 294, 299-301, 305-6, 307n-8n, 309n; Hancock's misunderstanding with, **14**: 275, 539; introduces John Coffin Jones to TJ, **14**: 410; acquaintance with Cutting, **15**: 219; characterized by Franklin, **15**: 316; memoir sent to, **16**: 39; pamphlets sent to, **16**: 252; Andriani introduced to, **16**:

ADAMS, JOHN (*cont.*)

254n; Read introduced to, **16**: 289n; recommends Dumas, **17**: 210n; served by Petit in Paris, **17**: 315; praised by Stiles, **17**: 444; Corbet (seaman) defended by, **18**: 312n; introduces Cutting to TJ, **18**: 313n; mentioned, **3**: 374; **4**: 310; **6**: 261, 268; **7**: 8, 413, 439, 550, 552, 647n, 651; **8**: 30, 33, 66, 70, 84, 95, 142, 175, 235, 243, 251, 259, 285, 303, 308, 321, 322, 330, 358, 376, 398, 424, 479, 498, 499, 522, 541, 561, 567, 587, 597, 605, 649, 654, 669, 680; **9**: 16, 26, 77, 78, 126, 136, 137, 225, 226, 312, 329, 337, 352, 408, 409, 433n, 447, 449, 557, 610; **10**: 73, 99, 114, 180, 209, 266, 393, 396, 400, 404, 455, 464, 489, 633; **11**: 20, 47, 130, 172, 174, 219, 293, 321, 384, 502, 515, 556, 585, 592; **12**: 10, 112, 172, 193, 225, 461, 485, 598, 657, 666, 690; **13**: 33n, 162, 185, 337, 440n, 461n; **14**: xxvi, 15, 49, 82n, 222, 315, 373, 494, 502; **15**: 230, 356, 475, 508, 614, 638; **16**: 62n; **17**: 240, 601; **18**: 556; **20**: 428, 693n

Continental Congress

signs Continental Association, **1**: 153; and Articles of Confederation, **1**: 180n; signs second petition to king, **1**: 222; and Lord North's conciliatory proposal, **1**: 230n; signs agreement of secrecy, **1**: 253; and committee on Canadian campaign, **1**: 296n; and resolution for independence, **1**: 298n, 311; and Declaration of Independence, **1**: 300n, 306n, 307n, 313, 335n, 405n, 414n, 427n-8n, 432; debates taxation of slaves, **1**: 321; debates state representation, **1**: 325; proposes colonies take over governments, **1**: 330n; proposal for U.S. seal, **1**: 495n, 497n; and Drummond's peace proposals, **1**: 502n; and Howe's peace proposal, **1**: 520-1; and committee of inquiry on Esek Hopkins, **15**: 581n-2n; proposes medal for Washington, **16**: 54n

Diplomatic Career

departs for France, **2**: 121n; arrival in America expected, **3**: 65; opinion on possibility of peace, **3**: 336; efforts to win aid for America, **3**: 382; effect of surrender of Charleston on, **3**:

[6]

ADAMS, JOHN (*cont.*)
ican Revolution, **13**: 155; introduces Barlow to Russian ambassador, **13**: 157n; account in Europe settled, **13**: 161; diplomatic expenses, **13**: 201-2, 552; **20**: 592; *Observations on the Whale-Fishery* sent to, **14**: 219, 334-5; arrêt on whale oil sent to, **14**: 442; receives medal from Netherlands, **16**: xli-ii, 55n, 366; role in U.S. boundary settlement, **16**: 326; receives gift from British government, **16**: 366; anecdote of Sarsfield, **17**: 437n. *See also* American Commissioners for Negotiating Commercial Treaties

Opinions

on governmental secrecy, **4**: 167n; on Franklin, **6**: 235, 241; **19**: 83; on Jay, **6**: 241; prejudice against France, **6**: 235; opposes solicitation in Europe for American colleges, **7**: 399; on Abbés Arnoux and Chalut, **8**: 92n; on anti-American propaganda, **8**: 678n-9n; on reimbursement of public expenses, **9**: 104; on French debts, **11**: 664; on pride of place, **12**: 220; on Society of Cincinnati, **13**: 11; on immigration to America, **13**: 432n; on speculation in foreign debt, **14**: 191-2; on transfer of U.S. debts to Netherlands, **14**: 194; on being out of politics, **14**: 411; on Mediterranean trade, **18**: 413; on danger of French interest, **19**: 103-4; on Tench Coxe, **19**: 126; on the whale and cod fisheries, **19**: 140-1, 154-5, 154n, 163; on assumption of state debts, **19**: 179

Other Correspondence

letter to, from Mazzei, quoted, **5**: 375; report of letters of, **6**: 400n; letter from, to Franklin, quoted, **7**: 310n; with Barclay, **7**: 310n; **8**: 622-3; **9**: 383-4, 566-7, 626; **10**: 141-2; **11**: 125; with Dumas, **7**: 310n; **8**: 37, 156n, 312-3, 459; **11**: 581n; **15**: 201n; letters from, to Souza de Coutinho, **7**: 419-20, 551; with Baron de Thulemeier, **7**: 421, 465n, 490-3, 611-2, 628n (quoted); **8**: 14-5, 26-33, 134-5, 311n; letters from, to Conde de Aranda, **7**: 423-4, 455-6; letters from, to Gerry, quoted, **7**: 426n, 652n; letter from, to Baron

ADAMS, JOHN (*cont.*)
Staël de Holstein, **7**: 428-9; with Francesco Favi, **7**: 430, 561-2; **8**: 104-10; with Duke of Dorset, **7**: 456-7, 457-8; **8**: 55-9, 153; letter from, to Samuel Adams, quoted, **7**: 468n; letter from, to Thomas Cushing, quoted, **7**: 469n; letters from, to president of Congress, **7**: 493-500, 573-4, 646-7; with John Jay, **7**: 608; **8**: 19-22, 36-8, 42, 80-3, 140-1, 606; **9**: 287n-8n, 357-9, 402, 403, 406-9, 468; **12**: 200n; **16**: 239n; **17**: 227n-8n; **18**: 374, 379n, 380n, 389, 394n, 396, 409, 429n-30n; letter from, to R. Cranch, quoted, **7**: 652n; with W. Gordon, **7**: 652n; **18**: 283n; with Storer, **8**: 58n; **17**: 349n; with Vergennes, **8**: 61-3, 120, 625-7; letter to, from Lafayette, **8**: 70-2; letter from, to Barrett, quoted, **8**: 144n-5n; with Short, **8**: 313-5, 459; with Higginson, **8**: 610n-1n; **14**: 599-602; letter from, to Emperor of Morocco, **8**: 619-21; with William Carmichael, **8**: 623-4; **9**: 244-9, 385-6; letter from, to Willink and van Staphorst, **8**: 656n; letter to, from Boylston, quoted, **9**: 26; letters regarding Barrett, **9**: 74n; with John Lamb, **9**: 283-4, 549-54; **10**: 96-7; letters to, from Paul R. Randall, **9**: 284-5, 525-6; letters from, to Lord Carmarthen, **9**: 327, 375; letters from, to Congress, cited, **10**: 213; letter to, from Sarsfield, cited, **10**: 289; with R. H. Lee, **12**: 205; **14**: xxxviii; letter to, from Fagel, quoted, **12**: 312; letters from, to Abigail Adams, quoted, **13**: 128n-9n; letters to, from Cutting, **13**: 210n, 291, 515; **16**: 415n; **18**: 314-5, 317n, 318n; letter from, to Tessier, cited, **13**: 281n; letter from, to Wooddrop, quoted, **13**: 432n; letter to, from Brush, **15**: 616-7; with Washington, **16**: 54n; letter to, from Van der Kemp, cited, **16**: 285n; letter to, from Price, cited, **16**: 294n; letters as President of the Senate, **16**: 674; **18**: 437; letters to, from French National Assembly, delivered to, **18**: 179; letter to, from Abigail A. Smith, quoted, **18**: 245n-7n; letter to, from W. S. Smith, quoted, **18**: 261-2, 273n; let-

ADAMS, JOHN (*cont.*)
ters to, from Coxe, **18**: 261n, 263, 268, 272; letter to, from Duke of Leeds, cited, **18**: 285; letter to, from Purdie, **18**: 317; letter from, to Richard Oswald, quoted, **19**: 140; letter to, from Lovell, quoted, **19**: 302; letter to, from Trumbull, quoted, **19**: 462n; letters to, from Jones, cited, **19**: 588

Political Theories
contributions to plan of government for Va., **1**: 332n-5n, 369n; advice on state constitutions, **1**: 333n; on Shays' Rebellion, **10**: 620, 621; on Constitution, **12**: 335, 396; on divided executive, **17**: 107; on political parties, **18**: 566; on definition of republic, **19**: 106n; monarchist views attributed to, **20**: 286-8

Vice-President
election, **13**: 502, 658; **14**: 4, 17-8, 275, 302, 339, 385, 529, 559, 595, 596, 599, 615, 619, 628, 666, 688; **15**: 4-6, 17, 50, 74, 87, 92, 104, 106, 116 (TJ's congratulations); favors title of honor for President, **15**: 147, 315-6; **19**: 97; consults with TJ, **16**: 357n, 359n, 380n; consults with Washington, **16**: 380n; and arrearages in soldiers' pay, **16**: 458n; and Philadelphia as seat of government, **16**: 474, 475; and consular appointments, **16**: 523; **17**: 247, 248, 254n; and war crisis of 1790, **17**: 49, 71, 77, 79, 131n, 137-40; advice on diplomatic establishment, **17**: 218, 220, 224-5, 227n, 228n; returns ciphers, **17**: 330; receives Calonne's pamphlet, **17**: 671n; and Smith's mission to England, **18**: 243-5; and Privy Council report, **18**: 268, 271; and impressed seamen, **18**: 314, 317; and Franklin's death, **19**: 78-9, 82, 83, 84, 99, 100; relationship with Tench Coxe, **19**: 125; and the fisheries, **19**: 140n, 143-4, 163; recommends Samuel R. Gerry, **19**: 156; attitude toward France, **19**: 302; attends Apr. 11, 1791, cabinet meeting, **20**: 87, 117-8, 144; role in cabinet, **20**: 118n; and controversy over Paine's *Rights of Man*, **20**: 158, 268-313 (editorial note and documents); criticizes Paine, **20**: 277n; leaves Philadelphia, **20**: 343

ADAMS, JOHN (*cont.*)
Writings
Thoughts on Government, **1**: 333n, 337n; **20**: 581; diary quoted, **9**: 351n, 643n-4n; *Defence of the Constitutions of Government of the United States of America*, **11**: 119n, 163, 175n, 177, 184, 189-90, 239-40, 364, 401-2, 622, 624; **12**: 56, 124, 206, 220, 291, 325, 329, 579, 602; **20**: 279, 279n, 297, 308; *Discourses on Davila*, **16**: 238n-9n, 246n, 429; **19**: 515-6; **20**: 284, 285, 286, 287, 291, 293, 297, 308, 567, 582; *Four Letters*, **19**: 148n; "Publicola" letters attributed to, **20**: 283, 284, 296, 297, 304, 309n, 581, 582
Adams, John (Va.): death of, **14**: 530
Adams, John Quincy: quoted on TJ's learning Spanish, **7**: 383n; TJ's opinion of, **8**: 44, 144, 148; returns to America, **8**: 133, 134, 151, 152, 420, 472, 498, 521; introduced to Hardy, **8**: 145; carries ciphers, **8**: 146, 149; delivers mail, **8**: 226, 227, 261, 381; correspondence with Abigail Adams Smith, **14**: xxxviii; **15**: 279n; marriage of, **14**: 530; "Report on Weights and Measures" (1821), **16**: 610n; letter to cited, **16**: 610n; letter to quoted, **16**: 611n; *Journal . . . of the Convention*, **19**: 547; "Publicola" letters, **20**: 280-3, 285, 298-9, 302, 306, 310-1, 567, 692, 703; mentioned, **8**: 43, 143, 151, 159, 160, 163, 180, 215, 424; **14**: 599
Adams, Littleton, **5**: 174
Adams, Louisa Catherine (Mrs. John Quincy Adams): settlement of father's accounts, **20**: 503n
Adams, Mrs. Margaret (innkeeper at Bladensburg), **17**: 465
Adams, Philip: signs nonimportation resolutions (1770), **1**: 47
Adams, Richard: letter to, **9**: 593; signs nonimportation resolutions (1770), **1**: 46; signs Virginia Association, **1**: 108; and nonimportation agreements, **1**: 110; signs letter to Va. HB, **1**: 111; candidate for Va. senate, **1**: 476; and construction of arms depot, **3**: 43, 144; furnace and canal affairs, **3**: 174, 175, 182; commissioner of Westham foundry, **3**: 188; protests payment in paper money, **5**: 387n-8n; director of Va.

247; distance from New York City, **7**: 83; Hogendorp plans visit to, **7**: 283; riot in, July 4, 1788, **13**: 549; visited by TJ and Madison, **20**: 436-7, 458

Albany Plan of Union: compared to Constitution, **12**: 335

Albemarle, George Monk, Duke of: land grants to, **1**: 136; **6**: 657

Albemarle barracks: British prisoners held in, **2**: 31-2; **3**: 424, 450; **5**: 71; Convention troops held at, **2**: 237; **5**: 409; cost of building, **2**: 238; healthfulness of, **2**: 241-2; troops for, **3**: 214, 537; **4**: 8; **5**: 97, 100; **6**: 22; illustration of encampment at Charlottesville, **4**: 266; suppliers of provisions for unpaid, **4**: 611-2; rendezvous for recruits, **5**: 146, 667n; **6**: 632; discharge of guard at, **5**: 323; debts of, **5**: 346-9; dismantled, **5**: 530; arms collected at, **5**: 537; British depredations at, **6**: 631, 633

Albemarle co., Va.: letter to commissioner of provisions for, **3**: 568n; letters to county lieutenant of, **5**: 443, 601-2, 616-7; letters to commissioners of the specific tax, **15**: 590-2, 594-5, 603-4; TJ commissioned as lieutenant of, **1**: 42; TJ commissioned as surveyor of, **1**: 99; adopts resolutions opposing Boston Port Act, **1**: 117-9; elects state senators, **1**: 476; **6**: 174-5; appoints infantry officers, **1**: 579; petition of dissenters in, **1**: 586-9; place of court of assize, **1**: 630; grand jury in, **1**: 638-9; militia of, **1**: 664-8; **2**: 130; **3**: 429, 600; **4**: 63, 295n, 308, 352, 371, 477, 659; **5**: 29, 35, 73, 214, 310, 443n, 475, 501, 561, 601-2, 607, 616-7, 646; **6**: 93, 119; **15**: 583; TJ's map of, illustrated, **2**: xxiii, 208; recruits soldiers, **2**: 9; **3**: 8; elects delegates to Va. GA, **2**: 10-1; **5**: 430; petition for division of, **2**: 14-5; signs Va. oath of allegiance, **2**: 128-30; fertility of, **2**: 240-1; senatorial district, **2**: 336; defends western frontier, **3**: 50, 51, 53; provision law in, **3**: 486, 573; **5**: 274; tobacco loan office certificates, **3**: 516; supply post for, **4**: 286; recommended site for harness manufacture, **4**: 509; fails to provide wagons, **5**: 274; arms in, **5**: 341; and Reuben Lindsay's refusal to serve as county lieutenant, **5**: 554; adopts instructions concerning Va. Constitution, **6**: 284-94; establishes grammar school, **6**: 432; climate

of, **6**: 545; land owned by TJ in, **11**: 641, 653; **13**: 328, 340; **14**: 358, 362; address of welcome from citizens to TJ, **16**: 110, 111n, 167-77 (editorial note), 177-8, 178-80 (response by TJ)

Albemarle Court House, Va.: time of holding court of assize, **1**: 628; proposed meeting of school overseers at, **2**: 529; arms at, **6**: 38n, 625n

Albemarle Sound: canal, **7**: 558; **8**: 556

Albenga, Italy: TJ describes, **11**: 441-2; TJ's travel hints, **13**: 271

Albert de Rions, François Hector, Comte de: naval command, **12**: 216, 224; arrested in Toulon, **16**: 42; insulted by mob at Brest, **17**: 525; resigns command at Brest, **17**: 611, 642

Alberte, Francis: signs Continental Association, **1**: 154

Alberti, Francis (musician): death of, **8**: 342

Albertus Magnus: Stiles' comment on, **7**: 365

albinos: found among Indians, **10**: 643

Albion Mill, **9**: 401n

Albon, Claude Camille François, Comte d': *Discours sur l'histoire, le gouvernement, les usages*, **9**: 333; **11**: 662

Alburg, Vt.: custom house at, **20**: 467; port collector at, **20**: 628n

Alciphron: *Epistolae*, **12**: 678; **13**: 290

Alden, Roger: letter to, **17**: 262; holds state papers, **15**: 519; **17**: 349n; as chief clerk in Dept. of State, **16**: 181n, 339n, 345n; **17**: 347, 349n-50n, 356n, 358n; letter from quoted, **17**: 262n; reimbursed for expenses, **17**: 361

aldermen, county: responsibility for care of poor, **2**: 419-23; to be in charge of public education, **2**: 527-8

Alderney (Channel Island): citizenship of inhabitants, **6**: 435; cattle, **14**: 543

Aleaume, M.: letter from, **13**: 520; letter from cited, **13**: 535n; sends letters of procuration, **13**: 641, 662

Alembert, Jean Le Rond d': and *Encyclopédie*, **4**: 211; **16**: 587; Rittenhouse compared to, **6**: 551n; Jefferson follows, **16**: 608; computations of, **16**: 652n

Alert (ship): depositions concerning, **5**: 588-92, 634n; seizure of, **5**: 590, 682n; mentioned, **5**: 559, 675n

Alessandro, Don. *See* Malaspína, Alejandro

Alexander, Charles: letter to, **3**: 543

Alexander, Hugh: signs petition, **1**: 588

Alexander, James: signs petition, **1**: 588
Alexander, John: signs nonimportation resolutions, **1**: 30, 46; signs petition, **1**: 588; **6**: 294
Alexander, Lewis. *See* Alexandre, Louis
Alexander, Philip: asked to prepare bill to prevent importation of slaves, **2**: 24n
Alexander, Robert: signs agreement of secrecy, **1**: 253
Alexander, Samuel: silver askos made for TJ, **15**: xxvi, xxxi, xxxii
Alexander, William: acts as agent for attorneys of Simon Nathan, **3**: 316n; provides funds for William Short, **7**: 253; on William Short's position in Paris, **7**: 254, 257; settles in Richmond, **7**: 256n; ships owned by, **7**: 322, 385, 395; **11**: 328; bills of exchange, **7**: 519, 647-8; letter sent by, **7**: 538; acts as agent for farmers-general, **7**: 614, 648; **8**: 429, 666; bill on Laval & Wilfelsheim, **8**: 90, 507, 564; arrival of daughter, **8**: 423; tobacco contract with farmers-general, **8**: 644, 660; **11**: 193; **12**: 347; mentioned, **10**: 108
Alexander, Sir William: Nova Scotia granted to, **1**: 136
Alexander of Jerusalem, **1**: 552
Alexander VI, Pope: grant to Spain, **6**: 488
Alexandre, D. (father of Louis Alexandre): and regulation of tobacco trade, **9**: 625; **10**: 125; and copying press, **10**: 634
Alexandre, Louis: letters to, **8**: 290; **9**: 598; **14**: 457; letters from, **8**: 221-4; **9**: 624-5; **10**: 125-6, 587; **15**: 169-70; letter from cited, **8**: 244, 291; desires American consulship at Bayonne, **9**: 625; TJ sends copy of order of Berni to, **10**: 196; tobacco shipped to, **11**: 496n; as consul in Bayonne, **14**: 60; remarks on tobacco quality, **17**: 441
Alexandria, Egypt: Ledyard describes, **13**: 517
Alexandria, Va.: defenses of, **3**: 194; **4**: 169; **5**: 335-6, 419, 423, 612-3; as depot for French goods, **3**: 372; terminus of communication line to Philadelphia, **3**: 445, 454; threatened by British, **4**: 91; **5**: 336, 406; as central point for truce ships, **4**: 160; as supply post, **4**: 285, 286, 592; **5**: 16, 77-8; naval skirmishes at, **5**: 393, 529; arrival of Lafa-

yette at, **5**: 477, 522, 523; races at, **6**: 337, 341; considered for permanent seat of Congress, **6**: 357, 365; **7**: 118; as port of entry, **7**: 26, 360, 503, 562; competition with Norfolk for trade, **7**: 215; growth of expected, **8**: 511; visited by Mrs. Trist, **10**: 167; advantages as main depot for Le Couteulx fur company, **10**: 531; **11**: 385-7; opposes Mason's attitude toward Constitution, **12**: 280; turnpikes in, **14**: 304, 529-30; fur trade, **14**: 548; address of welcome from mayor to TJ, **16**: 224, 225 (response by TJ); petitions for removal of courthouse, **17**: 458n; and capital site, **19**: 29, 30, 31, 40, 57, 61, 62, 64, 65, 70, 71; poverty of described, **19**: 47; postal service in, **20**: 666
Alexis and Justine. See Dezède, Nicolas
Alfred the Great: Anglo-Saxon translation of Orosius, **11**: 523
Algiers: treaties with, **6**: 396; **8**: 522; **9**: 618; U.S. treaty of amity and commerce, **7**: 263, 269, 496; **8**: 19, 46; **12**: 180-1; captures American vessels, **7**: 556, 634; **8**: 512, 525, 544, 555, 559, 577, 586, 607, 616-7; **9**: 14, 92, 93, 168, 553, 628, 646; **10**: 206-7; **19**: 355n; naval forces, **7**: 639; **8**: 81, 419; **9**: 533-5, 553, 616, 617; tribute paid to, **8**: 47, 71, 72; **9**: 506, 528-9, 546, 547, 551-2, 564, 568, 617, 667, 668; **10**: 151-2, 207, 251, 287, 386, 565n; **12**: 182; U.S. relations with, **8**: 61-2, 566-7, 571-2; **9**: 8, 14, 23-4, 75, 245-8, 364-5, 376-7, 383, 385, 515-6, 538-40, 567-8, 600, 611, 614-22, 648; **10**: 138, 149, 238, 241, 242, 287, 396, 542, 629, 631, 649; **11**: 163; **12**: 500; **20**: 679; treaty with France, **8**: 62; **9**: 531; Spanish expedition against, **8**: 65-6, 69; Spanish-Moroccan coalition against, **8**: 83; relations with Britain, **8**: 150; **10**: 413; **12**: 550; **15**: 181-2; **18**: 373-5; piracy of, **8**: 294; **9**: 84, 473; **10**: 132; **11**: 376; **18**: 369-70; relations with Spain, **8**: 321, 376, 399, 401, 419, 444, 455, 460, 567; **9**: 233, 244-9, 531, 539, 568, 595; **10**: 246, 248; **11**: 566-7; **12**: 100, 565; **14**: 502; **15**: 284; rumors of war against U.S., **8**: 334; takes American captives, **8**: 440, 544; **9**: 614-22, 648; **10**: 152, 412, 606; **11**: 118, 321-2, 369, 376, 512, 567,

619; **12**: 51, 115, 149, 151, 238, 341, 342, 549; relations with Naples, **8**: 567; **9**: 233, 244-5, 376, 377, 525, 527, 539, 619, 648; **10**: 179, 224; **11**: 322, 379, 512; **12**: 550, 565; **13**: 330, 500; **17**: 33; relations with Portugal, **8**: 567; **9**: 244-5, 246, 376, 377, 525, 527, 539, 619, 648; **10**: 179, 224, 266, 606; **11**: 512; **12**: 565; **17**: 33; **18**: 408, 414; U.S.-Portuguese alliance against proposed, **9**: 64; war with Portugal, **9**: 64; inhabitants of in Va., **9**: 197; treaty with Naples, **9**: 249; treaty with Spain, **9**: 249, 376, 377-8, 525, 590, 619; **10**: 137, 150, 266, 329, 412; possibility of war with Denmark, Venice, and Netherlands, **9**: 249; relations with Denmark, **9**: 527; **15**: 181; relations with Turkey, **9**: 527, 531, 550, 553, 595; relations with Venice, **9**: 527, 619; government of, **9**: 528, 533, 553; manner of declaring war, **9**: 528; revenue, **9**: 529, 534; list of captives taken by, **9**: 530-1, 532; defenses, **9**: 531; **12**: 551; relations with Austria, **9**: 532; relations with Russia, **9**: 532; **10**: 224; use of captives in navy, **9**: 535; blockade of proposed, **9**: 542-4, 568, 569, 617; **10**: 124; cost of war with, **9**: 551-2; **12**: 183; commerce, **9**: 552; languages, **9**: 553; ports, **9**: 553; religion, **9**: 553; relations with European countries, **10**: 150; TJ's policy toward as minister to France, **10**: 176-7; **14**: 688; **15**: 310; **18**: 371-3, 376-84, 389-98; fortification of harbor, **10**: 177; relations with Italian states, **10**: 266; relations with Morocco, **10**: 359; Emperor of Morocco recommends U.S. to, **10**: 391; Barclay's mission to considered unnecessary, **10**: 403, 405; Lamb's correspondence with minister of marine, **10**: 428; naval retaliation against, **10**: 536; proposed convention against, **10**: 566n, 569, 570; plague in, **11**: 321; **12**: 58, 184; attacks Va. ship, **11**: 334; depredations against Genoa, **11**: 338; captures Spanish vessels, **11**: 512; captures British seamen, **12**: 235; ransom of Russian captives of, **12**: 242, 313; Dr. Warner's notes on, **12**: 549-51; treatment of captives, **12**: 549-50; death of Prime Minister, **13**: 399; **14**: 288; political changes in, **13**: 399; Genoese captives of, **13**: 500; capture of Dr. and Mrs. Spence reported, **14**:

4; relations with France, **14**: 183; **15**: 284; **16**: 403, 573; **17**: 16; **18**: 374-8, 380-1; Jay urges treaty with, **14**: 288; Montgomery reports on conditions in, **14**: 288-9; **17**: 397-8; in Russo-Turkish war, **14**: 506, 516; **15**: 341; U.S. action against suggested, **14**: 506, 516; French vessels captured by, **15**: 213, 284; use of force in dealing with advised, **16**: 390, 600; **17**: 15; French captives of ransomed, **16**: 573; proposed concurrence of powers against, **16**: 600; slaves in, **17**: 30-3; demands reparation for French damage to vessels, **17**: 414; TJ's Report on American Trade in the Mediterranean, **18**: 230, 369-416 (editorial note), 423-30; declares war on U.S., **18**: 382; Lamb's mission to, **18**: 384-90, 410-1; anonymous proposal on, **18**: 406-8, 421, 422n; TJ's Proposal to Use Force against the Barbary States, **18**: 416-22; Cathalan's reflections on peace treaty with U.S., **18**: 587-91; and the fisheries, **19**: 159, 174; interest in purchasing American frigate, **19**: 333

Algiers, American captives in: ransom of, **9**: 546, 547, 549, 551, 565, 615; **10**: 96-7, 131-2, 597, 598, 650; **11**: 35-6, 66, 101; **12**: 173, 184, 266, 313, 413, 432, 448, 474, 565, 674; **13**: 134, 149n, 168-70, 192, 229, 500, 569, 575; **14**: 215, 437, 644-5; **15**: 455-6; **16**: 7n, 8n, 20-1; **17**: 19, 293-4; **18**: 434, 436n, 596; **20**: 254-5, 476, 547, 601n; Lamb negotiates for, **9**: 549-50; **13**: 630, 631n; **17**: 30-1; **18**: 384-90, 410-1; Carmichael's concern for, **13**: 142, 399; **14**: 502; plague among, **13**: 500; **19**: 332-4; subsistence for, **13**: 630, 631n; **14**: 581; **20**: 626-7, 690; aided by Chauvier, **14**: 395-6, 396n-7n, 401-2, 433, 594n; **15**: 430-1, 455, 461-2; **16**: 570-1; list of living and dead (Sep. 16, 1788), **14**: 396n-7n; petition Congress for relief, **14**: 396n-7n; **18**: 401, 403; Willink & Van Staphorst's payments for, **14**: 587, 593, 644-5; **15**: 112, 356-7; U.S. Treasury orders on, **15**: 112; account of payments for, **15**: 340-1, 342n, 419; Spanish consul responsible for, **16**: 6n; **17**: 19; Short corresponds with, **16**: 221, 222n, 288n, 334; **17**: 555; discussed by Washington and TJ, **16**: 288n; **18**: 221, 398; Short negotiates

Algiers, American captives in (*cont.*)
for, **16**: 316, 505, 507n, 570-1; **17**:
14-6, 19, 20n, 258, 280, 527; **18**: 24,
401, 403-4, 406-7, 501; *Julius Caesar*
and, **16**: 562-5; summary of case by
O'Bryen, **17**: 29-34; TJ's Report on,
18: 221, 230, 369-416 (editorial note),
430-6; Cathalan's inquiry on, **18**:
399n, 590-1n; details of capture, **18**:
400n; Senate resolution on, **18**: 444;
Washington's statement on, **18**: 444-5;
Reynolds' connection with, **18**: 642n-
3n; letters from cited, **19**: 541; Jones'
interest in, **19**: 591. *See also* Algiers:
takes American captives

Algiers, Dey of. *See* Muhammad ibn
Uthman; Ali Hassan

Algol (star): variations of light in, **7**:
602; **8**: 575

Alicante, Spain: Montgomery desires
consulship at, **11**: 620; American consulate at, **19**: 314, 317; climate of, **19**:
552

alienage: notes on British and American,
6: 433-6

alien enemies: property of, **2**: 279-85;
treatment of, **2**: 479-80; trade treaty
stipulations, **7**: 472, 484, 486, 620-1,
622; **8**: 108-9, 192; protection of, **9**:
63-4, 417

aliens: property rights of, **2**: 152n; **7**:
268, 481, 617-8; **8**: 107-8, 190-1,
318; **9**: 108, 414; **10**: 45-6, 424; Va.
bill concerning, **2**: 409-10, 479-80;
trade treaty stipulations and crimes by,
6: 395, **8**: 108, 192; punishment for
injuries by, **7**: 472; reciprocity between France and U.S. proposed, **7**:
472; **8**: 317-9, 354; **20**: 529, 535n,
651; duties, **8**: 332-3, 354; power of
Va. executive to imprison or banish, **9**:
197; status according to Calvin's case,
9: 259; state laws concerning, **11**: 559;
lease of western land to, **12**: 6; ineligi-
ble for U.S. consular positions, **19**:
312n

Ali Hassan: succession as Dey of Algiers,
14: 46; **20**: 669, 678

alimony: suits on to be tried before High
Court of Chancery, **2**: 567

Allaire, Peter: as British secret agent, **17**:
43n, 68n, 91n; **18**: 240, 241n; dispatches, **17**: 90-1; and Nantucket,
Mass. emigration to Great Britain, **19**:
161n

Allanby, John: accident, **12**: 377

Allegheny mountains: settlements west
of, **2**: 103; **6**: 660; as boundary of Augusta co., Va., **2**: 113, 114; alleged to
be western limit of Va., **6**: 176; Le
Maire's comments on, **8**: 123; geology
of, **8**: 566; Rev. James Madison's observations on, **14**: 534

Allegheny river: as boundary, **1**: 389n;
junction with Monongahela, **2**: 98; settlements on, **2**: 100; Le Maire's comment on, **8**: 123, 128

Allen, Lieut.: fires on British, **5**: 95

Allen, Mr.: Ramsay's history sent to TJ
by, **16**: 577; certificate of, **19**: 322;
mentioned, **18**: 131

Allen, Andrew: signs agreement of secrecy, **1**: 253; on committee to meet
with Lee, **1**: 286; sons in British army,
1: 659; deserts to British, **2**: 3

Allen (Allan), David: signs petition, **1**:
587; **6**: 294; signs Va. oath of allegiance, **2**: 128

Allen, Ebenezer: and Seneca land grants
to daughters, **20**: 131

Allen, Ethan: treatment as prisoner of
war, **1**: 276-7; **3**: 44-5; at Quebec, **1**:
446; proposal to Dorchester, **17**: 124n;
appeals to Lord Dorchester, **19**: 366;
death of, **19**: 368; mentioned, **1**: 460

Allen, James (British war prisoner), **2**:
32

Allen, John: deserts to British, **2**: 3; report of committee to Congress on letter of, **6**: 511-2

Allen, Capt. John: letter to, **4**: 625-6;
letter from, **5**: 126-8; requests new
commission, **4**: 425; in Va. artillery
regiment, **4**: 541; mentioned, **4**: 395,
593; **5**: 500

Allen, Levi: leaves for England, **19**: 368

Allen, Richard: imports slaves, **15**: 654

Allen, Thomas: supplies purchased from,
17: 362; mentioned, **5**: 294n

Allen, William: in Albemarle co. militia,
1: 664; deserts to British, **2**: 3

Allen's Creek Church, Hanover, Va.:
army hospital in, **6**: 54

Allen's Ordinary: Innes at, **5**: 506, 521,
528

Allentown, Pa.: visited by TJ and Madison, **20**: 461

Allesandro, Don. *See* Malaspína, Alejandro

Allexander, John: signs petition, **1**: 587

Amelia co., Va. (*cont.*)
    GA for, **5**: 585-6; recruits soldiers, **1**:
    249; **3**: 8; senatorial district, **1**: 476; **2**:
    336; appoints infantry officers, **1**: 579;
    place of court of assize, **1**: 630; militia
    of, **2**: 130; **3**: 599; **4**: 62, 63, 295n,
    318, 352, 371, 477, 645, 646-7, 664,
    669; **5**: 6, 7, 29, 35, 36, 310, 496n-
    7n, 501, 520-1, 546, 560, 561, 573,
    614-6, 646; tobacco loan office certifi-
    cates, **3**: 516; flour quota of, **3**: 609n;
    supply post for, **4**: 286; impressment
    of horses in, **6**: 51
Amelia Court House, Va.: ammunition
    and flints at, **5**: 480
Amelot, M. *See* Amyot, Joseph Marie
amercements. *See* fines
America: behavior of citizens of in Eng-
    land criticized, **7**: 521-2; as subject for
    Mrs. Cosway's landscapes, **10**: 447;
    women's life in described by TJ, **11**:
    123; resourcefulness of people, **11**:
    251; list of Spanish books on, **11**: 554;
    curiosity concerning in Siberia, **11**:
    638; histories of, **12**: 62; superiority
    over Europe, **12**: 601; admired by
    Germans, **13**: 449n; British aversion
    to, **13**: 461-2, 610; **14**: 13; Count An-
    driani's opinions on, **17**: 104n
America (ship): voyages, **14**: 10, 417; in
    China, **16**: 39-40
American (British ship): damaged in
    storm, **4**: 651
American Academy of Arts and Sciences:
    TJ elected to membership, **16**: 111-2,
    289; Dumas elected to membership,
    17: 209, 210n; and new system of
    penmanship, **19**: 120n; eulogy of Bow-
    doin, **20**: 599
American Atlas: lent by Baylor, **4**: 586;
    TJ receives, **11**: 108; desired by
    Moustier, **11**: 621, 622, 624
"American Citizen, The": quoted, **18**:
    88n-9n
American colonies: TJ's theory of rela-
    tions with Great Britain, **1**: 119; laws
    based on English civil code, **10**: 11;
    relations with Great Britain, **10**: 32
American Commissioners for Negotiating
    Commercial Treaties: TJ appointed, **7**:
    229, 233, 235; commission from Con-
    gress, **7**: 262-3; letter from Charles
    Thomson, **7**: 308-9; correspondence
    with Souza de Coutinho, **7**: 419-20,
    428, 551, 580; correspondence with
    Baron de Thulemeier, **7**: 421, 436-7,

490-3, 565-6, 611-2, 616-28, 649-50;
8: 14-5, 26-33, 134-5, 165-6, 234;
correspondence with Conde de Aranda, **7**: 423-4, 425-6, 455-6; letters
from Chevalier de Pio, **7**: 424, 612-4;
letter from Rivière, **7**: 424; letters from
Count Scarnafis, **7**: 425, 632-3; letter
from Chevalier Delfino, **7**: 427; correspondence with Baron Staël de Holstein, **7**: 428-9, 434-5; correspondence
with Francesco Favi, **7**: 430, 437-8,
533, 561-2, 649; **8**: 104-10, 187-8,
205; correspondence with Duke of
Dorset, **7**: 456-7, 457-8, 547, 560-1;
8: 55-9, 153; TJ's notes for, **7**: 478-9;
letters to the president of Congress, **7**:
493-500, 573-4, 646-7; need allowance for house rent, **7**: 564; letter from
papal nuncio, **7**: 575-6; correspondence with Jay, **7**: 606; **8**: 19-22, 36-8,
80-3, 140-1, 235-6, 606; **9**: 357-9,
406-9; **11**: 77-8; **18**: 379n; extract
from proceedings of, **7**: 645-6; **8**: 48n;
authority of questioned by Dorset, **8**:
55-6; trip to England discussed, **8**:
56n-7n; correspondence with Vergennes, **8**: 61-3, 120, 625-7; **18**: 376,
377n; letter from Lafayette, **8**: 70-2;
instructions to revised, **8**: 76, 217,
605; letter from Marquis de Castries,
8: 277; letter to Dumas, **8**: 312-3; letter to Short, **8**: 313-5; letter to the
Emperor of Morocco, **8**: 619-21; correspondence with Carmichael, **8**: 623-
4; **9**: 244-9, 385-6; expiration of appointment near, **9**: 166, 241; correspondence with Lamb, **9**: 283-4, 549-
54; **10**: 96-7, 218, 407; letters from
Randall, **9**: 284-5, 525-6; letter to
Carmarthen, **9**: 375; letters from Barclay, **9**: 383-4, 566-7, 626; **10**: 71-2,
141-2, 181, 220, 334-48, 357-62,
389-92, 418-9, 509-11, 535-6; **11**: 21-
2, 132-3, 582-4; submits projet of
treaty to Portugal, **9**: 412; observations
on proposed treaty with Portugal, **9**:
426-32; correspondence with Fennish,
10: 76-7; **11**: 79-80; powers, **10**: 286;
renewal of commission desired by Jay,
10: 488; pay accounts, **14**: 283; letter
from Brush, **15**: 616-7
American Committee. *See* Comité du
    Commerce avec les Etats-Unis
American Fabius (Va. navy brig), **5**: 557
American Museum: prints letter from TJ
    to Ramsay, **10**: 492n; sent to TJ, **11**:

289; sent to TJ by Hopkinson, **11:** 561; cited, **12:** 283; **16:** 412n, 615; **19:** 563, 588n; prints letter from Humphreys, **16:** 60n, 63n-4n; publishes treaties, **17:** 261n-2n; prints Coxe's article, **19:** 559; quoted, **19:** 567

American Philosophical Society: letter from, **4:** 544-6; seal of, **1:** 482; certificates of TJ's membership in, **4:** xxxvii, 107 (illus.); TJ elected member of, **4:** 544-6; **5:** 490; **6:** 142; **10:** 437; elects new members, **4:** 545n; **8:** 51; **11:** 111, 151; objectives of, **6:** 163; TJ moves orrery be presented to King of France, **6:** 418; building for, **7:** 20; and balloon experiments, **7:** 247n; Hopkinson's efforts in behalf of, **7:** 534-5; and animal magnetism, **8:** 15; inactivity of, **8:** 100; Rittenhouse's contributions to, **8:** 118; copy of *Notes on Virginia* promised to, **8:** 551; **10:** 249, 250n; Magellanic Fund, **9:** 131, 321; *Transactions* of, **9:** 320, 362, 440; **10:** 73, 77, 136n, 530, 624, 625, 637, 642, 643, 646; **11:** 72, 289, 293; **12:** 145; **13:** 157, 339, 413; **14:** 188; and medal for discovery in natural philosophy, **9:** 321; establishment of, **9:** 487; promised account of satellites by Herschell, **11:** 162; Lavoisier accepts membership, **11:** 197; Guichen accepts membership, **11:** 200-1; membership in, **11:** 301, 331; **20:** 476; *Mémoires* of Turin Royal Academy of Sciences requested for, **11:** 468; recommends description of Indian antiquities, **12:** 159; Ingenhousz' work on vegetables sent to, **15:** 119; and TJ's proposal on weights and measures, **16:** 617; receives Indian figure from TJ, **17:** xxx, 20n; Bonne's work on measures sent to, **17:** 636, 638n; cellars used for TJ's experiment, **18:** 457-8, 476; Barton reads paper to, **19:** 584; receives memorial on Panama canal from TJ, **20:** 211n; committee on Hessian fly, **20:** 245, 341, 395, 446-7, 461n-2n; lamp donated to by TJ, **20:** 420; mentioned, **3:** 149; **6:** 420, 542, 556; **14:** 701n; **18:** 528

American Revolution. *See* Revolution, American

American state papers: proposal to publish by Ebenezer Hazard, **19:** xxxv-vi, 348 (illus.)

American Traveller: sought by TJ, **11:** 523

American travels: books on, **8:** 410

"Americanus" (pseud. of John Nicholas, Jr.), **16:** 141n

American vessels. *See* vessels, American

Amery, Francis: passport issued by TJ, **15:** 485

Ames, Fisher: opposes commercial treaties, **16:** 516; relationship with George Beckwith, **17:** 44n; denies charge of British influence, **17:** 54; and residence bill controversy, **17:** 169, 173, 175-7; and response to Washington's address, **18:** 229n; on Algerian captives, **18:** 413-4; on Constitution, **18:** 518; and tonnage acts, **18:** 521; and capital site, **19:** 6, 7, 281n; and new system of penmanship, **19:** 120n; and the fisheries, **19:** 145, 155, 179; comments on national bank, **19:** 281n; mentioned, **17:** 183n; **18:** 135n

Ameshoff, Mr. (merchant at Amsterdam), **13:** 9

Amherst, Sir Jeffrey: appointed to replace Gen. Gage, **1:** 247; military plans of, **1:** 450; **4:** 606; false rumor of arrival in Philadelphia, **2:** 175

Amherst co., Va.: letter to commissioner of provisions for, **3:** 568n; letters to county lieutenant of, **5:** 204, 416; uses land as lottery prize, **1:** 22; senatorial district, **1:** 476; **2:** 336; appoints infantry officers, **1:** 579; petition of dissenters in, **1:** 586-9; **2:** 548n; place of court of assize, **1:** 630; militia of, **2:** 130; **3:** 599; **4:** 63, 295n, 308, 352, 371, 406, 477; **5:** 6n, 29, 35, 214, 310; **6:** 36, 93, 119; levies of soldiers in, **3:** 8; defends western frontier, **3:** 50, 52, 53, 79; provision law in, **3:** 486, 573; tobacco loan office certificates, **3:** 516; supply post for, **4:** 286; arms in, **5:** 341; Executive orders issued to, **6:** 106

Amiable Catherine (ship), **15:** 68

Amiable Elizabeth, L' (ship): claim for, **7:** 377-8, 497-8, 499n

"Amicus": opposes separation of executive and legislative buildings, **20:** 31-2

Amiens, France: merchants import wheat from U.S., **14:** 425-6, 446, 460

Amitié (ship): goods sent on, **11:** 283

Ammonet, Charles, **11:** 360n

Ammonet, Jacob: estate of, **11:** 360, 546

Ammonet (Ammonett, Amonit, Am-

Ammonet (*cont.*)
monit), John: letter from, **11**: 360; introduced to TJ, **11**: 319, 327, 330, 335; claims French estate, **11**: 327, 335, 360; **12**: 20-1; and Mary Jefferson on journey to France, **11**: 524; **15**: 636; mentioned, **12**: 370

ammunition: scarcity of, **1**: 288; **4**: 27, 473; **5**: 188, 231-2; for Transylvania settlers, **2**: 83, 109; for friendly Indians, **3**: 276; produced by Continental laboratory, **3**: 480; need of officers to supervise, **3**: 504-5; needed by western troops, **3**: 520; sent to Gloucester co., **3**: 533; for southern army, **3**: 576, 659; **4**: 319; **5**: 388, 416-8; accounting for, **4**: 165; for militia, **4**: 305, 419; **5**: 337; for Gen. Nelson, **4**: 313-4, 319n; Steuben's queries on, **4**: 357; for Va., **4**: 470, 486; **5**: 68; for Gen. Muhlenberg, **4**: 581; transport of, **5**: 389, 417; for defense of Chantilly, **5**: 435

Amory, Samuel: letter from, **8**: 168

Amoureux, M.: letter to, **13**: 428-9; letters from, **13**: 284-5, 657; **14**: 520, 648-9; letter to, from J. P. Jones, cited, **13**: 284, 585; Nesbitt asks for help, **13**: 562; letter from, to Nesbitt, cited, **14**: 520; payment to John Paul Jones, **14**: 686

amphictyony, **12**: 274

Amphitrite (British ship), **4**: 399

Ampthill (estate), **8**: 342; **10**: 107

Ampuys, France: TJ describes, **11**: 421

Amsterdam: imports from S.C., **8**: 202-3; Short's comments on, **8**: 446; defenses of, **12**: 166, 167, 205; banks in, **12**: 171, **19**: 531; U.S. funds at, **12**: 173; negotiations with Duke of Brunswick, **12**: 215; surrender to Prussia rumored, **12**: 243; "Het Wapen van Amsterdam," TJ's hotel, **13**: xxvi-vii, 16 (illus.), 264; TJ's sketches of, **13**: 8-9; TJ's notes on, **13**: 8-12, 264; British credit in, **13**: 129-30; U.S. Commissioners in, **16**: 328, 329n; American consulate at, **19**: 313, 317

Amsterdam (ship), **12**: 510

Amsterdam Westchurch: chimes of, **13**: xxv, 16 (fac.)

Amyot, Joseph Marie: book on travels into China, **8**: 111, 461; **11**: 663

Anabaptists, **6**: 289

Anacharsis. See Barthelemy, Jean Jacques

Anacostia: TJ's revival of name, **6**: 596n

Anacreon: Αι του Αναχρεοντος ωδαι

ordered by TJ, **9**: 153; TJ seeks information on best Italian translation, **11**: 159; mentioned, **8**: 407; **12**: 18; **14**: 491, 707n

Analyse da profissâo da fé do Santo Padre Pio IV, por A. Pereira de Figueiredo, **20**: 656-7

"An American" (pseud. used by Hamilton), **20**: 719

Anan, Rev. Mr., **7**: 316

An Answer to Paine's Rights of Man, **20**: 283n

anatomy: study recommended by TJ, **10**: 306; study by T. M. Randolph, Jr., **11**: 291

Anburey, Thomas: *Travels* cited, **2**: 244n

Ancenis, France: TJ describes, **11**: 459

Ancherville, M. de. *See* Hancarville

anchors: made at Hunter's iron works, **5**: 447

anchovies: sent to Eppes by TJ, **9**: 210; mentioned, **11**: 442

Ancona, Italy: Short describes, **14**: 380

Andernach, Germany: millstones, **13**: 15, 265, 447

Anderson, Capt.: bears letter from Colley, **19**: 260

Anderson, Mr.: and ferry on the Roanoke, **2**: 460; vessel of captured by enemy, **3**: 82; appointed commissioner for provision law, **3**: 485, 575; revaluates horses, **5**: 286, 287; serves as Paradise family agent, **19**: 354

Anderson, Adam: *Historical and Chronological Deduction of the Origin of Commerce*, **13**: 652; **19**: 208, 222n

Anderson, Alexander (of St. Vincent Botanical Gardens): report on rice seed, **14**: 707; Vaughan requests rice seed from, **16**: 274; letter from, to Vaughan, **17**: 514, 516n

Anderson, Maj. Archibald: letter from, to Stevens, cited, **4**: 217; killed, **5**: 156, 199

Anderson, Capt. Atcheson: tables carried by, **18**: 591; mentioned, **18**: 592n

Anderson, Sir Edmund: *Reports*, **10**: 518

Anderson, Garland: votes against bill for religious freedom, **2**: 549n

Anderson, George: letters cited, **4**: 196n, 306n, 483; and shipping corn to Bermuda, **4**: 196n, 376

Anderson, Henry: imports slaves, **15**: 654

Anderson, James (Md.): treason of, **3**: 644

Anderson, James (public armorer): proposes employment of Negroes, **3**: 284n; contract with Va. for labor, **3**: 324n; and appointment as public armorer, **3**: 505; **4**: 90-1; employs artisans, **4**: 224, 397, 566; **5**: 255; shop of, **4**: 434, 435n; **5**: 580; refuses terms offered, **4**: 479; concludes agreement for nailers, **4**: 566; on cooking and washing for workers at public expense, **5**: 255; wants to remove public workmen from Richmond, **5**: 516; repairs arms, **6**: 20-1, 27; mentioned, **4**: 314, 315, 578; **5**: 97n, 106

Anderson, James (Scotland): letter to, **18**: 111-2; letter from, **16**: 391-2; edits *The Bee*, **16**: 391n-2n; **18**: 112; letter to cited, **16**: 392n; *An Account of the Present State of the Hebrides*, **18**: 42, 43n; letter from, to Russell, cited, **18**: 399

Anderson, John: assumed name of Maj. André, **4**: 29

Anderson, John (Va.): signs petition, **6**: 294; letter from, to Washington, **19**: 405-6

Anderson, Joseph: signs petition, **1**: 588

Anderson, Joseph Inslee: judicial appointment of, **18**: 509n; **19**: 284n, 381-402 (editorial note), 402-8 (documents); correspondence with Washington, **19**: 385, 402-3, 406-8; letter to, from Vining, **19**: 404-5

Anderson, Matthew: supervises public shoe factory, **4**: 413, 416-7, 454n; refuses Council of State's proposals, **4**: 440; proposition on tobacco, **8**: 430; **9**: 445; **12**: 652; mentioned, **11**: 249

Anderson, Nathaniel: letter to, **17**: 262-3; mentioned, **16**: 196n

Anderson, R., **16**: 196n

Anderson, Richard: signs nonimportation resolutions (1769), **1**: 30; pledges to support clergyman, **2**: 7; signs Va. oath of allegiance, **2**: 128

Anderson, Maj. Richard, **3**: 652

Anderson, Robert: letters to, **5**: 166, 292; entertaining by, **1**: 237; case of, **8**: 662; **9**: 32-6

Anderson, Thomas: signs petition, **1**: 588; in Albemarle co. militia, **1**: 664; signs Va. oath of allegiance, **2**: 129

Anderson, William: signs Va. oath of allegiance, **2**: 129; votes for bill for religious freedom, **2**: 549n

Anderson, William (London merchant): letter from cited, **12**: 652; Mrs. Paradise's financial troubles with, **13**: 457;

14: 461-2, 580; **15**: 95; **16**: 137; John Paradise's debt to, **13**: 472-3, 522, 537, 544, 599-600, 602-3; **14**: 210, 277, 299, 313, 455-6; **15**: 95, 292; reports ratification of Constitution, **13**: 481; letter to, from Paradise, cited, **14**: 45, 209-10; letter to cited, **14**: 278n; as trustee of Mrs. Paradise's deed, **14**: 579; pays John Paradise's bill on Bancroft, **15**: 328, 333; mentioned, **2**: 26n; **13**: 571, 607; **14**: 9n, 52, 513, 516; **15**: 96, 130; **16**: 138, 198n; **17**: 483

Anderson's bridge: Lafayette's army marches toward, **6**: 26

Anderson's Tavern, Richmond: Independence Day celebration at, **10**: 110

Andes, Reinhard. *See* Antis, Richard

Andlau, Comte d', **8**: 359

Andrade, Gen. Gomes Freire de: introduction to TJ, **8**: 321; letter from cited, **8**: 402

André, Abbé: letter from, **10**: 436; recommended by James Smith, **10**: 402

André, John: capture of, **4**: 12, 29; **16**: 54n, 55n; plots with Arnold, **4**: 29; **17**: 41; execution of, **4**: 29

Andreani (Andriani), Paolo, Count: introduced to TJ by Rutledge, **16**: 266; introduced to TJ by Paradise, **16**: 294; introduced to Adams by Price, **16**: 294n; visits New York, **16**: 543; opinions on America reported, **17**: 104n; on Washington's administration, **18**: 532; ore sent to, **20**: 410

Andrew (ship), **9**: 52

Andrews, John: *History of the War with America, France, Spain and Holland*, **8**: 554; **10**: 166, 201, 294, 352, 377, 380; **12**: 115, 529-30

Andrews, Rev. Robert: letters to, **5**: 303-4, 373; **6**: 7-8, 72; letters from, **4**: 574; **5**: 339; signs nonimportation resolutions (1770), **1**: 47; signs Virginia Association, **1**: 109; serves as Va.-Pa. boundary commissioner, **3**: 18n, 77; **5**: 478n; **7**: 236; **15**: 605; quoted, **4**: 382n, 678n; signs honorary degree for TJ, **6**: 222; proposed for Maury school's board, **7**: 112; leaves ministry, **8**: 428; supports Constitution, **13**: 98; recommends Andrew Ellicott as U.S. geographer, **19**: 40n; **20**: 61n; mentioned, **4**: 262; **6**: 8

Andrews, William, **5**: 642n

Andriani, Count. *See* Andreani, Paolo

Andrier, Mr., **9**: 25

Antioch, Council of, **1**: 554

antipiratical confederacy. *See* Barbary States: concert of powers proposed against

Antiquités d'Herculaneum. See Maréchal, Pierre Sylvain

Antis, Richard (Reinhard Andes): deposition concerning Henderson's land claims, **2**: 101

Antoinette, L' (ship): carries letter to TJ, **18**: 584

Antoninus, Marcus Aurelius: TJ seeks information on best Italian translation, **11**: 159

Antwerp: surrender of, **16**: 305

Anville (Danville), Duchesse d'. *See* Enville, Louise Elisabeth de La Rochefoucauld

Anville, Jean Baptiste Bourguignon d': map of North America by, **6**: 600-1

Anyar, Edmund: Baptist enlisted in army, **1**: 662

Apalachicola river: as part of U.S. boundary, **6**: 458

Apicius, Coelius: *De Opsoniis et Condimentis*, **12**: 678; **13**: 290

Apling, David: in Albemarle co. militia, **1**: 666

Apling, Thomas: in Albemarle co. militia, **1**: 666

Apollinarians: TJ's notes on, **1**: 554

Apollo (Va. navy ship), **5**: 557; **8**: 548

Apollonia (ship), **12**: 448

Appalachian mountains: Le Maire's account of, **8**: 123

Appeals, Court of (Va.). *See* Virginia: Court of Appeals

appeals, legal: in common law courts, **2**: 610

Appenines: TJ describes, **11**: 440, 441; mentioned, **11**: 437

Appiani: alfresco painting by, **11**: 437

Appianus of Alexandria: *Romanarum Historiarum*, **12**: 678, 688; **14**: 491, 707n; works of, **13**: 290

Appian Way, **14**: 541

Appleby, Sir William: address by, **14**: 568

apples: French and American compared, **8**: 683; preservation of, **8**: 683; **12**: 533; at Monticello, **9**: 623; TJ wishes to have sent to France, **12**: 137; sent to TJ, **12**: 409, 528, 533, 568

Appleton, John: introduced to TJ, **10**: 160; knowledge of Col. Blackden, **11**: 519; **12**: 197; packet sent by, **11**: 592,

595; letter sent by, **12**: 613; passport issued by TJ, **15**: 484, 485; mentioned, **8**: 58n; **10**: 152; **12**: 291, 619, 668

Appleton, Nathaniel: letter from, **13**: 207; letter from cited, **17**: 644; loan to Cutting, **18**: 320; mentioned, **14**: 60

Appleton, Thomas: letters to, **13**: 429, 560; letters from, **13**: 367, 421, 543; **18**: 152; and French duties, **13**: 421, 429, 543; as consul in Rouen, **14**: 60; **15**: 374; **18**: 359; signs Fourth of July tribute to TJ, **15**: 240; proposed appointment as Lisbon consul, **20**: 161n; mentioned, **10**: 491; **13**: 207; **17**: 655

Applin, Thomas: signs petition, **1**: 588

Appling, Joel: signs petition, **6**: 293

Appling, Thomas: signs petition, **6**: 294

Appling, Thomas, Jr.: signs petition, **6**: 293

Appomattox river: post service on, **2**: 389; ferries across, **2**: 458; impressment of vessels on, **4**: 635; **5**: 51, 55; **5**: 401; boats on, **5**: 124; skirmish on, **5**: 580

appraisers: of estates, law regarding, **2**: 401

apprentices: Va. bill concerning, **2**: 485-8; complaints of, **2**: 488

apprenticeship of seamen, **2**: 383-4

appropriating money: and powers of Committee of the States, **6**: 523-4

apricots: at Monticello, **9**: 623; French and American compared, **10**: 641

apricots, melon, **12**: 29

apricot stones: planting, **16**: 194

Apsley, Henry Bathurst, first Baron of: TJ terms "cypher" on British Board of Admiralty, **13**: 462

Apuleius, Lucius: *Opera Omnia*, **15**: 223; **20**: 634n

Aquago Indians: land purchase from, **8**: 85, 95

Arabic language: dialect spoken in Morocco, **10**: 346

Aragon, M. d' (Rochambeau's secretary), **15**: 417n

Aranda, Pedro Pablo Abárca y Boléa, Count: letters to, **7**: 423-4, 455-6; **8**: 657; **12**: 186-7; **14**: 700; letters from, **7**: 425-6; **8**: 658; **12**: 186, 187; TJ wishes conference with, **8**: 93; asked to intercede for Watson's release, **8**: 341; asked for passports for emissaries to Barbary States, **8**: 670; recall to Spain from Paris, **11**: 174; **12**: 151, 190,

arms (*cont.*)
  ported from France to U.S., **12**: 469, 470; **13**: 70; seized in France, **14**: 68. *See also* bayonets; muskets
arms, coat of. *See* coat of arms
Armstead, Mr. (of Hampton), **5**: 691; **8**: 35, 36
Armstrong, Col., **20**: 594
Armstrong, Col. James: at battle of Camden, **3**: 597n
Armstrong, John, **3**: 5n
Armstrong, Gen. John, Jr.: in command of Pa. troops in French and Indian Wars, **2**: 100, 103; appointed temporary judge of western territory, **12**: 256; Moustier comments on, **12**: 590
Armstrong, Col. Martin: in charge of prisoners taken at King's Mountain, **4**: 177-8
Armstrong, Robert: petition from, **5**: 349
army, Continental. *See* Continental army
army, standing: kept by king in American colonies, **1**: 317; power over retained by Congress, **12**: 425; protection against, **12**: 440; TJ's suspicion of, **12**: 558, 571; **20**: 215, 235-6; restrictions on in Bill of Rights, **12**: 583; **13**: 442-3
army clothing. *See* clothing for military
army officers: qualifications of in Va. Constitution, **1**: 354; promotions, **3**: 166; transfers between regiments, **3**: 229-30, 236; form of parole for captives, **3**: 253-4; for western battalions, **3**: 274; commissions, **3**: 377-8; **5**: 79; shortage of, **3**: 478, 489; pay, **3**: 540, 616; **4**: 350; **5**: 147; rank, **4**: 72, 168, 247; **5**: 145; importance of, **4**: 131; rank of exchanged prisoners, **4**: 199; list of resigned and supernumerary asked, **4**: 243-4; right of dismissal, **4**: 281-2; draft of letter to retired officers, **4**: 290-1; distressed by currency depreciation, **5**: 100; replacement of, **6**: 293; appointment by Va. GA, **6**: 298; power of Committee of the States over, **6**: 523-4; efforts to obtain land north of the Ohio, **6**: 572n; half pay, **8**: 269, 276. *See also* clothing for military
army paymasters: and irregularities of accounts, **5**: 245
army quotas, state: within powers of Committee of the States, **6**: 523-4
army supplies: transport of, **5**: 301, 326
Arnal, Abbé Etienne d': letter to, **11**: 563-5; and steam mill at Nîmes, **14**: 374; **15**: 67; steam engine used for navigating French rivers, **14**: 374; **15**: 67, 81n, 82n
Arnaud (Arnoud), Abbé François: name confused with Abbé Arnoux, **8**: 92n; recommends M. de Sasserno to TJ, **13**: 271
Arnet, Mr.: recommended for federal office in N.C., **16**: 477
Arnold, Benedict: letter to, **5**: 227-8; and Canadian campaign, **1**: 248, 252, 264, 269, 270, 293, 397, 434, 437, 438, 440, 442, 443, 444, 445, 447, 448, 452; **10**: 352, 370-1, 377; **13**: 194n; **17**: 573, 575; forced to sign cartel at the Cedars, **1**: 398-9, 400-4, 459; **15**: 576; dissatisfaction of troops with, **1**: 435, 436; characteristics as officer, **1**: 450, 488, 489; commands fleet on lakes, **1**: 499, 520, 589; charges against, **2**: 20; relieves Fort Stanwix, **2**: 29; and troop casualties, **2**: 197; orders destruction of munitions foundry at Westham, Va., **3**: 147n; treason of, **4**: 7, 12-3, 28-9, 38n; **17**: 41; invades Va., **4**: 258-77, 335, 336, 351, 399, 436, 607, 637, 639, 641, 661n; **5**: 50, 92, 204, 235, 312, 351, 474n, 507, 624; **6**: 636; plan of raid on Richmond, **4**: xxxviii, 267 (illus.); denounced, **4**: 270, 291, 671; replies to request for flag of truce, **4**: 330-1; efforts to capture, **4**: 487-8, 651n, 676n; **5**: 107n, 684n; pays Mr. Buchanan, **4**: 507; leaves New York, **4**: 567; and exchange of prisoners, **4**: 622; **5**: 293, 330; offended by TJ's proclamation, **4**: 623; quarrels with British officers, **5**: 73, 74; strength of forces, **5**: 75, 350, 370; on parole violations, **5**: 228n; reinforcements for, **5**: 260; superseded as commander of Va. invasion, **5**: 261; Steuben on strategy of, **5**: 277n; shortage of supplies reported, **5**: 305; paroles American prisoners, **5**: 329, 365; retaliation for Hare's detention, **5**: 331n; returns slaves to Loyalists, **5**: 425n; captures Richmond, **5**: 634; **6**: 105; and Westover affair, **5**: 671n, 673n, 675n, 676n, 677n, 678n, 682n, 685n, 686n, 704, 705; letter from sent to Steuben, **5**: 697; letter from, to Gen. Muhlenberg, **5**: 699; joined by Cornwallis, **6**: 25, 32; letter of published, **6**: 108, 109n; commercial speculation by, **9**: 3-4; reported at Detroit,

Artois, Marie Thérèse de Savoie, Comtesse d', **12**: 502n

Arton: drawing by, **13**: xxvi, 16 (illus.)

arts: introduction into America, **8**: 469; in Europe, **13**: 269

Arundel, Capt. Dohickey, **1**: 289, 469

Arzilla, Morocco: harbor of, **10**: 340

"A Sailor": letter from, to Washington, quoted, **19**: 158n

Asalto (Assalto), Francisco González de Bassecourt, Conde de: letter to cited, **9**: 248

Ascheraden, Baron Schultz d': letter from cited, **11**: 405n

Aselby, Capt. John, **1**: 165; **15**: 649, 651, 662, 664, 667, 668

Ash, Robert (British war prisoner), **2**: 32

Ashburnham, Mr.: introduced to TJ, **13**: 119-20

Ashby, Mr.: rice sent to Constantinople by, **15**: 13

Ashe, John B.: opinions on N.C. candidates for federal offices, **16**: 477-8; letter from, to Washington, cited, **17**: 293n

Ashley, Feilding: petition from, **5**: 349

Ashley, Lord. *See* Shaftesbury, Anthony Ashley Cooper, third Earl of

Ashley river, S.C.: enemy shipping in, **3**: 400

Ashlin, Joseph: TJ's accounts with, **10**: 614

ash tree: seeds asked by TJ for France, **9**: 255; plants asked from John Banister, **11**: 121

Asia: U.S. trade with, **12**: 470, 481

Askew, John, **4**: 20

Askin, John: prisoner of war, **5**: 432

askos, bronze, at Nîmes: copied as gift for Clérisseau, **15**: xxvii-xxxi, 172, 280 (illus.); silver copy for TJ, 1801, **15**: xxxi-ii, 280 (illus.); Short obtains copy for TJ, **15**: xxvii, xxx, 67, 125n; copied by Souche, **15**: xxviii, xxx-ii, 124, 187

asparagus: in France, **11**: 428; **13**: 26

Asquith, Lister: letters to, **9**: 52-3, 169-70, 314, 517, 551-2, 558, 627; letters from, **8**: 492-8, 500-1, 527-9, 560, 578, 639-40, 661-2; **9**: 31, 66, 77-8, 98, 135, 177, 290, 348, 393-5, 439, 537; letters from, to Adams, cited, **8**: 492-8; case of, **8**: 597, 628, 647; **9**: 12-3, 32-6, 37n, 98-9, 119, 314, 317, 318n, 629-30; letters from cited, **9**: 72; **10**: 99; draws bill on Grand, **9**:

650, 656. *See also William and Catherine* (ship)

Asquith, Mrs. Lister, **8**: 527

assault: extradition for, **6**: 513-5; English law regarding, **9**: 5-6

Asselin, Capt. (master of *Vendangeur*), **19**: 261

assemblies: projects for, in Europe, **12**: 413

assemblies, provincial (France): established, **11**: 490; mentioned, **12**: 8, 32, 59, 67, 246, 350, 490, 682

assemblies, unlawful. *See* riots

Assembly of Notables: called by Louis XVI, **11**: 31-2; agenda of, **11**: 42, 46-7; postponed, **11**: 48, 118, 128, 141; convened, **11**: 169; puns and bon mots about, **11**: 174, 182; proceedings of, **11**: 176-7, 179-80, 231, 257, 258-9; adopts rule of secrecy, **11**: 184; Lafayette's presence at, **11**: 199; Mme de Tessé's comments on, **11**: 207; results, **11**: 227, 470, 489-90; **12**: 32, 34, 36, 59, 67, 490; recessed, **11**: 269; compared to Federal Constitutional Convention, **11**: 286; concerned about revenue, **11**: 325, 345; adjourned, **11**: 399; discusses American debt, **11**: 517, 595; mentioned, **11**: 238, 241, 303, 362-3, 374

"Assenisipia" (TJ's name for new state), **6**: 604

asses: sent Washington by king of Spain, **7**: 549, 567; **9**: 172; TJ proposes to buy females, **7**: 567; Mazzei wishes to send to Va., **8**: 678; taken from Minorca by Lamb, **11**: 366; prices in Provence, **11**: 427; export from Bayonne permitted, **11**: 627

assignats: proposed, **16**: 161, 302; value of, **16**: 420; **17**: 652; proposal to pay public debt with, **17**: 523-4; burning of, **20**: 168

assize, courts of. *See* Virginia: District Courts

Associated Company of Irish Merchants, **8**: 672; **9**: 27

Association: nonimportation resolutions of 1769, **1**: 27; nonimportation resolutions of 1770, **1**: 43-8, 71; signed by members of Va. HB against Boston Port Act, **1**: 107; and Va. Convention of 1774, **1**: 137-44; of Congress, **1**: 149-54; and Bermuda, **1**: 239-40; violation by Upshur, **1**: 653

assumption bill: approved by Washington, **16**: 245n; discussed in Congress, **17**: 162; editorial account of, **17**: 163-71, 182-3; and connection with residence bill, **17**: 163-72, 182-3, 205-8, 217n, 390-1, 459; votes for, **17**: 355n; opposed by Va. HD, **17**: 459

Ast, William Frederick: letters to, **12**: 5, 45-6, 575, 625; **13**: 256-7; **14**: 279; letters from, **12**: 371-2; bill received by TJ, **11**: 669; presents drafts to Grand, **12**: 10; clerical affairs of, **12**: 378, 475, 497, 573; letters from missing, **12**: 658; **14**: 339; salary arrears of, **12**: 674; payment to, **13**: 168, 170, 256-7; **14**: 279; delivers Barclay's papers and books, **13**: 307, 574; letter to cited, **15**: 371n

Astrea (ship): Purdie's service on, **18**: 318, 338

Astrée, L' (French frigate), **5**: 433

Astrolabe (ship): and scientific expedition, **8**: 587

astronomical instruments: for surveying Va.-Pa. boundary, **6**: 7; timekeepers, **10**: 73; **11**: 162

astronomical observations: to determine Va.-Pa. boundary line, **5**: 304, 478, 650; **6**: 76; **8**: 117

astronomy: information about found in almanacs, **8**: 298-9; comments on by the Rev. James Madison, **9**: 355-6; study recommended by TJ, **10**: 306; books on, **13**: 638; Cassini sends observations to Rittenhouse, **14**: 51

Asturias, Prince of. *See* Charles VI

asylum, right of: and Brazil, **9**: 64

Atkins, Capt. Joseph (master of the *Esperance*), **10**: 181

Atkins, Thomas: and bill establishing ferries, **2**: 460

Atkinson, Roger: signs nonimportation resolutions (1770), **1**: 47; marriage of, **14**: 530

Atkyns, James Tracy: *Reports of Cases* cited, **11**: 548; **16**: 481; **19**: 542-3

atlas, American: lent to TJ, **4**: 586

atmosphere: density of, **9**: 356; humidity of, in Europe and America, **13**: 396, 397

attachments, legal: Va. bill for granting, **2**: 633-4

attainder, bills of. *See* bills of attainder

Attakullaculla (Little Carpenter, Cherokee Chief): represents tribe at parley with Henderson & Company, **2**: 68, 71, 73-4; mediates with northern Indi-

ans, **2**: 75; and Cherokee land claims, **2**: 77-81; signs deeds of sale, **2**: 89, 108; and Cherokee archives, **6**: 141n

Attorney General, U.S., The. *See* Randolph, Edmund

attorney general, Va.: provisions in TJ's drafts of Va. Constitution, **1**: 360. *See also* Randolph, John

attorneys general, deputy, Va.: form of commission, **3**: 21

attorneys: regulation of practice, **2**: 235; Va. bill for licensing, **2**: 587-9; appointed by court to act for poor, **2**: 600

Aubagne, France: TJ describes, **11**: 429

Aubenton. *See* Daubenton, Louis Jean Marie

Aube river, France, **11**: 447

Aubert, C.: chargé d'affaires of Netherlands in Spain, **13**: 239n

Auberteuil. *See* Hilliard d'Auberteuil, Michel René

Aubery, M. d': chargé d'affaires of France at Warsaw, **14**: 604n

Aubuchon (Aubuniere), Gabriel: memorial to Arthur St. Clair, **18**: 210-1

Auckler, G. A.: letter to, **11**: 559; letter from, **11**: 360; introduction by TJ, **12**: 49

auction sales: Va. bill to prevent, **2**: 561-6; of debtors' chattels, **2**: 643-4

Audibert, Dominique: letter to, **14**: 279-80; letters from, **14**: 354-5, 507-9; TJ's introduction to, **11**: 261; vineyard of, **11**: 445; Frontignan wine produced by, **11**: 621; potash in soap manufacture, **14**: 279-80, 354-5, 508-9; mentioned, **11**: 463n

Audibert-Caille, Steffano di: influence with Emperor of Morocco, **8**: 21

Auditors, Virginia Board of. *See* Virginia: Board of Auditors

auditors of public accounts: bill to establish, in Va., **1**: 654-5

Auger (rebel leader in Saint-Domingue), **18**: 504

August Damian Philipp Karl, Baron von Limburg-Stirum, Archbishop of Speyer: agitates imperial Diet, **17**: 312; conflicts with National Assembly, **19**: 534

Augusta, Ga.: captured by Americans, **4**: 68; in British hands, **5**: 552; Greene on way to, **6**: 52; Col. Elijah Clarke at, **6**: 80; treaty with Cherokees at, **6**:

Baffin Bay: proposed voyage to, **18**: 492-3

Bagnols, France: TJ describes, **11**: 423

Bagwell, Charles: letter from, **5**: 651

Bahama Channel: instability in, **17**: 542

Bahama islands: reduction of, **10**: 559; **12**: 100; expedition against, **11**: 301n

Baiban, John, **3**: 542n

bail: Va. bill on, **2**: 481; in common law courts, **2**: 601-3; in criminal cases, **2**: 613

Bailey, Francis: *Pocket Almanac for 1785*, **6**: 594n; *Freeman's Journal*, **6**: 652n; sells subscriptions to *National Gazette*, **20**: 755

Bailey, James: signs petition, **6**: 290

Bailey, John: signs petition, **1**: 588; **6**: 294; in Albemarle co. militia, **1**: 666; signs Va. oath of allegiance, **2**: 129

Bailey, Robertson: signs petition, **6**: 290

Bailey, Thomas: signs nonimportation resolutions, **1**: 30, 46; mentioned, **5**: 22, 106n

Bailli de Suffren (ship): arrives in France, **11**: 110, 138n

Baillie, Mr. (nephew of William Hunter): introduced to TJ, **13**: 112

Bailly, Jean Sylvain: *Rapport . . . du projet d'un nouvel Hôtel-Dieu*, **11**: 42; *Histoire de l'astronomie*, **13**: 638; presents cockade to Louis XVI, **15**: xxxiv, 289; confirmed as Prévôt des Marchands, **15**: 289; conspiracy to assassinate, **16**: 50, 106, 134; in *Journée des dupes*, **16**: 107; mentioned, **15**: 554; **17**: 28

Baily (Bayley), Dr.: Angelica Church sends tea by, **14**: 515, 554; passport issued by TJ, **15**: 486

Baine, Alexander: signs nonimportation resolutions (1770), **1**: 46

Baird, James: signs nonimportation resolutions (1770), **1**: 47; and boundary of Rockingham co., Va., **2**: 113

Baird, John: account of seizure of goods by British, **5**: 660-1; guard for, **6**: 14n

Baker, Benjamin: signs nonimportation resolutions (1770), **1**: 46; David Ross comments on, **6**: 14n

Baker, Elijah: in Albemarle co. militia, **1**: 666

Baker, Evan: letter to, **3**: 567; supplies for militia, **3**: 421, 448, 562, 572, 655n, 667; **4**: 34, 120; **5**: 359; as commissary and quartermaster for Washington co., **3**: 613

Baker, Sir George: attends George III, **14**: 50

Baker, James: signs nonimportation resolutions (1770), **1**: 47

Baker, Jerman: letter to, **15**: 670-1; signs nonimportation resolutions (1770), **1**: 46; supports American state papers series, **1**: 145; on committee for land office bill, **2**: 136n; on committee reviewing sale of property of enemy aliens, **2**: 283n; on committee to prepare bill on religious freedom, **2**: 547n; on committee to examine Short's qualifications, **6**: 122n; in Wayles estate debt, **15**: 648, 649n, 670-1

Baker, Richard: signs nonimportation resolutions, **1**: 30, 46; in Albemarle co. militia, **1**: 666, 667

Baker, Samuel: signs nonimportation resolutions (1769), **1**: 31

Baker, William: as reputed murderer of LeBrun, **10**: 470n

Baker & Thompson, **6**: 198

balance of power in Europe, **3**: 118; **10**: 650

balance of trade: Conn., **7**: 337; N.H., **7**: 345; effect of doctrine on Britain, **8**: 216; in Britain's favor, **8**: 341

Balbastre, Claude Louis, **11**: 203

Baldwin, Mr.: inn of rated by TJ, **20**: 471

Baldwin, Abraham: letters to, **12**: 49, 572-3; letters from, **13**: 96-7; **14**: 285; member of Constitutional Convention, **11**: 401; letter from, to Fanning, cited, **13**: 96, 430; **18**: 496; letter from cited, **14**: 533n; reports on executive compensation, **15**: 263n; congressman from Ga., **17**: 665; and Cherokee Indians, **17**: 665; on trade with Britain, **18**: 522-3, 525; recommended as commissioner of Federal District, **19**: 59; recommends Chipman, **19**: 378

Baldwin, George (British consul at Cairo): Ledyard's death described by, **15**: 198

Baldwin's Regiment, **5**: 576

Balfour, James: signs nonimportation resolutions (1770), **1**: 46; mentioned, **1**: 39

Balfour, Col. Nesbitt: letter to, from Cornwallis, intercepted, **3**: 664; **4**: 16

Balieu, Peter: signs Va. oath of allegiance, **2**: 129

Ball, Gen.: slaves of and lead mines, **5**: 265

Ball, Col. Burgess: mentioned, **3**: 652; **4**: 278

Ball, George: signs nonimportation resolutions (1769), **1**: 30

Ball, James: letter from, **5**: 424-5; desires flag of truce, **5**: 445

Ball, James (d. 1781): as commissioner of provision law, **4**: 89, 351; death of, **5**: 196, 197; mentioned, **5**: 643

Ball, John: signs nonimportation resolutions (1770), **1**: 47; petition to Va. GA, **5**: 57n

Ball, Moses: signs nonimportation resolutions (1770), **1**: 47

Ball, Moses, Jr.: signs nonimportation resolutions (1770), **1**: 47

Ball, Spencer M.: signs nonimportation resolutions (1770), **1**: 46

Ball, William: signs petition, **6**: 290

Ball, Williamson: votes for bill for religious freedom, **2**: 549n

Ballantine, John: bad management of cannon foundry, **1**: 591

Ballard, Byram, **4**: 15

Ballard, Francis: taken prisoner, **5**: 294n

Ballard, Lieut. William: in Albemarle co. militia, **1**: 668n; signs Va. oath of allegiance, **2**: 130; in Va. artillery regiment, **4**: 542

Ballards creek, **3**: 239

ballarmonic: Hopkinson's invention, **11**: 562

ballast: Va. bill for unlading, **2**: 467-8

ballast masters: fees of, **2**: 433; bill on, **2**: 467

Ballendine, John: letter from, **5**: 19-20; and dealings with Va. GA, **3**: 43-4, 126-30; rights to canal, **3**: 135-6; lent money by state, **3**: 138-9; payment of damages to, **3**: 144-5; iron purchased from, **3**: 189; land appropriated for magazine and laboratory, **3**: 535; house burned by British, **4**: 263

Ballendine, William: signs nonimportation resolutions (1770), **1**: 47

balloons: ascensions, **6**: 542; **7**: xxvii, 57, 132 (illus.), 602, 603, 604, 608; **8**: 64, 110, 233, 237, 241, 245, 342; ascension planned by the Rev. James Madison, **7**: 133; experiments with, **7**: 134-6, 246, 280, 504, 514, 518; **8**: 551, 553, 559, 576, 599; **9**: 356, 379; **15**: 610-1; history of, **7**: 538; and screw propulsion, **7**: 643; **8**: 576; treatise on, **8**: 640

Ballow, Charles (TJ's steward), **15**: 625, 628; **16**: 210

Ball's landing: ferry at, **2**: 456

Ballston Spa (Balltown), N.Y.: mineral springs of visited by Stiles, **10**: 585

Balsamum canadense: sent to Deville, **16**: 306, 445; **17**: 506; Arnoux's memorandum on, **20**: 429n

Baltic countries: U.S. import of hemp and sailcloth, **9**: 20

Baltic Sea: control of entrance to, **7**: 405; Swedish naval action against Russians, **13**: 483, 489, 491, 496, 503, 579; **15**: 357, 513n; **17**: 209, 313-4

Baltimore, Cecilius, second Lord: charter, **1**: 595; **7**: 36

Baltimore, Charles, third Lord: boundary agreement with William Penn, **1**: 463

Baltimore, George Calvert, first Lord: Maryland granted to, **1**: 136; **6**: 657

Baltimore, Md.: merchants support war effort in Chesapeake, **3**: 565; reported British objective, **4**: 90, 92; agreement of Va.-Pa. boundary commissioners at, **5**: 650; TJ's visit to, **6**: 211n; as permanent seat for Continental Congress, **6**: 357; rumors of British invasion of Ireland in, **6**: 419; trade at, **7**: 50; **19**: 131; stage line in, **7**: 280; commercial rivalry with Va., **7**: 380; immigrants, **10**: 13; attitude toward Constitution, **12**: 281; proposed seat of U.S. government, **13**: 498, 591, 612n, 620, 625; **16**: 487-95, 577; **17**: 167, 168, 176; **19**: 17, 20-1; and the fisheries, **19**: 192; postal service to, **20**: 666

Baly, John: death of, **5**: 96

Balyal, Mr. *See* Belew, Peter

bamboo: introduction in America suggested, **17**: 515

Banana Islands: Mr. Cleveland at, **17**: 4-5

Bancroft, Edward: letters to, **9**: 295-6, 299-300; **11**: 351; **13**: 543-5; **14**: 492-4, 602-3, 605-6, 657-8, 692; **15**: 8-9, 39, 70, 160-1, 183, 270-1, 332-3, 476; letters from, **8**: 522; **9**: 40-1, 280-1; **11**: 242; **13**: 285-6, 606-8; **14**: 578-80, 629-32; **15**: 3-4, 59-60, 73-4, 200-1, 292, 352-3; notice of *A Summary View* in *Monthly Review*, **1**: 676; suggested as emissary to Barbary States, **8**: 347, 400, 544; arrives in London, **8**: 400; assists J. P. Jones, **8**: 597, 603; **9**: 10-1; **10**: 209; **13**: 186; **14**: 606, 630, 692; as British spy, **9**: 41n; letter from cited, **9**: 274; aids John Paradise, **9**: 454, 517; **10**: 69, 75, 120-1, 174, 256; **13**: 472-3, 522, 537, 543-5, 599, 602-3, 606-7; **14**: 455, 461, 629-30; **15**: 59-60, 73-4;

8; Hamilton proposes, **18**: 232, 534n; **19**: 38-40; TJ's views on, **19**: 275-82; **20**: 297-8; criticized by Madison, **20**: 299; subscriptions to, **20**: 602-3, 616-7, 670, 690, 717; directors of, **20**: 617; and land as security for loans, **20**: 705

bankers, Dutch: avarice of, **12**: 581-2; handling of American loan, **12**: 698

bank notes, American: replacement of gold by, **7**: 190; discount in France, **12**: 52-3, 61

bank notes, private: Va. bill to prevent circulation of, **2**: 435

Bank of England: and discount rates, **1**: 93; **14**: 568

Bank of North America: aid to public financing, **7**: 214; abolition of, **7**: 20; **8**: 99, 248, 562, 581, 672; **9**: 321; **10**: 314; Hogendorp desires information on, **10**: 191; becomes private institution, **10**: 299

Bank of St. Charles: proceedings of (1784), **8**: 665; mentioned, **13**: 93

bankruptcy: in Philadelphia, **7**: 393; in U.S., **8**: 632-3; laws on, **12**: 513, 523; Va. bill on, **12**: 602; **15**: 264n; in London, **13**: 209, 210n; predicted after declaration of war, **13**: 379; in France, **13**: 500, 530, 564; **15**: 455-6, 459

banks: TJ recommends establishing in Europe, **2**: 224; as rival national bank, **7**: 20; and loan to Continental Congress, **7**: 53, 85; in Spain, **8**: 252

Banks, Alexander: signs nonimportation resolutions (1770), **1**: 46

Banks, Henry: letter from, to John Jay, **10**: 183; letters from, to Richard Claiborne, **11**: 412-3; mentioned, **12**: 602; **14**: 360

Banks, John, **5**: 294n

Banks, Sir Joseph: and Ledyard, **10**: 548; **14**: 455, 568; **15**: 128n, 137, 193-4, 274; letter from cited, **12**: 374; as inspector of wheat for insect control, **13**: 663; **14**: 567; and Hessian fly, **14**: 567; **20**: 445-6; investigates rice culture, **14**: 673, 674, 707-8; **16**: 274; **17**: 565; letters from, to Paine, quoted, **15**: 193-4, 197-8; praises Paine's bridge, **15**: 193-4; letter to, from Beaufoy, on death of Ledyard, **15**: 198; London residence of, **15**: 449; suggests importation of Chinese bamboo, **17**: 515; on quality of Shetland

wool, **18**: 367n; mentioned, **15**: 147n, 152, 182; **16**: 580n

Bankson, Benjamin (Dept. of State clerk), **17**: 356n-8n, 361, 381

Bankson, Benjamin, Jr., **6**: 580

bank stock: rise of in England, **12**: 692

Banneker, Benjamin: participates in laying out national capital, **19**: 41n-3n

Bannel, William: signs petition, **1**: 588

Banton, Jesse: signs petition, **1**: 588

Baptiste, M. (express rider), **3**: 263

Baptiste, Jean, **11**: 463n

Baptists: petition against Acts of Toleration, **1**: 525n; declaration of Virginia Association of, **1**: 660-1; military service of, **1**: 662; and education in Va., **2**: 247; in Ky., **8**: 125

Barail, Mme Frimont de. *See* Frimont de Barail

Barbados: rumors of French at, **3**: 75, 411; taken by Marquis de Bouillé, **6**: 110; ports of, **7**: 348

Barbançon, M.: orders plants and seeds, **17**: 558

Barbary States: privateering, **7**: 231-2, 469n, 574, 577-8, 629, 634, 636, 639, 640, 644, 649; **8**: 43, 46-7, 69, 81, 119, 254-5, 294, 309, 440, 512, 622; **9**: 91-2, 319n, 602, 609, 628; **10**: 84, 173, 207, 403; **15**: 22; **18**: 369-70; protection of U.S. citizens from, **7**: 471; tribute demands, **7**: 496; **8**: 19-21, 37, 38n, 46-7, 62, 65-6, 69, 70-2, 80-2, 120, 150, 321, 399, 401, 418-9, 460, 473-4, 614, 655, 664; **9**: 168, 285-8, 358-9, 364-5, 448, 465, 469, 473, 500, 546, 568, 611, 649; **10**: 123, 177, 386, 560n-1n; **11**: 101; **12**: 448; TJ recommends war against, **7**: 511-2, 571, 639; **9**: 525, 568; **10**: 123-4, 176-7; information on sought from Carmichael, **7**: 630; relations with Christian powers, **8**: 46, 150; U.S. treaty with, **8**: 47, 246, 266, 347-54, 400, 521-2, 542, 614, 624; U.S. relations with, **8**: 61-2, 77, 95, 134, 137, 138, 140, 145, 152, 154, 169, 170, 235, 246, 247-8, 261, 317, 320-2, 376, 465, 512, 526, 555, 606-7, 626, 631, 665; **9**: 13-4, 176, 186, 187, 295, 329, 468, 504, 590, 594, 651; **10**: 137, 178, 222, 509-10; **11**: 78, 187, 329, 442, 466, 500; **15**: 46; **18**: 378-81, 384-7, 390-8, 406-11; Congress consulted on, **8**: 88; stimulation of privateering by foreign govern-

Barbary States (*cont.*)
  ments, **8**: 196, 572; truce with Spain rumored, **8**: 253; U.S. emissary to, **8**: 394, 400, 401, 425, 444, 465, 604, 605; papers relating to, **8**: 603; mission of Barclay and Lamb to, **8**: 610-24, 657-8, 670; **10**: 68; navy of, **8**: 621; ports, **8**: 621; U.S. trade with, **8**: 621; **10**: 142; languages, **8**: 622; relations with France, **8**: 626, 631; TJ fears capture of *Polly* by, **9**: 159; relations with Spain, **9**: 245; **10**: 535-6; proposed blockade of, **9**: 318-20, 500; **18**: 380, 408-9, 414; relations with Turks, **9**: 567-8, 595, 611; cost of war with, **9**: 611; American captives in, **9**: 614-22; **12**: 550; concert of powers proposed against, **10**: 88, 124, 224, 486, 559, 560-70; **11**: 22; **12**: 177n; Adams opposes war against, **10**: 177; Carmichael's views on, **10**: 178; Jay's views on, **10**: 598; alliance with Portugal against, **10**: 607; TJ opposes tribute to, **10**: 560n-1n; delay of Congress in deciding on negotiations, **11**: 130; editorial notes on, **18**: 369-416; "A Proposal to Use Force against the Barbary States," **18**: 416-22; "Report on American Trade in the Mediterranean," **18**: 423-30
Barbauld, Anna Laetitia Aikin: poetry of praised, **8**: 522, 523
Barbauld, Rochemont: introduction to TJ, **8**: 522, 523
Barbé de Marbois, François: letters to, **5**: 58-9; **6**: 141-2, 171-2, 373-4; **7**: 645; **12**: 31; letters from, **6**: 149-50, 177-8, 535; **7**: 205, 568-9; and clothing drive for Continental troops, **3**: 442n; interest of in Va., **4**: 166-7; **6**: 171-2, 177-8, 203, 339, 467; **7**: 381; **8**: 16; **11**: 558; and American Philosophical Society, **4**: 545; and Adams' Feb. 1783 letter to Congress, **6**: 268; relays information on Turkish-Russian relations, **7**: 5; as chargé d'affaires, **7**: 115, 120, 139; **8**: 523; borrows books from TJ, **7**: 240n-1n; marries, **7**: 308n; transcribes Indian treaty talks, **7**: 447n; consults TJ on Beaumarchais claims, **7**: 553; translates Chastellux' *Travels in North America*, **7**: 584; quoted on extradition, **7**: 599n; letters from quoted, **8**: 33n, 360n-1n; judges harpsichord experiment, **8**: 50; antagonism toward R. Morris, **8**: 99; letter

to, from Vergennes, cited, **8**: 139n; and Ramsay's history of S.C., **8**: 210, 359; promoted to intendancy of Saint-Domingue, **8**: 228; discusses Jay's objections to consulate convention, **8**: 384n; receives Mme Grégoire's land claim, **10**: 239; letter from cited, **12**: 623; Nourse's debt to, **14**: 37; criticizes Chilleau's action in Saint-Domingue, **15**: 456; mentioned, **4**: 168; **6**: 142, 143, 163, 165, 170n, 176, 542, 556; **7**: 114, 134, 362, 438, 439, 440, 449n, 580, 581, 585, 628; **8**: 36, 148, 293, 294, 472; **14**: 86, 284, 285, 341; **16**: 201. *See also* Longchamps, Charles Julien
Barbé de Marbois, Pierre François, fils: as vice consul in Philadelphia, **14**: 65n, 66n; information on Saint-Domingue, **20**: 240
Barbee, Thomas: expedition against Indians, **20**: 481
Barber, Mr.: in Nathaniel Cutting's diary, **15**: 490, 491, 493-5
Barber, Col. Francis: warrant drawn up by, **19**: 385, 388
Barber, Thomas: signs nonimportation resolutions (1770), **1**: 46
Barbeyrac, Jean: translates work by Bynkershoek, **6**: 550; cited by Hamilton, **17**: 144
Barbour (Barber), Col. James: letter to, **5**: 353; letters from, **5**: 251-2, 318, 587-8; appointed commissioner for Ky., **3**: 17; mentioned, **5**: 123, 278, 407
Barbour, Thomas: signs nonimportation resolutions (1769), **1**: 30
Barboutin, Capitaine: executor for Pelcerf estate, **10**: 92, 127
Barcia Carballido y Zuñiga, Andrés González de: *Ensayo cronologico para la historia general de la Florida*, **11**: 554, 668
Barclay, Francis, **1**: 455n
Barclay, James: passport issued by TJ, **15**: 484
Barclay, John: letter to, **20**: 414
Barclay, Mary (Mrs. Thomas Barclay): letters to, **10**: 126-7, 384; **11**: 108; **12**: 308, 379; **13**: 435, 478-9; letters from, **11**: 119; **12**: 150, 343, 507; **13**: 474; payment of account to, **7**: 547; proposes assignment of property, **11**: 535; TJ promises to visit, **11**: 670; applies to TJ for funds, **12**: 507; returns to

America, **13**: 253, 416, 435, 474, 478-9, 485, 492-3, 526; letters sent by, **13**: 467, 496, 499, 529, 564; Mlle Langat complains about, **14**: 479; mentioned, **7**: 574; **9**: 278, 327; **10**: 254, 282, 313, 396, 638; **11**: 21, 478, 560, 625, 669; **14**: 180, 274, 444
Barclay, Robert: aids Rumsey, **15**: 404
Barclay, Thomas: letters to, **7**: 500, 574; **8**: 73, 552; **10**: 313-5, 396, 637-8; **11**: 163-4, 347-8, 477-9, 544-5, 669-71; **12**: 130-1; **13**: 492-3; **19**: 247-8; letters from, **7**: 533-4, 579; **9**: 174-5, 209-10, 298, 327, 348-9, 352-3, 365-6, 376-7, 383-4, 390-3, 566-7, 580-1, 626, 629; **10**: 71-2, 141-2, 181, 220, 334-48, 357-62, 389-92, 403-4, 418-9, 509-11, 535-6, 573; **11**: 20-1, 21-2, 132-3, 133-5, 466-7, 467, 504-6, 534-8, 552, 560-1, 582-4, 584-5, 593-4, 625-7, 643-4, 662; **12**: 385; **13**: 253-4; **16**: 471-2; **19**: 535; **20**: 239; settles claims against U.S., **6**: 398; report of letters of, **6**: 400n; agent at Nantes, **6**: 421; negotiates naval prizes, **7**: 270; investigates *L'Amiable Elizabeth* case, **7**: 498; and appointment of consuls, **7**: 510; **10**: 200; **12**: 70, 122, 462; **14**: 59-60, 62n; letters from cited, **7**: 576; **8**: 253, 566; **9**: 359, 407, 515, 590, 645; **10**: 92, 126, 241, 266, 291, 294, 302, 315, 362, 393, 472, 479, 606, 618; **11**: 30, 108, 110, 118, 184, 236; **13**: 435; and TJ's china, **8**: 8, 60; letter to, from Adams, quoted, **8**: 56n; purchases arms for Va., **8**: 67, 68, 213, 507; **9**: 213, 381, 540-1, 581; **10**: 290-1, 304, 309-10, 331, 497; arrives at Paris, **8**: 163; and bust of Lafayette, **8**: 214-5, 422; criticizes TJ's estimate of tobacco duties, **8**: 390n-1n; aids Contée in sale of tobacco, **8**: 394; mission to Barbary States proposed, **8**: 394, 400, 424, 444, 473-4 **10**: 349; consulted on *Alliance* claims, **8**: 452-3; **10**: 192; appointed consul general in France, **8**: 466; **12**: 155, 244; case of Lister Asquith, **8**: 493-6, 628; aids crew of *William and Catherine*, **8**: 518; mission to Morocco, **8**: 521-2, 526, 542, 543, 572, 604, 605, 607, 610-24, 626, 631; **9**: 14, 91, 117, 152, 187, 210, 214, 234, 298, 378, 539, 546-7, 564, 621, 626, 629, 666; **10**: 71, 76, 84, 99, 138, 141, 178, 181, 207, 220, 265, 300, 313, 329, 334-

48, 420, 425, 649; **11**: 66, 77, 79, 133, 582-5, 669; **18**: 389, 401; **20**: 397-401, 406; suggests clerk for Lamb, **8**: 544; expense account, **8**: 572, 573; **9**: 210; letter of credit, **8**: 622-3; recommended to Carmichael, **8**: 623; Spanish passport asked for, **8**: 657-8, 670; draws bills, **8**: 658; French passport, **8**: 680; cipher, **9**: 13, 250; **12**: 175n-6n, 238, 424; **13**: 91, 142, 230, 398; **16**: 320; aids the Fitzhughs, **9**: 25, 52; settles Adams' account with Bondfield, **9**: 90, 116; and Beaumarchais claims, **9**: 91, 137-8, 234; offers to bring Mary Jefferson to France, **9**: 92; and Carmichael's financial affairs, **9**: 105; papers and books of, **9**: 128; **13**: 307, 394, 573-5, 604n, 632, 637, 661; **14**: 5, 40, 52, 55, 581; **15**: 46; letters carried by, **9**: 276; **20**: 622, 624; appoints Burrill Carnes American agent, **9**: 303; fails to pay bill, **9**: 308-10; and tobacco contract, **9**: 390-3; letter from sent to Adams, **9**: 506; proposes mission to Turkey, **9**: 566; letters from quoted, **9**: 581n; **16**: 320n; appointment of American agents, **9**: 625; **10**: 196; appoints vice consuls, **9**: 627-8; departs from Cadiz, **9**: 648; ships books, **9**: 667; **10**: 285, 471; praised by Taher Fennish, **10**: 77; mission to Algiers, **10**: 84, 238-9, 242, 287, 302, 313, 349, 392, 396, 403, 405, 428; **18**: 384; and prize money due American seamen, **10**: 88; TJ's debt to, **10**: 127; debt to Veuve Samuel Joly l'aîné et fils, **10**: 163-4, 172; **11**: 495n; recommended by Carmichael for mission to other Barbary States, **10**: 180; and British-Moroccan affairs, **10**: 180; and account with Grand, **10**: 229; **11**: 475; Thévenard's esteem for, **10**: 254; sends Spanish books, **10**: 285; letters to cited, **10**: 427; **11**: 65, 125, 479; **16**: 159n; arrives at Cadiz, **10**: 480, 481; departs for America, **10**: 510; **11**: 499n-500n, 611, 625, 671; **12**: 55, 175; converses with Floridablanca, **10**: 537; recommended by Adams to exchange Moroccan treaty, **10**: 557; and Lamb's accounts, **10**: 618, 633; fails to settle U.S. accounts with Delap, **11**: 22-3; and Schweighauser claim, **11**: 29; recommendations to Congress, **11**: 78; settles Franks' account, **11**: 108; Led-

Barclay, Thomas (*cont.*)
yard's friendship for, **11**: 216; disbursements for Mercier, **11**: 347; financial difficulties of, **11**: 365, 366, 377, 483, 491-500n, 504, 534-8, 606, 626-7; **12**: 71, 114, 150, 168, 565-6, 618; **13**: 95; **15**: 45, 109, 323-4, 409; **17**: 480; **18**: 584; **20**: 239; imprisoned for debt at Bordeaux, **11**: 366-7, 491-2, 493n, 506, 508, 611; **13**: 479n, 485n; **14**: 68; **16**: 233; Lamb regrets failure to meet, **11**: 369; leaves Bordeaux, **11**: 395, 537n, 538, 552; **16**: 233; illness of, **11**: 466; accusations against, **11**: 477-8; TJ's views on, **11**: 483, 492, 493n, 495n, 606, 671; **20**: 251; biographical note on, **11**: 493n-500n; and Congress' failure to pay salary, **11**: 494n; letters of protection for, **11**: 494n; account with Va., **11**: 560, 626; arrêt concerning, **11**: 596; account against U.S., **11**: 609; settles TJ's account, **11**: 625; **13**: 161-2; bill on Grand for Va. protested, **11**: 673; bills in favor of Ast, **12**: 5; settles account of Schweighauser & Dobrée, **12**: 12; negotiates on naval prizes, **12**: 336; arrives at New York, **12**: 378; account books, **12**: 395; arrives at Philadelphia, **12**: 437; settles accounts, **12**: 497; **13**: 161; removes consular papers to Paris, **12**: 575; safe conduct of requested, **12**: 587; memoir of, on tobacco trade, **13**: 89-90; pays Ast as secretary, **13**: 256-7; departs for Philadelphia, **13**: 401; objects to forbidding consuls to engage in trade, **14**: 69-70; Mlle Langat complains against, **14**: 479, 510; seeks position for negotiating loans, **16**: 472; recommended by Adams as consul, **16**: 523; **17**: 254n; advice of on diplomatic establishment, **17**: 220, 225-6, 228n; views on Lisbon, **19**: 247-8; appointed consul to Great Britain, **19**: 625; **20**: 87, 93; instructions from TJ, **20**: 397-400; admission of French jurisdiction, **20**: 689; mentioned, **7**: 226, 439, 521, 575, 587; **8**: 22, 24n, 54, 242n, 244, 251, 327, 547, 549, 564, 589, 594, 676; **9**: 54, 107, 154, 243, 287, 293, 385, 572, 649, 658; **10**: 82, 87, 229, 254, 282, 295, 328, 352, 413, 549, 634; **11**: 101, 117, 136, 141, 164, 358, 510, 524, 639; **12**: 8, 10, 28, 52, 118, 224, 372, 373, 534n, 636, 691;

13: 278, 416, 478, 479, 648n; **14**: 283, 537, 578; **15**: 61n-2n, 203, 303, 432, 628; **16**: 102, 473n; **17**: 577
Bard, M., **12**: 82
Barentin, Charles Louis François de Paule: as keeper of seals, **13**: 621, 633, 634; **15**: 279; in ministry, **15**: 280, 286, 299; released from prosecution, **16**: 124
Baretti, Giuseppe Marc Antonio: and English-Spanish dictionary, **8**: 408, 554; **10**: 72; **14**: 663; death of, **15**: 130
barges, armed: for western troops, **4**: 235; **6**: 46
Barham, John. *See* Bartram, John
Bariatinski, Prince Ivan Sergeevich: letter to, from American Commissioners, **7**: 424n
bar iron: purchase, **5**: 281
bark: for tanning, **5**: 296; as medicine, **6**: 26
Barker, Josiah: and the whale fisheries, **19**: 147
Barker's mill: Rumsey's improvement on, **15**: 504-5, 522; **16**: 591; **17**: 516; description of, **18**: 149n
Barksdale (Barksdill), Capt., **5**: 571
Barksdale, Hickerson: and bill establishing ferries, **2**: 460; votes for bill for religious freedom, **2**: 549n
Barksdale, Samuel: in Albemarle co. militia, **1**: 665
Barksdale, William: quarters British prisoners, **2**: 31; signs Va. oath of allegiance, **2**: 128
barley: Va. bill prohibiting exportation of, **2**: 348; taxes payable in, **3**: 250
Barley, Richard, **4**: 322
Barlow, James: in Albemarle co. militia, **1**: 664
Barlow, Joel: letter from, **11**: 473; *Vision of Columbus*, **11**: 473; **13**: 118, 157n, 344, 572; introduced to TJ, **13**: 118, 156; visits Europe, **13**: 157n, 288, 315, 360, 551; introduced to Price by TJ, **13**: 344; advises on Greene's education, **13**: 348; health of, **13**: 434; delivers books and catalogue for Trumbull, **13**: 564; promotes Scioto Company and Muskingum lands, **13**: 609, 612n-3n; **16**: 159; **18**: 160-2, 173-6, 364-5, 530; **19**: 593-5; **20**: 430-1; Price unable to entertain, **14**: 38; poem of in *Columbian Magazine*, **14**: 51; Paradise's creditor, **15**: 73,

200; signs Fourth of July tribute to TJ, **15**: 240, 241n; passport issued by TJ, **15**: 486; signs Bastille Day address, **17**: 214n; mentioned, **13**: 244; **14**: 532n; **15**: 40, 173

Barlow, Ruth Baldwin (Mrs. Joel Barlow): arrives in London, **17**: 240-1

Barlow, Thomas: Albemarle co. militia, **1**: 668n

Barlowe, Capt. Arthur: commands Sir Walter Raleigh's ship, **1**: 279

Barnard, Capt. Tristam: master of *Mary*, **18**: 326-7

Barnave, Antoine Pierre Joseph Marie: discusses royal veto, **15**: 355n; influence in National Assembly, **15**: 559; **17**: 504; **19**: 634; opposes Necker, **15**: 567; opposes power of king to make war, **16**: 437, 438; opposes Lafayette, **16**: 474, 508n; **20**: 350-1; and French tobacco cultivation, **18**: 76; and French colonial policy, **19**: 636; represents French commercial interests, **20**: 240

Barnes, John: signs deposition, **11**: 360n; letter from quoted, **18**: 685n

Barnes, Joseph: letter from, **16**: 590-1; letter from quoted, **16**: 591n; contributes to *National Gazette*, **20**: 733-4

Barnes, Joshua: edits Euripedes, **13**: 240

Barnet, Commodore Curtis: Le Poivre's papers held by descendant of, **14**: 708

Barnet, Ens. William, **4**: 531

Barnett, David: passport issued by TJ, **15**: 487

Barnett, Lieut. James, **3**: 8

Barney, Capt. Joshua: arrives in America, **6**: 238n, 253, 254; **7**: 12, 15; brings packages, **7**: 46, 58

Barnowl, Siberia: Ledyard describes, **11**: 637-8

Barnwell, Robert (congressman from S.C.), **18**: 52

barometer: stolen from Rev. Madison, **6**: 507; Madison lacks, **7**: 122; Short wants, **13**: 655

Barradelle, M.: letter to, **11**: 173

Barras-Saint-Laurent, Jacques Melchior, Comte de: portrait in Trumbull's "Surrender of Lord Cornwallis at Yorktown," **12**: xxxv, 60, 67 (illus.); letter from, to Washington, cited, **5**: 663n

barratry: and John Ferrière's case, **12**: 228, 249, 251; **14**: 82-3, 86; in American Revolution, **20**: 207n

Barraud, Daniel: signs nonimportation resolutions (1770), **1**: 46

Barré, Isaac: toasted by Virginians, **1**: 31

Barré, Jean Baptiste Henri: letters to, **8**: 176-7, 281-2, 573-4; **9**: 170; letters from, **8**: 168, 256-7, 529-30; **9**: 122; letter from cited, **9**: 173

Barrell, Colborn: letter from, **13**: 627

Barrell, Joseph: letter from, **12**: 379; letter from cited, **13**: 627; sends medals to TJ and Lafayette, **13**: 627n

Barrell, Joseph, Jr.: at Lisbon, **13**: 627

barrels: needed for cured fish, **5**: 234; export from S.C., **8**: 198

Barrère, J. Marc: lawyer for Derby and Nichols, **11**: 191

Barrère & Le Maire Cie.: affair of the *Nancy*, **11**: 69n

Barret, Capt. James (of Amherst co.), **4**: 531

Barret, Capt. Joseph (master of *L'Antoinette*), **18**: 584; **20**: 476

Barrett, Capt.: killed at Guilford Court House, **5**: 199

Barrett, Mr.: agrees on interest, **16**: 210

Barrett, James (of Albemarle co.): in Albemarle co. militia, **1**: 666

Barrett, Margaret Hunt (Mrs. Nathaniel Barrett): dines with TJ, **10**: 507; ill health of, **11**: 174, 276; death of, **11**: 476

Barrett, Nathaniel: letters to, **11**: 625; **12**: 214; **15**: 149; **17**: 285, 423-5; **20**: 401-2; letters from, **10**: 630; **11**: 578-9; **12**: 210, 401-2, 491-2; **13**: 523-4; **14**: 411, 618-9; **16**: 102; **17**: 285n, 583; **20**: 701; sale of whale oil in France, **8**: 662-3; **9**: 46n, 73-5, 89, 116-7, 127, 142, 183, 262-4; **10**: 349, 403; **12**: 388, 418-9, 604, 687; **14**: 234n; introduced to TJ, **8**: 670-1; letters sent by, **9**: 273; **17**: 656n; **20**: 672; and education of son, **10**: 436; proposals for American commerce, **10**: 541; **11**: 265; **12**: 300; letters from cited, **11**: 10; **18**: 330; presses Short to have interview with Colonia, **11**: 210, 234; TJ's opinion of, **11**: 247; and petition for making Honfleur a free port, **11**: 315; letters to cited, **11**: 511; **16**: 102n; knowledge of Col. Blackden, **11**: 519; **12**: 197; letter to, from Brailsford & Morris, quoted, **12**: 302n; letter from, to Lafayette, cited, **13**: 523, 524n; letter from, to Mme de Vaas, cited, **13**: 523, 524n; letter from,

sword presented to, **16**: 55n; Rittenhouse asks TJ's patronage for, **17**: 350n; letter from quoted, **17**: 350n; letter to cited, **17**: 357n; reads paper to American Philosophical Society, **19**: 584

Bartram, John: letter to, **9**: 228-30; letter from, **10**: 593; TJ recommends to Hopkinson, **9**: 149; letter from cited, **11**: 563

Bartram, John, Jr.: letter to, **9**: 228-30

Bartram, William: taken into partnership by brother, **9**: 230n; information on Hessian fly, **20**: 341

Barziza, Antonio, Count: letter to, **13**: 314; letters from, **12**: 670; **14**: 428; marries Miss Paradise, **11**: 242; and Paradise family, **13**: 522, 537; **14**: 298-300, 313, 384, 419, 611-2; **15**: 95; plans trip to Venice, **14**: 273, 312-3; characterized by wife, **14**: 298-9; mentioned, **11**: 501; **13**: 571n; **14**: 9, 43, 453

Barziza, Lucy Paradise, Countess: letters to, **13**: 314-5; **14**: 384; letters from, **12**: 669-70; **14**: 298-300, 611-2; children of, **12**: 669; **14**: 611; **16**: 294n, 446; title, **13**: 302; complains of parents, **14**: 298-300, 611-2; annuity promised by father, **14**: 300, 384; TJ offers to help, **14**: 384; Va. estate as inheritance, **14**: 419, 456; letter from cited, **14**: 694; mentioned, **11**: 501; **13**: 270, 571n; **14**: 273; **16**: 447n; **17**: 241. *See also* Paradise, Lucy

Bascomb, Benjamin: and bill establishing ferries, **2**: 457

Basel, Switzerland: American medals sent to, **16**: 67

Bason & Sawyer: bankruptcy of, **7**: 393

Basset, Mr. (of Lyons), **14**: 388

Basset (Bassett), Col. Burwell: signs nonimportation resolutions, **1**: 30, 46; signs Virginia Association, **1**: 108; mentioned, **6**: 206

Basseterre, Martinique, **11**: 336n

Bassett, Richard: attends Constitutional Convention, **11**: 400; senator from Del., **14**: 339, 394, 529, 560, 615; recommends Peery, **19**: 384

Bassline (Basseline), Capt.: influence in Algiers, **9**: 618, 621

Bassville, Nicolas Joseph Hugon de: letter to, **10**: 295-6; letters from, **10**: 269-70, 295; letter of recommendation to Dumas, **10**: 295-6, 297; visits Le Havre, **10**: 328; letters sent by, **10**: 404

Bastard, John Pollexfen: in House of Commons, **14**: 664

bastards: inheritance by, **2**: 393; **6**: 152-3; concealment of death by mother, **2**: 494n

Bastille: as political prison, **11**: 238, 334; Lafayette's imprisonment in rumored, **11**: 363; capture of commemorated, **16**: 506; key and picture of, sent by Lafayette to Washington, **16**: 531n-2n

Bastille Day (Fête de la Fédération): planned, **16**: 506, 572, 586; **17**: 17-8, 27-8, 208-9; Dumas considers honor for Lafayette, **17**: 209; described, **17**: 212-3, 214n; Saint-Domingue celebrates, **17**: 299-300

Batavia, Dutch East Indies: government changed, **20**: 478; prohibition of U.S. trade with, **20**: 629-32; letter to governor and council of, from Shaw, quoted, **20**: 631n-2n

Batavia (ship): carries tobacco to L'Orient, **9**: 391

Batbedat, Pierre & Léon: refusal of tobacco shipment, **10**: 327; mentioned, **10**: 204

Bates, Ezra: passport issued by TJ, **15**: 484

Bates, Thomas, **4**: 385

Bates, Thomas F., **4**: 21n

Bath, Va.: Convention troops at, **5**: 100

Bath, William Pulteney, Earl of: purchases land from Robert Morris, **20**: 127

Baton Rouge, La.: free port proposed at, **7**: 407

Battaile's Landing, Va.: ferry at, **2**: 456

Batte, Henry: and bill establishing ferries, **2**: 458

batteries: garrison duty for, **2**: 179-81

battery carriages, **4**: 609

Battery Creek, Va.: ferry at, **2**: 459

Battle of the Kegs. See Hopkinson, Francis

Battle of the Saints, **6**: 191

Battora, Mr., **3**: 57n, 69

Batty (Batie), Capt. George: deposition concerning the *Alert*, **5**: 589, 590

Baudeau, Abbé: article on tobacco for *Encyclopédie Méthodique*, **11**: 599

Baudin, François: letter to, **12**: 155; letters from, **12**: 70, 432-3; as consul, **17**: 248, 252, 254n, 573

Bauer, John Joshua: introduced to TJ, **11**: 145

Baugh, Peter: and bill establishing ferries, **2**: 458

Baugh, Richard: imports slaves, **15**: 654

Baum, Col. Friedrich: attacked by Gen. Stark, **2**: 29

Baumgarten, John: bookbinding of, **1**: 75

Bauque, Louis de, **9**: 607

Bauvais (Bovay), Rago, **5**: 387n

Baux, Jean & David: letter to, **14**: 397-8; letter from, **14**: 352

Bavaria: dispute over succession, **2**: 200, 209, 215; exchange for Austrian Netherlands rumored, **7**: 637, 641, 643, 649; **8**: 39, 42, 149, 226, 236, 237-8, 300, 321, 373, 399, 418, 553, 592; **9**: 151; **12**: 446; foreign relations, **8**: 302; desire of Joseph II to annex, **12**: 311

Bavaria, Karl Theodor, Elector of. See Karl Theodor

Baville. See Lamoignon de Baville, Nicolas

Bay, J. C. de, **8**: 328

Bayard, M.: letter from, **15**: 54-5; claim against Ga., **6**: 399-400; **7**: 271; claim against U.S., **6**: 399-400; **7**: 270-1

Bayard de La Vingtrie, M.: letter to, **12**: 586-7; letters from, **12**: 585-6; **15**: 514; *Notes on Virginia* sent to, **15**: 514

Bayard, Susannah: biographical note, **20**: 271n

Bayens, John: signs petition, **1**: 588

Bayens, Robert: signs petition, **1**: 588

Bayens, William: signs petition, **1**: 588

Báyer. See Pérez Báyer, Francisco

Bayley, Benjamin: packages committed to, **19**: 581

Baylor, Col. George: regiment under, **1**: 662; **3**: 154, 156, 204, 244, 248, 294, 365, 457n, 494; **5**: 187n; capture of, **2**: 216; **3**: 390; victory at Ninety-six, **4**: 322

Baylor, Lieut. John: letter from, **4**: 586; mentioned, **4**: 540

Baynham, John Jeffries Pratt, Viscount: termed "cypher" on British Board of Admiralty, **13**: 462

Baynton, Mr.: letter to cited, **20**: 294

Bay of Biscay: and the fisheries, **19**: 175n, 191

bayonet belts: needed, **3**: 496; **4**: 82, 402; supplied to Gen. Gates' army, **3**: 526, 529; purchased, **5**: 331

bayonets: patterns specified in contract with Penet, Windel & Co., **3**: 132; prices, **3**: 135; needed, **4**: 402; **5**: 68,

109; **11**: 83, 344, 673; **12**: 3; available, **5**: 621

Bayonne, France: American trade with, **8**: 223; **11**: 487; **15**: 169-70; U.S. agent at, **9**: 598, 625, 627; **10**: 196; **14**: 60; free port, **9**: 625; **20**: 632; merchants of, demand duty on imported fish, **10**: 126; and whale oil, **13**: 119, 433; **14**: 297-8; in Necker's speech to Estates General, **15**: 113

Baytop, James: recommended for commission as lieutenant colonel, **4**: 497

baywood: U.S. import of, **10**: 147

Bazen, Thomas: in Glaubeck case, **18**: 686n

Baziège, France: TJ describes, **11**: 449

Bazin, M., **10**: 203

Beache, Mme. See Bache, Mrs. Richard

beads: manufacture of, **9**: 361-2

Beal (Beall), Mr.: consults with Thomas Smith, **3**: 101; mentioned, **10**: 483

Beale, Thomas: insurance against being drafted, **5**: 220-3

Beall, George: letter to auditors, **5**: 515; signs petition, **17**: 471

Beall (Beal, Beale), Samuel: sells army supplies, **3**: 337; **5**: 484; warrants to, **4**: 444; owns gunpowder and lead, **5**: 411; letter from cited, **11**: 256; letter from, to McCullum, quoted, **11**: 256n; mentioned, **6**: 138

Beall, Thomas (of Georgetown): signs petition, **17**: 471; letter to, from Washington, quoted, **19**: 69n-70n

Beam, Messrs. (book dealers), **10**: 201

Bean, William: killed, **5**: 96

beans: imported to France from U.S., **8**: 250; **12**: 469, 480; cultivated in northern Italy, **11**: 442; sent to Benjamin Hawkins, **20**: 89, 360

Beard, Jonas: assaulted by Va. citizen, **6**: 513-5; affidavit in Hancock case, **7**: 38

bears, **6**: 342

Beatey, Capt., **5**: 152n

Beattie, James, **12**: 19

Beatty, Charles: and land survey for capital, **20**: 73, 74

Beatty, John: American commissary of prisoners, **3**: 86, 87; motion on Va. land cession, **6**: 575n; and Conn.-Pa. territorial dispute, **6**: 483n; and Ordinance of 1784, **6**: 612n; member of Congress from N.J., **7**: 7n

Beauchamp, Francis Ingram Seymour Conway, Lord: letter to, from Duke of Würtemberg, cited, **14**: 440, 514

Beaufils, M., **7**: 396

Beaufort, M.: letter from, **12**: 320

Beaufoy (Bufoy), Henry: speech on fisheries, **13**: 291, 663; letter from, to Banks, on death of Ledyard, **15**: 198, 274; mentioned, **9**: 363n

Beaujolais, France: TJ describes, **11**: 214, 418-20; climate, **11**: 247

Beaujon, M.: death of, **10**: 624

Beaulieu, Leroux de: lead, sheet, price list, **14**: xxxv

Beaulieu, Louis Joseph de: letters to, **9**: 479, 571; letters from, **9**: 328-9, 541; **13**: 254-5; biographical note, **9**: 329n; land claim, **9**: 479; Loan Office certificates, **9**: 479

Beaumarchais, Pierre Augustin Caron de: commercial transactions with, **3**: 14, 199; ill treatment by U.S., **3**: 15-6; disposition toward America, **4**: 524; claim against Va., **7**: 550, 553-4; **8**: 35; imprisoned, **8**: 265; claim against U.S., **9**: 91; **11**: 664; settles accounts, **9**: 137-8, 234; **13**: 161; mentioned, **9**: 555; **12**: 537

Beaumard, M.: dictionaries, **8**: 412, 629

Beaumont, Antoine François, Vicomte de: arrives in Brest, **12**: 308

Beaumont, Elie de. *See* Elie de Beaumont, Jean Baptiste Jacques

Beaumont, James: paid by Department of State, **17**: 375

Beaune, France: Dumas' birthplace, **10**: 558; wines of, **11**: 417; **13**: 635-6; wine cooper at, **11**: 601-2; Short and Paradise family in, **13**: 635

Beauport, Que., **1**: 445

Beauregard, Luis Toutant: claim against Va., **3**: 320, 482-3

Beausace, M. de: vineyard of, **11**: 422

beausprits: Portugal's desire to import, **9**: 19

Beausset, Comte (Abbé) de: in attack on Aix, **15**: 322, 323

Beauties of Shakespear: ordered by TJ, **10**: 617

Beauvau, Charles Juste, Prince de: TJ's introduction to, **7**: 414; in council, **15**: 333

Beauzée, M., **12**: 504n

Beaver, Dr. (owner of "Enfield Chase"), **9**: 372

Beaver, George: in Albemarle co. militia, **1**: 667

Beaver, John: in Albemarle co. militia, **1**: 667, 668

Beaver creek, Va.: plans for defense of, **3**: 55; Indians killed near, **20**: 122

beavers: French import of skins, **10**: 475; **12**: 469, 480; **13**: 69; at Karlsruhe, **13**: 25

Beawes, Wyndham: *Lex Mercatoria Rediviva*, **11**: 548

Beccaria, Cesare Bonesana, Marquis: cited on murder, **2**: 494n; cited on suicide, **2**: 496n; cited on buggery, **2**: 497n; use of by TJ, **2**: 505n; *Essay on Crimes and Punishments*, **16**: 481

Beck, James: in Albemarle co. militia, **1**: 666

Beckett, M., **11**: 531

Beckley, John: letter from, **6**: 88-90; and bill on escheats, **2**: 283n; signs Va. documents, **2**: 290; **3**: 632; **5**: 52n, 62n, 230n; **6**: 37n, 134, 136n, 188; **9**: 204; **10**: 409; **16**: 335n; and revisal of the laws, **2**: 311n-2n, 333n; and TJ's text of Statute for Religious Freedom, **2**: 552n; defends TJ, **4**: 273n; furnishes extract of TJ letter to *Va. Gazette*, **5**: 104n; petition from, **5**: 349; and notification of Va. GA's investigation of TJ, **6**: 105n; and 1781 act of cession, **6**: 574; boards with Mrs. House, **11**: 405; and Federal convention, **11**: 631; discusses British politics with TJ, **18**: 227n; in Reynolds case, **18**: 632, 658-9, 660n; in controversy over *Rights of Man*, **20**: 271, 290, 291, 293, 295-6, 298, 302; mentioned, **4**: 223; **16**: 196; **18**: 649

Beckwith, George: in war crisis of 1790, **17**: 36-46, 51n, 52-85, 90-9, 103-7, 352n; TJ's memorandum on, **17**: 38n; interviews with Hamilton, **17**: 45, 55-7, 59-64, 68-70, 80-5, 92-8, 105-6, 132n-4n, 161n; **18**: 221-2, 234-7, 256, 259, 262, 266n, 278, 280, 282, 536, 549n; **20**: 107, 108, 111-2, 138, 145, 252; reports to Grenville, **17**: 64, 102n, 106-7, 387n; **18**: 221n, 222, 226n, 235n, 238n, 239-40, 245n, 251, 262n, 263, 270n, 275, 548n, 549; **20**: 107n, 116; relations with Dorchester, **17**: 67-8, 71n, 72-5, 77, 83-4, 85n, 88, 90, 92-8, 104, 132n-4n, 387n; **18**: 396n; **20**: 107n, 110, 111, 116n; on model of Arkwright's cotton mill, **17**: 387n; **18**: 123n; in British commercial and diplomatic relations, **18**: xxxiv-v, 221-4, 226-7, 234-40, 243, 245, 259; **20**: 117; views on monarchy in U.S.,

Beckwith, George (*cont.*)
18: 396n, 520n; and navigation bill,
18: 544; and tonnage acts, 18: 546;
letters from, to Grenville, quoted, 18:
557; 19: 454n, 568-9; informed by
Hamilton of political divisions, 19: 88;
quoted on effect of revolution on New
England seafarers, 19: 143; fears U.S.
elections, 19: 171; schemes of, 19:
367; and Society for Establishing
Manufactures, 19: 453; and U.S.-Brit-
ish boundary dispute, 19: 626; portrait
by S. W. Reynolds, 20:
xxxii, 384 (illus.); and Indian supplies,
20: 87; as diplomatic intermediary, 20:
106, 132, 133, 143, 145; interviews
with Knox, 20: 133-6, 138; letter
from, to Knox, quoted, 20: 135n; interviews with Madison, 20: 136-7,
145, 147-50, 251-2; TJ refuses to deal
with, 20: 137, 148-9; and controversy
over *Rights of Man*, 20: 274-6, 293-4;
criticizes Gouverneur Morris, 20: 299;
confers with Jay, 20: 435; confers with
Schuyler, 20: 435; confers with Wadsworth, 20: 435; confers with W. S.
Johnson, 20: 435; reports on TJ and
Madison's northern journey, 20: 435,
438-9; mentioned, 17: 290n; 18: 242
bedding: loss of, by Anderson's men, 4:
578; lack of, for hospitals, 6: 54
Bedel (Beadel), Col. Timothy: in charge
of defense works at the Cedars, 1: 396;
Cedars affair, 1: 451; court-martial, 1:
500
Bedford (British ship): damaged in
storm, 4: 651
Bedford, Francis Russell, fifth Duke of:
pisé buildings, 15: 185n; as physician,
15: 385
Bedford, Gunning, 6: 407n
Bedford, Gunning, Jr.: attends Constitutional Convention, 11: 400; shoots
wife and her lover, 16: 351, 386
Bedford co., Va.: letter to commissioner
of provisions for, 3: 568n; letters to
county lieutenant of, 5: 275-7, 617;
appoints infantry officers, 1: 579; court
of assize in, 1: 629; grand jury in, 1:
638-9; petitions for new county, 2:
118n; militia, 2: 130; 3: 599; 4: 63,
295n, 301, 352, 371, 637, 638, 641;
5: 7n, 29, 35, 36, 103n, 123, 212n-3,
275-7, 310, 402-3, 617, 646; 6: 3, 77;
removal of John Goodrich from, 2:
173; senatorial district, 2: 336; troops

for, 3: 8, 50, 52, 53, 79; tobacco loan
office certificates, 3: 516; Tory conspiracy, 3: 519-20, 523; commissioner
of provisions for, 3: 573; disaffection
in, 3: 648; 4: 14; 5: 213; 6: 77; supply
post for, 4: 286; justices of the peace
recommended for, 6: 55; visited by
TJ, 6: 113; land owned by TJ in, 11:
641, 653; 13: 340, 342; 15: 660; 17:
600; land in marriage settlement of
Martha Jefferson Randolph, 16: 154
Bedford Court House, Va.: court of assize in, 1: 628; 7: 589
Bedinger, Henry (prisoner of war), 3:
390
Bee, The: prospectus for, 16: 391n-2n;
TJ subscribes to, 18: 112
Bee, Thomas: letter from, 4: 483; in
committee on medals, 16: 57n; mentioned, 3: 401; 12: 505
beef: prices, 2: 264; 4: 437; 5: 101; 15:
361-2; 20: 717; Va. bill to prohibit exportation of, 2: 348; Va. bill on frauds
in, 2: 444-7; for Continental army, 3:
335, 409, 528; 4: 8, 10, 13, 27, 209,
219, 235, 239, 375, 442, 533-4, 586;
5: 157, 290, 291-2, 312; 6: 11; 15:
594-5; for Va. troops, 4: 41, 348, 379,
508; 5: 3, 373, 464, 561, 647-9; 15:
592; for Convention troops, 4: 46, 65,
182, 255; impressment, 4: 73; taken
by British, 4: 111; supplies in west, 4:
199; supply in Jefferson co., 4: 365;
shortage, 4: 565, 666; 5: 467; difficulty of collecting tax on, 4: 664; for
Greenbrier co. militia, 5: 445; U.S.
export of, 7: 334, 335, 336-7, 349,
372; produced in S.C., 8: 198; for TJ,
12: 660; 13: 138, 184, 472; Swan's
proposals on, 13: 243, 244n, 278,
313, 383-6, 387n, 425; 15: 361-2,
483n; 17: 504-5, 529, 557, 561-4;
Irish packers and curers sent to Mass.,
13: 437; Limozin advises on, 13: 472;
commercial importance, 14: 416;
French import of, 15: 220-1, 311,
344-5, 481-2, 502; 16: 374, 444; 17:
611, 617; 18: 22, 586; Short negotiates with Necker and Lafayette on, 15:
537n; 16: 374-5; 17: 16; woodland,
17: 324, 325n
beer: N.Y. imports, 7: 330; U.S. import
of, 10: 147
beeswax: Va. export of, 7: 373; U.S. import of, 10: 147; duty reduction suggested, 12: 436

beggars: France, **8**: 437; **13**: 28, 616; Germany, **13**: 26

Begouën, Desmeaux & Cie., **15**: 521, 526

Belches, Dr. James, **7**: 418

belette: comparison with weasel, **9**: 661-5

Belew, Peter: peaches grown by, **9**: 252-3; place of, **9**: 624

Belfast: and U.S. commercial policy, **19**: 134

Belgioiosa Casa, Milan, **11**: 437

Belgrade: Austrian attack on, **12**: 464, 482, 483, 564, 682; **13**: 190-1; in Rutledge's plans for travel, **13**: 358; capture reported, **16**: 7n

Belidor, Bernard Forest de, **3**: 342

Belin, Capt. (master of *Juno*), **15**: 378

Belinda. *See* Burwell, Rebecca

Belisarius. See Marmontel, Jean François

Belknap, Jeremy: errors regarding U.S., **12**: 579; and new system of penmanship, **19**: 120n

Bell, Capt. (master of the *Ann*), **9**: 4, 391

Bell, Alexander: testimony on killing of Frenchmen by British, **3**: 114n

Bell, Henry: signs Virginia Association, **1**: 109

Bell, Lieut. Henry: impresses Page's horse, **15**: 604; mentioned, **5**: 321

Bell, John: signs nonimportation resolutions (1770), **1**: 46

Bell, John: *Bell's Edition of Shakespeare's Plays*, **10**: 201; **11**: 522; **13**: 177

Bell, Joseph: letter from, **5**: 3-4

Bell, Robert (printer), **6**: 542; **7**: 288; **12**: 488

Bell, Capt. Thomas, **4**: 310

Bell, Col. Thomas: letter to, **20**: 758-9; at Charlottesville, **16**: 26; **18**: 42; signs address, **16**: 178; TJ sends regards to, **17**: 324; biographical note on, **17**: 325n; letter from, to Monroe, cited, **18**: 509; delivers letter, **19**: 74; subscribes to *National Gazette*, **20**: 759; mentioned, **1**: 40

Bellanger, Mme Plumard de. *See* Plumard de Bellanger, Mme

Bellefonds, Chevalier de: affidavit for, **14**: 489-90

Bellegarde, François Eugène Robert, Marquis de: claims Oglethorpe estate, **9**: 108, 114n, 181

Belle Isle, Newfoundland: and the fisheries, **19**: 196

Bellenden, William: preface to works, **14**: 512

Bellfuille, Antoine, **3**: 541n

Bellini, Carlo (Charles): letters to, **7**: 230; **8**: 568-9; **9**: 593; **13**: 415-6; **18**: 485-6; letters from, **5**: 572; **6**: 150-1, 173-4; **8**: 458-9; **9**: 591; **12**: 634; **17**: 21-3; supports American state papers series, **1**: 145; reports on finances of Duke of Tuscany, **2**: 28n; and Va. clerkship for foreign correspondence, **2**: 182n, 295n; letter from, to Fabbroni, cited, **2**: 198n; recommended by TJ as U.S. agent in Italy, **2**: 224, 226n; signs honorary degree for TJ, **6**: 221-2; teaches Italian to Maury's pupils, **7**: 112; as professor at William and Mary College, **8**: 635; **13**: 372; urges Peter Carr to study Italian, **10**: 648; books sent to, **11**: 229; copy of *Notes on Virginia* sent to, **12**: 130; spectacles sent to, **12**: 130; **13**: 416; interprets for Va. admiralty court, **17**: 22; mentioned, **2**: 206n; **3**: 149, 201, 237; **6**: 114, 508; **8**: 119; **9**: 277

Bellini, Gaspara Farolfi (Mrs. Charles Bellini): ill health of, **8**: 568; **9**: 591; **17**: 22; mentioned, **8**: 458, 569; **12**: 634; **13**: 416; **16**: 486

Bellon, M.: letters from, **11**: 302

Belloni, Gerolamo: banker in Rome, **14**: 451

bells: Hopkinson's invention for drawing tone by friction, **11**: 562

Belvedere (ship): Reynolds captain of, **18**: 643n

Belvidere: estate of the Harvie family, **1**: 67

Ben, Tom: and Indian land claims, **2**: 97

Benbury, Thomas, **4**: 611

Bender, Blassius, Baron von: as Austrian commander, **18**: 85, 86, 114, 354, 609; letter from cited, **19**: 117-8; letter to, from Pilsack, quoted, **19**: 118

Benedictine monks: wine of, **11**: 456; **13**: 635; **20**: 405

benefit of clergy: abolished in Va., **2**: 325; mentioned, **10**: 46-7

Benge, M. Lewis: Albemarle co. militia, **1**: 668n

Benge, Samuel: signs Va. oath of allegiance, **2**: 129; paid by Department of State, **17**: 372

Benge, William Lawrence: signs Va. oath of allegiance, **2**: 128

Benge, William Lewis: on Albemarle co. militia roll, **1**: 667

Benière, Jacques Michel Guillaume, Curé: sends account of proceedings honoring Franklin to American government, **19**: 81, 83, 107

Benjamin, Mr.: and Hessian fly, **20**: 458; inn of rated by TJ, **20**: 471

Benn, James: and bill establishing ferries, **2**: 457

Benn, Thomas: chosen to report on Sycamore Shoals conference, **2**: 72

Bennet's creek: ferry at, **2**: 457

Bennington, Vt.: visited by TJ and Madison, **20**: 441-4, 458, 465, 466

Bensberg, Germany: Elector's palace, **13**: 265, 445-6

Benson, Mr.: land claims, **1**: 26

Benson, Egbert: sends money to Wooster, **1**: 442, 443; as assistant deputy commissary, **1**: 453; N.Y. delegate to Hartford Convention, **4**: 139; as N.Y. delegate in Congress, **7**: 572; and motion on R.I., **15**: 263n, 297

Bentalou, Paul: letter to, **10**: 296; letters from, **10**: 204-5, 326-7; introduced to TJ, **9**: 516

Bentalou, Mme Paul: desires to bring slave to France, **10**: 205, 296, 326

Bentivoglio, Guido, Cardinal: *Relationi*, **11**: 523; *Della Guerra di Fiandra*, **12**: 688; **14**: 491, 707n

Bentley, Mr.: quarrel with Brown, **8**: 52

Bentley, Thomas: recommended to TJ, **5**: 574; complaints of Kaskaskia inhabitants against, **5**: 599; bills countersigned by Gen. Clark, **6**: 86

Bérard, Jean Jacques, & Cie.: letter to, **10**: 205-6; letters from, **9**: 390-3; **10**: 290; letters from cited, **11**: 187; **12**: 295; and rice, **11**: 590-2, 659; **13**: 367-8, 377; **14**: 633; **15**: 12; tobacco trade, **12**: 77n; letter from, to farmers-general, **12**: 78-82; agency for S.C. products proposed, **12**: 300; letter to, from Brailsford & Morris, quoted, **12**: 302n-3n; bill of exchange on, **12**: 631; money to be sent to, **13**: 138; mentioned, **9**: 393, 505, 509; **10**: 210; **11**: 173; **12**: 250, 298, 299, 380, 505, 676; **13**: 55n, 149, 264; **14**: 60, 392; **15**: 135, 150, 158, 543

Bérard, Simon: letters to, **11**: 156-7; **12**: 626; letters from, **9**: 457-61; **11**: 157; **12**: 599-600; putative author of notes on trade with French colonies, **9**:

135n; opposes tobacco monopoly, **9**: 292n; on U.S.-French trade committee, **9**: 338n; possible aid in speech before the Comité du Commerce, **9**: 345n-6n; biographical note, **9**: 458n; *Observations* on the tobacco trade, **11**: 513-4; **12**: 82-93; ally to TJ in tobacco negotiations, **12**: 76n-7n; proposals on rice trade, **12**: 250; mentioned, **11**: 142, 157, 173; **13**: 136n

Berber language: spoken in Morocco, **10**: 346

Berckel, M. van (son of Pieter Johan): criticizes Dumas, **13**: 408n

Berckel, Franco Petrus van: letter to, **20**: 629; sails for U.S., **14**: 519; mentioned, **17**: 340n

Berckel, Pieter Johan van: preparations for reception of, **6**: 276; statement of Netherlands claim, **8**: 79; esteem for Dumas, **9**: 237; letter to cited, **9**: 462; protests Va.'s exemption of duty on French brandy, **10**: 492n; **11**: 222; arrives in England, **12**: 413; letter from cited, **12**: 696; medal, **16**: 367, 368n; **19**: 583; mentioned, **7**: 84; **9**: 301, 304; **13**: 175

Bérenger, Laurent Pierre: *Le Peuple instruit par ses propres vertus; ou Cours complet d'instructions et d'anecdotes*, **11**: 597

Bérenger de Beaufain, Hector de: letter to, **12**: 433; letter from, **12**: 402-3; career in America, **12**: 402; claims property in S.C., **12**: 402, 433; epitaph, **12**: 403n

Beresford (ship), **9**: 392

Beresford, Richard: attends Congress from S.C., **6**: 437; **7**: 7n, 461; mentioned, **6**: 465

Bergamo, Italy: Paradise's financial arrangements in, **13**: 599-600, 602-3; Rutledge in, **14**: 273

Bergasse, H. & L., Frères: letter from, **13**: 648

Bergasse, Nicolas: introduction to TJ, **11**: 261-2; wine cellar of, **11**: 428; TJ wants to visit, **11**: 463n; report on judicial authority, **16**: 116

Bergen, Germany, **13**: 18, 48, 266

Berger, M.: vineyard, **11**: 422

Berger, Alexandre: requests passports and letter to America, **13**: 97; introduced to Francis Lewis by TJ, **13**: 121; **14**: 325

Bergius, Peter J.: letter to, **11**: 111-2;

Biddle, Edward: signs Continental Association, **1**: 153; signs Congress' second petition, **1**: 223; signs agreement of secrecy, **1**: 253

Biddle, Capt. Nicholas: takes transport, **1**: 407, 454

Biddle, Owen: appointed to confer with Va. delegates, **1**: 466n; secretary of American Philosophical Society, **4**: 544

Bidon, M., **11**: 290

Bidpai (Pilpay): *Les Fables politiques et morales de Pilpai*, **13**: 651

Big Beaver river: navigation of, **7**: 26, 558; and canal connecting with Cuyahoga, **13**: 124; **15**: 117; **17**: 445n; Heart's report on, **17**: 444-8; mentioned, **12**: 489

Big Bone Creek, **9**: 477

Big Bone Lick, Ky., **2**: 74

Big Buffalo Lick: plans for defense of, **3**: 55

Big Creek, **2**: 96

Bigelow, Mr.: inn of rated by TJ, **20**: 471

Big Island, Va., **2**: 79

Bignonia sempervirens: sample to be sent to France, **10**: 227

Big Rock: plans for defense of, **3**: 55

Big Sandy Creek: plans for defense of, **3**: 55

Big Sandy river: plan for regimenting and stationing western battalion on, **3**: 54; detachment of soldiers at, **3**: 78-9; as boundary, **8**: 124

Bilbao (Bilboa), Spain: market for fish, **7**: 340; letter from cited, **17**: 18

billets d'achat: use of, **16**: 44

billets de la caisse: use of, **16**: 44; forgery attempted, **16**: 46

Billing, Sir Thomas: cited, **2**: 502n

Billings, John Gregory (captive in Algiers): ransom of, **17**: 32

Billings, Thomas: captured by Algerians, **14**: 395, 397n

Bill of Rights: supported by George Mason, **12**: 280; Adams' desire for, **12**: 335; TJ's views on, **12**: 440, 557, 558, 569, 571; **13**: 6n, 128, 208, 232, 378, 442-3, 490, 502; **14**: 188, 328, 370, 385, 529, 596, 605, 615, 650, 659-61, 673, 678-9, 688; **15**: 367-8, 388; **17**: 354n; Va.'s insistence on, **12**: 583-4; Henry's speech opposing, quoted, **13**: 354n-5n; Va. Constitutional Convention, **13**: 482, 619; N.C.

proposal, **13**: 659-60; **15**: 106; Madison on, **14**: xxxix, 18-21; **15**: 181; passage by Congress predicted, **14**: 344; **15**: 337; Congress discusses, **15**: 154, 229

billon (coinage metal): usage of, **18**: 454-5; TJ's notes on, **18**: 458-9

bills of attainder: Josiah Philips and others, **2**: 189-93; TJ's attitude toward, **2**: 192n-3n; in TJ's notes of acts of General Assembly, **2**: 661n; mentioned, **2**: 283n, 503n; **6**: 281n

bills of credit: Va. bill concerning, **2**: 434, 507-10; supplied to states, **3**: 531; appointment of commissioners to endorse, **4**: 25; as legal tender, **5**: 216; report concerning, **7**: 221-4; mentioned, **11**: 51

bills of exchange: rate on foreign debts, **2**: 434n-5n; Va. bill on, **2**: 501, 629-30; payment of, **4**: 375-6; **5**: 61, 87-9, 110-1, 152-3; **13**: 429-30; purchase of, **4**: 523-4, 672; of Convention troops, **5**: 19; for American war prisoners, **5**: 38-9; speculation in, **6**: 321n; not accepted by Laval & Wilfelsheim, **7**: 647-8; British loss on, **8**: 341

Billy (German soldier): hired to work at Monticello, **5**: 244n

Billy (slave): sentenced to death for treason, **5**: 640-3

Binasco, Italy, **11**: 440

Bingham, Anne Willing (Mrs. William Bingham): letters to, **11**: 122-4; **13**: 151-2; letter from, **11**: 392-4; seeks appointment for husband, **9**: 563n; beauty of, **11**: 95; letter to cited, **13**: 207; passport issued by TJ, **15**: 484; mentioned, **15**: 56, 476-7

Bingham, William: letters to, **8**: 359; **15**: 476-7; letters from, **8**: 328-9; **15**: 55-6; **16**: 591n; letter from, to Congress, **2**: 34, 36n; letters from cited, **3**: 63, 411; **7**: 90; departs The Hague, **8**: 448; on Dutch resentment at navigation acts, **9**: 43; departs Paris, **9**: 146, 228; as possible U.S. minister to Netherlands, **9**: 563n; **11**: 244, 245n, 275-6, 277n; delays return to U.S., **10**: 114; TJ's opinion of, **11**: 95; passport issued by TJ, **15**: 484; letter from quoted, **17**: 391n; and Reynolds' letters to Hamilton, **18**: 677-9; and address to National Assembly, **19**: 96; introduces Brown to TJ, **19**: 252n; favors Philadelphia capital site, **20**: 5n;

Bingham, William (*cont.*)
mentioned, **3**: 656-7; **7**: 310n; **9**: 128, 153, **10**: 351, 593; **11**: 124; **12**: 230; **18**: 260
Bingham family, **9**: 241
Birch, Capt. Robert (master of *Amiable Catherine*), **15**: 68
birch bark: used for writing by TJ, **20**: 462-4
Bird, Mr. (brother-in-law of Benjamin Vaughan): investigates rice culture, **14**: 673
Bird, Abner: signs petition, **1**: 588
Bird, Bartlet: signs petition, **1**: 588
Bird, Fort, **3**: 206
Bird, George: letter to, **5**: 464; letter from, **5**: 411
Bird (Byrd), Henry: prisoners taken by, **3**: 561
Bird, James: signs Va. oath of allegiance, **2**: 129
Bird, John: discoveries of, **16**: 570
Bird, John, Sr.: signs petition, **1**: 588
Bird, Richard: Washington mentions papers on his arrest, **3**: 216
Bird, Thomas: signs nonimportation resolutions (1769), **1**: 31
birds: foot and feathers sent TJ, **11**: 289, 656; aviaries in Europe, **13**: 9-10, 24; TJ brings to America, **14**: 45; **16**: 321; different species in America and Europe noted, **14**: 699; appearance of swallows and martins, **16**: 492; seasonal arrival of whip-poor-wills, **16**: 492
Bird's tavern: express station, **4**: 372
Birmingham, England: debased guineas coined at, **7**: 162-3; manufacture of copper coins at, **7**: 196; visited by TJ, **11**: 521; riots in, **20**: 712
Biron, Comte de, **15**: 399
Biron, Armand Louis de Gontaut, Duc de: letter to, **10**: 384; letter from, **10**: 353; death of, **14**: 48, 276; mentioned, **17**: 555
births: Va. bill for registering, **2**: 491-2
Bisdom, Mr., **8**: 37n, 46
Bishop, Abraham: passport issued by TJ, **15**: 485
bishops. *See* episcopacy
bison: in Ky., **8**: 126
Bisson, M., **12**: 20
Bissy, M. de (French consular official in Boston), **14**: 64n
Bivins, Capt. James: as master of *Prince of Wales*, **15**: 651, 653, 656, 663; let-

ter to, from Wayles, **15**: 655; loan to Richard Randolph, **15**: 655n
Black, Mr., **10**: 148
Black, Alexander: in Albemarle co. militia, **1**: 664
Black, James: signs petition, **1**: 587
Black, John: signs petition, **1**: 588; **6**: 294; in Albemarle co. militia, **1**: 664; signs Va. oath of allegiance, **2**: 129
Black, John, Jr.: in Albemarle co. militia, **1**: 664
Black, Joseph: writings sent Madison, **7**: 288; in Edinburgh scientific society, **11**: 293
Black, William: in Albemarle co. militia, **1**: 664; and bill establishing ferries, **2**: 460; signs petition, **6**: 294
Blackband, Col. *See* Blackburn, Thomas
Blackburn, Col.: and landlord bill, **2**: 263
Blackburn, Thomas: letter from, **3**: 369; and nonimportation agreements, **1**: 110; declines appointment to Executive Council, **3**: 349n, 369, 371; negotiations with Md. on navigation of Potomac, **7**: 589, 591
Blackburn, William, **4**: 322
Blackburne, Thomas: signs letter to Va. HB, **1**: 112
Blackden (Blagden), Col. Samuel: letter to, **12**: 582-3; letters from, **12**: 554-5; **14**: 462; **16**: 247-51; **20**: 430-2; knowledge of Canadian campaign, **1**: 446-7; **10**: 378, 381, 382; recommended to Famin and Garvey, **10**: 517; in Paris, **10**: 610; **11**: 277, 383; **15**: 173; possibility of sending Moroccan treaty by, **11**: 36; letter sent by, **11**: 373; Claiborne's relations with, **11**: 411, 469, 486, 519, 579; **14**: 359-60, 402; land sales of, **12**: 197, 601-2, 630; **15**: 478; **16**: 434n; **18**: 364; letter from, to Lafayette, cited, **12**: 311; at Dunkirk, **12**: 601; proposals for supplying Paris with flour and wheat, **13**: 659; **15**: 245-7, 249; signs Fourth of July tribute to TJ, **15**: 239-40; assists Paradise, **15**: 282; passport issued by TJ, **15**: 486; letter from, published in *Gazette of the United States*, **16**: 241n-2n, 247-51, 387n (cited); describes revolt in Flanders, **16**: 247-51; Bastille Day address signed by, **17**: 214n; visits Champagne, **17**: 528; criticized by G. Morris, **18**: 364
Blackden, Mrs. Samuel: in Paris, **15**:

173; assists Paradise, **15:** 282; arrives in London, **17:** 241

Blacket, Sir Thomas: interested in Paine's bridge, **14:** 566

Blackfish (Shawnee Indian), **4:** 442

Blackfriars Bridge, London: steam mill at, **9:** 401n; failure of, **13:** 589

Blackie, Mr., **15:** 47

Blackmore's Fort, Clinch river: Indian attack on, **4:** 499, 546

blacks: incited to insurrection, **1:** 378; not eligible as witnesses, **1:** 633; **2:** 607; extension of protection of certain laws to, **2:** 23n; penalties for remaining in Va. once freed, **2:** 471; colonization proposed by TJ, **2:** 472n; inferiority to whites argued by TJ, **2:** 472n-3n; marriage with whites prohibited, **2:** 557; purchased by Va., **3:** 284; as workmen at Westham foundry, **4:** 438-9; on escheated property, **4:** 439; for work at Hoods, **5:** 55, 127, 207, 499-500; illness among, **5:** 74; employed by Va., **5:** 127; manning of river craft by, **5:** 152n; sought for lead mines, **5:** 265; captured by British, **5:** 371, 393, 406, 424, 430, 435, 529; **6:** 268-9; **8:** 199; **10:** 604; **18:** 285; celebrate holidays, **5:** 500; used in military operations, **5:** 570; TJ's opinion on inheritance of, **6:** 145-6; remarks on fossils, **6:** 208; in Dabney's legion, **6:** 430n-1; inferiority of disputed by TJ, **8:** 186; change in color and features predicted, **9:** 441; TJ's views on separate creation of, **9:** 441; population, **10:** 18; French inquiries on, **11:** 51; preference for Brazilian tobacco among, **11:** 514; TJ seeks copy of Somersett case, **11:** 523; citizenship of in French West Indies, **16:** 280; sold by Potawatomi Indians, **17:** 132n; status in French West Indies, **20:** 367, 385, 427, 658; seek asylum in U.S., **20:** 551-5; settlement in U.S. opposed by TJ, **20:** 558. *See also* slaves

Black Sall (slave): taken by British, **6:** 224

Black Sea: place of origin of English fruits, **11:** 70; J.P. Jones' naval action on, **13:** 126, 134, 404, 427-8, 436-8, 454-6, 458-9, 461, 465, 471, 483, 488-9, 491, 497, 503, 580; third Russian victory, **13:** 529, 580; TJ on exaggerated accounts of action, **13:** 632-3, 650; free navigation of, **14:** 516;

Russian naval action renewed (1790), **17:** 593, 627-8

Blacks Fort, Va., **1:** 573

blacksmiths: to repair arms, **4:** 397; for work at Hoods, **4:** 626; sent to Lafayette, **5:** 144; contract conditions for, **5:** 391; employment of, **6:** 83; wages, **7:** 297, 327 (N.Y.), 332 (Conn.), 338 (R.I.), 339 (R.I.), 342 (Mass.), 343 (N.H.)

Blackstone, Sir William: criticized by TJ, **2:** 41n, 57-9; *Commentaries on the Laws of England,* **2:** 50; **7:** 415; **11:** 547; **12:** 519, 576; **15:** 615; **16:** 393, 481; **20:** 378; suggested as model of Va.'s revisal of laws, **2:** 314n; cited on capital crimes, **2:** 493n; cited on suicide, **2:** 496n; cited on kidnapping and polygamy, **2:** 497n; cited on maiming, **2:** 498n; cited on burglary, **2:** 500n; cited on pleading, **2:** 503n; cited on contracts, **6:** 490; cited on assault, **6:** 514; basis of law lectures at William and Mary College, **7:** 303; influence on Court of Chancery, **9:** 71; quoted by Démeunier, **10:** 46; *Analysis of the Laws of England,* **11:** 547; works by, **16:** 277; and common law doctrine on impressment, **18:** 311, 312

Black Water river, Va., **3:** 611; **5:** 299, 614

Blackwater swamp: land granted to College of William and Mary, **2:** 536

Blackwell, Mr.: and bill establishing ferries, **2:** 457

Blackwell, David: in Albemarle co. militia, **1:** 665

Blackwell, Capt. George: exemption requested, **5:** 295

Blackwell, Jacob: as clerk in Dept. of State, **17:** 357n, 358n, 363, 597

Blackwell, Col. John: appointed deputy to John Browne, **5:** 373

Blackwell, Capt. John E., **4:** 481

Blackwell, Samuel, **5:** 295n

Blackwell, Capt. Samuel, **4:** 541

Blacon, Henri François Lucretius d'Armand de Forest, Marquis de: discusses royal veto, **15:** 355n

bladder senna: seeds sent to Monticello, **10:** 616

Bladen, Gov. Thomas, **1:** 21n

Bladensburg, Md.: Shippen visits, **17:** 464-5; and capital site, **19:** 45; **20:** 75-6, 82

Blagden, Col. *See* Blackden, Col. Samuel

Blagge, John: signs testimonial, **18**: 627

Blagrove, Benjamin: signs Virginia Association, **1**: 109

Blain, Alexander: signs petition, **1**: 588

Blain, George: signs petition, **1**: 588

Blaine (Blane), Ephraim (Commissary General of Purchases): signs petition, **6**: 294; mentioned, **3**: 494; **4**: 70, 177

Blaine, James: Mlle Langat's complaint against, **14**: 479, 510

Blaine, John: in Albemarle co. militia, **1**: 666

Blaine, Samuel: in Albemarle co. militia, **1**: 666

Blair, Capt. (master of the *Rising Sun*), **12**: 180

Blair, Miss, **12**: 187

Blair, Mr.: Richmond property, **8**: 344; sermons, **8**: 641; mentioned, **1**: 18

Blair, Anne. *See* Banister, Anne Blair

Blair, Archibald: letter to, **16**: 82-3; docket of, **1**: 69; attests Council order, **2**: 294; **3**: 13n; signs Va. documents, **3**: 103-4, 160, 333-4, 420-1, 423-4, 653; **4**: 82-4, 405-6, 536-7; **5**: 211; deposition respecting TJ's conduct during Arnold's invasion, **4**: 271; sends blank commissions, **5**: 385; mentioned, **1**: 72; **6**: 648n; **7**: 400

Blair, Hugh: *Lectures on Rhetoric and Belles Lettres*, **6**: 537, 544; **7**: 288; **8**: 536; **16**: 481

Blair, James: as first president of the College of William and Mary, **2**: 536

Blair, John (1678-1771), **1**: 25

Blair, John: letters to, **9**: 593; **12**: 27-8; letters from, **1**: 103; **11**: 248-50; signs nonimportation resolutions (1770), **1**: 46; relations with Mazzei, **1**: 157-8; **20**: 713-4; and revisal of Va. laws, **2**: 313n, 323n; **10**: 576; and examination of Short to practice law, **6**: 122n; delegate to Congress, **6**: 137n; proposed examiner of Maury's school, **7**: 112; Mazzei gives power of attorney to, **8**: 677; on committee to amend unpassed Va. bills, **11**: 153; delegate to Constitutional Convention, **11**: 154, 219, 310, 312, 331, 352, 363, 401, 626; Constitution supported by, **13**: 98, 352, 620; TJ's opinion of, **14**: 659; in Wayles estate debt, **15**: 649n; justice of Supreme Court, **16**: 27; TJ consults, **16**: 307-9; Gilmer dines with, **16**: 433; proposed arbitrator in Edgehill

boundary dispute, **20**: 165; mentioned, **1**: 39; **3**: 341; **7**: 273; **9**: 154; **17**: 422

Blair, Mrs. John, **12**: 28

Blair, John, Jr.: signs nonimportation resolutions (1769), **1**: 30

Blair v. Blair, **6**: 123n

Blake, Joseph: departs London, **11**: 520; mentioned, **9**: 363n

Blake, John: testimony on Canadian campaign, **1**: 433-4; mentioned, **1**: 443

Blake, Thomas, Jr.: letter to, **12**: 107-8; letter from, **12**: 56

Blakely, John: passport issued by TJ, **15**: 484

Blakey, Smith, **5**: 37

Blakey's mill: uninsurability of, **6**: 515

Blan, M.: letter from, **13**: 604-5

Blanc (gunsmith): improvements on manufacturing, **18**: 69

Blanc, Pierre, **9**: 193

Blanca, Conde de Florida. *See* Floridablanca

Blancan, Mr., **7**: 555

Blanchard, François: and travels in balloon, **7**: 601, 602, 603, 604, 608

Blanchard, Jonathan: member Committee of the States (1784), **6**: 484n; **7**: 299, 432; succeeds TJ as chairman of Grand Committee, **6**: 506n; and papers on Vt., **7**: 282; replaced in Congress, **7**: 572

Blanchard, Thomas: letter to, **12**: 108; letter from, **12**: 28; employed by British firm, **12**: 161

Blancherie, M., **12**: 598

Bland, Dr., **8**: 119

Bland, Edward: votes against bill for religious freedom, **2**: 549n

Bland, John: signs nonimportation resolutions (1770), **1**: 47

Bland, Richard: signs nonimportation resolutions, **1**: 30, 46; signs Virginia Association, **1**: 108; appointed to Continental Congress, **1**: 141; signs Continental Association, **1**: 153; on committee to investigate land grants, **1**: 162n; collection of state papers, **1**: 164, 176; and bill to abolish entail, **1**: 561n; and bill to revise Va.'s laws, **1**: 563n; papers of, **1**: 591; and establishment of Va. courts, **1**: 606n; and TJ's suggestion to extend legal protections to blacks, **2**: 23n-4n; Duché's opinion of, **2**: 39n

Bland, Col. Theodorick: letters to, **2**:

286-7, 299; **3**: 263; **4**: 566-7; **5**: 152-3, 251, 367-8, 395, 440, 632-4, 634-5, 650-1; letters from, **2**: 291-2; **4**: 12-3, 136-8, 203, 214, 292-3, 436-7, 462-3, 483-4, 567-9, 605-6, 606-7; **5**: 193, 266, 334-5, 481-3, 550-2, 566-7, 586-7, 620-1; **6**: 9-10, 39, 72-3; and Mazzei's agricultural co., **1**: 158; as captain of Va. cavalry, **1**: 386; and Johnson case, **2**: 43n; and case of Henry Hamilton, **2**: 287n; **3**: 25, 31-2, 65; asks to rent Monticello, **2**: 291; and flag of truce, **2**: 299; **3**: 14-4, 24; and Convention troops, **3**: 41, 74, 253; criticized by Gen. Phillips, **3**: 74, 97; as commander of regiment, **3**: 154, 156, 191-2, 204, 214, 228, 229n, 244, 250, 265, 294, 316, 365; and translation of German letters, **3**: 339; qualification as delegate to Congress, **4**: 121; on committee to quell army mutiny, **4**: 326; letter to, from Arthur Lee, quoted, **5**: 671; finances of, **6**: 72-3; and reappointment of TJ as peace commissioner, **6**: 202n, 206, 207n; motion to prepare list of books for use of Congress, **6**: 216; opposes releasing TJ as peace commissioner, **6**: 259n; sends thermometer to Zane, **6**: 347; **7**: 41; elected to Va. GA, **9**: 519; fails to be elected governor or speaker, **10**: 577; opposes Constitution, **12**: 410; **13**: 98; revises Va. resolution on second Constitutional Convention, **14**: xxxix, 558; antifederalism of, **15**: 6; as congressman from Va., **15**: 6, 78; letter to cited, **15**: 573; illness of, **16**: 450; and resolution on soldiers' pay, **16**: 456n-8n, 461n; **18**: 611, 613, 616, 620-3, 653, 656, 657, 686, 687; **18**: 620-3; death of, **16**: 475; mentioned, **3**: 75, 86n, 514n; **4**: 179; **5**: 587n; **6**: 538; **18**: 633

Bland, Mrs. Theodorick, **2**: 291
Bland, William: marriage, **1**: 16, 17; signs Virginia Association, **1**: 109
Blandford, Va., **5**: 550n; **6**: 44
Bland's Ordinary (near Petersburg, Va.), **5**: 510, 511, 527, 545
Blane (Blare?), Mr., **1**: 286
Blane, Alexander, Sr.: signs petition, **6**: 294
Blane, Ephraim. *See* Blaine, Ephraim
Blane, George: signs petition, **6**: 294
Blane, John: signs petition, **6**: 294

Blane, Samuel: signs petition, **6**: 294
Blaney, Capt., **10**: 352
Blank, Mr.: and bill establishing ferries, **2**: 460
blankets: scarcity of, **1**: 294; **3**: 261; **4**: 16, 27, 40, 150-1, 195-6, 445, 496, 565; for army, **1**: 658; **3**: 517, 587-8, 619; **4**: 188, 219, 358, 402, 453, 471, 591, 592, 607, 679; **6**: 13; requisitions for, **3**: 536; to be provided by counties, **3**: 602; obtained from prize ship, **3**: 646, 658; to be supplied by militia, **4**: 59; manufacture in France desirable, **11**: 263; **12**: 338; **14**: 253, 284, 292
Blanton, Mr.: and bill establishing ferries, **2**: 460
Blanton, Jesse: and Indian treaties, **2**: 86
Blard, M.: plants to be sent to, **13**: 138
blasphemy: Va. resolutions on, **1**: 530n-1n
Blaton, Haley: imports slaves, **15**: 654
Blaye, France: TJ's description, **11**: 457
bleaching: linen and paper, **14**: 367
Bledsoe, Col. Anthony: to dispense Va. HD claims, **2**: 63; mentioned, **5**: 552
Bledsoe, Isaac: and case of Thomas Johnson, **2**: 42n
Bleibtrear, F. W.: letter from, **8**: 242-3
"Bleig's cart," **11**: 607
Bleiswyck, Pieter van: Adams' contact with, **6**: 128
Blenheim, England: garden of described by TJ, **9**: 372
Blenheim, Va. (home of E. Carter): rented to Gen. Phillips, **2**: 252n
Bligh, Capt. William: account of mutiny on the *Bounty* sent to TJ by Vaughan, **16**: 274-6, 578; rice seed brought from Timor by, **16**: 274, 276n, 492, 495, 496n, 578; **17**: 564-5; **18**: 97
Bliss, Capt. Theodore T.: delivered as hostage to British, **1**: 399
blockade: stipulations in trade treaties, **6**: 395; against Barbary States proposed, **10**: 177, 561n
Blodget, Samuel, Jr.: and the Federal City, **20**: 68
Blois, France: TJ's description of, **11**: 462
Blome, Otto, Baron von: letters to, **8**: 157-8; **10**: 270-1; **13**: 294; letters from, **10**: 622; **12**: 523; negotiations with American Commissioners, **9**: 514; letter to cited, **10**: 281, 282; absence from Paris, **10**: 329; books received

Blome, Otto, Baron von (*cont.*)
from, **10**: 624; negotiation on prize
money for J. P. Jones, **13**: 47n, 258;
conversations with Short, **20**: 386;
mentioned, **13**: 282, 299; **16**: 585; **17**:
433, 655

Blonde (British ship), **4**: 90, 92

Blondel, Antoine Louis: on American
Committee, **9**: 338n; mentioned, **10**:
94

Blondin (valet at Nîmes), **15**: xxx, 67

Bloodworth, Timothy: opposes decimal
system of coinage, **7**: 158n; recommendations for federal offices in N.C., **16**:
476-8; **17**: 293n; and residence bill,
17: 182

Blooms, Mr.: and Indian land claims, **2**:
91

Blount (Blunt), William: letters to, **17**:
292-3; **19**: 535-6, 605-6; letters from,
19: 284; **20**: 639, 681; expected arrival in Baltimore, **6**: 243; as member
of Constitutional Convention, **11**: 401;
as governor of Southwestern Territory,
16: 477, 478n; **17**: 293n; **19**: 354
(proceedings); letters from cited, **17**:
293n, 644; treaty with Indians, **20**:
481

Blue Licks, Ky., **2**: 84, 90, 91

Blue Ridge mountains: supplies for territory beyond, **4**: 286; grant to land beyond, **6**: 659; Rev. James Madison's
observations on, **14**: 534; mentioned,
2: 114

Blumendorf, M. de (Zigeiner, Joseph):
letter from, **11**: 575; mentioned, **9**:
167, 234, 235, 515

Blunt, Mr.: draft of, **3**: 85, 182

Blunt, Benjamin: letter from, **5**: 665

Blunt, James: letter from cited, **8**: 285n

Boardman, Capt. (master of *Mary*), **4**:
310; **18**: 5

Board of Treasury, U.S.: expenses, **6**:
562

Board of War, Continental: letters to, **2**:
300-1; **3**: 513; **4**: 374; **5**: 542-3; letters
from, **3**: 78; **4**: 181-2, 197, 199; **5**:
239-40, 414-5; **6**: 15, 39; and John
Harvie, **2**: 35; refers subject of Convention horses to Va., **3**: 322; TJ's
disgust with, **3**: 501; letter from, to
Phillips, on flags, **5**: 509; Va. delegates
plead before, **5**: 551; letter from, to
Steuben, quoted, **6**: 27n; letter from,
to Weedon, quoted, **6**: 28n; mentioned, **4**: 142

Board of War, Virginia. *See* Virginia:
Board of War

boat boards: Conn. export to West Indies, **7**: 334

boat carriages: requisitioned by Lafayette, **5**: 666

boats: abandoned, law concerning, **2**:
441; lack of for army, **3**: 392; **5**: 638;
required for army, **3**: 582; **4**: 375,
384, 533-4, 626; **5**: 50, 75, 86, 130,
253, 666; impressment of, **4**: 80-1,
384, 393-4, 405-6, 626, 635, 636; **5**:
121, 124, 133, 592; **6**: 4; on Ohio, **4**:
149, 162; use for transporting supplies
from one post to another, **4**: 286-7;
portable, **4**: 380; building of, **4**: 666;
5: 645; shortage of, in Virginia, **5**: 92;
hire for, **5**: 93; for landing men and
cannon, **5**: 129, 131; lookout, **5**: 132,
199, 203, 401; destroyed to prevent
use by British, **5**: 614; screw propulsion, **7**: 642-3; **8**: 299, 576; **9**: 356;
spring-block propulsion, **10**: 78; self-
propelling, invention of, **11**: 293;
canal, in Netherlands, **13**: 9; on Rhine,
13: 12, 16, 19, 34n; bridge supported
by, **13**: 18, 22, 267; Italian bucentaur,
14: 378, 383n; jet-propelled, Bernoul-
li's proposal, **15**: 23n

boatwrights: pay of, **4**: 548, 552

Bob (slave): delivers letter from TJ, **7**:
401; **15**: 615; employment of, **13**: 343;
bears letter for Fitzhugh, **17**: 241; to
carry supplies for TJ, **17**: 327; TJ inquires whereabouts of, **17**: 417, 418n;
mentioned, **7**: 356, 375, 386; **14**: 362

bobac. *See* marmot

Bockerie, Joseph Cowen: in ransom of
American captives in Algiers, **16**: 21

Bocock, Samuel: signs petition, **1**: 588

Bode, Mr.: observes Herschel planet, **8**:
575

Bodenheim, Germany, **13**: 21

Bodin, Jean: cited in support of privilege
of foreign minister, **11**: 495n

Boerum, Simon: signs Continental Association, **1**: 153

Boethius: *De Consolatione Philosophiæ*,
13: 652; **20**: 634n

Bogert (Bogart, Rogert), John J.: bill
on, **7**: 251, 392

Bohannon (Bohannan), Capt. Ambrose:
preparations for Portsmouth expedition, **5**: 47; mentioned, **7**: 256

Bohemia: revolutionary spirit in, **16**: 96

Bohemia, Elector of: American medals sent to, **16**: 67

Bohlen, B.: paid by Department of State, **17**: 368, 373

Boileau, Gilles: works of, **8**: 411

Boileau-Despréaux, Nicolas, **4**: 118

Boilly, Louis: painting of Houdon in his studio, **8**: xxvii, 215 (illus.)

Boine, M. de: letter from cited, **20**: 352

Boinod & Gaillard: letters to, **6**: 529-30, 541, 544; **7**: 124; books bought from, **6**: 550; catalogue of, **7**: 37; bill paid, **7**: 56, 57; accused of stirring anti-French feeling, **7**: 307n; offer to print Marbois' version of Longchamps affair, **7**: 308n; mentioned, **7**: 280, 281, 288, 290

Bois de Boulogne: TJ's praise of, **11**: 509; view of Mont Calvaire from, **12**: xxxv, 482 (illus.); TJ rides in, **13**: 422

bois de lit: ordered from London, **11**: 531

Boisgelin de Cucé, Jean de Dieu, Raymond de (Archbishop of Aix): rumor of effort to imprison, **11**: 363

Boissel, François: letter from, **12**: 685-7; *Le Catéchisme du genre humain*, **12**: 686n-7n

Bolek, Capt. A. (master of *William Elizabeth*), **13**: 483n

Bolingbroke, Henry St. John, Viscount: *Philosophical Works*, **12**: 18-9; TJ recommends style of, **16**: 481

Bolling, Mr.: and bill establishing ferries, **2**: 458; mentioned, **8**: 45

Bolling, Archibald: plaintiff, **15**: 587n

Bolling, John: letters to, **16**: 157-8, 207-8; marries TJ's sister, **1**: 6n; **20**: 157n; manages land lottery, **1**: 22; public papers stored at house of, **5**: 579; copy of Catesby's *Natural History*, **6**: 220; TJ's opinion of, **11**: 612; deaths in family of, **15**: 618, 620; in estate settlement of TJ's sisters, **16**: 192n, 194, 195n, 207-8; visited by Mary Jefferson, **16**: 436; mentioned, **15**: 621, 634; **17**: 656; **20**: 157

Bolling, John, Jr. (nephew of TJ): copy of *Notes on Virginia* sent to, **12**: 133; marries, **15**: 627; mentioned, **11**: 612

Bolling, Mary Jefferson (sister of TJ): letters to, **11**: 612; **17**: 656; letter from, **20**: 156-7; marries John Bolling, **1**: 6n; **20**: 157n; health of, **15**: 613; **20**: 633; deaths in family of, **15**: 618, 620, 640-1; mentioned, **6**: 220; **9**: 397; **15**: 621, 637; **16**: 158

Bolling, Nancy: Negro girl sent to, **10**: 615

Bolling, Robert (Buckingham co., Va.): signs nonimportation resolutions (1769), **1**: 30; death of, **1**: 238; defendant, **15**: 587n

Bolling, Capt. Robert (Petersburg, Va.): letter to, **5**: 412; death of wife, **12**: 654; mentioned, **5**: 660

Bolling's point, Va.: ferry at, **2**: 458

Bolling *v.* Bolling, **15**: 586

Bologna, Italy: Short in, **14**: 378-9

Bolton, Mr.: and bill establishing ferries, **2**: 460

Bon, François, & fils, **14**: 388

Bon, Pierre: letter from, **11**: 506-7

Bond, Capt. (master of *Washington*), **15**: 265

Bond, Phineas: letter from, **16**: 83; and appointment of George Miller, **13**: 249n; consular activities of, **17**: 42; **18**: 280; **19**: 306; reports of, **17**: 43, 339n-40n; **18**: 223n, 549; letters from, to Duke of Leeds, **17**: 333n-4n; **18**: 235n, 238n, 240; as a loyalist, **18**: 254; letter from, to Grenville, cited, **18**: 279; and TJ's report on the fisheries, **19**: 165n, 166; mentioned, **15**: 147n; **17**: 91n

Bond, Dr. Thomas: vice president of American Philosophical Society, **4**: 544

Bond, Dr. Thomas, Jr.: educational fees, **20**: 474

Bonde (Bongé, Swedish chargé at The Hague), Mr., **13**: 221n

Bondfield, Haywood & Co., **3**: 551

Bondfield (Bonfield, Bonfeild), John: letters to, **7**: 578; **8**: 73, 158; **9**: 210-1, 540-1, 599; **10**: 196-7, 503, 508, 554; **11**: 36, 524; **12**: 108-9, 294, 351-2, 434, 616, 640; **13**: 171-2; **14**: 45-6, 353, 457, 621-2; **15**: 42-3, 218-9, 276-7, 371; letters from, **7**: 415-6; **8**: 93-5, 116, 250-1, 294, 412-3; **9**: 581-2, 627-8; **10**: 66-7, 136-7, 191-2, 399-400, 461, 492-3, 516, 589-91; **11**: 47, 255, 538-9, 596; **12**: 28-9, 117-8, 161, 210-1, 226, 235-6, 248-9, 385-6, 514-5, 648-50; **13**: 96, 296-7, 416-7, 485, 526; **14**: 336-7, 444-5, 549-51, 585; **15**: 63-4, 71, 74, 84-5, 147, 264, 383, 400-1, 464-5; **17**: 573-80; testimony on Canadian campaign, **1**: 453-4; wine ordered through, **9**: 54, 212, 298; **12**: 541, 560, 658; **13**: 96, 171;

Bondfield, John (*cont.*)
14: 589; account against Adams, **9:**
90, 116; letters from cited, **10:** 81,
292, 483; **13:** 435; as vice consul at
Bordeaux, **10:** 200; arms for Va.
shipped by, **10:** 229, 310, 331; **11:** 62;
forwards letters to TJ, **11:** 363, 373,
381; **15:** 85; part in Barclay affair, **11:**
499n, 537n; letter from, to Barclay,
quoted, **11:** 585n; recommended to
Wilson Miles Cary, **12:** 23-4; vouches
for Thomas Blanchard, **12:** 28; arranges Mrs. Barclay's return to Amer-
ica, **13:** 416; letter to cited, **14:** xxxiv;
considered for consul at Bordeaux, **14:**
59, 62n; **17:** 247, 254n, 476, 580n;
19: 55; and shipment of plants for TJ,
14: 286; **15:** 310; aids American seamen, **14:** 549, 622; TJ inquires about
ships for America, **15:** 42; Short introduced to, by TJ, **15:** 43; Cutting introduced to, by TJ, **15:** 218-9; and
proposal on wheat importation, **15:**
464-5; financial difficulties of, **16:** 233;
letter from, to Short, cited, **16:** 270;
complains of injustice, **17:** 573-80; letter to, from William Lee, **17:** 576; letter from, to Jay, cited, **18:** 382n; loses
business of TJ, **19:** 55n; mentioned, **3:**
92; **10:** 82; **11:** 365, 467, 510, 607;
12: 353, 435, 501, 618; **13:** 171, 296;
15: 51, 77, 277; **17:** 212
bonds: punishment for theft of, **2:** 501;
for sheriffs, **2:** 583-4; for debts, **2:** 606-
7; custom house, **9:** 542; **10:** 206, 292,
333, 473, 547, 588; **11:** 38, 55, 67,
88. *See also acquits-à-caution*
Bondville, M.: letter from, **9:** 390-3
Bône (Bona), Algeria: plague, **11:** 22
Bonelli, Mr.: Carmichael recommends,
12: 100
bones: exported from Mass., **7:** 339-40.
See also animals, prehistoric
Bongé. *See* Bonde
Bonhomme Richard (ship): prize money,
6: 398; **7:** 266, 270; **8:** 279n, 327,
680; **9:** 22, 44, 294, 378, 443, 471,
563; **10:** 94; **12:** 266, 336-7, 430,
494; Wuibert's position on, **9:** 78; **10:**
501; roll of crew, **10:** 253; Laurent's
wages as volunteer, **13:** 432; on medal,
13: 586; **16:** xl, 52 (illus.), 55n; Bondfield procures cannon for, **17:** 577;
Coram's service on, **19:** 409
Bonn (Bonne), Germany: palace at, **13:**
447; mentioned, **13:** 15, 48, 265

Bonnay (Bonnai), Charles François,
Marquis de: at Bastille Day, **17:** 213
Bonne, Rigobert: letter from, **17:** 636-8;
Principes sur les mesures, **17:** 636,
638n; **18:** 359n
Bonnel, William: signs petition, **6:** 294
Bonner, Frederick: warrants issued to, **5:**
142n, 164n; disobeys orders, **5:** 661
Bonnet, Charles: *Contemplation de la nature*, **20:** 329
bonnetery: exported from France to U.S.,
12: 470
Booker, Mr.: and bill establishing ferries,
2: 460
Booker, Col. Edmund: arrest demanded
by Steuben, **4:** 358; court-martial ordered, **4:** 499
Booker, Richard: signs nonimportation
resolutions (1770), **1:** 47
Book of Common Prayer: American revision, **10:** 78; TJ seeks copy of, **15:**
406
books: ordered by TJ, **1:** 34; **8:** 365; **10:**
165-6, 362, 384, 398, 417, 471, 478,
518, 545; **11:** 522-3, 642, 643; **12:** 35,
227, 488, 518, 678, 687, 688-9; **13:**
177-80, 182, 200, 203-4, 240, 240n,
280, 288, 289-90, 300, 345, 362,
391, 411, 420, 421, 536, 650-2, 656;
14: 364, 468, 469n, 491, 511-2, 647,
663, 706-7, 707n; **15:** 163, 223-4,
260, 350, 406, 615; **16:** 388, 389n;
20: 210, 382, 417, 633-6, 647-8;
burning of TJ's at Shadwell, **1:** 35,
37; TJ's agreement to acquire John
Randolph's, **1:** 66; advice on sought by
Robert Skipwith, **1:** 74, 76-81; purchased for Madison, **7:** 233, 288, 506-
7; **8:** 111, 416, 461, 462-4; **9:** 264,
517-8; **10:** 604; **11:** 483, 629, 662-3;
12: 136, 270; TJ's plan of reading for
Peter Carr, **8:** 407, 408, 411-2; **12:**
18-9; sent to Va. by TJ, **8:** 513, 565,
570, 575, 638-9; cost of in France, **8:**
560; **11:** 672; TJ requests permission
to bring from England to France, **9:**
313; sent to the Rev. James Madison,
9: 355; **14:** 533; **16:** 82n; Spanish
purchased for TJ, **9:** 629, 649; **10:**
285; ordered for Peter Carr, **10:** 72;
12: 414; **15:** 156; sent to Currie, **10:**
107; sent to Edmund Randolph, **10:**
133; U.S. import of, **10:** 147; shipped
by Charles Dilly, **10:** 291; duty exemption, France, **10:** 476; **12:** 469,
480-1; **13:** 70; American colleges seek

Boston (*cont.*)
393; Démeunier describes, **10**: 36; evacuation of, **10**: 352; communication of selectmen to Washington, **10**: 373, 376n-7n; disbursements for, **11**: 602; fire of 1787, **12**: 93, 94, 119; approves Constitution, **12**: 280; and foreign trade, **13**: 221; **17**: 434n-5n; **19**: 129; medal on evacuation of, **16**: xxxvi, 52 (illus.), 54n, 55n; Charles River Bridge, **16**: xliii, 53n (illus.); receives National Assembly's reaction to Franklin's death, **19**: 81n-2n; postal service, **20**: 666

Boston (frigate), **6**: 399

Boston Navigation Acts. *See* navigation acts, American

Boston Port Act: Va. opposition to, **1**: 106n, 107, 117-9, 138; Continental opposition to, **1**: 152, 153

Boswell, Benjamin: signs nonimportation resolutions (1770), **1**: 47

Boswell, Capt. Machen (Machere), **4**: 539

Boswell, William: carries express, **5**: 60; discharged, **5**: 72, 226

botany: TJ's interest in, **2**: 196; **10**: 108; Crèvecoeur's interest in, **8**: 155; American interest in, **8**: 636; **10**: 306; T.M. Randolph, Jr., studies, **11**: 291; Mme de Tessé seeks plants, **13**: 476-7, 484

Botany Bay, Australia: convicts sent to, **11**: 74; Tench's account of, **15**: 182, 183n

Botetourt, Norborne Berkeley, Baron de: dissolves Va. GA, **1**: 26-7; toast to, **1**: 31; commissions TJ as lieutenant of Albemarle co., **1**: 42; and western frontier, **2**: 67, 78, 79; death of, **6**: 648n; statue of, **7**: 378-9

Botetourt, Va., parish of: divided, **1**: 575-6; election of vestry, **2**: 117

Botetourt co., Va.: letters to county lieutenant of, **3**: 503-4; **4**: 85-6; **5**: 275-7; **6**: 24-5; and Indian relations, **1**: 508; **3**: 356; **4**: 301; troops of, **1**: 579; **3**: 50, 51, 53, 79, 420; **4**: 16, 301, 621, 669; **5**: 7, 36, 103, 275-7; petition from religious dissenters in, **1**: 589n; place of court of assize, **1**: 629-30; division of, **2**: 113-8; collection of public dues or fees in, **2**: 115; jurisdiction over lawsuits in newly formed counties, **2**: 116; militia, **2**: 130; **3**: 422, 479, 503, 533, 600; **4**: 63, 82-4, 362-3, 458, 614, 622, 638, 641; **5**: 20,

310, 449-50; **6**: 24-5, 56, 93; land commissioners for, **2**: 165n; senatorial district, **2**: 336; gunpowder in, **3**: 422; defense of lead mines, **3**: 480; tobacco loan office certificates, **3**: 516

Botetourt Court House, Va.: proposed meeting of school overseers at, **2**: 529; council of officers at, **3**: 398; provisions post at, **3**: 537

Botidour (Botidoux), Mlle: letters from, to Martha Jefferson, cited, **16**: 130, 135n, 273, 386, 388; remains at Pentemont, **20**: 670

Bottom, Michaja, **4**: 322

Bottom's Bridge, Va.: express station at, **4**: 372; Continental army at, **5**: 598, 601

Bottsworth, Mr.: Paradise's creditor, **15**: 73

Bouchault, François, **8**: 55

Boucher, John: signs nonimportation resolutions (1770), **1**: 47

Boudinot, Elias: letter to, **16**: 581; letter from quoted, **6**: 347n; reports on Danish treaty, **7**: 467n; aid solicited by Washington, **12**: 325n; and residence bill, **17**: 166n; House conferee on excise bill, **19**: 37; objects to replying to the French, **19**: 84; chairs committee on trade legislation, **19**: 559; mentioned, **6**: 215, 218, 257n, 410n

Bouébe, M.: letter to, **12**: 196-7; letters from, **12**: 119, 164; letter from cited, **12**: 217

Boufflers, Louis François, Duc (Chevalier) de: captured at Namur, **3**: 48

Boufflers, Stanislas Jean, Marquis (Chevalier) de: TJ's account of, **8**: 242n

Bougainville, Louis Antoine, Comte de: *Voyage autour du monde*, **8**: 411; commands fleet at Brest, **17**: 642

Bouillé, François Claude Amour, Marquis de: victories in West Indies, **6**: 110; friendship for Bingham, **11**: 95; proposed as member of marine council, **12**: 683; son seized, **17**: 396; and mutiny of garrison at Nancy, **17**: 490-1, 504, 524; and king's flight to Varennes, **20**: 574, 585-6, 611, 620; opposes Revolution, **20**: 651; flees France, **20**: 575, 655

Boullongne, Jean Nicolas de, Comte de Nogent-sur-Seine: on U.S.-French trade committee, **9**: 338n, 458n; **12**: 142, 143

Bowdoin, James (*cont.*)
introduces foreign visitors to Franklin, **15**: 64n; signs certificate of TJ's election to American Academy, **16**: 112n; and desalination of sea water, **19**: 609, 620; eulogy of, **20**: 599; mentioned, **10**: 70, 240

Bowdoin, John: signs Virginia Association, **1**: 108; Mazzei's debt to, **7**: 273, 274, 357; **16**: 307; **17**: 422

Bowen, Jabez: TJ's acquaintance with, **7**: 312n; replies to TJ's queries on R.I. commerce, **7**: 337-9; and memorial to king of France, **10**: 463n; letter to, from Washington, quoted, **10**: 533n-5n; letters from cited, **17**: 477n, 644; mentioned, **7**: 157

Bowie, Cyrus (gardener), **13**: 110n

Bowie, James: and bill establishing ferries, **2**: 456

Bowler, Thomas, **3**: 606n

Bowles, Carington: map of, **6**: 601

Bowles, Henry: letter from, to Mrs. Wright, quoted, **9**: 101n

Bowles, William Augustus: brings Indians to England, **17**: 665, 666n; **18**: 7n; correspondence with Lord Dorchester, **17**: 666n; intrigues of in London, **18**: 14, 25n

Bowling, John: signs nonimportation resolutions (1770), **1**: 47

Bowling Green, Va., **4**: 420; **5**: 554

Bowman (ship): at Le Havre, **12**: 561; sale to Brown, **16**: 236; at Norfolk, **16**: 382; mentioned, **12**: 348, 428, 592, 594, 630

Bowman, D.: letter from, **5**: 651

Bowman, Maj. Issac: killed by Chickasaw Indians, **3**: 416; mentioned, **2**: 256

Bowman, Col. John: letter to, **3**: 160-1; commands expedition against Shawnee, **2**: 298; **3**: 6; county lieutenant of Ky., **3**: 161n; Todd criticizes, **5**: 462; commission as sheriff of Lincoln co., **6**: 645; mentioned, **3**: 421; **4**: 498; **5**: 467

Bowman, Joseph: appointed justice of Harrodsburg, **2**: 110

Bowman, William: signs petition, **6**: 290

Bowyer, Charles: in Albemarle co. militia, **1**: 665

Bowyer, John: signs Virginia Association, **1**: 108; on committee to divide Fincastle co., **1**: 566n; appointed commissioner to investigate land claims, **2**:

65n; on committee for dividing Augusta and Botetourt counties, **2**: 117n

Bowyer (Boyer), Col. John: letter to, **4**: 486; serves against Arnold, **5**: 507; mentioned, **4**: 420; **5**: 329, 350, 454n, 622

Bowyer, Michael: votes for bill for religious freedom, **2**: 549n

Bowyer, Col. William, **4**: 239

box elder: plants asked from John Banister, **11**: 121

Boyd (ship): Purdie's service on, **18**: 318; arrives off Foulstone, **18**: 338

Boyd, Andrew: and Henderson's land claims, **2**: 82; and bill establishing ferries, **2**: 459

Boyd, Archibald: letter and miniatures sent to, by brother, **15**: 487-8, 503; **16**: 311; TJ's advice on aid to, **16**: 311-2, 489-90; debts, **16**: 428-9

Boyd, Edmund: signs petition, **6**: 293

Boyd, John: and bill establishing ferries, **2**: 461

Boyd, Ker & Co.: letters to, **15**: 9-10; letters from, **13**: 149; **14**: 11; **15**: 63, 78; forwards letters from Rutledge, **13**: 138; and financial affairs of Rutledge, **13**: 264, 368, 374; **14**: 276, 481, 538; **16**: 319; bills of exchange for, **13**: 615; and U.S. debt to France, **20**: 202n; mentioned, **15**: 158

Boyd, Margaret: and bill establishing ferries, **2**: 460

Boyd, Patrick: and bill establishing ferries, **2**: 461

Boyd, Robert: signs testimonial, **18**: 627

Boyd, Walter: letters to, **15**: 503; **16**: 311-2, 387, 388n, 429n; letters from, **15**: 487-8, 499n; **16**: 312n; signs nonimportation resolutions (1770), **1**: 47; letter and miniatures sent to brother, **15**: 487-8, 503; **16**: 311; and debts of brother, **16**: 311-2, 428-9, 489-90

Boyd, Mrs. Walter: portrait, **15**: 487

Boyd's Creek: battle of, **4**: 359-63

Boyds Ferry, on Dan river: Cornwallis at, **5**: 12; mentioned, **5**: 429

Boyds Hole: British depredations at, **5**: 399, 548; mentioned, **2**: 454

Boyer, Gazaigner de: letter to, **9**: 86

Boyer, Col. John. *See* Bowyer, Col. John

Boyetet, Edouard: letter to, **10**: 172-3; letter from, **10**: 163-4; on U.S.-French trade committee, **9**: 338n; **12**: 142; letter from cited, **12**: 328; "Rapport sur le commerce des Etats-Unis" attributed to, **13**: 53n, 75n; opposes trade treaty with Britain, **13**: 54n; in whale oil negotiations, **14**: 261; mentioned, **13**: 52n, 65, 73, 194n; **15**: 169

Boyle, Robert: donation to College of William and Mary, **2**: 538, 543n; works of, **20**: 635n

Boylston, Thomas: letters from, **9**: 26, 275, 299, 307-8, 601-2; **11**: 5-6; introduced to TJ, **8**: 550; description of, **8**: 550n; **9**: 117; commercial ventures, **9**: 29-31, 42, 45n-7n, 72-3, 73n, 75n, 88-9, 127, 140, 183, 262-3, 359; **10**: 140, 349; **11**: 26-7, 55, 116; **12**: 334-5; **13**: 221; **14**: 183, 217-8, 234n; letters sent by, **9**: 41; letter quoted, **9**: 45n; and TJ's memoranda on the fisheries, **14**: 232; mentioned, **9**: 82

Boze, Joseph: miniature of Martha Jefferson, **14**: xli-ii, 361 (illus.); portrait of Lafayette, **16**: 318; **18**: 32, 356, 359n, 450

Braam Houckgeest, A. E. van: letter from, **11**: 283; letter from cited, **11**: 295

Brabant: camp near, **11**: 517; revolution in, **11**: 490, 611, 632, 636, 672; **15**: 559, 567; **16**: 8n, 49, 234, 488; **18**: 85-6, 114, 354; **19**: 363; relations with Austria, **12**: 153, 215; union with Flanders, **16**: 104-5; opposition to Belgic States, **16**: 220. *See also* Netherlands, Austrian

Brac de la Perrière, Jacques Joseph de: letters from, **14**: 390-1; **15**: 247, 250-1; on U.S.-French trade committee, **9**: 338n; and circular to farmers-general on whale oil, **14**: 391n, 398n; statistics on wheat and flour, **15**: 250-1

Brack, Charles: letter to, **12**: 638; Brissot dines with, **10**: 514

Bracken, Rev. John: leaves William and Mary College, **16**: 25; rector of Bruton parish, **18**: 313

Brackenridge, Mr.: at Charlottesville, **16**: 27

Brackenridge, William: expense account as express rider, **5**: 581

Bracton, Henry de: cited, **2**: 230; suggested as model of Va.'s revisal of laws, **2**: 314n; cited on suicide, **2**: 496n; cited on kidnapping, **2**: 497n; cited on maiming and counterfeiting, **2**: 498n; cited on arson and robbery, **2**: 499n; cited on escape, **2**: 502n; cited on clergy, **2**: 503n

Bracton Grammar School. *See* Brafferton Grammar School

Braddock, Edward: defeat of, **2**: 104; Franklin assists, **9**: 487, 496

Braddocks Road: as Va.-Pa. boundary line, **1**: 389n, 594; Andes' plantation near, **2**: 101

Bradel, J. B.: prints description of medal, **16**: 55n

Bradford, Mr. (Boston): buildings burned, **12**: 94

Bradford, Mr. (England), **8**: 523, 634; **9**: 40, 65

Bradford, Lieut. Charles, **5**: 504

Bradford, David: votes for bill on religious freedom, **2**: 549n

Bradford, John: letter from, **18**: 490; report to Congress on copper, **7**: 153n; publishes *Kentucky Gazette*, **17**: 509n; mentioned, **4**: 557

Bradford, Maj. Samuel Killett (aide-de-camp to Weedon), **5**: 457

Bradford, Thomas: supports American state papers series, **1**: 145; mentioned, **6**: 381; **13**: 6n

Bradford, William (Philadelphia): letter from, **4**: 138-41; supports American state papers series, **1**: 145; as Continental agent at Boston, **4**: 139; Franklin's connection with, **9**: 487, 495; and case of W. Green, **20**: 502n; mentioned, **5**: 529n

Bradford, William (R.I.): delegate to Hartford Convention, **4**: 139

Bradford, William, Jr.: arbiter in Nathan case, **6**: 323n; Pa. commissioner in dispute with Conn., **6**: 476n, 484n

Bradley, Capt. James, **4**: 54, 541

Bradly, Stephen Rowe: Wadsworth's opinion of, **19**: 377

Bradshaw, John: epitaph of, **1**: 511n, 677-9

Brady, Richard: prisoner of war, **5**: 432

Brafferton Grammar School, **7**: 302, 303n

Bragg, Thomas: action against Mc-Clenachan, **7**: 435-6

Brahm, Frederick F. S. de: letter to, **11**: 111-2

Brahm, John de: letter from, **14**: 627-8; asks payment for service in Revolution, **14**: 628

Brailsford & Morris: letters to, **13**: 367-8; **15**: 99-100; **16**: xxxi, 52 (fac.); letters from, **12**: 298-303, 505, 676; **14**: 632-4; Rutledge praises, **12**: 250, 264;

Brailsford & Morris (*cont.*)
  ship rice to France, **12**: 287; **14**: 633;
  15: 99-100; Gadsden praises, **12**: 296;
  letters from quoted, **12**: 302n-3n; olive
  trees sent to, **12**: 380; **13**: 369; **14**:
  463; **15**: 43, 46n, 100, 101; **18**: 584;
  20: 332-3; make payment, **13**: 138;
  and financial affairs of Rutledge, **13**:
  374; letter to cited, **13**: 415; letter
  from cited, **15**: 12, 70n; correspondence with Vernes, **15**: 538, 543-4; **16**:
  95; acts for Agricultural Society of
  South Carolina, **16**: 318
Brandenburg, Prussia: commerce of, **8**:
  606; *Mémoires de*, **11**: 666; American
  medals sent to elector of, **16**: 67
Brandon, David: and bill establishing
  ferries, **2**: 460
Brandon, Col. Thomas: at King's Mountain, **4**: 32n
Brandon, Va.: British at, **4**: 395; **5**:
  231n, 613, 614, 624
brandy: price for soldiers and sailors, **2**:
  379; supplied to army, **3**: 609; distilled
  from potatoes, **6**: 509; TJ orders, **7**:
  501, 533-4; U.S. imports, **8**: 309; **10**:
  147; **11**: 353, 617; **12**: 301, 385;
  French trade in, **10**: 474; **14**: 550; import duty on reduced in Va., **10**: 492n;
  11: 146, 147n, 222, 241; TJ comments on production of, **11**: 457; sent
  to H. Skipwith, **16**: 91
Branham, Mr.: and bill establishing ferries, **2**: 456
Branham, James (interpreter for Cherokees), **2**: 75
Branham, William: signs petition, **6**: 294
Branhem, Barnet: signs petition, **1**: 588
Branhem, John: signs petition, **1**: 588
Brant, Charles: citation to published, **16**:
  552
Brant, Joseph: letter to, from Peter
  Otchikeita, cited, **9**: 337; rouses Indi-
  ans, **15**: 218; and proposed peace mis-
  sion, **20**: 124; criticizes Cornplanter,
  20: 127; meets Dorchester, **20**: 138-9
Brantley, Joseph: parole of, **5**: 148
Brantsen (Brantzen), Gerard: letters sent
  by, **11**: 14n, 27, 109
Bras de Fer, Rhone River, France, **11**:
  450
brass: U.S. import of, **10**: 147
Brattan, Adam: loan to Va., **3**: 386
Brattan, Capt. Robert: loan to Va., **3**:
  386
Braxton, Carter: letters to, **7**: 95; **18**:

488n; letters from, **3**: 406; **5**: 656-7;
  signs nonimportation resolutions
  (1769), **1**: 30; and sale of Moore's estate, **1**: 60, 64-5; signs TJ's commission, **1**: 246; signs agreement of secrecy, **1**: 253; and Continental
  Congress, **1**: 286, 391n, 404n, 407,
  412, 472, 475, 483; and plan of government for Va., **1**: 332n, 334n-5n,
  368n; signs Declaration of Independence, **1**: 432; on Va. HD Committee
  on Religion, **1**: 527n; on Va. HD committee to divide Fincastle co., **1**: 566n-
  8n, 576n; and establishment of Va.
  courts, **1**: 606n; buys tobacco from
  TJ, **2**: 4n; and Va. representation in
  Congress, **2**: 16n; encomiums of
  Duché, **2**: 39; on land committees, **2**:
  135n, 138n; and bill for care of poor,
  2: 423n; votes for bill for religious
  freedom, **2**: 549n; vessels of, **3**: 57,
  184-6; **4**: 467; payment to Congress,
  4: 122, 123; warrants to, **4**: 444; and
  army supplies, **4**: 453, 553; remittances to troops, **6**: 73, 93-4; opposes
  federal control of commerce, **9**: 198,
  199; sponsors Va. bill for postponing
  tax, **9**: 199-200; on Va. Executive
  Council, **9**: 202; on Va. committee to
  prepare resolution on Congress, **9**:
  204n-8n; TJ's accounts with, **10**: 614;
  13: 341; sells horse, **17**: 243n, 418n;
  mentioned, **1**: 240, 488
Braxton, Corbin (son of Carter Braxton):
  Donald recommends to TJ, **16**: 592;
  17: 473, 626
Braxton, Elizabeth Corbin (Mrs. Carter
  Braxton): misconduct of, **1**: 475
Braxton Plan. *See* Virginia: Constitution,
  Braxton Plan
Brazier, Mr., **1**: 441, 442
Brazil: paleontology, **6**: 538, 544; whaling, **7**: 328, 329, 338; **8**: 445; exports,
  7: 352; **9**: 20, 62-3; **11**: 514; exclusion
  of Americans from, **9**: 18; desires independence, **10**: 546-7; **11**: 339-42; interest in American Revolution, **10**:
  546-7; racial composition, **11**: 339-40;
  resources, **11**: 340-1; U.S. trade with,
  14: 646; **15**: 22; TJ's interest in, **17**:
  249, 258-9; **20**: 209
Brazil, Prince of. *See* Joâo Maria José
  Luis, Prince of Brazil
bread: need of in army, **3**: 336; **5**: 189,
  233, 522; price of, **9**: 660; **15**: 502;
  U.S. export of, **10**: 146, 147; and Ge-

nevan revolution, **14**: 603-4; and French Revolution, **14**: 676; **15**: 44, 104, 243-4, 284, 314, 316, 358, 364, 445, 450, 452, 459, 510-1, 513n, 531, 533; **16**: 5n; English government distributes to poor, **15**: 180; French government distributes to poor, **15**: 243-4; French experiment with American wheat, **15**: 401

breadfruit (bread tree): Bligh brings plants from Tahiti, **15**: 134; **16**: 275, 276n

Brearly, David: appointed commissioner in Conn.-Pa. dispute, **6**: 477n, 478n; member of Constitutional Convention, **11**: 400

Breck (Brick), Samuel: letter to, from Lafayette, cited, **10**: 294n; returns to America, **11**: 317, 318n

Breckinridge, John: drafts address from citizens of Albemarle Co., **16**: 170n, 171n, 178n; signs address, **16**: 178

Brede's Hill. *See* Bunker Hill

breeches: leather, for Nelson's cavalry corps, **3**: 100; TJ orders, **10**: 479, 518

breeding of animals: bill concerning, **2**: 443

Bref du Pape Pie VI, **20**: 368

Breglio, Italy, **11**: 432

Bréhan, M. (son of Mme de Bréhan): education of, **12**: 219; mentioned, **15**: 555, 564, 568

Bréhan, Marquis de: remains in France, **12**: 219; enquiry about his wife's arrival in U.S., **12**: 657-8

Bréhan, Marquise de: letters to, **12**: 222; **13**: 149-50; **14**: 552, 655-6; **18**: 117-8, 120n; letters from, **12**: 75, 251-2, 294, 308-9, 645-6; **14**: 399-401; **16**: 424-5; TJ characterizes, **12**: 66; **13**: 492; voyage to America, **12**: 69, 207, 252n; **13**: 149-50; promised a copy of Trumbull's "Bunker Hill," **12**: 139; introduced to Jay, **12**: 217; introduced to Madison, **12**: 219; health of, **12**: 591, 663, 665; letter to quoted, **13**: xxxi; sketches New York harbor, **13**: xxxi, 481 (illus.); Washington entertains at Mount Vernon, **14**: 24n, 294, 303, 341, 399; relationship with Comte de Moustier, **14**: 291, 341; Humphreys characterizes, **14**: 303; criticized by American women, **14**: 303, 399; disillusioned with America, **14**: 303, 341, 399-400, 446; Madison characterizes, **14**: 341; Angelica

Church introduced to, **14**: 515, 552, 553-4; favorable opinions of, **15**: 148, 154; and rumors to replace TJ as Secretary of State, **15**: 564; reacts to French Revolution, **15**: 568; recommends Madison as minister to France, **16**: 424; mentioned, **10**: 453; **12**: 225, 248, 307; **13**: xxx, 295; **14**: 652, 654; **15**: 142; **16**: 102; **17**: 260

Breidbach Burrhesheim, Baron, **13**: 15-6

Breining, George: paid by Department of State, **17**: 368, 371, 372, 373

Breintnall, Joseph, **9**: 486

Bremen: imports from U.S., **7**: 370; **8**: 202-3; and the fisheries, **19**: 178

Bremner, Robert: letter to, from Francis Hopkinson, **6**: 359; letter to mentioned, **6**: 418; on pianofortes, **7**: 57; illness of, **7**: 246

Bremo, Va.: pisé buildings, **15**: 185n-6n

Brent, Cornet, **3**: 573

Brent, Daniel: recommended as clerk, **17**: 354, 355n

Brent, Daniel Carroll: votes for bill for religious freedom, **2**: 549n

Brent, Lieut. George P.: member of court-martial, **3**: 350; resignation of, **4**: 218

Brent, William: British burn property of, **1**: 480, 481; new commission issued to, **3**: 56n, 77; and Petersburg expedition, **3**: 342, 439; supplies for regiment, **3**: 387, 427; proposal to put regiment under Gates' command, **3**: 498, 501, 527; and reorganization of army, **3**: 641; and question of rank, **4**: 168; death of, **8**: 345; **9**: 195; debts, **15**: 644; mentioned, **4**: 529, 539, 557; **5**: 641

Brentford, Conn., **10**: 36

Brescia, Italy: Short describes, **14**: 311

Brest, France: J.P. Jones at, **2**: 207; harbor blocked by British, **3**: 571; naval armament, **12**: 28; consular agent recommended, **14**: 61; disorders at, **17**: 524-5, 557, 611-2, 614, 639-40

Breteuil, Louis Charles Auguste Le Tonnelier, Baron de: letter to, **9**: 613; resignation of, **9**: 470; **13**: 455, 464, 492; and bust of Lafayette, **10**: 145, 415; **11**: 104, 171n; retains office, **12**: 70, 72; favors alliance with Russia, **12**: 174, 190; favors war, **12**: 218; firmness of position, **12**: 314; attitude toward Dutch, **12**: 315; reappointed to ministry, **13**: 573; **15**: 273, 275, 279,

Brook's Point, Va.: ferry at, **2**: 457
broom: Loire valley, **11**: 460
Broom (Groom), Jacob: delegate to Federal Convention, **11**: 400; letter to cited, **11**: 663; and case of John Burke, **12**: 136, 283, 408
Broome, Samuel: letter from, **15**: 92; Smith introduces to TJ, **14**: 560; letter from cited, **14**: 560n; summarizes votes for Washington and Adams, **15**: 92; delivers pictures and books, **15**: 157, 176; TJ issues passport, **15**: 486; on William Green's losses, **20**: 505n; mentioned, **7**: 238; **15**: 160, 240n; **16**: 130; **17**: 482
Brossier, James I.: letters to, **14**: 537-8; **15**: 316-7; letters from, **14**: 532; **15**: 237, 354; seeks Le Havre consulship, **14**: 532, 537-8; **15**: 237, 316-7, 354; Mme de Bareil supports application of, **15**: 283, 284n, 369-70; letter from cited, **15**: 284n; letter to cited, **15**: 284n; petition to Jay, **15**: 354n, 374
Brothers (ship), **15**: 400
Broucq, Frères & Soeurs: letter from, **13**: 151; plants sent to, **13**: 123
Broughton, Thomas: TJ cites, **1**: 555
Broutin, Mme Denise: letter to, **15**: 272-3; letter from, **15**: 278-9
Brown, Andrew: paid for articles in *Federal Gazette*, **17**: 363; paid by Department of State, **17**: 364, 368, 369, 372; Rush recommends to TJ, **17**: 391; presents *Federal Gazette* to TJ, **17**: 391n, 509n; letters from quoted, **17**: 391n; **18**: 78; newspaper quoted, **18**: 100n; publishes laws in *Federal Gazette*, **18**: 66n, 135n; TJ reports on memorial of, **19**: 251; prints *Rights of Man*, **20**: 272n; payment to, **20**: 420
Brown, Bernis (Bernice): in Albemarle co. militia, **1**: 665, 667; account of, as guard for British prisoners, **2**: 32-3; signs Va. oath of allegiance, **2**: 129
Brown, Bristol, **5**: 625
Brown, Henry: lawsuit, **1**: 86; purchase of rum for troops from, **3**: 294
Brown, James: letters to, **16**: 80-2; **17**: 321-2, 653-4; **18**: 3, 306-7; **19**: 541; letters from, **16**: 38-9; **17**: 571-2; **18**: 69; and financial affairs of Donald, **16**: 29, 90, 264; **17**: 566; **18**: 478; merchandise delivered by, **16**: 38-9, 80-1; letters to cited, **16**: 94n; **17**: 324, 327; **18**: 479, 480n; Heth's dispute with, **16**: 236, 382, 565, 593-4; **17**: 322n,

481; bills of exchange, **16**: 331n; returns from Norfolk, **16**: 566; letters from cited, **17**: 322n, 572n; **18**: 346, 480n; **20**: 555; letters to quoted, **17**: 572n; books and supplies forwarded to, **18**: 42, 307; TJ's opinion of, **18**: 72; declines appointment, **19**: 404; ships furniture, **19**: 592; **20**: 95, 211; cloth sent to, **20**: 380; receives TJ's merchandise, **20**: 417; handles Short's funds, **20**: 545-6, 644; mentioned, **16**: 91, 387; **17**: 482, 488, 497; **19**: 521; **20**: 602, 604, 671, 706
Brown, John: killed by Indians, **5**: 535
Brown, Capt. John (master of *Polly*), **16**: 353n-4n; **17**: 417
Brown, Dr. John: and bill establishing ferries, **2**: 460; in Franklin's autobiography, **9**: 486; in Nathaniel Cutting's diary, **15**: 492, 494, 495
Brown, John (Ky.): letter to, **13**: 211-3; letter from, **13**: 494-5; and formation of Ky. constitution, **6**: 283, 284; **14**: 22n; letters from, to Madison, quoted, **6**: 283n; **19**: 437; quarrel with Bentley, **8**: 52; copy of *Notes on Virginia* sent to, **12**: 133; and admission of Ky. to union, **13**: 248n, 249n, 620; **19**: xxxiv, 482; letters from cited, **13**: 496; **17**: 322n; leaves for Ky., **13**: 620; **19**: 505; as congressman, **15**: 6, 154, 337; **17**: 24n; on TJ as Secretary of State, **16**: 170n; on nominees for federal office, **16**: 476-8; **17**: 293n; and navigation of the Mississippi, **17**: 77; **19**: 17; and mission to Madrid, **17**: 87, 89; miniature portrait of, by John Trumbull, **19**: xxxiv, 348 (illus.); education of, **19**: xxxiv; and location of capital, **19**: 4n, 14, 17; and publication of congressional journal, **19**: 115; leaves Philadelphia, **19**: 465; accused of dealing with Gardoqui, **19**: 470; relations with J. M. Marshall, **19**: 470; mentioned, **1**: 8, 103; **4**: 321, 338, 342; **7**: 157n; **15**: 6; **20**: 480
Brown, John (Mass.): printer of handbill making charges against Arnold, **2**: 20n
Brown, John (R.I.): cited on West Indies ports, **7**: 338, 348; commissioner for permanent seat of Congress, **8**: 99
Brown, John (Va.): in Albemarle co. militia, **1**: 665
Brown, Mary: testimony on killing of Frenchmen by British, **3**: 114n
Brown, Mather: portrait of TJ, **1**: lvii, 3

Brown, Mather (*cont.*)
(illus.); **11:** 169, 531; **12:** 597, 647; **13:** 199; **14:** xxxvi, 365n; portrait of John Adams, **10:** 479; **12:** xxxvii, 297, 358, 514 (illus.), 558, 597, 622, 630, 647; **13:** 178, 199, 281n; **14:** 365n; opinion of statue of Washington, **12:** 36; portrait of Paine, **12:** 207, 307, 405; payment to, **13:** 280; pictures of sent to TJ by Trumbull, **13:** 519

Brown, Morgan: bills against Va., **3:** 604-5; **5:** 390-1

Brown, Peter: testimony on British killing of Frenchmen, **3:** 114n

Brown, Lieut. Robert, **4:** 542

Brown, Samuel: letter from, **4:** 469

Brown, Thomas: books consigned to, **8:** 639; letter from, to B. Randolph, quoted, **16:** 520n

Brown, Col. Thomas: orders defense against Indian attacks, **5:** 256

Brown, William: letters to, **16:** 349-50, 486; **18:** 487; **19:** 579-80; **20:** 98-9; letters from cited, **16:** 349, 350n, 486n; letter to cited, **16:** 350n; letter on Mediterranean trade attributed to, **18:** 401n; TJ's account with, **20:** 98-9, 100, 174, 214

Brown, William (flutist): quarrels with Bentley, **8:** 52

Brown (Browne), Capt. Windsor: as commissary of military stores, **4:** 531, 619, 658; **5:** 65, 97, 139; pay, **4:** 658; to be supplied with horse, **5:** 27; to go to Hoods, **5:** 90; mentioned, **4:** 539; **5:** 183

Brown College: solicits funds in Europe, **7:** 399n; **10:** 461-3; seeks French books, **11:** 609-10; condition of, **16:** 453

Browne (Brown), John (commissary of purchases): letters to, **4:** 284, 508-9, 509, 586-7, 587, 686; **5:** 194-5, 441; letters from, **4:** 324; **5:** 274; and provisions, **3:** 246, 402; **4:** 297, 301, 419, 450, 491, 574, 685; **5:** 176, 177, 290, 342, 452, 458-9, 464, 533, 537; **6:** 34; assists Steuben, **4:** 326, 328, 338, 352; impressment of wagons, **4:** 405-6; **5:** 279, 340, 465n; Carrington criticizes, **4:** 492; appoints deputies, **4:** 508-9; **5:** 151, 289, 373, 444; provisions for Convention troops, **4:** 607, 672; Davies criticizes, **5:** 48-9; uses wagons, **5:** 215, 278; and execution of

provision law, **5:** 242; warrants for, **5:** 339; Mason's charges against, **5:** 647-9; mentioned, **4:** 510; **5:** 428, 434, 450

Browne (Brown), Col. Thomas (Georgia Loyalist): treatment of captives by, **5:** 63

Browne, Capt. William: mentioned, **5:** 13

Browne (Brown), William S.: holds property of Thomas Burke, **12:** 136-7; and Madison, **12:** 408; letter to cited, **12:** 611; Madison inquires about, **13:** 413; in case of Thomas Burke, **14:** 4

Browne (Brown), Mrs. William S.: letter from quoted, **12:** 611-2

Browning, Absalam, **4:** 322

Browning, Francis: signs Va. oath of allegiance, **2:** 129

Brownson, Dr. Nathan: signs agreement of secrecy, **1:** 253; purveyor general to hospital of southern department, **4:** 365; money for, **4:** 576

Brown *v.* Tucker, **1:** 86

Bru, Juan Bautista: and work with megatherium, **14:** xxv, xxix-xxxiii, 41 (illus.)

Bruas, Mr.: and bill establishing ferries, **2:** 460

Bruce, Rev.: endorses Pearce's loom, **20:** 243n

Bruce, George: and treatment of John Goodrich, **2:** 4; subscribes to *National Gazette*, **20:** 759

Bruce, Jacob, **1:** 477

Bruce, John: teaches logic, **15:** 205n

Bruce, Robert and Peter: letter to, **20:** 151; TJ rents house from, **16:** 279n; **17:** 495, 554-5, 596; TJ's account with, **20:** 151

Bruce, William, **4:** 332

Bruff, William, **4:** 309, 494

Bruges, Belgium: imports from S.C., **8:** 202-3

brugnols (brugnoles or brugnons): TJ sends to Eppes, **9:** 210; ordered for S.C., **13:** 508; **14:** 183

Bruhl, Germany: Elector's palace, **13:** 447

Bruhl, Count von, **9:** 363n

Bruin, Maj. Peter Bryant, **5:** 576, 577n

Brunneau, Charles (wine merchant), **11:** 457

Brunswick, Karl Wilhelm Ferdinand, Duke of: and troops in America, **5:**

259; negotiations with Amsterdam, **12**: 215; honors bestowed on Unger by, **12**: 524-5

Brunswick, Prince of. *See* Frederick, Prince of Brunswick

Brunswick co., Va.: letters to county lieutenant of, **4**: 646-7; **5**: 416, 614-6; militia, **1**: 160; **2**: 130; **3**: 599; **4**: 62, 63, 97-8, 295n, 352, 371, 477, 645, 646-7, 669; **5**: 6, 29, 35, 36, 310, 315, 614-6, 646; appointment of infantry officers, **1**: 579; place of court of assize, **1**: 629; senatorial district, **2**: 336; levies of soldiers, **3**: 8; tobacco loan office certificates, **3**: 515; collections under provision law, **4**: 7; impressment of supplies and horses for army, **4**: 42; **6**: 51; supply post for, **4**: 286; mentioned, **5**: 175

Brunswick Court House, Va.: assembling of soldiers at, **3**: 8; arms at, **5**: 480; place of court of assize, **7**: 588

Brunswick regiments: among Convention troops, **5**: 100, 184

Bruny, Mlle de: letter from, to Mrs. Randolph, cited, **20**: 377

Brush, E.: letter from, to American Commissioners, **15**: 616-7

Brush, Ebenezer: letters to, **17**: 423-5; **20**: 401-2; consul at Surinam, **17**: 247, 319

Brussels: Trumbull describes, **10**: 440; Dumas desires to be sent to, **12**: 258; disorders in, **16**: 32-3, 41, 220-1, 247-8; Congress of United Belgic states assembles in, **16**: 120; in Flemish revolt, **18**: 114; mentioned, **13**: 146; **18**: 502

Brutus: Italy cited as land of, **11**: 199

"Brutus": criticizes "Publicola," **20**: 297, 302

Bruzatin, Dom, **11**: 463n

Bryan, Mr., **5**: 579n; **12**: 231n

Bryan, A. S.: pledges to support clergyman, **2**: 7

Bryan, Anderson: letter to, **16**: 83-4; letter from, **16**: 93; signs Continental Association, **1**: 154; in Albemarle co. militia, **1**: 667; as surveyor with TJ, **16**: 84n; and Shadwell-Edgehill boundaries, **16**: 97-8, 99, 99n-100n, 136; **19**: 75; **20**: 163-5

Bryan, Andrew: signs Va. oath of allegiance, **2**: 129

Bryan, George: signs nonimportation resolutions (1770), **1**: 47; Pa. bound-

ary commissioner, **3**: 77; councillor of American Philosophical Society, **4**: 545; Hopkinson's caricature of, **7**: 20, 538n; defeated in 1785 election, **8**: 672; opposes federal government, **13**: 39

Bryan, John, **6**: 65n

Bryan, Justice, **7**: 305

Bryan, Samuel, **12**: 231n

Bryan, Samuel (Loyalist officer): movements, **3**: 620

Bryant, Lieut. (British officer): at battle of Camden, **3**: 597n

Bryant, Lieut. Thomas (provost marshal): salary, **3**: 570; mentioned, **3**: 541n; **4**: 540

Bryant's Fort, **4**: 442

Brynberg & Andrews: paid by Department of State, **17**: 371

bucentaur (Italian boat), **14**: 378, 383n

Buchan, Earl of: and gift to Washington, **16**: xxxii; miniature of Washington commissioned for, **16**: xxxiii; letter to, from Washington, cited, **16**: 392n

Buchanan, Miss, **15**: 417n

Buchanan, Mr.: passport issued by TJ, **15**: 485, 486

Buchanan, Mrs.: TJ inquires about, **16**: 300

Buchanan, Archibald: signs nonimportation resolutions (1770), **1**: 47

Buchanan, George: letter to, **16**: 487; letter from, **18**: 472; *Rerum Scoticarum Historia*, **10**: 592; recommends treatment for TJ's headache, **16**: 487n

Buchanan, James: letters to, **6**: 538; **7**: 114, 242, 601; **8**: 207, 366-8, 539; **9**: 220-3, 636-7; **10**: 632; **15**: 592; letters from, **8**: 48-50, 648; signs nonimportation resolutions (1770), **1**: 46; director for Va. public buildings, **8**: 19n; **8**: 343, 534, 537; paid by Gen. Arnold, **4**: 507; books sent to, **6**: 127, 186, 192, 261; **7**: 288; **8**: 565; TJ consults, **6**: 195; forwards plants to Crèvecoeur, **7**: 355; forwards cheese and wine to Eppes and Skipwith, **7**: 384; letters to cited, **9**: 267, 652; **10**: 67; instructions from, **10**: 229; illness of, **11**: 330, 333; mentioned, **3**: 270n; **6**: 321, 567; **7**: 239; **8**: 147, 643; **9**: 652; **11**: 183, 641

Buchanan, John: minister of Richmond church, **8**: 345; and contract with William Green, **20**: 505n

Buchanan, Neill: signs nonimportation resolutions (1770), **1**: 47; administers Banister estate, **14**: 593

Buchannon, John: and bill establishing ferries, **2**: 459

Buchara, Mr.: character of, **20**: 679

Bucheti, Abbé, **16**: 446

buck horns: Banister asked to send, **11**: 121; sent to Buffon, **12**: 194

Buckingham, George Nugent-Temple-Grenville, Marquess of: title conferred on, **7**: 571, 577; owns estate at Wotton, **9**: 370; owns "Stowe House," **9**: 371; dealings with South American agents, **9**: 555; relations with Ledyard, **10**: 98

Buckingham (Rockingham) co., Va.: letter to commissioner of provisions for, **3**: 568n; letters to county lieutenant of, **5**: 204, 275-7, 617; senatorial district, **1**: 476; **2**: 336; petition from religious dissenters in, **1**: 589n; militia, **1**: 579; **2**: 130; **3**: 599; **4**: 63, 295n, 352, 371; **5**: 6n, 29, 35, 275n, 310, 617, 646; place of court of assize, **1**: 629; levies of soldiers, **3**: 8; iron furnace, **3**: 43, 126-7, 188; **5**: 19; troops for defense of western frontier, **3**: 50, 52, 53, 79; state trust in certain lands in, **3**: 138; commissioner of provisions for, **3**: 573; supply post for, **4**: 286; arms, **5**: 341

buckles: manufactured in Conn., **7**: 336

Buckner, Maj. Aylett: resigns commission in Fauquier militia, **5**: 424, 449

Buck-Row (Col. Seldon's place), **5**: 95

Bucks co., Pa.: conspiracy in, **2**: 4

Bucktrout, Benjamin: powder mill, **1**: 288-9

Budden, Mrs.: house in Philadelphia, **17**: 211, 236-7

buffalo: Clark promises TJ bones of, **6**: 159; weight of, **6**: 343; in Italy, **14**: 543

Buffon, Georges Louis Leclerc, Comte de: letters to, **11**: 111-2; **12**: 194-5; letters from, **9**: 130-1; **11**: 243; **15**: 635; TJ asks correction of his notes on, **6**: 339; works by, **6**: 377; **7**: 37; **8**: 111; **11**: 610; **16**: 321; **18**: 580; **19**: 329; theory of central heat, **6**: 378, 436-7; character of Indians, **6**: 427; Hopkinson's fanciful interpretation of his solar system, **6**: 443-4; hypothesis, **6**: 541; *Epoques de la nature*, **6**: 544; **10**: 642; opinion on gold chain from Siberia, **7**: 123; theory on identity of

American mammoth with elephant, **7**: 304, 312; **8**: 632; **13**: 593; works sent to College of William and Mary, **8**: 74, 575; theories on degeneracy in America disputed, **8**: 174-5, 184-5; **12**: 35, 240-1; copy of *Notes on Virginia* sent to, **8**: 184; *Histoire Naturelle, générale et particulière*, **8**: 411; **15**: 398n; refutation of errors hoped for, **8**: 502-3; desires pamphlet by Colden, **9**: 148; notes on American deer and elk, **9**: 158, 520; TJ's acquaintance with, **9**: 218; errors concerning America, **9**: 441, 664-5; **10**: 625; **11**: 71; **13**: 397; describes marmot and mole, **9**: 521-2; respects Morveau's article on chemical elements, **9**: 661; heron sent to, **10**: 78; price of colored plates, **10**: 606; cited on humidity of American climate, **10**: 646; and pigmentation of American Indians, **10**: 643; *Minéraux*, **11**: 43; **12**: 137; Hawkins sends plants to, **11**: 414; natural history specimens sent to, **11**: 656; **12**: 194-6, 197, 208, 287; letter from, to Franklin, cited, **12**: 505; death of, **13**: 152, 382; compares chemistry with cookery, **13**: 381; moose unknown to, **13**: 567, 593; describes reindeer, **13**: 593; TJ uses demographic figures, **15**: 394, 399; T. M. Randolph, Jr. reads, **19**: 556; mentioned, **3**: 342; **6**: 418; **8**: 537; **9**: 261, 357; **10**: 642; **14**: xxvi, xxix; **15**: 307, 394, 399; **20**: 381, 417

Buffon, Marie Françoise de Saint-Belin Malain, Comtesse de, **15**: 555

Buford (Bluford), Col. Abraham: letter from, **5**: 187; at battle of Hampton, **1**: 256-7; reenlisting soldiers, **3**: 7; troops under, **3**: 152, 433, 498, 501; **4**: 112; **6**: 30; equipment for, **3**: 282, 316, 527; **4**: 554, 591; defeated in S.C. campaign, **3**: 415; supplies for troops, **3**: 621; **4**: 471, 472; lodges complaint against Epaphroditus Rudder, **5**: 196, 357; mentioned, **3**: 526

Bufoy. *See* Beaufoy

buggery: discussion of penalties for, **2**: 497n

Bugiasco, Italy: oranges grown at, **11**: 441

Bugniet, Pierre Gabriel: design for Richmond prison, **9**: 222n; TJ desires to visit, **11**: 463n

Builder's Price-Book: TJ orders, **13**: 651

Bukaty, Mr., **9**: 363n

Bulfill, Robert: quoted, **4**: 109n

Bulfinch, Charles: passport issued by TJ, **15**: 484, 485; mentioned, **10**: 211, 393; **12**: 559, 619

Bulkeley, John: letter from, to R. Morris, quoted, **18**: 408n; seeks Lisbon consularship, **19**: 314, 315n; **20**: 161n; TJ's recommendation on, **19**: 317; letter from cited, **20**: 327; vice consular appointment recommended, **20**: 362n

Bulkeley, John, & Son: letter to, **20**: 622-3; letter to, from Johnson, cited, **18**: 50; letters from cited, **20**: 210, 211n, 623n; payment to, **20**: 622

Bull, Frederick: TJ rates inn of, **20**: 471

Bull, John: recommended as commissioner of Federal District, **19**: 59

Bullington, William, **4**: 322

bullion: inconvenience of, **7**: 162; valuation and price of, **7**: 196, 197

Bullitt, Alexander Scott: member of Va. committee to prepare resolution on Congress, **9**: 204n-8n

Bullitt, Cuthbert: and bill to abolish entail, **1**: 561n; member Va. HD Committee on Fincastle co. bill, **1**: 567n-8n, 576n; and establishment of Va. courts, **1**: 606n; and Va. bill on Congressional representation, **2**: 18n; member Va. HD committee on Thomas Johnson case, **2**: 42n, 47n; on committee on court houses in Fluvanna and Cumberland counties, **2**: 122n; on committee on sale of unappropriated lands, **2**: 135n; on committee to adjust titles to unpatented lands, **2**: 138n; votes for bill for religious freedom, **2**: 549n; as attorney for Prince William co., **5**: 641

Bullitt, Capt. Thomas: in French and Indian Wars, **2**: 102; mentioned, **1**: 259

Bulloch, Archibald: signs agreement of secrecy, **1**: 253

Bullock, Leonard Hendley: proprietor of Transylvania colony, **2**: 72, 109

Bullock Pens, **1**: 389n; **2**: 101

bulls: measurements of, **7**: 281n

Bumgarten, **1**: 81

Bunch, Martin: in Albemarle co. militia, **1**: 666

Bunch, Samuel: in Albemarle co. militia, **1**: 668n

Bunker, Capt. (master of *Sally*), **14**: 273

Bunker, Samuel: letter from, **9**: 386-7

Bunker Hill, battle of: TJ's report on, **1**: 175, 184-5, 185-6; Gilmer's comment

on, **1**: 236; reports on, in England, **1**: 247; referred to by TJ, **1**: 488; number of Americans at, **10**: 352, 377; TJ criticizes Andrews' account of, **10**: 377; mentioned, **2**: 198n

Bunyan, Capt. (master of *Montgomery*), **15**: 515, 553

Burbeck, Capt. Henry: letters from, to Knox, quoted, **17**: 472n-3n; reports to Henry Knox, **20**: 98n

Burbeck, Col. William: ordered dismissed from army, **1**: 395

Burd, Mr., **5**: 446

Burd, Edward: letter to, **8**: 151

Bureau de Pusy, Jean Xavier: letter from, **20**: 524-6; and Pa. legislature's address, **19**: 102

Burger, Nicholas: on Albemarle co. militia roll, **1**: 668

Burges, H. J.: signs Virginia Association, **1**: 109

Burges, J. B.: silence of, **18**: 4; in British Foreign Office, **18**: 5n, 323, 324n, 363, 367-8; conversation with Gouverneur Morris, **20**: 700

Burgess, John, **3**: 542n

Burgh, James: *Political Disquisitions*, **16**: 449

burglary: punishment for, **2**: 499-500

Burgoine, Chevalier de. *See* Bourgoing

Burgoyne, Gen. John: pursues Gen. Sullivan's army, **1**: 412; plans attack on Va. and Md., **2**: 14; marches to Fort Edward, **2**: 29; surrender at Saratoga, **2**: 36n, 37, 127; **11**: 43; **14**: 487; **16**: 55n (medal commemorating); and troop casualties, **2**: 197; correspondence with Sir William Howe, **3**: 259; mentioned, **1**: 469; **2**: 201; **3**: 47, 304. *See also* Saratoga, battle of

Burgsdorf, Ludwig Traugott, **3**: 73n

Burgundy, France: TJ describes, **11**: 214, 415-6; soil of, **11**: 284; prosperity of, **11**: 420; nobles opposed to government, **14**: 597, 604, 615

burial, rights of: trade treaty stipulations, **7**: 474, 477, 482, 619, 626

burial at sea: Va. bill for, **2**: 467-8

Burk, John Daly: *History of Virginia*, **6**: 635-7

Burke, Ædanus: pamphlet on Society of the Cincinnati, **7**: 88, 107, 116; **10**: 50; as congressman from S.C., **14**: 666; **15**: 51; **18**: 52; opposes Hamilton, **16**: 456n; in residence bill contro-

Burke, Ædanus (*cont.*)
versy, **17**: 172, 173n, 176; criticized, **19**: 21

Burke, Edmund: speech on economical reform, **3**: 343; Mazzei cites, **5**: 380; quoted on Adam Smith's economics, **8**: 59n; speech against Hastings, **12**: 606; Paine's relations with, **13**: 589; **14**: 454, 564; **18**: 287; **20**: 294; political prospects, **14**: 482; speech on regency, **14**: 580; T. L. Shippen introduced to, **14**: 664; Paine shows him TJ's letters on French Revolution, **15**: 269n-70n; opinion of Dr. Gem, **15**: 386; speech on French Revolution published in *Gazette of the United States*, **16**: 241n, 242n, 252, 255n, 260-2; TJ's comments on, **16**: 242n; **20**: 391; dispute with Fox, **16**: 259; *Reflections on the Revolution in France*, **17**: 671n; **18**: 7; **20**: 266, 268-9, 291, 296, 391, 410, 422, 425; criticism of, **20**: 422, 478; mentioned, **12**: 18

Burke, Henry: in Albemarle co. militia, **1**: 665

Burke, James: property of, **11**: 663

Burke, John: bequest to Thomas Burke, **12**: 136; as master of *Good Hope*, **20**: 361n

Burke, Thomas: letters to, **1**: 72, 85; **4**: 3-4, 39; letters from, **1**: 55-9, 69-70, 73-4, 81-3, 84-5; letter from, to Jamieson, on Tucker case, **1**: 52-5; statement of Tucker case, **1**: 74; signs agreement of secrecy, **1**: 253; TJ's notes of speech before Va. HD on Transylvania land claims, **2**: 66-8; cited on peace terms, **3**: 76; case of, **11**: 663; **12**: 136-7, 283, 408, 439, 611; in committee on medals, **16**: 57n

Burke, Mrs. Thomas: lives in France, **12**: 137; case of, **14**: 4, 437

Burke, William: TJ recommends works by, on George III, **16**: 481

Burkinhout, Dr. *See* Berkenhout

Burk's Bridge, Va.: express at, **5**: 195

Burlamaqui, François Charles, Chevalier de, **1**: 450

Burlington, Earl of: as executor of College of William and Mary, **2**: 539

Burn, Richard: *Justice of the Peace, and Parish Officer*, **11**: 547; *Ecclesiastical Law*, **11**: 548

Burnes, David: sells land for capital, **20**: 8, 13, 14, 20, 78, 79, 82; signs landholders agreement, **20**: 85n

burnet: experiments in cultivation, **8**: 197

Burnet, Bana: signs petition, **1**: 588

Burnet, Durand & De La Marche: letter of credit for TJ, **11**: 184-5; TJ desires to visit, **11**: 463n

Burnet, Gilbert: *History of his own Time*, **12**: 18; **16**: 481

Burnet (Burnett), Maj. Ichabod (Gen. Greene's aide-de-camp), **4**: 561

Burnet, Gov. William, **9**: 486

Burnett, Mr.: publishes falsehoods about U.S., **12**: 637

Burnett, Edmond: in Albemarle co. militia, **1**: 667

Burney, Charles: letters to, **10**: 117-8; **11**: 140-1; letter from, **11**: 58-60; *General History of Music*, **7**: 19; TJ's acquaintance with, **9**: 579; letter from, to John Paradise, **10**: 75-6; letters from cited, **10**: 120; **11**: 90, 168; aids TJ in purchase of harpsichord, **10**: 175, 211, 393, 417, 516

Burnley, Garland (in Regiment of Guards for Convention troops), **3**: 155, 121

Burnley, Mrs. Hardin: permitted to go to Hanover co., **3**: 487; **4**: 47n

Burnley, Richard, **4**: 413

Burnley & Brackenridge (B & B), **15**: 652, 663, 665

Burnly, Richard: state agent purchases goods from, **3**: 19

Burns, Robert: *Poetical Works*, **13**: 651

Burr, Aaron: trial of, **16**: 15n; and Reynolds affair, **18**: 628n, 632, 677n; as intermediary in Hamilton's threatened duel with Monroe, **18**: 670-3; correspondence with Monroe quoted, **18**: 671; as senator from N.Y., **19**: 249n; confers with TJ and Madison, **20**: 434-5; supports *National Gazette*, **20**: 731

Burrell, Jonathan, **3**: 494

Burrhesheim, Baron Breidbach. *See* Breidbach Burrhesheim, Baron

Burroughs, Capt. George: petition from, **5**: 405; reply to, **5**: 405n

Burrow, Sir James: *Reports of Cases in the Court of King's Bench*, **11**: 548; **16**: 277, 481

Burrus, Peter: signs Va. oath of allegiance, **2**: 129

Burrus, Robert: signs Va. oath of allegiance, **2**: 129

Burt, Richard, **5**: 294n

Burton, Forbes, & Co., **14**: 283, 293

Burton, James: signs petition, **1**: 588

Burton, Capt. James: officer in Regiment of Guards for Convention troops, **3**: 121, 155-6

Burton, John: signs nonimportation resolutions (1770), **1**: 46; signs Virginia Association, **1**: 108

Burton, Robert: partner of Alexander Donald, **11**: 193; **12**: 347; letter from, to Jones, cited, **19**: 591

Burwell, Mr.: and bill establishing ferries, **2**: 455

Burwell, Mrs. (of the Grove): death of, **14**: 530

Burwell, Frances (Fanny): courted by John Page, **1**: 16; mentioned, **1**: 14, 34. *See also* Page, Frances Burwell

Burwell, Jonathan, **17**: 585n

Burwell, Judy, **1**: 11

Burwell, L. (of Kingsmill): death of, **9**: 65

Burwell, Col. Lewis (Gloucester co.): letter from, **4**: 612-3; signs nonimportation resolutions, **1**: 30, 46, 47; signs Virginia Association, **1**: 109; and nonimportation agreements, **1**: 110; signs letter to Va. HB, **1**: 112; money collected from, **1**: 237; quarrel with Peyton Randolph, **1**: 250; and bill establishing ferries, **2**: 457; estate of, **4**: 274; **8**: 34, 117; **12**: 650, 652; commissioned lieutenant of Mecklenburg co., **6**: 642; death of, **8**: 345; **9**: 65

Burwell, Mrs. Lewis: death of, **1**: 38

Burwell, Lewis, Jr.: TJ courts sister of, **1**: 6n; leaves William and Mary College, **1**: 12

Burwell, N., **4**: 262

Burwell, N., of the Grove: marriage, **16**: 25

Burwell, Nathaniel: letters to, **5**: 30; **13**: 570-1; **20**: 710-1; letters from, **4**: 294; **5**: 10, 284; attorney for John Paradise, **13**: 472-3, 522, 537, 570; manages Paradise's Va. estate, **13**: 543-4; **14**: 418, 461; **15**: 34, 52; **16**: 84-6; Mrs. Paradise requests TJ to write to, **15**: 164; **16**: 197; mentioned, **15**: 230, 434; **16**: 198n

Burwell, Rebecca (Mrs. Jacquelin Ambler): TJ's courtship of, **1**: 5-11, 13-4; marries Jacquelin Ambler, **1**: 16; mentioned, **1**: 13

Burwell, William Armistead: letter to, from William Tatham, **4**: 273-7

Burwell & Thompson: in Wayles estate debt, **15**: 649n

Burwell's Ferry, Va.: British ships at, **4**: 294, 351, 373; **5**: 344, 496, 499, 502, 506; TJ desires information about, **4**: 338, 339; British landing at, **5**: 506, 521, 527-8, 546; mentioned, **1**: 258, 260, 455; **5**: 166, 318, 489, 538, 624

Burwills Bay, **5**: 486

Bury, Mr., **12**: 73

Busby, James, **4**: 20

Bush, Mr.: conversations with Vining, **19**: 404-5

Bush, George: port collector of Wilmington, **19**: 388

Bush, Philip: in Albemarle co. militia, **1**: 668n

Bush (Boush), Philip (commissary and quartermaster at Winchester), **3**: 613; **4**: 647, 649; **5**: 288n

Bush, Capt. Thomas, **5**: 583, 584n

Bush, Ens. Thomas (Baptist army officer), **1**: 662

Bushara, Abraham: in ransom of Algerian captives, **17**: 29, 30, 32

Bushill, William: killed, **5**: 96

Bushnell, Capt. (master of the *John*), **18**: 307

Bushnell (Bushnel), David: letter from, **12**: 303-5; *Connecticut Turtle*, **7**: 643; **8**: 299, 301, 557; **9**: 150

Busoni, Giovanni Maria Gaspare, **5**: 381

Busset, Mme G.: portrait of Monroe, **18**: xxxvi-vii, 268 (illus.)

Buster, Claudius: signs petition, **6**: 294

Butay, M. A.: fits out privateer, **12**: 44

Bute, John Stuart, Earl of: rumored patron of Hawkesbury, **13**: 291; mentioned, **8**: 525

Butler, Mr.: possible minister to Netherlands, **17**: 508

Butler, D. (master of the *Bowman*), **12**: 561, 592, 630

Butler, Dennis: citizenship of, **16**: 236, 382, 565, 593-4; **17**: 626

Butler, Edward: in Albemarle co. militia, **1**: 666, 668; pledges to support clergyman, **2**: 7; signs Va. oath of allegiance, **2**: 129

Butler, John: aid refused by Indians, **1**: 500; land purchase from Indians, **8**: 85

Butler, Capt. John: albino slave of, **6**: 473

Butler, Gen. John: safe after battle of Camden, **3**: 596; commissioners meet with, **5**: 116; at Guilford Court House,

Butler, Gen. John (*cont.*)
5: 156; letter to, from Pierce, quoted, 5: 570n

Butler, Pierce: as member of Federal Convention, 11: 401; as senator from S.C., 14: 394; bonds sent to, 16: 324, 325n; cooperates with N.Y. delegation, 17: 169n; Drago di Domenico and, 18: 359, 360n; and capital site, 19: 17, 34-5; and Franklin's death, 19: 78-9

Butler, Pinckney: as S.C. delegate to Federal Convention, 11: 219

Butler, Richard: Indian commissioner, 7: 8, 11, 396, 444; 8: 79; complains of mismanagement, 19: 464; mentioned, 4: 325; 8: 442

Butler, Lieut. Samuel, 4: 542

Butler, Zebulon: petitions Congress, 6: 479, 482, 483, 484, 498-500, 501-5; TJ's report on petition, 6: 571

Butte aux Cailles: balloon flight to, 7: xxvii, 132 (illus.)

butter: price of, 2: 264; not included in army ration, 3: 324; U.S. export of, 10: 147; making, 11: 438-9

Butterfield, Maj. Isaac: and Cedars affair, 1: 396-8, 401, 403, 451; conduct at Cedars condemned by TJ, 1: 459; court-martial of, 1: 500

butternut: sample to be sent to France, 10: 227

Buttler, Charles: parole of, 5: 148

Buxton, Charles: "Bowling-Green Washington," 16: xxxiii-iv, 52 (illus.)

Buxton, James: and bill establishing ferries, 2: 457

Bynkershoek, Cornelius van: TJ examines writings of, 6: 550; works ordered by Madison, 7: 37, 288

Byram, William: imports slaves, 15: 654

Byrd, Mr.: ferry from estate on Rappahannock, 2: 455

Byrd, Abigail, 5: 705n

Byrd, Anne Willing, 5: 705n

Byrd, Charles, 5: 705n

Byrd, Evelyn, 5: 705n

Byrd, Francis Otway, 1: 268

Byrd, J., 4: 322

Byrd, Jane, 5: 705n

Byrd, Maria Horsmanden, 5: 705n

Byrd, Mary Willing (Mrs. William Byrd): letters to, 3: 112-3; 5: 31-2; letter from, 4: 690-2; and management of property, 3: 111; 4: 682; letter from cited, 4: 668; and flag of truce, 4: 680-1; 5: 677n, 693; restitution of prop-

erty, 4: 688; and Westover affair, 5: 121n, 671-705 (editorial note and documents); described by Chastellux, 5: 671n; family connections, 5: 677n; correspondence with Steuben, 5: 679n, 680n, 688, 689-91, 691-2, 693-4; letters from, to Hare, cited, 5: 695; letter from, to Thomas Nelson (?), 5: 703-4; letter from, to Sir Guy Carleton, 5: 704-5; mentioned, 1: 252

Byrd, Otway, 5: 679n, 688; 10: 109

Byrd, Richard, 5: 705n

Byrd, William: lead mines of, 2: 388n; as auditor of College of William and Mary, 2: 536

Byrd, Col. William III: Innes' attack on, 1: 289; library of, 1: 596; 2: 207; 6: 220n; 20: 635n; involved in scheme to purchase land from Cherokee, 2: 69, 70, 82; land entries, 3: 111, 113; excerpt from family Bible, 5: 671n; characterized by David Meade, 5: 677n; TJ's Richmond lot bought from, 7: 636; death of, 9: 65; Wayles' transactions with, 15: 653-4, 661, 671; mentioned, 1: 39; 5: 677n

Byrd, William IV, 5: 705n

Byrd ordinary: TJ arrives at, 16: 51

Byron, Adm. John: squadron of joins Adm. Howe, 2: 212, 214; naval actions in American Revolution, 3: 75

Cabanis, M.: letter to, 13: 110-1; banker of Lambert, 11: 596; and wine purchase, 12: 226-7, 353

Cabarrus, Dominique, 8: 35

Cabarrus, Francisco, Count: appointed director of royal treasury, 12: 153, 162; arrives in Paris, 12: 168; refuses appointment as treasury director, 12: 170, 175, 180, 190, 216; pays servant of Carmichael, 18: 597, 600n

Cabarrus, Peyrinault & Cie.: account with Mainville, 11: 655

Cabbage, Capt. (master of *Volunteer*), 14: 31

Cabbin, Mr., 9: 486

Cabeen, John: letter from, 6: 68-9

Cabell, John: and bill establishing ferries, 2: 459

Cabell, Col. Joseph: manages lottery, 1: 22; signs nonimportation resolutions, 1: 30, 46; and Rivanna river, 1: 87; signs Virginia Association, 1: 108; and bill establishing ferries, 2: 459; forces under, **3**: 364; elected to Va. GA from Albemarle, **5**: 430; mentioned, **3**: 204; **6**: 49n

Cabell, Samuel Jordan: votes for bill for religious freedom, **2**: 549n; signs petition, **3**: 652

Cabell, William: letter to, **1**: 94; letter from, **1**: 388; manages lottery, **1**: 22; and Rivanna river, **1**: 87; and Dickey *v.* Cabell, **1**: 94; signs Virginia Association, **1**: 108; runs for Va. senate, **1**: 476; and conference on Johnson case, **2**: 43n; and bill establishing ferries, **2**: 459; elected member of Va. Executive Council, **6**: 89n, 93; declines election to Executive Council, **6**: 98n; opposes Constitution, **12**: 284; **13**: 98; attacked for Antifederalist views, **16**: 143n

Cabell, William, Jr.: signs nonimportation resolutions, **1**: 30, 46; on Va. committee to welcome TJ, **16**: 11n; attacked for Antifederalist views, **16**: 143n

Cabell family: opposes Constitution, **12**: 284

cabinet, U.S.: meeting of Apr. 11, 1791, **20**: 87, 117-41, 144-5; role of vice president in, **20**: 118n; authorized to meet in Washington's absence, **20**: 123, 142

Cabinet des modes, **13**: 151; **16**: 322

cabinet work: U.S. import of, **10**: 147

Cabin Point, Va.: rendezvous of troops at, **4**: 64; identified, **4**: 98n; Mathews ordered to march to, **4**: 473; desertions from, **5**: 114; Muhlenberg at, **5**: 511

Cabot, Mr.: letter to, **7**: 383

Cabot, Francis: and Potomac capital site, **20**: 20n; relations with L'Enfant, **20**: 36n, 701; identified as "Spectator," **20**: 54-5; purchases capital lot for Lear, **20**: 55; criticized by Washington, **20**: 55n; introduced to TJ, **20**: 701-2

Cabot, George (senator from Mass.), **20**: 55

Cabot (Gabot), John: and discovery of North America, **6**: 488, 492

Cabot, Sebastian, **11**: 199

cabriolet and phaeton: TJ's drawings for Geismar, **13**: 528; **14**: 582-3; **15**: xxvii

cacao: imported from Brazil, **9**: 62-3; not grown in U.S., **10**: 33

Cacciapiatti, Marquis di: Clerici recommended to, **11**: 585, 586

cadavers: means of acquiring, **13**: 233

Cadiz, Spain: commerce of, **7**: 550; imports from S.C., **8**: 203; Spanish fleet sails from, **13**: 114, 143, 173, 174, 191; U.S. consulate at, **19**: 313, 317; **20**: 160, 563

Cadogan, Charles, Lord: estate at Caversham sold, **9**: 370

Cadusch, Marquis de: in Saint-Domingue revolt, **17**: 306, 309

Cadwalader, Gen. John: failure to cross Delaware, **2**: 3; **6**: 61; death of, **10**: 288, 412; mentioned, **6**: 351

Caen, France: U.S. agent at, **20**: 676

Caermarthen, Marquis of. *See* Carmarthen

Caesar, Caius and Lucius: building of Maison Carrée, **8**: 535, 537

Caesar, Caius Julius: TJ seeks information on best Italian translation, **11**: 159; TJ recommends works by, **12**: 18; *Commentaries*, **13**: 655; mentioned, **14**: 380

Cagliostro, Mme: acquittal, **9**: 606

Cagliostro, Alessandro, Count: in Bastille, **9**: 447, 470; acquitted, **9**: 606, 634; mentioned, **10**: 283

Cahierre, Mme Paul, **15**: 174, 183, 184

Cahierre, Paul: letter to, **15**: 183; letter from, **15**: 174; introduced to TJ, **15**: 86; introduced to Curson by TJ, **15**: 184

Cahokia, Ill.: French settlement at, **6**: 61; land claims from, **18**: 167; described, **18**: 196-7; TJ reports on, **18**: 207-8

Caillard, Antoine Bernard: as French chargé at The Hague, **9**: 279; letter to quoted, **10**: 208

Caillot, Mme: mistress of Temple Franklin, **18**: 87n

Cain, Capt. Alexander: letters from, **9**: 386-7; **14**: 668-70; as master of *Marquis de Lafayette*, **9**: 392; **13**: 297; receives papers for wheat cargo, **14**: 668-71, 690; letter from cited, **14**: 690; mentioned, **15**: 63, 64n

Cairnes, Burrill. *See* Carnes

Cairo, Egypt: Ledyard in, **13**: 594, 596

caisse de l'extraordinaire, **16**: 44

Calais, France: TJ visits, **9**: 542

Calaway, James. *See* Callaway

Caldwell, Henry: introduced to TJ, **13**: 657-8

Caldwell, Margaret: McHenry's courtship of, **6**: 405n

Caldwell, Samuel: certificate to Bondfield for clothing, **17**: 578

Caloogee (Cherokee town), **4**: 362

Calton, John: in Albemarle co. militia, **1**: 668n

Calvaire, Mont: hermitage on, **12**: xxxv, 482 (illus.)

Calvert, Benjamin: pledges to support clergyman, **2**: 7; quarters British prisoners, **2**: 32; mentioned, **4**: 672

Calvert, Christopher: letter to, **5**: 214; letter from, **5**: 4

Calvert, Cornelius, Sr.: signs address to TJ, **15**: 556

Calvert, John, **1**: 82

Calvert, William: in Albemarle co. militia, **1**: 666

Calvil, Charles: reports on conditions of Americans in Algiers, **19**: 332

Calvinistical Reformed Church: subscription to support clergyman of, **2**: 6-8

Calvinists: compared with Arminians, **1**: 554

Calvin's case: Coke's decision in, **9**: 259

Cambden, William. *See* Camden

Cambray (Cambrai), Archbishop of. *See* Rohan-Guemené, Prince de

Cambray (Cambrai), Comte de: letters to, **9**: 171, 191-2; **10**: 73-4; **13**: 215, 259-60, 662; **15**: 345-6, 407-8; letters from, **9**: 164; **10**: 142; **13**: 244, 479-80, 641; **15**: 347-8; marriage of, **9**: 164, 171; pays claim, **9**: 191; presses claims of French officers, **12**: 286-7; **15**: 345-6; letters of procuration attested for, **13**: 520, 535, 641, 662; papers sent to Petry, **13**: 535, 662; **15**: 347-8, 407-8; **16**: 52; on French Revolution, **15**: 348; mentioned, **9**: 272; **14**: 389n

Cambrésis, Estates of: protests appropriation of church property, **15**: 548

cambric: ordered for Mrs. Adams, **9**: 278; **12**: 202; for Mrs. Smith, **10**: 211; **12**: 619

Cambridge, Mass.: military headquarters at, **1**: 243

Cambridge, N.Y.: visited by TJ and Madison, **20**: 458

Camden, battle of (Aug. 1780): described by Gen. Stevens, **3**: 558-9, 563, 576; role of Va. militia in, **3**: 592; **4**: 20, 46; **5**: 298; TJ's narrative of, **3**: 593-7; strength of opposing forces, **3**: 597n; First Continental Regiment of Artillery in, **3**: 636; mentioned, **4**: 536, 611

Camden, Charles Pratt, Earl of: as presi-

dent of privy council, **7**: 577; and Franklin's autobiography, **9**: 487; and case of *Mentor*, **20**: 638n

Camden, S.C.: Cornwallis' army near, **3**: 403, 415; British garrison at, **3**: 462, 465, 620; fortified by British, **4**: 86; Greene's army near, **5**: 624; evacuated by British, **6**: 19, 26, 52

Camden (Cambden), William: cited by TJ, **1**: 553; *Annales Rerum Anglicarum et Hibernicarum, Regnante Elizabetha*, **12**: 18

Camden, William (Va.): in Albemarle co. militia, **1**: 666

camels (for lightering ships), **13**: 9

Cameron, Alexander: and relations with Cherokee, **2**: 79, 93, 107; and Henderson's land claims, **2**: 91; and Cherokee archives, **6**: 141n

"Camillus" (pseud.): writings of, **18**: 660

Camm, John: signs commission, **1**: 99

Camp, Ichabod: signs Virginia Association, **1**: 109

Campana in die. *See* Burwell, Rebecca

Campanula americana and perfoliata: sample to be sent to France, **10**: 227

Campbell, Lieut.: travel permit sought for, **2**: 299; seeks permit to go to flag, **3**: 14, 15

Campbell, Maj.: commands riflemen in N.C., **4**: 562

Campbell, Mr.: possible minister to Denmark, **17**: 433

Campbell, Mrs.: sale of effects of, **15**: 50

Campbell, Archibald: signs nonimportation resolutions (1770), **1**: 46

Campbell, Col. Arthur: letters to, **3**: 534-5; **4**: 634-5; **5**: 476; letters from, **4**: 359-63, 457-8, 499-500, 546-7, 587; **5**: 20, 267-8, 339-40, 552-3; **6**: 79, 80, 94, 98-9, 201, 208-9; **15**: 596-7; interest in Transylvania, **1**: 566n; member Va. HD Committee on Fincastle co. bill, **1**: 567n-8n; supports Richard Henderson, **1**: 568n; appointed commissioner to investigate land claims, **2**: 65n; witnesses deposition, **2**: 96; letter to, from Muter, quoted, **4**: 179; campaigns against Cherokee, **4**: 407-8; **5**: 562; **6**: 141, 172-3; proposes building fort at confluence of Holston and Tennessee rivers, **4**: 640; **5**: 6; aids Greene, **4**: 683; **5**: 112; commissioned to negotiate with Cherokees, **5**: 395, 396n; letters to, from Joseph Martin, **5**: 534-5; **6**:

send to France, **9**: 160; Whipple asked to send to France, **9**: 161; horns sent to TJ, **11**: 296, 359; horns sent to Buffon, **12**: 194

Carleton, Sir Guy: relations with Indians, **1**: 175, 217, 244, 500; and British strategy, **1**: 247; retires to Quebec, **1**: 248; leads army from Montreal to Quebec, **1**: 264, 269; banishes Canadians refusing to fight, **1**: 434; accused of giving smallpox to Continental army, **1**: 435, 437, 448; fleet of, **1**: 442; ill feeling of Canadians toward, **1**: 499; evacuates Crown Point, **1**: 597-8; plan for campaign, **2**: 13; orders expedition against western settlers, **2**: 256; as commander in chief for Detroit, **2**: 292; treatment of prisoners of war, **3**: 45; Mrs. Byrd seeks damages from, **5**: 686n; letter to, from Mrs. Byrd, **5**: 704-5; and arrangements for executing provisional treaty, **6**: 268, 269n; letter from, to Washington, cited, **6**: 328; refuses to return American slaves, **6**: 430n; **9**: 111; alleged instructions to harass Americans, **10**: 221, 596; rule in Canada, **12**: 226; mentioned, **1**: 446. *See also* Dorchester, Lord

Carleton, Joseph: letter from, **6**: 530; mentioned, **3**: 494; **6**: 510n

Carlisle, Mr.: mentioned, **7**: 20

Carlisle (Carlyle), Frederick Howard, fifth Earl of: British commissioner to Congress, **2**: 200, 205

Carlisle, Pa.: petitions from, **19**: 6; possible site of capital, **19**: 12

Carlos VI (Prince of Asturias): illness of son, **9**: 24, 48; influence of, **16**: 254; mentioned, **10**: 179

Carlos Clemente (son of Carlos VI): illness of, **9**: 24, 48

Carlotta Joaquina (Infanta of Spain): marries prince of Portugal, **8**: 66, 69, 84; birth of daughter, **12**: 324; mentioned, **10**: 179

Carlsruh. *See* Karlsruhe

Carmack, John: petitions Va. HD for care of livestock, **2**: 41n-2n; claim against Va., **2**: 63

Carmarthen (Caermarthen), Francis Godolphin Osborne, Lord: letter to, **9**: 436; letter to, from American Commissioners, **9**: 375; on trade negotiations between Britain and U.S., **8**: 57n; **9**: 281; receives John Adams, **8**:

166, 167, 170, 176; on consuls, **8**: 302; rumored appointment as ambassador to France, **8**: 317; letter to quoted, **8**: 362n-3n; official entertaining, **8**: 594; on western posts, **9**: 184; as possible ambassador to Spain, **9**: 241; letter to, from Adams, **9**: 327; TJ's comments on, **9**: 364n; confers with Adams and TJ, **9**: 406; on release of American prisoners, **10**: 62; on prospects for war, **12**: 292; mentioned, **7**: 547; **8**: 301; **9**: 363n, 405; **10**: 266

Carmichael, James: letters to, **8**: 73; **13**: 532; letters from, **8**: 92; **14**: 285; mentioned, **15**: 378, 490

Carmichael, William: letters to, **7**: 396, 462, 575, 630; **8**: 93, 134, 247-9, 401-2, 648-9, 670; **9**: 13-7, 85-6, 171-3, 448-9, 665-7; **10**: 284-8, 396-7, 632-5; **11**: 164-5, 378, 469-70; **12**: 172-9, 423-7, 552; **13**: 229-35, 502-3; **14**: 385-8, 615-7, 700-1; **15**: 103-5, 307-8, 336-8, 418-9; **16**: 329-30, 450-1; **17**: 111-7, 318-20, 472-3; **19**: 522-3; **20**: 203-9, 417-8, 563; letter to, from American Commissioners, **8**: 623-4; letters from, **7**: 548-50; **8**: 64-7, 69-70, 95-6, 137-9, 251-6, 320-2, 464-7, 566-7, 570, 665-6; **9**: 23-4, 25, 103-6, 223, 250, 538-40, 546-7, 647-9; **10**: 137-9, 149-51, 178-81, 265-7, 329-30, 411-3, 427-9, 536-8, 606-8; **11**: 236-8, 565-7; **12**: 50-2, 99-101, 238-42, 323-5, 361-5, 539; **13**: 91-5, 113-4, 142-4, 176-7, 215-7, 239, 398-400, 509, 576-9, 643; **14**: 46-7, 353-4, 498-505, 642-3; **15**: 340-2; **18**: 597-600; letters from, to American Commissioners, **9**: 244-9, 377-8, 385-6; and instructions from Maryland on western lands, **3**: 628; letters from quoted, **4**: 605-6; **11**: 118; **20**: 95-6; on European situation, **6**: 9; complains of neglect by Congress, **7**: 548; letters from cited, **7**: 574; **8**: 80-1; **9**: 407, 515, 547, 590; **10**: 142, 196, 238, 241, 302, 396, 403, 480; **11**: 553; **12**: 204; **13**: 137n; **14**: xxv-vi, xxxi-iv, 388n; **15**: 360, 405; **20**: 327, 566; cipher, **7**: 630; **8**: 134, 247, 321, 402, 649; **9**: 13, 250; **10**: 287; **11**: 470, 567; **12**: 175n-9n, 238, 424; **13**: 91, 142-3, 144n, 176, 217n, 230, 398-9; **14**: 288, 289n; **15**: 338n; **16**: 496; **17**: 320, 330n; **18**: 597-8; intercedes with

Carmichael, William (*cont.*)
Spain for American vessel, **8**: 43; and
Barbary States, **8**: 80; **9**: 14-5, 565n;
10: 619; **11**: 22, 102, 163; **13**: 527;
letter from, to Benjamin Franklin, **8**:
83-4; letter to, from Louis Goublot, **8**:
253-4; letter to, from Alcaid Driss, **8**:
255-6; asked to intercede for Watson's
release, **8**: 341; draws bills, **8**: 589; **9**:
56, 57, 85-6, 171-2, 243, 250; **10**:
237, 257, 411; letters to be sent
through, **8**: 615; **11**: 380, 395; letters
to cited, **9**: 89, 138, 383, 615; **11**:
494n; **12**: 151; **13**: 237; **14**: 503n; **15**:
342n; **16**: 310n, 408n, 450; **17**: 120-
1, 281n, 319, 341n; **18**: 162n, 241-2,
377n, 505; **19**: 573; **20**: 254, 345n,
530, 653; expenses, **9**: 104-5, 172,
648; **11**: 609; **19**: 586; **20**: 592; opinions of, **9**: 236-7; **11**: 95; **18**: 599n-
600n, 602; **20**: 208n; confers with
Floridablanca, **9**: 349; **19**: 254; letter
to, from Lamb, cited, **9**: 376; salary, **9**:
481; **11**: 185, 469, 474-5; **12**: 72,
147, 341; **14**: 56, 581; **15**: 41, 105;
letter from sent to Adams, **9**: 506; relations with John Lamb, **9**: 547, 550,
621; **10**: 480, 510, 556, 649; **11**: 368-
9; **12**: 176n, 181; orders books for TJ,
9: 580; **11**: 667; letter to, from
O'Bryen, quoted, **10**: 132n; financial
difficulties, **10**: 137, 180, 284-5; **13**:
94; **14**: 502-3; **15**: 341, 418-9; sends
map to TJ, **10**: 214n; drafts on Grand,
10: 237, 257; seeks diplomatic information from TJ, **10**: 330; wishes to be
sent to The Hague, **10**: 412; and
Spanish political affairs, **10**: 428; **13**:
576-9; **14**: 500-2; **18**: 599; and Mississippi negotiations, **10**: 457; copying
press sent to, **11**: 53n, 384; letter to,
from Congress, cited, **11**: 240; W. S.
Smith introduced to, **11**: 366, 511;
copy of *Notes on Virginia* sent to, **12**:
175; and political intrigue, **12**: 178n-
9n; books sent to, **12**: 186, 187; owed
money by Littlepage, **12**: 334; **13**: 94,
230, 399; on Constitution, **13**: 91-2,
95; letters from, to Jay, cited, **13**: 93,
94, 114n; **14**: 47n; investigates Panama canal project, **13**: 93-4, 399, 577;
14: 499, 503n; and American captives
in Algiers, **13**: 142, 399; **14**: 502; **15**:
340-1, 342n; **20**: 624; payment to, **13**:
149, 230, 509, 552, 568, 576, 600;
correspondence with G. Morris, **13**:

164n; **14**: 531n-2n; **15**: 241n, 340; introduces Trotti to TJ, **13**: 643; sends
drawing and description of megatherium to TJ, **14**: xxv-vii, xxxi-iv, 40 (illus.); letters to, from Jay, cited, **14**:
288, 289n; **16**: 329, 330n; **17**: 472;
letter to, from Chiappe, cited, **14**:
503n; introduces Ventura Caro to TJ,
14: 642; Rutledge introduced to, **14**:
700-1; Huger introduced to, **15**: 307,
308n; letters from, to Short, **15**: 338n;
16: 273, 403-4, 425, 440, 585; **18**:
506-7; letter to, from Roberts, quoted,
15: 342n; letter to, from Short,
quoted, **15**: 551n; letter of credence
for, **16**: 329, 330n, 450-1; suggested
as minister to France, **16**: 423, 424n;
commission as chargé d'affaires, **16**:
450, 451n; retirement doubtful, **16**:
585; and Humphreys' mission to
Spain, **17**: 111, 125; **18**: 472-5, 498,
597, 599; **19**: 293; and war crisis of
1790, **17**: 111-7, 125; **18**: 472-5, 498,
597, 599; Report on Weights and
Measures sent to, **17**: 320; letters to,
from Montgomery, cited, **17**: 397; letter for sent to TJ, **17**: 558; Short
comments on TJ's letter to, **18**: 14;
navigation bill sent to, **18**: 241-2; **19**:
571, 574-5; letters to, from O'Bryen,
18: 410-2, 437-44; correspondence
with Washington, **18**: 597, 599n-
600n; **19**: 522; letters intercepted, **18**:
597-8; relations with Gouverneur
Morris, **18**: 598; **20**: 95-6; account of
Natural Bridge, **19**: xxxi, 299n; health
of, **19**: 254; **20**: 538; received by
Charles IV, **19**: 269; aided by Littlepage, **19**: 417; and fugitive slaves, **19**:
430; letter to sent to Short, **19**: 528;
return to U.S., **20**: 96; irregularity of
letters, **20**: 203-4, 209; in *Dover* case,
20: 208n; confers with Duke of Leeds,
20: 212; lack of communication with
Short, **20**: 365, 587; supported by
French, **20**: 531; mentioned, **3**: 234; **6**:
265; **7**: 395, 579; **8**: 48n, 140, 244,
376, 443, 474; **9**: 284, 298, 365, 525,
526, 564, 566, 619, 620, 625, 646,
667; **10**: 71, 349, 618, 638, 651; **11**:
20, 21, 257, 512; **16**: 288n; **17**: 19,
34n, 560
Carminice, Prince, **12**: 43n
Carnes (Cairnes), Burrill: letters to, **9**:
599; **12**: 9, 109, 164-5, 294, 493,
497, 640; **14**: 457, 553; **17**: 423-5;

20: 600; letters from, **9**: 303, 628; **11**: 601-3; **12**: 52, 191, 222, 475, 515-6; **13**: 249, 657-8; **14**: 31, 483-4, 528, 532, 588-9; **17**: 573; letters sent by, **8**: 371; **11**: 143; suggested as clerk to Lamb, **8**: 544; delay in forwarding seeds, **11**: 233; letters from cited, **11**: 234; **12**: 598; letter to cited, **11**: 268; visits London, **11**: 277; verifies vouchers, **13**: 295; consul at Nantes, **14**: 59; **17**: 246, 252, 253n, 280, 573; recommends Gallwey to take charge in his absence, **14**: 588-9; visits America, **14**: 589; passport issued by TJ, **15**: 485; in Banister's debt to TJ, **16**: 31; mentioned, **8**: 409; **10**: 227, 303; **11**: 174, 175, 188, 395; **12**: 12, 493, 495; **14**: 61; **15**: 43n, 66

Carnes, Burrill, & Co.: formation of, **11**: 602

Carnes, Edward, **17**: 573

Carney, Lieut. Richard: member of court martial, **3**: 350

Caro, Annibale: translation of Virgil, **6**: 173

Carolina: grant by Charles II, **6**: 657

Carolina campaign: Va. troops in, **3**: 432, 439, 480, 500; **5**: 54; reports on, **3**: 432-4; Gates commands American forces in, **3**: 438; TJ plans line of communication for, **3**: 445, 446, 471; Congress orders Va. militia to support southern army, **3**: 457; British operations in southern N.C., **3**: 462-4; strategy for proposed by Monroe, **3**: 465-6; strength of British and American forces in, **3**: 472, 477; reports of American success in, **3**: 553; Greene commands southern army in, **4**: 60-1; Morgan reports on engagements in, **4**: 495-6; reinforcements from Va. requested, **4**: 504; Washington comments on, **4**: 543; Greene retreats before Cornwallis, **4**: 561-4, 576; Greene's strategy in N.C., **5**: 111, 361; progress in reported to Va. HD, **5**: 182; mentioned, **2**: 264; **3**: 415. *See also* southern army, and under names of generals (e.g., Cornwallis, Gates, Greene) and battles (e.g., Camden, Charleston, King's Mountain)

Carolina Planter (ship): sails for Charleston, **15**: 538; **16**: 94

Caroline co., Va.: letter to commissioner of provisions for, **3**: 569n; letters to county lieutenant of, **5**: 128, 443, 601-

2, 616-7; **6**: 34-5; letter to members of GA for, **5**: 585-6; appoints infantry officers, **1**: 580; place of court of assize, **1**: 629; militia, **2**: 130; **3**: 239, 599; **4**: 63, 304, 554; **5**: 128, 141, 181, 191, 271, 273, 309n, 310, 329n, 332-3, 443n, 475, 501, 561, 601-2, 616-7, 646; senatorial district, **2**: 336; levies of soldiers, **3**: 7; tobacco loan office certificates, **3**: 516; supply post for, **4**: 286; resolves on connection between U.S and France, **19**: 105

Caron, André: letter from, **10**: 256; case of, **10**: 650

caroubier tree, **11**: 442

Carp, Mathey: signs nonimportation resolutions (1770), **1**: 47

Carpenter, John, **4**: 531, 532

carpenters: needed to repair damage at Richmond and Westham, **4**: 373; for public work, **4**: 609; for work at Hoods, **4**: 626; **5**: 500; salary of, **5**: 126-7; **7**: 297, 327 (N.Y.), 332 (Conn.), 339 (R.I.), 342 (Mass.), 343 (N.H.); tools, **5**: 127; housing conditions of, **5**: 322; superiority of English over French, **8**: 367

Carr, Mr. (coachmaker), **20**: 555

Carr, Mr. (Va.): in settlement of TJ's father's estate, **16**: 157

Carr, Dabney (Currus): TJ comments on domestic happiness of, **1**: 36; death of, **1**: 97; **15**: 571; education of sons of, **6**: 166-7; **7**: 233-4; TJ's affection for, **6**: 168; estate of, **11**: 623; **17**: 677; sale of books, **15**: 627; mentioned, **1**: 38; **16**: 205

Carr, Dabney, Jr.: education of, **7**: 224, 233-4, 361-2, 408, 500, 504, 597-8; **8**: 96, 114; **9**: 39, 520, 550, 648; **10**: 614; **11**: 155, 299, 402, 623; **12**: 414; **15**: 157, 618, 620, 623; **16**: 89; **20**: 331, 378; health of, **15**: 618, 627, 640; Maury as teacher, **16**: 89; payment to, **16**: 114, 115, 128, 129n, 138, 157; books received by, **17**: 3; mentioned, **7**: 356; **11**: 668; **15**: 633; **16**: 277

Carr, Garland: letter to, **17**: 672-3

Carr, Jack, **15**: 640

Carr, John: legal dealings with Sam Carr, **19**: 337

Carr, Lucy, **11**: 624

Carr, Martha Jefferson (Mrs. Dabney Carr): letters to, **6**: 370, 391, 470; **7**: 224, 500; **8**: 413; **11**: 623-4; **15**: 620-

master department, **4**: 285-8, 340-2,
464, 510, 511; **5**: 5, 341; letters from,
to Davies, quoted, **4**: 297n; **5**: 465n;
warrants for, **4**: 444; letters from cited,
5: 5, 240-1; **13**: 339n; **16**: 456n; **18**:
162n; letter from, to Pickering, **5**:
574-8; letter to, from Greene, quoted,
5: 577n-8n; as Va. delegate in Congress, **9**: 191, 202, 242, 479; **10**: 577;
11: 328; TJ characterizes, **10**: 225;
correspondence with Short, **11**: 50n;
13: 414n, 496, 558n; attitude toward
Confederation, **11**: 311; forwards
packages, **11**: 328; on Constitution,
12: 254-5; **13**: 100-1, 103, 156-7; introduces Barlow to TJ, **13**: 156; sends
Federalist to TJ, **13**: 157, 158n, 245,
495, 498; **14**: 188; letter to, from
Madison, cited, **13**: 157; introduces
George Washington Greene to TJ, **13**:
172; inquires about parcel for TJ, **14**:
280; bust of J. P. Jones sent to, **15**:
122, 438; on Va. HD committee to
welcome TJ, **16**: 11n; marshal of U.S.
District Court, **16**: 27; letter to, from
Hamilton, cited, **17**: 391n-2n; sends
Northwest Ordinance to TJ, **18**: 162;
letter to cited, **18**: 162n; and Northwest Territory, **18**: 165; and Scioto
Company, **18**: 176; views on commercial policy, **18**: 525; letter from, to
Madison, quoted, **18**: 615n; sends
Tench Coxe's pamphlet to TJ, **19**:
123n; rejects commission as federal su-
pervisor, **20**: 99; on Va. census, **20**:
295; mentioned, **11**: 414; **12**: 269,
270, 283; **13**: 50, 413; **14**: 281
Carrington, George: on committee to
bring in land office bill, **2**: 136n
Carrington, George, Jr.: letter from, **5**:
82; mentioned, **6**: 225
Carrington, Joseph: and Johnson case, **2**:
43n; payment of British debts by, **2**:
171n
Carrington, Paul: letter from, **1**: 388;
manages land lottery, **1**: 22; signs nonimportation resolutions, **1**: 30, 46;
signs Virginia Association, **1**: 109; and
nonimportation agreements, **1**: 110;
signs letter to Va. HB, **1**: 112; signs
TJ's commission, **1**: 246; and Johnson
case, **2**: 43n; appointed commissioner
to investigate land claims, **2**: 65n, 68-
9; member committee on court houses
in Fluvanna and Cumberland counties,

2: 122n; nominated to Committee of
Revisors, **2**: 313n; letter from cited, **4**:
619; attitude toward Constitution, **12**:
284
Carrol, Capt., **8**: 429, 430
Carrol, Buucer. *See* Carrell, Booker
Carroll, Mr.: book sent by, **9**: 302
Carroll, Charles, of Carrollton: letters to,
20: 100-1, 214-15; letter from, **20**:
174; signs agreement of secrecy, **1**:
253; signs Declaration of Independence, **1**: 432; resigns from Constitutional Convention, **11**: 401; news of
desired, **12**: 485; in Md. Constitutional Convention, **13**: 332; as senator
from Md., **14**: 302, 394, 529, 560,
615; **17**: 208n; federalism of, **14**: 394,
529; letters sent by, **16**: 349, 350n,
486n; moves to introduce capital bill,
19: 34; and bank bill, **19**: 39; moves
to honor Franklin, **19**: 78; defends
France, **19**: 88; concludes tobacco deal
with Leiper, **19**: 342; represents William Brown, **20**: 99n, 174; on commercial policy, **20**: 174; on French
Revolution, **20**: 174; criticizes Joshua
Johnson, **20**: 486
Carroll (Carrol), Daniel: letters to, **17**:
467-8; **19**: 63-4; letters from, **19**: 62-
3, 67; **20**: 84, 593, 701-2; signs Articles of Confederation, **4**: 389n; as delegate to Congress from Md., **5**: 42; letter from cited, **5**: 55; and land
speculation, **6**: 164; asked to find accommodations for TJ at Annapolis, **6**:
355; opposes Annapolis Convention, **9**:
519; attends Constitutional Convention, **11**: 400; receives copy of Franklin's Federal Convention speech, **12**:
233n; and residence bill, **17**: 167n,
175-6, 182, 191n, 200-1, 208n; and
diplomatic establishment, **17**: 218,
220; recommends Sloane as consul,
17: 253n; and Potomac capital site,
17: 455-6, 461-3, 465, 466n; **19**: 4n,
13n, 18n, 24; **20**: 4, 6, 7, 16, 18, 20n,
22n, 37, 39n, 42n, 45, 84-5; appointed Federal District commissioner,
19: 63; **20**: 9; unable to serve as Federal District commissioner, **19**: 67-
8; **20**: 11; drafts L'Enfant's instructions, **20**: 12; purchases land for capital site, **20**: 31, 73; house destroyed,
20: 44-51, 71; letter to Madison, **20**:
84-5; recommends Christopher Rich-

Carter, Mrs. Robert, **2**: 206

Carter, Robert W.: TJ sends money by way of, **19**: 246

Carter, Robert Wormeley: signs nonimportation resolutions (1770), **1**: 46; signs Virginia Association, **1**: 108; and nonimportation agreements, **1**: 110; signs letter to Va. HB, **1**: 111

Carter, William: in Albemarle co. militia, **1**: 667

Carteret, Sir George: land grants to, **1**: 136; **6**: 657

Carter's creek, Va.: post service on, **2**: 389

Carters Ferry, Va.: supply post, **4**: 285, 286; supply of lead at, **5**: 600; mentioned, **5**: 414, 429, 581n; **6**: 631, 633

Carter's Valley, **2**: 96, 106

Carthage: theory of American settlement from, **12**: 264

Carthaginians: Indians descended from, **13**: 377-8; **15**: 14-5, 451; language of, **13**: 378; Turnbull's conjectures on colonies in America, **15**: 14-5, 451

cartouche boxes: procured for army, **3**: 398, 406; **4**: 126, 467, 553, 612, 634, 657; **5**: 65, 67, 109, 620; shortage, **3**: 427, 433, 471, 496; **4**: 68, 82, 443; **5**: 28; type used in British army, **3**: 479-80; poor quality of, **3**: 499n; **4**: 219; supplied to Gen. Gates' army, **3**: 526, 529; TJ requests from Congress, **4**: 76; production of, **4**: 402, 535, 609; **5**: 38n, 52, 53, 331; **6**: 76n; TJ requests from Steuben, **5**: 66; needed for Va. defense, **5**: 68; **6**: 75; purchased in France by Va., **9**: 174-5; **10**: 164, 198, 228, 261, 542; **11**: 375, 673; shipment delayed, **10**: 223; passports for, **10**: 504; TJ orders, **15**: 587; mentioned, **6**: 75-6; **9**: 174

cartridge blocks: destroyed by enemy, **4**: 553

cartridge paper: shortage of, **3**: 427, 433; **4**: 68, 467; **5**: 472; TJ requests, **4**: 76, 398; **15**: 587; for Va. navy, **5**: 151, 152, 178, 558; needed by southern army, **5**: 199; import desired, **5**: 266; for defense of Chantilly, **5**: 435; purchased in France by Va., **10**: 472, 523

cartridges: supplied to Gen. Gates' army, **3**: 531; for Gen. Nelson, **4**: 315, 318; scarcity of, **4**: 443; **5**: 594; for Gen. Greene, **5**: 343

Cartwright, Edmund: mills erected by William Pearce, **20**: 315n; relations with William Pearce, **20**: 318n

Carver, Mr., **6**: 22

Carver, James: in Albemarle co. militia, **1**: 666

Carver, John: in Albemarle co. militia, **1**: 668

Carver, Richard: in Albemarle co. militia, **1**: 666

Cary, Capt. (master of the *Comtesse d'Avaux*), **10**: 80

Cary, Col. (British officer), **3**: 594; **4**: 47, 622; **8**: 342

Cary, Mr.: demands payment, **10**: 483; mentioned, **4**: 306n; **8**: 560

Cary, Archibald: letters to, **1**: 154-6; **7**: 8, 40, 383; **9**: 158-9, 260, 593; letters from, **1**: 249-50; **3**: 43-4, 75-6, 230-1; **4**: 378-9, 463, 596-7; **6**: 96-8, 342-5; signs nonimportation resolutions, **1**: 30, 46; signs Virginia Association, **1**: 108; and North's conciliatory proposal, **1**: 174n; and Mazzei's agricultural company, **1**: 158; reports plan of government for Va., **1**: 384n; runs for Va. senate, **1**: 476; and Johnson case, **2**: 42n; approves U.S.-French treaty, **2**: 290; director for Va. public buildings, **3**: 19n; **8**: 343; signs resolution appointing TJ governor, **3**: 410; slaves employed at Hoods, **5**: 127; letter to, from Steuben, **6**: 75-6; and inquiry into conduct of TJ, **6**: 88n, 89n, 105n; criticizes Steuben, **6**: 621n; receives game from England, **7**: 500; indebtedness to Wayles estate, **9**: 396; **11**: 651; health of, **10**: 109; death of, **11**: 223, 304, 310, 329; **12**: 104; estate of, **11**: 650; **17**: 458; mentioned, **1**: 257; **3**: 73; **6**: 19, 362n; **7**: 12; **8**: 687

Cary, Mrs. Archibald, **3**: 75

Cary, Edward: petition from, **5**: 404-5n

Cary, Jane Barbara Carr (Jenny, TJ's niece): birth of son, **7**: 302; **15**: 611, 613; health of, **15**: 627, 633; children of, **15**: 635; mentioned, **12**: 23, 24; **15**: 620

Cary, Polly: marriage of, **15**: 641

Cary, Richard: letters to, **9**: 444; **10**: 226-8, 635-8; **12**: 29; letters from, **9**: 120; **11**: 228-30; signs Virginia Association, **1**: 109; box sent to, **10**: 602; seeds and plants sent to, **11**: 48; copy of *Notes on Virginia* sent to, **12**: 130; death of, **16**: 25

Cary, Richard, Jr.: votes against bill for religious freedom, **2**: 549n

Cato (ship): puts into English port, **16**: 125; books shipped on, **16**: 495n; mentioned, **14**: 352; **15**: 438n, 524; **16**: 126n

cats: weight of, **6**: 343; Angoras imported by W. T. Franklin, **9**: 180; TJ orders Angora from France, **16**: 322

cattle: taxed in Va., **2**: 218; Va. bill on infection of, **2**: 442-3; for Continental army, **3**: 58; for southern army, **3**: 501, 525, 610, 658; **4**: 132, 133; impressment of, **3**: 506, 611-2; **5**: 411, 647-9; **6**: 3-4; purchased by Samuel Lewis, **3**: 527, 528; for Albemarle barracks, **3**: 537, 569, 573; for Portsmouth expedition, **5**: 75-6, 189; Va. counties to provide, **5**: 242; for Fort Pitt, **5**: 492; on Eastern Shore, **5**: 619; seized by British, **5**: 627; **6**: 3-4; price of, **5**: 648-9; in Italy, **14**: 42, 381; Short recommends use of Alderney, **14**: 543

cattle, engrossing. *See* engrossing

"Catullus" (pseud. of Hamilton): attacks on TJ, **18**: 640, 644, 650; **20**: 286n, 635n; Monroe replies to, **18**: 666

cauliflower seeds: TJ sends to Cary, **10**: 228

Causennage Kaznadji. *See* Yusuf Khodja

causeways: contracts for, **2**: 451-2

Causin, M.: letter from, **20**: 352

cautery: abolished, **2**: 325

Cavallo, M.: Madison comments on experiments of, **9**: 356; copying press made by, **9**: 570; **10**: 116

cavalry: in Va., **2**: 194; **4**: 54, 64, 460, 485, 615-6, 617; **5**: 479; for western frontier, **3**: 277; difficulty of supporting, **3**: 485; remounts, **4**: 6; equipment for, **4**: 40, 301, 343; **5**: 300, 319, 548, 575; **6**: 6, 31, 44, 48; importance of, **4**: 288-9, 392; **5**: 99, 360, 405, 569; **6**: 103; impressment of horses for, **5**: 229-31, 533; swords for, **5**: 274, 284-5, 296-7; illegal in militia, **5**: 434; officers in, **5**: 69, 567

cavalry, volunteer: recruitment, **3**: 492, 539; **5**: 491, 501, 566, 583, 631, 645; pledge of service, **4**: 353-4; plan for proposed by Gen. Lawson, **4**: 460-1, 485; equipment, **4**: 612; **6**: 15-7; for expedition against Portsmouth, **5**: 40; in Gloucester co., **5**: 41; to rendezvous at Petersburg, **5**: 412; called to meet invasion, **5**: 520, 536, 615-6; in Fairfax co., **5**: 630; mentioned, **5**: 514

Cave, William: in Albemarle co. militia, **1**: 665

caveats: entered in Va. Land Office, **2**: 144-5, 151n-2n, 162

Cavelier (Cavallier), M., fils: letters to, **9**: 599 (circular); **15**: 310-1, 423; letters from, **10**: 181, 507; **12**: 226; **15**: 203, 303, 336; consul in Dieppe, **14**: 60, 62n; TJ introduces Morris to, **15**: 311

Cavenaugh, Philemon: and bill establishing ferries, **2**: 456

Cavendish, Henry: experiments with air, **11**: 289; **15**: 610; on scientific instruments, **13**: 460

Cavendish, John, Lord: political strategy, **14**: 665

Caversham, England: garden described by TJ, **9**: 370

caves: temperature of, **6**: 347-8

Cavetta river: as proposed boundary of S.C., **6**: 602

Cawsey, Capt. (master of *Planter*), **15**: 649

Cayahoga creek, **1**: 662

Cayahoga river: navigation, **7**: 26, 558; distance from Niagara, **7**: 83; source of, **12**: 489. *See also* Cuyahoga river

Cayla, M.: *Notes on Virginia* sent to, **13**: 628, 643

Cayo Romano, Cuba: and desalination of sea water, **19**: 614n

Cayry (?), Col., **8**: 121

Cayuga Indians: land claimed by, **2**: 77; in French and Indian Wars, **2**: 104; and land grants, **20**: 130

Cazalès, Jacques Antoine Marie de: in aristocratic party, **16**: 437

Cazeau, Francis: claim against U.S., **12**: 406, 420, 683; **13**: 113, 192, 194n, 247, 248n; mentioned, **7**: 224

Cazenove, Théophile: speculates in U.S. debts, **13**: 323n; introduced to TJ by Van Staphorst & Hubbard, **15**: 562-3; recommends Greenleaf as consul, **17**: 250; represents Amsterdam in New York banking houses, **17**: 255n; as attorney for Van Staphorst & Hubbard, **17**: 487; on capital site, **18**: 534n; **19**: 281n; business dealings with Duer, **19**: 453-62; and Society for Establishing Useful Manufactures, **19**: 453n; relations with Hamilton, **19**: 454-5; **20**: 173n, 192-3; letters to, from Hamilton, quoted, **19**: 456-7; describes statue of Washington, **20**: 66n; introduced to James Currie, **20**: 331-2; in-

Charlotte (sloop) (*cont.*)
400; Shippen's letter carried on, **13**: 564

Charlotte, N.C.: menaced by British, **3**: 463; grain taken by enemy, **4**: 5; strength of British forces at, **4**: 14n; rendezvous for recruits, **5**: 361; mentioned, **3**: 466, 621

Charlotte co., Va.: letters to county lieutenant of, **5**: 275-7, 617; appoints infantry officers, **1**: 580; place of court of assize, **1**: 629; grand jury in, **1**: 638-9; militia, **2**: 130; **3**: 599; **4**: 63, 294-5, 352, 371, 620, 669; **5**: 6, 7, 29, 35, 36, 275-7, 310, 344-6, 371, 400, 598, 617, 646; senatorial district, **2**: 336; levies of soldiers, **3**: 8; tobacco loan office certificates, **3**: 516; collections under provision law, **4**: 7; impressment of supplies for army, **4**: 42; supply post for, **4**: 286; resolution of militia officers, **5**: 571-2

Charlotte Court House, Va.: time of holding court of assize, **1**: 628; proposed meeting of school overseers at, **2**: 529

Charlotte Sophia, Queen of Great Britain: meets Adams, **8**: 176, 179, 183; and king's will, **14**: 454; role under regency, **14**: 482, 531; **15**: 4; proposed journey to Hanover with George III, **15**: 105, 110; political influence, **18**: 299-300; caricature of, **20**: xxxi, 384 (illus.)

Charlottesville, Va.: prison at, **1**: 60; subscription to support clergyman and clerk of the congregation in, **2**: 6-9; mills near, **2**: 241; postal service to, **2**: 389; **18**: 488; **20**: 618, 641, 664-5, 711; seat of government temporarily moved to, **4**: 260, 261; **5**: 629n, 640, 645, 651; GA driven from, **4**: 264; raided by British, **4**: 265; **6**: 77n, 78n, 84, 85n, 90, 627n; **13**: 363; supply post, **4**: 285, 286; British prisoners of war sent to, **4**: 438; harness factory, **4**: 500, 509; Steuben's headquarters in, **5**: 667n; housing shortage, **6**: 21n; place of court of assize, **7**: 589; Monroe buys land near, **14**: 558; Marks' property in, **15**: 93-4; prices in, **20**: 717; mentioned, **3**: 639; **5**: 429. *See also* Albemarle barracks

Charlottina: name proposed for new colony, **6**: 596n

Charlton, Edward: TJ's debt to, **17**: 388n

Charlton, Jane: letter from, **17**: 388n

Charming Polly (ship): prize, **10**: 209, 210

Charnock, Robert: contract with William Green, **20**: 505n

Charollois canal, France: TJ's description, **11**: 418

Charon (British ship), **4**: 399; **5**: 73, 294n, 343n

Charpentier, François Philippe: letter from, **15**: 16; recommended for making copying press, **10**: 218; copying press ordered from, **16**: 323; **17**: 212, 412, 507

Charrier de la Roche, Abbé, **11**: 463n

Charsenay, M. de, **12**: 560

Charteressi, Prince. *See* Czartoryski, Adam Jerzy

charter of rights (for France): proposed by TJ, **15**: 165-8; TJ's draft, **15**: 167-8, 389; suggested, **15**: 209n-10n. *See also* Declaration of Rights (France)

Charton, M.: letter from, to Jay, **10**: 183-4

Chartres, Duc de: treasury of, **9**: 241. *See also* Orléans, Louis Philippe Joseph, Duc d'

Chas, Jean: letter to, **10**: 580; letters from, **10**: 442-3, 571; *Histoire politique et philosophique de la Révolution en l'Amérique Septentrionale*, **10**: 442-3, 571, 580

Chase, Jeremiah Townley: and western territory, **6**: 164, 585n, 594, 598n, 599n, 605n; in Md. Constitutional Convention, **13**: 333-4, 336; mentioned, **7**: 235n

Chase, Samuel: letter from, **10**: 82; signs Continental Association, **1**: 153; signs Congress' second petition, **1**: 223; signs agreement of secrecy, **1**: 253; debates taxation in Congress, **1**: 320; debates representation in Congress, **1**: 323; signs Declaration of Independence, **1**: 432; serves on Committee of the States (1784), **7**: 299; as Md. delegate in Congress, **7**: 572; confers on Potomac navigation, **8**: 113; opposes Constitution, **12**: 281, 409, 423, 425, 609; serves in Md. Constitutional Convention, **13**: 332-3, 336

Chastain, Charlotte J., **11**: 360n

Chastel: letter from, **13**: 640

chemical box: sent to Madison, **11**: 97
chemistry: researches, **8**: 559; study of, **8**: 636; **10**: 306; books on, **9**: 217; Madison's interest in, **9**: 661; Lavoisier's nomenclature, **13**: 381; **14**: 366-7, 698; TJ's interest in, **13**: 381; **14**: 366-7, 698
Chenesta (Cherokee chief): and Transylvania land claims, **2**: 73
Chenier de St. André, M.: letter from, **10**: 550
Chenosa river. *See* Kentucky river
Cheraw (Cherraws), S.C., **3**: 403, 465
Cheraw Hill, N.C., **3**: 462
Cherbourg, France: harbor, **8**: 592; **9**: 646; **10**: 241, 245, 247-8, 251; **11**: 32; Louis XVI visits, **10**: 68, 111; works reported destroyed, **13**: 405, 572; consular agent for recommended, **14**: 61
Cherbury, Edward Herbert, Baron of: *History of King Henry VIII*, **12**: 18
Cheriton, Va.: battery at, **3**: 215
Cherokee Indians: hostilities with U.S., **1**: 386, 480, 485; **4**: 217, 254, 301, 457, 499; **6**: 80; **7**: 606; **8**: 124; **15**: 596-7; **20**: 481; and western Va., **1**: 508; and sale of lands, **1**: 565n; **2**: 67, 68-110, 142, 148n, 150n; **3**: 266, 273; expeditions against, **2**: 41n, 77, 298; **3**: 5, 6, 544-5; **4**:359-63, 407-8, 546, 634, 639; **5**: 5n, 20, 267-8, 304n-5; **6**: 99; **15**: 589; **19**: 467; negotiate with northern Indians, **2**: 75; land claimed by, **2**: 76, 78-9, 81, 82, 92; at Lochaber, **2**: 78; letter to, from Lord Dunmore, cited, **2**: 82; disagreement with Wyandot, **2**: 84; ordered by Cameron to rob white hunters, **2**: 107; support British, **2**: 256, 259; **4**: 200-1; **5**: 552; treaties with, **2**: 285; **4**: 362, 657-8; **5**: 234, 236-7, 268, 395-6, 398, 476-7; **9**: 504, 642n; **17**: 389n, 430-1; **19**: 467; **20**: 481, 639; supplies for, **3**: 125, 160, 175-6, 179-80, 295; relations with Va., **3**: 448; **4**: 587; invited to visit Congress, **4**: 25, 53; chiefs visit Richmond, **4**: 36n; invited to visit Gen. Washington, **4**: 53; archives captured, **4**: 362-3; **5**: 562; **6**: 141, 172-3; support of prisoners, **4**: 551; defense against, **5**: 421; Overhill tribe, **7**: 280; language, **9**: 640; **11**: 201; population of, **9**: 641; cattle, **9**: 641-2; Rev. Madison's contact with, **15**: 593; chiefs visit England, **17**: 664-

5, 666n-7n, 673; strength of, **18**: 6-7; mentioned, **1**: 494; **2**: 80, 91, 97, 109; **3**: 79; **6**: 79. *See also* Chickamauga Indians
Cherokee river: plans for defense of, **3**: 55; floods in, **6**: 536; mentioned, **2**: 76, 81, 84; **4**: 360; **6**: 208
"Cherronesus" (TJ's name for new state), **6**: 595n, 604
cherry: French and American compared, **8**: 683; Monticello, **9**: 623
Cherry, John: testimony on killing of Frenchmen by British, **3**: 114n
cherry, wild: seeds requested by TJ for France, **9**: 254; plants requested from John Banister, **11**: 121; trees, **16**: 36
Cherry, Capt. William: appointed captain of western battalion, **3**: 51, 52; member of court-martial, **3**: 350; complains about rank, **3**: 377; account of expenses, **5**: 354-5; note on, **5**: 355; mentioned, **5**: 143, 504
Cherrystone, Va.: postal service to, **2**: 390
Cherryton's, **3**: 339
Chesapeake Bay: settlement on, **1**: 280; British operations in, **2**: 30; **3**: 217, 238n, 366, 406, 475, 500, 549; **4**: 55, 57, 58, 59-60, 61, 64, 65, 81, 258, 606; **5**: 90, 129, 131, 423, 440, 652; **6**: 236; ferries across, **2**: 454-5; provision for returning runaways across, **2**: 476; defenses of, **3**: 215; Barron asked to station galley in, **3**: 485; British depredations in, **3**: 565, 578; naval cooperation between Va. and Md., **3**: 578-9, 591, 642; French fleet in proposed, **3**: 647, 658, 661; **4**: 28, 309, 494-5, 568; Barron appointed commissioner for provision law in, **3**: 672; British blockade of, **4**: 502; **5**: 368, 488; conditions of, **5**: 308; naval engagements on, **5**: 334; place on considered for permanent seat of Congress, **6**: 357; jurisdiction over, **8**: 113; extent, **10**: 38; relationship to capital site, **19**: 9
Cheselden, William, **12**: 18
Chesepians, **1**: 279
Cheshire's, N.Y.: transportation to, **1**: 393
chess: Currie hopes to play with TJ, **8**: 641; figures sent to Eppes, **9**: 395; **15**: 632
Chessaway Indians: and G. R. Clark, **2**: 258, 259

Chester, John: letter to, **19**: 363-4; letter from, **20**: 215; nomination of, **14**: 525; appointed excise commissioner, **20**: 215

Chester, Peter, **18**: 495

Chesterfield, Philip Stanhope, fifth Earl of: recalled, **9**: 241

Chesterfield, Va.: ferry at, **2**: 458; recruits rendezvous at, **3**: 363, 588, 589, 592, 594; sick troops moved to, **3**: 371; hospital at, **4**: 504; Davies at, **5**: 290; military stores removed from, **5**: 453n, 465n

Chesterfield co., Va.: letter to commissioner of provisions for, **3**: 569n; letters to county lieutenant of, **4**: 646, 654; **5**: 104-5, 416, 496n-7n, 618; **6**: 3-4, 46; letter to members of GA for, **5**: 585-6; militia, **1**: 160; **2**: 130; **3**: 599; **4**: 62, 63, 295n, 297, 303n, 318, 352, 371, 379, 477, 645, 646, 669, 680, 682; **5**: 7n, 9n, 35, 36, 104n-5, 114, 119-20, 181, 310, 496n-7n, 501, 520-1, 546, 560, 561, 618; recruiting in, **1**: 249; senatorial district, **1**: 476; **2**: 336; appoints infantry officers, **1**: 580; place of court of assize, **1**: 630; prisoners at, **2**: 298; levies of soldiers, **3**: 8; tobacco loan office certificates, **3**: 516; flour quota, **3**: 609n; supply post for, **4**: 286; impressments in, **5**: 194-5; commissioner of provision law, **5**: 196; wagons not furnished by, **5**: 274; impressment of horses in, **6**: 51

Chesterfield Court House, Va.: proposed meeting of school overseers at, **2**: 529; militia at sent to Greene, **4**: 163, 622, 638; supply of arms at, **4**: 302; arms removed from, **4**: 306; recruits rendezvous at, **4**: 401; **5**: 18, 30; **6**: 632; tents removed from, **4**: 527; destitution of troops at, **4**: 591; troops at, **5**: 103; Davies quits charge at, **5**: 234; British depredations, **5**: 579

Chester river, Md.: Indian antiquities on, **12**: 241

Chestertown, Md.: Shippen visits, **17**: 464

Chesterville, Va., **6**: 144

Chetam, Pete: signs petition, **6**: 293

Chetwood, Mr.: and bill establishing ferries, **2**: 455

Chevalier, M.: departs for France, **10**: 550; letters sent by, **10**: 574; **14**: 414

Chevalier d'Luzerne (Lauzun) (Continental cutter), **6**: 115

Chevallié, Jean Auguste Marie: letter from, **11**: 55

Chevallié, Pierre François: letter from, **8**: 34-6; claim against Va., **7**: 546-7, **7**: 550, 553-4; **8**: 34-6; **11**: 55

Chevaux de frise, **2**: 38

Chevremous, M., **12**: 455

Chew, Mr., **9**: 364n

Chew, James: settlement on Indiana claim, **2**: 103

Chew, Lieut. John, **4**: 76

Chezelles (saddler), **15**: 150

Chianti river, Italy, **14**: 381

Chiappe, Francisco: letters to, **12**: 121-2; **15**: 405; **20**: 400-1; letters from, **12**: 644; **13**: 526-7; handles Emperor of Morocco's correspondence, **9**: 626; **13**: 526-7; **15**: 341, 342n; **18**: 402; Barclay and Franks recommended to, **9**: 648; American agent at Morocco, **10**: 361, 418; **11**: 619; **12**: 122, 150, 239; **14**: 46; **15**: 341, 360; **17**: 226n, 228n, 229n; letters from cited, **13**: 94, 95n; **14**: 47n; **19**: 325; **20**: 612; letter from, to Carmichael, cited, **14**: 503n; letter from, to Giuseppe Chiappe, cited, **15**: 342n, 405; letters to cited, **15**: 342n, 418; TJ questions status of, **17**: 320; letter from, to Washington, cited, **18**: 402n; correspondence with Jay, **18**: 402n; **19**: 325n; assists Barclay's mission to Morocco, **20**: 398, 400-1; mentioned, **17**: 518

Chiappe, Girolamo (American agent at Tangier), **11**: 619; **12**: 122, 150; **17**: 226n

Chiappe, Giuseppe: letter to, **13**: 508-9; letters from, **12**: 462-3, 626-7, 644-5; **13**: 200-1, 400-1; **14**: 545, 577-8; **18**: 512-3; letters from cited, **10**: 536; **13**: 95, 134, 137n; as American agent at Mogador, **11**: 619, 626; **12**: 122; as American agent in Morocco, **11**: 626; **12**: 150; **18**: 402n; letters to cited, **15**: 342n, 405n, 418; **20**: 239; letters to, from Francisco Chiappe, cited, **15**: 342n, 405; letter from, to Washington, quoted, **16**: 441n

Chiappe, Jacome Geronimo, **15**: 342n

Chiappe brothers: appointments in Morocco confirmed, **12**: 462

Chichester, Richard: letter from, **6**: 34

Chickahominy river: act for clearing, **1**: 88n; ferries across, **2**: 457; extension of navigation on, **3**: 140; impressment of boats on, **4**: 393; **5**: 124; armed vessels

Chickahominy river (*cont.*)
in, **5**: 39, 144, 181; British movements
on, **5**: 519, 521, 532, 538, 543n, 546,
549; Long Bridge on, **5**: 544n, 545n,
549

Chickahominy River Road: British march
up, **5**: 539, 540

Chickahominy River Shipyard: letter to
superintendent of, **5**: 135; taken by
British, **5**: 539, 546; mentioned, **5**:
144, 645

Chickamauga (Chuckamagga), Ga.
(Cherokee town), **4**: 362; **5**: 305, 535

Chickamauga Indians: peace overtures, **2**:
285; expeditions against (1780), **3**: 5,
6, 420-2, 447-8, 479n, 517-8,
544-5; **15**: 588-9; mentioned, **3**: 79; **4**:
361

Chickasaw Indians: support British, **2**:
256, 259; TJ's advice on treatment of,
3: 276; anger at establishment of Fort
Jefferson, **3**: 279n; hostilities with
U.S., **3**: 416, 444; **7**: 45; **8**: 124; treaties with, **5**: 268, 395; **9**: 642n; **17**:
389n; language, **9**: 640; population of,
9: 641; cattle, **9**: 641-2

Ch'ien Lung, Emperor of China: medal
presented to, **12**: 106n; medals sent to,
16: 65n

Child, Sir Josiah: works by, **19**: 208,
212

Child & Loudon (printers), **17**: 485

children: binding out of, **1**: 590; inheritance by, **2**: 394; employed by state as
nailors, **5**: 255; protection of in enemy
countries, **7**: 486, 622; **9**: 419, 426;
TJ on, **11**: 57, 415

children's books: TJ requests, **10**: 545;
Stockdale requests, **11**: 577, 597

Childrens' Friend, The, **10**: 545

Childress, John: signs petition, **6**: 290

Childs, Francis, and Swaine, John: letters from, **18**: 307; **19**: 115-6; sell sets
of *Daily Advertiser*, **17**: 360, 362; paid
by Department of State, **17**: 365, 369,
373; desire to set up press in Philadelphia, **17**: 397; print laws, **17**: 509n;
18: 66n, 307; print report on cod fisheries, **19**: xxxii, 165n, 348 (illus.); and
publication of congressional journal,
19: 115; partnership with Freneau, **20**:
667, 726, 748, 754; criticism of, **20**:
719n; mentioned, **16**: 238n, 615

Chiles, Micajah: in Albemarle co. militia,
1: 665; signs Va. oath of allegiance, **2**:
128

Chilhowee (Cherokee Indian town), **4**:
360, 362

Chilleau (Chillon), Marie Charles, Marquis de: recalled from Saint-Domingue, **15**: 456

Chillicothe (Chelecauthy), Ohio, **3**: 560

Chillingworth, William: cited by TJ, **1**:
553

China: trade with, **7**: 336; **8**: 154, 520n,
656-7; **11**: 146; **13**: 3-4; **14**: 275, 601-
2; American voyages to, **8**: 656-7; **9**:
137; **10**: 135; **11**: 306, 313; French
ships with American colors in, **16**: 39-
40; *America* visits, **16**: 39-40

China, Emperor of. *See* Ch'ien Lung

Chinault, William: signs Va. oath of allegiance, **2**: 129

chinaware: purchased by TJ, **7**: 533-4,
579, 586; **8**: 8, 60, 73; **9**: 313; **10**:
436-7, 479-80, 497, 578; **11**: 26; **13**:
47, 138, 183-5, 420; **15**: 563; ordered
from Macarty, **12**: 498, 512, 522, 527,
535; German, **13**: 18; marks of manufacturers, **13**: 18. *See also* porcelain

chinch bug: effect on Va. crops, **7**: 402

Chingoteague, Va.: defenses at, **3**: 215

Chinie, M.: treatment by Morocco, **10**:
357-8

Chipindall, Mr.: creditor of Gearey, **9**:
622, 630-1, 640

Chipman, Darius, **19**: 377, 378

Chipman, Nathaniel: letter to, **20**: 627-8;
meets with Washington, **19**: 368-9;
letter from, to Hamilton, **19**: 371; recommended by Wadsworth, **19**: 377;
appointed federal judge, **19**: 381; **20**:
627-8; Vt. commissioner, **20**: 444

Chisholm, William: claims TJ in debt to,
13: 342

Chistowee (Cherokee Indian town), **4**:
361, 362

Chiswell, Fort, Va., **1**: 573; **5**: 504

Chiswell, John: lead mines of, **1**: 262-4;
76, 78, **2**: 388n; **17**: 24n; daughter of,
2: 33n

Chiswell, Elizabeth Randolph (Mrs.
John Chiswell), **2**: 33n

Chiswick, England: TJ visits, **9**: 369

Chittenden, Thomas: letter to, **19**: 379-
80; and Vt. intrigues, **19**: 368; letter
from, to Washington, quoted, **19**: 369

chocolate: manufacture in Conn., **7**: 336;
imported to U.S., **9**: 62; **10**: 147

Choctaw Indians: TJ's advice on treatment of, **3**: 276; language, **9**: 640; **11**:
201; population of, **9**: 641; improvi-

dence, **9**: 642; treaties with, **9**: 642n; **17**: 389n

Choczim, Russia: siege of, **13**: 633

Choiseul-Praslin, César Gabriel de Choiseul, Duc de Praslin: rumored to favor war, **1**: 488; death of, **9**: 45; quoted on U.S. commerce, **18**: 376, 519; mentioned, **9**: 488

Choiseul-Stainville, Etienne François, Duc de: death of, **8**: 143; and whale fishery, **14**: 256; *Mémoires*, **16**: 47; and cession of Louisiana, **16**: 556; mentioned, **3**: 305; **12**: 314

Chort, M., **11**: 604

Chotank (Joetank), Va.: British landing at, **5**: 529, 530n

Chote (Cherokee town): council place of Cherokee, **2**: 91, 93; mentioned, **4**: 360, 362

Chowan river, N.C., **3**: 611, 659

Chowning, William: property plundered by British, **5**: 394; appointed deputy for impressing cattle, **5**: 411

Chrage, Charles: signs nonimportation resolutions (1770), **1**: 47

Chrestien & Co., **12**: 634n

Chrétien, Gilles Louis: physiognotrace portrait of TJ, **14**: xlii-iv, 361 (illus.)

Christian VII, King of Denmark: invites Franklin to dinner, **9**: 488; letter from, to Jones, quoted, **19**: 589-90

Christian, Fletcher: in mutiny on the *Bounty*, **16**: 275

Christian, Maj. Gilbert: destroys Cherokee Indian town, **4**: 361

Christian, Capt. John, **4**: 531

Christian, Peter: deserts British army, **4**: 89

Christian (Christy), Gen. William: letters to, **5**: 236-7, 476-7; letter from, **5**: 395-6; involved in scheme to purchase land from Cherokee, **2**: 69; deposition concerning Henderson's land claims, **2**: 82, 89; at Long Island treaty, **2**: 92; appointed to confer on western defense, **3**: 51, 53; to command volunteers, **3**: 653; resigns lieutenancy of Jefferson co., **4**: 420; negotiates with Cherokees, **5**: 234, 236, 396n; TJ accused of rejecting offer of troops, **6**: 106; retires from Va. Council, **7**: 597; killed by Indians, **9**: 519; **10**: 110; mentioned, **4**: 365

Christine of Saxony, Princess: TJ's account of, **8**: 242n

Christopher, John, **4**: 181

Christy, Col. *See* Christian, Gen. William

chronometers: means of transporting to Fort Pitt, **5**: 374; and Rittenhouse's inventions, **12**: 145

Chuccamogga. *See* Chickamauga

Chunn, Capt. John T., **5**: 424n

Church, Mr.: letters sent by, **8**: 498

Church, Angelica Schuyler (Mrs. John Barker Church): letters to, **12**: 600-1; **13**: 422-3, 520-1, 623-4; **14**: 553-4; **16**: 549-50; letters from, **12**: 656; **13**: 391; **14**: 210-1, 515; Trumbull paints miniature of TJ for, **10**: xxix, 466 (illus.); **13**: 391, 520; **14**: xxxvi; Trumbull's portrait of, **10**: xxx, 467 (illus.); departs from England, **12**: 405; **13**: 241; Mrs. Cosway's friendship for, **12**: 459; **13**: 391, 520, 525; **14**: 9; sends trunk to Hamilton, **12**: 483; TJ praises, **12**: 539-40; coach of admired by TJ, **12**: 598; loses trunk, **12**: 603, 612-3, 629, 647; arrives in England, **12**: 622; sent *Federalist* by Mrs. Hamilton, **13**: 158n; health of, **13**: 200; **17**: 261; chariot made for, **13**: 280; and book on Herculaneum, **13**: 361n, 623; sends tea vase to TJ, **13**: 361n, 391, 520; returns to America, **13**: 391, 521, 639; **14**: 211, 515, 554, 591, 634, 667; TJ urges to visit Paris, **13**: 423, 623; TJ's friendship for, **13**: 520-1, 546; tries TJ's carriage, **14**: 365; sends tea to TJ, **14**: 515, 554; introduced to Mme de Bréhan by TJ, **14**: 552, 553-4; letters to cited, **14**: 561; **16**: xxxi; issued passport by TJ, **15**: 485; returns to England, **15**: 517, 520, 521; mentioned, **12**: 406, 502n, 540, 551, 607, 613, 643, 645, 694; **13**: 115, 179, 214, 289, 301, 597; **14**: 365n, 441, 446, 514, 525; **15**: 143, 152, 554

Church, Catharine (Kitty): letter to, **14**: 28; letter from, **14**: 44; with TJ in Paris, **13**: 301, 422-3, 521, 546, 623; writes to mother, **13**: 422, 623; receives book of ancient moralists, **14**: 28, 44; returns to mother, **14**: 211; Mary Jefferson writes to, **14**: 293, 663; **15**: 152; worried by Mary Jefferson's illness, **14**: 514; letter to, from Mary Jefferson, **16**: xxxi, 52 (fac.); lack of correspondence, **17**: 261; mentioned, **12**: 600, 601, 613, 646, 656; **13**: 179; **14**: 554; **16**: 549, 550

Church, Edward: letters to, **17**: 423-5;

Church, Edward (*cont.*)
20: 401-2; letter from, 20: 681-2; consul at Bilbao, 17: 246, 247, 250, 253n, 280; 20: 681-2; commission for, 18: 365; consul at Lisbon, 20: 161n; vice-consul in Lisbon, 20: 362n

Church, John Barker: leaves London, 13: 200; TJ comments on, 16: 549; letters from, to Hamilton, quoted, 17: 36; 18: 272; entertains Fox, 17: 101n; Hamilton sends dispatches to, 17: 126n, 654, 656n; member of Parliament, 17: 261; and stock speculation, 17: 604; warns of possibility of war, 17: 651; in Monroe's meeting with Hamilton, 18: 663; mentioned, 14: 211; 15: 551n; 16: 550; 17: 615, 616, 639

Churchill, William: letter from, 5: 285-6

Churchman, John: letters to, 12: 5-6; 15: 439-40; 18: 68; letters from, 11: 397-9; 12: 374-5; 15: 129-30; 18: 61, 492-3; memorial on magnetic declination, 11: 398-9; method of ascertaining longitude, 11: 403, 562; letters from cited, 12: 161; 15: 419n, 440n; memorial on magnetic variation, 15: 129-30, 439-40; *An explanation of the Magnetic Atlas or Variation Chart*, 18: 61, 68; mentioned, 15: 419

Church of England: disestablishment of, in Va., 1: 525-58; rough draft of resolutions for disestablishing, 1: 530-1; petition of dissenters against establishment in Va., 1: 586-9; relation to College of William and Mary, 2: 536, 543n; Va. bill for saving property of, 2: 553-5; bill for dissolution of vestries, 3: 467; support of, 6: 289. *See also* Protestant Episcopal Church

Ciandola, Italy: TJ describes, 11: 432-3

Cibber, Mr., 9: 486

Cicé, Jerome Marie Champion de, Archbishop of Bordeaux: letter to, 15: 298; letter from, 15: 291; consults TJ on constitution, 15: 291, 298, 354n; *garde des sceaux*, 15: 333

Cicero, Marcus Tullius: works of, 8: 323; reading by Peter Carr, 8: 407, 408; 9: 38, 201; 11: 299; 12: 18; *Opera omnia* sought by TJ, 10: 72; *Cato Major, or Discourse on Old Age*, 10: 518; TJ seeks information on best Italian translation, 11: 159; *Tusculanarum disputationum*, 11: 523; 15: 223; Dumas quotes, 13: 512n; *De Senectute*,

15: 223; *Orations*, 20: 634n, 635n; *Epistles*, 20: 635n; mentioned, 11: 199, 258

cider: made by Francis Eppes, 12: 133; efforts to obtain, 16: 90; ordered by TJ, 20: 95; mentioned, 12: 428; 18: 307

Cimitière, Pierre Eugène. *See* Du Simitière

Cincinnati, Society of: Washington's queries concerning, 7: 88-9; TJ's opinion of, 7: 105-8; 10: 53-4; objections to, 7: 106-7, 109n, 116, 225; French membership in, 8: 121; 9: 79; 12: 521-2, 677, 694, 695n; Adams' opinion of, 8: 250n; 13: 11; W. S. Smith's opinion of, 8: 250n; attitude of Congress toward, 9: 77; payment for badges, 9: 160; Mazzei asks TJ for account of, 9: 257; article on, in *Encyclopédie méthodique*, 9: 382; 10: 5n, 6n-7n, 532; origin of, 10: 48-9; 13: 11; TJ's account of, for Démeunier, 10: 48-54; medals, 10: 186; danger of hereditary aristocracy through, 10: 532; Washington re-elected president general, 10: 533n-5n; 11: 389; Washington's attitude toward, 11: 388-9; objections to medal for Gates, 16: 61n-2n; governor of Martinique requests honorary badge, 20: 718; mentioned, 16: 56n, 59n

Cincinnatus: Washington's reputation as, 19: 47

Cincinnatus (ship), 9: 645

Cinque Ports, England: British guarding of, 3: 106

ciphers: proposed to John Page, 1: 15; in Madison correspondence, 6: 226; 7: 417, 444; 8: 147, 579-80; 11: 203; 12: 102; 13: 133n; 15: 149n, 154n-5n, 316n, 369n; in Monroe correspondence, 6: 233; 7: 278, 291-2, 379, 459, 508, 562, 607, 637-8; 8: 43-4, 75, 149, 215, 217; 17: 233; returned by TJ, 6: 273, 318; in Short correspondence, 7: 149, 235-7; 16: 310, 320, 363n, 440, 496; in Carmichael correspondence, 7: 630; 8: 134, 247, 321, 402, 649; 9: 13, 250; 10: 287; 11: 470, 567; 12: 175n-9n, 238, 424, 552; 13: 91, 142-3, 144n, 176, 217n, 230, 398-9; 14: 288, 289n; 15: 338n; 16: 496; 17: 320, 330n; 18: 597-8; in Williamson correspondence, 7: 641, 643n; in Jay correspondence,

8: 146; **14**: 521n-3n; **15**: 120n-1n, 191n; **16**: 6n; in Adams correspondence, **8**: 173, 333, 355-6, 395; recommended for American foreign ministers, **8**: 251; in Lamb correspondence, **11**: 368; in Jay-Adams correspondence, **11**: 512n; in Smith correspondence, **12**: 71, 146; in Barclay-Lamb correspondence, **12**: 190n; in Jones correspondence, **12**: 685; in British intelligence reports, **17**: 44n; mentioned, **6**: 243n-4n, 318, 569

Cipières, Louis Antoine, Marquis de: nominated for Estates General, **15**: 45

Circello, Signore: letter from, **10**: 468

cities: TJ on, **12**: 442

citizenship: provisions in TJ's drafts of Va. Constitution, **1**: 344, 353, 363; Va. bill on, **2**: 476-9; restoration of to Americans held by British, **6**: 324-33; exchange of between states advocated by TJ, **7**: 466n; rights of Americans to British, **9**: 182; legal aspects of, **9**: 259; honorary for friends of St. John de Crèvecoeur, **13**: 547n

Citoyen (ship), **17**: 435-6, 437n

City Point, Va.: ferry at, **2**: 458; British landing at, **5**: 550n, 558n, 623, 631

civil authority: and military authority, **1**: 317; **5**: 276n-7n, 301-2, 356, 568, 636; **6**: 304, 403n, 619n; **7**: 116; **11**: 49

civil liberty: protection in U.S., **11**: 409

civil office: military rank a bar to, **5**: 481, 489

civil officers, Va.: qualifications of in Va. Constitution, **1**: 354; salaries of, **5**: 78-80; removal from office, **6**: 280n; commissions for, **6**: 644-5

civil rights. *See* rights, civil

civil service: report on needed, **6**: 533; expenses of, **6**: 559-63; committee on reductions in U.S., **7**: 12-5; arrears of interest for U.S., **7**: 65; in N.Y., **7**: 327; in Conn., **7**: 331; in R.I., **7**: 337; in Mass., **7**: 339; in N.H., **7**: 343

civil suits: stay during militia service, **2**: 359

Civita Castellana, Italy, **14**: 381

Clagett, Mr.: letter sent by, **15**: 400, 429; passport issued by TJ, **15**: 486

Claiborne, Messrs.: payment to, **3**: 486; mentioned, **3**: 495

Claiborne, Ferard, **11**: 412

Claiborne, Herbert: authorized to purchase horses, **3**: 420

Claiborne, Maj. Richard: letters to, **4**: 393, 509, 547-8, 628, 635; **5**: 10-1, 60-1, 224-5, 286-7, 388, 596; **6**: 10-1; **11**: 518-9; **12**: 6; letters from, **4**: 340-2, 393-4, 464-5, 500, 547, 580, 627, 635-6, 636, 674; **5**: 4-5, 72, 82-3, 124, 136, 142, 195, 225-6, 226-7, 240-1, 287-8, 288, 318-9, 319, 340-1, 358, 389, 414, 428-9, 429, 442, 581-2, 594, 665-8, 668, 669-70; **11**: 411-3, 468-9, 485-6, 579-80; **12**: 197, 601-2; **13**: 308; **14**: 359-60, 402-3; **15**: 107-8; appointed deputy quartermaster for Va., **3**: 608n; **4**: 340, 374, 510, 521-2; **5**: 60, 575, 576-7; recommended to TJ, **4**: 158; plan for Quartermaster's Department in Va., **4**: 285-8, 340-2, 464; and ammunition for Gen. Nelson, **4**: 315, 318; describes conditions in Quartermaster Department, **4**: 340; **5**: 340; letters from, to Davies, quoted, **4**: 341n; **5**: 465n, 517n; supplies request of, **4**: 378; duties of, **4**: 478; letter from, to Charles Pettit, **4**: 510-4; allows wagon hire, **4**: 642; impressment of supplies, **4**: 665; **5**: 114, 120, 121n; forwards letter of TJ, **4**: 696; pays assistants, **5**: 52; Greene's opinion of, **5**: 60n; TJ sends supplies to, **5**: 132, 476; boats delivered to, **5**: 135; on Standley case, **5**: 237n; appointed Continental quartermaster for Va., **5**: 288; letters from, to Steuben, quoted, **5**: 289n, 578n, 667n; **6**: 10n-1n; and Wagon Act, **5**: 298; resigns from office, **5**: 340; lacks wagons, **5**: 417; refuses forage to Armand's corps, **5**: 480n; applied to for wagons, **5**: 516; letters from, to Russell, quoted, **6**: 10n; property of sold, **11**: 486, 519; letter from cited, **12**: 630; Va. land grants, **14**: 402-3, 434-5, 476; financial affairs, **20**: 380; mentioned, **4**: 407, 665, 696, 697; **5**: 27, 48, 121n, 132, 145n, 166, 280n, 356, 459n, 476, 638n; **6**: 54

Claiborne, Thomas: signs nonimportation resolutions (1769), **1**: 30; and bill establishing ferries, **2**: 457; votes against bill for religious freedom, **2**: 549n; sends wagons to John Green, **4**: 611

Claiborne, William: authorized to purchase horses, **3**: 420; extract of letter from, to R. Claiborne, **5**: 594; mentioned, **3**: 494; **4**: 412, 458

Clansmate, Charles. *See* Clinchsmith

Clapham, Col. John, **15**: 602

Clara (ship): wreck of, **20**: 242

"Claremont": garden described by TJ, **9**: 370

Clarendon, Edward Hyde, first Earl of: land grants to, **1**: 136; **6**: 657; *History of the Rebellion and Civil Wars in England*, **12**: 18

claret: ordered by TJ, **7**: 501, 601; sent to Eppes, **10**: 483; **11**: 256; ordered by Donald, **12**: 428, 561

Claret, Charles Pierre, Comte de Fleurieu: Spanish expedition recommended by, **14**: 503n; as minister of marine, **17**: 619, 640; **20**: 370; opposes plans to supply navy, **20**: 523-4

Clark, Maj., **2**: 38

Clark, Mr.: permit to go to flag-of-truce ship, **3**: 322; mentioned, **1**: 40

Clark, Abraham: signs agreement of secrecy, **1**: 253; signs Declaration of Independence, **1**: 432; member of Constitutional Convention, **11**: 400; member of committee on TJ's expenses, **14**: 291n

Clark, Bowling: payment to, **20**: 155n

Clark, Daniel, **5**: 587n

Clark, David: repairs Washington's carriage, **20**: 94n

Clark, Francis: repairs Washington's carriage, **20**: 94n

Clark (Clarke), George Rogers: letters to, **2**: 132-3, 246; **3**: 258-9, 273-8, 316-8, 354, 356-7, 613-4, 667, 670-1; **4**: 31, 233-8, 348, 413-4, 414, 424-5, 597-8, 653-4; **5**: 503-4; **6**: 139, 204-5, 218-9; **7**: 8-9; **9**: 395; **11**: 487; letters from, **3**: 88-9, 560-1; **4**: 394, 414, 420, 574-5; **5**: 252-4; **6**: 11-2, 86, 159-60; **15**: 609-10; **20**: 583-4; supports anti-Transylvania settlers, **1**: 565n-6n; letter from, to Patrick Henry, **2**: 256-60; captures Gov. Hamilton, **2**: 270, 287n, 292; **3**: 26-7, 48; victory at Vincennes, **2**: 270, 298; **3**: 5, 6, 26, 30; Indian warfare, **2**: 289; **3**: 421, 560-1; prisoners taken by, **2**: 301; thanked by Congress, **3**: 5n-6n; and defense of Illinois, **3**: 72, 154, 169n, 272, 415, 416, 444, 480; bills protested, **3**: 158, 168, 270-1, 316, 317, 320; **4**: 207-8, 283; **5**: 504; **6**: 320; choses site for Fort Jefferson, **3**: 278, 279n; TJ's opinion of, **3**: 279n, 292-3; **4**: 237; **19**: 521; to command proposed expedition against Detroit, **3**:

291-2, 312, 665-6, 670; **4**: 204-6, 641; **5**: 492; supplies for, **3**: 302; **4**: 467, 589, 598-9; **5**: 280; **6**: 69; asked for list of bills on New Orleans, **3**: 317; to aid Preston, **3**: 325-6; Gov. Reed aids, **3**: 353; and defense of falls of the Ohio, **3**: 521; authority over Crockett's expedition, **3**: 667; **4**: 238; letter from, to John Gipson, quoted, **4**: 172; and western defense, **4**: 226, 230, 231, 232, 233-8, 239, 247, 352, 573, 688-9; **5**: 142-3, 455; commands Continental troops, **4**: 246; sent to Steuben, **4**: 326-7; land grant to, **4**: 387; **6**: 579; skirmish with British at Hoods, **4**: 399; commissioned as brigadier general, **4**: 424; reinforcements, **4**: 451, 469, 628; **5**: 256, 461, 467; nails for, **5**: 97n; respect of Ky. settlers for, **5**: 467; preparations at Fort Pitt, **5**: 548; Kaskaskia inhabitants profess loyalty to, **5**: 599; TJ urges Indians to join western forces, **6**: 61, 63; resents lack of appreciation, **6**: 204-5; claims against Va., **6**: 321n, 356; and Nathan case, **6**: 322n; and western exploration, **6**: 371; **15**: 609-10; conquests in west, **6**: 557; as Indian commissioner, **6**: 568; **7**: 8, 11, 250; commission to recruit soldiers, **6**: 641-2; relationship with James O'Fallon, **19**: xxxiii; TJ's instructions to, **19**: 442; proposed history of expeditions of, **20**: 481; mentioned, **3**: 70, 71, 266, 268, 328; **4**: 148, 149, 172, 180, 188, 198, 199n, 216, 249, 321, 355, 356, 365, 375, 391, 397, 596; **5**: 37, 386, 574

Clark, John: signs petition, **2**: 15n; invoice for services, **4**: 223; seeks treasury auditorship, **20**: 230n

Clark, Jonathan (prisoner at Charleston), **3**: 652

Clark, Joseph: recommended as architect for capital, **20**: 9-10

Clark, Robert: votes for bill for religious freedom, **2**: 549n

Clark, Samuel: carries rice to TJ, **17**: 5

Clark, William: signs petition, **2**: 15n; mentioned, **10**: 614

Clarke, Capt., **4**: 310

Clarke, Gen.: attitude toward U.S., **9**: 398-9; comment on U.S. cited, **9**: 467

Clarke, Mr., **7**: 338

Clarke, Benjamin: in Albemarle co. militia, **1**: 665

375; aid sought by Knox, **20**: 124-5; Indian policy of, **20**: 125; opposes Cayuga land grants, **20**: 130; fails to meet TJ and Madison, **20**: 440; mentioned, **15**: 74

Clinton, Sir Henry: joins Lord Howe, **1**: 386, 485, 493; reduces Fort Montgomery, **2**: 34; letter from, to Congress, cited, **2**: 200; camp on Staten Island, **2**: 207; speculation on movements of, **2**: 217, 265; reinforcements for, **2**: 236; operations in New York, **3**: 30-1; and Henry Hamilton, **3**: 31; treatment of American prisoners, **3**: 199; captures Charleston, **3**: 335, 343, 399-400, 403, 426; **15**: 586; paroles American prisoners, **3**: 374; anticipated strategy of, **3**: 405; returns to New York, **3**: 437, 461, 465, 477, 478; proclamation to citizens of S.C., **3**: 466, 473; **4**: 360; ordered to attack N.C. and Va., **3**: 499; reportedly sends reinforcements south, **3**: 620; **4**: 6; invitation to loyalist refugees, **3**: 654; issues general orders from Charleston, S.C., **4**: xxxvii, 90 (illus.); rumored to have gone to Halifax, **4**: 66; encourages American mutineers, **4**: 325; and prisoners of war, **5**: 329-30, 461n, 606, 633, 634n; expected to command reinforcements in Va., **5**: 369; reported embarkation from New York, **5**: 423, 475, 495, 586; **15**: 608; reported landing in N.C., **15**: 575; mentioned, **1**: 388; **3**: 397, 647, 662; **4**: 436; **17**: 41

Clinton, Col. James: quells mutiny at Quebec, **1**: 435

Clitumnus river, **14**: 381

Clive, Robert, Lord, **9**: 370

clocks: TJ asks Rittenhouse to make, **2**: 202; manufactured in Conn., **7**: 335; black marble ordered by TJ, **16**: xxxiii, 52 (illus.), 321, 324n, 501; **17**: 316; pendulum vibrating half seconds, **16**: xxxiii, 320; stolen from TJ's study in Paris, **16**: xxxiii, 321; self-winding invented by Read, **16**: 111

Clopton, Capt.: deserts, **5**: 214

cloth: purchased for Va. army and navy, **3**: 17, 90, 184; **4**: 4; ordered in France, **3**: 90; paid for in cannon, **3**: 195; for making uniforms, **4**: 445, 453, 471, 493, 565; for Col. Buford's troops, **4**: 591; plentiful in Philadel-

phia, **4**: 657; offered in exchange for flour, **5**: 546-7

clothier, state (Va.): duties of, **3**: 174; **4**: 674; **5**: 125, 137; salary for, **3**: 209-10; discussed, **4**: 692-3; advice of Council concerning, **5**: 200-1

clothier general, Continental: authority of, **4**: 500, 514

clothing: lack of in colonies, **1**: 288; not subject to execution, **2**: 649; prices of, **3**: 152; abundance in Philadelphia, **4**: 589; TJ orders from Cannon, **14**: 467, 468n, 514, 634, 640, 663, 668. *See also* women: fashions for

clothing for military: for soldiers in Canada, **1**: 390; scarcity of, **3**: 260-1, 507, 660, 670; **4**: 27, 150-1, 206-7, 210, 445-6, 453, 659, 694, 700; **5**: 66-7, 75; boots for officers, **3**: 265; uniforms for officers, **3**: 316, 347, 517, 547; for hospital and medical staff, **3**: 357; for southern army, **4**: 38, 219, 495, 502, 503; **5**: 620; states asked to supply, **4**: 89; importance of, **4**: 131-2; transportation of, **4**: 140; for western forces, **4**: 188, 235; for Col. Lee's legion, **4**: 188-9, 190, 191; preservation of, **4**: 446; imported from Ireland, **4**: 466; taken off *Le Comité*, **4**: 467; repair of, **4**: 516; not brought by Capt. Jones, **4**: 656, 670-1; in French ships, **4**: 683; for American war prisoners, **5**: 38; increase in allowance for asked, **5**: 65; for navy, **5**: 223; distribution proposed by Davies, **5**: 245, 269; for Convention troops, **5**: 259, 359; for Lomagne's corps, **5**: 601; mentioned, **2**: 126, 128n, 194; **3**: 172, 352-3, 639; **4**: 4-5, 172, 183, 185, 284, 493-4, 514-6, 549, 558, 565, 604, 622, 623, 668-9; **5**: 23, 34, 100, 143, 173, 175, 268, 362, 373, 484. *See also* Continental army: clothing; Virginia: Troops, clothing

Clouet, Jean Charles: letter to, **8**: 18; letter from, **7**: 628-9; ordered to pay prize money to J. P. Jones, **8**: 326, 327; **10**: 501; daughter of, **10**: 395n

Clousier, Jacques Gabriel: prints Consular Convention, **14**: 88; prints *Observations on the Whale-Fishery*, **14**: 218, 254n

Clugny, Nicolas Marc Antoine, Baron de: as governor of Guadeloupe, **17**: 587

provision law (Va.): commissioners of commissioners of the specific tax: for Essex co., **3**: 606; **4**: 43; King William co., **3**: 606n; for Albemarle co., **15**: 590-2, 594-5, 603-4

Commissioners of the Treasury, British: in *Rachel* case, **20**: 508n

Commissioners of the Treasury, U.S.: letters to, **7**: 608; **9**: 225-7, 471; **10**: 237-8; **11**: 108, 474-6; **12**: 12-4, 149, 472-3, 573-4, 698-700; **13**: 123, 168-70, 574-5, 637; **14**: 593-4, 656-7; **15**: 125; letters from, **9**: 80, 479-81; **11**: 159-61; **12**: 341-3, 357-8, 395-6; **13**: 307-8, 393-4; and establishment of mint, **7**: 159n; organization, **7**: 226; **8**: 15; administration, **8**: 248; displeasure with Ferdinand Grand, **8**: 684; La Rouerie blames for slow payment of debts, **10**: 401; pay Loan Office certificates, **11**: 51; appeal for payment from French officers, **11**: 82; shortage of funds, **11**: 469, 471; letters forwarded to, **11**: 613; letter from expected by TJ, **12**: 417; lack of support from, **12**: 444; permission necessary for payment of Fizeaux loan, **12**: 457, 471, 472-3; correspondence with Willink & Van Staphorst, **12**: 545-8; **14**: 586, 593, 609, 683; **15**: 20, 41-2, 474-5; letter from quoted, **12**: 548n-9n; suspension of remittances to Europe, **12**: 671, 672; letters from cited, **12**: 696; **13**: 633; letter to, from Franklin, quoted, **13**: 394n; letters to cited, **13**: 467, 575; Barclay's papers and books sent to, **13**: 573-5, 604n, 632, 637, 661; **14**: 5, 40, 52, 55, 581; inspect wheat for insect control, **13**: 662-3; order on payment for Algerian captives, **15**: 112; interest on loan from France, **15**: 456

Commissioners to Negotiate Trade Treaties. *See* American Commissioners for Negotiating Commercial Treaties

commissioners to settle Va.-Pa. boundary dispute: proceedings of, **3**: 77-8; complaints of, **3**: 206-8; background of, **3**: 286-9

commissions, military: issued by Henderson, **2**: 109; for Convention troops guards, **3**: 121; for western battalions, **3**: 161; **5**: 436; for Va. militia officers, **6**: 641-4

commissions, naval, **3**: 152

Committee (ship). *See Comité, Le*

Committee of Albany, **2**: 38

Committee of Congress at Headquarters: letters to, **3**: 476-7, 500; letters from, **3**: 391-7, 397, 406-10, 434-6, 455-6, 461, 483, 502, 552-3, 554-7; appointment, **3**: 379-80; call on states for supplies, **3**: 424

Committee of Correspondence (Va.): and Fast-Day resolution, **1**: 106n; urged to call for general Congress, **1**: 108; and Virginia Association, **1**: 109

Committee of Merchants (British), **9**: 281

Committee of North American Merchants: and American debts to British creditors, **8**: 56; **9**: 403-5, 433-4, 474-5

Committee of Safety (Va.). *See* Virginia: Committee of Safety

Committee of Secret Correspondence, **8**: 340

Committee of South Whalers: opposes Greville plan, **19**: 203n

Committee of the States: Va. bill for annual appointment of member for, **2**: 367-70; TJ's efforts to establish, **6**: 516, 522; **11**: 480; powers of, **6**: 516-29; **7**: 226, 292; appointed, **6**: 522; **7**: 299-300; chairman of, **6**: 526; and coinage, **6**: 528-9; **7**: 181; TJ's opinion of, **6**: 546-7, 567; meetings of, **7**: 21, 306, 309, 310; forbidden to appropriate money, **7**: 35; Monroe unable to attend, **7**: 381; orders to American commissioners, **7**: 394; lacks quorum, **7**: 413, 417, 446; ineffectiveness of, **7**: 431-2, 433n; adjourns, **7**: 432; **8**: 39, 41n, 414; letters from, to American Commissioners, cited, **7**: 497

committees: Fleming's criticism of, **3**: 33; Harrison's criticism of, **6**: 420

committees for regulating prices: Meriwether Smith's criticism of, **3**: 59

committees of correspondence: inspection of Custom House entries by, **1**: 152; origin of, **1**: 671

common law: and Va.'s revisors of the laws, **2**: 314n, 325; Va. bill for regulating proceedings in courts of, **2**: 599-612; TJ's history of, **9**: 67-72

Common Sense (Paine), **7**: 289; **20**: 269, 270, 272, 277, 291, 293

Commonwealth *v.* Caton, **6**: 279n

Commonwealth *v.* Reynolds and Clingman, **18**: 655-6

communications: plans for in case of in-

draft of, **1**: 177-82 (annotated by TJ), 180n, 182n (TJ's amendment to); **10**: 372-3, 376n; report on to Congress, **1**: 274-5; debated by Congress, **1**: 320-7, 477; **2**: 39; representation of colonies under, **2**: 18-9, 21, 22n; ratification of, **2**: 111-2, 120-1, 202, 205, 208, 269, 289; **3**: 484, 625-36; **4**: 389n, 534; **5**: 167-8; **6**: 447-8; Md.'s contingency for ratifying, **3**: 626-7; Va. resolution on, **4**: 386-91, 483; adopted by Congress, **5**: 41-2; increasing power over states urged, **5**: 469-72, 473-4; and territory of states, **6**: 120-1, 131-2; and ratification of Definitive Treaty, **6**: 424-6; completion of, **6**: 454; Article IX discussed, **6**: 475n; **8**: 215, 230, 296; and private right of soil, **6**: 485n; new states to be under, **6**: 608, 614; treaty making power, **7**: 33; provision for Committee of States, **7**: 292; change in proposed, **8**: 76, 80; **10**: 14; **18**: 395-7; TJ on, **10**: 19-20; **15**: 577; and power to use naval force, **18**: 372

confiscated property: ordered to be sold, **1**: 391; restoration of in Peace Treaty, **6**: 384, 459, 464n; Va. act on, **6**: 429, 566; by British, **7**: 541; N.Y., **8**: 482

confitures: U.S. import of, **10**: 147

Congaree river, S.C., **4**: 80

Congress (ship), **9**: 387, 392

CONGRESS, CONTINENTAL: letter to, from S.C. delegates, **4**: 483; letters from, to president, from American Commissioners, **7**: 493-500, 646-7; letter to, from Ga. delegates, **10**: 280-1; letter from, to R.I. delegates, **11**: 609-10

Authority

report on powers of committee to sit during recess, **1**: 272-3; to make treaties and alliances, **2**: 120; **6**: 424; **8**: 55-6, 230, 266-7; **10**: 286; increase of, **2**: 194; **12**: 42-3; increase in financial urged, **4**: 140; **7**: 251, 257, 258, 273, 277, 630-1; and impost, **4**: 559-61; **7**: 596-7; **12**: 446; control over states urged, **5**: 469-72, 473-4, 585; **6**: 149, 248; jurisdiction over surrounding district discussed, **6**: 368, 370n; exemption from taxation of public property, **6**: 369; strengthened by Va. acts (1783), **6**: 428; appeals to, **6**: 449-50, 452-5; to decide cases between states, **6**: 547; new states to be subject to, **6**:

CONGRESS, CONTINENTAL *(cont.)*
608, 614; over commerce, **7**: 102, 123, 225, 226, 231, 232, 356, 470n, 573, 651; **8**: 56, 76, 133, 149, 215, 229, 230-2, 266-7, 296, 309, 325, 328, 382, 402, 413, 460, 483-4, 579-80, 633; **9**: 84, 95, 183, 185, 188, 190, 197-8, 203-9, 235, 264, 449, 519, 666; **10**: 15-6, 41, 110, 286-7, 293, 313-4, 397; **11**: 672; to deal with international offenses, **7**: 307n; to requisition troops, **7**: 412; **10**: 58; mutiny against (1783), **7**: 541; **10**: 41, 42; powers, **8**: 53, 215-6, 579-80; **9**: 349, 519, 666; **10**: 58, 135-6, 234, 297; **11**: 220; **12**: 391; jurisdiction over western territory, **8**: 123; weakness of, **8**: 520, 579-80, 641; **9**: 179, 504; lacks over education, **9**: 121; to tax urged, **9**: 612; **12**: 439; to veto state laws proposed, **11**: 480-1; to enforce decisions, **12**: 43; to produce medals, **16**: 53n

Confederation
Franklin's proposed Articles of, **1**: 177, 180n; TJ's notes of debate on, **1**: 320-9; resolution adopting Articles of, **5**: 42. *See also* Confederation, Articles of

Delegates
draft instructions to Va. (*A Summary View*), **1**: 121-37, 669-76; TJ as, **1**: 169n; **6**: 256n, 335; **7**: 244; wages of, **1**: 407; **2**: 425; **4**: 6; **7**: 120; **10**: 27; from Transylvania, **2**: 109; from Ga., **5**: 317, 324; move to Princeton, **6**: 318-9, 334; meet at Annapolis, **6**: 348, 349; **7**: 57; leave Philadelphia, **6**: 376, 466; **7**: 272; convene slowly, **6**: 381, 419, 469; **12**: 100; attendance of, **6**: 437, 471; **7**: 25, 31, 41, 47, 60-1, 84, 90, 130, 276; **8**: 516; **9**: 185, 349, 451, 504, 510, 652, 666; **10**: 143, 294; **11**: 220-1, 619; **12**: 267, 412; matters before, **6**: 468-9, 470-1; lack full representation, **6**: 545, 546; TJ recommends young statesmen for, **6**: 549; president's expenses, **6**: 560; meet at Trenton (1784-1785), **7**: 41, 111, 118, 572; attitude toward Society of the Cincinnati, **7**: 107; **9**: 77; adjourn, **7**: 115, 120, 121, 136, 139, 225, 248, 306, 309, 310; **8**:

CONGRESS, CONTINENTAL (*cont.*)

Six Nations, **1**: 486, 494; land purchase from Indians, **8**: 324, 401-2, 514; ineffectualness in, **9**: 641

Military and Naval Affairs

orders raising of troops, **1**: 175; committee to confer with Gen. Schuyler, **1**: 275; draft declaration on British treatment of Ethan Allen, **1**: 276-7; committee to confer with Gen. Lee, **1**: 286; report of committee on Cedars cartel, **1**: 400-4; resolution on case of Gen. Sullivan, **1**: 478-9; takes over expresses to southern army, **3**: 536, 541; resolutions on Convention troops, **4**: 248; **5**: 56, 136, 239; **6**: 15; quells army mutiny, **4**: 325; rules on quartermaster for invaded states, **4**: 327, 337-8, 351-2; reorganizes army, **4**: 349-50; resolution on establishing hospital in Virginia, **5**: 35; resolution on funding Elliott, **5**: 35; resolution on supplying southern army, **5**: 77-8; and military rank of William Davies, **5**: 246, 251; resolution on arms for southern army, **5**: 269; ordinance on maritime prizes, **5**: 292-3; requires warrants for purchases, **5**: 356; recommends removal of public stores from Eastern Shore, **5**: 392, 488; establishes courts of admiralty, **5**: 497-9, 626; resolutions to form magazines, **6**: 39; and Washington's resignation as Commander-in-Chief, **6**: 402-14, 419; TJ's sketch of reply to Washington's resignation, **6**: 410-1; reception for Lafayette, **7**: 573; and French claims to prize money, **8**: 452-3; commands generals to defend territory, **10**: 381; authorizes TJ to settle *Alliance* claim, **13**: 390; and case of William Klein, **14**: 487-9; resolution on payment to French officers in Revolution, **14**: 680-1, 702-3; **15**: 19-20; authorizes medals, **16**: 53n-66n; American medals sent to, **16**: 67; and Spanish seizure of *Dover*, **20**: 205n-9n

Other Correspondence

letters from, to Louis XVI, cited, **8**: 315; **11**: 240; **13**: 247, 248n; letter to, from TJ, cited, **9**: 169; letter to, from Adams and TJ, cited, **10**: 213; letter from, to King of Spain, cited, **12**: 240; letters to, from Emperor of

CONGRESS, CONTINENTAL (*cont.*)

Morocco, cited, **13**: 527n; **14**: 46; letters to, from Dumas, cited, **13**: 639n-40n; **14**: 32

Permanent Seat

discussed, **6**: 319, 336-7, 345, 349, 371, 546; **7**: 248, 275, 278, 290, 306, 535, 568, 651; **8**: 78, 99, 228; votes on, **6**: 351-3, 365-6; Harrison's views on, **6**: 357-8; documents concerning, **6**: 361-70; and site on the Potomac, **6**: 362n; comparative table of distances for, **6**: 366-7

Procedure

meeting suggested by Association of Va. HB, **1**: 108; agreement of secrecy, **1**: 252-4; report of committee on unfinished business, **1**: 274-5; proposed resolution for rotation of membership, **1**: 411; report of committee on rules of, **1**: 456-8; form of prayer, **1**: 486; open debates advocated by Stephen, **1**: 660; first proposal for meeting, **1**: 671; Journals, **2**: 19, 21; **6**: 515; **7**: 248, 261, 281, 518; **8**: 78, 215, 499; **9**: 655; **11**: 619; **17**: 386; resolution on state papers, **5**: 562; resolution to publish state documents, **5**: 603n; TJ given access to offices, **6**: 211n; TJ asks perusal of Madison's notes on, **6**: 336, 337; peacetime organization, **6**: 338; TJ's draft resolution for erecting public buildings, **6**: 367-8; TJ's resolution on privileges and immunities, **6**: 368-70; TJ's view of length of session, **6**: 374; report of committee to revise files of reports, **6**: 438-9; interim organization, **6**: 516-29; numbers necessary for business, **6**: 526; chaplains, **6**: 560; secretary's expenses, **6**: 560; doorkeeper, **7**: 13; annual sessions approved by Washington, **7**: 51-2; debates in, **7**: 272; **11**: 308-9; majority concurrence on important questions, **10**: 20-2; reconsideration of questions, **10**: 22-3; delay in transacting business, **10**: 271; executive committee proposed by TJ during recess, **10**: 603; information sent to promptly, **11**: 66; Adams' discussion of functions, **11**: 177, 190; representation in, **11**: 220; **12**: 284, 440; lack of privacy in communications to, **11**: 312-3; organizes new federal government, **13**:

CONGRESS, CONTINENTAL (cont.)
498, 535, 540, 591, 593, 594,
612n, 620, 625. See also Committee
of the States

Relations with States
and Va.-Pa. boundary dispute, 1: 234-
6; requisitions on states, 2: 290; 3:
425; 5: 216; 7: 66-72; 8: 383, 519;
9: 9, 334; 12: 444; dependence on
states, 3: 370, 379-80; asks states to
report transactions, 3: 457; approves
of TJ's line of communication, 3:
472; resolutions on state quotas, 3:
508-13; aid to Va., 4: 58, 471; 5:
265, 266; urges compliance with
requisitions, 4: 140; Va. GA appoints Harrison to confer with, 4:
468n; calls upon states for utmost
exertions, 6: 65-6; resolution on Ky.
independence, 13: 495, 550-1

Reputation
Harvie criticizes members, 2: 35; ven-
ality criticized by Cyrus Griffin, 2:
216; Madison comments on lack of
statesmanship, 3: 335; TJ's comments on, 6: 61, 569; lack of popular esteem, 8: 99

Western Lands
prejudice against Va., 3: 262; report
on claims to, 3: 625-36; resolution
on, 3: 633-4; territorial cessions, 6:
120-1, 131-2, 164, 170-1, 176-7;
committee on, 6: 131-2, 147-9; evaluation of, 6: 234; accepts Va.'s land
cession, 6: 572n, 575n; debates TJ's
report on, 6: 598n; report of committee on temporary government of,
6: 603-7; report of committee on
Va.'s cession, 6: 650n; ordinance on
sale of lands, 8: 317; land sales, 12:
27, 173, 283
Congress, President of. See Griffin, Cyrus; Hancock, John; Huntington,
Samuel; Jay, John; Lee, Richard
Henry; St. Clair, Arthur
Congress, Secretary of. See Thomson,
Charles
Congress, U.S. See United States: Congress, House of Representatives, Senate
Congressional library: report of plan for,
6: 212n; 16: 605n; report of committee to prepare list of books for, 6: 216
Congressional Register: Madison criticizes, 15: 114

"Cong-ss Embark'd on board the Ship
Constitution of America bound to
Conogochegue by way of Philadelphia"
(cartoon), 17: xxxvi-vii, 427 (illus.)
Coni, Italy: TJ describes, 11: 433
Coningham, W.: letter from, to Wilson,
quoted, 16: 548n
conjuration: punishment, 2: 502
Connaissance des Temps: sought by TJ,
6: 544; sent to Rittenhouse, 8: 566;
12: 136, 144; sent to Stiles, 9: 476;
mentioned, 7: 133, 508, 514, 517; 8:
117, 298, 419, 575; 9: 355; 12: 31,
130
Connaux (Connault), France: TJ describes, 11: 423
Connecticut: apportions men and money
for Continental army, 1: 182; votes for
independence, 1: 314; votes against
Chase's taxation plan, 1: 323; asked to
send militia to aid N.Y., 1: 395; Tories in, 2: 13; supplies quota of money
and commodities, 3: 370; mutiny of
two regiments, 3: 412; approves new
currency act of Congress, 3: 527-8,
531; Continental requisitions of food
on, 4: 107; at Hartford Convention, 4:
138; quota for army pay, 4: 369; cedes
western lands, 6: 147, 485n; 9: 609,
652-3; 20: 595; votes on permanent
seat for Congress, 6: 365; delegates at
Congress, 6: 461n; 7: 572; boundaries
of, 6: 476n, 489-90; western land
claims, 6: 480n, 495n, 497, 575n;
charter (1662), 6: 489, 494; 10: 33;
settles lands patented to Lord Say and
Sele, 6: 493; purchases land from Indians, 6: 493, 495; settles western
lands, 6: 494-5; incorporates Westmoreland co., 6: 499; quota to national
treasury, 7: 5, 55, 70-1; 10: 34, 35,
54-6; attitude toward Society of the
Cincinnati, 7: 109n, 110n; attitude toward impost, 7: 114, 226, 232, 596-7,
630; 9: 608; ox teams hired in, 7: 128;
value of pound in, 7: 178; government
of, 7: 331; commerce of, 7: 331-7,
349; 19: 136-8, 139; population of, 7:
332; 10: 34, 35, 54-6; debts to other
states, 7: 336; troops for western posts,
7: 412; article on in *Encyclopédie Méthodique*, 9: 155; duties on imports from
Mass., 9: 198; free ports in, 9: 334;
revises laws, 10: 12; public debt, 10:
12, 45; agricultural character of, 10:
16; and emission of paper money, 10:

232; attitude toward Federal Convention, **10**: 232; **11**: 252, 309-10, 311; governorship of, **10**: 314; troops in vicinity of New York, **10**: 370, 375n; popular disturbances in, **10**: 633; delegates to Constitutional Convention, **11**: 154, 400, 470, 526; attitude on Mississippi navigation, **11**: 309; attitude toward Constitution, **12**: 281; opposes overseas embassies, **12**: 282; ratifies Constitution, **12**: 406, 409, 425, 490, 608, 620; **13**: 100-1, 205, 370; whale fishery, **14**: 227; elects senators, **14**: 302, 339, 344, 385, 394, 525, 529; nominates representatives for Congress, **14**: 525; votes for Adams as Vice President, **14**: 559; electoral votes (1789), **15**: 92; laws sought by TJ, **17**: 647; **20**: 326, 388

Connecticut Courant: requested by TJ, **17**: 509n; and Webster's satire, "A Pendulum without a Bob," **18**: 480-2

Connecticut Farms, N.J.: British raid on, **3**: 436n

Connecticut-Pennsylvania boundary dispute: discussed, **1**: 248; **3**: 634n; **6**: 474n-507, 575n; **7**: 432, 439; costs of, **6**: 477n-8n; decision in, **6**: 478n, 480n; arguments on by James Wilson and William Samuel Johnson, **6**: 488-98

Connecticut River, **6**: 494

Connecticut Turtle. See Bushnell, David; submarine: Bushnell's *Connecticut Turtle*

Connelly, Maj.: takes possession of Fort Pitt, **2**: 99

Conner, Edward: prisoner of war, **5**: 432

Connolly, John: and Va.-Pa. boundary dispute, **1**: 235n; captured, **1**: 389n; British agent in Northwest Territory, **17**: 39, 55; activities discovered by Innes, **19**: 437n; mentioned, **6**: 12

Conococheague River: and capital site, **17**: 453-4, 456-7; **19**: 18, 19, 23-4, 25, 27, 65

Conquérant, Le (ship), **10**: 257

Conroe, Miss: marriage to Samuel House, **10**: 169

conscience, liberty of: TJ's views on, **1**: 530, 532, 535-9, 544-50, 553-8; **2**: 545-7; in trade treaty stipulations, **7**: 474, 477, 482, 618; **8**: 108; **9**: 415, 425, 432

Considerations on the Present State of Virginia (John Randolph?), **1**: 106n, 107n

Consolver, James: in Albemarle co. militia, **1**: 665

Consolver, Martin: in Albemarle co. militia, **1**: 665

Consolver, Micajah: in Albemarle co. militia, **1**: 668n

conspiracy: Va. bill concernng, **2**: 320n, 520. *See also* Hickey Plot

Constable, Rucker & Co., **11**: 375

Constable, William: letter from, **5**: 369; handles Paine's funds, **15**: 274; Duer represents, **16**: 329n; books sought by Donald from, **16**: 406; and speculation in U.S. foreign debt, **20**: 177; owner of *Nancy*, **20**: 238n; mentioned, **5**: 295, 475; **6**: 18-9, 36n; **14**: 280

Constable & Co.: owners of *Nancy*, **20**: 237

constables: fees of, **2**: 431

Constantine, Algeria: plague in, **11**: 21-2

Constantine, Bey of. *See* Salih, Bey of Constantine

Constantine I: quoted by TJ, **1**: 553

Constantinople: Mazzei's knowledge of, **2**: 211; key to Asia, **12**: 128; probable fall to Russia, **12**: 161; **13**: 436; plague in, **13**: 212; Rutledge plans travel to, **13**: 318, 358, 359, 506, 530; imports rice, **15**: 13, 22, 37, 372, 408-9, 444, 450, 451; insurrection in, **16**: 254

Constitution, British, **2**: 49; **12**: 189

Constitutional Convention: Washington named head of Va. delegation to, **10**: 533n-5n; **11**: 389; results expected from, **10**: 574-5; **11**: 219-20, 279, 471, 672; **12**: 34, 36, 230, 335; Va. delegates at, **10**: 593n, 622; **11**: 154, 263, 331; purpose, **10**: 634; **11**: 289, 304, 407-10, 526; **12**: 27, 39, 42; Va.'s role in calling, **11**: 201; delegates to, **11**: 219, 252, 302, 309, 311, 363, 470, 549, 626; Otto labels an "Assemblée des Notables," **11**: 286; Jay's attitude toward, **11**: 313; Madison reports on, **11**: 400; strengthening of, **11**: 409; proceedings of, **11**: 409, 414, 561, 600, 619; **12**: 10, 69, 102, 173, 228-34, 271-80; Monroe's hopes for, **11**: 630-1; probable effects of, **12**: 105; TJ comments on, **12**: 113; TJ's advice asked, **12**: 128; text of Constitution sent to TJ, **12**: 149; Pa. delegates to, **12**: 229, 231n; liberal conduct of, **12**: 230, 308; divisiveness in, **12**: 232n, 233n; Madison's argument for power of negative over states, **12**: 273-9;

Constitutional Convention (*cont.*)
Verme inquires about, **12**: 588; and foreign commerce, **18**: 517. *See also* Constitution of the United States

Constitutional Convention, second: TJ on, **12**: 426; **14**: xxxix, 188, 344, 529, 673, 689; **15**: 50; Madison opposes, **14**: xxxviii-ix, 340, 352; Henry favors, **14**: xxxviii-ix, 673, 689; **16**: 145n, 173n; Va. resolution on, **14**: xxxviii-xl, 329 (fac.), 558, 615; Clinton favors, **14**: 689

Constitutional Conventions, state: violence in, **13**: 331-2; opposition in, **13**: 333, 359; TJ on, **18**: 132-4

constitutional law. *See* law

Constitutional Party (Pa.): hostility to the Bank of North America, **8**: 99, 562; **9**: 321; and revision of Test Law, **9**: 320-1; defeated in 1785 election, **8**: 672; **9**: 320; and Constitution, **12**: 281, 409; congressional candidates, **14**: 473

Constitutional Society: Dumas on, **13**: 161n

CONSTITUTION OF THE UNITED STATES: Madison on, **12**: 102-3, 271-82; **13**: 98-9, 160, 412-3, 539-40, 624-5; sent to TJ, **12**: 149, 185, 236, 252, 266, 357n, 489; Franklin's speech on, **12**: 229-30; William Lewis on, **12**: 230; merits debated, **12**: 252-5, 280-1, 295, 296, 297, 335, 423, 425, 428; Carrington on, **12**: 254-5; **13**: 100-1, 103, 156-7, 244-5, 414n; Executive under, **12**: 272; John Trumbull on, **12**: 308; Crèvecoeur hopes for success of, **12**: 332; Va.'s attitude toward, **12**: 335, 345, 602; Adams on, **12**: 335, 396; effect on money quotas of states, **12**: 342; TJ on, **12**: 350-1, 356-7, 425, 439-41, 446, 476-9; **13**: 6n-7n, 128, 174, 208-9, 232, 378, 442-3, 489-90, 502, 508; **14**: 385, 420, 529, 583, 605, 639, 650-1, 678-9; **20**: 709; W. S. Smith on, **12**: 390-1, 518; Uriah Forrest on, **12**: 416, 475, 479n; attacked in American newspapers, **12**: 425; Gilmer on, **12**: 453; Lafayette on, **12**: 460; **13**: 348; news of in *Gazette de Leide*, **12**: 562; **13**: 408n, 409n, 411n, 436n-7n, 474, 558n-9n; **14**: 348n-9n; news of in Europe, **12**: 616-7; Page defends, **12**: 650-2; Paine on, **13**: 6n-7n; Wilson's speech on, **13**: 6n-

CONSTITUTION OF THE U.S. (*cont.*)
8n; opposition to, **13**: 38-9, 98, 333, 359; **14**: 559-60; **16**: 293; **19**: 50-3; Hopkinson on, **13**: 38-9, 370; pamphlets on, **13**: 39, 40n-1n, 337, 338n, 354n; Washington on, **13**: 42n-3n, 160, 536n, 556-7; Carmichael on, **13**: 91-2, 95; Mason's objections to, **13**: 204-5; Henry cites TJ's opinions on, **13**: 353, 354n-5n, 412, 414n; celebration of on July 4, 1788, **13**: 370, 371n, 551; French attitude toward, **13**: 409n-1n, 466-7, 490-1, 546; **20**: 263-4; Cutting on, **13**: 480-1, 645-6; Louis XVI on, **13**: 490-1; Catherine the Great receives from J. P. Jones, **13**: 583; J. P. Jones on, **13**: 583; sent to Verme, **13**: 605; revision of, **13**: 624-5; **14**: 340; Franklin on, **14**: 36; cited, **16**: 357n, 407; authorizes navy, **18**: 397; British trade and, **18**: 518; Hamilton on, **18**: 520. *See also* Bill of Rights; individual states

Amendments

TJ on, **12**: 426, 558, 569-70, 571, 583-4; **13**: 208; **14**: 615, 688; Va. recommends, **12**: 583-4; **13**: 205-6, 351-2, 354n-5n, 412, 550, 619; **14**: 385, 615; **16**: 13; Mass. proposes, **13**: 205, 208, 315; **14**: 385; ratification before, **13**: 205-6, 232, 277, 315, 351-2; Md. proposes, **13**: 333-6; European reports of, **13**: 408n, 409n, 539, 571-2; N.Y. recommends, **13**: 413, 591, 608, 610n-1n, 619; **14**: 557-8; Madison on dangers of, **13**: 497-8; **14**: 340; Va. rejects, **13**: 542; Washington on, **13**: 556; N.C. proposes as condition of ratification, **13**: 644, 659-1; **14**: 48, 385; method of adoption, **14**: 344; Donald on, **14**: 458; Adams asks for TJ's opinions on, **14**: 599; Congress discusses, **15**: 154; Madison proposes, **15**: 181, 229, 324-5; votes of six states on, **16**: 470-1; progress of, **18**: 119; ratified by states, **18**: 595-6

Ratification

state conventions for, **12**: 409, 443-4, 489-90, 608-9; **13**: 41-2, 164, 254; Madison on, **12**: 443-4, 608-9; **13**: 412-3; Washington on, **12**: 489-90; TJ's summary of, **12**: 557; **13**: 159-60, 231-2, 357, 359, 489-90,

consuls, American (*cont.*)
581; **17**: 423-4; **18**: 101, 107; uniforms of, **17**: 423-4; taxes on, **17**: 475-6; fees for, **17**: 668; Maclay rejects salaries for, **19**: 303; regulations governing, **19**: 319-20; problems of, **19**: 338-42; Cutting's comments on, **20**: 241; reporting form, **20**: 244, 246-9; dealing with seamen, **20**: 249, 403n; list of needed by Hamilton, **20**: 647; expenses, **20**: 708-9

consuls, American, in France: service in, **10**: 200; **11**: 627-9; **12**: 244, 250-1; needed in ports, **10**: 273; need for, **13**: 641; appointment of, **14**: 58-9; **16**: 288n; TJ's list, **14**: 59-60; Barclay's list, **14**: 62n; engaging in trade, **14**: 68-70; Vernes' suggestions on, **15**: 541-2; Cathalan appointed, **19**: 74

consuls, British: in Algiers, **9**: 528-9, 617-8; **12**: 550; mentioned, **10**: 150

consuls, foreign: duties on goods imported by, **12**: 266

consuls, French: Va. proclamation on, **3**: 251-2; Moustier on, **14**: 63n-6n; mentioned, **14**: 67-8

Contee, Benjamin: letters to, **8**: 291, 394; letters from, **8**: 303, 329; as delegate for Md., **13**: 535; passport issued by TJ, **15**: 484

conte-pas. *See* pedometer

Conti, Louis François Joseph de Bourbon, Prince de: returns from exile, **16**: 303

Continental accounts: settlement of, **3**: 110

Continental army: financial and military estimates for, **1**: 182-4; mentioned in Declaration of Causes, **1**: 203, 212; desertions from, **1**: 244, 444, 446-7; needed for defense of Va., **1**: 268; post of physician to Va. troops sought by McClurg, **1**: 286-7; not to be disbanded in Canada, **1**: 392; officers for, **1**: 392, 412, 579-82; **2**: 359; **3**: 56; **4**: 247; **10**: 49; pay of, **1**: 395; **3**: 392; **4**: 141-4, 229, 242, 367; **7**: 214; **10**: 45; lacks supplies in Canadian campaign, **1**: 434; lacks discipline in Canadian campaign, **1**: 450; numbers, **1**: 458, 473, 506, 508; **6**: 97; courage praised by TJ, **1**: 459; officers' rank, **1**: 461, 478; recruitment of, **1**: 477, 483, 581; **2**: 184; **3**: 39, 245, 393; **4**: 18; Va. troops in, **1**: 482, 491, 493, 577-84; **2**:

18, 20, 176, 177, 194, 213-4; **3**: 6, 107, 154, 157, 204-5, 244-5, 294, 312, 455, 456, 492, 500, 506, 508, 530, 546, 584; **4**: 193-5, 197, 212-4, 469, 483, 499, 697; **5**: 268, 289, 398, 603, 621; **6**: 4-5, 30, 49, 75; clothing for, **1**: 578; **2**: 126, 128n; **3**: 7, 77, 167, 172, 260-1, 353; **4**: 89, 140, 188-9, 190, 191; **5**: 334; needs blankets, **1**: 658-9; **3**: 261; drafts for, **2**: 14; plague reported in, **2**: 20; provisioning of, **2**: 125; **3**: 35, 72, 155, 303-4, 336, 368-9, 392, 461, 465-6, 471, 500, 502, 552-3, 572, 584-5; **4**: 105-8, 284-7; land bounties for, **2**: 140; **3**: 266, 631; **6**: 572n-4n, 579; superiority in marksmanship, **2**: 195; enlistments for, **3**: 66; Steuben's book of regulations for, **3**: 108, 110; on Eastern Shore of Va., **3**: 215; state quotas of supplies for, **3**: 222, 305, 395, 406-9, 417; TJ recounts Va.'s services to, **3**: 224-7; state quotas of troops for, **3**: 290, 313, 434-5, 454, 461, 554-7, 571; **4**: 45-6, 139, 222; **5**: 458; **7**: 67, 214; uniforms, **3**: 306; Va. quotas of supplies, **3**: 334-5, 455, 456, 476, 529; **6**: 39; medical affairs, **3**: 357; **4**: 242; discontent fostered by British, **3**: 393; low morale of, **3**: 412; cavalry, **3**: 420, 427; **4**: 6; Washington demands more infantry, **3**: 485; wagons for, **3**: 513; vouchers for arms of Va. troops in, **3**: 514; difficulties of supplying northern army from south, **3**: 565; artillery regiments, **3**: 636, 641; reorganized by Congress, **4**: 17, 69-70, 349-50, 604; lack of magazines, **4**: 27; Pennsylvania line in, **4**: 325; **5**: 351, 354, 423, 453, 482, 495, 552, 662; **6**: 52, 103, 636; regulations for issue of liquor, **4**: 488-9; inferior to British, **4**: 501; reimbursement of officers in, **4**: 501-2; bounty money for recruits, **4**: 601-2; pay of civilian staffs, **5**: 26-7, 52; retirement of officers, **5**: 179; issuing commissary general for, **5**: 418, 452-3; French forces in, **5**: 639; French deserters in, **6**: 34; demobilization of, **6**: 263, 334; **7**: 542; mutinies against Congress, **6**: 318, 336, 338; **7**: 541; **10**: 41, 42; Washington's Farewell Orders to, **6**: 402n-3n; Hand's plan for dismissal and enlistments, **7**:

252; TJ's defense of, **10**: 45; payment of arrearages to, **11**: 388

Continental Board of War. *See* Board of War, Continental

Continental certificates: payment in Europe, **12**: 581-2

Continental currency. *See* money, Continental

Continental laboratory: in Va., **3**: 505; mentioned, **3**: 480; **4**: 9

Continental Loan Office. *See* Loan Office, Continental

contraband: trade treaty stipulations, **6**: 395; **7**: 472, 477, 483, 490, 619, 626-7; **8**: 30-1, 108, 191, 274; **9**: 63, 415-6, 429-31, 432; **10**: 104; **12**: 164; U.S. definition of, **7**: 267-8; enumeration of, **7**: 473, 474; and tobacco, **8**: 388; and Moroccan treaty, **10**: 423; snuff seized as, **11**: 283

contracts: actions for breach of in common law courts, **2**: 606; Va. bill concerning breach of, **2**: 624-5; violations of, **12**: 276

convent: TJ's views on daughter being educated in, **10**: 628

Convention troops: sent to Va., **2**: 212; division of officers and men contrary to Convention, **2**: 237-8; **4**: 79; TJ protests removal from Albemarle barracks, **2**: 237-44; advantages to neighborhood from, **2**: 238-40; provisioning of, **2**: 239-41; **3**: 74, 94, 108, 341, 436, 486, 554, 562, 567-9, 580-1, 581-2, 648-9, 661; **4**: 26, 95, 165, 181-2, 195, 210-1, 248, 319, 369-71, 467, 483, 532-3, 549, 550-1, 605, 607, 664-5, 672; **5**: 302-3, 306-7, 565; low mortality of, **2**: 241; guarding of, **2**: 241; **3**: 95, 239; **5**: 271, 404, 661-2; officers' quarters for, **2**: 242; described, **2**: 244n; TJ's protection of requested, **3**: 3; desertions from, **3**: 41; **4**: 93, 95, 110-1, 113; **5**: 239; problems with bills of exchange, **3**: 64; removal from Albemarle barracks, **3**: 66, 80, 240, 253, 423-4, 428, 446, 449-50, 453, 648; **4**: 14-5, 58, 60, 65, 78, 88, 92-3, 93-4, 100-2, 105, 120, 160, 248, 299, 308, 466, 500, 625, 640, 649, 652, 656, 660, 666, 671-2; **5**: 6, 15; Regiment of Guards for, **3**: 121, 154, 155-6, 192, 214-5, 250; **4**: 23, 73, 252, 303; **5**: 322-3, 334, 341, 403-4, 408-9; Riedesel commends Brunswick troops to TJ's protection, **3**: 212; attempts at rescue reported, **3**: 217, 453, 654; supplied by flag of truce, **3**: 227, 318, 322; **5**: 97-8, 257, 511, 633; TJ's notes and queries concerning proposed removal of, **3**: 255-7; and examination of German letters, **3**: 339; recall of officers to barracks, **3**: 449-50, 453; Tory scheme to arm, **3**: 533; permits for sending letters, **3**: 561, 562; removal to Frederick, Md., **3**: 650-1; **4**: 70-1, 72-4, 80, 109, 181-2, 255; Albemarle barracks at Charlottesville, view of, **4**: xxxviii, 266 (illus.); strength of, **4**: 93, 94; officers' horses, **4**: 101; debts of, **4**: 101; **5**: 484-5; exchange of, **4**: 154-5; horses for, **4**: 154-5, 157, 160; money for, **4**: 164, 698; orders of Congress on, **4**: 196, 197; **6**: 15; complain of meal, **4**: 249, 252; need of clothing, **4**: 278; express post for, **4**: 285; cooperation with invaders feared, **4**: 308; bills of exchange, **5**: 19; transferred to Pa., **5**: 56, 301, 306; movement of, **5**: 131, 136, 147; Md.'s provision for, **5**: 168; British officers ordered to Conn., **5**: 239, 545n; supplies for, **5**: 414; at Winchester, **5**: 432-3; Va. unable to provide for, **5**: 542-3; Geismar's friendship with, **9**: 81; mentioned, **3**: 339; **5**: 271. *See also* German prisoners in American Revolution; prisoners of war, British

conveyances: Va. bill for regulating, **2**: 405-9; of land to Congress, **6**: 428

convict labor: Va. bill governing, **2**: 513-5

Conway, Capt. (officer of Alexandria artillery company), **5**: 336

Conway, Edwin: letter from, **6**: 81

Conway, Francis: and bill establishing ferries, **2**: 456

Conway, Capt. Joseph, **4**: 5

Conway, Gen. Thomas: takes Trincomalee, **13**: 465; letter from cited, **15**: 478; mentioned, **11**: 536

Conway river: post service on, **2**: 389

Conway's landing, Va.: ferry at, **2**: 456

Conyngham (Cunnyngham), Capt. Gustavus: prizes taken to Coruña, **11**: 20, 133

Conyngham & Nesbit: lawsuit, **1**: 70-1; William Pearce recommended to, **20**: 314, 316n

Cook, Mr. (of Stafford co.): and bill establishing ferries, **2**: 454

Cook, Capt. James: maps of voyage desired by TJ, **8**: 554; accompanied by John Ledyard, **9**: 273; **12**: 159; voyages, **11**: 146; **16**: 329; mentioned, **5**: 378; **10**: 259, 316

Cook (Cooke), John: taken prisoner by British, **4**: 311, 421

Cook, Joseph Platt: Conn. delegate in Congress, **7**: 572; recommendation of John Lamb, **8**: 60; mentioned, **18**: 386n

Cook, Lodowick: in Albemarle co. militia, **1**: 665

Cook, Nicholas: as governor of R.I., **15**: 579, 581n

Cook, Rutherford: in *Dover* case, **20**: 207n

Cook, Samuel: in *Dover* case, **20**: 207n

Cook, William: signs nonimportation resolutions (1770), **1**: 47

Cooke, Bowler: hires out slaves, **4**: 583

Cooke, John (of Petersburg): letter from, to George Washington, **19**: 626-7; "Description of a new standard for Weights and Measures," **19**: 626-7; mentioned, **5**: 152n

Cooper, Capt. (master of *Nancy*), **16**: 95

Cooper, Mr. (express at Harrisburg), **4**: 49, 77

Cooper, James: legal suit of, **20**: 499n-500n

Cooper, John: letter from, **8**: 336; introduced to TJ, **8**: 70; passport issued by TJ, **15**: 485; distributes *Gazette de Leide*, **17**: 499, 541

Cooper, Capt. John, **20**: 435

Cooper, Mrs. John: passport issued by TJ, **15**: 485

Cooper, Roe, **3**: 345

Cooper, Dr. Samuel: sermon mentioned, **6**: 191; grandson of recommended for consular appointment, **20**: 376

Cooper, Thomas: letter to quoted, **16**: 605-6; letter to cited, **16**: 610n, 615n

Cooper, William: produces maple sugar, **20**: 343-4

Cooper river, S.C., **3**: 399, 400, 401

coopers: wages in R.I., **7**: 339

Coote, Capt.: permission to change quarters, **4**: 15

Copeland, Henry: signs Va. oath of allegiance, **2**: 129

Copinger, Mr. (wine merchant), **11**: 457

Copley, John Singleton: and statue of Washington, **12**: 36; mentioned, **8**: 160

copper: U.S. trade in, **10**: 147; sent to Tunis by Emperor of Morocco, **12**: 626

copper coinage: bill for altering rates of in Va., **1**: 597; table of, **7**: 172; regional variations in value of, **7**: 178; debasement of, **7**: 196-7; value of, **7**: 200; name of, **7**: 202; Durival's inquiry on, **10**: 499-500; alleged to be struck in U.S., **10**: 500; TJ's Report on, **16**: 335-42 (editorial note), 345-9; **17**: 534n; Boulton's proposals for, **16**: 335n-42n; **18**: 139-41; Mitchell's negotiations on, **16**: 336n-41n; costs, **16**: 338n, 342n; **17**: 535; designs suggested by Mitchell, **16**: 342-5; letter to Speaker of the House of Representatives on, **16**: 345; Paine's thoughts on, **17**: 534-40; **20**: 308-9; Hamilton's plan for, **17**: 534n; mentioned, **7**: 153n, 163, 167, 190, 195, 196, 197-8; **10**: 511; **18**: 454-5. *See also* cent

copper mines: purchase by Va. for Penet, Windel & Co., **3**: 135

copying devices, mechanical: TJ's interest in, **6**: 373

copying paper: ordered by TJ, **10**: 398, 479; **12**: 694

copying press: ordered by TJ, **7**: 575; **8**: 22; **10**: 211, 400, 620; **11**: 55, 168; **12**: 95, 559; **15**: 608-9; **17**: 212, 412, 507; shipped to TJ, **7**: 586, 587; **8**: 93, 103, 159; **9**: 555, 557; **10**: 116, 393, 417, 471, 478; **11**: 91; TJ's use of, **8**: 177n, 461, 576; **10**: 318n; **15**: 521n; Madison lacks, **9**: 333; delivered to W. S. Smith, **9**: 570; cost of, **9**: 655; **10**: 92; **11**: 97; Charpentier recommended for making, **10**: 218; ordered for Lafayette, **10**: 294, 312; **12**: 529-30; passport for import of asked, **10**: 467, 508; *acquits-à-caution* for, **10**: 588; given to Carmichael, **10**: 634; **11**: 52-3, 237, 384; sent to Madison, **11**: 97, 307; ordered from Woodmason, **11**: 365, 506, 607; **12**: 356; sent to Lardizábel, **11**: 553; ordered for Ethis de Corny, **12**: 430; taken to Holland, **12**: 655n; Dugnani's, **14**: 326n-7n; Franklin's use of, **15**: 608, 609n; Mary Jefferson's use of, **16**: xxxi, 52 (fac.); for State Dept., **16**: 288n, 323, 324n;

left in Paris, **16**: 323; used as duplicating machine, **17**: 339n, 346; sent from Paris, **18**: 36n-7n

copyists: application of Dubosq, **12**: 375

copyright: infringement of, **8**: 211; Secretary of State receives books, **17**: 598

Coram, Robert: letter from, **19**: 409-10; *Political Inquiries*, **19**: 409-10

Corancez, Guillaume Olivier de: quoted, **8**: 242n

Corbet, Michael (seaman): defended by Adams, **18**: 312n

Corbin, Col.: death of, **16**: 475

Corbin, Alice, **1**: 5

Corbin, Betty Tayloe. *See* Turberville, Betty Tayloe

Corbin, Francis: opposed to bill for religious freedom, **2**: 548n, 549n; opposes federal control of commerce, **9**: 198, 199; supports Constitution, **12**: 410; **13**: 98, 352, 620; on committee to welcome TJ, **16**: 11n; interest in U.S. Senate, **16**: 319; mentioned, **15**: 664

Corbin, Gawen: death of, **9**: 65

Corbin, Col. George: letter to, **5**: 137; letters from, **3**: 81-2; **5**: 21-2; **6**: 44-7; swivels to be left with, **3**: 215; letter from cited, **3**: 544; threatens to resign, **5**: 137n; efforts to curb draft riot in Accomac, **5**: 653

Corbin, John Tayloe: signs nonimportation resolutions (1770), **1**: 47; loyalism of, **1**: 476n

Corbin, Richard: money collected from, **1**: 237; loyalist, **1**: 476n; mentioned, **1**: 289

cordage: U.S. import of, **7**: 330; **10**: 147

Corderius, *Colloquies*, **6**: 166

Córdoba (Cordova), Luis de: commands Spanish squadron, **3**: 306

Cordon, Victor Amédée, Marquis: letter from, **13**: 312

cork: import from S.C., **8**: 203

Cork, Ireland: and U.S. commercial policy, **19**: 134

cork acorns. *See* acorns, cork-oak

cork trees (cork oaks): ordered for S.C., **13**: 508; shipped from France by TJ, **15**: 376, 377n

Corke fleet: reported fallen, **5**: 551

corkwood: used for shipbuilding, **10**: 343

Cormier, J., **14**: 648

corn: Va. bill on exportation of, **2**: 348; export to Bermuda, **3**: 13n; **4**: 466; quota levied on Va. by Congress, **3**:

222, 511; exchanged for salt, **3**: 238, 326, 376; **4**: 502; taxes payable in, **3**: 250; **5**: 256; for Continental army, **3**: 334, 585, 586; **4**: 413; for southern army, **3**: 496, 611, 659; **4**: 8, 9; sale of, **3**: 539; danger to stock on Eastern Shore, **3**: 544; hoarding of, **3**: 562; notice to commissioners of the provision law on, **3**: 609; for Va. militia, **4**: 41; impressment of, **4**: 73; supplies in west, **4**: 170, 199; **5**: 467; price fixed by Va. GA, **4**: 342; supply in Jefferson co., **4**: 365; dishonest transactions in, **4**: 391-2; captured by British privateer, **4**: 416; purchased at Cumberland, **4**: 426, 450; for proposed Detroit expedition, **4**: 442; cost of moving, **4**: 458; transportation from N.C. to Va., **4**: 503; for Lafayette's troops, **6**: 34; exported from Conn., **7**: 335, 336; exported from N.H., **7**: 345; exported from Pa., **7**: 347; trade statistics on, **7**: 349; exported from Va., **7**: 372; **8**: 250; crops of, **7**: 402, 592; **8**: 508, 642, 660; **10**: 577, 588; **11**: 601; **12**: 283; exported from U.S., **7**: 406; **10**: 147; prices of, **7**: 604; **8**: 115; **9**: 202, 335-6, 519; **10**: 108; **20**: 717; production in S.C., **8**: 198; exported from S.C., **8**: 201, 202, 203; damaged by insects, **8**: 344, 415; grist mills for, **10**: 262; cultivated by TJ in France, **11**: 373, 383; **12**: 135, 486; **13**: 298, 343; seeds sent to U.S., **12**: 466; in France, **12**: 469, 480; **15**: 409; French and Italian compared to American, **13**: 343; hominy, **13**: 343; imported by Britain, **20**: 567, 704; in Guinea, **20**: 602. *See also* planting of crops

Corneille, Pierre: works, **8**: 411

Corneille, Thomas: works, **8**: 411

Corneillon: paper bought from, **15**: xxvii

Cornelius Nepos: TJ seeks information on best Italian translation, **11**: 159; mentioned, **20**: 634n

Cornell, Ezekiel, **5**: 620

Cornish, Adm. Samuel: West Indian expedition, **19**: 324; **20**: 251; mentioned, **17**: 650; **18**: 504

corn law, British: opposition to, **20**: 100-1, 590; mentioned, **20**: 567

corn meal: supplied to Convention troops, **4**: 182; supplied to army, **4**: 419, 426, 449

Cornplanter (Seneca chief): audience

Corsica: French annexation of, **15**: 567; **16**: 123

Cortez, Hernando: copy of portrait desired by TJ, **12**: 245; portrait in Florence copied for TJ, **14**: 440, 467-8; **15**: xxxv-vi, 152, 157, 425 (illus.)

Cortlandt, Mr., **1**: 54

Coruña, Spain: goods belonging to U.S. at, **10**: 536; Barclay's business at, **11**: 20; mentioned, **11**: 22, 133

Cosby, William, **4**: 20, 21n

cosmogony: Whitehurst's theory of, **10**: 104, 604, 608; TJ's views on, **10**: 608

Coste, Jean: transports wine for TJ, **11**: 465n

Coster (Koster), Janszoon: claim to invention of movable type, **8**: 447

Cosway, Maria Hadfield (Mrs. Richard Cosway): letters to, **10**: 431-3, 443-55, 458-9, 542-3, 555, 627-8; **11**: 519-20; **12**: 539-40; **13**: 103-4, 423-4, 435, 638-9; **14**: 445-6; **15**: 142-3, 305-6, 413-4, 521; **16**: 550-1; letters from, **10**: 393-4, 433, 441, 494-6, 538-40, 552; **11**: 3-4, 148-51, 567-9; **12**: 387, 403, 415, 459-60; **14**: 372, 525-6; **15**: 339, 351, 513-4; **16**: 312-3; TJ's left-handed letter to, **10**: xxix, 435 (fac.); and Trumbull's miniature of TJ, **10**: xxix, 466 (illus.); **12**: 645, 647; **13**: 391, 525; **14**: xxxvi; miniature portraits of by husband, **10**: xxx, 467 (illus.); **13**: xxix, 449 (illus.); might visit Hoffman, **10**: 320n; TJ visits, **10**: 367n; intends to visit TJ, **10**: 393-4; departs Paris, **10**: 432, 433, 443; arrives at Antwerp, **10**: 438; conversation about, **10**: 444; TJ describes, **10**: 446; and landscape painting, **10**: 447; letters sent to by Trumbull, **10**: 460; letters to cited, **10**: 506, 610, 611; **11**: 531; letters from cited, **10**: 556; **11**: 182; **13**: 289; **14**: 524n, 525; sends *Songs and Duets* to TJ, **10**: 556, 627; messages to, **11**: 181; visits Paris, **12**: 60, 69, 139, 207, 358, 393; invited to dinner by TJ, **12**: 387; returns to England, **12**: 406, 415, 459, 539-40; popularity of, **12**: 540; anger at TJ, **12**: 622; letters to quoted, **13**: xxvi, xxix; "The Hours" engraved by Bartolozzi, **13**: xxix, 424, 449 (illus.), 525; TJ tells of German tour, **13**: 103-4; TJ neglects to write, **13**: 287-8, 360-1, 435, 524-5; and Angelica Church,

13: 391, 520, 525; **14**: 9, 525-6; TJ asks for picture of, **13**: 424, 525; visiting card for TJ, **13**: 424, 638-9; asks TJ to visit, **13**: 525; **14**: 372, 526; will go to Italy, **13**: 639; TJ advises to go to America, **13**: 639; **16**: 550-1; introduces Mrs. Cowley to TJ, **14**: 372, 510-1, 524; relationship with TJ, **14**: 446; **15**: 143, 306; Mrs. Paradise criticizes, **15**: 95; encourages Jerningham's poetry, **15**: 96; and Gouverneur Morris, **15**: 305-6, 351; brother presented to TJ, **15**: 351, 413; illness prevents from seeing TJ, **15**: 513; birth of daughter, **16**: 198, 550, 551n; desired by TJ to paint Natural Bridge, **19**: 301n; mentioned, **11**: 156, 578; **12**: 139, 297, 643, 694; **13**: 214, 241, 301, 546, 597; **14**: 211, 365n, 441, 514, 515; **15**: 200, 504

Cosway, Richard: miniature portraits of wife, **10**: xxx, 467 (illus.); **13**: xxix, 449 (illus.); might visit Hoffman, **10**: 320n; to go to England, **10**: 433; arrives at Antwerp, **10**: 438; conversation about, **10**: 444; purchase of paintings, **10**: 506; mentioned, **10**: 393, 441, 453, 459, 495, 543, 555n; **11**: 149, 150, 569; **12**: 139, 415, 540, 647; **13**: 525; **15**: 504, 513; **16**: 551n

Côte, La, France: TJ's description of, **11**: 416-8

Côte Rôtie, France: TJ's description of, **11**: 421

Cotolendi, Charles: edition of Columbus' life, **20**: 210

Cotter, John: Mazzei's creditor in Ireland, **3**: 311

Cotton, Mrs., **7**: 358, 411

cotton: price of, **8**: 511; not grown north of Md., **10**: 33; imported from West Indies, **10**: 148; produced in southern states, **10**: 262; export to France proposed, **10**: 303; duty on, **13**: 543; production encouraged, **14**: 546; **15**: 452; Edward Rutledge experiments with, **15**: 13; British restrictions on importation, **16**: 548n; improved loom for weaving, **20**: 242-3

cotton manufacture: in Mass., **7**: 341; in Md., **8**: 511; in Va., **8**: 511; **13**: 153-4, 183-4, 260-1; in Ireland, **13**: 153; in U.S., **14**: 546; Philadelphia, **15**: 55-6; models of machinery requested, **15**: 56; carding and spinning machinery at

cotton manufacture (*cont.*)
La Muette, **15**: 476, 477n; Fielding's interest in, **15**: 528; Pollard's project, **16**: 582; model of Arkwright's machine, **17**: 387n; **18**: 123n

cotton textiles: imported by U.S., **8**: 309; **9**: 62; **12**: 470; in Portugal, **9**: 20; in U.S., **10**: 262

Couedic de Kergoualec, Charles Louis, Vicomte du: Louis XVI's message to widow of, **3**: 344

cougar. *See* puma

Coughnowaga, Que., **1**: 399

Coulaux la Vigne (Vigna), J.: cargoes consigned to, **5**: 395; mentioned, **4**: 143-4

Coulomb, Charles Augustin de: on committee on weights and measures, **20**: 353

Coulon, M.: letter to, **13**: 548-9; mentioned, **14**: 557

Council of State: proposed in Dickinson's draft Articles of Confederation, **6**: 517n-8n

Counsel, Michael, **5**: 294n

counselors at law: Va. bill for licensing, **2**: 587-9

Count Belgioso (ship): commanded by Bauer, **11**: 145

Count de Cobensel (ship): commanded by Bauer, **11**: 145

counterfeiting: punishment for, **2**: 44n, 185n, 498n-9, 507-10; of bill of health, **3**: xxxiii, 254 (illus.), 257; precautions against, **7**: 162

county courts. *See* Virginia: County Courts

county lieutenants (Va.): letters to, **3**: 161-2, 518-9, 601-3, 603-4; **5**: 243-4, 289, 415-6, 614; duties of, **2**: 359-60; and punishment of deserters, **4**: 279; fail to make returns of militia, **4**: 508; called together by Gen. Nelson, **6**: 108; commissions for, **6**: 642

county rates: Va. bill for levying, **2**: 418-9

Coupland, Joseph: British war prisoner, **2**: 31

Courier de l'Europe (newspaper): influence of British opinion on, **7**: 544n; TJ's opinion of, **8**: 226; reports seizure of forts, **10**: 65; extract from, **10**: 500; account of U.S. coinage, **10**: 511; mentioned, **7**: 552; **8**: 420; **10**: 171; **19**: 644

Courier de l'Europe (ship): chased by enemy into Boston harbor, **4**: 556; carries wine for TJ, **10**: 290; and plants for TJ, **11**: 112, 142, 156, 157; Humphreys sails on, **16**: 59n

"Cours la Reine," Paris: TJ's accident on, **10**: 432n

Courtenay, John: *Philosophical Reflections on the Late Revolution in France*, **16**: 244n

Court of Appeals (Va.). *See* Virginia: Court of Appeals

Court of Appeals (U.S.): Cyrus Griffin serves on, **3**: 425, 483; powers of, **6**: 447-8, 450; established by Congress, **6**: 453; decisions of, **6**: 455n; expense of, **6**: 560; judges' salaries, **7**: 13-4

Court of Commissioners in Connecticut-Pennsylvania dispute: appointment of, **6**: 476-8; arguments in by James Wilson and William Samuel Johnson, **6**: 479, 488-98; decision of, **6**: 480, 481-6; and petition of Zebulon Butler, **6**: 484, 498-505; TJ on proceedings of, **6**: 505-7

courts, county (Va.). *See* Virginia: County Courts

courts, federal: jurisdiction in territorial disputes, **6**: 505; **7**: 19, 35

courts, general (Va.): in TJ's drafts of Va. Constitution, **1**: 361

courts-martial: law respecting, **2**: 353-4, 360-1; Va. bill constituting, **2**: 578; request for writs compelling witnesses to appear, **3**: 194; proceedings of, **3**: 350-1; invasion law on, **4**: 358; **5**: 509, 512; for deserters, **5**: 175; difficulty of holding, **5**: 197

Courts of Admiralty: jurisdiction enlarged, **1**: 172, 194; mentioned in Declaration of Causes, **1**: 207, 214

courts of equity: Va. bill for regulating proceedings in, **2**: 592-9

courts of justice (Va.): drafts of bills establishing, **1**: 605-52

courts of oyer and terminer, **2**: 189n

couscous (kuskus): slave diet of, **12**: 556

Cousin, Louis: cited by TJ, **1**: 554; translations, **8**: 411

Coutts (Coutt), Patrick: signs nonimportation resolutions (1770), **1**: 46; and bill establishing ferries, **2**: 458; mentioned, **3**: 144

Couturier, Guillaume: letter from, to Chalon, **16**: 18-20

Couwee Warrior (Cherokee chief): designates lands of tribe, **2**: 91

Coventry, Robert: letter from quoted, **20**: 573n

Coverley, Thomas: prisoner of war, **3**: 390

covin. *See* collusion

Cowell, Ebenezer: contract for repair of arms, **5**: 567n

Cowell, William: master of the *Machias*, **12**: 462; trade with Morocco, **14**: 578; **18**: 401-2

Cowes, Isle of Wight: TJ arrives at, **7**: 384; port for American goods, **11**: 40-1; rice depot, **11**: 516; **12**: 300; TJ boards *Clermont* at, **15**: 467-9, 471, 520, 527, 530; TJ and daughters at, **15**: 496-8; Auldjo as vice consul at, **17**: 246, 247, 251, 253n, 280, 673; **18**: 316; U.S. consulate at, **19**: 316; U.S. trade with, **20**: 607

Cowley, Hannah Parkhouse: letter from, **14**: 510-1; introduced to TJ by Maria Cosway, **14**: 372, 510-1, 524; letter sent by, **14**: 526

Cowling, Mrs.: asks flag to go to Portsmouth, **5**: 635

Cowne, Lieut. Austin, **4**: 542

Cowne, Capt. Lieut. Robert, **4**: 542

Cowpens, battle of: description of, **4**: 440-1; effect on Tarleton, **5**: 115; medals of, **16**: xxxvii-xl, 52 (illus.), 55n-7n, 59n-61n, 64n, 66; mentioned, **4**: 437, 496n, 575-6, 577; **5**: 24n, 507

Cowper, Capt., **9**: 90

Cowper, John, Jr.: recommended for consular appointment, **16**: 523; **17**: 326

cows: prices of, **20**: 717

Cox, Mr., **6**: 138

Cox, Mrs., **5**: 658

Cox, Isaac: appointed lieutenant colonel, **5**: 465; mentioned, **5**: 439n

Cox, James, **15**: 417n

Cox, John, **6**: 655n

Cox, Lemuel: builds Charles River Bridge, **16**: xliii, 53 (illus.), 579, 580n; uses cod-liver oil to preserve timber, **16**: xliii, 579-80

Cox, Samuel: letter to, **5**: 444

Cox, William: signs petition, **6**: 290; letter from, to Rochambeau, quoted, **15**: 417n

Coxe, Mr.: printer of Va. map, **12**: 164

Coxe, Tench: letters to, **18**: 102; **19**:

350; **20**: 234, 244; letters from, **12**: 93; **16**: 531; **17**: 261-2; **18**: 62, 268, 461; **19**: 116-7, 118-9, 195-6, 237-8, 360-1, 410-11, 553, 587-8; **20**: 215-8, 232-3, 244, 246-7, 563-4, 589-90, 591, 623, 646, 647; relations with James Wilson, **6**: 476n; *An Enquiry into the Principles on Which a Commercial System for the United States of America Should Be Founded*, **11**: 661, 662n; **13**: 338n; **14**: 50n; **19**: 123, 566; recommended to TJ, **12**: 47; part owner of *Canton*, **13**: 4n; *Address to an Assembly of the Friends of American Manufactures*, **13**: 338; introduced to TJ by Rush, **16**: 411; "Notes on the State of Pennsylvania," **16**: 412n; as Assistant Secretary of the Treasury, **16**: 412n; **17**: 350n; correspondence with Jay, **16**: 576, 604-5, 618-9; and residence bill controversy, **17**: 168; application for position, **17**: 351n-2n; letters from cited, **17**: 352n, 451n; and the fisheries, **18**: 62; **19**: 158-9, 161, 167, 182-95 (Notes), 223, 227n; W. S. Smith visits, **18**: 261; correspondence with Adams, **18**: 261n, 263, 268, 272; on British commercial policy, **18**: 262-3; letter to, from W. T. Franklin, cited, **18**: 267-8; and Privy Council report, **18**: 267-71; and Otto, **18**: 539n, 540n; and overseas freight costs, **19**: 116-7; and export duties, **19**: 118-9; and return of exports, **19**: 119n; and commercial policy, **19**: 121-7, 168; *A Brief Examination of Lord Sheffield's Observations on the Commerce of the United States*, **19**: 122, 559, 562, 587-8; **20**: 101n, 217n, 668, 682n, 708, 715; solicits recommendation from Benjamin Rush, **19**: 123n; relationship with TJ, **19**: 125, 126n, 127; biographical sketch of, **19**: 125-6; solicits federal appointment from Madison, **19**: 127; on succession to presidency, **19**: 167n; Notes on the Dutch and Prussian Fisheries, **19**: 175-82; letter to, from Joseph Anthony, **19**: 196-7; and shipping insurance rates, **19**: 199-200; letter from, to Madison, quoted, **19**: 234n-5n, 438n; "Thoughts on the Navigation of the United States," **19**: 411-6, 560; proposals concerning capital site, **20**: 10; proposed appointment as comptroller of treasury, **20**: 146,

Coxe, Tench (*cont.*)
219-34 (editorial note and documents), 667-8, 682, 707-8; manufacturing plan, **20**: 216-8; letter from, to Washington, **20**: 234; "Greene" and "Sherman" articles, **20**: 287n; relations with William Pearce, **20**: 319n-20n, 623; partnership with George Parkinson, **20**: 339-40; encourages maple sugar production, **20**: 344n

Coxe, William: part owner of *Canton*, **13**: 4n

Coxe, William, Jr.: letter from, to Cutting, **13**: 3-4

Coxes Dale (Coxendale, Cock and Dale, Osborne's), Va., **5**: 557, 558n, 588, 590, 658-9

Crénis, Martial Jean Antoine Crozat de: recommended to TJ, **1**: 519; bears letter from Fabbroni, **2**: 195

crab apple: Izard requests, **7**: 131; plants requested from John Banister, **11**: 121; TJ orders cider made from, **19**: 592

crabs, **11**: 442

Crabtree, Capt.: burns Cherokee Indian town, **4**: 360

Craddock, Lewis: pledges to support clergyman, **2**: 7; property leased to, **16**: 309

Crafts, William. *See* Graves, Boonen, & William Crafts

Cragy, James: court-martial of, **3**: 351

Craig, Adam, **4**: 187

Craig, Alexander: signs petition, **6**: 290; attorney to Polson, **13**: 389

Craig, Elijah, **1**: 662

Craig, Frederick, & Co.: publishers of *Delaware Gazette*, **17**: 509n; letter from cited, **17**: 598n

Craig, Maj. James Henry: commands British troops on Cape Fear river, **4**: 583, 590

Craig, John: signs petition, **1**: 588

Craig, Thomas: signs petition, **1**: 588; signs Va. oath of allegiance, **2**: 129

Craig, William: in Albemarle co. militia, **1**: 665

Craigie, Andrew: correspondence with Parker, **13**: 322n; **14**: 193-4; speculation in U.S. foreign debts, **14**: 193-4; **20**: 177; letter from cited, **16**: 264n; Scioto Company speculations, **18**: 173, 174, 176

Craik, Dr. James: visits Mount Vernon, **10**: 535n; **11**: 390n

Crainy Island, Va., **1**: 297; **5**: 186

cranberries: Sarsfield advised to eat in England, **11**: 515; sent to TJ, **12**: 137, 409, 528, 533, 568

Cranch, Richard: introduces Read to Adams, **16**: 289n

Cranch, William: letter from, to Simpson, quoted, **18**: 674n

Crane, Stephen: signs Continental Association, **1**: 153; signs agreement of secrecy, **1**: 253

Cranmer, Mr., **5**: 440

Crapper, Isaac (impressed seaman), **18**: 333

Craufurd (Crawford), George: negotiates for Anglo-French treaty, **8**: 341, 361, 362n-3n; mentioned, **9**: 126, 183

Craven, William, Earl of: land grants to, **1**: 136; **6**: 657

Crawford, Mr.: escapes from Cherokees, **6**: 80, 94; mentioned, **9**: 241; **20**: 596

Crawford, Adair: theory of physics, **6**: 420, 427, 507; writings on air and fire, **7**: 288; *Experiments and Observations on Animal Heat*, **13**: 37, 38n, 395; **15**: 612; experiments on cancer, **15**: 103; mentioned, **3**: 149

Crawford, David: signs petition, **6**: 293

Crawford, Edward: signs petition, **6**: 294

Crawford, French: and escheated property, **2**: 284n

Crawford, James: loan to state, **3**: 386

Crawford, Thomas: commands ship with American crew, **12**: 237, 244, 250

Crawford, Col. William: deposition concerning Henderson's land claims, **2**: 102-4; praised by G. R. Clark, **4**: 575; mentioned, **4**: 574

Crawford's Point, Va.: ferry at, **2**: 457

crayons: TJ asked to purchase for Hopkinson, **7**: 286; **8**: 563, 672; **9**: 132, 146, 224, 439-40, 482

Creasey, Mr., **16**: 511

creation. *See* cosmogony

credit, bills of. *See* bills of credit

Creech, Thomas: edition of Lucretius, **11**: 523

Creek Indians: hostilities against U.S., **1**: 386; **7**: 45; **10**: 293, 301, 314; **12**: 284, 317; rumor of massacre by, **1**: 480; support Cornwallis, **4**: 664; threatened invasion by, **6**: 80; population of, **9**: 641; cattle of, **9**: 641-2; resemblance to Carthaginians, **12**: 264; chiefs and Trumbull's portrait of Washington, **17**: xxix; portraits of chiefs by Trumbull, **17**: xxix-xxx, 218 (illus.); treaty with, **17**: 127n, 289n-90n, 321, 340n-1n, 388n-9n; Mc-Gillivray brings chiefs to New York, **17**: 269, 271; McGillivray's monopoly of commerce with, **17**: 288-91, 389n; reception for chiefs, **17**: 341n; chiefs visit England, **17**: 666n; **18**: 6, 7n; Ga. discontented over 1790 treaty with, **19**: 431n

Crescent (ship): Purdie's service on, **18**: 317-9, 338-41; American crewmen on, **18**: 331-2

Cresswell, Nicholas: journal quoted, **15**: 582-3; introduced to TJ by Mason, **15**: 583

Crèvecoeur, Guillaume Alexandre: education of, **15**: 259n; mentioned, **12**: 668

Crèvecoeur, Michel Guillaume St. John de: letters to, **7**: 113, 355, 604; **8**: 421-2; **10**: 127-8, 300-1, 509, 583; **11**: 43-5, 188; **13**: 485-7; **15**: 139-41; letters from, **6**: 508-9; **7**: 376-7, 413-5; **8**: 155-6, 381, 450; **10**: 92-3, 591, 601; **11**: 294-5; **12**: 332-3; **14**: 28-31, 273-4, 414-7; biographical note, **6**: 509n; fish sent to, **7**: 355; plants to be sent to, **7**: 356; publishes Lafayette's speech to Indians, **7**: 447n; *Letters from an American Farmer*, **8**: 155-6; **11**: 43, 105, 295; **12**: 290, 586; **14**: 64n; and French packets, **8**: 227; **9**: 137; **14**: 309n; and article on America in *Encyclopédie Méthodique*, **10**: 5, 8; considers Abbé André as tutor for son, **10**: 436; receives report from Coffyn, **10**: 627; account of battle of Wyoming, **11**: 110; efforts to make Honfleur a free port, **11**: 126; presses Short to meet with Colonia, **11**: 210, 234; requests map of Va., **11**: 233, 253, 275; copy of *Notes on Virginia*, **11**: 253, 275, 350; opinion of Mrs. Barrett's health, **11**: 276; petitions Harcourt and others, **11**: 315-6; departs for America, **11**: 317, 356; letters sent by, **11**: 326, 344, 345; **16**: 443, 445n, 475; **17**: 13n, 14, 485; rumored to be authorized to treat on postal service, **11**: 492; letter to cited, **12**: 471; as French consul in N.Y., **12**:

483; **14**: 64n; sons of, **13**: 157n, 486; **14**: 31, 274, 611n; **15**: 140, 259n; honorary American citizenship for French friends, **13**: 547n; reports N.Y.'s adoption of Constitution, **13**: 558-9, 566; correspondence with Short quoted, **13**: 558n; **16**: 238n, 279n; **17**: 13n-4n, 412, 413n; **18**: 536n; on French politics, **14**: 28-9, 414, 416; on American government, **14**: 29-30, 415-6; on manufactures and industries, **14**: 30, 416; appoints consul, **14**: 65n; in *L'Aigrette* case, **14**: 85; condemns Quesnay's plan for academy, **14**: 627n; and Fitch's steamboat, **15**: 80n, 641; letter to, from Franklin, cited, **15**: 82n; TJ sends pamphlet to, **15**: 127n; letter to, from Mme d'Houdetot, cited, **15**: 432; books sent to by Valady, **15**: 483; praised by La Vingtrie, **15**: 514; letter from cited, **16**: 272; health of, **16**: 292; daughter marries Otto, **16**: 356n; letter from quoted, **17**: 13n; sends watch to TJ, **17**: 412, 413n; uses "St. John" as signature, **17**: 413n; advises Osmont, **18**: 30; on Northwest Territory, **18**: 159; mentioned, **7**: 357; **9**: 330, 363; **10**: 638, 639; **11**: 6, 37, 255; **13**: 207; **14**: 16, 21n, 303, 354; **15**: 478; **16**: 159, 445

Crew, John, **5**: 208, 265; **6**: 14n

Crew, Robert: letters to, **7**: 609; **15**: 410-1; letters from, **7**: 434; **15**: 353; **18**: 309; biographical note, **18**: 309n; letters from cited, **18**: 309n; mentioned, **4**: 354

Crew & Allport: imports tobacco, **18**: 309n

Crillon-Mahon (Grillon), Louis de Berton de Balbes de Quiers, Duc de, **13**: 578

Crimea: Turks demand restitution of, **13**: 404; cession to Turkey predicted, **14**: 366, 370, 375, 387, 429

crimes and punishments: TJ's outline of bill for proportioning, **2**: xxiv, 305 (illus.), 663-4; Va. bill proportioning, **2**: 310n, 322n, 492-507; **10**: 483, 575, 604; **12**: 283; failure of Va. GA to pass revised bill, **11**: 152

criminal cases: in Va. courts, **2**: 226-7

criminal intent: as factor in law, **6**: 326

criminal law (Va.): system of, **1**: 490, 636-3; **9**: 195; bill for the trial of of-

criminal law (Va.) (*cont.*)
fenses committed out of Va., **1**: 655-7; plan of Committee of Revisors, **2**: 325; bill concerning process, **2**: 612-6
criminal law, French: reformed, **13**: 189
criminals: desirability of rehabilitation, **2**: 493; percentage of in American population, **10**: 30
criminal trials: removal to England, **1**: 128, 153, 172, 194, 200, 207, 214; **10**: 369-70, 374n; and Lord North's Proposal, **1**: 228; bill to speed up, **2**: 189; and Moroccan treaty, **10**: 424
Cripps, John: S.C. agent, **15**: 32
Critical Review: TJ requests issues of, **10**: 166; **13**: 177, 367, 376
Critta (slave): to work for Randolph as house servant, **18**: 29
"Croatoan": and Roanoke Island, **1**: 282
Crocco, Giacomo Francisco: representative of Emperor of Morocco, **8**: 21
Crockett, Col. Hugh, **3**: 533
Crockett (Crocket), Joseph: letters to, **3**: 667-8; **4**: 238; **6**: 531; letters from, **4**: 303-4; **5**: 142-3; appointed lieutenant colonel commandant of western battalion, **3**: 51, 52; and western expedition, **3**: 161, 422, 521, 613, 623, 667, 670; supplies for, **3**: 302-3; **4**: 34-5; recruits for, **3**: 357; battalion of, **3**: 421, 480; **4**: 62, 73, 234, 366; leather for, **3**: 506; letter to officers of his battalion, **3**: 540-1; meat provision for troops under, **3**: 567; orders to, **4**: 15; battalion ordered to remain in Albemarle co., **4**: 65; battalion to guard Convention troops, **4**: 93, 95-6, 100; and Detroit expedition, **4**: 235, 236; arrival hoped for, **4**: 442; joins Greene, **4**: 683; **5**: 44; irregularities of regimental paymaster, **5**: 245, 269; returns home, **5**: 438; joins Clark, **6**: 12; sends powder and lead, **15**: 588; mentioned, **3**: 350; **4**: 74, 170, 498
Crocketts & Harriss: owners of the *Minerva*, **9**: 387
Croft, Lieut., **4**: 120
Crofts, Thomas: on the whale and cod fisheries, **19**: 154
Croghan, Col. George: and Indian treaties, **2**: 76; and Henderson's land claims, **2**: 78, 81, 84-5; settlement of, **2**: 100, 102-4; collects fossils, **6**: 209n; mentioned, **1**: 389n, 464
Croghan, Maj. William, **3**: 652; **5**: 38

Cronstedt, Axel Fredrik, Baron: work on mineralogy, **3**: 237
Crook, Pennel, **5**: 294n
Crooks, Robert: signs nonimportation resolutions (1770), **1**: 47
Cropper, Col. John: appointment as county lieutenant of Accomac, **6**: 47
crops: Va. (1784), **7**: 503, 604; U.S. (1785), **8**: 571; Va. (1785), **8**: 604, 660; U.S. (1786), **10**: 230; Va. (1786), **10**: 577; Va. (1787), **12**: 283
Crosby, Sampson: messenger in Department of State, **17**: 358n; paid by Department of State, **17**: 365, 367, 368, 370, 371, 372, 375
Cross Creek, N.C.: Cornwallis at, **5**: 403; mentioned, **3**: 403, 428, 501; **5**: 215, 303
cross posts. *See* postal service
Crosthwait, James William: signs Va. oath of allegiance, **2**: 129
Crouch, Richard, **4**: 275
Crow, Nathaniel, **4**: 520
Crow, William: and bill establishing ferries, **2**: 459
Crowder, Jesse, **5**: 430
crown, French: value of, **7**: 200
Crown Point, N.Y.: defense of, **1**: 394, 450; army from Canada stationed at, **1**: 412, 459; **15**: 577; evacuated by American army, **1**: 473, 483, 589; evacuated by Carleton, **1**: 598; visited by TJ and Madison, **20**: 466; mentioned, **1**: 499, 520; **20**: 465
Crozier, Capt.: legal suit against, **20**: 491-2
cruet: TJ describes, **11**: 441; **13**: 16 (sketch)
Cruger, Henry: in *Rachel* case, **20**: 483, 519
Cruger, John Harris: in N.C., **15**: 596
Crul, Adm. Willem: death reported, **5**: 193
Crump, Capt. Abner, **4**: 539
Crusca vocabulary (Italian), **14**: 382, 383n, 483, 540
Cruse, Englehart: applies for steam engine patent, **16**: xlii-iii, 53 (illus.), 412-3; **17**: 320; letter from, to Washington, cited, **16**: xlii-iii, 413n; introduced to TJ by McHenry, **16**: 413n; letter from cited, **16**: 413n; letter to cited, **16**: 413n
Cruz Cano y Olmedilla, Juan de la: *Mapa Geográfico de America Meri-*

Cunningham, Timothy (*cont.*)
Law of Bills of Exchange, **11**: 547; **16**: 481

Cunningham, William: letter to, **11**: 99; letter from, **11**: 88; mentioned, **5**: 294n

Cunningham and Co.: house used by Va. GA, **2**: 284n; inquisition against, **4**: 186; ships flour to Le Havre, **19**: 262n

Cunningham & Nisbett. *See* Conyngham & Nesbit

Cunningham's Branch, Va., **2**: 113

Cupressus disticha: sample to be sent to France, **10**: 227

Cupressus thyoides: sample to be sent to France, **10**: 227

Curaçao: reportedly taken by British, **5**: 176, 177, 193; tobacco exports, **7**: 369, 370

Curd, Capt. Edmund, **4**: 21n

Curd, John, **4**: 21

Curiatii, **3**: 405

Curle, Col. William Roscoe Wilson: letter from, **5**: 11; and establishment of Va. courts, **1**: 606n; captured by British, **5**: 96, 294n, 331n, 685n; exchanged, **5**: 293-4, 324, 330, 352, 365, 366, 367, 384; in charge of Ellegood's parole, **5**: 428

Curles, R. Randolph: death of, **11**: 329

Curling, Capt. (master of *London*), **13**: 563

Currell, Capt., **6**: 81n

currency: problems of redemption, **3**: 17; exchange of for British prisoners of war, **3**: 64; recall of Continental, **3**: 321, 336, 493, 506, 528, 531; **6**: 97; emission, **3**: 441, 484. *See also* coinage; coins; copper coinage; depreciation of currency; money

Currey, Charles: signs nonimportation resolutions (1770), **1**: 47

Currie, Anne Inglis (Mrs. James Currie): visits Monticello, **20**: 675

Currie, Dr. James: letters to, **6**: 372, 427; **7**: 44, 133, 242, 500, 604-6, 635; **9**: 239-40, 593; **14**: 365-8; **17**: 621; **18**: 488; **19**: 600-1; **20**: 331-2, 411-2, 613-4; letters from, **7**: 538-9; **8**: 342-7, 640-4; **10**: 107-11; **11**: 327-30; **15**: 562; **17**: 621n; **19**: 553-4; **20**: 161-2, 675; deposition respecting TJ's conduct during Arnold's invasion, **4**: 272; medical practice, **6**: 340-1; **20**: 166; TJ's present to, **7**: 44, 538; let-

ters from cited, **7**: 635; **8**: 539, 540; **9**: 159; **15**: 624, 625; shares in James River Company, **8**: 343; purchases coal mine, **8**: 643; letters from quoted, **9**: 59n; **19**: 553n-4n; subscribes to *Encyclopédie*, **9**: 237, 239, 499; **11**: 327; bill of lading for, **9**: 636; losses in Richmond fire, **11**: 209, 329; **15**: 634; exchanges books with William Hay, **11**: 318; wants books in English, **11**: 319; letter to cited, **14**: 356n; marriage, **16**: 25; letter to quoted, **16**: 28n; notes TJ's need of Richmond map, **16**: 187; bond, **16**: 210, 211; and Hay's subscription to *Encyclopédie Méthodique*, **18**: 113; **19**: 256-7, 286-7; introduces J. Hamilton, **19**: 553; payment to, **20**: 103; financial affairs, **20**: 211, 420, 555, 613-4, 675; mentioned, **6**: 342; **7**: 18; **8**: 380; **9**: 58, 219, 252, 253, 397; **10**: 72; **11**: 311; **12**: 572; **14**: 186; **15**: 616; **16**: 28n, 136

Currie, William: *An Historical Account of the Climates and Diseases of the United States,* **20**: 408; biographical note, **20**: 409n

Currus. *See* Carr, Dabney

Curson, Mrs.: letter from cited, **16**: 385

Curson, Richard: letters to, **6**: 531; **7**: 16, 62, 110, 117, 242; **15**: 184; letters from, **7**: 95-6, 242-3; account, **7**: 292; letter to cited, **15**: 183; Cahierre introduced to, **15**: 184; mentioned, **7**: 206, 241, 252

Curtis, Mr. (English agent at Morocco): hostility toward U.S., **8**: 69

"Curtius" (pseud.): writings of, **18**: 660

Curtius Rufus, Quintus: Delphin edition of, **11**: 523; mentioned, **8**: 407, 408

Cushing, Capt. (master of London packet), **13**: 610

Cushing, Thomas: letter to, **9**: 263; letter from, **8**: 670-1; signs Continental Association, **1**: 153; signs Congress' second petition to king, **1**: 222; signs agreement of secrecy, **1**: 253; delegate to Hartford Convention (1780), **4**: 139; recommends Nathaniel Barrett, **9**: 89; recommends Winslow Warren, **9**: 127; aid solicited by Washington, **12**: 325n

Cushing, William (justice of Supreme Court), **16**: 27

cusk: in N.H., **7**: 346

Cussy-les-Forges, France, **11**: 415-6

Custine-Sarreck (Gustine), Adam Philippe, Comte de: letter from, **4**: 249; introduced to TJ, **4**: 214, 215n; **15**: 598, 599; mentioned, **4**: 255n

Custis, Mr.: grievances against France, **20**: 569

Custis, John Parke: leader of anti-draft mob, **6**: 45; mentioned, **5**: 311

customs. *See* duties

Cuthbert, William: ships hams, **16**: 566; letters from quoted, **16**: 566n; letters to quoted, **16**: 566n-7n

Cutler, Ammi Ruhamah: petition of, **6**: 448-52

Cutler, John: in *Rachel* case, **20**: 516

Cutler, Manasseh: *Explanation of the Map which Delineates . . . Part of the Federal Lands*, **18**: 159-61; and Scioto Company, **18**: 174-7; describes Benjamin Franklin, **19**: xxxiv-v; and site for capital, **19**: 6; mentioned, **18**: 530

Cutter, Capt. M. (master of *Eliza*), **17**: 541

Cutting (Cotting), Capt. (master of *Louise*), **13**: 221

Cutting, John Brown: letters to, **13**: 315-6, 403-7, 427-8, 471, 538-9, 565-6, 579-80, 632, 649-50; **14**: 47-8; **15**: 173, 277, 411, 469-70, 523-4; **18**: 330; letters from, **12**: 321-2; **13**: 290-3, 331-8, 401-3, 461-3, 480-1, 509-11, 514-5, 535-6, 549-51, 571-3, 608-13, 629-30, 643-6, 658-63; **14**: 12-6, 393-5; **15**: 144-5, 159-60, 175, 264-5, 293-6, 401-2, 414, 427-8, 440-3, 465-7, 499-501, 514-5; **16**: 251-8, 262-3; **18**: 324-9; introduced to TJ, **12**: 124, 138, 145-6; **18**: 313n; visits Paris, **12**: 139; letters sent by, **12**: 189, 192, 201, 202, 206, 235, 297; **15**: 11, 14, 16n, 21-2, 193, 264, 274, 443, 451, 469; gift for Abigail Adams, **12**: 193, 554; attorney for claimants against S.C., **12**: 204; **13**: 608; **14**: 15-6; **15**: 218-20, 257, 450, 452, 463, 464n; introduced to Rutledge, **12**: 225; letter to, from Coxe, **13**: 3-4; correspondence with Adams, **13**: 210n, 291; **18**: 317n, 318n; **16**: 415n; **18**: 314-5; on Md. Constitutional Convention, **13**: 331-7; letters to cited, **13**: 415, 428; **15**: 370n; **18**: 321, 322n; illness of, **13**: 434; **15**: 515, 516; letters from cited, **13**: 452n; **14**: 276; **16**: 165n, 387n, 415n; **17**: 645; **18**: 160n, 313n-4n, 321, 322n; on British politics, **13**: 462-3, 510, 515; **15**: 175; **16**: 252-3;

on ratification of Constitution, **13**: 480-1; plans return to America, **13**: 510, 519, 536, 563-4, 608, 646; **14**: 15; **16**: 251; introduced to Ramsay by TJ, **13**: 538, 542; **15**: 37; on American politics, **13**: 549-51, 644-6, 659-61; apologizes for failure to report news, **13**: 571; on British newspapers, **13**: 572-3, 610; **15**: 401-2; TJ sends news to, **13**: 597; on American trade with Spain, **13**: 609; papers for Commissioners of the Treasury sent by, **13**: 632; on revision of Constitution, **13**: 645-6; on British whale fisheries, **14**: 13-5, 218, 219; summarizes elections of 1788, **14**: 394-5; letters from, to John Rutledge, Jr., cited, **14**: 481n; leaves S.C. for London, **15**: 14, 16n; on funding of foreign debt, **15**: 33n; returns to London from America, **15**: 144-5; introduced to Bondfield by TJ, **15**: 218-9; on French Revolution in Bordeaux, **15**: 293-6; returns foreign debt estimate to TJ, **15**: 411, 440, 443n; letter to Pinckney sent to Van Staphorst, **15**: 414; suggests loan from U.S. to France, **15**: 440-1; rice trade statistics sent to, **15**: 446n, 469; suggestions on election, **15**: 465-6; passport issued by TJ, **15**: 487; correspondence with Short, **15**: 529-30, 551n, 558; **16**: 168n, 205n, 415n, 440n-1n, 507n-8n, 509n; **18**: 314n, 318, 333; at Cowes with TJ and Trumbull, **15**: 530; sends Short address to TJ at Norfolk, **16**: 161, 162n; letter from published in *Gazette of the United States*, **16**: 244n, 251-8; letter to, from Short, sent to TJ, **16**: 252, 255n, 258-60, 508n; sends Burke's speech to TJ, **16**: 255n, 262n; sends newspaper to Washington, **16**: 405n; letter from, to Washington, quoted, **16**: 541n; sends newspapers, **16**: 542; aids impressed seamen, **17**: 19, 489, 583, 594, 630; **18**: 287, 313-22, 326-9, 339-41, 364; on relations with Britain, **18**: 276; TJ's regard for, **18**: 313; *Facts and Observations . . . in a Letter Addressed to the Secretary of State*, **18**: 315-7, 318n-21n; correspondence with Purdie, **18**: 318-9, 334-6; letter from, to Lords Commissioners of the Admiralty, **18**: 333; letter from, to Hunt, **18**: 334; correspondence with Stephens, **18**: 334, 336; Morris refuses

Dalling, Thomas: petition of, **6**: 448-52

Dalrymple, Mr.: secretary to British legation in Paris, **9**: 126, 128

Dalrymple, Adm. John, **18**: 328

Dalrymple, Sir John: *Essay towards a General History of Feudal Property in Great Britain*, **11**: 547; **16**: 481; **17**: 3; works by, **16**: 277, 393

Dalrymple, Gen. Richard, **15**: 263

Dalton, Gen. *See* Alton, Gen. Richard d'

Dalton, Mr.: letter carried by, **16**: 102

Dalton, Bradley: in Albemarle co. militia, **1**: 668n

Dalton, David, Jr.: in Albemarle co. militia, **1**: 664

Dalton, Mass.: visited by TJ and Madison, **20**: 458

Dalton, Michael: cited on arson, **2**: 496n

Dalton, Samuel: in Albemarle co. militia, **1**: 668n

Dalton, Tristram: on Va. commercial policy, **7**: 468n; on Lafayette's commercial policy, **9**: 74n; senator from Mass., **14**: 339, 394, 529, 560, 615; federalism of, **14**: 394, 529; and the fisheries, **19**: 155, 167n

Dalton, Capt. William: in Albemarle co. militia, **1**: 665; petition from, **5**: 349; mentioned, **6**: 133

Dal Verme, Francis. *See* Verme, Francesco

Dalzan, M.: letter from, **15**: 233-7

Daman, Capt. John (master of the *Adventure*), **7**: 587; **10**: 471; **11**: 506

Damas, Gen. Claude Charles de: in Martinique, **17**: 587, 588

Damas (Dames), Joseph François Louis Charles César, Comte de: introduced by Washington, **4**: 190; **5**: 231

damask. *See* table linen

Damieta, Egypt: captured in Crusades, **8**: 447

Damme, Pieter Bernhard van: letters to, **12**: 678, 687, 688-9; **13**: 181, 420; **14**: 490-1; **15**: 88; letters from, **13**: 289-90; **14**: 40-1, 474, 706-7; **15**: 462; sends book catalogues to TJ, **12**: 689; **14**: 40-1, 474; **15**: 462; TJ seeks books from, **13**: 284, 289-90, 420-1; **14**: 491 (list), 706-7, 707n (list); **15**: 42; payment to, **15**: 88-9, 126; mentioned, **13**: 477

Damon, Capt. (master of the *Adventurer*), **10**: 291n

dams: roads over, **2**: 452-3; Va. bill concerning, **2**: 464-7; Penet, Windel &

Co. empowered to erect, **3**: 142

Dana, Mr.: mentioned, **1**: 18

Dana, Francis: secretary of embassy in France, **3**: 459; letter from, to R. R. Livingston, cited, **6**: 213; mission to Russia, **6**: 275, 334, 390; report on letters of, **6**: 400n; member Committee of the States (1784), **6**: 522n; **7**: 299, 432; letter to, from Adams, quoted, **8**: 56n; Mass. delegate to Federal Convention, **11**: 219; and postage allowance, **17**: 227n; mentioned, **5**: 376; **6**: 259n, 275, 522n; **8**: 414

Dancarville, M. *See* Hancarville

dancing: in England, **11**: 150

Dandridge, Bartholomew: signs Virginia Association, **1**: 108; death of, **8**: 116, 345; imports slaves, **15**: 654

Dandridge, Harry Bolling: former judge of Va. General Court, **8**: 345

Dandridge, Nathaniel, **6**: 96

Dandridge, Patsy, **1**: 13, 16

Dandridge (Danderidge), Col. William, **5**: 344

Dane, Nathan: efforts to prohibit slavery in western territory, **6**: 612n; delegate to Congress from Mass., **10**: 144; opposes Constitution, **12**: 282; and admission of Ky., **13**: 248n-9n; opposes appointment of TJ as minister in London, **14**: 82; **18**: 260n; and Northwest Ordinance, **18**: 163n, 165; Jay's recommendations referred to, **19**: 495

Danekert and Krohn (bankers), **10**: 209

Dangerfield, Miss, **1**: 16

Dangerfield, William: marries Mary Willis, **1**: 8

Dangirard, Jean Baptiste François, **9**: 219, 457

Dangirard & Vernon: letter to, **10**: 267-8; letter from, **10**: 279-80; funds under care of Marck, **9**: 513, 514

Dangivilliers, Comte. *See* Angiviller, Charles Claude

Danican, François André: letter from, **20**: 371-2; *L'Analyse des échecs*, **20**: 372

Daniel, Mr.: extraction of sulphur by, **1**: 289; mentioned, **5**: 259, 312

Daniel, Capt. Beverley: nominated for colonel, **5**: 285

Daniel, Col. George: commissioner of specific tax for Middlesex, **5**: 411

Daniel, John: votes for bill for religious freedom, **2**: 549n

Daniel, Walker: killed by Indians, **8**: 345

Davies, Benjamin: in Albemarle co. militia, **1**: 664

Davies, David: signs nonimportation resolutions (1770), **1**: 47

Davies, Francis: in Albemarle co. militia, **1**: 664

Davies, Gressitt, **3**: 494

Davies, Isaac: in Albemarle co. militia, **1**: 665

Davies, John: signs petition, **1**: 588; in Albemarle co. militia, **1**: 664

Davies, Nicholas: and bill establishing ferries, **2**: 459

Davies, Samuel: in Albemarle co. militia, **1**: 665

Davies, Rev. Samuel: advocate of religious liberty in Va., **3**: 69n

Davies, Thomas: in Albemarle co. militia, **1**: 665

Davies, Col. William: letters to, **3**: 536, 587-8, 619-20; **4**: 288, 453-4, 492-3, 500, 527, 549, 674; **5**: 72, 137, 178, 196, 204-5, 244, 269, 291, 299, 300, 341, 342, 359, 396-7, 404, 428, 516, 537-8, 594-5, 618-9; **6**: 15, 48-9; letters from, **4**: 312-3, 328-9, 337, 342, 364, 379, 406-7, 445-7, 493-4, 514-6, 557-8, 692-3; **5**: 90-1, 125, 173-6, 196, 197, 244-6, 255, 278-80, 290-1, 298-300, 300, 341-2, 358-60, 391-2, 392, 396-7, 404, 416-8, 418-9, 429, 465, 515-7, 517, 537-8, 538, 618-9; in Albemarle co. militia, **1**: 665; reports on Va. quota of troops, **3**: 107; equipment for troops of, **3**: 527; as deputy quartermaster for Va., **4**: 48; **5**: 143, 183, 238, 264, 426, 661; **6**: 23, 634; letters to, from Muter, **4**: 161, 296-7; receives recruits, **4**: 194; **6**: 50; letter to, from William Armistead, **4**: 300; disperses arms, **4**: 314, 316-7, 318, 319; letter to, from Fleming, **4**: 329; correspondence with Greene, **4**: 661n-2n; **5**: 539; TJ's instructions to, **5**: 192, 293; advice on clothier's department, **5**: 200; as member of Va. War Office, **5**: 204-5, 233, 247, 251, 481, 489, 536, 645; **6**: 31n, 68; on Standley case, **5**: 237n; procures entrenching tools, **5**: 249; on lack of lead, **5**: 368; plans to publish lists of deserters, **5**: 386n; correspondence with Steuben, **5**: 389n, 452, 480n-1n, 544-5, 581n, 667n-8n; **6**: 38n, 78n, 631-2, 633; Greene on, **5**: 418n; accusations against Munford, **5**: 419n;

asked to furnish workmen and supplies for Hoods, **5**: 428; letter from, to Phillips, **5**: 459-60, 634n; letter to, from Gamble, quoted, **5**: 459; memorandum to, from Senf, cited, **5**: 500; letter to, from Claiborne, quoted, **5**: 517n; letter to, from Dudley, quoted, **5**: 517n; plan for moving artillery, **5**: 528; letters to, from Syme, quoted, **5**: 528n-9n; letter from, to Hume, cited, **5**: 548; letter to, from Lindsay, quoted, **5**: 555n; correspondence with Young, **5**: 580-1, 614, 643, 646n-7n, 651; **6**: 8n, 14n, 84-6, 105n; letter from, to Downie and Thompson, quoted, **5**: 597n; letter to, from Posey, quoted, **5**: 605n; correspondence with Taylor quoted, ♦ 608n; **6**: 67n; letter from, to commissioners of Accomac and Northampton counties, **5**: 619-20; correspondence with Ross, **5**: 634n; **6**: 23n; letter to, from Reid, **5**: 643; letter from, to Weedon, quoted, **5**: 647n; note to, from Nelson, quoted, **5**: 662n; letter to cited, **6**: 5; correspondence with Patteson quoted, **6**: 13n, 22-4; letter to, from Peyton, quoted, **6**: 21; correspondence with Corbin, **6**: 47n; letter to, from Southall, quoted, **6**: 49; letter to, from Lind, quoted, **6**: 54n-5n; letter to, from Pryor, quoted, **6**: 94n; opinion of Steuben, **6**: 622n; orders tent poles, **15**: 600; in possession of Va. Executive journals, **19**: 245; seeks treasury auditorship, **20**: 230n; mentioned, **4**: 216, 284, 297, 409, 523; **5**: 90n, 527, 606

Davies, William John: affidavit on slaves quoted, **16**: 451n

Davila. See González de Ávila, Gil

Davin, Henri, Abbé: in Estates General, **15**: 45

Davis, Capt. (commander of *Le Darth*): on Deane's death, **15**: 500; mentioned, **5**: 430

Davis, Col.: number of militia under, **4**: 263

Davis, Mr. (prisoner of war), **5**: 432

Davis, Amos: signs nonimportation resolutions, **1**: 31

Davis, Augustine: letter to, **20**: 664-6; letters from, **16**: 52; **18**: 112-3; **20**: 711; prints Revisal of the Laws (1794), **2**: 324n; and edition of journal of Va. convention, **13**: 393n; postage paid to, **16**: 81, 82n; letter to cited,

Davis, Augustine (*cont.*)
16: 82n; and *Virginia Independent Chronicle*, **16**: 141n; paid by Department of State, **17**: 363, 365, 368, 370, 373, 509n; and proposal for postal service in Va., **20**: 711-2; mentioned, **16**: 91, 172n; **18**: 66n, 596

Davis, Caleb: imports slaves, **15**: 654

Davis, Edward: signs nonimportation resolutions (1770), **1**: 47

Davis, Isaac: signs nonimportation resolutions (1769), **1**: 31; in Albemarle volunteers, **1**: 237; signs election certificate, **2**: 11; signs Va. oath of allegiance, **2**: 128; letter to, from Twyman, **5**: 192; elected to Va. HD, **5**: 430; **6**: 134n; mentioned, **6**: 135n

Davis, Isaac, Jr.: signs Va. oath of allegiance, **2**: 129

Davis, John: signs petition, **6**: 294

Davis, M. L. & W. A.: letter to cited, **16**: 610n

Davis, Robert: in Albemarle co. militia, **1**: 666; signs petition, **6**: 290

Davis, Thomas: brings gunpowder and arms for Va., **1**: 500; letter from, to John Hancock, on the whale and cod fisheries, **19**: 173-5

Davis, Walter: loan to state, **3**: 386, 442

Davis, William: supports American state papers series, **1**: 145; in Albemarle co. militia, **1**: 664; petition from, **5**: 349

Davison, Nathaniel: appointed consul, **18**: 374-5

Davis' Strait: and the fisheries, **19**: 176, 181

Dawsey, Capt., **3**: 604

Dawson, John: signs petition, **1**: 588; opposes Constitution, **13**: 98; on Va. HD committee to welcome TJ, **16**: 11n; recommended as assistant to TJ, **16**: 182; recommended by Monroe, **16**: 597; letter from, to Madison, cited, **18**: 616n; letter to, from Monroe, cited, **18**: 670n; comments on Hamilton, **18**: 685n; opinion on Md. legislature, **19**: 15; sends Madison copies of Va. act of cession, **19**: 18n; seeks treasury auditorship, **20**: 230n

Dawson, William Jones: letter from, **15**: 256-7

Day, Benjamin: letter to, **3**: 525-6; as state agent, **3**: 323, 645; **4**: 283; as deputy field quartermaster, **5**: 5, 225; **6**: 19; supply of horses, **5**: 225, 288n

Day, John: signs Va. oath of allegiance, **2**: 128

Day, Thomas: *The History of Sandford and Merton*, **10**: 545, 586, 617; **13**: 376

Deakins, Francis: promotes Monocacy River capital site, **19**: 24n

Deakins, William, Jr.: and Potomac capital site, **17**: 455-6, 461-3, 465, 466n, 471; **20**: 4, 6, 7, 8, 13, 14, 15, 16, 22; correspondence with Washington, **17**: 457n; **19**: 33, 285-6, 358-9; **20**: 73-4, 78-9

Dean, Capt., **4**: 43

Dean, Mr., **3**: 85

Dean, John: violates pardon, **4**: 694-5

Deane, Mr.: inn rated by TJ, **20**: 471

Deane, Barnaby: dispatches to, **13**: 227

Deane, Silas: letter to, **2**: 25-6; signs Continental Association, **1**: 153; signs Congress' second petition, **1**: 222; signs agreement of secrecy, **1**: 253; appointed commissioner to France, **1**: 521-4; additional instructions as commissioner to France, **1**: 576-7; concludes treaties with France, **2**: 177n; discredited by enemies, **2**: 217; attacks William Lee, **2**: 263n; dispute with Arthur Lee, **2**: 263n; **3**: 65, 105; accused of apostasy from principles, **6**: 132; *Paris Papers*, **7**: 37, 134, 288, 299, 357, 401; in favor in England, **8**: 302; on need for British trade, **9**: 4; reports about U.S. less reliable than Clunie's, **10**: 263; purchases arms, **11**: 488; **12**: 13; Paine disagrees with, **13**: 224n, 227-8; dispatches from, **13**: 227; letterbooks held by Foulloy, **13**: 308, 323; **14**: 364n, 523, 606, 658; **15**: 4; letterbooks lent to TJ, **13**: 308, 316, 323-4, 466, 467n-9n; bills of exchange for peace commissioners, **13**: 430; letterbooks copied, **13**: 468n; letterbooks purchased by TJ, **14**: 287, 606, 644, 658; TJ on immorality of selling official secrets, **14**: 606; Bancroft's account of misfortunes, **14**: 630-2; **15**: 3-4, 353; letterbooks allegedly stolen, **14**: 631-2; refuses to sell letterbooks, **15**: 3-4, 39; plans return to America, **15**: 353, 368, 500; letterbooks taken to America, **15**: 353, 524n, 553; death of, **15**: 500, 501n; and gift from French government, **16**: 365, 366; expenses of, **17**: 220n; supplies Lord

De la Cruz, Juan. *See* Cruz Cano y Olmedilla, Juan

De La Forest. *See* La Forest

Delagarde, Fanny: letter to, **12**: 94-5; letters from, **12**: 93-4, 119-20

Delahaie, M.: letter from, **9**: 629

Delahais, M.: letter from, **11**: 337

Delahante, Jacques: letter to Chalon, **16**: 18-20

Delahaye, Guillaume: letter to, **11**: 559; letter from, **11**: 603-4

Delaire, James, **14**: 410

Delaire, Thomas: letter to, **14**: 490; letters from, **14**: 410, 643; **15**: 547; **19**: 596-7; asks help for crew of *Clementina*, **14**: 410, 490; arrêt on whale oil sent to, **14**: 490, 643; asks for consulship, **15**: 547

Delamarche, Charles François: *Etats-Unis de L'Amérique Septentrionale*, **6**: 595n

Delamotte, M. (French naval officer). *See* Picquet de La Motte.

Delamotte, M. (vice consul at Le Havre). *See* La Motte, M. de

Delamotte, Lair. *See* La Motte, Lair de

DeLancey, Maj. Oliver: succeeds André, **17**: 41

Delany, Mr.: stores TJ's wine, **20**: 420

Delany, Sharp: letter to, **18**: 493-4

Delap, M.: report on trade of Bordeaux, **11**: 627

Delap, Samuel & John H.: letter to, **11**: 51; letter from, **11**: 22-3

Delaplaine, Joseph: letter to quoted, **15**: xxxv, xxxvi

DelaRocque, Capt. *See* La Rocque, Capt. de

Delaville, M.: reply to Bérard, **12**: 78

Delaware: population of, **1**: 182; **10**: 34, 35, 54-6; and independence, **1**: 310-4; votes for Chase's taxation plan, **1**: 323; criticized by Harvie, **2**: 125-6; delays ratifying Articles of Confederation, **2**: 205, 208; asked to aid N.C., **3**: 403; Va. asked to aid, **3**: 426; troops from sent south, **3**: 433, 435; and Continental requisitions, **4**: 107; quota of provisions for southern army, **5**: 77-8, 101; Congress recommends removal of public stores from Eastern Shore, **5**: 392; refuses to comply with embargo, **5**: 473; Va. asks cooperation in transporting supplies southward, **5**: 483; and protecting Delaware bay, **5**: 551; forces from to be sent to Va., **6**: 74n; attitude on Congress' proposed budget,

6: 334; vote for seat of Congress, **6**: 352, 366; **7**: 118; financial quota to national treasury, **7**: 5, 55, 71; **10**: 34, 35, 54-6; **12**: 444; unrepresented in Congress, **7**: 31; attitude toward Society of the Cincinnati, **7**: 110n; value of pound, **7**: 178; currency in, **7**: 200; delegates in Congress, **7**: 276; duties on foreign goods, **8**: 581; free ports in, **9**: 334; and impost, **9**: 510; **10**: 234; votes power over commerce to Congress, **9**: 666; Démeunier's errors on corrected, **10**: 37; delegates to Annapolis convention, **10**: 232; flour mills in, **10**: 262; appoints commissioners for Chesapeake-Delaware canal, **10**: 512; delegates to Federal Convention, **11**: 154, 400; attitude toward Constitution, **12**: 409; and ratification of Constitution, **12**: 423, 443, 490, 608; **13**: 100-1, 205, 370; follows Pa.'s lead, **12**: 425; elects senators, **14**: 339, 394, 529; ratification of constitutional amendments, **18**: 595; and exports, **19**: 136-9; laws of sought by TJ, **20**: 91

Delaware (ship): leaves L'Orient for Philadelphia, **15**: 150, 158

Delaware bay: probable British objective, **5**: 551; mentioned, **6**: 494

Delaware Gazette: edited by Coram, **19**: 409; mentioned, **17**: 509n

Delaware Indians: reportedly disposed to peace, **1**: 244, 493-4; tenants on land of Six Nations, **2**: 76, 77, 80; in French and Indian Wars, **2**: 99, 100, 101, 102, 104; reportedly hostile toward U.S., **3**: 561; furnished goods for service to U.S., **4**: 114; as independent nation, **7**: 10; treaty with, **19**: 585; hostilities against U.S., **20**: 122; mentioned, **2**: 84

Delaware river: naval engagement on, **1**: 292, 293; and Pa.-Va. boundary dispute, **1**: 463; **3**: 77; held by Americans above Fort Island, **2**: 34; discussed as permanent seat of Congress, **6**: 352, 357, 366; territory to west of, **6**: 501, 503, 504; fortifications on, **10**: 38; falls of, *see* Trenton

Del Campo (Campa), Don. *See* Campo, Bernardo, Marquis del

De Lessart. *See* Lessart, Antoine de Valdec de

Deleurieux, Prevost: letter from, **5**: 430

Deleuze, Abbé, **11**: 464n

Delfino. *See* Dolfin, Daniele I

Denney, Samuel: signs petition, **1**: 588

Denning, William: appointed commissioner of accounts, **7**: 413

Dennistone, James: signs nonimportation resolutions (1770), **1**: 46

Denny, Robert, **18**: 657n

Denny, Capt. Samuel, **5**: 424, 425

Denny, Lt. Samuel (?), **1**: 469

Denny, Capt. William: accompanies Monroe on western trip, **7**: 381; introduced to Franklin, **9**: 487

Dent, George: British depredations on estate of, **5**: 393, 406

Denton, Achilles: in Albemarle co. militia, **1**: 668n

Denton, Charles: in Albemarle co. militia, **1**: 666, 668

Denton, David: on Albemarle co. militia roll, **1**: 668

Dents, M., **12**: 456

Denyver, Jan Baptiste van, **11**: 364

Department of Finance, U.S.: criticism of, **6**: 338; expenses, **6**: 561; appropriation reduced, **7**: 13-4; efforts to avoid bankruptcy, **7**: 53; states' payments of interest to be reported to, **7**: 67; negotiations for loan, **7**: 85; payments for ox teams, **7**: 138; bills discounted, **7**: 139; commissioners appointed, **7**: 299, 535; **8**: 79, 86; reorganization, **7**: 461

Department of Foreign Affairs, U.S.: disorganization, **6**: 276; secretaryship, **6**: 336, 338, 546; papers of, **6**: 427; expenses, **6**: 562; cut in appropriation, **7**: 13-4; secretaryship desired by Mercer, **7**: 119; office suppressed, **16**: 27. *See also* Jay, John: Secretary for Foreign Affairs

Department of State, U.S.: establishment of, **15**: 428n; **17**: 349n; appropriation for, **16**: 479; estimate of expenses, **16**: 512-3; **18**: 150-1; diplomatic establishment, **17**: 216-31; removal to Philadelphia, **17**: 330n, 379-81, 474, 596-7, 598n; personnel and services, **17**: 343-87 (editorial note and documents); translators in, **17**: 351, 352n-3n; **20**: 725-30; salary account, **17**: 356-9; contingent expenses, 1790-1793, **17**: 359-79; passports issued by, **17**: 376n-7n; library of, **17**: 378n; offices in Philadelphia, **17**: 378n. *See also* United States: Secretary of State

Department of the Treasury, U.S.: establishment of, **15**: 217, 228; employees increased, **17**: 350n; interferes with

Department of State, **17**: 351n-3n; removal to Philadelphia, **17**: 597; appointment of comptroller, **20**: 146, 219-34 (editorial note and documents), 667-8, 682, 707-8; auditor appointed, **20**: 221, 230n-1n, 636-7. *See also* Hamilton, Alexander; soldiers' pay: arrearages in pay

Depeyster (Depeister), Col. Schuyler: British commander at Niagara, **7**: 459

DePonthiere, Capt. *See* Ponthiere

depreciation of currency: and difficulty of supplying army, **2**: 22, 267; **3**: 379; **5**: 548; remedy for, **2**: 27-8, 268, 298; **6**: 87; and frontier traders, **2**: 259; effect on rents, **2**: 263; effect on negotiating foreign loan, **3**: 382; conversion to new system of finance, **3**: 405; mandated by Congress, **3**: 474-5; scale of, **3**: 475; prevention of, **3**: 584; compensation for, **4**: 217-8; **5**: 79, 80; Nathan's claims against Va., **4**: 283; **6**: 320, 322n-4n; payment of bills of exchange in, **5**: 61, 87-9, 110-1, 152-3; and army pay, **5**: 100, 147, 427; **6**: 40; rates of exchange with new currency, **5**: 608, 620; debts incurred by public agents, **5**: 669-70; **6**: 69, 138; inquiry on, **11**: 51; claims for not allowed, **12**: 130-1

deputy surveyors, county, **2**: 142-4

Derby (Darby), Elias Hasket: letter from, **11**: 191-3; letters sent by, **8**: 554; **10**: 518; **12**: 8, 41n; claim against France, **11**: 68-9, 191; complaint on condemnation of vessel, **12**: 31; and duties on whale oil, **13**: 119, 433; passport issued by TJ, **15**: 485

Derby, Elias Hasket, Jr.: represents father in France, **11**: 192

Derieux, Justin Pierre Plumard: letters to, **12**: 125-6, 126-7, 379; **13**: 418-9; **17**: 400-1; **19**: 601-2; letters from, **6**: 555; **11**: 394; **12**: 536-8; **16**: 192-3; **17**: 233-6; **18**: 45-7; **19**: 249-50; **20**: 253; arrives at Charleston, **7**: 134; letter from cited, **12**: 9; letter to, from Plumard de Bellanger, **12**: 125; letters to cited, **12**: 134; **17**: 324; **19**: 358; **20**: 671; aided by Mme de Bellanger, **12**: 155; mismanagement of affairs, **12**: 486; TJ arranges aid for, **13**: 166-7, 418; asks TJ to be child's godfather, **13**: 418; TJ sends news of, **16**: 299; correspondence with Mme de Bellanger, **16**: 299n; **17**: 263-4, 265n; offers

diplomatic service (*cont.*)
9; Short comments on, **17**: 394. *See also* consular establishment

diplomatic immunity: in treaty proposal, **8**: 318; English law, **9**: 5-6; and case of Dumas, **12**: 200n-1n

Diquem, M. de. *See* Yquem

Diriks, Jacob Gerrit: letters to, **13**: 303; **15**: 184; letters from, **13**: 302; **15**: 173-4; and Patriot Party in Netherlands, **13**: 296; negotiates loan, **13**: 302; payment for services in Revolution, **15**: 173-4, 184

Dischong, Peter: merchandise of seized, **8**: 181-2, 205, 207, 238-9, 242-3; nationality of, **8**: 243

Dismal Swamp, Va.: exempt from title act, **2**: 163n; obstructs Continental army movements, **4**: 92; canal in, **7**: 46, 293, 558, 569, 591, 642; **8**: 280, 660; **9**: 150, 201

dissection: of bodies of criminals, **2**: 494

dissenters: and fight for religious freedom in Virginia, **1**: 525-58; petition against reestablishment of Church of England, **1**: 586-9; not excluded from Transylvania, **2**: 109; attitude of Episcopalians toward, **7**: 558. *See also* Baptists

distemper: kills oxen, **7**: 127

district attorneys (U.S.): circular letter to, **17**: 338-40

District of Columbia. *See* seat of U.S. government on Potomac

Divers, Mr.: proposes to provision troops, **4**: 35; to serve with Newton, **4**: 136; refuses office of deputy quartermaster, **4**: 374

Divers, George: signs address, **16**: 178; and subscriptions for extending navigation of Rivanna river, **18**: 40; purchase of mill, **20**: 606, 671; subscribes to *National Gazette*, **20**: 759

Divers & Lindsay: subscribe to *National Gazette*, **20**: 759

dividers, brass: ordered by TJ, **9**: 153

Divoux, J. David: letter from, **12**: 377-8; seeks appointment at L'Orient, **12**: 359, 371-2, 377

Dix, Mr.: and bill establishing ferries, **2**: 461

Dixon, Capt.: master of *Louisa*, **13**: 519; mentioned, **4**: 527n

Dixon, Mr.: Richmond property of, **8**: 344

Dixon, Anthony Tucker: at Charles City, **5**: 87

Dixon, Haldenby: signs nonimportation resolutions (1770), **1**: 47

Dixon, Col. Henry: letter to, **5**: 412; at battle of Camden, **3**: 595-6

Dixon, J., **17**: 546

Dixon, John: letters from, **5**: 41, 583; supports American state papers series, **1**: 145; death of, **20**: 293, 405; mentioned, **3**: 432

Dixon, R.: signs Va. oath of allegiance, **2**: 129

Dixon, Tilman: and Henderson's land claims, **2**: 108

Dixon & Nicolson: invoice for printing Va. documents, **5**: 211-2

Dnieper (Nieper) river, Russia: navigation restrictions on, **7**: 405

Dniester (Niester) river, Russia: navigation restrictions on, **7**: 405

Doane, Elisha: claimant to the *Lusanna*, **6**: 448-9, 453, 454; mentioned, **6**: 450, 451

Doane, Isaiah: claimant to the *Lusanna*, **6**: 448-9

Dobbyns (Dobbyn, Dobyn, Dobin), Mr.: introduced to TJ, **13**: 285; introduced to Madison, **13**: 469; mentioned, **13**: 606; **14**: 187, 360

Dobel, Capt. (master of *Commerce*), **20**: 248

Dobie, Mr., **10**: 133

Dobrée (Dobrie), Pierre Frédéric: representative of Schweighauser, **11**: 134-5; **14**: 61; claims, **11**: 475, 488; **12**: 342; Carnes' business with, **11**: 601-2; **12**: 52

Dobson, John: letters to, **20**: 597-8, 666; TJ's debt to, **16**: 211; **17**: 592, 657; **20**: 326, 666; and sale of lands, **18**: 308; payment to, **20**: 103, 572; letter from cited, **20**: 666n

Dobson, Thomas: publisher in Philadelphia, **14**: 33; **17**: 598; **18**: 131; **20**: 418; paid by Department of State, **17**: 369

doctors: taxed in Va., **11**: 153

Dodds, John: paid by Department of State, **17**: 368

Dodds, William: British war prisoner, **2**: 32

Dodge, John: letter from, **3**: 520-2; treatment as British captive at Detroit, **2**: 293, 295n; Henry Hamilton's opinion of, **3**: 96n; agent in Ill., **3**: 416; complaints against, **4**: 188; **5**: 599; inquiry into conduct of, **4**: 355, 413-4;

5: 253; arrests Winston, **5**: 600n; mentioned, **3**: 11; **4**: 170, 443n; **5**: 574

Dodsley, Mr.: bookshop of, **10**: 78

Dodson, Daniel: pay due, **5**: 141-2; warrants issued to, **5**: 164

Doeg's Neck, Va.: ferry at, **2**: 454

Doglass, John: signs petition, **6**: 293

dogs: weight of, **6**: 343

dogs, shepherd: brought by TJ from France, **15**: 499n, 509, 552, 553; **16**: 30, 576; **18**: 350n; **20**: 606; sent from France by La Motte, **15**: 499n; **16**: 18, 575-6; **17**: 559, 646

dogwood: sample to be sent to France, **10**: 227; plants asked from John Banister, **11**: 121; sent to Mme de Tessé, **13**: 187; **18**: 608-10

Dohm, Christian Conrad Wilhelm von: Prussian minister, **18**: 608-10; letter to, from Maréchal Bender, cited, **19**: 117-8

Dohrman, Arnold Henry: appointed agent at Lisbon, **8**: 208n; **18**: 49; efforts on behalf of Americans, **19**: 421

Dohrman (Dorman), Jacob: Mazzei's claim against, **11**: 402, 601; **13**: 166, 167n, 499; **18**: 218; **20**: 335-6, 657, 667, 678, 713; acts as deputy to agent at Lisbon, **18**: 49; business setbacks, **19**: 421; and British minister to U.S., **20**: 327; letter from cited, **20**: 361; recommends Samuel Harrison, **20**: 361, 361n, 362n; mentioned, **9**: 257; **12**: 104; **16**: 307, 308; **18**: 49

Dohrman, John Henry, **3**: 92

Dolce (Dolci), Carlo: paintings of, **13**: 103, 444

Dolfin, Daniele I.: correspondence with American Commissioners, **7**: 424n, 427; visited by Short, **14**: 312

Dollains, William: signs petition, **6**: 294

dollar: weights, **7**: 159n, 174; as money unit, **7**: 159n, 175-8, 183-4, 193-4, 195, 205; **8**: 295n, 445; **9**: 15, 190; **10**: 511, 634; value, **7**: 166, 179-80; **18**: 454-6; Spanish, **7**: 169, 197; **18**: 455-6; alloy, **7**: 181; assay, **7**: 182, 183; money of account, **7**: 189; Mexican, **7**: 197

Dollins, Presley: in Albemarle co. militia, **1**: 668n

Dolly's Chop House: TJ's dinner at, **9**: 350-2

Dolomieu, Dieudonné Sylvain Guy Tancrède, Chevalier: letter from, **8**: 560; introduction to John Adams, **8**: 585;

mentioned, **9**: 364n

Dolphin (ship). *See Dauphin*

Domenger, M.: manages wine estates, **19**: 267

Domenick, Capt. (master of N.Y. packet), **16**: 196

Dominica, B.W.I.: falls to French, **2**: 214

Dominis, Marcantonio de: theory of rainbow, **13**: 380

Donald, Alexander: letters to, **11**: 632-3; **12**: 132-4, 570-2, 594-5; **14**: 185-7; **16**: 222-3, 325, 331, 488-9; **17**: 473; **18**: 27n, 71-2; **20**: 404-6; letters from, **11**: 193-4; **12**: 345-8, 427-9, 486-7; **14**: 280-3, 457-8; **16**: 28-30, 90-2, 236-7, 263-4, 382-4, 406, 565-7, 591-4; **17**: 481-2, 566-7, 626-7; **18**: 477-8; **20**: 601-2; Richmond property of, **8**: 344; tobacco shipment by, **11**: 632, 640; books sent to, **12**: 136; letters from cited, **12**: 561; **15**: 574n; **16**: 81, 410, 523n; **17**: 26; owner of the *Bowman*, **12**: 561; wine ordered for, **12**: 593, 594-5, 661, 684; TJ's orders for payment of debts, **13**: 341; **16**: 211, 212, 213n; letter to cited by Patrick Henry, **13**: 353, 354n-5n, 412, 414n; correspondence with Short, **14**: 186n-7n; **15**: 512, 537; **16**: 91n-2n, 228, 230n; ships flour and wheat to France, **14**: 187n; **15**: 245; letters to cited, **14**: 190n; **15**: 245, 247, 379n, 381, 400; **16**: 495n; shipments to TJ lost, **14**: 280; wine sent to, **14**: 281; **17**: 322n; letters sent in care of, **15**: 523; **16**: 13, 31, 443; **18**: 604; on sale and prices of tobacco, **16**: 29-30; sends merchandise to TJ, **16**: 90-1; sends packet to Short, **16**: 91; tobacco sold to, **16**: 211, 492; Heth's dispute with, **16**: 236, 237n, 263-4, 325, 382-3, 565, 593-4; **17**: 322n, 481, 626; letters from missing, **16**: 237n, 325n; ships hams, **16**: 406, 492, 566, 591-2; asks for appointment as consul in London, **16**: 523, 592-3; **17**: 256; papers from cited, **17**: 321; Short advises, **17**: 566, 626-7; handles Short's funds, **20**: 545-6; mentioned, **12**: 537

Donald, Andrew: letter to, **19**: 541-2; TJ requested to write to, **16**: 594; letter from, to Short, cited, **19**: 541; letter to cited, **19**: 541

Donald, James: signs nonimportation resolutions (1770), **1**: 47; and Mazzei's agricultural co., **1**: 158

ters from cited, **8**: 82, 88, 167; letter quoted, **8**: 153n; letter to cited, **8**: 235; TJ's London newspapers put under cover to, **8**: 247, 398, 578; TJ asks assistance for Franklin, **8**: 303, 308; praised by TJ, **8**: 317; letters from, to Carmarthen, quoted, **8**: 362n-3n; in Paris, **10**: 545; and Barclay affair, **11**: 497n; honesty of, **12**: 40; TJ borrows book from, **12**: 246; conference with French court, **12**: 310; communication of secret declarations to TJ, **12**: 315, 316n; reports on threat of war with France, **12**: 461; succeeded as ambassador to France, **15**: 175; denies British interference in French Revolution, **15**: 315; letter from, to Leeds, quoted, **15**: 315n; leaves Paris, **15**: 537; marriage of, **16**: 385; inquires about TJ, **20**: 159

Dorsey, Edward: case against Mildred, **19**: 428

Dorsey, John: letter to quoted, **16**: 611; letter from cited, **16**: 617n; letter to cited, **16**: 617n

Dossenheim, Germany, **13**: 23, 267

Dot, Capt. (master of *La Virginie*), **20**: 477

double stars. *See* stars

Douglas (Duglass), James: appointed justice of Harrodsburg, **2**: 110

Douglas, Katherine Sprowle: letters to, **8**: 259-60, 364; letters from, **8**: 243-4, 329-30; claim against Va., **8**: 243-4

Douglass, John: in Albemarle co. militia, **1**: 666; denounced by Congress, **3**: 66

Douglass, Robert: in Albemarle co. militia, **1**: 664

Douglass (Douglas), William: *Summary, Historical and Political . . . of the British Settlements in North-America*, **6**: 489, 491, 493; **12**: 18

Douw, Volkert, **1**: 274

Dove (ship), **4**: 310; **6**: 115

Dover, England: TJ's detention by weather, **9**: 446

Dover (ship): seized by Spanish, **20**: 204, 205n-9n

Dow, John: British war prisoner, **2**: 31, 32, 33

Dowell, Maj.: in Albemarle co. militia, **1**: 664

Dowell, John: petition from, **5**: 349

dower. *See* widows: dower

Down, Capt., **1**: 452

Downie, James: letter from, **5**: 597; instructions on, **5**: 597

Downman, Col. Rawleigh P.: militia under command of, **5**: 82

Downs, Mr.: and Hessian fly, **20**: 460; inn rated by TJ, **20**: 471

Dowse, Edward: letter to, **16**: 286-7; letter from, **15**: 563; on *Montgomery*, **15**: 527n; letters from cited, **16**: 52n, 286n-7n; porcelain ordered from, **16**: 286

draft (Va.): recommended by R. H. Lee, **2**: 14; attitude toward, **2**: 18, 175; Adams' comments on, **2**: 20-1; method of determining subjects of, **3**: 182; resistance to, **4**: 18-9, 693; **5**: 14, 153, 318, 409-10; TJ advises postponement of execution of law, **4**: 614; **5**: 336; exemptions from, **4**: 627, 635; **5**: 219-23, 237n, 241n, 243n, 353, 449-50; need for, **4**: 662; time fixed by law, **4**: 669; Syme requests information on, **5**: 126; suspended, **5**: 128; reports on fraud, **5**: 173-5; in Bedford co., **5**: 212; insurance against, **5**: 220-3; suspended for Spotsylvania, **5**: 224; substitutes, **5**: 289; in Fairfax co., **5**: 336; in Fauquier co., **5**: 373; in Northumberland co., **5**: 430; in Fayette co., **5**: 462; in Jefferson co., **5**: 462, 466; in Hampshire co., **5**: 513; in Gloucester co., **5**: 596, 605-6; in Augusta co., **5**: 603-5; in Rockbridge co., **5**: 621-2; in Northampton co., **5**: 652; in Accomac co., **5**: 653; **6**: 45; difficulty of executing law, **6**: 30-1

Dragging-Canoe (Cherokee chief): sale of land to Henderson, **2**: 74, 85, 97, 105, 106; withdrawal from conference, **2**: 86-7; land claims of, **2**: 96

Dragging-Canoe's Town, **4**: 360

Drago di Domenico, Gaetano: letters from, **15**: 89-90, 205; letter from, to Washington, **18**: 359-60; letter from cited, **18**: 360n

Dragon (ship): Board of Trade requests service of, **3**: 315; transferred to Board of Trade, **3**: 331; repaired and manned for service, **3**: 488, 491; ordered to shipyard, **4**: 554, 602; proposed use by Capt. Joel, **4**: 569-70; put into service, **5**: 344

dragoons. *See* cavalry

Drake (British warship): captured by J. P. Jones, **2**: 207

Drake, Sir Francis: touches at Roanoke Island, **1**: 279

Drake, Jonathan: petition to Va. HD for care of livestock, **2**: 41n-2n; claims against Va., **2**: 63

Drake, William: prisoner of war at New York, **4**: 34

draperies: export from France to U.S., **12**: 470

drawing: as an accomplishment, **6**: 542, 543; Martha Jefferson's efforts at, **11**: 282

Drayer, Baron. See Dreyer

Drayton, Col. Stephen, **3**: 550

Drayton, William: letters to, **9**: 461-2; **11**: 119-20, 644-50; **12**: 507-8, 567; **13**: 368-9; **15**: 101-2; **20**: 332-3; letters from, **9**: 53; **11**: 374-5; **12**: 380-2; seeds sent to, **9**: 498; **13**: 368-9; rice sent to, **11**: 520; **12**: 148, 464, 500, 509, 534; **13**: 107, 368-9; letters to cited, **11**: 588, 659; **12**: 338; **13**: 415; **15**: 46n; **16**: xxxi; **18**: 585n; package sent to, **11**: 592; **12**: 112, 569, 591; TJ's plans for sending olives to, **13**: 369; **14**: 463; **15**: 43, 100, 101; fruit trees sent to, **15**: 101-2; payment to TJ, **17**: 422; olive trees sent to, **18**: 584; **20**: 332-3; seeks treasury comptrollership, **20**: 230n; mentioned, **12**: 112; **18**: 584

Drayton, William Henry: death of, **11**: 120

dress, women's: TJ's advice to his daughter, **6**: 417

Drew, Thomas: and bill establishing ferries, **2**: 460

Drew, Capt. Thomas H. (master of *Liberty*), **1**: 165; **4**: 40, 539; **5**: 288n; **15**: 670

Drew, Maj. Thomas Haynes, **5**: 582

Drew, William: witnesses TJ's agreement with J. Randolph, **1**: 67; attests revisal report, **2**: 312n; attests resolutions as clerk of Senate, **5**: 62n, 230n; **6**: 136n, 189; mentioned, **5**: 218

Dreyer (Drayer), Christopher Wilhelm, Baron: recommended to Carmichael, **8**: 649; **9**: 24; mentioned, **9**: 449

Driesbach, Simon: runs for Congress from Pa., **14**: 473

Driss, Alcaid: letter from, to Carmichael, **8**: 255-6

drivers. See wagon drivers

droit d'aubaine: Americans exempted from, **3**: 264; abolition of, **17**: 434n-

5n, 618, 641; **18**: 353, 452, 604; **19**: 258, 362, 539, 635-6; **20**: 256-7, 365, 392-3, 588

Drost. See Droz

Drouais, Mme, **11**: 187

Drouais, François Hubert, **11**: xxxi

Drouais, Jean Germain: painting of Marius at Minturnes, **11**: xxxi, 187-8, 198-9, 259, 270, 414 (illus.); death of, **13**: 150

drought: in Va., **1**: 476; in France (1785), **8**: 160, 161, 163

Drouilhet, Etienne, & Cie.: bill drawn for, **8**: 84; Carmichael's transactions with, **13**: 509

Droz, Jean Pierre: execution of coins, **11**: xxxi, 414 (illus.); and coinage method, **11**: 30, 100; **16**: 335n-6n, 339n, 368-9; **17**: 412; letter from, to Grand, quoted, **11**: 102n-3n; biographical note, **11**: 103n; in TJ's plan to establish mint, **16**: 335n, 337n-9n, 368-9; **18**: 452, 458; **20**: 213, 255, 256n, 534, 578-9, 587, 652, 675, 684; extract of letter sent to, **17**: 450; note from, to Hamilton, cited, **18**: 68; mentioned, **17**: 451n; **18**: 141n

drugs: U.S. import of, **10**: 147

Drummon, Col., **5**: 454n

Drummond, Mrs.: letter from, **1**: 65-6; mentioned, **1**: 585n

Drummond, Thomas Lundin, Lord: and peace proposals, **1**: 501-2

drums: for Va. militia, **2**: 127

drunkenness: unknown in France, **8**: 569; in U.S., **10**: 262-3

Drury, Capt.: impresses U.S. seamen, **20**: 243n

dry goods: for army, **4**: 543; imports by S.C., **8**: 199

Duane, James: signs Continental Association, **1**: 153; signs Congress' second petition, **1**: 222; signs agreement of secrecy, **1**: 252; member of committee on Canadian campaign, **1**: 296n; chairman of committee on powers of Committee of the States, **6**: 518n-20n; chairman of committee dealing with Indian affairs, **6**: 582n, 583n, 584n, 586n; supports Steuben's claims, **7**: 100n; report on coinage cited, **7**: 152n; member of committee of Congress on coinage, **7**: 155n; supports ratification of Constitution, **13**: 413; in *L'Aigrette* case, **14**: 85; proposed as senator from N.Y., **14**: 519; **15**: 427;

551; **17**: 161-2, 502, 598n, 644; letter from, to Humphreys and Short, **9**: 463-4; recommended by TJ to Congress, **9**: 468; seeks appointment as U.S. minister to the Netherlands, **9**: 503, 561-3; usefulness to France and Holland, **9**: 562; correspondence with Jay, **9**: 562n; **10**: 435n, 482, 558n; **11**: 510n; **13**: 160n-1n, 613n-4n; **14**: 6n-7n, 32n, 348n, 484n-5n, 613n, 622, 647n, 694n; **15**: 21n, 79n, 201n, 443n; letters to cited, **10**: 99; **16**: 238n, 240n, 243n, 282n; drafts on Grand, **10**: 237; payment of bills, **10**: 285; letters of recommendation for Bassville and Robert Morris' sons, **10**: 295-6, 297; death of daughter-in-law, **10**: 354, 397; and Démeunier's *Essai sur les Etats-Unis*, **10**: 434, 468; correspondence with William Short, **11**: 195-7, 243-5; **15**: 201; correspondence with Congress, **11**: 240; **13**: 639n-40n; **14**: 32; bills paid by Grand, **11**: 474-5; attitude of Congress toward, **11**: 482; **12**: 695; and purchase of French debt in Netherlands, **11**: 517; letter from, to Hubbard, cited, **11**: 582n; account against U.S., **11**: 609; and Geraud and Roland affair, **11**: 669; **12**: 224; and fear of violence, **12**: xxxviii; and political intrigue, **12**: 178n-9n; protection of, **12**: 199, 217, 257, 312; dismissal asked by States General, **12**: 200n, 292, 312; position with relation to U.S., **12**: 200n; attitude of Dutch toward, **12**: 289; **14**: 6n-7n, 348n, 484n-5n; **20**: 558; desires mission to Brussels, **12**: 359, 376, 383, 388-9, 394, 407, 449, 483; accounts sent to Ast, **12**: 372; letter to, May 15, 1788, published, **13**: 160n-1n, 221n, 409n, 411n; letter from, to John Rutledge, Jr., cited, **13**: 312n; States General of Netherlands, documents on, **13**: 440n; expenses of, **13**: 552; assistance with TJ's accounts, **13**: 576; reports on Dutch loan to U.S., **13**: 613n-4n; **18**: 592-3; letters from, to Fagel, cited, **13**: 614n; Washington on, **13**: 640n; status of, **13**: 640n, 647; **14**: 32; letters to, from Luzac, cited, **14**: 6, 7n; **17**: 209, 210n; letter from, to Willink & Van Staphorst, cited, **14**: 7n; daughter marries, **14**: 623; correspondence with Washington, **15**: 201n; **16**: 243n; **17**:

498-9; assists in sending *Gazette de Leide*, **16**: 243n; **18**: 595; sends books, **17**: 361; Rymer's *Fœdera* presented to E. Randolph, **17**: 378n; suggestion on packet boats, **17**: 543; **18**: 63-4, 137; allowances of, **19**: 586; letter to quoted, **20**: 404n; mentioned, **7**: 428, 462; **8**: 431, 435, 447, 593; **10**: 650; **11**: 491; **12**: 103; **14**: 297

Dumas, Mrs. Charles William Frederick: health of, **12**: 689; mentioned, **11**: 244; **12**: 679

Dumas, Guillaume Mathieu, Comte de: J. P. Jones praises, **13**: 584

Dumbar, Jesse. *See* Dunbar

Dumez, M.: drafts in favor of, **10**: 461n, 493, 508

Dumfries, Va.: possible object of British raid, **5**: 393; place of court of assize, **7**: 589

Dumoulin de Seille & Son: letter to, **10**: 200-1; letter from, **10**: 164-5

Du Moussy, M., **9**: 78

Du Muy, M., **11**: 109

Dunari, Keith & Co., Genoa, **14**: 591

Dunbar (Dumbar), Jesse: ill treatment as prisoner of war, **8**: 653-4; **9**: 4-5, 16; attack on Capt. Stanhope, **10**: 62

Dunbar, John: letter to, **16**: 30-2; manager of Banister estate, **16**: 23, 30-1; **17**: 657

Dunbar, Mrs. John, **16**: 32

Duncan, Mrs. (mother of William), **18**: 642n-3n

Duncan, Dr. Andrew, **14**: 351

Duncan, Charles: signs nonimportation resolutions (1770), **1**: 46

Duncan, James: petition to Va. HD, **2**: 42n; resolution in Va. HD respecting claim of, **2**: 63

Duncan, John: British war prisoner, **2**: 31

Duncan, Joseph, **5**: 154

Duncan, William: in Algerian captivity, **18**: 642n-3n; **20**: 677-8

Dundas, Henry, first Viscount Melville: minister for India, **15**: 175; and Smith's mission to England, **18**: xxxiv, 246, 248-9, 256, 259; **20**: 113; portrait, **18**: xxxv, 268 (illus.); in trade negotiations with U.S., **18**: 246; letter to, from Colquhoun, quoted, **18**: 248; reports to Pitt, **20**: 140; mentioned, **13**: 461; **17**: 43n; **18**: 254

Dundas (Dundass), Col. Thomas: near Hampton, **4**: 588-9; **5**: 293-4; quarrel

Dundas (Dundass), Col. Thomas (*cont.*) with Gen. Arnold, **5**: 74; commands plundering detachment, **5**: 95-6; horse killed under, **5**: 96; mentioned, **4**: 330, 405n; **5**: 331n

Dundas, Sir Thomas: former owner of "Moor-Park," **9**: 373

dung: lack of in Aix-en-Provence, **11**: 248; price in Provence, **11**: 426

Dungeness (estate of Thomas Randolph), **1**: 410n

Dunham, Aaron: letter to, **19**: 363-4

Dunkard's Creek, Pa.: Indian attack on, **15**: 218

Dunkirk (Dunkerque), France: consul in, **8**: 441; **14**: 60, 62n; harbor, **8**: 592; in whaling industry, **13**: 66, 67; **14**: 218, 220-5, 235-41, 334; and Nantucket, Mass. emigration to, **19**: 163; free port, **20**: 632. *See also* Nantucket whalers at Dunkirk

Dunlap (Dunlop), Maj. James, **5**: 552

Dunlap, John: prints broadside of Declaration of Independence, **1**: 417n; prints *A Summary View*, **1**: 673; accounts of, **2**: 213; **5**: 157-8; engaged as public printer for Va., **3**: 579-80; claim for loss of printing apparatus, **3**: 580n; sets up printing press in Va., **4**: 534; **6**: 92, 93; weekly gazette of, **5**: 386; denied flag, **5**: 686; prints proclamation of ratification of Peace Treaty, **6**: xxxvi, 463n, 604 (illus.); paid by Department of State, **17**: 369, 373; mentioned, **7**: 282, 518

Dunlap, Robert: loan to state, **3**: 386, 442

Dunmore, Charlotte Stewart, Lady: arrives at Williamsburg, **1**: 104

Dunmore, John Murray, fourth Earl of: dissolves Va. HB, **1**: 106n; attitude toward land grants, **1**: 115n; prorogues Va. HB, **1**: 119n; and Mazzei's agricultural co., **1**: 157-8; and Lord North's conciliatory proposal, **1**: 174n; **10**: 371-2, 376n; and Va.-Pa. boundary dispute, **1**: 235n, 463; at Norfolk, **1**: 238; **15**: 574-6; violations of private property, **1**: 243; enlists support, **1**: 247, 267; Pendleton's comment on, **1**: 261; proclamation of emancipation, **1**: 261n, 265, 266; **10**: 372; victory at Norfolk, **1**: 265, 266; attempts to burn Hampton, **1**: 269; departure from Va., **1**: 296-7; **15**: 96; on Gwynn's Island, **1**: 297; property sold, **1**: 387, 455; de-

feat at Fort Sullivan, **1**: 462; fleet at mouth of Potomac, **1**: 468, 471, 472, 476, 480, 481; **15**: 578, 581n; flight from Gwynn's Island, **1**: 482; reported en route to New York, **1**: 485; fleet in Hampton Roads, **1**: 491; at Staten Island, **1**: 497-8; and Indian relations, **2**: 82; **15**: 573; spirit level of, **2**: 175; raid on Alexandria, **5**: 424; and Cherokee archives, **6**: 141n; characterization of, **8**: 329; debts of, **16**: 197; Jamieson's connection with, **16**: 522; sends Bowles to incite Indians, **17**: 665; mentioned, **1**: 264; **2**: 5n; **3**: 5

Dunmore co., Va.: appoints infantry officers, **1**: 580; place of court of assize, **1**: 630; militia, **2**: 35, 131; name changed to Shenandoah, **2**: 117

Dunn, James: Albemarle co. militia, **1**: 668n

Dunn, Capt. James (master of the *James*), **12**: 235, 297, 323

Dunn, Nathaniel: commission as justice of the peace, **6**: 644

Dunn, O., **15**: 97

Dunn, William, **5**: 294n

Dunscomb, Andrew: letter from, to John Hay, **10**: 183; Ewell sends certificates to, **17**: 585

Dunwoody, John: paid by Department of State, **17**: 374

Dupaty, Charles Marquerite Jean Baptiste Mercier: death of, **13**: 621

Dupeuty, (DePauly), M.: letter from, to Topham, Ross, and Newman, cited, **12**: 564

Du Pin d'Assarts, M.: letter to, **11**: 476

Duplessis, Gen. *See* Mauduit du Plessis, Thomas Antoine, Chevalier de

Du Plessis, Pierre: manuscript sent to Franklin, **8**: 303, 308, 585; **9**: 349

Duplessy, Mme: letter from, **12**: 701

Du Ponceau, Peter Stephen: letter from, to John Jay, **10**: 184-5; letter to quoted, **13**: 235n; "Indian Vocabularies," **20**: 450n, 470n; mentioned, **5**: 572n

Dupont, M.: letter sent by, **20**: 546

Dupont, François: goes to America, **13**: 600, 601n; Crèvecoeur gives pamphlets to, **14**: 31

Dupont, Victor Marie: letter to, **12**: 212-3; introduction to R. R. Livingston, **12**: 213; accompanies Moustier to U.S., **12**: 314; Washington entertains at Mount Vernon, **14**: 24n, 303; recommended for consular appointment, **14**: 65n; mentioned, **13**: 42

Dupont de Nemours, Pierre Samuel: letters to, **12**: 211-2, 325, 328-9, 595-6; letters from, **12**: 325-7, 328; **15**: 421; on U.S.-French trade committee, **9**: 338n; **12**: 76n, 77n, 142; **13**: 52n; possible author of speech before Comité du Commerce, **9**: 345n; biography of Turgot, **12**: 213; favorable attitude toward U.S., **12**: 314; comments on government, **12**: 326, 329; and son's arrival at New York, **12**: 697; **13**: 262n; "Rapport sur le commerce des Etats-Unis" attributed to, **13**: 53n-4n; promotes trade treaty with Britain, **13**: 54n; report on tobacco trade, **13**: 61; supports arrêt of December 1787, **13**: 194n; **16**: 505; **18**: 353; and American trade, **13**: 196n; *Lettre à la Chambre du Commerce de Normandie*, **13**: 441, 443n; **14**: 16, 40n; friendship with Turgot, **14**: 40; in whale oil negotiations, **14**: 261; mémoire cited, **14**: 263-4; characterization of Necker, **15**: 191n; report on wheat shortage presented to National Assembly, **15**: 244; rice trade statistics from, **15**: 446n; on farmers general, **17**: 395; opposes assignats, **17**: 524; mentioned, **14**: 266, 267

Duport, Adrien Jean François: discusses royal veto, **15**: 355n; position in National Assembly, **15**: 559; in radical party, **16**: 437; opposes Lafayette, **16**: 474; **20**: 350-1

Duportail, Louis LeBègue de Presle, Chevalier: letter to, **10**: 73-4; letters from, **8**: 234; **10**: 85-6; Treasury certificate to, **8**: 87, 227; recommends Castaing, **10**: 81; esteemed by Washington, **12**: 258; dines with TJ, **12**: 265; becomes minister of war, **17**: 698; **18**: 85; characterized by Gouverneur Morris, **20**: 698; mentioned, **7**: 398; **9**: 78, 481

Duport du Tertre, Marguerite Louis François: appointed keeper of the seals, **18**: 114; characterized by Gouverneur Morris, **20**: 698

Dupré, M.: creditor of Nesbitt, **14**: 555n, 584

Dupré, Augustin: letters to, **14**: 413, 545-6, 554-5, 588; letter from, **14**: 418; medal for Greene, **9**: 241; **14**: 555; **16**: xxxvii, 52 (illus.), 61n-2n,

67n; medal for Morgan, **14**: 545, 555; **16**: xxxvii-xl, 52 (illus.); makes medals, **14**: 545-6, 554-5, 588; **16**: 60n, 65n, 68, 74n, 361n, 505; **20**: 368; medal for Jones, **14**: 687; **16**: xl, 52 (illus.); medal for Franklin, **16**: xxxv, xlii, 52 (illus.), 65n; diplomatic medal of 1790, **16**: xli-ii, 52 (illus.); letters to cited, **16**: 65n, 69n, 73n-5n; TJ compliments, **16**: 396; finishes engravings, **17**: 527; engraver general of French mint, **18**: 583; **20**: 652; observations on Droz' proposal for mint, **20**: 534

Dupris, St. George, **1**: 446

Du Prunel, M.: vineyards, **11**: 421

Duquesnay, M.: engineering experiments of, **11**: 234

Duquesne, Fort, **2**: 98, 99, 101

Duquesne, Lieut.: letter sent by, **13**: 637

Durand, M., **11**: 463n

Durazzo, Count: gardens of, **11**: 441; **13**: 270; **14**: 705

Durazzo, Jean Luc, Marquis, **11**: 464n

Durazzo, Palazzo Marcello, **11**: 440

Durfort, Louis, Comte de: appointed ambassador to Venice, **19**: 637

Durham, Bishop of, **1**: 67

Durival, Jean: letters to, **10**: 511; **11**: 52; **15**: 49-50; letters from, **10**: 499-500; **11**: 60

Durnford, Elias, **18**: 495

Durocher, Jean Baptiste, **12**: 626

Du Roi, August Wilhelm: returns books borrowed from TJ, **4**: 117

Du Roy, M. (president of *Cours des Aides*): vineyard, **11**: 456; wine recommended by TJ, **20**: 406

Dushield, Capt., **5**: 210

Du Simitière, Pierre Eugène: and design for U.S. seal, **1**: lviii, 495-6, 550 (illus.); design for coat of arms for Va., **1**: lviii, 551 (illus.); design for Va. seal, **1**: 483n, 510-1, 679; curator of American Philosophical Society, **4**: 545; as art tutor of Martha Jefferson, **6**: 381, 417, 444-5, 465, 542, 543; **7**: 44, 62; death of, **7**: 535; papers of, **7**: 535; designs medal, **16**: 54n

Dussault, J., **12**: 527

Dussaut, M.: letter to, **14**: 459; letter from, **14**: 458

Düsseldorf, Germany: Trumbull describes, **10**: 440; TJ admires paintings in, **13**: 14, 103-4; TJ's notes on, **13**: 14, 264-5; Shippen describes paintings, **13**: 444-5

Dutch. *See* Netherlands
Dutch East India Company. *See* East India Company, Dutch
Dutch loans. *See* Netherlands: loan to U.S.
Dutens, Louis: *Itinéraire des routes les plus fréquentées*, **13**: 268, 276n; recommendations of, **13**: 653
duties, French: on American products, **8**: 86, 370n-1n; **9**: 498; **10**: 474-6; **11**: 540; **12**: 106, 163; arms exports subject to, **10**: 67; documents on, **13**: 57-74, 197-8; admiralty, report on, **13**: 71-2; on spermaceti oil, **13**: 221; Appleton on, **13**: 421, 429, 543; Marseilles riots caused by, **15**: 44; on salt beef, **15**: 220-1, 311, 344-5; **17**: 611, 617; on rice, **15**: 544; on meats, **17**: 480; mentioned, **12**: 106, 110, 368-9, 648; **13**: 191-2, 194n-7n; **17**: 610-1; on tobacco, *see* tobacco trade: with France; on whale oil, *see* whale oil: duty on, in France
duties, U.S.: Hogendorp's queries on, **7**: 297; in N.Y., **7**: 330; in Conn., **7**: 332; in R.I., **7**: 337; **15**: 275-6; in N.H., **7**: 346; trade treaty stipulations, **7**: 471; state, **7**: 471 (TJ's notes for treaties); **8**: 483-4; **10**: 15; reciprocal agreements, **7**: 480, 616-7, 624, 652; **8**: 27, 105, 188-94, 231-2, 310; levy, **7**: 573; freedom from, of vessels not unloading, **8**: 29-30, 107, 190, 481; **9**: 414, 424-5; most-favored-nation clause, **8**: 188-94, 318; in S.C., **8**: 201; aliens compared to nationals, **8**: 332-3; on French goods, **8**: 577; collected in U.S. ports, **9**: 110-1; imports from other states, **9**: 198; foreign ships, **9**: 203; and Portuguese, **9**: 412, 424; and Morocco, **10**: 335-6, 345; proposed on exports from New Orleans, **10**: 457; definition of terms, **11**: 539-40; **15**: 25; in Va., **12**: 411; Congress deliberates on, **15**: 114-5, 153-4, 175, 225-7; Britain as favored nation, **15**: 115, 225-7; bill on, **15**: 148, 153, 225, 263, 264n, 275-6, 277, 337, 418; N.C. imports and exports, **15**: 276; Le Havre merchants complain of, **17**: 314; **18**: 526; French communications on, **17**: 395-6; TJ on, **19**: 210-1. *See also* impost; tonnage acts
Du Val, Mr.: reported killed by Indians, **9**: 209n, 236n; **10**: 183; mentioned, **4**: 275

Duval, Lewis: warrant for expenses from Monongalia, **4**: 525-6
Du Val, Samuel: signs Virginia Association, **1**: 109; mentioned, **8**: 643
Du Val, William: attorney for Yancey, **2**: 45n
Duval d'Eprémesnil, Jean Jacques IV: arrest and imprisonment, **13**: 188-9, 193n, 633, 634, 642, 649
Duvall, John Pierce: letter from, **4**: 454; appointed to confer on western defense, **3**: 51, 53
Du Verget, M. (wine merchant): in Bordeaux, **11**: 457; shell collection, **11**: 461
Du Vernet, Théophile Imarigeon: *Vie de Voltaire*, **11**: 666
Duveyrier, Honoré Marie Nicolas: letter sent by, **20**: 655; and king's flight to Varennes, **20**: 674
Duvivier, Pierre Simon Benjamin: letters from, **14**: 417, 588; **15**: 42, 174; and medal for Washington, **9**: 241; **16**: xxxvi, 52 (illus.), 62n, 65n; vineyards, **11**: 421; medals made by, **14**: 555; **16**: 60n, 65n, 68, 74n; and medal for Fleury, **16**: 56n, 74n-5n; TJ compliments, **16**: 396
Dwight, Timothy: poem in *Columbian Magazine*, **14**: 51; criticizes Freneau, **20**: 723
Dyer, Eliphalet: signs Continental Association, **1**: 153; signs Congress' second petition, **1**: 222; signs agreement of secrecy, **1**: 253; Conn. commissioner in dispute with Pa., **6**: 476n, 477n, 478n, 481n; mentioned, **1**: 286; **4**: 139
Dyer, James: cited, **2**: 497n
dyewood: U.S. import of, **10**: 147

Eadmer: Selden's edition of *Historiae Novorum*, **15**: 406
Eads, Abram: signs Va. oath of allegiance, **2**: 129; signs petition, **6**: 290
Eads, Bartlet: signs petition, **1**: 588
Eads, John: signs petition, **6**: 290
Eads, Thomas: signs petition, **1**: 588
Eads, William: signs petition, **1**: 588
eagle (coin): name, **7**: 159n; alloy, **7**: 181; mentioned, **7**: 182; **15**: 585n
Eagleston, James (master of *Betsey*), **20**: 361n
Earl, Mr.: uncle of Nicholas Trist, **10**: 168

Earl, Capt. John (master of *Pennsylvania Packet*), **19**: 588

Earles, Samuel: and bill establishing ferries, **2**: 455

Early, Joshua: and petition on organization of military service, **6**: 55-60

earth: diameter of, **6**: 378; probable effects of sudden change of position of, **10**: 104; origin of, *see* cosmogony

"Earth Belongs in Usufruct to the Living": editorial note on, **15**: 384-91; Gem's proposition, **15**: 391-2; TJ comments on, **15**: 392-9; Madison and, **16**: 146n-54

earthenware: manufactured in Conn., **7**: 336; U.S. import of, **10**: 147

earthquakes: in Va., **1**: 104; at Monticello, **18**: 500

East Augusta co., Va.: appoints infantry officers, **1**: 579; omitted from senatorial districts bill, **2**: 336n

Easterbrooks, Capt. Joseph: at the Cedars, **1**: 397, 399; death of, **1**: 452

Eastern Shore (Md.): transportation of 18-month men from, **4**: 694; as British objective, **5**: 392-3; removal of provisions from, **5**: 551; public stores on, **5**: 618-20; British depredations, **6**: 46; antiquities of, **12**: 241

East Florida. *See* Florida, East

East Haven, Conn.: plundered by British, **3**: 31

East India Company, Austrian: forming at Trieste, **3**: 447

East India Company, British: and tea act, **1**: 127; boycott of, **1**: 138; mentioned in debate, **1**: 324; regulated by Parliament, **7**: 6, 8, 16, 42; **9**: 184; purchase of tea from Portugal, **9**: 20; and Senegal, **12**: 455; suppression, **12**: 481, 627, 641; Morris on, **18**: 300

East India Company, Dutch: commerce, **7**: 354-5; and spice trade, **7**: 367; negotiations with, **14**: 12; proposed takeover by Dutch government, **20**: 478

East India Company, French: trade, **7**: 354-5; carriage of ginseng to China, **7**: 374; French decision on, **16**: 301-2

East Indies: U.S. trade with, **7**: 330, 353-5; **8**: 154; **9**: 238; **10**: 147; **12**: 322, 368; **13**: 3; **14**: 304, 416, 599-602; trade with France, **7**: 354; Danish possessions in, **7**: 478; British difficulties with, **7**: 638, 649; imports through Portugal, **9**: 62; U.S. prisoners in, **9**: 115, 173; **10**: 62; U.S. sea

letters, **12**: 107-8; European possessions in, **12**: 681; British troops sent to, **13**: 173, 175; French troops sent to, **13**: 173, 175, 191; British possessions in, **15**: 50; **18**: 609; goods imported from sold in Netherlands, **17**: 540-1; Dutch trade restrictions in, **20**: 591, 629-32

Easton, Col. James: stores taken by, **1**: 453

Eastwood, Capt., **5**: 589

Eaton, William: letters to, **3**: 610-1, 611-2; letter from, **4**: 13; appointed commissioner of provision law, **3**: 610-2; directed to collect cattle, **3**: 637; mentioned, **3**: 246, 402; **4**: 10, 41

ebony: U.S. import of, **10**: 147

Ebrens, H.: account of bones found at Schartsfield, **7**: 316

Eccleston, Thomas: opposes corn bill, **20**: 101n

Echecs, Salon des: TJ's membership in, **11**: 23

eclipses: Rittenhouse's observations, **8**: 565. *See also* solar eclipse (1778)

Ecole des Ponts et Chaussées: prospectus of, **13**: 211n

écu: and coining, **10**: 626

Eddin, Capt. Samuel: artillery company of, **4**: 675; mentioned, **4**: 531; **5**: 70

Eddy, Mr.: letter from, to Cutting, cited, **13**: 644

Eden, Robert, Baronet: and Washington's resignation, **6**: 407n; succeeded by Johnson, **16**: 522

Eden, William: British commissioner to Congress, **2**: 200, 205; negotiations with France, **9**: 96, 447; **12**: 171, 202, 310, 362; changes party, **9**: 118-9; biographical note, **9**: 448n; attitude toward U.S., **9**: 467; **12**: 174-5, 424; part in Barclay affair, **11**: 477, 497n; appointment as ambassador to Spain, **11**: 491; **12**: 40, 52, 363; Carmichael's opinion of, **12**: 240; letters from cited, **12**: 361, 461; TJ's conversation with, **12**: 424; in Spain, **13**: 95, 114, 142-3, 216, 577; **16**: 253-4; **17**: 398; journal of quoted, **13**: 217n; ridicules French political situation, **13**: 577; recall predicted, **14**: 387; peerage for, **15**: 175, 441; at The Hague, **16**: 254; in British intelligence, **16**: 522, 523; **18**: 226; mentioned, **9**: 183, 281

Edenburgh, Sewell, **4**: 542

Edenton, N.C.: tent cloth at, **3**: 501;

Ellicott, Andrew (*cont.*)
355-6; **20**: 9, 13, 17, 29, 33, 80, 81; applies for post of U.S. geographer, **19**: 40n; **20**: 61n; offers scientific assistant post to cousin, **19**: 41n; employs Benjamin Banneker, **19**: 41n-2n; describes poverty of Alexandria, Va. and Georgetown, Md., **19**: 47; doubts Washington's motives, **19**: 47-8; recommended as commissioner of Federal District, **19**: 59; sketch of capital site, **20**: 25; maps Federal City, **20**: 33-4, 34n, 42, 60-9; and destruction of Daniel Carroll's house, **20**: 45; celestial observations, **20**: 58; falls into disfavor, **20**: 58n; criticized by L'Enfant, **20**: 70; advises Washington, **20**: 82

Ellicott, Benjamin: maps Federal City, **20**: 34n; relations with L'Enfant, **20**: 59, 70

Ellicott, George: declines appointment, **19**: 41n

Elligood, Capt. (master of the *Betsy*), **9**: 391

Ellington, Jeremiah: imports slaves, **15**: 654

Elliot, Mr.: unfamiliar with new hygrometer, **13**: 460; with J. P. Jones at Copenhagen, **13**: 582-3

Elliot, Andrew: appointed British minister to U.S., **18**: 106, 226-7, 259, 368; **19**: 338, 607; **20**: 146, 237

Elliot, Gilbert: attachment to Eden, **18**: 226n

Elliot, Robert, **3**: 8

Elliott, Gen., **10**: 413

Elliott (Elliot), George: letters to, **4**: 674-5; **5**: 155-6, 214-5; letters from, **4**: 216, 342-3, 396, 484, 611, 665; **5**: 205-6; payment, **3**: 486; as commissioner of army provisions, **4**: 89, 175; willing to act as deputy field quartermaster, **5**: 5; and letters on William Boswell, **5**: 226; bills against Va., **5**: 390-1; as Continental quartermaster, **5**: 404; succeeded, **5**: 414; mentioned, **3**: 494, 495, 668; **4**: 218, 409, 454n, 549, 643, 650, 664, 674; **5**: 27, 45, 72, 97n, 120n, 166, 195n, 225, 288n, 341, 442; **15**: 601

Elliott, Grace Dalrymple: describes Dr. Gem's imprisonment, **15**: 386

Elliott, Hugh: warning to Denmark, **14**: 212; in Paris on diplomatic mission, **17**: 640

Elliott, James: death of, **4**: 361

Elliott, Richard: letter from, **4**: 97-8

Elliott (Elliot), William: property of, **1**: 389n; deposition concerning Henderson's land claims, **2**: 101

Ellis, Charles: and bill establishing ferries, **2**: 458

Ellis, John: warrant in favor of, **4**: 518

Ellis, Sir Wellbore: garden of described by TJ, **9**: 369-70

Ellsworth, Oliver: appointed commissioner of accounts, **7**: 413; member of Federal Convention, **11**: 400; as senator from Conn., **14**: 302, 339, 385, 394, 525, 529, 560, 615; federalism of, **14**: 394, 529; and case of Isaac Williams, **18**: 311n; and tonnage acts, **18**: 524, 526, 541, 546-8, 554; and arrearages of soldiers' pay, **18**: 611, 616, 617n, 624, 625; and capital site bill, **19**: 17, 34; appointed Senate conferee on excise bill, **19**: 37; and Franklin's death, **19**: 78, 84, 90; attacks France, **19**: 99; and bill on consular establishment, **19**: 307; on committee on Vt., **19**: 374; settles Conn. accounts, **20**: 221-2; praises Wolcott, **20**: 222; mentioned, **17**: 218, 444; **18**: 167, 410

Ellyson, John: and bond given Va. governor, **6**: 65

Ellzey, N.: signs nonimportation resolutions (1769), **1**: 31

Ellzey, William: and conference on Johnson case, **2**: 43n; nominated to Committee of Revisors, **2**: 313n; and certification of Charles Lee to practice law, **5**: 518

Elmer, Jonathan: signs agreement of secrecy, **1**: 253; as senator from N.J., **14**: 339, 394, 529, 560, 615; federalism of, **14**: 394, 529

elm trees: used for arbors, **11**: 455

Elott, John: signs nonimportation resolutions (1770), **1**: 47

Elsinore, Denmark: free port, **20**: 590

Elsworth, Vandine and Dorothy: payment to, **20**: 560, 566, 581; forwards seeds to TJ, **20**: 603

emancipation. *See* slavery: proposed abolition

embargoes: and Del.'s refusal to comply with, **5**: 473; trade treaty stipulations, **7**: 474, 477, 484, 620; **8**: 192; **9**: 417, 431

embargoes (Va.): bill empowering governor to lay, **2**: 348-9; resolves of Congress on, **3**: 87, 222; proclamation of Nov. 1779, **3**: 208-9; **4**: 406; **5**: 248; TJ's plan for, **3**: 492; repeal of acts on (1781), **5**: 483

embezzlement of arms: penalty for, **2**: 358

Embree, Thomas, **5**: 40, 41

Emden, Germany: free port, **7**: 566, 611, 649; **8**: 14; and the fisheries, **19**: 188

Emeraude (French frigate), **6**: 246

emergency powers: TJ's opinion on, **5**: 356

Emerson, William, **16**: 543, 569

Emery, Samuel: letter to quoted, **18**: 655n

Eminence (Va. state sloop), **5**: 152n

Emlen (Œmlan), George, **7**: 20

Emmes, Capt. (master of *Virginian*), **15**: 651, 661, 662, 664

Empey, Sir Elijah: proceedings against, **12**: 602

Empress of China (ship): voyage to China, **8**: 657n

Encyclopédie, ou Dictionnaire raisonée: TJ desires, **4**: 168, 211; **5**: 15, 311-2; **6**: 25; data on foreign coins, **20**: 546n; mentioned, **3**: 342

Encyclopédie Méthodique: motion to acquire for Congress, **6**: 216; TJ orders, **6**: 258; **16**: 388, 389n; **18**: 600; Madison's interest in, **6**: 508; **7**: 507; **9**: 333, 518; **10**: 604; **15**: 122; prospectus of, **7**: 281; Hopkinson's subscription, **7**: 285; **9**: 224, 232, 321, 362, 439, 482; **10**: 249, 624, 625; **11**: 563, 657; **12**: 236; **13**: 145; **14**: 345, 369, 370; **15**: 17; **16**: 490n, 581-2; subscription open, **7**: 504; Monroe's subscription, **7**: 511; **8**: 79, 233; **9**: 237, 499, 511; **10**: 115, 277, 612; Thomson's interest in, **7**: 518; **8**: 16; purchase for College of William and Mary, **8**: 74; **9**: 357; Franklin's subscription, **8**: 263; **9**: 224, 232, 439, 482; **10**: 247, 249, 624, 625; **11**: 301, 657; **12**: 236; **14**: 370; Currie's subscription, **8**: 342, 559, 641; **9**: 237, 499; **10**: 107; **11**: 327; TJ comments on, **8**: 537; ordered for the Rev. James Madison, **8**: 575; Démeunier's article on the U.S., **9**: 150, 155, 192, 382; **10**: 3-61, 288, 297, 299, 302-3, 317, 365n, 397, 532; **10**: 9n; **12**: 579-80; notes on publication of, **9**: 155n-6n; TJ offers to get for Madison, **9**: 265; article on chemistry in, **9**: 661; Va. act establish-

ing religious liberty printed in, **10**: 200, 604; Hay's subscription, **11**: 318; **18**: 113; **19**: 286; article on tobacco, **11**: 599; volumes presented to Congress, **11**: 667; copies received in U.S., **12**: 423; publication of, **14**: 367, 369; price increased, **14**: 649-50; E. Randolph receives, **16**: 13; **17**: 388; volumes available, **16**: 417; W. T. Franklin receives, **16**: 581; measures in, **16**: 587; copy for T. M. Randolph, Jr., **18**: 579; **19**: 329, 556; **20**: 381, 415; TJ cites, **19**: 212; sale of, **20**: 418; mentioned, **9**: 146; **15**: 356

Encyclopaedia Britannica: *Notes on Virginia* quoted in, **14**: 412n

Encyclopaedia; or, A Dictionary of Arts, Sciences, and Miscellaneous Literature: TJ cited in, **14**: 412n

Endeavour (ship), **20**: 316n

Enderby, Mr., **8**: 17

enemy aliens. *See* alien enemies

"Enfield Chase": garden described by TJ, **9**: 372-3

engineering: and road building, **8**: 4-5; profession of, **12**: 339; study of, **13**: 372-3

engineers, French: in Dutch service, **12**: 482

England. *See* Great Britain

England, David, **4**: 20

Englehard, Nicholas: letter to, from Shaw, **20**: 631n

English Channel: French and Spanish fleet in, **3**: 82; naval engagement in, **3**: 152; discomforts of crossing, **8**: 436-7

"Englishman's Turn." *See* New Orleans

engraving: improved method, **9**: xxvii, 386 (fac.); with ink on copper plates, **9**: 216, 232, 240, 267; Trumbull's works, **10**: 248, 250, 251; of map of Va., **11**: 207-8

engrossing: condemned by R. H. Lee, **2**: 215; Va. bill to prevent, **2**: 561-6; of cattle, **5**: 3

Enis (Ennis), James, **4**: 147

enlistment: of Va. forces, **2**: 378-81; length of, **3**: 490; **4**: 213; disadvantages of short, **3**: 548, 572; **4**: 27, 45-6; **5**: 173-5; for duration of war, **4**: 70

Ennery, M. d', **3**: 149

Ennis, George: death sentence and remission, **3**: 350, 351

Enos, Col. Roger: in Quebec campaign, **1**: 437

Ensign, Mr.: inn of rated by TJ, **20**: 471

entail: Va. bills to abolish, **1**: 104, 560-2; abolished in TJ's drafts of Va. Constitution, **1**: 344, 353; repeal of Va. laws of, **2**: 308n

Enterprise (frigate): impressed sailors on board, **18**: 326

entrepôts: for American exports, **8**: 142, 515; right of in French ports, **12**: 469-70, 481

envelopes: TJ's habit of destroying, **11**: 560

Enville (Anville, Danville), Louise Elisabeth de La Rochefoucauld, Duchesse d': letters to, **10**: 332-3; **16**: 290-1; letters from, **15**: 454; **17**: 286-7; Mazzei praises, **7**: 386; TJ excuses himself from dining with, **10**: 445; health of, **10**: 530; friendship for TJ, **16**: 48; TJ's farewell to, **16**: 290-1; TJ sends regards for, **16**: 297; introduction to, **16**: 377; wants seeds from America, **16**: 503, 504n; **17**: 558; **18**: 600; letter from cited, **17**: 317; requests sugar sample, **20**: 645; mentioned, **11**: 174; **13**: 486; **15**: 250, 256; **16**: 377

Enys, Lieut. John: British intelligence agent, **17**: 45

Eolus (ship): sails, **8**: 541, 570, 584; carries books to Va., **8**: 565, 639; mentioned, **9**: 52

Epernay, France: Trumbull's journey through, **10**: 438; TJ comments on, **13**: 28

Eperson, David: signs petition, **1**: 587

Ephemerides societatis meteorologicae Palatinae: ordered by TJ, **11**: 350, 464n

Ephraim: arrested, **20**: 649; letters from, to Frederick William II, cited, **20**: 649, 654; released, **20**: 654

Epictetus: TJ recommends works to Peter Carr, **8**: 407; TJ seeks information on best Italian translation, **11**: 159

episcopacy: TJ's notes on, **1**: 551-3

Episcopalians. *See* Protestant Episcopal Church

Epperson, James: signs Va. oath of allegiance, **2**: 129; petition from, **5**: 349; signs petition, **6**: 294

Epperson, John: signs petition, **6**: 290

Epperson, Richard: petition for pension, **2**: 42n; resolution in Va. HD respecting his claim, **2**: 63

Epperson, Sorrel, **4**: 274

Epperson, Thompson: in Albemarle co. militia, **1**: 665

Eppes, Mr.: and cavalry equipment, **4**: 343, 344; mentioned, **4**: 262; **5**: 293; **6**: 99n

Eppes, Bolling: illness of, **7**: 441, 539

Eppes, Elizabeth (Betsy) Wayles (Mrs. Francis Eppes): letters to, **6**: 198-200, 372, 427, 470; **7**: 113, 224, 500; **8**: 539-40; **10**: 594; **11**: 634-5; **13**: 347-8; **14**: 355-7; **15**: 624-5; **16**: 208-9, 489; **17**: 265-6, 658; **20**: 157, 413; letters from, **7**: 58; **8**: 517; **11**: 260, 356; **12**: 497-8; **15**: 628-9, 637; **16**: 209n; **17**: 331-2; marries Francis Eppes, **1**: 87; **15**: 658; attends Mrs. Jefferson, **6**: 199n; health of, **6**: 253, 416; TJ describes latest fashion for, **6**: 350; children of, **6**: 415; **13**: 347-8; **15**: 370; requests TJ to send seeds, **7**: 122; letters to cited, **9**: 91; **11**: 654; **14**: 349n; **16**: 332n; **18**: 7n; letters from cited, **9**: 211; TJ praises, **9**: 212; **10**: 600; **11**: 634; relations with Martha Jefferson, **9**: 560; **11**: 524; **14**: 355; **18**: 500; relations with Mary Jefferson, **10**: 111; **15**: 613, 616, 618, 621, 629, 632, 634, 636, 639; **16**: 208, 435, 436; receives anchovies from TJ, **10**: 483; Mary and Martha Jefferson remember, **13**: 347; Mrs. Carr praises, **15**: 627, 632; invited to Monticello, **17**: 266, 267, 331; letter from missing, **17**: 266n; mentioned, **1**: 175, 185, 247, 249, 252, 264, 458, 460, 473, 488; **6**: 220, 360; **7**: 110, 636; **8**: 121, 451; **9**: 92, 159, 396; **11**: 352, 379; **15**: 370, 622, 633; **16**: 36, 598; **17**: 581, 582; **18**: 579

Eppes, Francis: letters to, **1**: 174-5, 184-5, 246-7, 248-9, 252, 264, 458-60, 472-3, 487-8; **6**: 219-20, 244-5, 252-3, 349-50, 372, 470; **7**: 3, 113, 115, 355, 396, 500-1, 601-2, 635-6; **8**: 141-2, 451; **9**: 91-3, 159, 211-2, 395-7; **10**: 160-1, 594-6; **11**: 378-9, 524-5, 650-4; **13**: 327-9; **14**: 357-9; **15**: 370, 621-3; **16**: 35-6, 598; **17**: 266-7, 581-2, 584, 656-7; **18**: 578-9; **19**: 554-5; **20**: 412-3; letters from, **6**: 415-6; **7**: 3, 59, 422, 441-2; **8**: 518; **9**: 385, 567; **10**: 483; **11**: 255-7; **15**: 572-3, 574-6, 615-6, 623-4, 625-6, 628, 631-2, 636; **16**: 447; **17**: 592; **20**: 151-2, 313; signs bond for TJ's marriage license, **1**: 86; marries Elizabeth Wayles, **1**: 87; **15**: 658; and sale of Wayles' lands, **1**: 100, 103; signs Continental Association, **1**: 154; ordered to Portobello, **1**:

238; TJ sends book to, **1**: 294; manages TJ's affairs, **6**: 210; **7**: 239, 605; **9**: 389; **11**: 10-2; **13**: 340; and Nash's land scheme, **6**: 245; letters from cited, **6**: 381; **7**: 18, 538, 539n, 594; **10**: 615; **11**: 210, 640; **13**: 325; **14**: 359n; letters to cited, **7**: 376; **8**: 539; **11**: 48; **13**: 339; **14**: 16; **16**: 98, 125, 126n; **17**: 571n; **18**: 7; and Wayles' estate, **7**: 384, 423; **11**: 14, 329; **13**: 325, 327-8; **14**: 362; **15**: 161, 626, 645-7, 671n, 674, 676; **17**: 592; **19**: 542; **20**: 167; presents from TJ, **7**: 384, 501; articles shipped to, **7**: 578; **8**: 94; **9**: 210-1; **10**: 67, 136; **11**: 396; **12**: 428; seeds for, **8**: 122; **15**: 621, 624, 631; kindness toward Le Maire, **8**: 640-1; sends seeds, **11**: 246; **15**: 621, 632; makes cider, **12**: 133; *Notes on Virginia* sent to, **12**: 133; daughters of, **12**: 454; letters from missing, **13**: 329n; **16**: 209n; **17**: 332n; seeks tutor for children, **15**: 624, 631; chessmen sent to, **15**: 632; letters to quoted, **15**: 647; wants son to study law, **16**: 37-8; package for, **16**: 39; TJ gives note on harpsichord, **16**: 81, 90; receives payment, **16**: 211; sells slaves, **18**: 579n; health of, **19**: 295; and Hylton's debt, **20**: 714; mentioned, **6**: 199, 342; **7**: 17, 386, 559; **8**: 121, 517; **10**: 228; **11**: 260, 331, 404; **14**: 662; **15**: 132, 633; **16**: 16, 309, 489; **17**: 331, 488; **20**: 103, 157

Eppes, John Wayles (Jack): letter to, **11**: 635; letter from, **9**: 560; marries Maria Jefferson, **1**: 87n; projected visit to TJ, **6**: 199; education, **6**: 416; **9**: 560; **16**: 37-8; **17**: 581-2; **20**: 152, 157, 323, 412, 413, 636n; letters from cited, **11**: 379, 634; letter to cited, **11**: 654; in Philadelphia with TJ, **17**: 656-7, 658; **20**: 250, 313; advised by TJ to avoid girl with city education, **17**: 658; transcribes Madison's notes on Federal Convention, **19**: 549-51; baggage, **20**: 381, 417; mentioned, **17**: 592; **18**: 578-9; **20**: 214

Eppes, Lucy: death of, **7**: 441-2, 539, 635

Eppes, Tabby: indecision of, **16**: 27

Eppes family, **8**: 345, 643; **10**: 111; **11**: 209; **12**: 187

Eppington, Va., **6**: 199; **14**: 358

Eprésmesnil, Duval d'. *See* Duval d'Eprémesnil, Jean Jacques IV

Equoam river. *See* French Broad river

Erasmus, Desiderius: described by TJ as Arian, **1**: 554; mentioned, **3**: 64

Eraut river. *See* Herault river

Erfurt: giant teeth found at, **7**: 315

Eridanus: Po river called, **14**: 378, 383

Erie, Lake: American effort to take possession of, **4**: 234, 236; and U.S. boundary, **6**: 458, 583n, 600n, 602, 614; harbors on, **7**: 26; navigation on, **7**: 26; Indian attack on shore of, **7**: 459; connection with Ohio river, **12**: 488; **14**: 547; **15**: 117; **17**: 445n; canals affecting commerce on, **13**: 124; mentioned, **6**: 547, 603, 607

ermine: comparison with weasel, **9**: 661-5

Erskine, Henry: advice in Crozier case, **20**: 492

Erskine, Thomas: attorney general of Great Britain, **14**: 482

Ervin, Capt. James: captured by Barbary pirates, **8**: 254, 255

Erving, John: theory of need for British trade, **9**: 4

Escamaze, France: TJ describes, **11**: 448

escheats: use in Va., **2**: 282-3; purchase recommended, **2**: 284; Va. bills concerning, **2**: 410-2; **6**: 153-6; **9**: 200; **11**: 168; suspension considered, **3**: 492; payment for, **3**: 587; mentioned, **2**: 279-81, 285; **4**: 186-7, 439, 447; **12**: 453

Escorial, Spain: shortage of lodgings in, **12**: 323

Esdale, John: signs nonimportation resolutions (1770), **1**: 47

"Esher place": garden described by TJ, **9**: 370

Eskredge, Samuel: signs nonimportation resolutions (1770), **1**: 46

Esnauts and Rapilly: publish Paris map, **11**: 414

Esopus, N.Y.: Hogendorp plans visit to, **7**: 283

Espagnol (TJ's servant): employed by TJ, **10**: 213n; **11**: 248; **16**: 500; health of, **11**: 362, 395; expenses of, **13**: xxv

Esperance (ship), **10**: 181

Espilly, Count d'. *See* Expilly

Espinay de Laye, Mme de: TJ praises, **11**: 215; hospitality to TJ, **11**: 232, 287; mentioned, **11**: 463n; **12**: 291

Espinay de Laye, Chateau de: TJ visits, **11**: 215; Diana sculpture admired by

Espinay de Laye, Chateau de (*cont.*)
TJ, **11**: 226, 420; TJ describes, **11**: 418-20

Espinay de Laye, Marquis d': letter from, **13**: 97; relations with Short, **13**: 97n, 634, 636, 652-5; recommendation from, **13**: 121

Espion Anglois, L': TJ comments on, **11**: 663; TJ sends to Madison, **11**: 665

Essenberg, Germany, **13**: 13

"essence d'Orient": Hopkinson's method of distilling, **9**: 361-2; **11**: 288-9; sent to TJ, **11**: 290-1, 655-6; mentioned, **10**: 625

Essex co., Va.: letters to county lieutenant of, **4**: 526-7; **5**: 255, 612; **6**: 34-5; appoints infantry officers, **1**: 580; place of court of assize, **1**: 629; grand jury in, **1**: 638-9; militia, **2**: 131; **3**: 600; **4**: 63, 554; **5**: 255, 309n, 310, 329n, 612n, 646; senatorial district, **2**: 336; petition from on religious freedom, **2**: 548n; levies of soldiers, **3**: 7; tobacco loan office certificates, **3**: 516; specific tax, **3**: 606; **4**: 43; supply post for, **4**: 286; rioters in, **6**: 421; opposition to British subjects in, **7**: 116

Essex Court House, Va.: time of holding court of assize, **1**: 628

Estaing, Charles Henri Théodat, Comte d': letter to, **14**: 649; letter from, **9**: 542-4; commands French squadron in America, **2**: 204-5, 206, 208, 209, 213; actions in West Indies, **3**: 75, 76; **4**: 671; reported on southern coast, **3**: 90, 106; engagement with Barrington, **3**: 117; defeated at Savannah, **3**: 218, 231-3, 343, 382; French opinion of, **3**: 218, 232-3; takes command of fleet, **3**: 306; victory of, **5**: 55, 74, 86; sends news of peace settlement to America, **6**: 238n; Humphreys' letter of introduction to, **7**: 301n; and Order of Cincinnati, **9**: 161; **12**: 521; **14**: 489; given land by Ga., **9**: 266; **16**: 355; proposed blockade of Barbary States, **9**: 318, 319n, 500; **10**: 561n; **18**: 377, 380, 409, 410; letters from cited, **9**: 569; **10**: 310, 351; **14**: 649n; **18**: 378n, 380n, 430n; service in America, **9**: 604; medals for, **12**: 106n; **14**: 687; **16**: 65n, 67; J. P. Jones praises, **13**: 585; permits Short and Rutledge to visit Toulon, **14**: 649, 667; **15**: 29; praises Lafayette, **16**: 256n; corre-

spondence with Washington, **16**: 301, 305n, 555; **17**: 125n, 619; TJ advises Short on dealing with, **17**: 123; command of Brest fleet sought for, **17**: 611; Short confers with, **18**: 14; mentioned, **6**: 254; **9**: 129, 223

Estampes, France: TJ describes, **11**: 462

estates, personal: law of, **2**: 327

Este, Hinton: sends rice seed to TJ, **16**: 274; mentioned, **16**: 578

Estill, Mrs. (widow), **5**: 446

Estrada. *See* Strada, Famianus

estrays: Va. bill concerning, **2**: 440-1

Estrechy, France: TJ describes, **11**: 462

ethics: plan of reading for Peter Carr, **8**: 407

Ethis de Corny, Anne Mangeot (Mme Ethis de Corny): letters to, **11**: 509-10; **12**: 246-7; **14**: 37-8; **15**: 520; **16**: 289-90; letters from, **11**: 569-70; **12**: 551; **15**: 554-5; **17**: 259-61; failure to meet Mrs. Cosway in Paris, **10**: 542-3; introduced to Mrs. Adams, **10**: 557; invited to visit TJ's house, **11**: 268; acquainted with Marquise de Chambaraud, **11**: 269, 275; acquainted with Mrs. Cosway, **11**: 568; health of, **11**: 570; **14**: 37-8; concerned for husband, **12**: 539; TJ visits, **12**: 600; asks permission to visit TJ's daughter, **12**: 668; Mrs. Cosway's regard for, **13**: 116; reports TJ's plan to leave France, **13**: 391; meets Mrs. Church, **13**: 521; injured in carriage accident, **13**: 623; sends glass to TJ, **14**: 36; letter to quoted, **14**: 368n; and Martha Jefferson's romance with Randolph, **14**: 368n; **16**: 290; letters from cited, **15**: 568; **16**: 48, 550; TJ's farewell to, **16**: 289-90; household disrupted, **17**: 545; mentioned, **10**: 495; **11**: 269; **12**: 220, 502n, 645; **13**: 593; **14**: 554; **17**: 546; **18**: 358; **19**: 578

Ethis de Corny, Louis Dominique: letters to, **10**: 470; **11**: 165; **12**: 430-1; letter from, **11**: 170-2; and bust of Lafayette, **10**: 409n, 415; Shippen introduced to, **12**: 233n; health of, **12**: 539; **17**: 260; in carriage accident, **13**: 623; transmits Swan and Blackden proposals on flour and wheat for Paris, **13**: 659; **15**: 245-6; at fall of Bastille, **15**: xxxiii, 287-8; at Invalides to demand arms, **15**: 287; death of, **18**: 358; mentioned, **11**: 510; **12**: 551; **13**: 593; **14**:

454, 528n, 566; **15:** 520, 555; **16:** 290

Etorion (ship), **9:** 392

Etruscan language: derivatives, **11:** 254

Eubanks, John: in Albemarle co. militia, **1:** 665

Eubanks, William: in Albemarle co. militia, **1:** 665, 667

Euchee Indians, **9:** 641

Euclid, **20:** 331

Euler, Leonhard: and lunar tables, **8:** 73, 299

eunuchs: in Italy, **14:** 451

Eupen, Pierre Jean Simon van: heads aristocratic party, **16:** 220, 404; amnesty of, **18:** 86; fall of, **18:** 135, 354

Euripides: TJ seeks information on best Italian translation, **11:** 159; TJ urges Peter Carr to study, **12:** 18; *Tragœdiae*, **13:** 204; edition by Barnes, **13:** 240; works of, **13:** 300

Europe: U.S. trade with, **2:** 210; **7:** 334, 469n; **19:** 131, 135, 138n; commercial negotiation abandoned, **3:** 111; attitude toward U.S., **5:** 585; **7:** 250, 540, 542-3, 629; **8:** 461; **9:** 217-8, 380, 441; **11:** 400; **12:** 617; peace negotiations, **8:** 261; education in, **8:** 409-10, 412n, 636; **9:** 58-9, 60, 465; **11:** 299; TJ's opinions of, **8:** 569-70n; and possessions in America, **9:** 235; fauna and flora of, **11:** 70; ferment in, **12:** 117, 413; **18:** 295; politics of, **12:** 311, 447; **13:** 269; **17:** 593-5, 603-6, 627-30; in Russo-Turkish war, **13:** 124-6, 191, 215-6, 388, 404-5, 455, 458, 486, 489, 529, 531, 538; climate of, **13:** 397; and spermaceti candles, **19:** 129; and balance of power, **19:** 143; and the fisheries, **19:** 182-3, 193

European war: probability of, **2:** 30, 34; **7:** 501, 506, 509, 514, 515-6, 517, 518, 546, 559-60, 563, 566, 571, 577, 602, 607, 609-10, 636, 637, 639, 641, 643; **8:** 5, 39, 89, 119, 143, 145, 149, 196, 226, 228, 236, 237-8, 245, 252, 280, 287, 399; **10:** 613; **11:** 529, 533, 636, 641-2, 659-60; **12:** 31, 33, 34, 37, 70, 100, 108, 109, 110, 128, 131-3, 134, 145, 152-3, 160-1, 202, 205, 210, 214-6, 223-4, 226, 293, 339, 407, 464, 486, 486n, 568, 570, 571; **13:** 404-5, 555; **14:** 29, 623, 639, 645-6, 652-3, 661, 672, 677-8; **15:** 116, 121; **20:** 386; possible

effects of, **12:** 412, 424, 427, 490-1, 532; preparations for, **13:** 173-5, 191, 209, 212, 263, 288, 295, 360, 373, 378-9

Eusebius, Pamphili, bishop of Caesarea: cited by TJ, **1:** 553

Eustace, John Skey: letter to, from Jay, quoted, **16:** 8n; Vernes meets, **16:** 97n; plan for release of Algerian captives, **18:** 398

Eutaw Springs, battle of: Greene describes, **6:** 638; medal, **16:** xxxvii, 52 (illus.), 55n, 57n

Eutropius, **20:** 635n

Evans, Dr., **4:** 275, 411

Evans, Mr.: carries letter for TJ, **1:** 154-6; TJ offers bonds to, **11:** 15; and Cruse's patent for steam engine, **17:** 320

Evans, John: agent of Farrell & Jones, **15:** 649, 650, 653, 656, 657, 661-5, 668, 669, 673

Evans, Lewis: *General Map of the Middle British Colonies in America*, **6:** 601; **10:** 166, 201

Evans, Capt. Thomas: signs petition, **1:** 588; *Old Ballads, Historical and Narrative*, **11:** 523; imports slaves, **15:** 654; mentioned, **4:** 663, 691

Eveillé, L' (French ship): reported in Lynhaven Bay, **5:** 8; mentioned, **4:** 631n; **5:** 327

Eveleigh (Evely), Col. Nicholas: letter from, **4:** 153-4; draft of, **10:** 176; letter to, from Short, quoted, **10:** 514n; death of, **20:** 146, 220, 235-6, 417, 419, 555; as comptroller of treasury, **20:** 220; mentioned, **9:** 506

Eveleigh, Mrs. Nicholas: letter sent by way of, **16:** 544

Evelyn, John: *Terra*, **11:** 522

Evening Herald: sent to TJ, **9:** 131

Everard, Mr.: death of, **9:** 65

Everard, Thomas: signs nonimportation resolutions (1770), **1:** 47; witness, **1:** 67; mentioned, **1:** 91, 261; **3:** 262; **4:** 302; **5:** 35

Ewell, Capt. Charles, **4:** 539

Ewell, Maxcey: letters to, **17:** 599; **20:** 380; letters from, **17:** 584-5; **19:** 321-2; petition from, **5:** 349; correspondence with Madison, **18:** 617n; **19:** 322; financial claim of, **20:** 380

Ewell, Capt. Thomas W., **4:** 539

Ewing, James: fails to cross Delaware, **2:**

Ewing, James (*cont.*)
3; suggestions to Wolcott, **18**: 655-6; seeks treasury auditorship, **20**: 230n

Ewing, Rev. John: Pa. boundary commissioner, **3**: 77; as secretary of American Philosophical Society, **4**: 544; and newspaper quarrel with Rush, **8**: 52; recommends Andrew Ellicott as U.S. geographer, **19**: 40n; **20**: 61n

Ewing, Robert: letter from, **4**: 587-8

Ewings, Charles: express rider, **5**: 403

exceptions, bill of: Va. bill concerning, **2**: 640

exchange, bills of. *See* bills of exchange

exchange, rate of: between paper money and gold, **2**: 267; for state money, **5**: 607; decimal coinage, **7**: 201; U.S. and Britain, **14**: 296-7; mentioned, **6**: 270; **7**: 169-70

excise: definition of, **15**: 25; Hamilton's support of bill on, **19**: 38-40; Carrington's comments on tax, **20**: 99; Washington's view of tax, **20**: 100n; resistance to act, **20**: 560

excise, supervisors of: letter to, **19**: 363-4

execution of judgments: in Va. revisal of laws, **2**: 327; Va. bill concerning, **2**: 641-50; in different counties, **2**: 647

executive powers: in TJ's drafts of Va. Constitution (1776), **1**: 341-3, 349-51, 359-61; shared between governor and Council in Va., **6**: 281n; in TJ's draft of Va. Constitution (1783), **6**: 298-300; and committee of states under Confederation, **10**: 22-3; in states, **10**: 29; checks on, **11**: 410; in France, **15**: 337-8, 358-9, 365

executors and administrators: sureties, **2**: 327; Va. bills concerning, **2**: 394-405, 412-3

exercise: recommended to Peter Carr, **8**: 407-8; TJ comments on health and, **11**: 251

Expilly (Spilly), Count d': accompanies Algerian ministers, **8**: 465; **9**: 14; reception of American mission to Algiers, **8**: 573; **9**: 376; friendship for Carmichael, **9**: 244, 245; **10**: 149; **15**: 341; letter to cited, **9**: 248; Randall comments on, **9**: 284; letters from cited, **9**: 377, 407, 538; negotiates with Algiers, **9**: 378, 526, 529; aids American captives in Algiers, **9**: 530-1, 535, 620; **10**: 606; **11**: 118, 567; **12**: 173, 238; letters from quoted, **9**: 539n-40n; letters from, to Carmichael,

cited, **9**: 547, 566; relations with Lamb, **9**: 550, 620; **11**: 368; **12**: 238-9; advice on negotiating with Turkey, **9**: 590; **10**: 329, 396, 405, 536; knowledge of Algerian politics, **9**: 618; ransom of American captives proposed, **9**: 619; **10**: 150; returns to Algiers, **10**: 428; **11**: 133; Barclay's interview with, **10**: 510, 537; **11**: 21; recommends English consul in Algiers, **12**: 550; payments for Algerian captives, **14**: 502; **15**: 342n; mentioned, **9**: 246, 533; **12**: 181, 365

exports: via Bermuda, **1**: 239-40; restrictions on, **1**: 653; taxed in Va., **2**: 221; permits on, **2**: 376; U.S., **7**: 297; **8**: 308, 309, 621; **10**: 145-8; **19**: 136-8, 139; N.Y., **7**: 330; Conn., **7**: 334; Mass., **7**: 339-40; N.H., **7**: 345; agreement between U.S. and Prussia, **7**: 617; **8**: 27; S.C., **8**: 198-9, 201, 202-4; duty on proposed by Adams, **8**: 355; policy on suggested, **14**: 331. *See also* nonexportation agreements; treaties of amity and commerce; United States: Commerce

ex post facto laws, **6**: 281n

express posts: between Hampton and Williamsburg, **4**: 378; mentioned, **4**: 372; **5**: 45, 138

express riders: pay of, **2**: 371; **3**: 536, 541; **4**: 548, 552; duties of, **2**: 389; free ferriage provided, **2**: 462-3; between Richmond and Cape Henry, **3**: 404; to take news of arrival of French ships to Philadelphia, **3**: 418n; **6**: 107; suspected treachery, **4**: 39-40; TJ comments on, **4**: 115, 129; delays in reaching Congress, **4**: 128; difficulties in Va., **4**: 153; criticized by Gen. Nelson, **4**: 307; sent by Gen. Greene, **4**: 650; **5**: 138; for Gen. Gregory, **4**: 665, 674; accused of negligence, **4**: 699; abuses among, **5**: 72, 198, 226; offenders dismissed by Claiborne, **5**: 195; accounts of expenses, **5**: 252n, 446; from Lafayette's camp to Charlottesville, **5**: 645; mentioned, **3**: 431; **4**: 127, 381; **5**: 179. *See also* communications; postal service

extortion: Va. bill concerning, **2**: 521

extradition: Va. bills on, **2**: 478; **7**: 593-4; **8**: 93; provided in Articles of Confederation, **6**: 513-5; of Hancock demanded, **7**: 38-9, 260

eyes: diseases of, **11**: 164

house, **4**: 14n; killed at King's Mountain, **4**: 32n; describes campaign of 1780, **15**: 596

Ferguson, Robert, **3**: 514, 515

Fergusone, Capt.: permitted to change quarters, **4**: 15

Fergusson, James, **18**: 268 (illus.)

fern: as fruit preservative, **8**: 683

Fernán-Nuñez (Fernand-Nuguès), Carlos José, Count: letter to, **14**: 372; letters from, **12**: 242; **14**: 371-2; appointed Spanish minister of war, **8**: 83; appointed to Paris, **11**: 174; criticizes TJ, **15**: 355n; intervention in U.S.-Spanish relations sought, **19**: 528n, 530; conversations with Short, **20**: 364-5; mentioned, **12**: 365

Ferrara, Italy: Short in, **14**: 378

Ferreira, Antonio José: orders flour, **18**: 157; **19**: 309

Ferri, M., **9**: 279

Ferriere, Capt. John: commits barratry, **12**: 228, 249, 251; **14**: 82-3, 86

ferries: on Fluvanna river, **1**: 105; Va. bill concerning, **2**: 454-63; required for Gen. Gates' army, **3**: 582; in Rhine valley, **13**: 12, 16, 34n; and pendulum boat, **13**: 16, 34n

Ferrol, Spain, **13**: 114

Fersen, Axel, Comte de: and king's flight to Varennes, **20**: 605, 620

Fetyplace, Edward: signs petition, **19**: 226

Fevret de Saint-Mémin, Charles Balthazar Julien: physiognotrace portraits, **14**: xliv

Few, Mr. and Mrs., **15**: 430

Few, William: letters to, **12**: 49, 572-3; letter from, **10**: 280-1; attends Federal Convention, **11**: 401; presents congratulations to Washington, **16**: 168n; and diplomatic establishment, **17**: 218

Fez, Kingdom of, **10**: 359

Fiat, Marquis de. *See* Lafayette, Marquis de

fiction: TJ's remarks on, **1**: 76

Field, Capt., **5**: 513

Field, Henry: signs Virginia Association, **1**: 108

Field, Reuben: prisoner of war, **3**: 390

Field, Robert: signs petition, **6**: 290

Field (Fields), Lt. Theophilus: recommended as lieutenant in navy, **3**: 60; mentioned, **5**: 172

Fielding, Joseph: letter from, **15**: 528

Fierer, Charles: letter from, **18**: 348-50. *See also* Powell & Fierer

fieri facias, writs of: use in executions, **2**: 641, 642, 643, 644, 646

Fier Roderique (ship), **3**: 341, 376; **8**: 35

Fife, James Duff, second Earl of: letters from cited, **12**: 182

figs: sent to Eppes, **9**: 210; cultivated in southern France, **11**: 266, 647; in Marseilles, **11**: 428; in Toulon, **11**: 429; in Provence, **11**: 431; culture of, **11**: 433; **12**: 127; **13**: 263, 274, 369, 375; in Milan, **11**: 437; effect of altitude on, **11**: 650; trees ordered for S.C., **13**: 508; **14**: 183; **15**: 100, 101

Fille, M.: orange grove of, **11**: 430

Fillotte, M. de: vineyard of, **11**: 456

Filson, John: *Discovery, Settlement and Present State of Kentucky*, **7**: 568n; *Histoire de Kentucke*, **10**: 5n; **11**: 666

Finale, Italy: oranges grown in, **11**: 441

finance, public. *See* United States: Public Finance; Virginia: Public Finance

Fincastle (ship): Jamieson flees on, **16**: 522

Fincastle, Lord (son of John Murray, Earl of Dunmore), **18**: 313

Fincastle co., Va.: TJ's map of portion of, **1**: lviii, 567 (illus.); Mason claims lands in, **1**: 112; and Cherokees, **1**: 508; editorial note on division of, **1**: 564-69; division of, **1**: 569-76; **2**: 64n, 118n; appoints infantry officers, **1**: 580; militia, **2**: 131; omitted from senatorial districts bill, **2**: 336n; lead mines in, **2**: 388n

Finch, Sir Henry: cited on sodomy, **2**: 497n; cited on maiming, **2**: 498n; *Law, or, a Discourse Thereof*, **11**: 547

Finck, Jacques: letter from, **12**: 485-6

Findlay, Samuel: prisoner of war, **3**: 390

Findley, William: candidate for Congress from Pa., **14**: 473

fines: Va. bills concerning, **2**: 625-6, 627-8

Finguerlin, M., **11**: 463n

Finguerlin & Scherer: letter of credit for TJ, **11**: 184-5; mentioned, **11**: 211, 212, 257, 485

Finland: Swedish hostilities in, **13**: 472, 482, 491

Finley, William: loan to state, **3**: 386; mentioned, **3**: 442

Finney, Capt. William: arrest of, **4**: 358n, 499

Finnie, Col. William: letters to, **3**: 536, 544; TJ criticizes, **2**: 239, 244n, 299; employs workmen, **3**: 199; responsible for Convention troops, **3**: 257; commands expresses, **3**: 541; as deputy quartermaster for Va., **3**: 608; **4**: 48; makes payments, **5**: 300; debts of, **5**: 367, 482; mentioned, **3**: 8, 248, 406, 494, 496, 513, 526, 527, 536, 542, 646, 668, 669; **4**: 9, 10, 450, 470, 577; **5**: 577n

firearms. *See* arms

fire companies: Franklin establishes, **9**: 487

fire engines: in Paris, **8**: 574

fire ship: attempted use of at Quebec, **1**: 447

fish: southern Europe as market for, **2**: 210; U.S. export of, **7**: 339; **8**: 308, 309, 479, 515-6; **9**: 19, 50, 143, 145, 633; **10**: 146, 631, 633; **11**: 353; N.H. prepares for market, **7**: 346; prices of, **7**: 346; trade statistics on, **7**: 349; French bounties on, **9**: 11; French duties on, **9**: 11, 625; **11**: 317, 549; **12**: 468, 480; French production of, **9**: 141; in Rhine, **13**: 19; trade in salt, **18**: 371; consumption of promoted, **19**: 191; improved preservation sought, **19**: 191

fish bones: U.S. export of, **10**: 147

Fish creek: plan for western battalion at, **3**: 54

Fisher, Mr.: applies for clerkship with TJ, **15**: 528

Fisher, Daniel: letter to, **5**: 547; letter from, **5**: 531; letter to, from Kelly, quoted, **5**: 489n

Fisher, John: signs nonimportation resolutions (1770), **1**: 47; mentioned, **3**: 340

Fisher, Mier: *Brief of the Titles of Robert Morris*, **20**: 126n

Fisher, William: passport issued by TJ, **15**: 486

fisheries: in Declaration of Causes, **1**: 215; U.S. rights to, **3**: 63; and Treaty of Paris (1763), **6**: 213; and Definitive Peace Treaty, **6**: 243, 458; southern interest in, **7**: 48; Hogendorp's queries on, **7**: 296-7; in N.Y., **7**: 328-9; in Conn., **7**: 334; in R.I., **7**: 338; in Mass., **7**: 340-1; in N.H., **7**: 344, 345; profit to crew, **7**: 345; season, **7**: 345; Netherlands, **7**: 350; trade treaty stipulations, **7**: 471; French rights off

Newfoundland, **7**: 478; in France, **9**: 512; U.S., **10**: 33; **12**: 683; effect of rum and molasses duty on, **15**: 114; TJ queries Hancock on, **17**: 419-20; **19**: 173n; Coxe on, **18**: 62; **19**: 175-95; TJ's report on, **18**: 231; **19**: 140-237 (editorial note and documents), 425; Anthony's comments on, **19**: 196-9; U.S. vessels engaged in, **20**: 244. *See also* codfish; Newfoundland fisheries; whale fisheries

fishermen: protection of in enemy countries, **7**: 267, 486, 492, 622; **9**: 419, 426

Fishing creek: military post at, **3**: 259; mentioned, **8**: 125

fishing tackle: U.S. import of, **10**: 147

fish oil: U.S. export of to France, **8**: 222; **9**: 330-1; **10**: 146; **11**: 488; **15**: 46; **18**: 497, 503, 587, 604-5; **19**: 289-90; French duty on, **9**: 73, 76, 359-60, 582; **10**: 113; **11**: 488, 516, 540-1; **12**: 106, 163, 468, 480, 491, 595, 691; **13**: 72, 74, 95, 191, 195n, 250; **19**: 229; French regulations on sale of, **12**: 373; used for street lighting, **12**: 401. *See also* whale oil

Fisk, Jonathan: favors moving capital to Philadelphia, **19**: 20n

Fitch, John: letter from, **15**: 641-2; steamboat invention of, **11**: 561; **15**: 17, 80n, 82n, 641-2; Rumsey as rival, **15**: 17, 80n, 171; Crèvecoeur encourages, **15**: 80n, 641

Fitzgerald, John: letters to, **5**: 15; **15**: 587; letters from, **4**: 4-5; **5**: 311-2; receives guns from public foundry, **3**: 387; visits Mount Vernon, **10**: 535n; **11**: 390n; Washington recommends for appointment, **11**: 387-8; William Pearce recommended to, **20**: 314, 316n; relations with Thomas Digges, **20**: 317n; mentioned, **5**: 423; **6**: 25n; **16**: 491

Fitz-Gerald, Lord Robert: letter from, **15**: 129; letter from, to Martha Jefferson, cited, **15**: 512, 537

Fitzherbert, Alleyne, Baron (1753-1839): as British peace commissioner, **6**: 231; as British ambassador to Spain, **15**: 175; **16**: 254, 430, 586; **18**: 10, 473; and Spanish convention with Britain, **18**: 48

Fitzherbert, Maria Anne Smythe (Mrs. Thomas Fitzherbert): as mistress to Prince of Wales, **14**: 430

Fitzhugh, Mr.: recommended as commissioner of Federal District, **19**: 59; mentioned, **8**: 413; **9**: 658; **17**: 327

Fitzhugh, Daniel, Sr.: Weedon asks commission for, **5**: 109, 122; member Va. GA, **10**: 550; election to Va. HD, **15**: 621

Fitzhugh, Daniel and Theodorick: letter to, **9**: 27; letters from, **9**: 25, 657-8; depart America, **8**: 393, 584; **9**: 8, 27; **10**: 114; mail sent by, **8**: 452, 456, 534, 539, 540, 575, 585, 602, 603, 629; **9**: 91, 94, 95, 123, 211, 332, 349, 452, 466, 472; **10**: 166; **15**: 628; deliver diplomatic documents, **8**: 544, 606, 610n; financial problems of, **9**: 52, 59, 67, 333; **10**: 605; **11**: 154, 663, 665; mistreatment, **9**: 554; seeds sent by, **10**: 594; **15**: 621, 624, 631; passport issued by TJ, **15**: 484; mentioned, **8**: 8, 333, 452, 461; **11**: 483

Fitzhugh, William: letters to, **16**: 223; **17**: 241-3; letter from, **16**: 223n; TJ visits, **1**: 19; elected Va. delegate to Congress, **3**: 4n; federalism of, **15**: 5; Presidential elector from Va., **15**: 5; sells horse (Tarquin) to TJ, **16**: 223n; **17**: 241-2, 243n, 417, 418; correspondence with cited, **17**: 21n, 242n, 509n; **18**: 219, 509, 514; correspondence with quoted, **17**: 243n, 418n-9n; mentioned, **1**: 475; **17**: 243n

Fitzpatrick, John: signs Va. oath of allegiance, **2**: 129

Fitzpatrick, Capt. Patrick: payment for whiskey, **5**: 342

Fitzsimmons, Thomas: member of committee on public debt, **6**: 263n-5; member of committee on coinage, **7**: 153n, 155n; wins 1785 election, **8**: 672; Pa. member of Federal Convention, **11**: 400, 626; **12**: 231n; asked to support Baudin's appointment as consul at Ile de Ré, **12**: 433; congressman from Pa., **14**: 395, 473; **16**: 516, 517; and residence bill, **17**: 166-70, 173; consuls recommended by, **17**: 247, 250, 251, 254n-5n; opinion of Tench Coxe, **19**: 126; and the whale fisheries, **19**: 145; criticizes national bank, **20**: 602-3; mentioned, **12**: 302n; **18**: 237, 238n, 521, 634

Fitzwilliams, William Wentworth, second Earl of: Paine meets, **14**: 564

five-cent piece: proposed by TJ, **7**: 179; alloy, **7**: 181

five-per-cent tax. *See* impost

Fizeaux, Henri, & Cie.: letters to, **11**: 613; **12**: 420-1, 463, 471-2; letters from, **9**: 129; **11**: 5; **12**: 397, 421; seeks payment of U.S. debt, **11**: 24; **12**: 397, 417-8, 420-1, 421-2, 429, 432, 457-8, 463, 471, 472-3, 474, 485, 495, 506-7, 508-9, 510, 542-9, 566, 573-4, 623-4, 672, 674, 699, 700. *See also* Hogguer, Grand & Cie.

FizPatrick, William: signs petition, **1**: 588

flag-of-truce ships: in Chesapeake, **3**: 265; not permitted to carry merchandise, **3**: 308n, 327; and supplies for Convention troops, **3**: 318-9; **5**: 97-8, 302-3, 363, 400-1, 414, 511, 564-5, 635; in Westover affair, **4**: 330-1; **5**: 31, 98-9, 117-9, 250-1, 676n, 677n, 686-8, 697, 699; principle of, **4**: 669, 675n-7n; for American prisoners at Charleston, **5**: 243, 363, 400-1, 460, 606, 632-3, 634n; **6**: 20-1, 27, 42; sent by Riedesel, **5**: 257; to recover slaves, **5**: 424, 425n; prevention of abuse of, **5**: 625; passports for, **6**: 41; TJ suggests for voyage to peace conference, **6**: 231, 232, 234, 242, 251; mentioned, **2**: 299; **3**: 74; **4**: 15, 33-4, 46-7, 104-5, 160, 195, 624, 625n, 680, 688, 690-2; **5**: 27, 38, 39, 49, 180, 503, 509, 526-7, 573, 579, 588-92

flags: for French ships, **20**: 325-6

flags of truce: rules of, **5**: 445, 555; sought by Mrs. Sheed, **5**: 493

flagstaff: fastening of, with TJ's drawing, **13**: 8

Flamsteed, John: catalogue of stars, **8**: 299

Flanders. *See* Netherlands, Austrian

Flannagan, Wittle: signs Va. oath of allegiance, **2**: 129

flatboats: construction of, **4**: 241; **5**: 647n; for removing stores, **5**: 517

Flat Hat Club: called Society Spring, **1**: 32n

flax: Conn. export of, **7**: 336

flaxseed: U.S. export of, **7**: 334, 339-40, 345; **8**: 203; **10**: 147; **19**: 351-3; trade statistics, **7**: 349; French duty on, **12**: 469, 480

Fleeson, Plunket: affidavit quoted, **20**: 629n

Fleet, Mr.: and bill establishing ferries, **2**: 456

ish subdue British garrisons, **3**: 419; **7**: 570; position in regard to entering U.S., **6**: 121; Spain accedes to territorial limit, **6**: 265

Floridablanca, José Monino y Redondo, Conde de: letter from, **19**: 269-70; attitude toward U.S., **7**: 548, 549; **8**: 138; **9**: 378; **10**: 179; letters from cited, **7**: 650; **8**: 65, 80, 137, 138n, 320; **10**: 138, 178, 265, 310-1; **12**: 151, 204; audience with Barclay, **8**: 64; **9**: 245-8, 327, 348-9, 352; **10**: 537; aids American mission to Morocco, **8**: 83; **9**: 377, 384; **10**: 535; relations with Carmichael, **8**: 253, 464, 567; **10**: 607; **11**: 95; **12**: 177n; **13**: 113, 576; **16**: 329, 330n, 450-1; **19**: 254; instructions to Expilly, **9**: 244-5; **11**: 21; on relations with Naples, **9**: 546; health of, **10**: 266; **15**: 341; letter to Lafayette cited, **10**: 312; advice on treaty with Turkey, **10**: 329, 396, 405; views on treaty with U.S., **10**: 606; presentation of W. S. Smith to, **11**: 566; influence in Spanish government, **12**: 50-1; **14**: 500-1; **20**: 96; relations with England, **12**: 240; **13**: 216; **18**: 48; **20**: 700; letter from, to Zinovieff, cited, **13**: 114n; character of, **13**: 143; **20**: 532; relations with Netherlands, **13**: 239n; in Spanish political crisis, **13**: 578; sends d'Argès to America, **14**: 388n; letter to cited, **16**: 450; influence of Spanish exclusionary principles on, **16**: 557; attempted assassination of, **16**: 586; letter intended for, **18**: 242; and Humphreys' mission to Spain, **18**: 472-5; **20**: 538; sends instructions to Jaudenes, **19**: 509; on navigation of Mississippi, **20**: 95; mentioned, **8**: 252, 321, 465, 466; **11**: 236, 567; **12**: 100, 324, 362, 365; **18**: 597

Florus, Lucius Annaeus: Stirling's edition of, **11**: 523; mentioned, **20**: 635n

flour: Va. bills on, **2**: 348, 444-7; Congress permits exporting from Md. to Va., **3**: 100; purchased in Md., **3**: 171, 279, 303-4; cargo detained by Board of War, **3**: 231; for Continental army, **3**: 334, 363, 409, 511, 525, 609; **4**: 8, 9, 27, 220, 235, 239, 284, 375, 412-3, 419, 426, 449, 586; **5**: 101, 178, 189, 233, 253, 533; supplies of, **3**: 543, 550, 554, 670; **4**: 134-5, 147-9, 365, 565; **5**: 441, 452, 467; for Con-

vention troops, **3**: 573; **4**: 182; impressment of, **4**: 73; plans for inspection of, **4**: 227-8; price of, **4**: 481; **7**: 348; **14**: 585; **20**: 600; sent to prisoners at Charleston, **4**: 481; Pa. act removing embargo, **5**: 251; export to Haiti sought, **5**: 430; as exchange medium, **5**: 546-7; **6**: 9; imported by West Indies, **7**: 334; Conn. export of, **7**: 334, 335; trade, **7**: 349, 352, 454-5; Va. export of, **7**: 372; U.S. export of, **7**: 454-5; **9**: 19, 20, 61, 408, 411n, 426-8, 449, 633; **10**: 146, 147; **11**: 353; **14**: 646; French production of, **9**: 141; transport of, **10**: 104; L'Hommande proposal for manufacturing, **11**: 391; preservation of, **12**: 11; French duty on, **12**: 469, 480; French market for, **13**: 659; **15**: 104, 187n, 245-7, 249, 250-1, 255-6, 305n-6n, 315, 323, 327, 369, 386, 409-10, 425-6, 428, 460, 551, 565, 597; **16**: 7n; seized for French navy, **14**: 68; French bounty on, **14**: 551, 585, 622; **15**: 565; **16**: 7n, 18, 126; British market for, **15**: 146; export prohibited by R.I., **15**: 297; American government does not meddle with commerce, **15**: 311; Mirabeau proposes payment of U.S. debt in, **16**: 7n; Portugal prohibits U.S. exports, **20**: 710

flour mills: Ky., **8**: 129; Va., **10**: 262

Flower Gap, Va., **4**: 99

flowers: Cary seeks roots and seeds, **9**: 444

Floyd, Mr.: and bill establishing ferries, **2**: 454

Floyd, Catherine (Miss Kitty): Madison courts, **6**: 267, 333, 335, 336; marries William Clarkson, **6**: 335n; mentioned, **6**: 226, 251, 262, 265

Floyd, John: letters from, **4**: 199-200, 364-5; **5**: 465-8, 547-8; biographical note, **4**: 200n; appointed lieutenant of Jefferson co., **4**: 420-1; appointed colonel of Jefferson co. militia, **5**: 465; mentioned, **4**: 355; **5**: 439n, 493

Floyd, Sir John: defeated in India, **20**: 343

Floyd, Maria (Polly): letter to cited, **6**: 318; mentioned, **6**: 240, 273, 361n

Floyd, William: signs Continental Association, **1**: 153; signs Congress' second petition, **1**: 222; signs agreement of secrecy, **1**: 252; signs Declaration of Independence, **1**: 432; biographical note,

Floyd, William (*cont.*)
6: 240n; family, 6: 264; marriage of, 8: 438; and Hessian fly, 20: 447, 460; hospitality to TJ and Madison, 20: 449
Flucker, Thomas: claims against estate of, 19: 450
Flushing, N.Y.: visited by TJ and Madison, 20: 460
Fluvanna co., Va.: letter to commissioner of provisions for, 3: 568n; letters to county lieutenant of, 5: 443, 601-2, 616-7; letter to members of GA for, 5: 585-6; place of court of assize, 1: 630; created, 2: 15n; election writ issued to sheriff, 2: 24-5; Va. act for new court sites, 2: 121-2; militia, 2: 131; 3: 599; 4: 63, 295n, 352, 371, 477, 659; 5: 29, 35, 73, 310, 443n, 475, 501, 561, 601-2, 616-7, 646; 6: 119; opposition to draft in, 2: 175; senatorial district, 2: 336; levies of soldiers, 3: 8; defends western frontier, 3: 50, 51, 53; provision law in, 3: 486; tobacco loan office certificates, 3: 516; commissioner of provisions for, 3: 573; supply post for, 4: 286; arms, 5: 341; Marks' land in, 15: 94
Fluvanna river, Va.: ferry bill, 1: 105; post service on, 2: 389; ferries at, 2: 458, 459; mentioned, 2: 15; 6: 636
Fly (ship), 15: 578-80, 581n
"flying camp": on N.J. coast, 1: 467-8, 473
Folger, Capt.: master of the *Maryland*, 9: 391; master of *Harmony*, 20: 560; mentioned, 9: 299; 13: 227; 14: 183
Folger, Capt. Frederick, 3: 644
Folger, Capt. Robert (master of *Hudson*), 15: 303, 336
Foligno, Italy, 14: 381
Foljambe, Francis Ferrand: and plans to erect Paine's bridge, 14: 562, 564
Follenare, M. de, 9: 228
Folsom, Nathaniel: signs Continental Association, 1: 153; petition of, 6: 448-52
Folwell, Richard: in Reynolds case, 18: 647n, 675-7, 679, 684
Fombelle, M.: French translation of William Vaughan's book sent to, 15: 102-3; sends documents, 15: 182
Fondate, M. de: relations with Lucy Paradise, 13: 534; 15: 95; TJ agrees to meet, 13: 537
Fontaine, Rev. James: TJ recommends

as chaplain of Va. HB, 1: 23
Fontaine, Rev. John Maury, 8: 428; 12: 654
Fontaine, Nicolas Valentin: claim against S.C., 11: 300, 332
Fontaine, Col. William: absent from militia, 4: 443; procures horses, 5: 512; 15: 607
Fontainebleau: French court moves to, 8: 362; TJ describes, 8: 681; TJ visits, 9: 51n, 54; Short in, 13: 635
Fontaine de Vaucluse. *See* Vaucluse
Fontana, Félice, Abbé: letter to, 11: 111-2; works of, 3: 342; TJ presents works to American Philosophical Society, 6: 418; writings on air and fire, 7: 288
Fontenille, Fremyn de: letter to, 12: 265; letter from, 12: 258-9
food: Va. bill on selling, 2: 521-2; from France, 15: 375; 16: 322; for Monticello visit, 1790, 17: 321-2, 324. *See also* provisions
foot-bass, 10: 625
forage: shortage of, 3: 392, 483, 502; for army, 3: 500, 582; 4: 133; 5: 189, 480n-1n, 601; from wheat residue, 3: 609; at Shenandoah, 5: 100; mentioned, 4: 318, 508
foragemasters: pay of, 3: 583
Forbes, James: and western lands, 3: 628
Forbes, Gen. John: and establishing Fort Pitt, 2: 99
Forbis, Archler: signs petition, 1: 588
Forbis, William: signs petition, 1: 588
forcible entry: Va. bill concerning, 2: 655-6
Ford, Col.: quoted on embarkation of British troops, 2: 265
Ford, Mr.: letters sent by, 13: 137, 173, 184; mentioned, 4: 449; 9: 621
Ford, Col. Benjamin, 3: 620
Ford, Henry: signs Va. oath of allegiance, 2: 129; signs petition, 6: 290
Ford, Hezekiah: advised to seek hearing from Va. Council, 3: 65; defended by Arthur Lee, 3: 83; mentioned, 3: 87, 105
Ford, Milton: and Va. public works, 4: 425, 530; 5: 516; mentioned, 5: 580
Ford, Samuel, 4: 530, 578
Fordyce, Mr.: business failure of, 13: 210n
Foreign Affairs, U.S. Dept. of. *See* Department of Foreign Affairs, U.S.
foreign agents (U.S.): employment of, 7:

30, 63-4; trade treaty stipulations, **7:** 486, 623; **9:** 420; salary payment to, **11:** 475-6; **12:** 341
foreign correspondence: Va. bill establishing clerkship of, **2:** 181-2
foreign debt: transfer to Netherlands proposed, **13:** 127, 130-1, 556; **14:** 194, 195, 197-201; **15:** 472n-3n, 474-5; **17:** 425; speculation in, **13:** 319-23; **14:** 191-4, 531n; TJ's plan for funding, **14:** 189, 190-209 (editorial note and documents); S.C. ordinance on, **15:** 31-2, 32n-3n; TJ's estimate of, **15:** 411, 440, 443n; bill for funding in Congress, **16:** 316, 317n, 476, 536-7, 553; **17:** 25, 26, 162, 278-9, 319; transfer to Genoa proposed, **20:** 173n; Schweitzer, Jeanneret & Cie.'s proposal to purchase, **20:** 175-203 (editorial note and documents), 523. *See also* United States: Public Finance
foreign ministers (U.S.): authorized to make treaties, **6:** 468; and Committee of the States, **6:** 526; salaries of, **7:** 13-4, 426n, 512-3; **8:** 582, 664; **9:** 277-8; **14:** 610, 641-2, 644-5, 656, 681-3; **17:** 222-4, 229-31; attitude of Congress toward, **7:** 99; **11:** 483; secrecy of letters, **7:** 207; expenses of, **8:** 242n; **9:** 172; need of, **8:** 511; appointment of consuls by, **9:** 97, 127; immunity of, **11:** 495n-6n; payment of debts required, **11:** 544-5; Claiborne's recommendations on, **15:** 107-8; mentioned, **7:** 148; **12:** 103. *See also* consular establishment; diplomatic service (U.S.)
foreign ministers to U.S.: rights and immunities discussed, **6:** 276, 368
foreign service. *See* consular establishment; diplomatic service (U.S.)
foreign trade. *See* trade; treaties of amity and commerce
Foreman, Mr.: and bill establishing ferries, **2:** 455
Forest, Mr., **9:** 364n
Forest, The (Wayles estate), **1:** 74
forestalling: of clothing from France, **2:** 194; Va. bill to prevent, **2:** 561-6
forests: in Germany, **13:** 25; in France, **13:** 26
forfeiture of property: in TJ's drafts of Va. Constitution of 1776, **1:** 353; bills for applying, **2:** 56; in Ireland, **2:** 60; of enemy aliens, **2:** 279-85; and widow's dower, **2:** 503
Forgarson, Peter: signs Va. oath of allegiance, **2:** 129

giance, **2:** 129
forgery: Va. bill concerning, **2:** 507-10; impossibility of using polytype for, **10:** 321n; of letter from TJ, **15:** 142n
Forgurson, John: signs nonimportation resolutions (1770), **1:** 47
Forgurson, William: signs nonimportation resolutions (1770), **1:** 47
Forli, Italy, **14:** 380
Formidable (ship): at Gosport, **16:** 427
forms, legal: Pendleton desires simplification of, **2:** 266
Fornier (Fournier), Feliz Joseph: boards at Ginter's, **3:** 616
Forrest, Col. Uriah: letters to, **7:** 452; **12:** 475-9; **16:** 489-90; letters from, **7:** 435-6; **11:** 60; **12:** 416-7, 436; letters to be sent through, **8:** 615; letter from cited, **12:** 384; letter to cited, **16:** 312n; letter from quoted, **16:** 429n; consular appointment recommended, **17:** 254n; signs petition of Georgetown landowners, **17:** 471; signs landholders agreement, **20:** 85n; seeks treasury comptrollership, **20:** 226, 230n; mentioned, **8:** 358; **17:** 465, 466n
Forrest & Stoddert: letter from, **16:** 428-9; letter from cited, **16:** 312n
Forrester, Capt. (master of the *Good Hope*), **12:** 599
Forster, Capt. George: and the Cedars affair, **1:** 397-404, 451, 452, 459; **10:** 380
Forster, Israel: signs petition, **19:** 226
Forster Frères: claims against U.S., **6:** 398; **7:** 269-70, 496; **11:** 593
Forsyth, Alexander: captured by Algerians, **14:** 397n; **20:** 625; ransom of, **17:** 32; on crew of *Maria*, **19:** 333
Forsyth (Foresyth), Maj. Robert: letter to, **3:** 537-8; as deputy commissary general to southern army, **3:** 494; **4:** 352, 374; **5:** 59; and provisioning of Convention troops, **3:** 542, 581-2; **4:** 369; letter to, from Dudley Digges, **3:** 554; letter from, to agent superintending state supplies, **4:** 182-3; as deputy quartermaster for Va., **4:** 209, 338, 351, 513, 521-2, 533; Carrington criticizes, **4:** 492n; **5:** 576; mentioned, **4:** 8, 181, 577, 598; **5:** 196n
Fort Chartres, Northwest Territory: map of, **18:** 205n, 215
Fort Edward, N.Y.: visited by TJ and Madison, **20:** 453-6, 458

forte-piano. *See* pianoforte

Fortescue, Sir John: works by, **16:** 277

Fort George, N.Y.: visited by TJ and Madison, **20:** 458, 465, 466

Fort Henry: Cherokee treaty with Virginia, **6:** 141n

fortifications, prehistoric, **10:** 584-5

Fortin, Jean Baptiste: bequest of, **8:** 584n

Fortin, Joseph: suit to recover French inheritance, **8:** 371, 533-4, 541, 583, 598, 625; **9:** 123

Fortis, Alberto: *Viaggio in Dalmazia*, **13:** 656

Fort Island, **2:** 34

Fort McIntosh, treaty of, **19:** 585

Forton, John: signs petition, **1:** 588

Forton, Thomas: signs petition, **1:** 588

Forton, Zackary: signs petition, **1:** 588

Fort Point, Va.: ferry at, **2:** 457, 463

Fort-Royal, Martinique. *See* Martinique

Fortunatus: TJ wishes for cap of, **10:** 627

Fortune (ship), **7:** 533, 576

Fossard, France: Short in, **13:** 635

Fosset, William: in Albemarle co. militia, **1:** 666

Fossetts, William: signs Va. oath of allegiance, **2:** 129

Fossier (Fusieu), M.: draws prehistoric animal, **14:** 504, 505n

fossils: G. R. Clark promises to procure, **6:** 159, 204; sent to England, **6:** 208; found on Ohio river, **9:** 477; uncovered in French shell-pit, **11:** 460, 461; in Siberia, **11:** 638

Foster, Mr.: TJ declines invitation of, **2:** 275n; and drilling apparatus, **16:** 370, 448; mentioned, **11:** 457

Foster, Abiel: letter from, **8:** 60; letter from, to Weare, quoted, **6:** 452n, 454n; N.H. delegate in Congress, **7:** 572; mentioned, **6:** 452n

Foster, James: TJ's accounts with, **10:** 614

Foster, Sir Michael: cited on treason, **2:** 493n, 495n

Foster, Robert: prisoner of war, **3:** 391

Foster brothers. *See* Forster Frères

Foster, William, & Co.: owners of the *Maria*, **8:** 440, 610n

Fothergill, John: and Franklin's negotiations with Britain, **18:** 94n-5n

Foucault, Mme de: family of, **13:** 120n

Foulis, Andrew: catalogue of sent to TJ, **1:** 38; type used by, **11:** 45; Greek authors published by, **12:** 632

Foulke, Mr.: testifies about Maj. Hughes, **1:** 473-4

Foulke, Dr. John: and balloon experiments, **7:** 246

Foulke, Capt. Joseph (master of the *George and Patty Washington*), **10:** 189

Foulloy, M.: letters to, **13:** 308-9, 323-4; letters from, **13:** 313, 316; and Deane's letter books, **13:** 224n, 308, 323, 469n; **14:** 364n, 523, 606, 631-2, 658; **15:** 4

Foulon (Foullon), Joseph François: in ministry, **15:** 279, 280, 286; killed by mob, **15:** 300-1, 302, 314, 316

Fourcroy, Antoine François de: *Elémens d'histoire naturelle et de chimie*, **11:** 665; **12:** 18, 31, 130, 136, 144; **14:** 533-4; chemical nomenclature, **14:** 366

Fourmile creek: British encampment at, **4:** 259, 263

Fournier, Daniel: *A Treatise of the Theory and Practice of Perspective . . . by Dr. Brook Taylor*, **10:** 384

Fourqueux, Michel Bouvard de, II: as minister of finance, **11:** 316, 338, 345; **12:** 153; resigns, **11:** 346, 356

Fourth of July. *See* Independence Day

Foushee, Mr.: and bill establishing ferries, **2:** 460

Foushee, William, **3:** 498; **4:** 272; **5:** 590

Foushee, Dr. William: appointment approved, **3:** 439; to receive cavalry equipment, **4:** 343, 344; services requested, **4:** 473; house burned, **11:** 209; mentioned, **3:** 440, 619; **4:** 47, 486

Fowey (British ship), **4:** 399

Fowle, Daniel: supports American state papers series, **1:** 145

Fowler, Mrs., **7:** 87

Fowler, Henry: in Albemarle co. militia, **1:** 668n

Fowler, Samuel: in Albemarle co. militia, **1:** 668n

Fowler, Theodosius: public contractor, **19:** 444

Fowler, William: case of, **8:** 662; **9:** 32-6

Fowlkes, John: Baptist enlisted in army, **1:** 662

Fox (ship), **12:** 402, 419, 449

Fox, Mr.: and bill establishing ferries, **2:** 456, 460; letters sent by, **9:** 47; **10:** 87

Fox, Charles James: Laurens' opinion of, **6:** 275; ministry of falls, **6:** 568; **7:** 3, 6, 8, 12, 16, 31, 41, 42; opposes Pitt

ministry, **7**: 93; **18**: 309n; **20**: 556; attitude toward U.S., **7**: 102; **8**: 59n; relations with the Prince of Wales, **7**: 121; **14**: 430; political prospects, **7**: 293; **13**: 462; **14**: 186, 454; TJ fears ministry of, **10**: 202; speech against Hastings, **12**: 606; quarrels with Sheridan and Duke of Portland, **14**: 482; illness of, **14**: 519; criticized, **14**: 665; dispute with Burke, **16**: 259; encourages war with Spain, **16**: 427; and Gouverneur Morris, **17**: 97, 98, 100, 101n; Madison compared to, **20**: 436, 573; mentioned, **16**: 414; **18**: 523
Fox, Edward: letter to, **6**: 431; letter from cited, **6**: 538
Fox, George C.: letter sent by, **20**: 327
Fox, George C., & Sons: letters from, **18**: 42, 48n; letter to, from Johnson, cited, **18**: 50
Fox, Samuel: introduction to TJ, **8**: 220; Rush recommends, **8**: 653; stay in Paris, **11**: 317
Fox, Samuel M.: passport issued by TJ, **15**: 484
foxes: weight of, **6**: 343
Fox Indians: support G. R. Clark, **2**: 258
Foy, Edward, **1**: 289
Fraissmet & Cie.: letter from, **14**: 509
Fraize, M. (Fraise), **12**: 483, 494
Fraizer, John: killed, **5**: 96
Framery, Mr.: letter from, **13**: 116; letter from, to J. P. Jones, cited, **13**: 581, 582n
François, Cape. *See* Cape François
François l'Union (ship), **10**: 129
Franc, M., **11**: 463n
FRANCE: relations with Indians, **6**: 61, 62; **7**: 440, 445; bones of prehistoric animals found in, **7**: 312; rivers, **7**: 405; cost of trip to, **7**: 559; climate, **8**: 160; naturalization procedures, **8**: 513; TJ outlines essay on, **8**: 637n-8n; TJ advises T. M. Randolph, Jr. to study law in, **10**: 307; plan of travel for T. M. Randolph, Jr., **12**: 21-3; TJ tours, **13**: 26-33, 36n; TJ's travel hints, **13**: 271, 273-5; hailstorm as disaster, **13**: 486-7; militia, **15**: 279, 280, 287, 294-6, 300, 366

Army
at Brest, **11**: 517, 533; troops sent to East Indies, **13**: 173, 175, 191; mob attacks, **15**: xxxiii, 273, 275, 280, 287, 300; condition of, **15**: 196-7,

FRANCE (*cont.*)
272; **20**: 672-3; refuses to fight against citizens, **15**: 221-2, 267-8, 271, 294; marches toward Paris, **15**: 267, 273, 285-6, 299; wears revolutionary cockades, **15**: 294; Swiss troops in, **15**: 333, 358, 364; as civil weapon, **15**: 338; reorganization proposed, **16**: 302; officers oppose Revolution, **20**: 549. *See also* French Army in American Revolution; French officers in American Revolution

Assembly of Notables
convocation of and Estates General, **14**: 47, 48, 52, 186, 188, 212, 414; nobles and clergy oppose third estate, **14**: 276, 277, 287, 305, 329-30, 333, 343, 374, 386, 422-3, 431; opposes Calonne, **14**: 421; Necker advises, **14**: 422

Colonies
queries concerning U.S. trade with, **9**: 134-5; commercial advantages of, **9**: 631-2; *droits d'aubaine* abolished in, **17**: 431-3, 618, 641; **18**: 353, 452, 604; **19**: 258, 362, 539, 635-6. *See also* Guadeloupe; Martinique; Saint-Domingue; West Indies, French

Constitution
TJ and, **13**: 486, 489, 492, 506, 538-9; **15**: 291, 298, 326-7, 354n-5n; **16**: 296; **18**: 119; plans for, **14**: 366, 370, 677; charter of rights suggested, **15**: 165-7, 167-8; National Assembly proposals, **15**: 268-9, 317, 358-9, 366, 424, 425, 426; veto in, **15**: 354, 355n; powers of king under, **16**: 333-4, 375; National Guard supports, **16**: 506-7, 508n; delay in finishing, **17**: 613; Franklin's name used symbolieally to support, **19**: 80-1; Moustier comments on, **20**: 263; Arnoux and Chalut comment on, **20**: 423-4; completed, **20**: 684; presented to king, **20**: 712. *See also* Declaration of Rights (France)

Economy
effect of paper money on trade, **5**: 383n; restrictions on West Indian trade, **7**: 351-3; **10**: 83; trade with the Orient, **7**: 354; **9**: 458n; fishery rights off Newfoundland, **7**: 478; manufactures, **7**: 511; **10**: 303; use

FRANCE (*cont.*)

of Iberian ports, **8**: 70; commercial policy, **8**: 332; **19**: 162n, 164; agriculture, **8**: 335-6, 553; **9**: 445; **11**: 283-5; **13**: 26-32, 654; prohibition on British manufactures, **8**: 341; orders against importation of foreign manufactures, **8**: 361; trade treaty with Britain, **8**: 361-3; **9**: 447; **11**: 66, 78; **13**: 54n, 584; orders against British imports, **8**: 444; exports, **9**: 614; market for oil, **10**: 140; and exportation of wines, **10**: 486; merchant marine, **11**: 265; commerce, **12**: 649-50; marine council proposed, **12**: 682; trade with Ireland, **13**: 278

Estates General

plans for calling, **12**: 37, 350, 352, 448; **13**: 126, 174, 190, 263, 359, 458, 464, 483, 486, 492, 580, 633, 642; **14**: 47, 48, 186, 366, 370, 421-2, 432, 452, 463, 531, 623, 655, 661, 671, 689; **15**: 51; enquiry on, **12**: 482; financial situation, **12**: 682; TJ's comments on, **13**: 126, 263, 406, 441, 455, 489; **14**: 188-9, 213, 330, 375, 423, 597, 604, 605, 616, 639, 661-2, 676-7, 689; **15**: 105, 111-2, 122, 126, 136-41, 149, 188-91, 195-7, 205-10, 221-3, 224, 266-9, 271-2; order of Aug. 8, 1788 convoking, **13**: 499-500, 501n, 506; composition of, **13**: 538, 649-50; **14**: 212-3, 276, 277, 287, 305, 343, 374, 417, 422-3, 604, 616, 623, 639, 671; **15**: 334; Necker depends on, **13**: 565; Crèvecoeur comments on, **14**: 28-9, 414, 416; La Métherie's tracts on, **14**: 327n; third estate **14**: 329-30, 333-4, 386, 422-3; **15**: 105, 136, 138, 140, 141, 196, 213, 222-3, 267; vote by orders or by persons, **14**: 333-4, 376, 422-3, 432, 531, 623, 652, 661, 671, 677, 689; **15**: 105, 111-2, 116, 122, 126, 136-41, 188, 195-6; clergy and nobles threaten schism in, **14**: 374-6, 386, 431; representation of three estates equalized, **14**: 374-6, 422, 431, 444, 482, 676-7; Necker reports to king on, **14**: 376, 432, 443, 482, 689; Marseilles deliberates on, **14**: 410; **15**: 45; and legislation on whale fisheries, **14**: 443, 447; Paine

FRANCE (*cont.*)

comments on, **14**: 564; elections, **14**: 623, 638-9, 653, 655, 667, 671; **15**: 24, 30, 58; economic legislation of, **14**: 652, 661-2; **15**: 112, 136, 138, 140, 189, 196, 267; British attitude toward, **14**: 665; opening, **15**: 87, 91, 104-5, 111-2, 126, 139; lower clergy may join with third estate, **15**: 105, 111-2, 122, 136-41; nobles, **15**: 105, 110, 111, 122, 126, 188-9, 196; conflicting interests in, **15**: 111-2, 188-91, 195-7; meets in common chamber, **15**: 136, 138, 140, 166, 182, 191, 195-6, 206, 222, 266-7, 271, 299; in charter of rights, **15**: 167-8; motion on constitution of assembly, **15**: 189, 191; Saint-Domingue deputies in, **15**: 190, 221, 380n, 536; clergy in, **15**: 196, 206, 208; changes name to National Assembly, **15**: 197, 267-8; meets in church of St. Louis, **15**: 206, 209n-10n; meetings suspended, **15**: 206, 267; tennis court oath, **15**: 206, 267; moves to Paris, **15**: 289

Finances

public finance, **5**: 380; **11**: 182, 184, 259, 357, 363, 549, 660, 664; **12**: 67; money, **7**: 164, 165, 194; rate of exchange, **7**: 201; coinage, **8**: 90; regulates value of gold and silver, **9**: 137; financial affairs in Netherlands, **9**: 635, 636; **10**: 116, 153; **13**: 129-30; **14**: 613n, 646, 647n; **15**: 550, 565-6; taxes, **12**: 32, 34, 37, 39, 40, 152; **14**: 366, 370, 375, 376, 386, 421-3, 431-2, 677, 689; **15**: 44; subscription to loan, **12**: 564; crisis in, **13**: 499-500, 529-30, 564-5, 633; **14**: 421; **15**: 208, 209, 358, 457, 458; **16**: 199-200, 235, 260, 269; gold and silver standards, **15**: 26; Necker proposes reforms in, **15**: 111; Estates General and, **15**: 112, 136, 138, 140, 189, 196; loan proposed, **15**: 340n, 358, 364-5, 369, 373, 440-1, 457, 501, 503, 513n; Necker proposes converting *caisse d'escompte* into national bank, **15**: 549; **16**: 33, 42, 43-4; contribution from clergy proposed, **16**: 43; labor as direct tax, **16**: 132; *gabelle* abolished, **16**: 233, 374, 505-6; tax reforms proposed, **16**: 269-70, 505-6;

FRANCE (*cont.*)

Lafayette, **12:** 460; criminal law reformed, **13:** 189; civil war threatened, **13:** 373, 406; despotism moderated in practice, **13:** 405-6, 441-2; Moustier on, **13:** 505; **14:** 22n; Washington on, **13:** 555, 557; in British newspapers, **13:** 572-3; Carmichael on, **13:** 576-7; Paine reports on British attitude toward, **13:** 589; Crèvecoeur on, **14:** 28-9, 414, 416; Price on, **14:** 38-9; Shippen on, **14:** 517; Paine rejoices at progress of, **14:** 564-5; republicanism, **14:** 704n; **20:** 576-7, 585, 610, 648, 650; judicial powers, **15:** 337-8, 359, 365; **16:** 280-1, 302, 403, 420; powers of government, **15:** 337-8, 365; Short on, **15:** 547-50, 559; **16:** 3-8, 33-4, 42-7, 49-51, 86-7, 103-7, 119-24, 130-5, 160-1, 163-5, 199-202, 219-22, 234-6, 267-70, 302-4, 333-4, 371-6, 401-3, 420-1, 436-9, 508n, 571-3; **17:** 311-4, 413-5, 523-8, 555-7, 610-9, 639-42; **18:** 84-5, 114, 351-3, 451-2, 501-7, 604-6; elections of Protestants, Jews, and actors in, **16:** 44-5; Vernes on, **16:** 95-8; Littlepage on, **19:** 419. *See also* French Revolution

Society

British subjects in, **6:** 435; abjectness of people, **7:** 502; use of influence, **7:** 546; TJ on, **8:** 239, 404, 405n; **10:** 600; **13:** 307; conditions of, **8:** 568-9; **9:** 659-60; division of wealth in, **8:** 681-2; Mrs. Adams comments on, **9:** 54-5; compared to England, **11:** 262; frivolity of, **11:** 174; Abbés Arnoux and Chalut comment on, **11:** 303; discontent in, **12:** 32, 34, 37, 67, 117, 151, 442; religion, **12:** 557; **16:** 371-3, 376n; emigration from, **12:** 673; spoiled by politics, **13:** 150, 151; women in, **13:** 151-2; **14:** 330; winter of 1788-1789, **14:** 305, 343, 358-9, 363, 371, 377, 409, 429, 444, 446, 464, 483, 653, 656; **15:** 43; Mrs. Paradise comments on, **15:** 282

U.S. Relations

commercial alliance with urged, **1:** 288; attitude toward U.S., **1:** 310; **3:** 202; **4:** 525; **8:** 228, 423-4, 513, 656; **9:** 50, 569; **10:** 135, 406, 520;

FRANCE (*cont.*)

11: 96, 482-3, 595, 636; aid to U.S., **1:** 313; **2:** 126, 269; **3:** 405, 465, 474, 555, 574-5, 577, 663; **4:** 524, 576, 600; **6:** 39, 81; **7:** 138; **10:** 381, 383n; **12:** 141; American commissioners to, **1:** 521-4, 576-7; **2:** 126; treaty with sought, **1:** 522-3; alliance with U.S., **2:** 176-7, 221, 289; **3:** 33, 116, 117-8; U.S. treaty of amity and commerce, **2:** 176-7, 221, 289; **7:** 305, 308-9, 471-3, 494, 638; **8:** 266, 497-8, 577, 605, 608, 625-6; **9:** 42, 188; **12:** 424; **17:** 431-2; effect on West Florida of alliance with U.S., **2:** 260; Va. Assembly ratifies treaty with, **3:** 10, 11-2, 16; dislikes resolutions of Congress, **3:** 413; ready to sign Definitive Peace Treaty, **6:** 338; supplementary treaty with sought, **6:** 396; **7:** 269; instructions to Franklin regarding, **6:** 398; discussed, **7:** 269, 289, 291, 467n-8n, 597; **11:** 131n, 263; **12:** 248, 662-3; **13:** 106, 409n-11n; **15:** 366-7; **17:** 437; **18:** 239-43, 257, 277-8, 282; **19:** 258, 532; U.S. attitude toward, **7:** 307n; **10:** 386; **12:** 225; TJ's notes on treaty with, **7:** 471-3; aids U.S. in negotiations with Barbary States, **8:** 20-1, 62, 474; interest in American west coast, **8:** 373-4; minister to U.S. sought, **8:** 383; and Mezières case, **9:** 107-8, 122, 143, 144; attitude toward British surrender of western posts, **9:** 195, 326; inhabitants granted property rights in Ga., **9:** 259; Lamb desires intervention with dey of Algiers, **9:** 550; U.S. minister plenipotentiary to, not ambassador, **10:** 370. *See also* consular convention; Gérard, Conrad Alexandre; La Luzerne, Anne César; Mississippi river: right of navigation; Moustier, Eli Elenore François; Ternant, Jean Baptiste

U.S. Trade with

importation of goods from, **3:** 372; facilitates American trade with other nations, **3:** 413; debt due from Va., **3:** 551; discussed, **7:** 350, 352, 380; **8:** 354-5, 369, 385-93, 402, 444, 458, 512-3; **9:** 107, 112, 139, 141-3, 145, 458n-61n, 470-1, 474, 501-

FRANCE (cont.)

2, 627, 643, 650; **10**: 15, 145, 262, 465-6, 474-6, 484-5, 487, 493, 504, 517, 541, 579, 589, 590-1, 602-3, 612, 629; **11**: 25, 96, 153, 345, 516-7, 524, 539-42, 614-8, 627-9; **12**: xxxvi, 82-93, 118, 141-3, 162-3, 259, 263-5, 299-303, 352, 354, 366, 367-9, 385-6, 389, 399, 419, 443, 466-71, 479-82, 487, 492, 494, 497, 511-2, 516-7, 564, 570, 621n, 637, 648, 667, 683; **13**: 52-91, 191-2, 194n-8n; **14**: 331, 336-7; **16**: 259; **17**: 610-1, 617; **18**: 15-22, 503; **19**: 129, 161, 258, 345, 597; **20**: 366; tobacco import from Va., **7**: 368-9, 370; **8**: 650-3, 660, 666-7; trade wih S.C., **8**: 200, 201, 202-3; **12**: 301; exchange of tobacco for imports from, **8**: 213-4, 220-4, 244; U.S. payments, **8**: 287; protests American interference with commerce, **8**: 686; **9**: 43, 50, 110; rice import from U.S., **12**: 250; act of Council of State to encourage commerce with U.S., **12**: 468-70; regulates American vessels, **12**: 582; *Mémoire pour des négocians de l'Orient, intéressés au commerce des Etats-Unis, contre la ferme générale*, **13**: 51n, 54n-6n, 75-91; "Rapport sur le commerce des Etats-Unis de l'Amérique avec la France," **13**: 53n-4n, 57-75; order on (Dec. 29, 1787), **13**: 191, 194n, 451-2; **19**: 571; order on (Feb. 23, 1788), **13**: 194n-6n, 197-8, 451-2; regulations for entry of ships, **13**: 526; Washington on, **13**: 557; manufactures encouraged, **14**: 252-4; Bondfield reports on, **14**: 549-51; Higginson on, **14**: 599-602; to India and Mauritius, **14**: 599-602; proposal to limit trade with French colonies, **15**: 506; Moustier describes advantages of, **17**: 642; La Motte on, **18**: 51; and U.S. commercial policy, **19**: 129; order to encourage trade with U.S. (Dec. 29, 1787), **19**: 229; statement of U.S. vessels entering French ports, 1789, **19**: 233; G. Morris' observations on, **19**: 347-50; France proposes new treaty of commerce, **20**: 529, 547, 642-3, 651. *See also* tobacco trade; whale fisheries; whale oil; wheat

France, King of. *See* Louis XVI, King of France

Francfort, John. *See* Frankfort, John

Franche-Comté: opposition of nobles in, **14**: 597, 604, 615

Franchi, Peter de: letter from, to Robert Morris, **20**: 628-9; recommends Culnan for consular appointment, **20**: 628-9

Francis (TJ's servant): moves from New York to Philadelphia, **17**: 596, 597, 598n; payment to, **20**: 420; mentioned, **17**: 495, 518, 554; **20**: 555

Francis, Mr., **13**: 227

Francis, Richard: *Maxims of Equity*, **11**: 548

Francis, Tench, **5**: 704

Francy (Francey), Jean Baptiste Lazarus Théveneau de: negotiations on shipment of tobacco to France, **3**: 14, 315, 331, 376; **4**: 582; Smith recommends to TJ, **3**: 15; contracts with, **3**: 199, 268, 329, 372-3; **4**: 524; funds expected, **5**: 308; as agent of Beaumarchais, **7**: 553; **8**: 35

Frankfort, Germany: Trumbull describes, **10**: 438; TJ remarks on, **13**: 17-8, 266; fair at, **13**: 48; Rutledge in, **13**: 318, 454

Frankfort (Francfort), John: claim to prize money unwarranted, **9**: 130, 153, 156, 162-3

Franklin (independent state of): status, **8**: 287, 684; founding of, **8**: 483, 508; relationship with N.C., **8**: 659; **11**: 147; independence, **9**: 176, 186; admission to Confederation, **10**: 28; population grows, **12**: 426; proposed admission to union, **20**: 703; mentioned, **8**: 218-9, 280

FRANKLIN, BENJAMIN: letters to, **1**: 404; **2**: 26-7; **6**: 126, 216-7; **7**: 310-1, 424, 425-6, 427, 428, 434-5, 436-7, 437-8, 444, 533, 547, 550, 551, 553-4, 560-1, 565-6, 575-6, 580, 606, 612-4, 616-28, 629, 632-3, 649-50; **8**: 8-9, 303-4, 585-6; **9**: 232-3; **10**: 247-8, 624-5; **16**: 283-4; letters from, **5**: 610; **6**: 194; **7**: 546-7; **8**: 282, 308, 571; **9**: 349-50; **10**: 437; **11**: 301-2; **12**: 236-7, 596; **14**: 36; **16**: 326; letters to cited, **6**: 126; **8**: 34; **15**: 82n; **18**: 96n; letters from cited, **7**: 12, 15, 31, 41, 59, 227, 229, 250; **8**: 69, 209; **10**: 210; **11**: 570; **13**: 296; **14**: 482; **16**: xxxiv-v, 284n; **18**: 96n; letters from

FRANKLIN, BENJAMIN (cont.)
letters sent through, **9**: 271; leaves
Boston for New York and Philadelphia, **9**: 486; marriage, **9**: 486; voyage to England, **9**: 486; doctorate in
Britain, **9**: 487; death of son, **9**: 487;
visits France, **9**: 487; and Philadelphia Public Library, **10**: 38; news of
sent to Mme d'Houdetot, **10**: 66;
and Wednesday evening discussions,
10: 250; copy of Turgot biography
sent to, **10**: 354, 397, 404; books
sent to, **10**: 622, 642; **12**: 270; **14**:
369; **15**: 429, 436, 494; purchases
wine, **12**: 24; recommendation of
Dal Verme, **12**: 43n; butler's claim
against, **12**: 485-6; death of rumored, **12**: 642, 647, 657, 660,
680; La Blancherie's publication
sent to, **13**: 116; interest in cotton
manufacture, **13**: 153, 154n; printing and bookselling interests, **13**:
309; papers, **13**: 394; **17**: 590, 591;
18: xxxviii-ix, 87, 88n-97n; bills of
exchange paid by, **13**: 430; printing
and bookselling interests, **14**: 32;
and Society for Political Enquiries,
14: 50n; medal, **14**: 588; **16**: xxxv,
xlii, 65n, 69n, 70, 73n-5n; advises
TJ, **14**: 621; bust by Houdon, **15**:
xxxvii-viii, 457 (illus.); brochures
for, **15**: 470; uses copying press, **15**:
608, 609n; buys books for TJ, **15**:
615; last letter to TJ described by
Bache, **16**: xxxiv, 326n; map sent to
TJ, **16**: xxxiv-v, 52 (illus.); **18**: 86-
7, 96n; Société de quatre vingt neuf,
membership proposed, **16**: 133;
Vaughan's account of mutiny on the
Bounty sent to, **16**: 274, 276; TJ
visits, **16**: 292, 298, 306; death of,
16: 364, 369, 388, 578; Manasseh
Cutler describes, **19**: xxxiv-v; silhou-
ette of by Joseph Sansom, **19**: xxxiv-
v, 348 (illus.); recommends Andrew
Ellicott as U.S. geographer, **20**:
61n; books for College of Philadelphia, **20**: 432; purchases property in
France, **20**: 689; Philadelphia residence, **20**: 713

Political Career
and plan for imperial union, **1**: 166n;
proposed Articles of Confederation
(1775), **1**: 177-82; **6**: 517n; **7**: 33;
and draft of Declaration of Causes,

FRANKLIN, BENJAMIN (cont.)
1: 187n; signs Congress' second petition, **1**: 222; and Va.-Pa. boundary
dispute, **1**: 234; consulted on plan
for Bermuda, **1**: 238; appointed Indian commissioner, **1**: 245n; signs
agreement of secrecy, **1**: 253; participates in preparing Declaration of
Independence, **1**: 306n, 313, 404,
414n, 427n-8n, 432; president of
Pa. Convention, **1**: 466n; **15**: 577;
proposes U.S. seal, **1**: 494; and
statue of Washington, **7**: 378, 385,
567, 600; **9**: 150; consulted by TJ
on McClenachan case, **7**: 452; postal
convention proposed to, **8**: 45; presidency of Pa. Executive Council, **8**:
420, 562, 581, 672; **9**: 10, 96, 172,
180; bust for Va. Capitol suggested,
9: 267; delegate to Congress, **9**:
488, 497; connection with Putnam's
claim, **10**: 351; delegate to Federal
Convention, **11**: 310, 400, 626; **12**:
39, 43, 231n; speech on Federal
Constitution, **12**: 229-30, 233n; retirement announced, **13**: 262; **14**:
482; as possible vice president, **13**:
502, 531; and Passamaquoddy Bay
boundary dispute, **16**: xxxiv-v, 52
(map), 283-4; **18**: 86-7, 96n

Scientific Interests
influence on American Philosophical
Society, **4**: 544, 545n; **9**: 131, 320;
invents cylinder lamp, **7**: 518; cited
on relative humidity of cities, **8**:
186; subscribes to *Encyclopédie
Méthodique*, **8**: 263; **9**: 224, 482; **10**:
247, 249, 624, 625; **11**: 657; **12**:
236; **14**: 345, 370; **16**: 581; encourages textile manufacturing, **8**: 377;
brings Icelandic crystal to Philadelphia, **9**: 356; interest in polytype,
10: 318n-9n; engraving experiments, **10**: 324n; title of doctor, **10**:
370, 375n; seeds for, **10**: 641; observations on hygrometer, **10**: 646;
11: 72-5; **13**: 395, 396; **15**: 134;
aids English workman in making
wheel with single-piece circumference, **11**: 43-4; memoir of Turin
Royal Academy of Sciences requested for, **11**: 468; relations with
Ingenhousz, **12**: 191-2; **15**: 119; pa-
tronizes Rumsey, **13**: 346; **15**: 80n,

and papers sent by, **8**: 578, 654; **10**: 418, 509, 536, 618; **11**: 286; in Paris, **8**: 603, 610n; **11**: 97; relations with Carmichael, **8**: 623; **10**: 538; Spanish passport asked for, **8**: 657-8, 670; mission to Morocco, **9**: 152, 187; **11**: 582-5; letters to cited, **9**: 523, 524; **16**: 159n; leaves Cadiz, **9**: 648; returns to France, **10**: 404; at Barclay's interview with Expilly, **10**: 537; exchange of treaty by, **10**: 557; sends Moroccan treaty, **10**: 637, 649; settles accounts, **11**: 20; coins sent by, **11**: 30, 100; recommendations to Congress, **11**: 78; sends perspective machine, **11**: 90; introduced to Limozin, **11**: 127; and death of Vergennes, **11**: 313; loses box, **11**: 365; sends acorns, **11**: 650; and ciphers, **12**: 177n, 178n; **13**: 91, 95n, 142, 176; passport issued by TJ, **15**: 483, 484, 485; applies for position as TJ's secretary, **16**: 158; mentioned, **6**: 240; **8**: 547, 549, 572; **9**: 128; **10**: 314, 549; **11**: 68, 91, 121, 145, 383; **12**: 619

Frank's Tavern: Innes' position at, **5**: 532

Franque, F.: drawings of Pentemont, **14**: xl, 360 (illus.)

Fraser, Lieut., **4**: 359

Fraser, Charles Henry: letter from cited, **12**: 363; as possible British minister to U.S., **20**: 146

Fraser, John: letters from, **15**: 47-8, 296; and grass, **12**: 655n; **15**: 48n; discovers plants, **14**: 278; introduced to TJ by Limozin, **14**: 390; sends seeds, **15**: 47-8, 296; biographical note, **15**: 48n; *Short History of the Agrostis Cornucopiae*, **15**: 48n; mentioned, **3**: 542n; **14**: 427

Fraser, Gen. Simon, **1**: 498

Fraser (Frazier), William: confers with Adams and TJ, **9**: 406; mentioned, **8**: 302; **9**: 375; **18**: 226

frauds: Va. bills to prevent, **2**: 412-3, 444-7; punishment, **2**: 502

Fraunces, Andrew G.: and charges against Hamilton, **17**: 358n; **18**: 658, 658n-9n, 687n-8n; in Reynolds case, **18**: 630, 641n, 642, 656, 678; dismissed from Treasury, **18**: 656, 658n; in Glaubeck case, **18**: 687n

Fravel, Mr., **7**: 396

Frazer, Lieut.: appointment of, **2**: 5

Frazer, Miss: religious conversion of, **12**: 596

Frazer, John Grizzard: Monroe pays rent to, **7**: 241; Franklin introduces to TJ, **12**: 596; letters sent by, **14**: 467, 514

Frazer, William: letter to, **4**: 69; mentioned, **5**: 656

Frazier, Lieut.: deserter, **5**: 214

Frazier, Nalbro: part owner of *Canton*, **13**: 4n

Frazier, Phoenix: signs petition, **11**: 336

Frazier, William: and bill establishing ferries, **2**: 454, 458

Fredenheim, Carl Fredrik: excavations in Roman Forum, **14**: 453n

Frederick II, King of Prussia (Frederick the Great): relations with U.S., **2**: 30, 200, 209; **7**: 465n, 609; **8**: 314, 478; **12**: 450; relations with Austria, **2**: 215; **8**: 196, 252; Nathanael Greene studies, **5**: 570n; replies to Empress of Russia, **6**: 389, 437; Steuben claims service under, **6**: 623n; efforts toward improving river navigation, **7**: 6; quoted, **7**: 466n; attitude toward Bavarian exchange, **7**: 641; **8**: 39, 42; Voltaire criticizes, **8**: 89; permits Col. Smith to attend manoeuvres, **8**: 654n; interferes in Netherlands, **9**: 151; peace of Europe dependent on, **9**: 217, 233; illness of, **9**: 447, 465, 466, 468, 469, 470, 475, 580, 635, 636; **10**: 111, 115, 153, 224, 241, 246, 247, 251; arrangements with successor, **10**: 153; death of, **10**: 314, 317, 399, 405, 473; TJ seeks copy of *Mémoires pour servir à l'histoire de la maison de Brandenbourg*, **11**: 666; *Oeuvres posthumes*, **14**: 366, 367n, 437-8, 478-9, 485, 697; **15**: 114; *Oeuvres complètes*, **16**: 321

Frederick VI, Prince of Denmark: military ambitions, **17**: 628; meets with J. P. Jones, **19**: 590

Frederick, Md.: Convention troops at, **3**: 650-1; **4**: 70-1, 95, 100, 109, 160, 181-2, 248, 299; **5**: 97, 240; lack of barracks at, **4**: 92, 93, 95; glass factory near, **14**: 547

Frederick, Prince of Brunswick: leads army, **14**: 47; marries Princess of Orange, **17**: 542, 601

Frederick Augustus, Duke of York.

Frederick Augustus (*cont.*)
See York and Albany, Frederick Augustus, Duke of
Frederick co., Va.: letters to county lieutenant of, **3**: 601-3; **4**: 231, 627-8; **5**: 254-5, 403-4; letter to quartermaster of, **4**: 232-3; appoints infantry officers, **1**: 580; place of court of assize, **1**: 630; grand jury in, **1**: 638-9; militia, **2**: 131; **3**: 422, 598, 599, 643; **4**: 59, 63, 234, 573; **5**: 253, 254-5, 309n, 310, 329n, 383, 432n, 475, 501, 556, 561, 638n, 646, 661-2; **6**: 84, 93; construction of barracks at, **2**: 300; senatorial district, **2**: 336; levies of soldiers from, **3**: 6-7, 8; defends western frontier, **3**: 50, 51, 53, 420; **4**: 235, 627-8, 629, 653; **6**: 11, 12; tobacco loan office certificates, **3**: 516; beef supplies in, **4**: 46; and support of Detroit expedition, **4**: 575; discontent over taxes, **5**: 219; riflemen expected from, **5**: 644; county lieutenant of, **6**: 67n
Frederick Court House, Va.: time of holding court of assize, **1**: 628; proposed meeting of school overseers at, **2**: 530
Fredericksburg, Va.: Committee of Revisors meet at, **2**: 314n, 325-8, 405n; ferry at, **2**: 456; rendezvous of recruits at, **3**: 7, 181, 283, 351, 360; **4**: 401, 686; gun factory at, **3**: 199, 281, 617n; **4**: 119, 304, 327-8, 430-1, 549-50; **5**: 11, 355, 410-1, 517; hospital at, **4**: 242, 680; military supplies at, **4**: 285, 286, 491; **5**: 343, 472; defense of, **4**: 346, 347, 364, 376-7, 383, 398, 399, 448; **5**: 446-8, 451, 454, 483; entrenching tools to be made at, **5**: 87, 270; iron works at, **5**: 241, 446-8; importance of, **5**: 447; Lafayette arrives at, **5**: 553; possible objective of British, **6**: 26; Hunter's works at, **6**: 41; TJ ships articles to, **6**: 204, 219; competes with Norfolk for trade, **7**: 215; place of court of assize, **7**: 589; Monroe's residence at, **9**: 511; **10**: 457
Fredericksville parish, Va., **2**: 15n
Frederick William II, King of Prussia: character, **10**: 153; **16**: 263; interest in Stadtholder, **10**: 605, 613, 624, 629, 634; **11**: 42, 476, 490; attitude

towards Austria, Russia, and Britain, **10**: 650; **11**: 47; **14**: 429; importance in European situation, **11**: 127; letter to, from Mirabeau, cited, **11**: 572; resents insult to sister, **12**: 33, 34, 37, 41, 51; Smith comments on, **12**: 147; relations with France, **12**: 152; **13**: 125; relations with Poland, **12**: 215; **14**: 443, 661; **16**: 304; withdraws troops from Netherlands, **12**: 482; visits Guelderland, **13**: 220; views on Russo-Turkish war, **13**: 565; sends army toward Holstein, **14**: 46, 47; TJ characterizes, **14**: 48-9; **15**: 50, 460; relations with Sweden, **14**: 654, 672; changing attitude of, **15**: 110, 121; relations with Britain, **15**: 141-2; payment from Netherlands demanded, **15**: 441; in Flanders revolt, **16**: 41; **18**: 609; relations with Austria, **16**: 96, 404; **18**: 608; **20**: 695; in Reichenbach conference, **17**: 395, 439; in Silesia, **17**: 522; Humphreys comments on, **17**: 594-5; seeks cession of Danzig and Thorn, **18**: 294; and affair of Liège, **19**: 118; and the fisheries, **19**: 178; sultan desires to know intentions of, **19**: 418; Ephraim's letters to, **20**: 649, 654
Frederika Sophia Wilhemina (Princess of Orange): and letter to King of Prussia, **11**: 697, 701; stopped on way to The Hague, **12**: 33, 34, 37, 41, 51; avenge of insult to, **12**: 202, 243, 324n, 333n; marriage of, **17**: 542, 601
Frediani, Nicolao Lucchese: proposes mercantile venture to Va., **9**: 668, 669; letter to, from Giannini, cited, **16**: 319, 320n
"Free Citizen, A": quoted, **18**: 613
freedom of conscience. See conscience, liberty of
freedom of religion. See religion, freedom of
freedom of the press. See press, freedom of
freedom of the sea: trade treaty stipulation, **7**: 473; TJ on, **12**: 164-5
Freeland, James, Jr.: relations with Mary Williams, **6**: 152; estate of, **6**: 155-8
Freeland, James, Sr.: estate of, **6**: 155-8
Freeland, Mace: case of, **6**: 151-8; TJ's

statement and opinion of case, **6**: 152-4; petition to Va. executive, **6**: 155-6; petition to Va. HD, **6**: 156-8

Freeman, Capt.: horses of unsold, **20**: 245n

Freeman, Capt. John (master of the *Friendship*), **7**: 554

Freeman, Richard: *Reports of Cases in Law and Equity*, **20**: 375

Freeman, S.: portrait of Patrick Colquhoun, **18**: xxxv, 268 (illus.)

Freeman's Journal: Hopkinson criticizes, **9**: 131

free ports: in West Indies, **7**: 348; **8**: 608; **9**: 632; in Europe, **7**: 473; in France, **8**: 142, 370n; TJ's interest in, **9**: 643; needed for rice shipment to France, **12**: 263; mentioned, **7**: 338

free trade: and colonial rights, **1**: 123, 172; G. Morris argues for, **7**: 351; reciprocal agreement between U.S. and Prussia, **7**: 625; TJ's theory of, **8**: 94n-5n; Jay on prospects with France, **13**: 106. *See also* commerce: freedom of trade

freight carriage: Hogendorp's queries on, in U.S., **7**: 297; N.Y., **7**: 330; Conn., **7**: 335; Mass., **7**: 341; N.H., **7**: 345; Pa., **7**: 347, 348; British restrictions on, **7**: 468n; **8**: 40, 43; agreement with Denmark on, **7**: 480; agreement with Prussia on, **7**: 617, 624-5; **8**: 27, 28-9, 135; American vs. British, **7**: 634-5; **8**: 460-1; **9**: 472; **11**: 264; agreement with Tuscany on, **8**: 105-6, 188-94; S.C., **8**: 199; importance, **8**: 216; agreement with Britain on, **8**: 274; TJ comments on, **8**: 426; and American ships, **8**: 479; agreement with Portugal on, **9**: 63, 413, 424, 426-8; U.S., **11**: 353; **12**: 254-5, 481; and American advantage in European war, **12**: 210; and British ships, **12**: 234; West Indies, **12**: 451, 454-5

Freire, Cypriano Ribeiro, Chevalier: friendship for U.S., **15**: 131; Mrs. Paradise praises, **15**: 165; **16**: 197, 198n; **17**: 240; appointed Portuguese minister to U.S., **17**: 12, 213-4, 240, 394, 482, 606; **18**: 103-4; **19**: 320; mentioned, **15**: 130

Frejus, France: TJ describes, **11**: 431

French, Col., **9**: 486

French, George: letter from, **3**: 100

French, N. & P., & Nephew, **11**: 362

French, P. & V., & Nephew: letter to, **8**: 291-2; letters from, **8**: 244; **10**: 301; and Barclay, **11**: 466, 479, 495n-500n, 504-6, 508, 534-7, 626, 669, 670; **17**: 480; **20**: 239; mentioned, **1**: 519; **7**: 579; **11**: 365

French, Samuel: Baptist army officer, **1**: 662

French, Valentine: insults Barclay, **11**: 535

French and Indian wars: role of Six Nations in, **2**: 99; capture of Fort Duquesne, **2**: 101

French Army in American Revolution: lands at Shrewsbury, N.J., **2**: 206, 208; lays siege to Savannah, **2**: 233; sent to America, **3**: 378-9, 382, 383, 395-6, 411, 419; **15**: 602-3; provisioning, **3**: 383; **4**: 141; TJ seeks aid of in southern campaign, **5**: 421-2; second division to America, **6**: 80-1; Franks considers service in, **7**: 587; French disregard for, **10**: 247

French Broad (Equoam) river, **4**: 360

French commodore. *See* Destouches, Charles René Dominique Sochet, Chevalier

French East India Company. *See* East India Company, French

French in America: murdered in British raid on Portsmouth, **3**: 113-4; in Va., **3**: 162-6; Congress recommends privileges and immunities for, **3**: 264; in western territory, **3**: 276; **4**: 387, 390n; **6**: 579, 661; **7**: 511; **8**: 121; **19**: 19; in New Orleans, **7**: 404; in S.C., **12**: 299

French language: Martha Jefferson learns, **6**: 543; Peter Carr urged to learn, **8**: 408, 410; at Prussian court, **8**: 431; study of in U.S., **8**: 459; **11**: 557; **12**: 491; **16**: 89; study of in France and Canada, **15**: 204

French loan. *See* France: Loan to U.S.

French merchant ships: captured by British, **2**: 265; exemption for, **5**: 170

French Navy in American Revolution: letters to officer in command of squadron in Va. waters, **5**: 25-6, 55-6, 194; strength of, **2**: 30, 209; arrives in America, **2**: 204; **3**: 375-6, 378-9, 382, 383, 395-6, 411, 419, 490, 527, 549, 651, 654, 663; **4**: 6, 15, 105, 124, 146, 543; **5**: 49; **15**: 602-3;

fruit trees (*cont.*)
grown in Germany, **13**: 17, 24, 25; grown in France, **13**: 28, 32-3; planting of, **16**: 194
Fruzel, John: signs nonimportation resolutions (1770), **1**: 47
Fry, Henry: votes for bill for religious freedom, **2**: 549n
Fry, Joshua: in Albemarle co. militia, **1**: 664; votes for bill for religious freedom, **2**: 549n; map of Va., **4**: 41; **7**: 113; **9**: 300; **10**: 213; **11**: 519; in Va. GA, **8**: 113; **9**: 522n; **10**: 109; land sold to E. Randolph, **16**: 27; daughter marries, **16**: 139n
Fry, William: signs Va. oath of allegiance, **2**: 129
Führer (Fearer), Capt.: German prisoner in American Revolution, **14**: 487, 489n; **16**: 551
Fulgham, Charles: and bill establishing ferries, **2**: 457
Fuller, Mr.: orders rice from Jamaica, **14**: 674
Fumel, Philibert Henri, Marquis de: letter to, from Montmorin, cited, **11**: 496n-7n
Fumelle, Comte de: wine ordered from, **13**: 96, 171
funding of foreign debt. *See* foreign debt
Fundy, Bay of: and the Definitive Peace Treaty, **6**: 458; British pretensions to, **10**: 293
Funk, Jacob: lays out Hamburg, **20**: 6n
Fuqua, Joseph: and bill establishing ferries, **2**: 460, 461
fur: as medium of exchange, **3**: 317; U.S. export of, **7**: 334, 339-40, 345; **8**: 412; **10**: 147; **11**: 353, 617; Canadian duties on, **7**: 460; imported by Portugal, **9**: 19; imported by France, **9**: 112, 141; **11**: 41, 169, 617; imported by Sardinia, **11**: 353; French duties on, **12**: 156, 469, 480. *See also* fur trade
furloughs: not given by TJ, **4**: 594, 605
Furniss (Furness), Robert: petition of, **6**: 448-52
furniture: manufactured in Conn., **7**: 336; TJ's drawings of, **13**: 8, 22-3; TJ orders, **15**: 546-7; **16**: 475; **17**: 322, 327, 378n, 488; **18**: 591-2. *See also* Jefferson, Thomas: Personal Affairs
Fürstenberg (Ferstenbourg), Karl Egon, Prince von, **17**: 664
fur trade: treaties on, **7**: 48; statistics on,

7: 349; British interest in, **7**: 440; **9**: 569; **18**: 254-5; in Canada, **7**: 460; **8**: 78; in Ky., **8**: 129; **11**: 412-3; French interest in, **8**: 588; **9**: 582-3; **10**: 531-2; **11**: 385-8; and British posts, **11**: 387; **18**: 292, 293, 297-8; Parker recommended for handling, **12**: 322; in Far East, **12**: 379; in Alexandria, Va., **14**: 548
fusils. *See* muskets
Fusina, Italy: Short in, **14**: 312
fustic: U.S. import from West Indies, **10**: 148
Fynje, Mr.: and funds for swords and medals, **8**: 157; property in America, **8**: 655. *See also* Geyer, La Lande and Fynje; Lalande and Fynje

gabelle: debate on abolition of, **16**: 505-6
Gabriel, Don (Infante of Spain): marriage of, **8**: 95, 137, 321; on Barclay's mission, **9**: 365; daughter born to, **12**: 324
Gaceta de Madrid, **10**: 428
Gadsden, Christopher: letter from, **12**: 295-7; signs Continental Association, **1**: 154; signs Congress' second petition, **1**: 223; signs agreement of secrecy, **1**: 253; as Presidential elector from S.C., **14**: 666; **15**: 51; mentioned, **1**: 286; **15**: 579, 580
Gaelic language: TJ desires to learn, **1**: 97, 101-2
Gage, Thomas: and Mass. Bay proclamation, **1**: 142; and siege of Boston, **1**: 174-5, 196-7, 210, 217; mentioned in Declaration of Causes, **1**: 201-2, 209, 216; reportedly appointed governor general of America, **1**: 247, 249; substituted for Hutchinson, **10**: 369, 374n; mentioned, **1**: 248; **7**: 307n
Gaillet, M.: vineyard of, **11**: 422
Gaine, Hugh: paid by Department of State, **17**: 368
Gaines, Capt., **5**: 571
Gaines, Col. Daniel (?): TJ recommends to Steuben, **4**: 555
Gaines, Francis: in Albemarle co. militia, **1**: 668n
Gaines, Frank: works for TJ, **13**: 341
Gaines, Hierom: TJ owes for labor, **13**: 341-2
Gaines, Humphrey: in Albemarle co. militia, **1**: 666; mentioned, **2**: 175n
Gaines, Richard: in Albemarle co. mili-

tia, **1**: 667; pledges to support clergy-man, **2**: 7; signs Va. oath of allegiance, **2**: 129

Gaines, William: in Albemarle co. militia, **1**: 664

Gaines, Capt. William Fleming: gallantry at battle of Camden, **3**: 637

Gains, Heron: signs Va. oath of allegiance, **2**: 129

Gale, Capt., **3**: 91

Gale, George: letter to, **19**: 363-4; in Md. Constitutional Convention, **13**: 334; votes on compromise of 1790, **19**: 4n; and capital site bill, **19**: 18n

Galiffet, Marquis de: Col. Wuibert at residence of, **11**: 40

Galitzin (Gallitzin), Dimitri II, Prince: as Russian ambassador at Vienna, **13**: 427

Gall (de Gall), Gen. von, **2**: 255; **3**: 304, 322

Gallasby, David: signs Va. oath of allegiance, **2**: 129

Gallatin, Albert (Abraham Albert Alphonse): Tronchin's account of, **9**: 209n; slaying by Indians reported, **9**: 236n, 651; **10**: 182-6, 189, 221; letter from cited, **16**: 617n; letter to cited, **18**: 311n; opinion of Tench Coxe quoted, **19**: 126n; favors Potomac capital site, **20**: 4-5; *A Synopsis of the Indian Tribes . . . in North America*, **20**: 451

galleys: sale of, **3**: 9, 20, 331; sinking of the *Caswell*, **3**: 20; dismantling approved, **3**: 42n; abandoned on Eastern Shore, **4**: 599; in Chesapeake Bay, **5**: 22; for use in Portsmouth expedition, **5**: 75, 130; for state navy, **5**: 627

Gallimard, M.: letter to, **13**: 430-2; letter from, **13**: 303; plans for moving to America, **13**: 303; TJ sends Franklin's pamphlet to, **13**: 430-1

Gallipolis: French emigrants in, **18**: 162, 173-4, 176, 204, 206n

Gallois de la Tour, Charles Jean Baptiste des: captured, **15**: 322, 323

Galloway, John: with British army, **1**: 659

Galloway, Joseph: signs Continental Association, **1**: 153; in favor in England, **8**: 302; Franklin leaves papers with, **18**: 88n; letter to, from Franklin, quoted, **18**: 95n

Gallwey, John: letters from, **15**: 57, 383; Carnes recommends as substitute, **14**:

588-9; letters to cited, **15**: 43n, 371n

Galt, Mr., **4**: 480; **5**: 431

Galt, Gabriel: death of, **14**: 530; **15**: 50

Galt, Dr. John: appointed army surgeon, **4**: 429n; mentioned, **3**: 345, 515

Galvan, Maj. William: letter to, **3**: 399-401; sent to receive French fleet, **3**: 375-6; instructions to, **3**: 404; assisted by TJ, **3**: 432; return to Philadelphia, **3**: 618, 624; mentioned, **3**: 434, 494; **5**: 638n

Galves, Señor (Spanish minister to Berlin): Carmichael recommends, **10**: 138, 287

Galvez, Countess: exiled, **18**: 474

Gálvez (Galvis), Bernardo de: letter to, **3**: 167-70; letter from, **3**: 482-3; and Florida campaign, **3**: 419; **4**: 199; **5**: 551; **6**: 80

Galvez, José de, Marqués de Sonora: letter from cited, **7**: 433; consulted in treaty between Spain and U.S., **8**: 138; goes to Havana, **11**: 236; death of, **11**: 512, 567; **12**: 179n

Gambier, Adm. James, **2**: 208

Gambill, Henry: petition from, **5**: 349

Gambill, Matthew: petition from, **5**: 349

Gamble, Maj. James, **7**: 96, 242

Gamble, Robert: letter from, **5**: 5; on Davies, **5**: 205n; letter from, to Steuben, quoted, **5**: 557n, 581n; mentioned, **4**: 473, 532; **5**: 459n

gambling (gaming): Va. bill on, **2**: 559-61; Currie's discontinuance of, **8**: 641

game: sent to St. Barbe, **7**: 384; TJ attempts to import, **7**: 429; **8**: 17; French, **8**: 682, 683; German, **13**: 18

Gamelin, Antoine: settlement of account, **3**: 327; journal cited, **17**: 132n

gaming. *See* gambling

Ganander, Hendrik: *Grammatica Lapponica*, **15**: 223

Gannett, Caleb: certifies TJ's election, **16**: 112n

Garamond type: TJ's interest in, **11**: 45

Garat, Dominique Joseph, **15**: 169

Garbier (Gerbier), Thibert: letter to, **11**: 111-2

Garbutt, Richard: on Albemarle co. militia roll, **1**: 667

Garcilaso de la Vega, the Inca: *Comentarios reales de los Incas del Peru*, **11**: 554; *La Florida del Inca*, **11**: 554, 668

Garde-Meuble, Hôtel du: TJ on, **8**: 164; **20**: 86

ter from cited, **8**: 325
Garvey, Robert & Anthony: letters to, **10**: 269, 588-9; **11**: 55-6, 88-9, 501; **12**: 7, 95, 323, 366, 374; letters from, **11**: 26-7, 38, 67, 506, 607; **12**: 53-4, 327, 337, 366-7; parcels consigned to, **10**: 189; makes shipments, **10**: 248; mentioned, **10**: 206, 211, 223, 471; **11**: 625
Gascq, M. de: letter from, **11**: 112-6
Gaskins, Thomas: letters from, **4**: 693; **5**: 164-5, 430; house burned by British, **5**: 425, 430; battalion of, **6**: 75; mentioned, **5**: 592n, 667n; **6**: 31n, 54n, 634
Gastelier, René G.: letter to, **11**: 111-2
Gaston, Don Miguel, **3**: 306
gates: TJ's drawing of in Brittany, **11**: 459; TJ's drawing of in Düsseldorf, **13**: 14
Gates, Elizabeth Phillips (Mrs. Horatio Gates), **3**: 501; **6**: 110-1, 139
Gates, Gen. Horatio: letters to, **3**: 526-7, 549-50, 637-8, 658-9; **4**: 9-11, 39-42, 57, 77-8, 96, 108-9, 127, 206, 637-8; **6**: 138-9; **7**: 225, 571; letters from, **1**: 501n; **3**: 495-7, 498-9, 501, 524-5, 573-4, 604-5, 620-1, 646-7, 650, 662-3, 668-9; **4**: 5-6, 13-4, 16-7, 23-4, 32, 37-8, 44, 49-50, 53, 86-7, 91-2, 103, 501-2, 559; **6**: 110-1, 130; **7**: 396-8; appointed adjutant general, **1**: 175, 477, 478, 479; and Canadian campaign, **1**: 296n, 499, 500, 520; letter from, to Congress, quoted, **1**: 498-500; joins northern army, **2**: 29; victory at Saratoga, **2**: 34, 37-8; commands southern department, **3**: 438, 441, 486, 531, 537, 564, 650; **4**: 6, 8, 58, 60, 76, 81, 183; supplies for, **3**: 451, 513, 528, 582-3, 592, 644-5; **4**: 448; needs troops, **3**: 485, 539; **4**: 153; correspondence with Washington, **3**: 489, 502, 638; defeated in battle of Camden, **3**: 558-9, 576, 593-7; **6**: 111n, 139n; intends to send Va. militia to Guilford, **3**: 563; criticism of, **3**: 576, 656; letter from, to J. Mathews, cited, **3**: 585; letters from cited, **3**: 589, 593, 606, 650; **4**: 7, 23, 38, 53, 67; letter from, to Harrison, cited, **3**: 641; letter from, to T. S. Lee, cited, **3**: 648; letter to cited, **4**: 13; quoted, **4**: 37n-8n, 87n, 178n; letter from, to Huntington, cited, **4**: 67, 68; on treatment of prisoners, **4**: 84, 98-9, 178; letters to, from Weedon, cited, **4**: 94; letter from,

to Stevens, cited, **4**: 125, 126, 129; orders Senf to make observations, **4**: 169; money due, **4**: 637; Greene replaces, **5**: 23n; TJ recommends for Va. Executive Council, **6**: 549; visits Philadelphia, **7**: 62; and negotiations on navigation of Potomac, **7**: 589, 591; recommends Williamos, **8**: 270n; Houdon desires to sculpt, **8**: 289; medal commemorating, **9**: 77; **11**: 231, 233, 240, 280, 315, 343, 345, 356; **16**: xxxvi, 52 (illus.), 54n, 55n, 56n, 59n-61n, 63n, 64n, 67n, 69n, 70, 73n, 75n, 76n; bust for Va. Capitol suggested, **9**: 267; letter of introduction for Castaing, **10**: 81; resides in Va., **10**: 370, 375n; recommends Gordon, **11**: 172; favors Constitution, **13**: 98; mentioned, **3**: 663, 665; **4**: 43, 62, 65, 83, 92, 112, 217, 220; **5**: 356, 390-1; **6**: 71n; **7**: 357
Gatewood, William: votes for Va. bill for religious freedom, **2**: 549n; and tobacco taxes, **3**: 606n; elected to Va. HD, **7**: 116
Gatman, Mr.: Paradise's creditor, **15**: 73
Gatrick, John, Sr. *See* Goodrich, John, Sr.
Gattamelata de Narni, Erasmo: birthplace of, **14**: 381
Gatteaux, Nicolas Marie: letter from cited, **9**: 77, 96; paid for medal, **12**: 674; **13**: 168, 170; makes medals, **16**: 52 (illus.), 60n, 61n-2n, 65n, 67n, 68; mentioned, **9**: 241; **14**: 555
Gaubert, Abbé: letter to, **11**: 469; letter from, **11**: 377
Gautier, Mrs., **5**: 658
Gautier, Jean Antoine: letters to, **9**: 56, 548; **13**: 391-2; letters from, **9**: 548-9; **13**: 316-7; and TJ's interest in books, **13**: 316-7, 391-2; and miniature of Louis XVI, **16**: 363n; **20**: 346, 352n, 642; mentioned, **14**: 483; **17**: 316, 392
Gautier, Nicholas: medals designed by, **4**: 36n
gavelkind: in TJ's drafts of Va. Constitution, **1**: 353, 363; and western lands, **7**: 144. *See also* land tenure
Gay, Thomas: signs petition, **6**: 294
Gayoso, Manuel Luis: Spanish governor of Natchez, **14**: 499
Gayton, Commodore Clark, **4**: 90, 92
Gazaigner de Boyer, M.: letter from, **9**: 25
Gazette de France: comments on La Pé-

George III, King of Great Britain (*cont.*) of American colonization, **1**: 283; relations of American colonies to, **1**: 311; in Va. Constitution, **1**: 332n, 337n-40, 347, 356-8, 377-9; criticized in Declaration of Independence, **1**: 417-9, 420-1, 424-7, 430-1; comments on Howe and Cornwallis, **2**: 30; denounces Holland, **3**: 350; communications with Parliament, **6**: 237, 238, 239, 243, 247, 253; **13**: 338; **16**: 413, 414, 425; **18**: 106, 115, 343; **20**: 172; and ministerial politics, **7**: 42, 121; and Adams' address, **8**: 176, 179, 183, 525-6, 545, 546n, 577; and treaty with America, **9**: 259; characterizations of, **9**: 282; **10**: 369, 373n; **12**: 216; cited on Tripolitan ambassador, **9**: 287; attitude toward U.S., **9**: 398, 402, 433, 446, 474; **12**: 174, 311-2; **18**: 300; assassination attempt rumored, **10**: 202; supports Stadtholder, **11**: 476, 490, 672; friendship with Hastings, **12**: 606; letters on Morocco cited, **13**: 400-1; returns from Cheltenham, **13**: 515; health of, **14**: 50, 54, 186, 216, 276, 277, 305; **15**: 131, 141; insanity, **14**: 211, 276, 277, 287, 305, 327, 329, 333, 344, 350, 362, 363, 366, 370, 375, 386, 428, 429, 454, 463, 482, 518, 531, 565, 661, 662; **15**: 105, 110, 116, 121, 187-8, 195; recovery, **14**: 431, 567, 580, 597, 603-4, 616, 635, 646, 652, 658, 662, 664-6, 667, 673, 678, 689; **15**: 4, 50, 90, 96, 195, 282, 315; will of, **14**: 454; proposes journey to Hanover, **15**: 105, 110, 121, 126; conspiracy against reported, **15**: 351; reviews Guards, **17**: 650; prorogues Parliament, **18**: 293; Queen's influence on, **18**: 299-300; and possible war with Russia, **19**: 607; caricature of, **20**: xxxi, 384 (illus.); mentioned, **6**: 568; **18**: 296

George Island: French batteries on, **2**: 213

Georgetown, Md.: British flag of truce at, **5**: 414, 565; considered for seat of Continental Congress, **6**: 345, 349, 352, 358, 362, 364-8, 371, 391, 546; **7**: 35, 123, 232, 235n, 275, 278, 290; **8**: 78, 229; water transportation to, **7**: 50; commerce of, **14**: 549; considered for seat of U.S. government, **16**: 491, 493, 537, 541, 575, 577; **17**: 25, 455n, 456-7, 469-71; **19**: 5, 9, 25, 26, 30n, 45, 47, 56, 64, 69, 72, 73; **20**: 7,

8, 18, 19-20, 24, 33, 73, 79, 81-2, 84-5, 87-8. *See also* Residence Act; seat of U.S. government on Potomac

Georgetown, S.C.: recovered by Americans, **4**: 68; British post at, **4**: 323; mentioned, **3**: 397, 399

Georgetown Times and Patowmack Packet: cited, **17**: 456, 457

Georgia: letters to delegates in Congress, **9**: 121-2; **10**: 640; **12**: 49, 572-3; letter from delegates in Congress, **10**: 280-1; votes for independence, **1**: 314; attitude on slavery, **1**: 314; **8**: 667; **10**: 18; **12**: 279; divided on Chase's taxation plan, **1**: 323; seeks aid from Va., **2**: 234-5; British campaign against, **2**: 236; **4**: 150, 369; **5**: 421; European attitude toward, **3**: 93; and Continental Congress, **5**: 317, 324; **7**: 31; **9**: 179; and Indians, **6**: 99; **7**: 280; **9**: 641-2; **10**: 110, 294, 301; **12**: 284, 317; **13**: 283; **19**: 431n; recovers from British, **6**: 118, 126; votes on seat for Continental Congress, **6**: 366; **7**: 118; Bayard's claim against, **6**: 400; **7**: 271; western territory of, **6**: 594n; **8**: 124, 219; **13**: 96-7, 231; founding of, **6**: 596n, 658; and boundaries, **6**: 602; **10**: 39-40; quota to national treasury, **7**: 5, 55, 71; **10**: 35, 55-6; attitude toward Society of the Cincinnati, **7**: 110n; currency of, **7**: 178, 200; **10**: 232; and impost, **7**: 226, 232; **8**: 134; **9**: 510; **10**: 40; TJ offers services to, **7**: 283; grants property to Frenchmen, **9**: 259, 266; evacuation of loyalists from, **10**: 14; population of, **10**: 35, 55-6; attitude of toward Annapolis convention, **10**: 233; governorship of, **10**: 288, 314; at Federal Convention, **11**: 219, 401; rice culture in, **11**: 339; olive culture in suggested, **11**: 648-9; **13**: 263, 268; and U.S. Constitution, **12**: 254, 283, 412, 608; **13**: 100-1, 205, 370; elects senators, **14**: 395; cotton culture in, **14**: 546; Spanish government holds fugitive slaves from, **16**: 330n; **17**: 341n-2n, 638-9; **18**: 491-2; **19**: 429, 519, 520; TJ on land grants of, **16**: 406-9; confiscation acts of, **17**: 331, 334n, 335-7; laws of sent to TJ, **17**: 625-6; **18**: 360-1; **20**: 155-6; and appointment of commissioners, **19**: 59; annual exports of, **19**: 136-8; appoints health officer for Savannah, **19**: 331-2; Governors of, *see* Houstoun, John; Walton, George

son land claims, **2**: 98; regiment at Fort Pitt, **3**: 154; **6**: 320; commands western battalion, **3**: 186, 204, 244; joins Clark's expedition, **4**: 588, 596, 598-9, 653; **5**: 253-4; mentioned, **3**: 378; **4**: 31, 350, 385, 414, 595, 603; **6**: 11

Gibson's warehouse landing: ferry at, **2**: 455, 456

Giens (Geans), Château de, **11**: 431

gifts to foreign diplomats: TJ comments on, **16**: 318, 363, 366-8; editorial note on, **16**: 356n-68n; W. T. Franklin on, **16**: 364-6; mentioned, **18**: 601, 602n. *See also* medals: diplomatic medal of 1790

gifts to U.S. officials: Constitution forbids, **16**: 318

Gilbert, Mr.: and bill establishing ferries, **2**: 455; superintends public workers, **5**: 392, 516

Gilbert, Sir Geoffrey: *History and Practice of the High Court of Chancery*, **11**: 547; *Law of Devises, Revocations and Last Wills*, **11**: 547; **16**: 277, 481; *Law of Evidence*, **11**: 547; **16**: 277, 481; *Law of Uses and Trusts*, **11**: 547; **16**: 277, 481; *Treatise of Tenures*, **11**: 547; **16**: 481; *The History and Practice of Civil Actions, Particularly in the Court of Common Pleas*, **11**: 548; *Law and Practice of Ejectments*, **16**: 481; *Law of Distresses and Replevins*, **16**: 481; *Law of Executions*, **16**: 481; *Treatise on Rents*, **16**: 481; works of, **17**: 3; **19**: 337

Gilbert, Sir Humphrey: and expedition to take uninhabited countries, **1**: 277-8

Gil Blas: given Martha Jefferson to read, **6**: 374

Gilchrist, George: prisoner of war, **3**: 390

Gilchrist, James: creditor of Henry Tucker, **1**: 74

Gilchrist, John: signs nonimportation resolutions (1770), **1**: 46

Gilchrist & Taylor: creditors of Henry Tucker, **1**: 74

Giles, Mr.: Washington's postillion, **20**: 93

Giles, Maj. Edward: aide-de-camp to Morgan, **4**: 441n, 561

Giles, Thomas: enlists, **5**: 430

Giles, William B.: letter to, **16**: 22-3; letter from, **16**: 23-4; and resolutions on Hamilton, **18**: 658

Gilfillan, T., **7**: 394

Gilkinson (Gilkerson, Gilhison), Capt. (master of *Sally*), **13**: 214, 238, 255

Gill, Capt. (master of *Charlotte*), **13**: 564

Gill, Erasmus: prisoner of war, **3**: 391

Gill, John: supports American state papers series, **1**: 145

Gill, Nicholas: and case of *L'Amiable Elizabeth*, **7**: 498

Gill, Samuel: appointed captain of western battalion, **3**: 51, 52

Gillard, M., **9**: 12

Gillchrist, Capt. R. B. (master of *Grange*), **17**: 541

Gillchrist, Capt. Richard (master of *Rambler*), **18**: 55

Gillespy, Mr., **7**: 357

Gilliam, Mr.: settlement of Skelton estate, **7**: 17-8, 43

Gilliam, John: signs petition, **4**: 20

Gillies, John: *History of Ancient Greece*, **12**: 677

Gillon (Guillon), Commodore Alexander: leaves effects at Coruña, **11**: 20, 133; commands frigates for S.C., **11**: 236, 300; as master of *L'Indien*, **11**: 283; claim against S.C., **11**: 301n; commands frigate in Spanish service, **12**: 99; purchases clothing for S.C. soldiers, **12**: 633; in S.C. congressional election, **14**: 394; and S.C. bonds, **15**: 33n, 257-8, 264, 463, 464n; **16**: 324, 325n, 390; **17**: 487, 577; mentioned, **6**: 128; **7**: 428

Gilly's creek, **6**: 512

Gilman, John Taylor, **4**: 139

Gilman, Nathaniel: letter from cited, **17**: 598n; recommends W. Gardiner, **19**: 37n

Gilmer, Dr. George: letters to, **1**: 185-6; **3**: 538; **6**: 538-9; **7**: 237; **8**: 145; **12**: 24-6; **14**: 360-2; **16**: 574-5; **17**: 269-70; **18**: 28; letters from, **1**: 236-9; **5**: 430-2; **9**: 93-4; **11**: 27-9; **12**: 452; **16**: 433; **18**: 27; letter from, to John Morgan, introducing TJ, **1**: 18; supports American state papers series, **1**: 145; memorandum cited, **1**: 407; signs petition, **1**: 587; elected delegate from Albemarle co. to Va. GA, **2**: 11n; signs Va. oath of allegiance, **2**: 128; diary of, **2**: 130n; Purdie sends newspaper to, **2**: 207; D'Anmours dines with, **4**: 66; receives TJ's books from German Convention officers, **4**: 117; letter to, from Lind, cited, **6**: 55n; accounts, **6**:

Green, Col. John (*cont.*)
323, 471, 472, 485, 527, 558, 611; **5:**
246
Green, Joseph: address to Washington,
20: 551-5
Green, Samuel: organ builder, **11:** 59
Green, Thomas: in Albemarle co. militia,
1: 667
Green, Timothy: supports American
state papers series, **1:** 145
Green, William (R.I.): letters from, **18:**
580-2; **20:** 504-5, 519-22; in *Rachel*
case, **20:** 145, 483, 495-7, 500, 504-5,
508n, 519-22; East Indian losses of,
20: 501-2, 505n
Green, William (Va.): signs nonimportation resolutions (1770), **1:** 47
Green, Willis, **5:** 548
Greenbrier, parish of: election of vestry,
2: 117
Greenbrier co., Va.: letter to county lieutenant of, **4:** 230-1; letter from officers
of militia, **4:** 469; letter to officers of
militia, **4:** 641; formation of, **2:** 114;
administration of justice in, **2:** 114-5;
public dues or fees, **2:** 115; senatorial
district, **2:** 115, 336; lawsuits in, **2:**
116; land commissioners for, **2:** 165n;
post service to, **2:** 389; levies of soldiers from, **3:** 6-7, 8; defends western
frontier, **3:** 50, 52, 53, 420; position of
troops from, **3:** 55; communications, **3:**
79; directed by TJ to send militia
against Indians, **3:** 356; Indian depredations, **3:** 356; militia, **3:** 420, 422,
599; **4:** 225-6, 234; **5:** 256, 310, 445,
504; **6:** 35; tobacco loan office certificates, **3:** 516; supply post for, **4:** 288n;
danger from Indians, **4:** 469; express
from, **5:** 446; dissension in, **12:** 103
Greenbrier river: navigation, **8:** 3; possible waterway connection with Richmond, **11:** 385
Greene, Capt.: inquiry concerning captivity by Algerians, **10:** 206-7, 228
Greene, Benjamin: interview with TJ, **5:**
83n
Greene, Catherine Littlefield (Mrs. Nathanael Greene): supports American
state papers series, **1:** 145; concern
over lack of news about son, **16:** 166;
in Glaubeck case, **18:** 623n, 686n-7n
Greene, George Washington: admission
to Cincinnati, **12:** 220; educated in
Paris, **13:** 156, 157n, 172, 348; intro-

duced to TJ, **13:** 172; letter sent by,
13: 244; dines with TJ, **14:** 611n
Greene (Green), Griffin: case of, **9:** 233;
letter from cited, **10:** 70
Greene, Nathanael: letters to, **4:** 157-8,
240-1, 379-80, 575-6, 599, 647-8,
648, 654-5; **5:** 229-31, 291-2, 312-3,
313-4, 356; **9:** 167-9; letters from, **4:**
130-2, 183-5, 206-7, 253-4, 288-9,
365-6, 437-8, 455, 576, 615-6, 638;
5: 22-4, 111-3, 156-7, 215-6, 258-9,
301-2, 342, 360-2, 405, 567-70, 578-
9; **6:** 101-3, 103-4; **8:** 171, 205-6; illness of, **1:** 506; Gov. Reed's aid to, **3:**
354; **5:** 264; to command southern
army, **4:** 60-1, 84; supplies for, **4:** 133-
4, 151, 196, 219, 220, 291, 348, 448,
492, 666; **5:** 125, 175, 264; **6:** 631;
reinforcements for, **4:** 163, 184, 503,
546, 587, 618, 621, 624, 637, 638,
645, 647, 662, 682, 683, 687, 695n-
6n, 700; **5:** 6, 7, 8, 9, 36, 63, 66, 82,
103, 112, 213, 275-7, 309, 312, 344,
345, 350, 353-4, 361, 371, 385, 398,
402-3, 409, 437, 449, 453, 464, 492,
507, 524, 541, 542, 571, 573, 583,
584, 598, 613, 646, 657, 667n-8n; **6:**
3, 5, 30, 93; appoints deputy quartermaster, **4:** 250, 374, 522; **5:** 574,
577n-8n; views on furloughs, **4:** 279n;
number of troops, **4:** 323, 495; strategic retreat before Cornwallis (1781),
4: 561-4, 610, 613, 615-6, 625, 629,
637, 639; joins Morgan, **4:** 562; communications with TJ, **4:** 647, 649; **5:**
7, 8, 23n, 43n-4, 45n, 86n; advice on
militia officers, **4:** 681; at Halifax
Court House, **4:** 682; equipment
needed by, **4:** 697; **5:** 48; pursues
Cornwallis, **5:** 9, 12, 18; on need for
cavalry, **5:** 34; strategy of, **5:** 44, 570n;
6: 619-20, 626n; opinion of Maj. Claiborne, **5:** 60n; letters from, to Washington, cited, **5:** 102, 351, 494; reorganizes southern army, **5:** 116;
Bedford co. militia under, **5:** 123;
communications with, **5:** 138, 195,
227n, 303, 624; at Guilford Court
House, **5:** 162, 198; sends letter to
Washington, **5:** 185; views on Davies,
5: 205n; Steuben proposes to join, **5:**
262n-3n; **6:** 619-20, 626; and Steuben's plan against Cornwallis, **5:** 267;
6: 619n; appoints negotiators with
Cherokees and Chickasaws, **5:** 268,

395; on military vs. civil authority, **5:** 276n-7n; **6:** 619; march to south, **5:** 277n, 298; relations with TJ, **5:** 302n, 314n, 418n, 577n-8n; relations with Cherokees, **5:** 305, 476-7; support of and defense of Va., **5:** 338; needs ammunition, **5:** 343, 388, 416-8; impressment of horses, **5:** 357, 567-70, 626, 629n; **6:** 28; **15:** 604; correspondence with Steuben, **5:** 361n-2n, 418n, 440, 667n; **6:** 31n, 625n, 638; releases militia, **5:** 362; requisition for militia, **5:** 366; supported by Va., **5:** 421; orders carried out by Preston, **5:** 438; letters from, to Davies, quoted, **5:** 439n, 538n, 539; march from Deep river for S.C., **5:** 472; Lafayette to receive directions from, **5:** 477; sends prisoners to Halifax co., **5:** 495; characteristics of, **5:** 538n; importance to Va., **5:** 541; on emergency powers, **5:** 567-70; letter from, to Varnum, quoted, **5:** 570n; letter from, to Carrington, quoted, **5:** 577n-8n; letter from, to Pickering, quoted, **5:** 578n; cartel with Cornwallis, **6:** 26; orders Lawson to join him, **6:** 26-7; needs cartouche boxes, **6:** 75; at Orangeburg, **6:** 80; proposed as dictator for Va., **6:** 84; report of committee of Congress on letter of, **6:** 455-6; appointed commissioner in Conn.-Pa. dispute, **6:** 477n, 478n; and Steuben inquiry, **6:** 619-33, 636-8; letters intercepted by British, **6:** 639; as Indian commissioner, **7:** 8, 11; Houdon's desire to make statue of, **8:** 289; medal in honor of, **9:** 241; **11:** 144, 231, 233, 345; **14:** 555; **16:** xxxvii, 52 (illus.), 54n, 57n, 59n-64n, 67n, 69n, 72, 73n, 75n, 76n; bust for Va. Capitol suggested, **9:** 267; death of, **10:** 136, 170, 187, 294, 300, 311, 314; and admission of son to Cincinnati, **12:** 220; letter to cited, **18:** 379n; in Glaubeck case, **18:** 686n; N.C. land grant, **19:** 605; mentioned, **2:** 38; **3:** 474, 584, 650; **4:** 212, 217, 252, 279, 359, 440, 525, 588, 641, 667; **5:** 19, 43, 50, 86, 103, 150, 182, 269, 271, 285, 297, 316, 325, 368n, 369, 370, 403, 450, 529, 530, 538, 539, 576, 603, 657; **6:** 30, 75-6, 106, 281, 344; **11:** 401

Greene, William: letter to, from Howell, quoted, **7:** 156n

Greenesville co., Va.: letter to county lieutenant of, **5:** 614-6; supply post for, **4:** 286; militia, **5:** 310, 531, 614-6, 646

Greenhough, John: Richmond property of, **8:** 344

Greenhow, Mr., **3:** 152

Greenhow, John: signs nonimportation resolutions (1770), **1:** 47

Greenland Fishery (British whaling), **14:** 14-5, 228-9; **19:** 176, 181, 184n, 198n; **20:** 101

Greenleaf, James: consul at Amsterdam, **17:** 250, 253n, 256; consular applicant, **19:** 313; biographical note, **19:** 315n; TJ recommends, **19:** 317

Greenleaf, Thomas: publishes *New-York Journal*, **16:** 238n; paid by Department of State, **17:** 366, 373. *See also New-York Journal*

Green lick run, **1:** 389n

Green Mountain Boys: Wooster sends for, **1:** 438; lack of clothing and arms, **1:** 441

Green river, Ky., **2:** 90, 150n; **8:** 124

Green Spring, Va., **1:** 65

Greenup, Christopher: votes for bill for religious freedom, **2:** 549n

Greenvill, Sir Richard: commands *Sir Walter Ralegh*, **1:** 279, 280

Greer, Capt., **15:** 600, 601n

Greg, Admiral. *See* Greig, Adm. Samuel

Gregg, Archibald: passport issued by TJ, **15:** 484

Grégoire, Barthélemy de: petition to Mass. government, **12:** 318

Grégoire, Marie Thérèse de Lamotte Cadillac de: letter from, **10:** 239-40; land claim against Mass., **10:** 239, 264; **12:** 318

Gregory, Mr.: British consul in Barcelona, **9:** 618-9; **10:** 149

Gregory, Mr. (N.Y.): and Hessian fly, **20:** 458

Gregory (Grigorie), Alexander Frazier: introduced to TJ by Gen. Woodford, **3:** 657; **5:** 258n; permitted to land, **5:** 309

Gregory, Gen. Isaac: safe after battle of Camden, **3:** 596; forces under, **4:** 617; and express riders, **4:** 643, 665, 674; N.C. militia under, **5:** 103, 106

Gregory (Grigorie), James: kindness to Gen. Woodford, **3:** 657

dines with, **16**: 433; mentioned, **3**: 329, 330, 411; **13**: 98, 99; **16**: 158

Griffin, John Tayloe: financial affairs, **19**: 553; **20**: 162, 162n, 211, 212, 411-2, 420, 555; letter from quoted, **20**: 162n

Griffin, Samuel: letters to, **3**: 614-5; **5**: 166, 292, 412; **15**: 599; letters from, **3**: 85, 150-1, 166-7, 171, 173-4, 174-5, 183, 199, 209-10; on Va. Board of War, **3**: 4n, 58n; bill of exchange endorsed to, **3**: 323n; commissioned, **4**: 307; and cavalry corps, **4**: 343, 344, 422; evaluates horses, **5**: 214, 286, 287; congressman from Va., **15**: 6, 74; federalism, **15**: 6; as conduit for mail, **19**: 265; letter to quoted, **19**: 266n. *See also* Virginia: Board of War

Griffith, David: signs Virginia Association, **1**: 109

Griffith, Rev. David: elected bishop of Va., **10**: 110; and Washington, **18**: 396n

Griffiths, Dr., **10**: 625

Griffitts (Griffiths), Samuel Powel, **11**: 290

Grigg, Maj. John: petition from, **5**: 405; reply to, **5**: 405n

Grigsby, Hugh Blair: assessment of Nichols, **19**: 475

Grillemont, Chateau de, **11**: 460

Grillon. *See* Crillon-Mahon

Grills, William: petitions Va. HD, **2**: 42n, 63

Grimké, John Faucheraud: objects to Price's pamphlet, **8**: 258; Presidential elector from S.C., **14**: 666; **15**: 51

Grimm, Friedrich Melchior, Baron von: negotiations for Ledyard, **10**: 170-1, 188, 258; in Rousseau's *Confessions*, **15**: 568; memorandum to TJ on gifts, **16**: 359n; bears packets from Jones, **19**: 588; mentioned, **16**: 585; **17**: 558; **18**: 601

grindstones: U.S. import of, **10**: 147

Grinnell, Lieut.: on crew of *Indien*, **11**: 301n

Grinning, James: in Albemarle co. militia, **1**: 668n

Grinning, John: in Albemarle co. militia, **1**: 664

Grinning, Nehemiah: in Albemarle co. militia, **1**: 664, 667

Grippi, Count: letter from, to Carmichael, quoted, **9**: 648

grist mills: Va. bill concerning, **2**: 464-7; Ballendine offers for lease, **5**: 19; dri-

ven by steam power, **9**: xxviii, 387 (illus.), 400-1, 446; **11**: 424; U.S., **10**: 262; American method of described by TJ, **11**: 563-5 (illus.)

Griswold, Matthew, **18**: 385n, 386n

Grivel, Guillaume: letter to, **11**: 111-2

Groar (Groer), Capt.: engaged to teach duties of laboratory, **4**: 149-50; mentioned, **4**: 524, 530, 531

Grocers Company (London): supports Pitt the Younger, **7**: 139

Gronovius, Johann Friedrich: *Flora Virginica*, **12**: 129

Groom, Robert, **4**: 20

Gros, John Daniel: translates for Dept. of State, **17**: 352n, 361; **20**: 730

Grose, Francis: *Provincial Glossary*, **14**: 512

Gross, Alexander: imprisonment at Dunkirk, **10**: 70-1, 71n, 79-80, 105-6; **12**: 6, 44-5, 398-401, 646

Gross, Samuel, **10**: 79

"Grotius": pseudonym used by DeWitt Clinton, **20**: 707n

Grotius, Hugo: mentioned by TJ as Arian, **1**: 554; works sought by TJ, **6**: 541; *Histoire des troubles des Pays-Bas*, **7**: 288; **8**: 411; cited on extradition law, **7**: 593; cited on privilege of foreign ministers, **11**: 495n; *De rebus Belgicis*, **12**: 18, 678; **14**: 474, 491; *Mare Liberum*, **12**: 688; **13**: 290; cited by Hamilton, **17**: 144, 145

Grotjan, Peter A.: and soldiers' arrearages, **18**: 628n, 629

Groton, Conn.: fisheries, **7**: 334

Groubentall, Grouber de: letter to, **14**: 274; letter from, **14**: 50-1; *Théorie générale de l'administration politique des finances*, **14**: 50

ground hogs. *See* woodchucks

grouse: for Louis XVI's natural history museum, **9**: 148-9

Gruel, Jacques, **11**: 594, 669

Gruel, James, & Co., **3**: 91

Grymes, David: in Albemarle co. militia, **1**: 666

Grymes, John Dawson: debt to Monroe, **9**: 511

Grymes, John Randolph, **18**: 333n

Grymes (Grimes), Ludwell (Orange co.), **7**: 37, 123; **9**: 511

Grymes (Grimes), Mrs. Ludwell, **15**: 230

Grymes, Philip: defends TJ in Callender-Jones charge, **2**: 261n

needed at Quebec, **1**: 445; sent to Harrodsburg, **2**: 83; care for, **3**: 504; supplied by Va. to southern army, **3**: 592; for defense of York river, **4**: 69; for western expedition, **4**: 225, 235; purchase, **4**: 239, 585-6; **5**: 472; thrown into river by British, **4**: 270; removed from Hanover, **4**: 306; remanufacture, **4**: 336, 463; Va. requests from Congress, **4**: 398, 467; for Clark's expedition, **4**: 588, 589, 598; to be brought from Baltimore, **4**: 609; delay in sending to Fort Pitt, **4**: 655; brought by Capt. Jones, **4**: 671; transportation, **5**: 26; needed at Yorktown, **5**: 70; orders for, **5**: 80, 81, 246; **15**: 588, 589; for Portsmouth expedition, **5**: 89, 90, 130; import desired, **5**: 266; for privateer, **5**: 404; offered to Va., **5**: 411; needed for Montgomery militia, **5**: 437; needed in Jefferson co., **5**: 467; sent to Fredericksburg, **6**: 27, 50; spoilage, **6**: 49n; purchased in France for Va., **10**: 472, 476, 497, 523; export from France to U.S., **12**: 469, 470; **13**: 70; improvement in composition of, **14**: 367; mentioned, **4**: 142; **6**: 49

guns. *See* arms

gunsmiths: for public work, **4**: 609; employment of sought, **5**: 284, 293

Gurley, Rev. George (?), **7**: 386

Gurney, Mr.: house in Philadelphia, **17**: 238

Gustavus III, King of Sweden: influenced by France, **13**: 510; characterized by TJ, **14**: 659; **15**: 50, 121; arrests nobles, **14**: 672, 702; blames Britain for failure to aid him, **17**: 628; G. Morris comments on, **18**: 295; desires to become king of Poland, **19**: 418

Gustavus Adolphus (ship): burned by Russians, **13**: 579

Gustine, Comte de. *See* Custine-Sarreck, Adam Philippe, Comte de

Gutridge, John, Sr. *See* Goodrich

Guyot, Guillaume Germain: *Récréations physiques et mathematiques*, **11**: 61

Guys, Pierre Augustin: *Voyage littéraire de la Grèce*, **8**: 411; **12**: 129

Guyton de Morveau (Morveau), Louis Bernard, Baron: *Elémens de chymie* (*Le Necessaire chemique*), **9**: 661

Gwatkin, J.: signs nonimportation resolutions (1769), **1**: 31

Gwatkin, Thomas: signs commission, **1**: 99; appointed to preach Fast-Day sermon, **1**: 106, 107n; books for sale, **1**: 294, 455; professor at College of William and Mary, **15**: 572n; mentioned, **8**: 12, 635; **9**: 40

Gwinnett, Button: signs agreement of secrecy, **1**: 253; signs Declaration of Independence, **1**: 432

Gwynn's Island, Va.: sketch map of, by TJ, **1**: lviii, 566 (illus.); batteries at, **1**: 454-5; American success at, **1**: 474; mentioned, **1**: 297, 455, 469, 471; **15**: 575

Haagen, Baron van der: in Flemish revolt, **16**: 249

Haarlem, Netherlands: organ at, **8**: 447; attack on, **10**: 434; petition from bourgeoisie, **10**: 470

habeas corpus: Va. bill concerning writs of, **2**: 481-5; in TJ's revision of Va. Constitution (1783), **6**: 281, 304, 315; absent from Constitution, **12**: 440, 558, 571; TJ's suggestions for in Bill of Rights, **13**: 442; in France, **14**: 370, 375, 386, 423

Habington, Thomas: *Historie of Edward the Fourth*, **12**: 18

hackle (heckle): TJ's attempted purchase for Eppes, **1**: 487

Haddaway, Thomas: letter to, **11**: 99; letter from, **11**: 89

Hadfield, George (brother of Maria Cosway): introduced to TJ, **15**: 351, 413

Hadj, Abdurrahman. *See* Abdrahaman

Hagerstown, Md.: and capital site, **19**: 20, 21, 23

Haggard, Martin: signs Va. oath of allegiance, **2**: 129

Haggard, Nathaniel: signs Va. oath of allegiance, **2**: 128

Hagge Suliman Benchellon: character, **20**: 678-9

Haggord, John: signs petition, **1**: 588

Hagley Park, England: garden described by TJ, **9**: 372; TJ's drawings of, **13**: 17, 35n

Hague Gazette. See Gazette de la Haye

Hague, The: American agent at discontinued, **7**: 13-4; assassination attempt in, **9**: 360-1; Adams' visit to, **10**: 302; political corruption in, **11**: 576; disorders in, **12**: 168-9; **15**: 443n; conference at, **20**: 168

135; sent to TJ, **11**: 641; **12**: 135, 428, 486; Westphalia, **13**: 14, 265; Mainz, **13**: 18, 266; shipped by Donald, **14**: 280; **16**: 406, 492, 566, 591-2; from Mrs. Lewis, **17**: 324, 325n

Hambleton, Thomas. *See* Hamilton

Hamburg, Germany: treaty of amity and commerce, **6**: 393; **7**: 48, 263, 267, 495-6; cordage imported from, **7**: 330; tobacco imported from Va., **7**: 370; ships in Charleston harbor, **8**: 201; imports from S.C., **8**: 202-3; and the fisheries, **19**: 178, 180, 181

Hamburg, Md.: and capital site, **19**: 73; **20**: 6n, 13, 15, 37, 39, 78-9, 85

Hamer, Mr., **8**: 529

Hamilton, Mr.: brings Sir John Sinclair's book to TJ, **15**: 5; suggested for federal office in N.C., **16**: 477; letter sent by, **20**: 161; mentioned, **9**: 364n

Hamilton, Mr. (physicist): treatise on vapors, **6**: 508

Hamilton, Alexander: letters to, **16**: 483; **17**: 21, 409n, 474-5; **18**: 68, 459-60, 563-4; **19**: 536; **20**: 198, 570-1; letters from, **16**: 353-4, 479-80, 511-2; **17**: 451; **18**: 562-3, 564-5; **20**: 199, 200-2, 213-4, 377, 546-7; in American Philosophical Society, **4**: 545n; **19**: 100n; TJ's first meeting with, **6**: 217n; and public debt, **6**: 263-4; supports Steuben's claims, **7**: 100n, 101n; **11**: 494n; chairman of N.Y. branch of the Cincinnati, **7**: 110n; and coinage, **7**: 153n, 160n; **18**: 454-8; **20**: 546-7, 570-1; recommended to Upton, **8**: 482; elected to N.Y. assembly, **10**: 154; N.Y. delegate to Federal Convention, **11**: 219, 400; and Vt., **11**: 286; trunk sent to by Mrs. Church, **12**: 483; member of Congress, **13**: 42; *Federalist* papers, **13**: 157, 158n, 337, 498-9; **17**: 108; **18**: 220n, 231, 372n, 415, 516, 520, 523, 525, 526, 541, 556, 557; **19**: 494; misrepresents TJ's financial plan, **13**: 323n; **14**: 194; federalism of, **13**: 413, 414n; member committee on TJ's expenses, **14**: 291n; advises N.Y. allies, **14**: 416; in N.Y. convention, **14**: 519; Secretary of the Treasury, **15**: 153, 228, 336, 530, 545; **17**: 351n-3n, 358n, 359n; correspondence with Lear, **15**: 360n; **17**: 429n; correspondence with Short, **15**: 563, 567; **16**: 133, 165n, 273-4, 305n; **17**: 126n, 427n, 428n, 615,

639, 654, 656n, 672; **18**: 86, 114, 115n, 351, 355, 451, 500, 526, 603, 610n; **19**: 361, 539; proposal for debt to France, **15**: 566-7; TJ meets before Washington's house, **16**: xxxiv; **17**: 170; plan for revenue, **16**: 125-6, 183-4; loan from Willink, Van Staphorst & Hubbard, **16**: 134-5, 161-2; **17**: 425-30; in Heth's dispute with Donald, **16**: 236, 264, 325, 382, 383; **17**: 626; and *Gazette of the United States*, **16**: 245n, 519; *Report . . . relative to a provision for the support of the public credit of the United States*, **16**: 317n; plans for U.S. mint, **16**: 340n, 369n; **17**: 409n, 534n; letter to, from Lindsay, quoted, **16**: 353n-4n; TJ converses with, **16**: 387, 448; policy on Indian lands, **16**: 409n; and arrearages in soldiers' pay, **16**: 455-68 (editorial note and documents); **18**: xxxv-viii, 611-88 (appendix); Burke's attack on and rumor of duel, **16**: 456n; letter from, to Henry Lee, quoted, **16**: 461n; letters from quoted, **16**: 472n, 510n; **17**: 89, 350n; letters to, from Wolcott, quoted, **16**: 472n-3n; **18**: 647n, 662; and TJ's Report on Weights and Measures, **16**: 483, 511, 614, 643n, 645n; Estaing discusses Washington with, **16**: 558; engravings of Necker and Lafayette sent to, **16**: 559n; letters to cited, **16**: 607n, 614n; **17**: 318n, 429n; **18**: 455n; **20**: 173n; letters from cited, **17**: 21n, 417; **18**: 455n; letters to, from Church, quoted, **17**: 36; **18**: 272; and war crisis of 1790, **17**: 38, 44-5, 48, 51, 55-7, 59-65, 68-87, 89, 92-108, 126n, 130n, 143-61, 352n; Beckwith's interviews with, **17**: 45, 55-7, 59-64, 68-70, 80-5, 92-8, 105-6, 132n-4n, 161n; **18**: 221-2, 234-7, 256, 262, 266n, 278, 280, 282; **20**: 108, 111-2, 138, 145, 252; correspondence with Washington, **17**: 57, 97-8, 102, 161n, 427n, 428n; **18**: 100n, 272n, 277n, 638n; **20**: 141-2; correspondence with Jay, **17**: 77, 217n, 460n; letters to quoted, **17**: 89, 429n-30n; correspondence with Willink, Van Staphorst & Hubbard cited, **17**: 126n, 427n; and St. Clair's expedition against Indians, **17**: 132n-4n; **20**: 107; cites Barbeyrac, **17**: 144; cites Pufendorf, **17**: 144; cites Grotius, **17**: 144, 145; cites Vattel, **17**: 144, 145, 147; and assumption bill

616; criticizes Madison, **20**: 718-23; criticizes Freneau, **20**: 718-23, 727; "T. L." letters, **20**: 719; mentioned, **12**: 506, 590; **14**: 80; **16**: 238n; **17**: 321, 481, 564, 655; **18**: 396n, 529. *See also* Department of the Treasury, U.S.

Hamilton, Andrew (Pa.): in Franklin's autobiography, **9**: 486

Hamilton, Andrew (Va.): letter from, **4**: 469; loan to state, **3**: 386, 442

Hamilton, Elizabeth Schuyler (Mrs. Alexander Hamilton): sends *Federalist* to Mrs. Church, **13**: 158n; as bearer of news, **16**: 550; pregnancy, **18**: 669n

Hamilton, Gawin: votes for bill for religious freedom, **2**: 549n

Hamilton, Henry: plans expedition against Fort Pitt, **2**: 256; defeated at Vincennes, **2**: 256-8; as prisoner of war, **2**: 258, 270, 287n, 292-5; **3**: 5n-6n, 7n, 25-8, 30, 31-2, 34, 40-1, 44-9, 58-9, 61, 65, 86, 94-5, 97-8, 99, 101-2, 104, 198, 205, 245-6, 333, 488, 605n, 664-5; **5**: 365; excoriated by TJ, **2**: 286; sentence of appraised by TJ, **2**: 299; letter from, to Lieutenant Governor and Council of Va., **3**: 58-9; parole, **3**: 95-6; **4**: 24-5, 164; **5**: 429; exchange, **3**: 112-3, 605; **4**: 463n, 566-7; sent to New York, **4**: 33, 34, 47, 105; mentioned, **2**: 298; **4**: 28, 165

Hamilton, James: signs nonimportation resolutions (1769), **1**: 30

Hamilton, Gen. James: letter to, **4**: 517-8; letter from, **4**: 698; receives letters, **3**: 322; inquires about conditions of parole, **3**: 450; permitted to send express, **3**: 562; report of food deficiencies for Convention troops, **3**: 580-1; permitted to go to New York, **4**: 68; agrees to division of Convention troops, **4**: 100; endeavors to prevent desertions, **4**: 101; refuses to receive money for ration deficiencies, **4**: 664, 673; and supplies for Convention troops, **5**: 564, 565n; mentioned, **4**: 164; **5**: 147

Hamilton, John (British consul at Norfolk, Va.): consular activities of, **17**: 42; **19**: 306; describes Beckwith, **17**: 44n; letter from, to Duke of Leeds, quoted, **17**: 91n-2n; loyalist status, **18**: 254; received by TJ, **19**: 601

Hamilton, Col. John, **19**: 553

Hamilton, Joshua, **5**: 40, 41

Hamilton (Hambleton), Thomas: letter from, **5**: 432; and removal of public stores, **4**: 288n; wishes civilian employment, **5**: 116; retirement of, **5**: 178-9; appointed town major, **5**: 244-5, 269; authorized to pay arrears to soldiers, **5**: 387n, 396; mentioned, **4**: 539; **5**: 13

Hamilton, Sir William: *Observations on Mount Vesuvius*, **14**: 573

Hamlet: quoted, **8**: 586

Hammersly, William: passport issued by TJ, **15**: 486

Hammock (Hamock), John: in Albemarle co. militia, **1**: 667

Hammond, George: British minister to U.S., **17**: 40, 86; **18**: 222-3, 226-8, 263, 270n, 271, 276n; **20**: 594, 615; recalled from Madrid, **17**: 107; letters to cited, **17**: 334n; **18**: 281n, 471n; and U.S. debts to Britain, **17**: 340n; correspondence with Grenville, **18**: 243n, 263n, 273n, 280; and Lords of Trade report, **18**: 271n; in British-American relations, **18**: 277-82, 283n; presents credentials to Washington, **18**: 280; letters from cited, **18**: 281n; on controversy over *Rights of Man*, **20**: 287; arrival in London, **20**: 677

Hammuda Bey: letters to, from Sidi Muhammad, cited, **10**: 391; **13**: 527n; **14**: 46

Hamner, Henley: in Albemarle co. militia, **1**: 664

Hamner, Nicholas: signs Va. oath of allegiance, **2**: 129

Hamner, Richardson: in Albemarle co. militia, **1**: 668n

Hampden, John: portrait of sought by TJ, **14**: 467, 514; bust of, **14**: 525

Hampden-Sydney College: rector of, **2**: 249n; faculty and students of exempted from militia duty, **2**: 350; Dabney Carr, Jr., at, **9**: 39; **11**: 155, 402; **16**: 89; religion at, **16**: 26

Hampshire co., Va.: letters to county lieutenant of, **4**: 229-30, 629; **5**: 254; letter to quartermaster of, **4**: 232-3; appoints infantry officers, **1**: 580; place of court of assize, **1**: 630; bill to add part of Augusta co. to, **2**: 113; collection of public dues in, **2**: 115; petitions for new boundary, **2**: 118n; militia, **2**: 131; **3**: 420, 422, 598, 599, 643; **4**: 63, 234, 235, 688-9; **5**: 253, 254-5,

Hampshire co., Va. (*cont.*)
309n, 310, 329n, 455, 475, 501, 561, 565n, 638n, 646; **6**: 11, 12n, 84, 93; senatorial district, **2**: 336; levies of soldiers from, **3**: 6-7, 8; defends western frontier, **3**: 50, 51, 53; tobacco loan office certificates, **3**: 516; beef supplies in, **4**: 46; commissary and quartermaster for western defense, **4**: 235; insurrection in, **5**: 409-10, 455, 513-5, 566; **6**: 67n; riflemen expected from, **5**: 644

Hampton, James: translator of Polybius, **13**: 179

Hampton, Va.: British attack on, **1**: 249, 256-7; **4**: 57n, 67, 69, 78, 79; Lord Dunmore's attempt to burn, **1**: 269; battle at, **1**: 287; **15**: 572-3; ferry at, **2**: 457; hospital at, **3**: 269, 515; **4**: 25; arrival of *Patsy* at, **3**: 318; defenses, **3**: 327; **4**: 169; garrison at, **3**: 345, 537; difficulty of reaching, **3**: 445, 446; express post, **4**: 3, 372, 378; place of collection under provision law, **4**: 7, 8; medicine for, **4**: 47; embarkation of British at, **4**: 112; fortification by British rumored, **4**: 378; French ships at, **4**: 650; fear of British reprisals, **4**: 658; map of, **5**: 145; location, **10**: 602

Hampton Court, England: TJ visits, **9**: 369

Hampton Roads, Va.: hostile fleet reported, **3**: 475; British vessels in, **4**: 124, 424; **5**: 188, 250, 315, 344; mentioned, **5**: 25, 125

Hamtramck (Hamtranck), John Francis: testimony on Canadian campaign, **1**: 451-2; report on navigability of rivers in Northwest Territory, **17**: 448-9; letters to, from St. Clair, **18**: 213; **19**: 524-6

Hanau, Germany: regiment from, **3**: 304; TJ visits, **13**: 17, 48; mentioned, **13**: 266

Hanbury, Osgood: account against Wayles, **17**: 581, 592; supports Joshua Johnson, **20**: 487

Hancarville (Ancherville, Danquerville), Pierre François Hugues d': letter from, **11**: 182; accompanies TJ to St. Denis, **10**: 443-4; health of, **11**: 150, 182; invited to dinner by TJ, **12**: 387; lack of contact with, **14**: 446; mentioned, **10**: 453, 495

Hancock (British warship), **5**: 283

Hancock, Lieut.: prisoner of war, **3**: 391

Hancock, George: votes for bill for reli-

gious freedom, **2**: 549n; TJ's opinion on note asked, **6**: 188; assault on S.C. citizen, **6**: 513-5; **7**: 12, 38, 40n, 260

Hancock, John: letters to, **1**: 524; **2**: 224-6; **17**: 419-20; **19**: 237; letters from, **1**: 523-4; **2**: 37; **19**: 172-3; signs Congress' second petition, **1**: 222; signs resolutions on Lord North's proposal, **1**: 233; signs agreement of secrecy, **1**: 252; and Cedars report, **1**: 404n; signs Declaration of Independence, **1**: 417n, 432; letter from, to P. Henry, cited, **1**: 466; on Drummond peace proposals, **1**: 502n; as president of Congress, **2**: 34-5; **10**: 144n; absence from Congress, **2**: 37; **9**: 179; TJ's acquaintance with, **7**: 312n; Crèvecoeur dines with, **7**: 413; Storer recommended to, **8**: 58n; health of, **9**: 504; Mme Grégoire's land claim presented to, **10**: 239; as governor of Mass., **11**: 301, 307, 313, 383, 411n, 469; **13**: 337; seeks vice presidency, **13**: 502; **14**: 4, 17, 275, 302, 385, 596, 615, 688; **15**: 92; **20**: 284, 285, 307; Madison criticizes, **14**: 17; Adams' misunderstanding with, **14**: 275, 539; Moustier fails to visit, **14**: 341; and boundary of U.S., **16**: 283n; correspondence with Washington, **16**: 283n; **17**: 283n, 451-2; **19**: 304; and dinner invitation to Washington, **16**: 288n; letter to cited, **16**: 563n; letter from quoted, **16**: 563n-4n; and fisheries, **17**: 419-20; **19**: 144-5, 157, 158, 171, 172; and new system of penmanship, **19**: 120n; and assumption of state debts, **19**: 145n; and government protocol, **19**: 157; letter to, from Eben Parson, **19**: 173-5; letter to, from Peleg Coffin, Jr., **19**: 173-5; letter to, from Thomas Davis, **19**: 173-5; supports *National Gazette*, **20**: 731; mentioned, **8**: 294

Hancock, Va.: and capital site, **19**: 19, 23

Hand, Edward: battalion, **1**: 506; motion on Conn.-Pa. dispute, **6**: 483n, 484n, 486n; sends petition to Dickinson, **6**: 500n; plan for dismissing and enlisting troops, **7**: 252; member Committee of the States (1784), **7**: 299; and western lands, **9**: 151; **15**: 117

Handel, George Frederick: festival in London, **8**: 179

Handy, Thomas: letter from, **15**: 525-6

hanging. *See* capital punishment

Hanging-maw (Cherokee chief): friendly to U.S., **4**: 551-2; mentioned, **2**: 286n

Hannah (ship): discharges cargo at Cowes, **18**: 5

Hanna's Town, Pa., **1**: 235n

Hannibal: crossing of Alps, **13**: 272, 656n; victory at Lake Thrasymene, **14**: 381

Hannibal (slave): taken by British, **6**: 224

Hanno: and theory of American discovery, **12**: 264

Hannon, Lieut., **3**: 374

Hanover (ship), **9**: 330, 452

Hanover, Elector of: relations with Prussia, **8**: 316; and German Confederation, **8**: 460; vote for king of Romans, **14**: 565. *See also* George III

Hanover, Germany: relations with Prussia, **8**: 302, 373, 418; commerce, **8**: 606; prohibits import of U.S. wheat, **14**: 13

Hanover, Va.: and religious toleration, **1**: 526n; escheated property in, **3**: 313; removal of gunpowder from, **4**: 306

Hanover co., Va.: letter to commissioner of provisions for, **3**: 569n; letters to county lieutenant of, **5**: 128, 496n-7n, 612, 617; **6**: 4, 34-5, 48; letter to members of GA for, **5**: 585-6; militia, **1**: 160; **2**: 131; **3**: 599; **4**: 62, 63, 295n, 297, 303n, 312, 313, 326, 332, 385; **5**: 29, 128n, 141, 181, 310, 496n-7n, 501, 520-1, 546, 560, 561, 612, 617, 646; appoints infantry officers, **1**: 580; petition from religious dissenters in, **1**: 589n; place of court of assize, **1**: 629; senatorial district, **2**: 336; levies of soldiers, **3**: 7; tobacco loan office certificates, **3**: 516; flour quota, **3**: 609n; supply post for, **4**: 286; requests exemption, **5**: 91; letters from county lieutenant cited, **5**: 175; wagons not furnished by, **5**: 274

Hanover Court House, Va.: Henry Hamilton sent to, **3**: 96; rendezvous of recruits at, **4**: 452; need for arms at, **5**: 28, 70; British at, **6**: 26, 41; mentioned, **5**: 383, 554

Hanovertown, Va.: British at, **6**: 49

Hanseatic League: reduction of duty in France, **9**: 140, 142, 263; **11**: 540; **12**: 466; trade treaty with France, **9**: 538, 582; **11**: 488-9, 596; customs in France, **12**: 214; in whaling industry,

13: 67, 433, 450, 451; duties on fish oil, **13**: 72

Hansford, Cary H.: signs address to TJ, **15**: 556

Hanson, Alexander Contee: in Md. Constitutional Convention, **13**: 333; *Remarks on Proposed Plan of Federal Government*, **13**: 337; transacts judicial business, **16**: 432; recommends Joseph Clark to Washington, **20**: 9-10; appointed chancellor of Md., **20**: 9n; issues injunction to L'Enfant, **20**: 45; recommends Christopher Richmond, **20**: 226n

Hanson (Henson), John: signs Articles of Confederation, **4**: 389; delegate for Md., **5**: 42; British raid on property of, **5**: 406; warns Court of Commissioners, **6**: 478; mentioned, **5**: 55

Hanson, Richard: letters to, **18**: 28; **20**: 153-4; letter from, **20**: 326; letter sent by, **6**: 355; attorney in Wayles estate debt, **13**: 251, 252n, 324, 325; **14**: 357; **15**: 132, 161-2, 616, 643, 645-8, 673-4; **17**: 513; **20**: 597-8; TJ's payment to, **15**: 647; **16**: 183n, 212n; **17**: 581, 592; **20**: 103, 153, 568; memorandum of agreement with executors of John Wayles, **15**: 674-6; letter to, from William Jones, **15**: 676-7; tobacco proceeds to be sent to, **19**: 263

Hanson, Walter: British depredations at estate of, **5**: 393; son captured by British, **5**: 393

Harcourt, François Henri, Duc d': letter to, **11**: 40-2; letter from, to Crèvecoeur, quoted, **10**: 601; Crèvecoeur's influence with, **11**: 126; **15**: 80n; Short pressed to seek interview with, **11**: 210; petition addressed to, **11**: 315, 316; mentioned, **9**: 261; **10**: 591; **11**: 334

Hardaway, Mr., **5**: 391

Hardaway, Capt. William, **4**: 526

Harden, Edward: signs nonimportation resolutions (1770), **1**: 47

Harden, Isaac: signs petition, **1**: 588

Hardenbergh, Abraham: land speculation, **20**: 130

Harding, Capt.: master of *Pennsylvania*, **20**: 249; leaves France, **20**: 250

Harding, Commodore Seth: and troop casualties, **2**: 197

Harding, Thomas: enlistment, **5**: 430

hardware: export from France to U.S., **12**: 470

Hardy, Capt.: letter to, **5**: 369-70; mentioned, **5**: 214

Hardy, Mr.: recommendation from, **13**: 621

Hardy, J., **5**: 4n

Hardy, John (?) (naval officer), **3**: 37

Hardy, Richard: signs Virginia Association, **1**: 109

Hardy, Samuel: letters to, **7**: 285, 355, 384; **8**: 289-90; letters from, **7**: 150, 278-9; **8**: 425-6; elected member of Va. Executive Council, **6**: 89n, 93; opinion of Steuben, **6**: 97; elected to Congress, **6**: 318n; and report on brig *Lusanna*, **6**: 455; illness of, **6**: 468, 469n; **7**: 4; correspondence with B. Harrison, **6**: 510; **7**: 11-2, 18-9, 44-5, 61, 93, 103-4, 140, 248-50; signs Va. land cession, **6**: 577, 579, 580; supports Steuben's claims, **7**: 101n; letter from, to James Monroe, **7**: 150; on Committee of the States, **7**: 299, 306, 524n; reports on Rendon, **7**: 433n; on revision of Articles of Confederation, **8**: 296; recommends Stephen Sayre, **8**: 572; on control of trade by Congress, **8**: 580; death of, **8**: 685; **9**: 89, 96, 178, 191, 237, 257n-8n, 479; mentioned, **6**: 355, 391n, 455n; **7**: 46, 227, 230, 280, 291, 565, 573; **8**: 70, 641

Hardyman, Mr., **6**: 198

Hardyman, Lieut. John, **4**: 540

Hardy's Ferry: British fleet at, **4**: 382, 384

Hare, Mr.: letter to cited, **14**: 584

Hare, Lieut. Charles: in charge of British flag of truce ship, **4**: 624, 625n, 650, 690, 691; **5**: 331n; papers examined, **4**: 668, 669; comments on Virginians, **4**: 677; **5**: 679n-80n; impropriety of conduct, **4**: 680-1; **5**: 31; and Westover affair, **4**: 688; **5**: 98-9, 118-9, 180-1, 250-1, 677n, 682n-5n, 688, 690, 693, 694, 698; ordered released, **5**: 9; detention of, **5**: 49, 678n, 679n, 680n, 687, 692, 695; letters from, to Steuben, **5**: 688-9, 696-7, 702-3; investigation of conduct, **5**: 691; letters to, from Steuben, **5**: 693, 703; Gen. Arnold's letter concerning, **5**: 699; mentioned, **4**: 687; **5**: 173

Hare, Charlotte: letters from, **14**: 407, 584

Hare, Margaret Willing (Mrs. Robert Hare), **5**: 677n

Hare, Robert, **5**: 677n

hares: weight of, **6**: 343; TJ's effort to import, **8**: 17, 560; **9**: 158; in France, **8**: 682-3; **11**: 423

Harford, William, **6**: 407n

Hargrave, Francis: *Argument in the Case of James Sommersett, a Negro*, **11**: 523; edition of Coke's *Institutes of Laws of England*, **11**: 523; works, **13**: 177

Hargrave, Willis: recommendation of, **5**: 190

Hariot, Thomas: *Admiranda Narratio*, **12**: 688; **14**: 40, 491

Harison, Richard: letters to, **17**: 338-40; **20**: 88-9; letters from, **17**: 484-5; **18**: 125-30; letter to cited, **17**: 334n; sends N.Y. laws to TJ, **17**: 484-5; **18**: 125-30

Harlem, Ellis: chosen to report on Sycamore Shoals conference, **2**: 72; and Indian land claims, **2**: 97

Harlow, Michael: in Albemarle co. militia, **1**: 665

Harlstone, Maj. Isaac: reports on status of S.C., **3**: 401

Harmand, Anthony, **5**: 387n

Harmanson, John: letter to, **4**: 577; letter from, **4**: 416; signs nonimportation resolutions (1769), **1**: 30

Harmar (Harmer), Josiah: carries treaty to Europe, **6**: 461n, 545; **7**: 5; letter to, from Knox, quoted, **17**: 132n; expedition against Indians, **17**: 132n, 134n; **18**: 144n-5n; **19**: 439-41; **20**: 106, 108; Heart's report on Big Beaver river sent to, **17**: 445-9; Ste. Marie sends affidavit to, **19**: 505, 527

Harmer (Hamer), George: letter from, **4**: 447-8; slaves purchased by Va., **3**: 344; offers to lease slaves for public work, **4**: 438, 474-5, 518, 519; recovery of slaves, **4**: 447; warrant for, **4**: 663; wills of, **11**: 28; **12**: 25; estate of, **18**: 27, 28; mentioned, **3**: 492; **5**: 431

Harmer, John: estate of, **4**: 447n; **12**: 25, 453; in George Harmer's will, **11**: 28-9; imports slaves, **15**: 654; mentioned, **9**: 94

Harmer estate: legal opinions, **12**: 453

Harmon, Valentine: appointed justice of Harrodsburg, **2**: 110

harmonica: played with keys, **10**: 78; Hopkinson's improvements on, **10**: 625; **11**: 141, 289; price of, **12**: 235, 297, 308; bellarmonica, **13**: 145; glass, **13**: 145

Harmony (ship), **14**: 273; **20**: 560

harnesses: manufactured by German

Harrison, Ben (of Brandon): marriage of, **16**: 25

Harrison, Benjamin: letters to, **1**: 154-6, 158; **2**: 286, 290-1, 297-8; **3**: 109-11, 124, 125, 125-31, 153-5, 156, 162, 170, 193, 194, 195-6, 197-8, 199, 200, 213-4, 216, 241, 371-2, 398, 403, 417, 418, 423, 425, 436, 438, 443-4, 446, 450-1, 456, 458, 475, 481-2; **4**: 98, 118-9, 121, 134, 142, 150-1, 154-5, 163, 168-9, 179, 187, 197-8, 214, 238, 240, 248, 289-90, 296, 466-8, 550, 588-9; **5**: 532, 626-9; **6**: 4-5, 28-9, 49-50, 72, 175-6, 195-6, 197, 351-3, 383, 388-91, 419-20, 431-2, 468, 468-9, 510; **7**: 4-7, 42-3, 46, 59-60, 90-1, 102, 129, 138-9, 225-6, 227, 230, 400-1, 430-1, 599-601; letters from, **4**: 304-5, 589-90, 655-7; **5**: 518-9, 519; **6**: 200-1, 345-7, 347, 354, 357-8, 372-3, 392-3, 420-1, 438, 512-3, 551; **7**: 45-6, 91, 102-3, 114-5, 230-1, 251, 378-9, 519-20; signs nonimportation resolutions (1770), **1**: 46; signs Virginia Association, **1**: 108; appointed to Continental Congress, **1**: 141, 224n, 408n; **5**: 168n; supports American state papers series, **1**: 146; signs Continental Association, **1**: 153; and Mazzei's agricultural company, **1**: 158; signs Congress' second petition, **1**: 223; signs letter to Va. Convention, **1**: 224; and Va.-Pa. boundary dispute, **1**: 234; signs agreement of secrecy, **1**: 253; and Ethan Allen case, **1**: 277n; on committee to meet with Lee, **1**: 286; debate in Congress on taxation of slaves, **1**: 322; chairs committee on Canada campaign, **1**: 391n; not reelected to Congress, **1**: 407, 412, 472, 475; signs Declaration of Independence, **1**: 432; faction in Va. GA, **2**: 16n; eligibility to serve in Congress, **2**: 17n; praises Duché, **2**: 39; on committee for dividing Augusta and Botetourt counties, **2**: 118n; on committee to amend smallpox act, **2**: 124n; signs treaty approval for Va., **2**: 290; letter to, from TJ and Wythe, **2**: 301-2; signs resolution appointing TJ governor, **3**: 40; supplied with guns from public foundry, **3**: 387; affidavit of oath as Speaker, **3**: 482n; bricks bought from, **3**: 616; **5**: 126, 127n; letter to, from George Skillern, quoted, **4**: 44; lends Va. provisions, **4**:

284; mission to Congress, **4**: 371, 457, 468n, 495, 605, 637, 670; **5**: 37n, 56n, 246; and supplies for Va. soldiers, **4**: 592, 598; and pardon of treason, **4**: 642n; cannon sold to, **5**: 140n; on value of Va. money, **5**: 209; orders celebration of Definitive Peace Treaty, **5**: 464n; letter transmitted by Fleming, **6**: 14n; on TJ's retirement, **6**: 78n; letter to, from Josiah Parker, **6**: 83-4; discharges Mazzei from Va. service, **6**: 116n, 162n-3n; Mace Freeland's petition to, **6**: 155-6; proclamation on British subjects in Va., **6**: 250n, 328; on Nathan's claims, **6**: 321n, 322n; on Pollock, **6**: 323n, 324n; inquiry on seat of Congress, **6**: 361; letters from, to Va. delegates in Congress, **6**: 421-2; **7**: 103-4, 293-4; letter from, to Gov. Clinton, quoted, **6**: 430n-1n; correspondence with James Monroe, **6**: 539-40, 557, 564-5; **7**: 47-9; bill on Holker, **6**: 543; letters to, from Va. delegates in Congress, **6**: 552-5; **7**: 44-5, 248-50; and Va. land cession, **6**: 571, 572, 573, 575, 653; and national domain, **6**: 574; correspondence with Steuben quoted, **6**: 620-1; criticizes Steuben, **6**: 621; proclamation requesting records of Council of Virginia, **6**: 651; correspondence with Samuel Hardy, **7**: 11-2, 18-9, 61, 93, 140; on Hancock assault case, **7**: 39-40n; visits Mount Vernon, **7**: 46, 49; resents affront by Mercer, **7**: 103-4; agenda for 1784 Va. GA, **7**: 260; and statue of Washington, **7**: 413; **8**: 213; supports measure for compulsory religious teaching, **7**: 595; opposes bill on liquidating depreciated payments, **7**: 596; succeeded in governorship by Henry, **7**: 597; supports impost of 1783, **7**: 597; campaigns for election to Va. GA, **8**: 113, 154-5, 416, 641-2, 685; **9**: 518; **10**: 108-9, 577; **11**: 310; struggle for speakership of Va. HD, **9**: 194-5, 478-9; opposes Constitution, **12**: 410, 425; **13**: 98; Tatham's quarrel with, **13**: 622; **16**: 9; candidate for governor of Va., **14**: 282; on Marine Committee, **15**: 582n; letters to cited, **16**: xxxix; **18**: 517n; candidate for U.S. Senate, **16**: 319; **17**: 607, 644; death of, **20**: 293, 405; mentioned, **1**: 7, 19, 261; **3**: 494, 616, 632; **4**: 196,

Hawkins, William (lawyer) (*cont.*)
7: 37; *The Statutes at Large*, 11: 547; *Treatise of the Pleas of the Crown*, 11: 547; 16: 481; 20: 378; works by, 16: 277

Hawkins, William (soldier), 5: 294n

Hawks, Capt. (master of *Russel*), 15: 57

Hawks, John: architectural work in S.C. offered to, 7: 131

Hawles, Sir John: *Englishman's Right*, 15: 282

Haw river, N.C.: skirmish at, 5: 23, 44, 102-3

hay: for Continental army, 3: 334, 409; Languedoc, 11: 444; sparsette, 11: 444; prices, 20: 717

Hay, Mr.: recommended for district attorney, 16: 477

Hay, Anthony: meeting of members of Va. HB at home of, 1: 27

Hay, Charles: appointed clerk of Va. Executive Council, 5: 370n

Hay, Mrs. Charles: inn rated by TJ, 20: 471, 473n

Hay, George: *Treatise on Expatriation*, 18: 311n; mentioned, 6: 128

Hay (Hayes), Maj. Jehu: treatment as prisoner of war, 3: 75, 95, 205, 230, 333, 488, 665; 4: 28; parole of, 3: 95-6; 4: 25n; ordered to Chesterfield Court House, 3: 605n; permitted to go to N.Y., 4: 47, 68, 105

Hay, John: letter from, 3: 340; application to borrow gunpowder, 3: 340; warrants to, 4: 444

Hay, William: letters to, 8: 207, 366-8; 9: 220-3, 636-7; 10: 632; 16: 92; 19: 256-7; 20: 418-9; letters from, 5: 519, 519-20; 8: 48-50, 648; 11: 318-20, 332-3; 16: 92n; 18: 113; 19: 286-7; volunteers for duty, 4: 354; sends oil to Warwick, 5: 428; director of Va. capitol, 8: 343; 9: 222n; 20: 28; letter from cited, 8: 534, 537; discovers prehistoric bones and artifacts, 9: 202; letters to cited, 9: 267, 652; 10: 67; instructions from, 10: 229; finds trees in well, 10: 604; subscribes to *Encyclopédie Méthodique*, 11: 318; 18: 113; exchanges books with Currie, 11: 327; letter from cited, 11: 328; books sent to, 11: 597, 662; 12: 270; surveys Edgehill boundary, 16: 98, 100n; letter from quoted, 19: 257; supports Tatham map, 19: 265n; mentioned, 8: 643; 11: 667; 14: 367

Haye, Hugh: petition from, 5: 349

Hayes, Mrs., 8: 163

Hayes (Hays), Anne: petition for pension, 2: 42n; resolution in Va. HD respecting claim of, 2: 63

Hayes (Hays), James: letters from, 4: 396, 431-2; reputed printer of TJ's Va. Statute for Religious Freedom, 2: 550n, 552n; transports printing press to Va., 3: 580n; 4: 534, 671; 5: 158, 193; warrants to, 4: 444; TJ's memorandum on, 5: 158; newspaper of, 5: 386; 6: 93n; 7: 601; 8: 539; prints broadside for Va. HD, 9: 204n; mentioned, 7: 525

Hayes, Robert: recommended for federal office in Southwestern Territory, 16: 477

Hayes, Lieut. Thomas, 4: 540

Hayes, Thomas: relations with Arkwright, 20: 315n

Hayes, William: in Albemarle co. militia, 1: 665

Hayle, Mr. *See* Hailes, Daniel

Hayman, William: commissioner for settling land claims, 4: 454

Hays, Mr.: introduced to TJ, 13: 512

Hays, Capt. John: prisoner of war at N.Y., 3: 390; 4: 34

Hays, William: signs petition, 6: 290

Hayward (Heyward), Mr.: departs for South Carolina, 11: 573, 592; mentioned, 12: 112

Hayward, James: and TJ's recommendation, 10: 553; 11: 200n

Hayward, Nathaniel: and TJ's recommendation, 10: 553; 11: 200n

Haywood, William: testimony on Canadian campaign, 1: 453; with Bondfield in purchase of ships, 17: 578

Hazard, Ebenezer: letters to, 1: 164-5; 19: 287-9n; letters from, 1: 144-9, 176; 16: 188-9; 19: 284-5; collects state papers, 1: 144-9, 176; 5: 562-3; surveyor of the post office, 2: 21; in American Philosophical Society, 4: 545n; letter from, to Huntington, 5: 562-3; letter from, to Laurens, quoted, 5: 563n; letter from cited, 16: 102n; applies for position as clerk to TJ, 16: 102n, 188, 189n; in Purdie's impressment, 18: 317; *Proposals for Printing . . . a Collection of State Papers*, 19: xxxv-vi, 288n, 348 (illus.); and new system of penmanship, 19: 121n; *Historical Collections, Consisting of State*

3: 628; 9: 242; senator from Md., 14: 302, 394, 529, 560, 615; federalism of, 14: 394, 529

Henry, Patrick: letters to, 1: 460-1, 466-7; 2: 237-45; 7: 647-8; 8: 90-1, 151-2, 212-4, 282-4, 422-3, 564; 9: 212-5, 599-600; 10: 161, 206-7; letters from, 1: 236, 658-9; 2: 5-6, 9-10, 173; 3: 293-4; 8: 67-8, 214-5, 507, 508-10; 9: 544; signs nonimportation resolutions (1769), 1: 30; witnesses agreement, 1: 67; and legal fees, 1: 99; helps draft Fast-Day Resolution, 1: 106n; signs Virginia Association, 1: 108; and *A Summary View*, 1: 135n, 670, 672; appointed to Continental Congress, 1: 141; and resolutions on Stamp Act, 1: 149n; signs Continental Association, 1: 153; on committee to investigate land grants, 1: 162n; signs Congress' second petition, 1: 223; signs letter to Virginia Convention, 1: 224; and Va.-Pa. boundary dispute, 1: 234; recommends Edmund Randolph to Washington, 1: 236; appointed Indian commissioner, 1: 245n; in battle at Norfolk and Hampton, 1: 258; stationed at Williamsburg, 1: 260; and signing of Declaration of Independence, 1: 308n; and Va. Constitution, 1: 332n, 334n, 335n, 337n; 6: 283n, 284n; governorship of Va., 1: 454; 7: 431n, 597, 610, 630; 8: 154; 9: 479; 10: 108, 109, 133; 15: 576; illness of, 1: 455, 462, 470, 480, 482; and lead for weapons, 1: 467; moves to reduce Congressional delegation, 1: 475; interest in Transylvania, 1: 566n; draft of letter to, 2: xxiii, 209 (illus.); commissions Mazzei to obtain funds for Va., 2: 29n; deposition concerning Henderson's land claims, 2: 69-71, 110n; involved in scheme to purchase land from Cherokee, 2: 82; and Philips bill of attainder, 2: 191n-3n; correspondence with Clark, 2: 246n, 256-60; succeeded in governorship by TJ, 2: 278n; 3: 3; and alien property, 2: 283n; 12: 453; letter to, from Evan Shelby, 2: 285-6; and revision of Va. laws, 2: 323n; 11: 153; 12: 411; elected Va. delegate to Congress, 3: 4n; appoints Penet agent in France, 3: 36; and money for Convention troops, 3: 64; appoints William Lee agent in France, 3: 90, 551; advised by Arthur Lee, 3: 91; and supplies for Illinois, 3: 158; applies to

Spain for loan, 3: 167, 169; contract for Westham foundry, 3: 188; asks Congress to reimburse Col. Bland, 3: 228; scheme for fort at mouth of Ohio, 3: 279n; notifies TJ of reelection as governor, 3: 418n; asked by Greene to assist in raising troops, 4: 576; 5: 216n; and proposed remonstrance against Congress, 5: 76n; on committee on parole, 5: 294n; reports militia's reluctance to join Continental army, 5: 583, 584n, 599; defends Zachariah Johnston, 5: 623n; and dictator for Va., 6: 85n; and censure of TJ, 6: 89n; reports on petitions for pensions, 6: 140n; and Cherokee archives, 6: 141n; TJ's attitude toward, 6: 143, 205; 7: 558; TJ's characterization of, 6: 266; 19: 172; supports impost, 6: 273, 277; attitude toward Va.'s cession of western lands, 6: 415, 572n; relationship with Mazzei, 7: 63, 122, 124n, 273; antipathy toward British, 7: 116; opinions on Confederation, 7: 122; favors increasing powers of Congress, 7: 257, 258; leadership in Va. GA, 7: 260; opposes constitutional convention, 7: 360; supports general assessment for religion, 7: 361, 594-5; relations with Le Maire, 7: 431n; 8: 121, 132n; letter from, to Henry Martin, cited, 7: 522; and remonstrance to Great Britain, 7: 524n; letter to, from Henry Martin, 7: 527-9; contract with Francy for supplies, 7: 553; opposes establishing courts of assize, 7: 588; supports extradition act, 7: 593; opposes payment of British debts, 7: 595; 12: 602, 609-10; letters to cited, 8: 650, 666; and Littlepage mission, 10: 130, 357; correspondence with Monroe, 10: 278n; 19: 491-2; declines appointment to Federal convention, 10: 575; 11: 154, 219, 310, 312, 331; advocate of paper money, 11: 85, 223, 310, 402; on forfeiting Mississippi navigation, 11: 221; opposes Constitution, 12: 281, 284, 335, 410, 425, 444, 453, 490, 609; 13: 98, 100, 101, 352, 403, 412, 620; 16: 26; and importation of liquor, 12: 411, 444; opposes Peace Treaty, 12: 444; TJ's opinion cited by, 13: 353, 354n-5n, 412, 414n; calls Bill of Rights "despised thing," 13: 354n-5n; speech in Va. Constitutional Convention quoted, 13: 354n-5n; proposes southern con-

Henry, Patrick (*cont.*)
federacy, **13**: 359; favors revision of Constitution, **13**: 624; **14**: xxxviii-ix, 673, 689; **16**: 145n, 173n; opposes Madison's election to Senate, **14**: 302, 342, 529, 607; **16**: 143n; promotes Clinton's election, **14**: 339; manipulates election districts, **14**: 529, 531n; antifederalism of, **15**: 5; Presidential elector from Va., **15**: 5; debts, **15**: 644; leaves Va. Assembly, **16**: 26, 173n; tries to transfer revenues of William and Mary College to Hampden-Sydney Academy, **16**: 26; supports election of Charles Clay, **16**: 130n; and "Decius" letters, **16**: 140n-5n, 173n, 175n-7n; letter from, to Grayson, quoted, **16**: 145n; rejects Senate seat, **16**: 319; **19**: 48; retirement reported, **16**: 445; opposes federal government, **18**: 82, 83n; **19**: 53; denounces proposed federal titles, **19**: 51; Washington's comment on, **19**: 52n; opposition to, in Va., **20**: 252; mentioned, **1**: 259, 266, 569; **6**: 110, 187n, 644, 645, 651; **7**: 36; **8**: 35, 36, 660; **9**: 174
Henry, Walter: passport issued by TJ, **15**: 486
Henry co., Va.: letters to county lieutenant of, **5**: 275-7, 617; bill to establish places of holding courts, **1**: 592-4; place of court of assize, **1**: 629; petitions for new county, **2**: 118n; militia, **2**: 131; **3**: 599; **4**: 63, 614, 622, 637, 638, 641, 669, 682; **5**: 7, 36, 275-7, 310, 583, 598, 599, 617, 646; **6**: 93; senatorial district, **2**: 336; levies of soldiers, **3**: 8; defends western frontier, **3**: 50, 52, 53, 79; tobacco loan office certificates, **3**: 516; disaffection in, **3**: 648; **4**: 14; supply post for, **4**: 286; riflemen, **4**: 621
Hepburn, Mr., **3**: 661
Herald (ship), **15**: 495, 498
heraldry. *See* coat of arms
Hérault de Séchelles, Marie Jean: letter to, **11**: 547-9
Hérault (Eraut) river, **11**: 447, 450
Herculaneum: book on sent to TJ, **13**: 361, 623; Short visits, **14**: 574
Herd, Henry: signs Va. oath of allegiance, **2**: 129
Herd, John: in Albemarle co. militia, **1**: 666
hereditary honors: and government of western territory, **7**: 118, 205

Hereford, Mr.: and bill establishing ferries, **2**: 454
heresy: TJ's notes on, **1**: 553-5
Hermelin, Samuel Gustaf, Baron: in Philadelphia, **6**: 276
Hermet, James: captured by Algerians, **20**: 625
hermine. *See* ermine
Hermione, L' (ship), **6**: 236n; **10**: 257
Herndon, Edward: officer in Regiment of Guards for Convention troops, **3**: 121, 155-6
Hero (ship): Cutting departs on, **17**: 309
Herodianus: TJ recommends works of, **12**: 18
Herodotus: TJ sends works to Rev. James Madison, **8**: 323, 408; reading recommended for Peter Carr, **8**: 407; **11**: 299; **12**: 18; TJ seeks Foulis edition of, **10**: 72; TJ seeks information on best Italian translation, **11**: 159; criticized, **14**: 181; Wythe cites, **18**: 487
Heron (Va. state schooner), **5**: 152n
Heron, Lieut., **5**: 699
Heron, William (spy): obtains information for Parsons, **17**: 41
herons. *See* night heron
Herrera y Tordesillas, Antonio de: *Historia general de los Hechos de los Castellanos en las islas i tierra firme del Mar oceano*, **11**: 554, 668; *Description des Indes Occidentales*, **19**: 207; mentioned, **20**: 382, 417
Herries, Sir Robert: furnishes farmers-general with tobacco, **8**: 214, 507, 641, 642, 644, 650-1, 660, 667; letter for Trumbull sent to, **13**: 284, 366
Herries & Co.: TJ's bill, **13**: 213-4; copying press ordered through, **15**: 609n; mentioned, **6**: 373; **13**: 241; **15**: 543
herring: Conn. export to West Indies, **7**: 334; N.Y. exports, **20**: 453-6
Herring, Christopher: in Albemarle co. militia, **1**: 665
Herring, David: in Albemarle co. militia, **1**: 668n
Herring, George: in Albemarle co. militia, **1**: 665, 667
Herring, James: in Albemarle co. militia, **1**: 665
Herschel (planet). *See* Uranus
Herschel, William: discovers double stars, **7**: 602; **8**: 575; discovers Uranus, **8**: 419; discovers two satellites of

Uranus, **11**: 162; **12**: 30; discovers volcano on moon, **13**: 379; theories criticized by TJ, **13**: 379; studies Saturn's rings, **17**: 515

Hertel (Herstale, Harstall), Lieut. Daniel Arnold: letter to, **5**: 301; letter from, **5**: 259-60; request of rejected, **5**: 509

Hertzberg, Baron: criticized, **20**: 695

Hesse-Kassel, Friedrich II, Landgrave of: death of, **9**: 81; case of, **11**: 544

Hesse-Kassel, Wilhelm IX, Baron von: country seat, **13**: 17-8, 449n; Shippen and Rutledge presented to, **13**: 449n, 528

Hesse Hanau regiment: among Convention troops, **5**: 100

Hessian fly: infestation of, **11**: 319; in wheat, **13**: 414; **14**: 567; **15**: 134; Paine describes to Banks, **14**: 567; investigation of, **20**: 245, 341, 395, 445-9, 560; TJ's notes on, **20**: 456-62

Hessians: at Gibraltar, **1**: 247; in British Army, **1**: 498; left at Charleston, **3**: 620; propositions of Congress to, **10**: 381; service in Netherlands, **12**: 564; desertion of, **19**: 326-8

Hester (slave), **4**: 436, 521

Heth (Heath), Capt. Henry: letter from, **4**: 349-50; infantry regiment, **3**: 154; Continental regiments under, **3**: 204, 244; independent company at Fort Pitt, **4**: 603; to join Clark's expedition, **4**: 653

Heth, Will, **3**: 652

Heth, William: on Va. Executive Council, **12**: 445; Donald's complaint against, **16**: 236, 263-4, 325, 382-3, 565, 593-4; **17**: 322n, 481, 626; collector of customs, **16**: 237n, 279n, 352, 509; bill from presented to TJ, **19**: 243

Heukelom, John van, & Son: letter to, **12**: 114; letter from, **9**: 308-10; promissory note by Barclay, **11**: 494n

Heusman, Capt. (master of the *Batavia*), **9**: 391

Hewes, Joseph: signs Continental Association, **1**: 154; signs Congress' second petition, **1**: 223; signs agreement of secrecy, **1**: 253; signs Declaration of Independence, **1**: 432

Hewes, Thomas, **6**: 290

Hewes & Anthony: and the fisheries, **19**: 196

Hexham, Northumberland: bridges at fail, **13**: 589

Heylyn (Hielan), Peter: *Cosmography in Four Books*, **6**: 489

Heyward, Mr. *See* Hayward

Heyward, Thomas, Jr.: signs agreement of secrecy, **1**: 253; signs Declaration of Independence, **1**: 432; Presidential elector from S.C., **14**: 666; **15**: 51; and medal for Washington, **16**: 54n; recommended by TJ as comptroller of treasury, **20**: 146, 229

Hibernia (British sloop), **5**: 305, 306n; **15**: 57

Hickcock, William: signs Va. oath of allegiance, **2**: 129

Hickes, Mr., **6**: 641

Hickey plot, **1**: 412, 474

Hickling, Thomas: asks for consulship in Azores, **17**: 251

Hickman, James: land in Albemarle Co., Va., **16**: 97, 100n

Hickman, William, **16**: 195n

Hickman & Smith: lands in Albemarle co., Va., **13**: 340

hickory: seeds requested by TJ for France, **9**: 254; sample to be sent to France, **10**: 227; in Gloucester, **15**: 593; **16**: 370, 448; grafting experiments, **16**: 370

Hickory Hill, Westmoreland co., Va., **5**: 678n

Hicks (ship): Jamieson supercargo on, **16**: 524; arrival of, **16**: 528n

Hicks, Charles: passport issued by TJ, **15**: 484

hides: and taxes for William and Mary College, **2**: 537, 540; brought to Petersburg, **4**: 218; loss of, **4**: 520; use of, **4**: 578; order for, **5**: 171; Va. commissary for, **5**: 241; Continental commissary of needs oil, **5**: 429; export from S.C., **8**: 201, 202, 203; export to France, **8**: 222; **9**: 112, 141; Va. trade in, **9**: 184; U.S. import of, **10**: 148; French import of, **10**: 475; **13**: 69; **14**: 643; French duty on, **12**: 469, 480

Hiester, Daniel: congressman from Pa., **14**: 395

Higgenson, Col.: leader in pursuit of Mass. insurgents, **11**: 87

Higginbotham, Capt., **4**: 531

Higgins, Robert: prisoner of war, **3**: 390

Higginson, Stephen: Indian commissioner, **7**: 8, 11; member of committee of Congress on coinage, **7**: 155n; on commercial treaties, **7**: 467n-8n; on whale oil, **9**: 74n; letter from, to Ad-

11: 32; engineer for harbor, 10: 639; harbor approved, 10: 639; port for rice, 11: 516, 659; U.S. agent at, 20: 676

Honnoré, Lieut.: letter from, 12: 360

Hood, Adm. Sir Alexander, 16: 427

Hood, Jesse: arrest for desertion ordered, 4: 527n

Hood, Adm. Samuel: defeated in W. Indies, 5: 74; conquered at St. Lucia, 6: 97; engagement with De Grasse, 6: 164; in British Admiralty, 13: 462; in war crisis of 1790, 16: 427; to command English fleet in Baltic, 18: 504

Hoods, on James river, Va.: ferry at, 2: 458; battery at, 3: 301; 4: 169, 358, 475-6, 583, 584, 592-6, 596-7, 621, 625-6; 5: 68, 126-7, 413, 487, 499-500, 510, 516, 536, 543n; 15: 600; express rider posted at, 3: 404; 5: 163; magazine at, 3: 491; place of collection under provision law, 4: 7, 8; Senf's draft of works at, 4: 209; British at, 4: 333, 379, 399; boats sent to, 4: 398; defense of, 4: 609, 620; Negroes for work on fortification, 5: 55; vessels needed at, 5: 57, 89, 124, 125, 126, 132, 144, 136, 146, 150, 151, 181; need for battery at, 5: 68; artillery sent to, 5: 90; supplies sent to, 5: 178; garrison at, 5: 207, 249, 250; relief of guard at, 5: 322; British objective, 5: 486n; mentioned, 3: 530; 4: 524; 5: 39, 93, 173, 480, 545

Hooe, Col., 3: 454

Hooe, Gerard: British depredations on property of, 5: 371, 393, 399, 406, 529

Hooe, Robert Townshend: recommended by Washington, 11: 388

Hooe and Harrison (Alexandria), 13: 94

Hooes (Hoes) Ferry, 1: 477; 5: 210, 529

Hook, Mr.: and bill establishing ferries, 2: 455

Hook, John: letter from, 2: 233-4

Hoomes, John: mail contract, 20: 666

Hoop (Hope), Joan Cornelius van der: on tribute to Barbary States, 8: 38n, 46

Hooper, Robert, Jr.: recommends S. R. Gerry, 19: 156n; signs petition, 19: 226

Hooper, Samuel: signs petition, 19: 226

Hooper, William: signs Continental Association, 1: 154; signs Congress' second petition, 1: 223; signs agreement

of secrecy, 1: 253; signs Declaration of Independence, 1: 432; letter from cited, 4: 16

hoops: Conn. export to West Indies, 7: 334

Hoops, Adam: estimate of British forces at Camden, 3: 597n

Hope (British ship), 5: 64, 343n; 9: 391, 392; 14: 296, 474n; 20: 631n

Hope, Mr.: conversations with British ambassador, 18: 85

Hope, George, 5: 294n

Hope, Henry (banker): house in Haarlem, 13: xxvii, 10-2, 16 (illus.)

Hope, Henry, & Co., 20: 202n

Hopewell, Treaties of: compared with Creek treaty, 17: 388n-9n; Hawkins solicits TJ's views on, 19: 286

Hopkins, Mr.: garden described by TJ, 9: 370

Hopkins, Commodore Esek: charges against, 6: 274n; 15: 581n-2n; TJ's outline of argument concerning insubordination of, 15: 578-82

Hopkins, James: signs Va. oath of allegiance, 2: 128

Hopkins, John: votes for bill for religious freedom, 2: 549n; recommended as commissioner of Continental loan office for Va., 3: 381; certifies deserters' petition, 4: 21; Ewell applies to, 17: 585; refuses to provide payment, 18: 642; mentioned, 17: 599; 20: 380

Hopkins, Samuel (N.Y.): letter from, 20: 580; *Address to the Manufacturers of Pot and Pearl Ash*, 20: 580n

Hopkins, Samuel (Va.): electoral defeat, 7: 116; on Va. committee to welcome TJ, 16: 11n; mentioned, 3: 652

Hopkins, Stephen: signs Continental Association, 1: 153; signs Congress' second petition, 1: 222; signs agreement of secrecy, 1: 253; debates Congressional representation, 1: 326; signs Declaration of Independence, 1: 432; cited on S.C. debts to Britain, 7: 348; signs memorial to king of France, 10: 463n; on Marine Committee, 15: 582n; mentioned, 7: 338

Hopkins, William: signs Va. oath of allegiance, 2: 129

Hopkinson, Ann Borden (Mrs. Francis Hopkinson), 7: 603; 8: 264; 9: 149, 483; 10: 250, 626; 11: 657

Hopkinson, Francis: letters to, 6: 418-9, 541-3; 7: 58, 111, 205-7, 227, 502,

Houdetot, Elisabeth Françoise (*cont.*) respects to, **10**: 200; illness of, **13**: 486; sends letters to Franklin and Crèvecoeur, **15**: 431-2; writes to Mme Necker, **15**: 536, 537n; Rousseau's love for, **15**: 555, 568; TJ's farewell to, **16**: 292; on French Revolution, **17**: 485-6; praises Franklin, **17**: 486; recommends Osmont to TJ, **18**: 30; mentioned, **9**: 350; **10**: 172, 251

Houdon, Jean Antoine: letter to, **15**: 238; letter from, **12**: 348; statue of Washington for Va., **7**: 378, 385, 413-4, 519, 567, 599-601, 604; **8**: xxvii, 87 (fac. of first payment draft), 155, 213, 267, 279, 282-4, 288, 289, 295, 422, 507, 555, 671; **9**: 150, 172, 213, 265-6, 270n; **10**: 186, 414; **16**: xl-i; **17**: 421-2, 450; bust of Voltaire, **7**: 567; journey to America, **7**: 600-1; **8**: 151-2, 213, 267, 282, 307, 308, 571, 684; **9**: 172; reputation as sculptor, **7**: 600; life insurance, **8**: xxvii, 87 (fac. of premium), 283, 302, 317, 340, 362, 424, 546, 577, 594-5, 602, 653, 663-4, 668; **9**: 42, 47; **10**: 204; portrait by Louis Boilly, **8**: xxvii, 215 (illus.); letters sent by, **8**: 4, 598; **9**: 9, 84; illness of, **8**: 91, 279, 282; described by TJ, **8**: 279; TJ's recommendations to Congress on, **8**: 288; equestrian statue of Louis XV, **8**: 289, 290; proposed equestrian statue of Washington, **8**: 289-90; **9**: 138-9; **10**: 99; **15**: 319-20; busts of Lafayette, **8**: 422; **9**: 544; **10**: 407, 414, 470-1; **11**: 560; **13**: 419, 471, 533, 661; **14**: 52, 54-5, 182; **15**: xxxviii, 457 (illus.); Hopkinson's attitude toward, **8**: 671; bust of Washington, **8**: 671; **9**: 9-10, 440, 466; **15**: xxxviii-ix, 457 (illus.); **16**: xxxvi, 62n; letter from, to Grand, quoted, **9**: 57n; arrives in England, **9**: 115; returns to France, **9**: 146, 213, 241; bust of John Paul Jones, **9**: 305; **13**: 585, 587; **14**: 687-8; **15**: xxxviii, 122, 376, 437, 438, 457 (illus.), 551; **16**: xl, 125, 318; letter from cited, **9**: 379; arrival of sculpture in Philadelphia, **9**: 440; marriage of, **9**: 466; **10**: 248; recommends copyist for portrait of Washington, **10**: 304; bust of TJ, **15**: xxxvi-vii, 456 (illus.); bust of Franklin, **15**: xxxvii-viii, 457 (illus.); payments to, **15**: 238; **20**: 645n; letter from, to R.

R. Livingston, quoted, **15**: 319n-20n; suggests alabaster vase for pedestal, **15**: 506; busts, **16**: 36-7; **18**: xxxiii, 36n; plaster model of vase, **17**: 507; dress for TJ, **18**: 32; mentioned, **8**: 381; **10**: 435

Houghton, Thomas: deposition concerning Henderson's land claims, **2**: 107-8

hounds: weight of, **6**: 343

House, Mary: boarding house of, **6**: 226, 232, 252, 262n, 336, 341, 375, 538; **7**: 289; **8**: 169; **10**: 535n; **16**: 183; **18**: 30, 38n, 81; **19**: 546, 551n; mentioned, **6**: 276, 342, 373, 381, 438, 541; **7**: 40, 44, 98, 120, 229, 394, 417, 444, 447; **8**: 264, 403, 405, 438, 582; **10**: 169, 236, 600, 610; **11**: 290, 405; **20**: 85

House, Samuel: letters to, **6**: 373, 531, 543; **7**: 111, 356; **8**: 402-3; letters from, **7**: 392-4; **8**: 169; bill on, **7**: 356; marries Miss Conroe, **10**: 169; mentioned, **6**: 380, 537; **8**: 25; **9**: 314; **10**: 600; **11**: 404, 405

housebreaking: punishment for, **2**: 500

house joiners: needed by TJ, **2**: 212

House of Burgesses (Va.). *See* Virginia: House of Burgesses

House of Lords. *See* Great Britain: Parliament

House of Representatives. *See* United States: House of Representatives

houses: taxation in Va., **11**: 153

Houston, William Churchill: appointed commissioner in Conn.-Pa. dispute, **6**: 477n, 478n; indifference to coinage, **7**: 158n; N.J. delegate in Congress, **7**: 572; delegate to Federal Convention, **11**: 400, 401

Houstoun (Houston), John: letter to, **9**: 120-1; signs agreement of secrecy, **1**: 253; McGillivray's correspondence with, **17**: 321

Houstoun, William: letter to, **9**: 121-2; letter from, **10**: 280-1; Ga. delegate in Congress, **7**: 461

Houze, Baron de. *See* La Houze, Mathieu de Basquiat, Baron de

Howard, Mr., **12**: 590

Howard, Benjamin: signs nonimportation resolutions, **1**: 30, 46; and bill establishing ferries, **2**: 459

Howard, Carlos: letter to, from McGillivray, quoted, **17**: 290n

Howard, John Eager: governor of Md.,

14: 395, 529; medal, 16: xxxvii, 52 (illus.), 54n, 56n-7n, 59n-61n, 65n, 66, 67n, 72, 74n, 77n, 289n; sword proposed for, 16: 56n; letter from, to Washington, 18: 10; fowards capital site acts to Washington, 19: 63n; recommends Christopher Richmond, 20: 226n

Howard, Peter: on Albemarle co. militia roll, 1: 668

Howe, Adm. Richard: peace mission, 1: 297, 501, 520-1; 9: 497; arrives at New York, 1: 458, 473, 483; 15: 577; reinforcements for, 1: 477, 486, 493; size of army, 1: 488, 498; bribery by secretary of, 2: 13; fleet seen off Va. Capes, 2: 28; letters from, to Congress, cited, 2: 200; attacks French at Rhode Island, 2: 208, 209; joined by Byron, 2: 212, 214; forced out of Admiralty, 13: 462; commands Channel fleet, 16: 427; 17: 438; prepares fleet for service, 17: 502, 650; in Purdie's impressment, 18: 331; mentioned, 9: 488; 18: 91n

Howe, Robert: Indian commissioner, 8: 516

Howe, Sir William: interim command, 1: 247; awaits reinforcements in Boston, 1: 269; and treatment of Ethan Allen, 1: 276; peace mission, 1: 297n; arrives in New York, 1: 412; and battle of Sullivan's Island, 1: 469; plan for campaign, 2: 13; encamped near New Brunswick, 2: 14; George III's comment on, 2: 30; troops in Chesapeake Bay, 2: 30; abandonment of Germantown rumored, 2: 38; correspondence with Burgoyne, 3: 259; on banks of Schuylkill, 4: 55; treatment of American prisoners at Philadelphia, 10: 61-2; agreement with Washington, 10: 352; relationship with Tench Coxe, 19: 125; mentioned, 2: 3; 6: 318

Howell, Capt., 4: 128; 5: 152n

Howell, David: letters to, 9: 233; 16: 553-4; 17: 244; letters from, 16: 451-4, 483-4; 17: 8; intransigence of, 6: 263n-5; on Ky.'s petition for statehood, 6: 485, 597n; motion on debt, 6: 510n; motion to adjourn Congress (1784), 6: 521n; and Committee of States, 6: 527n; motion on Va. land cession, 6: 575n; letter from, to Jonathan Arnold, quoted, 6: 585n; on committees concerning western territory,

6: 585n, 594n, 598n, 605n, 611n; 7: 147n; quoted on new states, 6: 586n, 592n; R.I. delegate in Congress, 7: 7n, 572; supports Steuben's claims, 7: 101n; on coinage, 7: 156n-7n; copy of TJ's "Notes on Coinage," 7: 157n, 158n, 186n; demands roll call vote on money unit, 7: 159n; votes on secrecy of ministers' letters, 7: 207n; attitude toward impost, 7: 226n, 232, 432; borrows books from TJ, 7: 240n-1n; dispute with John F. Mercer, 7: 291; TJ's letter of introduction from, 7: 312n; nominates TJ minister to France, 8: 33n; writings in newspapers, 16: 452, 453n; sends pamphlet on Trevett v. Weeden to TJ, 16: 453n-4n; on Morris' papers, 16: 511; letter from cited, 16: 511n; recommends state printer for R.I., 17: 8, 244; proposes sale of Alliance, 18: 387-8; mentioned, 6: 426n, 464n, 606n; 10: 463n

Howell, Jeremiah Brown: speaks at Brown commencement exercises, 16: 453, 553, 554

Howell, Joseph: Paymaster General, 18: 621-3, 624n; certifies Knox report, 19: 387

Howell, T.: letter from, to Washington, quoted, 18: 121-2n

Howell v. Netherland, 2: 23n

Howland, Capt. John (master of the Mary), 11: 629, 657, 662; 12: 270

Hoyne, Kyran: letter from, 15: 374

Hubard, William: signs Virginia Association, 1: 109

Hubbard, B.: recommends John Glover, 19: 156n

Hubbard, Nicholas: letter to, 15: 86; letter from, 15: 119; partner of Nicolas & Jacob van Staphorst, 15: 19, 86; and U.S. debt to France, 16: 79; 20: 179; views on exchange rate, 18: 448, 450; and Society for Establishing Useful Manufactures, 19: 454n; mentioned, 13: 213, 301; 15: 464n; 16: 134. See also Willink & Van Staphorst

Huckstep, Samuel: signs Va. oath of allegiance, 2: 129

Hudson (ship), 15: 303, 311, 336

Hudson, Barzillai: publishes Connecticut Courant with G. Goodwin, 17: 509n

Hudson, Charles: signs Va. oath of allegiance, 2: 129

Hudson, Christopher: in Albemarle co. militia, **1**: 664, 668; warns TJ of approach of British, **4**: 261, 267n; deposition respecting Tarleton's raid (June 1781), **4**: 277-8

Hudson, Henry: discovers Hudson river, **6**: 489

Hudson, Capt. John, **4**: 539

Hudson, N.Y.: whale fishery, **20**: 559n

Hudson river: British men of war in, **1**: 459; naval battle in, **1**: 487; British maneuvers on, **3**: 30; permanent seat of Congress on discussed, **6**: 352, 362, 366; discovery, **6**: 489; commercial rivalry with Potomac, **7**: 26; mammoth bones found on, **8**: 300; visited by TJ and Madison, **20**: 435n, 456, 473n; mentioned, **1**: 393; **6**: 494

Huger, Benjamin: letter to, **15**: 308-9; letters from, **15**: 186-7; **17**: 332; introduced to TJ by Kinloch, **15**: 71-2; requests letters of introduction, **15**: 186; TJ introduces to Carmichael, **15**: 307, 308n; TJ introduces to Fabbroni, **15**: 308; passport issued by TJ, **15**: 487

Huger, Daniel: letter from, **13**: 107; congressman from S.C., **14**: 666; **15**: 51

Huger, Elizabeth (Mrs. Isaac Huger): son possibly in England, **11**: 521

Huger, Gen. Isaac: commands N.C. and Va. troops in S.C. campaign, **3**: 415, 496; **4**: 86, 279; **5**: 86, 163; safe after battle of Camden, **3**: 596

Huggart, Col. Thomas, **5**: 603

Hugguer, Grand & Cie. *See* Hogguer, Grand & Cie

Hughes (Hughs), David, **9**: 488

Hughes, Lieut. Pratt, **4**: 541

Hughes, Capt. Robert (master of the *Paragon*), **4**: 700; **9**: 392

Hughes, Maj. (Yousenne): and Canadian campaign, **1**: 473-4

Hughes, Stephen: in Albemarle co. militia, **1**: 666; account of as guard for British prisoners, **2**: 33

Hughes, Thomas, **5**: 622

Hughes, William: signs petition, **6**: 290

Hughs, Stephen, Jr.: signs Va. oath of allegiance, **2**: 129

Hughs, Thomas: signs petition, **6**: 290

Hughs river: missing on Peter Jefferson's map, **11**: 469

Hulett, Thomas Birch: seizure of horses by, **5**: 512

Hull, James: captured by Algerians, **14**: 395; ransom of, **17**: 32; on crew of *Dauphin*, **19**: 333

Hull, John: letter from, **5**: 445

Hull, Oliver, & Son, **20**: 429n

Hull, William: letter to cited, **20**: 121n

Hull, Col. William: deals with Gen. Haldimand on western posts, **7**: 412

Huls, Benjamin (seaman): suffers frostbite, **18**: 55-6; payment to, **20**: 675

Huls, Nathaniel: payments to, **19**: 261

Hume, Lord, **14**: 352

Hume, David: *History of England*, **1**: 75; **12**: 18; studied by T. M. Randolph, Jr., **11**: 292; essays of, **12**: 19; **16**: 449; errors of, **13**: 460; attacks mercantilism, **18**: 224

humidity: effect on animals, **8**: 186; in North America, **10**: 646; **11**: 72; European and American compared, **13**: 396, 397

Humphreys, Charles: signs Continental Association, **1**: 153; signs Congress' second petition, **1**: 223; and Va.-Pa. boundary dispute, **1**: 234; signs agreement of secrecy, **1**: 253

Humphreys, David: letters to, **7**: 311-2, 321, 363-4; **9**: 77, 152, 328, 469; **10**: 250-2; **12**: 32-3; **14**: 676-9; **17**: 125-7; **19**: 254-6, 572-4; **20**: 209-10, 210-1, 345, 406-7, 565-6, 624-5, 677-8; letters from, **9**: 96, 241-2, 311-2, 329-30, 376, 608-10; **14**: 300-4; **16**: 66-7; **17**: 593-5, 603-6, 627-30, 648-53, 663-7; **18**: 6-7, 48-50, 102-6, 342-3, 472-5, 497-8; **19**: 270-1, 421-3; **20**: 327, 421, 474-6, 539, 556, 592, 604-5, 620, 677; **20**: 168-9; and Society of the Cincinnati, **7**: 109n; **10**: 532; secretary to Commission to Negotiate Trade Treaties, **7**: 252, 279, 300, 302, 364; **8**: 445, 455; **9**: 241, 242n; Washington's letters of introduction for, **7**: 301n; letters sent by, **7**: 312, 493; **9**: 61, 347; **17**: 615, 639, 667; **20**: 254; copies data on Conn. commerce, **7**: 324n; invited to share TJ's quarters in Paris, **7**: 363; journey to Europe, **7**: 382, 414, 427; meets at Passy with American ministers, **7**: 420n; message from Duke of Dorset, **7**: 495; letter from, to Adams, quoted, **7**: 612n; and treaty with Prussia, **8**: 8, 302, 313, 314; poem by, **8**: 84; **9**: 105; **10**: 251; **11**: 230; secretary of legation at Paris, **8**: 133; illness of, **8**:

Hutchings, Daniel: signs nonimportation resolutions (1770), **1**: 46

Hutchings, John: signs nonimportation resolutions (1770), **1**: 46

Hutchings, Col. Joseph: signs nonimportation resolutions (1769), **1**: 31; signs Virginia Association, **1**: 108; taken prisoner, **1**: 265, 267

Hutchins, Thomas: letter to, **6**: 427; letter from, **6**: 535-7; *Topographical Description of Virginia*, **5**: 585n; **9**: 300; **18**: 159n; map, **7**: 113; **11**: 519; *Proposal for Publishing a Map of West Florida*, **7**: 280; map of new states, **7**: 284; TJ hopes for chart of Va.-Pa. boundary from, **8**: 417; mission to Indians, **9**: 176; map of western country, **10**: 213; survey of land purchased by Indians, **10**: 287; observations of position of rocks in America, **11**: 323; letter from cited, **17**: 123n; *An Historical and Topographical Description of Louisiana and West-Florida*, **17**: 123n-4n; affidavit on Scioto land, **18**: 161; U.S. geographer, **19**: 40n; urged by TJ to compile Indian vocabularies, **20**: 450; mentioned, **6**: 586n; **9**: 609

Hutchinson, James: letter to, **19**: 614; letter from, **19**: 616; on new system of penmanship, **19**: 121n; and desalination of sea water, **19**: 612, 614, 615, 616; committee on Hessian fly, **20**: 245n, 446; mentioned, **7**: 20; **12**: 231n

Hutchinson, Thomas: *History of the Colony of Massachusetts-Bay*, **6**: 489, 490; **12**: 18; replaced by Gage, **10**: 369, 374n; errors regarding U.S., **12**: 579; mentioned, **9**: 488

Hutchinson, William: cited, **6**: 493

huts: for army, **4**: 485, 486; lack of, **4**: 617

Hutton, Charles: *Mathematical Tables*, **10**: 384

Huveaune (Vaune) river, **11**: 428

Huveaune valley: TJ describes, **11**: 429

hydraulic rope, **7**: 508; **8**: 73, 574

hydrostatic waistcoat, **12**: 30

Hyères (Hieres), France: orangeries, **11**: 285; TJ describes, **11**: 287, 430-1; TJ's travel hints, **13**: 274

Hyginus, St., **1**: 552

hygrometer: Franklin's work on, **10**: 646; **11**: 72-5; **15**: 134; made by Rittenhouse, **10**: 647; manufacture, **11**: 74-5; Vaughan sends to TJ, **13**: 37,

395; TJ's design of, **13**: 395-7; Vaughan discusses, **13**: 459-60

Hylton, Daniel L.: letters to, **6**: 220-1; **18**: 7; **19**: 262-3, 353; **20**: 154-5, 414, 614; letters from, **5**: 293; **19**: 294-5, 537; **20**: 214, 478-9; and Mazzei's agricultural company, **1**: 158; and TJ's conduct during Arnold's invasion, **4**: 259, 263, 271-2; to be outfitted for cavalry service, **4**: 343, 344; imports slaves, **15**: 654; letter to cited, **19**: 263; ships TJ's tobacco, **20**: 102-4, 414, 568, 606, 641; note for, **20**: 155n; letter from cited, **20**: 571, 572, 573n; financial affairs, **20**: 713-5; mentioned, **8**: 122; **15**: 575

Hylton, Mrs. Daniel L., **6**: 221; **18**: 7

Hyrne, Edmund Massingbird: letter to, **4**: 649; letter from, **4**: 608; deputy commissary general of prisoners, **4**: 438, 645, 647

Ibbetson, Mr.: joint secretary of Admiralty, **18**: 325

Ibbetson, Barlow & Co.: refuse to act on Paradise's debt, **14**: 629-30

ice cream: TJ describes, **11**: 439

ice houses: at Rozzano, **11**: 439

Iceland: and the fisheries, **19**: 179n

idiots: Va. bills concerning, **2**: 417, 488-9

Ignatius of Antioch, St.: cited by TJ, **1**: 553

Ilchester, Henry Thomas Fox-Strangways, second Earl of: land grant to, **8**: 85

Île-aux-Noix: importance in attack on Canada, **1**: 412, 450, 498, 499

Île-de-Batz: landing of *William and Catherine* at, **8**: 493, 517-8; **9**: 35

Île-de-France: U.S. consul at, **20**: 593. *See also* Mauritius

Île-de-Ré: Baudin asks for consulship at, **12**: 70, 432-3

Île d'Orléans, Que., **1**: 445, 447

Île d'Ouessant (Ushant), **7**: 363, 382

"Illinoia" (TJ's name for new state), **6**: 605

Illinois: British proclamation to inhabitants of, **3**: 46; exposure to attack, **3**: 665; attack by enemy expected, **4**: 498; public purchases for, **6**: 321n; name, **6**: 596n; Le Maire's account of, **8**: 123

Illinois battalion, **4**: 234

Illinois co., Va.: form of government and laws for, **3**: 72, 272, 276; inability to provide supplies for garrisons, **3**: 89; cavalry troop for, **3**: 154, 268; supplies for, from New Orleans, **3**: 158; paper money not current in, **3**: 272, 275; protection of settlers, **3**: 275; withdrawal of Va. troops from, **3**: 320; reduction of number of posts, **3**: 415; expenses of establishing, **3**: 444; amendment of Illinois act, **3**: 492; Va. credit low in, **3**: 521; official misconduct in, **4**: 355; **5**: 574; militia, **5**: 310; complaints from, **5**: 462

Illinois Company, **4**: 137; **6**: 655n

Illinois Indians: support G. R. Clark, **2**: 258, 259

Illinois nuts. *See* pecans

Illinois river: proposed removal of Indians beyond, **3**: 259; floods in, **6**: 536; distance to New Orleans, **6**: 537; north boundary of proposed colony E, **6**: 602; north boundary of proposed colony F, **6**: 602; post at mouth of, **7**: 280; poverty of land on, **9**: 189; settlements on, **11**: 308; rich in furs, **11**: 386

Illinois-Wabash claim, **6**: 650n

Illinois-Wabash Company, **6**: 476n, 571n

Imbert de la Platière. *See* La Platière

Imlay, William Eugene: consul at Newry, **17**: 251, 253n, 256

immigration: TJ's plan for encouraging, **2**: 134n, 139-40, 141; from southern Europe, **2**: 210-1; Va. laws on, **3**: 381; **6**: 421; to western lands, **7**: 218; **11**: 580; **19**: 19; N.Y., **7**: 327, 330; Conn., **7**: 332; R.I., **7**: 337; Mass., **7**: 339; N.H., **7**: 343; European plans for, **7**: 502; British attempt to check, **8**: 632-3; European fears of, **8**: 678n-9n; U.S., **10**: 13, 31; **12**: 6; method of transferring money from France, **10**: 394-5, 636; and Le Couteulx, **10**: 395; Puisaye's desire for, **11**: 105, 139; Washington's views on, **12**: 491; Franklin's advice on, **12**: 586; from Amsterdam, **13**: 10; from Palatinate, **13**: 10, 48; Franklin's information on, **13**: 430, 431n-2n; Adams' advice on, **13**: 432n; TJ's advice on to Luttrell, **14**: 476. *See also* aliens: lease of western lands to; naturalization

impeachment: of Va. state officers, **1**: 368, 371-2, 382; of Va. justices of the peace, **2**: 581; Va. bill directing

method, **2**: 591-2; Va. court of, **6**: 301, 313-5; British law, **12**: 605; procedure for, **15**: 227-8

implied powers: Jones and Madison seek TJ's support for, **5**: 471n-2n

importation rights to waste lands, **2**: 139-40, 141, 142, 149n, 155, 156, 163n

imports: Hogendorp's queries on U.S., **7**: 297; N.Y., **7**: 330; Conn., **7**: 334, 335; Mass., **7**: 340; N.H., **7**: 345, 346; U.S., **7**: 406; **8**: 309, 621; **10**: 145, 147-8; reciprocal agreement between U.S. and Prussia, **7**: 617; **8**: 27; S.C., **8**: 199, 202-3; Va. duty on, **11**: 153; estimate of American (1785-1786?), **19**: 135

impost: Congress urges approval of, **4**: 559-61; Washington's circular letter on, **6**: 269n; P. Henry supports, **6**: 273; adopted by N.J. and Md., **6**: 334; Mason's attitude toward, **6**: 377; approved by Va., **6**: 392, 421, 428; approved by S.C., **7**: 130; state action on, **7**: 226, 232; **8**: 134, 149; **9**: 380, 510, 538, 557, 666; **10**: 40, 234, 277, 288; approved by N.C., **7**: 273; and R.I., **7**: 432, 597; **8**: 133, 402, 482; **9**: 608; proposition in Va. GA to authorize collection of, **7**: 596-7; difficulties in passing, **8**: 325, 374; **10**: 293, 298, 313; **11**: 129; and N.Y., **8**: 402, 482; **9**: 176, 504, 608; **11**: 161; payment from duties on foreign vessels, **9**: 203; revenue expected from, **10**: 40; definition of, **15**: 25; and U.S. Congress, **15**: 148, 153, 225, 263, 264n, 275-6, 277, 337, 353, 418; mentioned, **7**: 630. *See also* duties, U.S.

impressment: of military necessities, **2**: 357, 359; **4**: 97, 104, 328, 460, 477, 485; **5**: 82-3; procedure for, **5**: 180; Lafayette's views on, **5**: 189; unpopularity of, **5**: 189; of horses, **5**: 292; by Great Britain, **12**: 185

impressment of seamen. *See* seamen, impressment of

impressment of supplies: warrant for, **4**: 75-6, 172-3; **5**: 533; TJ's attitude toward, **4**: 635-6; dishonesty in valuation, **5**: 161, 166; Mason's interpretation of Va. laws, **5**: 647-9. *See also* impressment under names of specific supplies

imprisonment for debt, **2**: 647-8; **9**: 574-8, 595-6, 639; **11**: 273

Indians (*cont.*)
Spanish with, **7**: 570; punishment for aggression against, **7**: 594; theories on inferiority of disputed by TJ, **8**: 185-6; theories on origin of, **9**: 476; **10**: 316-7; **12**: 264; **13**: 306; Franklin's mission to, **9**: 487, 496; treatment of, **9**: 641; **10**: 240, 599; proportion of persons to warriors, **10**: 59; dissatisfaction with land cession, **10**: 135; ordinance of Congress relating to, **10**: 272; fortifications, **10**: 316; defense against, **10**: 586, 620, 633-4; **12**: 444; **15**: 218; white, **10**: 643; lack of government among, **11**: 49, 92; resemblance to Tartars, **11**: 638; prehistoric, **12**: 159; burial grounds, **12**: 241; attack Ga. plantations, **13**: 283; Carthaginians as ancestors of, **13**: 377-8; **15**: 14-5, 451; TJ's interest in, **13**: 378; **14**: 436; danger of war with, **13**: 495; attack Dunkard's Creek, Pa., **15**: 218; TJ's opinion on lands of, **16**: 406-8; sale of lands in Ga., **16**: 408n-9n; plan of structure on Elkhorn river, **17**: xxxi-ii, 20, 394 (illus.); St. Clair's expedition against, **17**: 131, 132n-4n; **18**: 82, 144n-6n, 308, 596; Randolph's proclamation on, **17**: 388n-9n; in England as ambassadors, **17**: 664-5, 666n-7n, 673; **18**: 6, 7n; Northwest Territory Executive Proceedings on, **18**: 188-90; Scott's expedition against, **19**: 466-7; **20**: 295, 303, 309, 387-8, 480-1, 563, 566, 614, 616, 657, 667, 670, 680, 682, 690, 703; and O'Fallon's scheme, **19**: 598; killed at Fort Pitt, **20**: 90; Washington's attitude toward, **20**: 93; unofficial diplomacy, **20**: 104-51 (editorial note and documents); grievances against U.S., **20**: 105; Harmar's expedition against, **20**: 106, 108; Washington's policy toward, **20**: 117, 131-2, 143, 480-1; Gov. Clinton's policy toward, **20**: 125; TJ's attitude toward, **20**: 145, 214-5, 235. *See also* under individual tribes
Indian Vocabulary: TJ orders, **13**: 651
Indien, L' (ship): claims of crew against S.C., **11**: 283, 300-1, 332, 492; renamed, **11**: 301n. *See also South Carolina* (ship)
indigo: as medium of exchange in Tuscany, **3**: 366; export to Sweden, **7**: 347; **9**: 633; export from U.S., **7**: 406; **8**: 309; **10**: 147; production in S.C., **8**:

197; **15**: 12; export from S.C., **8**: 198, 200; duty on, **8**: 310; in La., **8**: 412; Portuguese production, **9**: 19; export to France, **9**: 141; import by U.S. from West Indies, **10**: 148; export to Sardinia desirable, **11**: 353
Infanta of Portugal. *See* Mariana Victoria
Infanta of Spain. *See* Carlotta Joaquina
Infante of Spain. *See* Carlos Clemente
infants: Va. bills concerning, **2**: 485-8, 628-9
inflation: wages, **5**: 355; state currency, **5**: 607
Ingenhousz, Jan: letters to, **8**: 295; **11**: 570-1; **13**: 261-2; letters from, **10**: 641-2; **12**: 191-2, 529-30; **13**: 487-8; **15**: 119-20; writings on air and fire, **7**: 288; recommended to TJ, **8**: 282; *Nouvelles expériences et observations sur divers objets de physique*, **11**: 665; correspondence with Franklin, **13**: 261, 262n, 488n; theories on electrical fluid, **13**: 379; power of attorney for, **13**: 488; *Expériences sur les végétaux*, **15**: 119, 120n; experiments with air, **15**: 610-1; mentioned, **3**: 150; **11**: 575
Ingersol, Col. Joseph: TJ visits in Boston, **7**: 312n; money for Humphreys left with, **7**: 363
Ingersoll, Jared: Pa. member of Federal Convention, **11**: 400; **12**: 231n; attorney general of Pa., **18**: 655n
Ingersoll, William (impressed seaman), **18**: 328-9
Ingle, Henry: paid by Department of State, **17**: 364, 366, 373
Ingle, John: paid by Department of State, **17**: 364
Ingle, Joseph: paid by Department of State, **17**: 366
Ingles, William: and bill establishing ferries, **2**: 460
Inglis, Mr.: killed in duel, **20**: 550
Inglis, Samuel: letters to, **1**: 70-1, 91-2, 94-5; **15**: 571; mentioned, **5**: 677n; **6**: 261
Ingouf, François Robert: engraving of, **7**: xxviii, 453 (illus.)
Ingraham, Duncan: owner of the *Amsterdam*, **12**: 510; on William Green's losses, **20**: 505n
Ingram, Robert & Hugh: letters to, **15**: 327, 349; letter from, **15**: 339; Wayles estate debt payments to, **13**: 513; **15**: 212-3, 327, 328, 339; letter to cited, **15**: 328, 331

ish works, **13**: 588. *See also* Walker
Iron Works, Yorkshire; Westham
foundry
Iron Banks, **3**: 279n
Iron mountain, **1**: 572
ironware: manufactured in Conn., **7**:
336; manufactured by Abel James, **9**:
485-6; purchased in Holland, **12**: 693
Iroquois Indians: message from Congress
to cited, **1**: 486, 494; relations with
Cherokee, **2**: 76; Shawnee and Delaware tenants of, **2**: 76, 77, 80; land
claims of, **2**: 77; treatment of conquered tribes, **2**: 80; sells land to Sir
William Johnson, **2**: 84; permission to
erect trading post at Pittsburgh, **2**: 98;
in French and Indian Wars, **2**: 99,
100, 104; treaty with, at Lancaster
(1744), **2**: 250; Sullivan's expedition
against, **3**: 411; covenants of preemption with Pa., **6**: 492; land cessions, **6**:
666; TJ comments on, **7**: 280; treaties
with, **7**: 397, 412-3, 652; Madison's
and Lafayette's visit to, **7**: 439; relations with U.S., **7**: 440; predilection
for French, **7**: 445; Lafayette's speech
to, **7**: 446; land purchase from, **7**: 630,
652; Pickering mission to, **20**: 121-32,
144-5, 251, 617; land sought by Robert Morris, **20**: 125-32
Iroquois river: as part of U.S. boundary,
6: 458
Irvin, Carson & Semple (owners of the
General Mercer), **11**: 656
Irvin, William: letter from, **1**: 585; signs
petition, **1**: 587; signs Va. oath of allegiance, **2**: 129
Irvine, James, **1**: 274
Irvine, William (Pa.): letter to, **20**: 621;
letter from, **20**: 608; candidate for
Congress from Pa., **14**: 473; bust of J.
P. Jones presented to, **15**: 437; letters
from, to Madison, quoted, **15**: 529n,
560n; reports Benedict Arnold at Detroit, **17**: 77
Irvine (Irving), William (Scotland): writings on air and fire, **7**: 288; and desalination of sea water, **19**: 615, 619-20,
621, 623
Irving, Charles: in Albemarle co. militia,
1: 666; warrants to, **4**: 444
Irving, Paulus Æmilius: letter from, **3**:
363; assigned "Colle" as residence, **3**:
341

Irving, Thomas: and American imports,
19: 135n
Irwin, Gen. *See* Irvine, William (Pa.)
Irwin, Capt. Thomas: master of the
Morning Star, **7**: 634; vessel captured
by Morocco, **10**: 347
Irwin, Thomas: seeks auditorship of
treasury, **20**: 230n
Isaac (slave). *See* Jefferson, Isaac
Isaacks, Jacob: letter to, **19**: 623; letters
from, **19**: 622-23, 623-24; and desalination of sea water, **19**: 608-16, 618-
20, 622-24, 626
Isabel (Negro woman), **8**: 451; **15**: 622,
631, 633, 636
Isabella (ship), **4**: 310
Isbell, James: in Albemarle co. militia, **1**:
668n
Ishoven, P. van: letter from, **15**: 42
Isle of Sables: fishery, **7**: 340
Isle of Wight co., Va.: letters to county
lieutenant of, **5**: 32, 416; Page's trip
to, **1**: 17; appoints infantry officers, **1**:
580; place of court of assize, **1**: 629;
militia, **2**: 131; **3**: 239, 601; **4**: 62, 63;
5: 29, 47, 181, 310; senatorial district,
2: 336; levies of soldiers, **3**: 8; tobacco
loan office certificates, **3**: 516; appointment of cattle commissioner for, **3**:
612; British in, **4**: 424; petition for paroled citizens of, **5**: 148-50
Isle Royal, **6**: 458
Ismail: Russian acquisition of, **18**: 453,
504, 606; **19**: 290; Turks at, **18**: 593
Italian language: TJ's opinion of, **8**: 410;
12: 14; closer to Provençal than
French, **11**: 254; unnecessary for
American, **11**: 558; Adams' study of,
11: 575; Crusca vocabulary, **14**: 382,
383n, 483, 540; study of, **15**: 156
Italy: musical talents of people, **2**: 196;
Mazzei urges commercial relations
with, **3**: 366-7; postal service to U.S.,
7: 564; attitude toward U.S., **10**: 178;
TJ urges Banister, Jr. to visit, **10**:
307, 332; TJ urged to visit, **11**: 199;
TJ's tour in, **11**: 354, 356, 432-42,
519-20; dairies in, **11**: 438; rice production, **11**: 645; TJ's travel hints, **12**:
21-3; **13**: 270-2; expense of church in,
13: 272; Rutledge's comments on, **13**:
531; **14**: 404; agriculture in, **14**: 42-3,
310-1, 542-3; Short describes travels
in, **14**: 310-2, 377-83, 405-6, 448-52,
541-3, 571-4; TJ's proposed visit to,

JAY, JOHN (*cont.*)

118, 119n, 149, 195, 224, 245, 247, 250, 252, 284, 335, 342n, 354n, 400, 483n; **16**: 64n, 65n, 69n, 182n, 265n, 283n, 335n, 357n, 360n, 361n, 424n; **17**: 244, 349n, 580n; **18**: 83n, 378n, 380n, 383, 430n; letters to quoted, **6**: 211n; **9**: 113n; John Adams' hatred of, **6**: 241; letters from cited, **8**: 42, 472, 543, 587; **9**: 54; **10**: 178, 310-1, 618; **11**: 18, 35, 555, 566; **12**: 121, 122, 146, 415; **14**: 70n-1n, 73, 78, 79, 523n; **15**: 7, 191n; **16**: 65n, 69n, 450; **17**: 349n; **18**: 372, 377n, 383n-4n, 397, 517n; letters from quoted, **8**: 328; **10**: 274; copy of *Notes on Virginia* sent to, **12**: 136; and *Federalist* papers, **13**: 157, 338n, 498-9; wounded in riot, **13**: 233, 234n, 246, 277, 337; as federalist, **13**: 413, 414n; as candidate for Vice President, **13**: 502; **14**: 4, 344, 385; **15**: 74, 92; in N.Y. Constitutional Convention, **13**: 611n; considered for Secretary of the Treasury, **15**: 153, 336; TJ's packages from France sent to, **15**: 436-7, 524; wine sent to, **15**: 437, 494; Mazzei dislikes, **15**: 614; congratulates TJ on appointment as Secretary of State, **16**: 20; and controversy over *Rights of Man*, **20**: 297; confers with Beckwith, **20**: 435; mentioned, **7**: 467n; **8**: 381, 445, 474; **9**: 503; **10**: 464; **12**: 112, 363; **13**: 286; **14**: 341, 438, 661; **15**: 139, 146, 531, 536, 551n; **16**: 107, 108; **17**: 359, 449, 516, 620; **18**: 226n, 245, 261, 266, 415, 517, 529; **20**: 428, 693n

Continental Congress

signs Continental Association, **1**: 153; and draft of Declaration of Causes, **1**: 187n; signs Congress' second petition, **1**: 222; signs agreement of secrecy, **1**: 253; Indian letters sent to, **2**: 286n; money drawn on, **3**: 656; attendance in, **7**: 572

Diplomatic Career

as minister to Spain, **4**: 12; **8**: 137, 230; **13**: 201; as peace commissioner, **6**: 95, 114n, 210n, 213, 214, 215n, 397; **19**: 486; recommended as minister to England, **6**: 265; **7**: 570; signs Definitive Peace Treaty, **6**: 457, 461; visits London, **6**: 539, 546, 568; **7**: 8; plan to conclude

JAY, JOHN (*cont.*)

treaties, **6**: 546; departs for Paris, **7**: 12, 15, 31, 42; returns to America, **7**: 229, 233, 250, 312n; **15**: 467; approves Adams' draft treaty with Sweden, **7**: 466n; knowledge of British affairs, **7**: 638; Bondfield's services to, **17**: 579, 580; in *Dover* case, **20**: 206n-7n; and U.S. right to navigate Mississippi, **20**: 652

Other Correspondence

with Livingston, **6**: 218, 224; with Adams, **7**: 608; **8**: 498; **11**: 513n; **12**: 200n; **17**: 227n-8n; **18**: 374, 379n, 380n, 389, 394n, 396, 409, 429n-30n; with American Commissioners cited, **8**: 246, 379n; with Carmichael, **8**: 251; **10**: 265-6; **12**: 239; **13**: 93, 94, 114n; **14**: 47n, 288, 289n, 499; **16**: 329, 330n; **17**: 472; with Dumas, **9**: 230, 231, 279, 301, 304, 463, 464n; **10**: 435n, 482, 540n, 558n, 572, 631; **11**: 12, 128, 244, 275-6, 510n; **13**: 160n-1n, 279n, 440n, 453n, 511n-2n, 548n; **14**: 6n-7n, 32n, 348n, 484n-5n, 613n, 622, 647n, 694n; **15**: 21n, 79n, 201n, 443n; with Washington, **10**: 533n-4n; **18**: 226n, 395-7; **19**: 499; with Lafayette, **10**: 563n; **18**: 381n, 391-2; with Lotbinière cited, **11**: 18n; with Short, **11**: 231, 233, 253, 276, 317, 345-7, 549-50; **12**: 487-8, 681-4; **13**: 247; **15**: 512, 533, 549, 550, 563, 565, 568; **16**: 3-8, 28n, 32-4, 40-3, 43, 49-51, 63n, 79-80, 86-7, 87n, 103-5, 106, 109n, 119-25, 130, 135n, 162-5, 199-202, 219-22, 234-6, 267-71, 273, 279-81, 282, 301-5, 333-4, 361, 371-6, 400-5, 417, 419-21, 425-6, 430-2, 436-41, 445, 571; with Barclay, **11**: 583, 585, 626; with Madison, cited, **13**: 541n; with Otto, cited, **14**: 77-9; with Robert Montgomery, **14**: 288-9; with Eustace, quoted, **16**: 8n; with Franklin, cited, **16**: 60n; with Adams, copied by TJ, **16**: 239n; with Walton, quoted, **16**: 451n; with Coxe, **16**: 576, 604-5, 618-9; with Dorchester, quoted, **17**: 46; with Hamilton, **17**: 77, 217n, 460n; with Pinto, quoted, **17**: 355n; with G. Morris, quoted, **17**: 518; **18**:

JAY, JOHN (*cont.*)
cover to, **16**: 24; and war crisis of 1790, **17**: 44, 47-8, 57-61, 79-80, 131n, 134-7; advice on diplomatic establishment, **17**: 220, 225; actions on British debts, **17**: 334n; advice to Sir John Temple, **17**: 495; and Washington's message to Congress (1790), **18**: 100n; advises Washington on Federal City, **20**: 55; and case of William Green, **20**: 502n

Jay, Sarah Livingston (Mrs. John Jay), **6**: 218, 224; **12**: 217, 218; **13**: 286

Jeanneret, François: proposal to buy U.S. debt to France, **20**: 185-203 (editorial note and documents); bankruptcy, **20**: 186n

Jefferies, Dr. John: arrives in Paris in balloon, **7**: 601, 602, 603, 604, 608; visits Silas Deane, **14**: 631

Jeffers, William: signs Va. oath of allegiance, **2**: 129

Jefferson (ship): convoys vessels in Chesapeake Bay, **3**: 406, 642; repair of, **3**: 491; **4**: 290; clothing and pay for crew, **4**: 186, 198; cannon for, **4**: 426; **5**: 140n; preparations to aid French fleet, **4**: 640; **5**: 25; and Portsmouth expedition, **5**: 132, 135, 182, 344; mentioned, **4**: 47; **5**: 172, 557

Jefferson, Mr. (of Mecklenburg): and bill establishing ferries, **2**: 460

Jefferson, Anna Scott. *See* Marks, Anna Scott Jefferson

Jefferson, Elizabeth (sister of TJ): allowance for expenses, **16**: 115; estate of, **16**: 157-8, 191-2, 194, 195n

Jefferson, Fort: site discussed by TJ, **3**: 354-5; settlers encouraged at, **3**: 416; Dodge asks for provisions and arms for settlers, **3**: 520; cargo of goods at, **4**: 170; conditions at, **4**: 188, 319-21; commanding officer asked to supply ammunition, **4**: 429; difficulties in provisioning, **5**: 494n; mentioned, **3**: 89n, 279n; **4**: 199n

Jefferson, George: notice of land lottery, **1**: 21-3; names executors, **16**: 482n

Jefferson, Isaac (slave): quoted, **3**: 334n; **5**: 244n; **17**: 242n

Jefferson, Jane (sister of TJ): estate of, **16**: 157, 195n

Jefferson, Jane Randolph (Mrs. Peter Jefferson, mother of TJ): house at Shadwell burns, **1**: 34; death of, **1**:

409; allowance for support of children, **16**: 114-6; estate of, **16**: 157; **17**: 675-6

Jefferson, John: letter to, **16**: 181; letter from, **16**: 87-8; suit against Richard James, **16**: 88; payment to, **16**: 211; letter from cited, **20**: 419

Jefferson, John Garland: letters to, **16**: 480-2; **19**: 252-3; letters from, **17**: 10; **18**: 43-4; **19**: 336-8; TJ advises on law studies, **16**: 480-2; **19**: 253; may borrow law books from Peter Carr, **16**: 481, 487-8; TJ introduces to Nicholas Lewis, **16**: 482; TJ assumes responsibility for, **16**: 482; TJ introduces to Monroe, **16**: 483; **17**: 277; and Rind's scandal, **18**: 26, 43-4; education, **20**: 331

Jefferson, Lucy Elizabeth (first daughter of TJ): death of, **5**: 469n; **7**: 441-2, 538-9, 635; illness, **7**: 110

Jefferson, Lucy Elizabeth (second daughter of TJ): birth of, **6**: 186; described, **15**: 613; death of, **15**: 616; mentioned, **6**: 350, 381

Jefferson, Martha (Patsy, daughter of TJ): letters to, **6**: 359-61, 380-1, 416-7, 465-6, 543-4; **7**: 43-4, 62, 110-1; **9**: 318; **10**: 499, 507; **11**: 250-2, 277-8, 348-9, 369-70, 394-5, 472, 503; **15**: 638; letters from, **7**: 56, 93, 95; **11**: 203-4, 238-9, 281-2, 333-4, 380-1; invited to meet Riedesels, **2**: 252; TJ desires companionship for in Paris, **6**: 218; handwriting, **6**: 240; education, **6**: 336, 337, 355, 359-61, 374, 444-5, 542, 543; **7**: 43-4, 410-1, 500, 517, 576, 629; **8**: 25-6, 403; **9**: 93, 318; **10**: 543, 628; **11**: 203, 238, 250, 282, 634; dress, **6**: 417; health of, **7**: 364n, 384, 508, 602, 603, 636, 637; **8**: 145, 151, 152, 257, 421; **9**: 92, 149, 159, 217, 348, 454, 465; **10**: 246, 250; **11**: 235, 333-4, 357, 362, 395, 612, 623, 642; **12**: 26, 145, 676; **13**: 343; **14**: 355, 358, 359n, 441, 483, 514, 515, 524, 531, 538-9, 554; **15**: 370, 520, 521; **16**: 36; visits New England, **7**: 414; **8**: 517; correspondence with Eliza House Trist, **7**: 583; **8**: 436-9, 581; taken to see illuminations of Garde-Meuble, **8**: 164; Mrs. Adams' affection for, **8**: 180, 420; **9**: 278; **10**:

Jefferson, Martha (Patsy, daughter of TJ) (*cont.*)

162; letters from cited, **8**: 263; **10**: 626; **11**: 208, 383, 637; **12**: 646, 657; knowledge of French, **8**: 451; **15**: 620, 622; letter from, to Mary Hopkinson, cited, **8**: 563; invited to visit Adams family, **9**: 116; news of sent to TJ, **9**: 367-8; harpsichord for, **9**: 483; letter for cited, **10**: 277; address on letter to TJ, **11**: 240; Mrs. Barrett desires visit from, **11**: 276-7, 282; drawing efforts, **11**: 282; Short visits, **11**: 315; opposes slavery, **11**: 334; studies geography, **11**: 348; musical training, **11**: 395; **12**: 308; chided for extravagance, **11**: 472; height, **11**: 634; **14**: 355; cited on the Hermitage of Mont Calvaire, **12**: xxxvi; views of Ireland sent to, **12**: 656; Dr. Gem attends, **13**: 7n; **14**: 359n; friends send regards, **13**: 50, 353; **14**: 51, 211, 513; **15**: 17, 52, 95, 131, 151, 165, 230, 282, 350, 379, 403, 469, 508, 537, 561-3, 616; **16**: 15, 48, 137, 138; remembers Mrs. Eppes, **13**: 347; miniature by Boze, **14**: xli-ii, 361 (illus.); miniature of TJ by Trumbull sent to, **14**: xxxvi, 364, 365n, 440; at Pentemont school, **14**: xl-i, 356n; **18**: 579, 580n; considers becoming nun, **14**: xl, 356n-7n; Hopkinson's songs for harpsichord sent to, **14**: 33, 324; **15**: 16; letter to, from Miss Rittenhouse, cited, **14**: 352, 353n; writes to Mrs. Eppes, **14**: 355; **15**: 622; returns to America, **14**: 357, 434; **15**: 368-9, 468, 490-8, 560n-1n; romance with Thomas Mann Randolph, Jr., **14**: 367n-8n; **16**: 290; letter to, from Laborde de Méréville, **14**: 478; Hopkinson's songs played by, **14**: 649; Cutting describes, **15**: 498; letter to, from Lord Robert Fitz-Gerald, cited, **15**: 512, 537; sends greetings to Cutting, **15**: 552; invitation from Mme de Lafayette, **15**: 630; Mrs. Carr writes to, **15**: 641; letters to, from Mlle Botidour, cited, **16**: 130, 135n, 273; hat made for, **17**: 316; mentioned, **3**: 3, 304, 441; **4**: 157; **6**: 145, 198, 227, 252, 253, 263, 265, 271, 273, 335, 342, 370, 415, 416, 473, 474, 538, 555; **7**: 58, 87, 131, 296,

379, 398, 417, 427, 430, 433, 439, 441, 447, 462, 535, 538, 539, 584, 587, 598; **8**: 51, 86, 96, 100, 116, 120, 137, 169, 197, 206, 296, 310, 346, 381, 383, 430, 450, 458, 554, 566, 595, 643, 647; **9**: 82, 129, 132, 252, 322, 323, 331, 380, 514, 560; **10**: 73, 84, 105, 107, 236, 261, 309, 312, 389, 483, 512, 648; **11**: 61, 167, 181, 287, 290, 294, 306, 327, 330, 394, 631, 657; **12**: 340, 414, 497, 555, 613, 654, 658; **13**: 546; **14**: 53, 304, 456; **15**: 174, 183, 412, 512n, 530, 550, 613, 618, 628, 631, 632, 634, 647; **16**: 16. *See also* Randolph, Martha Jefferson

Jefferson, Martha (sister of TJ). *See* Carr, Martha Jefferson

Jefferson, Martha (Patty) Wayles Skelton (Mrs. Thomas Jefferson): courtship of, **1**: 63, 66, 78; marriage of, to TJ, **1**: 86; inquired for by father, **1**: 96; letter to cited, **1**: 246, 264; health of, **1**: 408n, 458, 477, 483, 486, 489, 508; **4**: 4; **5**: 580; **15**: 573-7; invited to meet Riedesels, **2**: 252; letter from, to Mrs. James Madison, **3**: 532-3; letters to, from D'Anmours, cited, **4**: 66-7; musical ability, **4**: 174; last illness, **6**: 186, 192, 193, 196n; copies lines from *Tristram Shandy*, **6**: 196-7; death of, **6**: 197, 198, 199n-200n, 203, 652n, 653n, 654n; **9**: 65; mourned by TJ, **6**: 199n; collects contributions for soldiers, **15**: 592n; Elk Island as dower, **15**: 659-60; mentioned, **1**: 84, 247, 249, 286, 292, 473, 488, 519, 585; **2**: 206, 267, 278, 279, 292; **3**: 3, 11, 24, 64, 66, 86, 113, 212, 291, 304, 338, 363, 368-9, 440, 441, 484; **4**: 19, 157, 173, 193, 224, 280; **5**: 98, 173, 184, 295, 431, 468, 572; **6**: 54, 95, 96, 98, 110-1, 119, 121, 125, 127, 129, 130, 133, 139, 145, 161, 165, 174, 179, 190, 191; **8**: 304, 523; **15**: 593

Jefferson, Mary (sister of TJ). *See* Bolling, Mary Jefferson

Jefferson, Mary (Maria, Polly, daughter of TJ): letters to, **7**: 113, 228; **8**: 532-3; **16**: 331-2, 405, 435, 491-2, 599; **17**: 271-2; **18**: 141-2, 476-7; **19**: 282-3n, 427; **20**: 250, 380-1, 462-3, 571,

706; letters from, **7:** 58; **8:** 517; **9:** 560-1; **11:** 260; **16:** 384, 435-6; **17:** 239, 332-3; **18:** 594n; **19:** 271, 423, 607; **20:** 238, 335, 479-80, 633; marries John Wayles Eppes, **1:** 87n; health, **6:** 381; **7:** 386, 441, 539; **8:** 96; **9:** 191n, 201; **10:** 648; **11:** 642; **12:** 26, 646, 657, 658, 665, 667, 668, 676; **14:** 349n, 355, 358-9, 441, 456, 461, 466, 475, 483, 514, 515, 523-4, 538-9; **15:** 616; **16:** 36; **17:** 399; **18:** 80; **20:** 241; letters to cited, **6:** 417; **16:** 351, 406n; letters from cited, **7:** 44; **9:** 211; **11:** 348, 380, 637; **16:** 416; **17:** 266n, 332n; **19:** 420n; name, **7:** 58-9n; TJ wishes to have in Paris, **7:** 602; **8:** 141, 145, 152, 404, 451, 532; **9:** 91-3; **10:** 161; plans for sending to France, **8:** 358, 451, 532, 539-40; **9:** 159, 211; **10:** 594, 621; **11:** 209-10, 256, 260, 331, 394-5; journey to France, **9:** 396, 397, 560-1; **10:** 111, 483; **11:** 27, 248, 260, 281-2, 351, 356, 503; **15:** 620-4, 625, 627, 628, 631, 633, 636, 637-9; and Mrs. Adams, **11:** 87, 503, 514, 551, 572; **12:** 66, 202, 351, 553, 572, 574; **12:** 65, 112; responsibility for placed on Martha, **11:** 278; arrives in Paris, **11:** 333, 370, 379, 509, 572, 592, 612, 623, 634; **12:** 24; arrives in London, **11:** 501, 524; homesickness, **11:** 502; characterized by Mrs. Adams, **11:** 551, 573; pleasure in reading, **11:** 552; Capt. Ramsay's praise of, **11:** 556; Maria Cosway regrets not meeting her, **11:** 568; Adams' praise of, **11:** 575; Trumbull's praise of, **11:** 578; TJ's praise of, **11:** 634; Mrs. Eppes' affection for, **12:** 497; Dr. Gem attends, **13:** 7n; **14:** 359n; friends send regards, **13:** 50, 353; **14:** 211, 513; **15:** 52, 95, 131, 151, 165, 230, 282, 350, 379, 403, 469, 508, 537, 561-3, 641; **16:** 137, 138, 446; **17:** 240, 520; Eppes child her namesake, **13:** 347; education, **13:** 347; **14:** 349n; **15:** 497, 498; **16:** 208, 209n; **20:** 479-80; tries to write letters, **13:** 347; and Kitty Church, **13:** 422; **14:** 293, 663; **15:** 152; moved by Hopkinson's song, **14:** 325n, 649; writes to Mrs. Skipwith, **14:** 355; returns to America, **14:** 357,

434; **15:** 368-9, 468, 490-8; Mrs. Paradise offers to care for, **14:** 456-7, 461; passport issued by TJ, **15:** 485; described by Cutting, **15:** 497, 498; sends greetings to Cutting, **15:** 552; with Eppes family, **15:** 613, 618, 621, 629, 632, 634, 636; **16:** 208, 435, 436, 489, 491, 549, 599; **17:** 657; letter from, to Kitty Church, **16:** xxxi, 52 (fac.); learns Spanish, **16:** 208, 209n, 331, 332n, 384, 393-4, 436; **18:** 500; **19:** 240, 598; caricatures sent to, **16:** 241n, 405, 436; TJ's advice to, **16:** 331; letter for, delivered by Sir John Temple, **16:** 351; at Monticello, **17:** 266, 272, 658; **18:** 29, 500, 594n; plans for in Philadelphia, **17:** 658; TJ's plan for writing to, **18:** 39n, 65, 110, 141, 142n; exchanges Christmas presents with sister, **18:** 594n; books for, **20:** 382, 417; needs sister, **20:** 413; mentioned, **6:** 145, 350, 415, 416n; **7:** 636; **8:** 122; **11:** 181, 329, 631, 655; **12:** 414, 613, 634, 654; **13:** 343, 546; **14:** 531, 554; **15:** 174, 183, 370, 412, 512n, 520, 521, 530, 550; **16:** 278, 290, 300, 352, 370, 384-7, 406, 450, 489, 560; **17:** 26, 260, 299, 327, 331-2, 402; **18:** 350, 580; **19:** 239

Jefferson, Nancy. *See* Marks, Anna Scott Jefferson

Jefferson, Peter (father of TJ): acquires Shadwell, **1:** 9n; and Transylvania land claims, **2:** 65n; map of Va., **4:** 41; **9:** 300; **11:** 468, 519; and shares in Loyal Company, **7:** 504; estate of, **16:** 112-5, 127-9, 156-8; **17:** 674-6; **20:** 390; land grant in western territory, **16:** 479

Jefferson, Randolph (brother of TJ): letters to, **14:** 433-4; **16:** 194-5; signs Continental Association, **1:** 154; in Albemarle co. militia, **1:** 666; pledges to support clergyman, **2:** 7, 9; signs Va. oath of allegiance, **2:** 128; and bill establishing ferries, **2:** 459; shares father's estate with TJ, **16:** 112-6, 127-9, 156-8; letter to cited, **16:** 192n; and settlement of Elizabeth Jefferson's estate, **16:** 194, 195n, 208; payment to, **16:** 211, 212n; mentioned, **16:** 88, 307; **17:** 600

JEFFERSON, THOMAS (*cont.*)

vance to Franks impossible, **8**: 225; debt to British creditors **8**: 326; **9**: 389-90, 395-6; **11**: 10-2, 14-8, 639-42, 650-4; bills drawn on as minister to France, **8**: 589-90; account with Adams, **8**: 602; **9**: 47; advice on bills of exchange, **9**: 85; loans to Americans in Paris, **9**: 107, 118, 657; account with Barclay, **10**: 127; **11**: 670; account with Mrs. Adams, **10**: 202, 203-4; **12**: 553, 554; purchase of land in Mohawk valley proposed to, **10**: 235-6, 458; credit in London, **10**: 417; tobacco crop purchased, **10**: 588, 595; **11**: 371; **12**: 207; efforts to borrow money for Potomac project, **10**: 605; debt to McCaul, **11**: 167; letter of credit from Grand, **11**: 184; sums drawn on Grand, **11**: 185; sale compared with rental of land, **11**: 640; money shortage, **12**: 331; account with W. S. Smith, **12**: 517, 559; payment for daughters' schooling, **12**: 697; expenses of tour through Netherlands and Rhine valley, **13**: 34n; debt to Kippen & Co., **13**: 324-6; **15**: 131-2; memorandum books, **13**: 342-3; interest in Potomac navigation project, **15**: 79; avoids giving advice on American funds, **15**: 382-3; letter of credit from Grand & Cie., **15**: 470; expenses as student at Williamsburg, **16**: 112-3; settles financial affairs of friends, **16**: 308n; account from Paris sent by Short, **18**: 30-2, 33n-9n, 450. *See also* Wayles estate debt

Character

description by German prisoner of war, **4**: 174; Page's estimate of, **4**: 192; Hogendorp's estimate of, **7**: 80-1; Va. delegates' opinion of, **7**: 249; Tyler praises public service of, **7**: 278; Ezra Stiles comments on, **7**: 302-4; **17**: 443-4; John Adams' tribute to, **7**: 382n, 652n; Chastellux' description of, **7**: 585n-6n; **8**: 467, 471; Mrs. Adams' opinion of, **8**: 181n; Fabbroni's praise of, **8**: 260; Sir John Sinclair's praise of, **9**: 405n; Lucy Paradise's estimate of, **9**: 454; Lafayette praises, **10**: 477n; **14**: 223; Thomas L. Shippen praises, **12**: 504n; Nathaniel Cutting describes, **15**: 498; Maclay describes,

JEFFERSON, THOMAS (*cont.*)

16: 381n-2n, 445n; assessment in *Maryland Journal*, **19**: 545

Continental Congress

elected to (1775), **1**: 169n; annotations on Franklin's draft of Articles of Confederation, **1**: 177-82; defense estimates, **1**: 182-4; subscribes to second petition to king, **1**: 219-23; reelected to (1775), **1**: 224n; resolutions on Lord North's proposal, **1**: 225-33, 501-2; and Va.-Pa. boundary dispute, **1**: 234-6; recommends Edmund Randolph to Washington, **1**: 236; arrives for (1775), **1**: 247; signs agreement of secrecy, **1**: 253; on committee concerning powers of, **1**: 272-3; on committee concerning business of, **1**: 274-5; declaration on British treatment of Ethan Allen, **1**: 276-7; advises recalling delegates for Va. constitutional convention, **1**: 292; and Canadian campaign, **1**: 295-6, 389-404, 433-54; notes of proceedings in, **1**: 299-329; character as delegate to, **1**: 304n; resignation from (1776), **1**: 407, 408, 475, 477; notes on rules of procedure in, **1**: 456-8; reelected to (1776), **1**: 475; resolution on Gen. Sullivan, **1**: 478-9; and U.S. seal, **1**: 494-5; plan to persuade foreign officers to quit British service, **1**: 509-10; report on value of gold and silver coins, **1**: 511-4, 515-8; resigns appointment as delegate to (1781), **6**: 137n; elected delegate to (1783), **6**: 317; and residence of, **6**: 361-70 (editorial note and documents); and ratification of Definitive Peace Treaty, **6**: 384-5, 423-6, 439-42, 456-65; report on letters from American ministers, **6**: 393-402; and Washington's resignation as commander in chief, **6**: 402-14 (editorial note and documents); report on Gerry's motion, **6**: 427; report on files of reports, **6**: 438-9; and case of J. Penhallow, **6**: 447-52; and case of *Lusanna*, **6**: 452-5; report on Gen. Greene, **6**: 455-6; and Conn.-Pa. dispute, **6**: 474-507 (editorial note and documents); **7**: 140; motion on expenses, **6**: 510; report on J. Allen, **6**: 511-2; report on the powers of the Committee of the States, **6**: 516-29 (edi-

JEFFERSON, THOMAS (*cont.*)

torial note and documents); and territorial cession by Va., **6**: 571-80 (editorial note and documents); plan for government of western territory, **6**: 581-617 (editorial note and documents); **7**: 205; and Va.'s western claims, **6**: 647-68; report on Indian commissioners, **7**: 9-11; report on civil list, **7**: 12-5; circular letter on finances, **7**: 53-6; report on national debt, **7**: 65-80; resolution on Steuben, **7**: 100-2; inadequacy of salary as delegate to, **7**: 120; report on Hugh Mercer, **7**: 132; report on land office, **7**: 146-8; and coinage, **7**: 150-203 (editorial note and documents); resolution on treaties of amity and commerce, **7**: 203-5; resolution on diplomatic letters, **7**: 207; report on bills of credit, **7**: 221-4; expenses as delegate to, **7**: 243; leaves (1784), **7**: 244; outline of argument concerning insubordination of Esek Hopkins, **15**: 578-82. *See also* Jefferson, Thomas: Writings

Correspondence

tracing over of press copies, **10**: 288; publication of letter to Ramsay, **11**: 279, 286; dots used in, **14**: 689n-90n; forged letter, **15**: 142n; impact of letter on Edmund Burke, **15**: 269n-70n; minuscule handwriting with shorthand abbreviations, **16**: xxxi-ii, 32 (fac.); seal, **16**: xxxii, 52 (illus.), 298n; aversion to publication of letters, **20**: 289-90; use of birch bark in, **20**: 462-4. *See also* ciphers; copying press

Designs

proposal for U.S. seal, **1**: 495; asked to plan statue of Washington, **7**: 378, 385; for cabriolet harness, **10**: 211-2; for silver coffee urn, **15**: xxvii-ix, 280 (illus.); for silver askos, **15**: xxxii, 280 (illus.); for silver goblets, **15**: xxxiv, 281 (illus.); for silver candlesticks, **15**: 335 (sketch), 400, 453-4, 504

Economic Theories

value of Mediterranean immigrants, **2**: 210-1; on European banking, **2**: 224-5; commerce, **8**: 633; inequality in division of wealth in France, **8**: 681-2; inheritance, **8**: 682; taxation,

JEFFERSON, THOMAS (*cont.*)

8: 682; superiority of agriculture over trade, **10**: 16, 262; **12**: 38; eventual solvency of U.S., **11**: 128; on English manufactures, **11**: 509; acquisition of wealth, **12**: 38; importance of U.S. manufactures, **20**: 563, 565

Educational Theories

legal studies, **1**: 23-4; views on, **2**: 526-35; **6**: 379-80; on diffusion of knowledge, **2**: 526-33; reform of William and Mary College, **2**: 535-42; on schools, **6**: 379; on education of Americans in Europe, **8**: 409-10, 636-8; **9**: 465; **11**: 299; on scientific studies, **9**: 58-9, 60; education as antidote for tyranny, **10**: 244; advice to T. M. Randolph, Jr., **10**: 305-9; politics as study, **11**: 557; advice to R. Izard, **13**: 372-3; advice to Peter Carr, **16**: 277; girl with city education a useless bauble, **17**: 658. *See also* Carr, Peter: education of; Jefferson, Martha: education; Jefferson, Mary: education; law, study of

Governor of Virginia

salary, **2**: 275n; election as, **2**: 277-8; **3**: 114-5; accepts office reluctantly, **3**: 15; proclamation expelling Tories, **3**: 22-3; dispute with Board of War, **3**: 122-3, 150-1, 195-6; résumé of GA dealings with John Ballendine, **3**: 125-31; bill for establishing a manufactory of arms and extending navigation of James river, **3**: 131-47; congratulated by Fabbroni, **3**: 148, 150n, 237; appoints day of thanksgiving and prayer, **3**: 177-9; proclamation of embargo, **3**: 208-9; proclamation concerning consuls, **3**: 251-2; calculations and returns of battalions, **3**: xxxiii, 254 (illus.); return of arms, stores, etc., **3**: xxxiii, 254 (illus.); returns of land and naval forces, **3**: xxxiii, 254 (illus.); annoyance at counterfeit bill of health, **3**: 258n; proclamation concerning northwest settlers, **3**: 266-7; criticized for establishing Fort Jefferson, **3**: 279n; removal from Williamsburg to Richmond, **3**: 334n; reelection as, **3**: 410, 417; rumor of impeachment, **3**: 430; desire to leave office, **3**: 643; **4**: 192; **5**: 58, 59n;

JEFFERSON, THOMAS (*cont.*)

reaction to reported resignation, **3:** 655; **4:** 19; preserves public records, **4:** 116n; charges against, **4:** 256n-8n; diary of Arnold's invasion, **4:** 258-68; retirement as, **4:** 260; **5:** 326, 431; **6:** 33, 77n-8n, 90; inquiry into conduct, **4:** 261-2, 264; **6:** 85n-6n, 88, 97, 104-9, 113-4, 118-9, 133-4, 143, 147; Gen. Lee's criticism of, **4:** 264-6, 267n; depositions on conduct during Arnold's invasion, **4:** 271-2; explanation of delay in starting battery at Hoods, **4:** 592-4; Steuben's criticism of, **4:** 652n; **5:** 107n; requisition of arms, **5:** 153; relations with legislature, **5:** 314n; and Gen. Phillips, **5:** 364, 633; plans to leave Richmond, **5:** 549; appointment of deputy quartermaster general, **5:** 577n-8n; reprieve of slave sentenced for treason, **5:** 640-3; administration praised by John Harvie, **6:** 133; resolution of thanks by Va. GA, **6:** 135-7, 143, 149, 160; bitterness over attempted impeachment, **6:** 184-7; signing of commissions, land grants, patents, licenses, Loan Office receipts, **6:** xxxvi, 640-6, 668 (illus.)

Health

headaches, **1:** 16, 292, 296; **6:** 570; **15:** 384; **16:** 411n, 416, 429, 432, 433, 443, 445n, 475, 486-95, 536, 600, 605-6; **20:** 417, 558; experiences hydrophobia, **1:** 19; illness in March 1776, **1:** 409; fall from horse, **4:** 261, 266; **6:** 112, 113; ill health in Annapolis, **6:** 438, 454n, 541-2, 543, 556; improvement in, **7:** 31; **9:** 92; ill health in Paris, **7:** 500, 502, 545, 602, 604, 636, 637; **8:** 43, 47n, 56n, 145, 152, 163, 381; **15:** 384, 407, 410, 413; seasickness not severe, **7:** 508; Gilmer's anxiety concerning, **9:** 83; re-establishment of, **9:** 465; injury to wrist, **10:** 367n, 394n, 397, 400, 402, 414, 417-8, 431-3, 438, 460n, 467, 478, 479, 503, 506, 542, 543, 556, 575, 594, 600, 602, 607, 608, 611, 620, 621, 624, 626, 628, 630, 632, 638; **11:** 12, 31, 86, 96, 163, 164, 267, 280, 289, 307, 323, 330, 350, 397, 403, 516, 553, 631, 636; **12:** 26, 453;

JEFFERSON, THOMAS (*cont.*)

14: 361; false reports of illness and death (1786), **15:** 626; seasickness as cure for headache, **16:** 475

Honors

membership in American Philosophical Society, **4:** xxxvii, 107 (illus.), 544; **10:** 437, 624; honorary degree from College of William and Mary, **6:** 221-2; recognition accorded in New England, **7:** 312n; proposed for faculty of College of William and Mary, **8:** 417; election to South Carolina Society for Promoting and Improving Agriculture and other Rural Concerns, **9:** 53; degree of LLD from Yale, **10:** 385-6, 594, 629; degree of LLD from Harvard, **13:** 637-8; **14:** 697; Fourth of July tribute from Americans in Paris, **15:** 239-42; address of welcome from officials of Norfolk, with TJ's reply, **15:** 556-7; address of welcome from Va. HD, with TJ's reply, **16:** 11, 168n-9n; address of welcome from Va. Senate, with TJ's reply, **16:** 11-3; address of welcome from citizens of Albemarle Co., with TJ's reply, **16:** 110, 111n, 167-80 (editorial note and documents); membership in American Academy of Arts and Sciences, **16:** 111-2, 289; membership proposed in Société de quatrevingt neuf, **16:** 133; address of welcome from mayor of Alexandria, Va., with TJ's reply, **16:** 224, 225; given miniature of Louis XVI by French government, **16:** 362n-3n, 366

Journeys

proposed trip to Europe (1763), **1:** 8-9, 13; trip north (1766), **1:** 18-21; abortive journey to Europe (1783), **6:** 216-8, 227-9, 230-2, 237, 241-2; from Philadelphia to Baltimore (1783), **6:** 225; voyage to Europe (1784), **7:** 234, 290, 321, 357-8, 363-4, 382, 384; **8:** 436-7; New England tour (1784), **7:** 311n-2n; proposed tour of France (1785), **8:** 43; visits Fontainebleau, **8:** 681; to England (1786), **9:** 295, 312-3, 325, 350-2, 362-4, 368-75, 395, 400-5, 433-4, 435-6, 446, 447, 651; proposed trip to Netherlands

JEFFERSON, THOMAS (*cont.*)
cyclopedias in, **14**: 412n; "biblio-manie," **15**: 163; work-sheet for catalogue of, **15**: 546n. *See also* books

Maps
Gwynn's Island, **1**: lviii, 566 (illus.); Kentucky region of Fincastle co., Va., **1**: 567 (illus.); Albemarle co., Va., **2**: xxiii, 208 (illus.)

Minister to France
appointment as, **7**: 115, 148, 570, 572, 652; **8**: 33, 54, 86, 133, 134, 140, 145-6, 150, 151, 153, 156n, 157, 158, 159, 171, 226, 328n-9n; importance to Va. of, **7**: 249; expenses, **7**: 512-3, 564; **8**: 230, 549, 590-1; **12**: 387; **13**: 161-4, 202-3, 625-6; **14**: 16-7, 290; **15**: 41; salary, **8**: 79; **11**: 611; **12**: 45, 55, 123, 546; **14**: 56, 581; **17**: 21, 318; sentiment for recall, **8**: 375n; secretarial aid, **8**: 445, 454, 547, 593; and mission of Barclay and Lamb to Barbary States, **8**: 610-28 (editorial note and documents); statement of case of the *William and Catherine*, **9**: 31-8; negotiations for treaty with Portugal, **9**: 410-33 (editorial note and documents); efforts to reduce errors concerning America in the *Encyclopédie Méthodique*, **10**: 4-60 (editorial note and documents); address on presentation of bust of Lafayette to Paris, **10**: 407-10, 414-5, 470-1; signs Moroccan treaty, **10**: 426; circular letters to U.S. agents in France, **10**: 493; **12**: 209-10, 474; **14**: 457; proposed concert of powers against Barbary States, **10**: 560-70 (editorial note and documents); Otto's tribute to, **11**: 147n; negotiations with Spain on Mississippi proposal, **11**: 309, 481; renewal of commission doubted, **11**: 483; observations on Calonne's letter concerning American trade, **11**: 539-42, 550; commissioned to treat with France concerning consuls, **11**: 628; and American tobacco trade, **12**: 76-93 (editorial note and documents); reappointment as, **12**: 266, 269, 282, 395, 432, 453; and American trade, **13**: 59-91 (editorial note and documents); plans return to America, **13**: 391, 521, 639; **14**: 45, 189,

JEFFERSON, THOMAS (*cont.*)
355, 357, 361, 362, 365-6, 369-70, 375, 387, 428, 434, 483, 554, 597, 605, 623, 673; Consular Convention negotiations, **14**: 66-180 (editorial note and documents); and funding of foreign debt, **14**: 190-209 (editorial note and documents); requests leave of absence, **14**: 214-6, 332, 335, 628-9, 639; **15**: 7, 118, 202-3, 224, 356; whale fishery negotiations, **14**: 217-69 (editorial note and documents); state of the case of Schweighauser & Dobrée, **14**: 315-23; refuses to authenticate writings, **14**: 389; memorandum on public accounts, **15**: 84; Mirabeau incident, **15**: 243-56 (editorial note and documents); and rice trade, **15**: 445-8 (editorial note and documents); passports issued by (1785-1789), **15**: 483-7; form letter for refusing requests for influence, **15**: 487; policy on gifts to foreign diplomats, **16**: 356n-68. *See also* Algiers; Algiers, American captives in; American Commissioners for Negotiating Commercial Treaties; Barbary States; farmers-general; France: Loan to U.S.; France: U.S. Relations; French officers in American Revolution; French Revolution; Great Britain: Relations with U.S.; Morocco; Portugal; Spain; tobacco trade; whale fisheries; whale oil

Music
orders clavichord, **1**: 62; agreement with John Randolph, **1**: 66-7; orders pianoforte, **1**: 71-2; acquires John Randolph's violin, **1**: 240-3; hopes to find musicians among Italian workmen, **2**: 196; desire for organ, **2**: 206; harpsichord and sticcado, **8**: 263; experiments in determining tempo, **9**: 146-8; interest in harpsichord, **10**: 75; **13**: 145, 200, 293; **16**: 81, 90; glass harmonica, **13**: 145; jacks for spinet, **16**: 490; **17**: 389-90

Opinions
on marriage, **1**: 16; utility of fiction, **1**: 76-8; on slavery, **1**: 129-30; **2**: 472n-3n; **9**: 9, 441; **10**: 58, 62, 63; **12**: 577-8; **14**: 492-3; **20**: 160; on need to preserve historical records,

JEFFERSON, THOMAS (*cont.*)
1: 145-9, 164-5; 19: 287-9; effect of
war on Va., 1: 409; on slave trade,
1: 426; 11; 589; attitude toward Indians, 1: 485-6; 2: 286; 3: 259; 5:
60-4; 10: 240; 20: 214-5, 235; on
deterring crime, 1: 505; 2: 230,
492-507; on genius, 2: 202-3; on
immigration to U.S., 2: 210; on
convict labor, 2: 515n; on meaning
of public library, 2: 544n; on curtailment of natural rights, 5: 356;
concept of public service, 6: 244-5,
255-6; 17: 344-6; on need to respect
women, 6: 379-80; on proper feminine attire, 6: 417; praise of America, 8: 233; freedom of opinion, 8:
260; trading without capital, 8: 399;
social conditions in France, 8: 568-9; writing and speaking, 8: 637; disadvantages of public service, 9: 215;
future power of U.S., 9: 218; separate creation of blacks, 9: 441; exercise and health, 10: 308; need of
congenial society, 10: 612; superiority of country life, 10: 613; children
as blessing for the autumn of life,
11: 57; better to have no ideas than
false ones, 13: 379; domestic felicity,
13: 490; 16: 386; minister of state
should not interfere in private suits,
14: 553; on love and friendships, 15:
143; ridicules titles of honor, 15:
315, 336-7, 367; public employment
as honorable exile from family, 16:
353; advice on friendships to Martha
Jefferson Randolph, 17: 215; need
for good neighbors, 20: 381; undesirability of free black settlement in
U.S., 20: 558

Personal Affairs
advised to go to college, 1: 3; courtship of Rebecca Burwell, 1: 5-11,
13-4; and family coat of arms, 1: 62;
courtship of Martha Wayles Skelton,
1: 63, 66, 71, 78; marriage of, 1:
86, 93n; petition to dock entail on
wife's property, 1: 104; Monroe
thanks for kindness, 3: 621-3; death
of wife, 6: 197, 198-200, 203, 652n,
653n, 654n; solicitude for daughters, 6: 198-200, 219; inoculation of
children, 6: 207; messages to children, 6: 350; reasons for melancholy, 7: 208; aids Beesly Edgar

JEFFERSON, THOMAS (*cont.*)
Joel, 7: 395-6; urges friends to settle
nearby, 7: 559; aids Learmonth, 8:
162; friendship with Adams family,
8: 164, 178; love of seclusion, 8:
500; loss of wife and children, 8:
500; 11: 57; interest in chess, 8:
641; refuses to ask personal favors,
9: 657; 12: 329, 587; acceptance of
criticism, 10: 113; 12: 439; aids
John Ledyard, 10: 259n-60n; daily
schedule, 10: 308; aids poor woman
in Philadelphia, 10: 451; change in
life brought about by ministry to
France, 10: 600; cook in Paris, 11:
98; against indolence and extravagance, 11: 250, 633, 636; love for
children, 11: 251-2, 277-8; conduct
of servants, 11: 298, 354; scrupulousness of conduct, 12: 116; sincerity of friendships, 12: 348; hospitality to young Americans in Europe,
13: 141n; social relationships not affected by political differences, 13:
141n; plainness of clothing, 13:
164n; thinks of friends while riding,
13: 422; mistaken for Englishman,
14: xxxviii; 15: 279n; relationship
with daughters, 14: 189, 215, 332,
335, 355, 357, 428, 434, 695, 697;
16: 300; on family life, 14: 433-4;
16: 353; weather preferences, 14:
446; plagued by friends of friends,
14: 703; passports, 15: xxxiv-v, 49-50, 424 (fac.); ambition "to glide
unnoticed thro' a silent execution of
duty," 15: 242; home in Paris
robbed, 15: 260-1; wants no office
away from home, 15: 369; discovers
suicide victim, 15: 509; household
furnishings sent from Paris, 16:
xxxiii, 229-30, 320-4, 500-1, 583,
590; 17: 11, 28-9, 212, 258, 282,
315, 392, 394-5, 402n, 410-2, 435-7, 506, 547, 559, 645-6; 18: xxxiii,
30-2, 33n-9n, 35n-7n, 65, 74n, 111,
306-8, 479-80, 600; 20: 94-5, 211;
desires news of friends, 16: 28n; sisters, 16: 113, 115-6, 127, 157-8,
191-2, 194, 195n; welcome at Monticello (1789), 16: 167n-8n; disdains
pseudonyms for attacks on opponents, 16: 247; appearance described
by Maclay, 16: 381n-2n, 445n; supplies ordered for, 17: 571-2; and exchanging letters with family, 18:

JEFFERSON, THOMAS (*cont.*)

9n, 660, 678, 687-8; sailing party with Washington, **16**: 475, 606n; recommendations for federal offices in N.C. and Southwestern government, **16**: 476-8; and U.S. commercial policy, **16**: 513-30; **17**: 109-11; **18**: 220, 276n; **19**: 121-39; desires to retire from public life, **16**: 560; war crisis of 1790, **17**: 35-161 (editorial note and documents); residence bill and assumption bill, **17**: 163-208 (editorial note and documents); plans for diplomatic establishment, **17**: 216-31 (editorial note and documents); and consular establishment (editorial notes and documents), **17**: 244-56; **19**: 301-20; notes on Brazil and Mexico, **17**: 258-9; opinion on McGillivray's monopoly of commerce with Creek Indians, **17**: 288-91, 389n; circular to district attorneys, **17**: 338-40; and departmental personnel and services, **17**: 343-87; salary account, **17**: 356-9, 596, 598n; paid by Department of State, **17**: 375; recording of letters and papers, **17**: 381-7; trip to R.I. with Washington, **17**: 390, 402; circular to American consuls, **17**: 423-5; opinion on fiscal policy, **17**: 425-30; seat of government on Potomac (editorial notes and documents), **17**: 452-71; **19**: 3-73; **20**: 3-88; memoranda for Washington, **18**: 98-9; items for Washington's message to Congress, **18**: 99-101; and form of address, **18**: 112n; opinion on proposed manufacture of textiles in Va., **18**: 120-4; and Northwest Territory, **18**: 159-218 (editorial note and documents); relations with Great Britain, **18**: 220-306 (editorial note and documents); relations with Spain, **18**: 242; **19**: 429-531 (editorial note and documents); opposition to, **18**: 260, 261, 266, 278-83; **19**: xxxii; and impressment of seamen, **18**: 310-42 (editorial note and documents); and Mediterranean trade, **18**: 369-445 (editorial note and documents); and Algerian captives, **18**: 369-445 (editorial note and documents); policy on Algiers, **18**: 371-3, 376-84, 389-98, 404-16, 431-6; naval policy, **18**: 372-3, 415-6; and

JEFFERSON, THOMAS (*cont.*)

coinage and unit of money, **18**: 454-60 (editorial note and documents); and tonnage acts, **18**: 516-77 (editorial note and documents); and fisheries, **19**: xxxii, 140-237 (editorial note and documents), 348 (illus.); and Franklin's death, **19**: 78-115 (editorial note and documents); report on memorial of Andrew Brown, **19**: 251; opinion on constitutionality of bank, **19**: 275-82; report on petition of Hessian deserter, **19**: 326-8; affidavit concerning Pickering and others, **19**: 361; circular letter to supervisors of excise, **19**: 363-4; and western disunion, **19**: 429-531 (editorial note and documents); and European concert on navigation law, **19**: 558-75 (editorial note and documents); estimate of expenses on foreign fund, **19**: 583; relations with L'Enfant, **20**: 12-72; and Indian affairs, **20**: 104-51 (editorial note and documents); attends Apr. 11, 1791 cabinet meeting, **20**: 117-8; and Schweitzer, Jeanneret & Cie.'s proposal to buy U.S. debt to France, **20**: 175-203 (editorial note and documents); and Tench Coxe's proposed appointment as comptroller of treasury, **20**: 219-34 (editorial note and documents); and controversy over Paine's *Rights of Man* (editorial note and documents), **20**: 268-313; instructions to Barclay, **20**: 397-400; circular letters to consuls and vice consuls, **20**: 401-4; and *Rachel* case, **20**: 482-522 (editorial note and documents); *Observations on the Whale-Fishery*, **20**: 559; relationship with Philip Freneau and *National Gazette*, **20**: 718-59 (editorial note and documents). *See also* Department of State, U.S.; France: U.S. Relations; Great Britain: Relations with U.S.; Jefferson, Thomas: Writings; Spain; United States: Secretary of State

Virginia Estate

burning of Shadwell, **1**: 35; desire to rent, **12**: 135; damaged in Revolution, **13**: 105, 363-5; land in Goochland and Cumberland counties to be sold, **13**: 325, 328, 340, 349; **14**: 358, 362; **15**: 132; **20**: 123; rental

JEFFERSON, THOMAS (*cont.*)
of land, **13**: 325, 328, 339-40, 349;
14: 358, 362; management of, **13**:
339-44; shares father's estate with
brother, **16**: 112-5, 127-9, 156-8;
sale of crops, **18**: 28, 29n; estimate
of yield (1790), **18**: 109-10. *See also*
Elk Hill; Jefferson, Thomas: Business and Financial Affairs; Monticello

Virginia Legislator
resolutions for an answer to Gov. Botetourt's speech, **1**: 26-7; amendments to Road Act, **1**: 88-90; notes
on status of bills, **1**: 104-5; and Fast-
Day Resolution, **1**: 105-6, 106n,
116; subscribes to association
against Boston Port Act, **1**: 107-12;
subscribes to nonimportation agreement between Va. and other colonies, **1**: 109-12; elected to Convention, **1**: 118; draft resolution on
N.Y. and the Association, **1**: 159-
60; report on militia, **1**: 160-2; resolution on land grants, **1**: 162-3; resolutions on Lord North's Conciliatory Proposal, **1**: 170-4; **10**: 371;
and disestablishment of Anglican
Church, **1**: 525-58 (editorial note
and documents); draft of bill for the
naturalization of foreigners, **1**: 558-
9; bill to abolish entails, **1**: 560-2;
and revisal of Va. laws, **1**: 563n-4n,
603-4; **2**: 266, 301-2, 305-665 (editorial note and documents); bills to
divide Fincastle co., **1**: 564-76 (editorial note and documents); leadership in western lands issue, **1**: 567n-
8n; skill as legislative leader, **1**:
569n; bill for raising six additional
battalions of infantry, **1**: 577-84; bill
establishing places for holding courts
in Pittsylvania and Henry counties,
1: 592-4; bill for altering rates of
copper coins, **1**: 597; bill for removal of seat of government of Va.,
1: 598-603; remodeling of Va. judiciary, **1**: 605n-7n; bill for High
Court of Chancery, **1**: 610-20; bill
for General Court, **1**: 621-44; bill
for Admiralty Court, **1**: 645-9; bill
regulating county courts, **1**: 650-2;
bill to establish auditors of public
accounts, **1**: 654-5; bill for suspending executions for debts, **1**: 657-8;

JEFFERSON, THOMAS (*cont.*)
elected to GA, **2**: 10-1; bill regulating appointment of delegates to
Congress, **2**: 15-8; possible author of
bill to prevent importation of slaves,
2: 22-4; and controversy over Senate's right to amend money bills, **2**:
40-63 (editorial note and documents); interest in western land, **2**:
64-6; and Transylvania land claims,
2: 64-111 (editorial note and documents); draft bill on Articles of Confederation, **2**: 111-2; bill for dissolving certain vestries, **2**: 112-3; bill for
dividing Augusta and Botetourt
counties, **2**: 113-8; bill on court
houses in Fluvanna and Cumberland
counties, **2**: 121-2; bill for smallpox
inoculation, **2**: 122-4; involvement
in Kaskaskia expedition, **2**: 132-3;
bills for establishing a land office, **2**:
133-67 (editorial note and documents); involvement with Land Acts
of 1779, **2**: 133n-8n; proposal on
cession of western territory, **2**: 148n;
bill for sequestering British property, **2**: 168-71; draft of resolution
concerning money due British subjects, **2**: 171-2; bill for locating General Court and High Court of Chancery, **2**: 172-3; bill for pardons to
Loyalists, **2**: 178-9; bill for garrison
duty, **2**: 179-81; bill for clerk of foreign correspondence, **2**: 181-2; bill
on defaulters against U.S., **2**: 182-3;
bill giving Chancery Court certain
powers, **2**: 183-4; bill on supply for
public exigencies, **2**: 184-6; bills to
amend act for raising money, **2**:
186-8, 217-24; bill concerning General Court judges, **2**: 189; bill of attainder against J. Philips, **2**: 189-93;
brought to HD in custody of sergeant at arms, **2**: 216n; bill to
amend act establishing General
Court, **2**: 226-9; bill for proportioning crimes and punishments, **2**: 229-
31, 492-507, 663-4; bill for legislative salaries, **2**: 231-2; bill regulating
practice of attorneys, **2**: 235, 587-9;
bill for removal of state capital, **2**:
271-2; bill for salaries of GA, **2**:
273-4; bill for salaries of state officials, **2**: 274-5; bill on securityship,
2: 275-7; bill on escheats from British subjects, **2**: 279-85; design of

INDEX, VOLUMES 1-20

JEFFERSON, THOMAS (*cont.*)
legislative method during Revolution, **2**: 306n; elected to HD, **6**: 133; accounts for attending Va. GA for Oct. 1781, **6**: 135; bill for relief of military prisoners, **6**: 140; obtains leave of absence from GA, **6**: 140n; delegate to HD for Albemarle co., **6**: 174-5; resigns from HD, **6**: 179, 184-7; HD refuses to accept resignation, **6**: 183-4; threat of seizure for declining to serve in HD, **6**: 184, 187n; and Va.'s western claims, **6**: 189; payment as revisor of laws, **7**: 361, 559, 597-8, 635-6; **9**: 211

Writings
Autobiography, **1**: 105n, 106n, 109n, 117n, 188n-9n, 299n-300n, 589n, 669; **2**: 23n, 231n, 305n-6n, 306n-7n, 308n, 314n, 316n, 317n, 472n, 478n, 480n, 505n, 515n, 534n, 542n, 543n, 545n, 547n, 552n, 598n-9n; **4**: 508n; **6**: 210n-1n, 426n, 441n, 516n; **10**: 560n, 562n; **15**: 209n-10n, 243-4, 354n-5n; **16**: 610n; **18**: 89n-90n, 376n, 377n, 381n; Declaration of Rights for Virginia Convention, **1**: 119-20; "A Summary View of the Rights of British America," **1**: 121-37, 669-76; **6**: 649n-51n; **19**: 482; Declaration of Causes and Necessity for Taking up Arms, **1**: 187-219 (editorial note and documents); refutation of argument that colonies were established at British expense, **1**: 277-85; Virginia Constitution (1776), **1**: 329-86 (editorial note and documents); Declaration of Independence, **1**: 413n-33 (editorial note and documents); report in *Virginia Gazette* of Arnold's invasion, **4**: 269-70; possible authorship of "Vindication of Virginia's Claim against the Proposed Colony of Vandalia," **6**: 649n, 656-63; reply to representations of affairs in America by British newspapers, **7**: 540; account of Stanhope affair, **9**: 4-7; answers to Démeunier's queries, **10**: 11-29; observations on Démeunier's manuscript, **10**: 30-61; comments on Soulès' *Histoire*, **10**: 364-83; notes on tour of France and Italy, **11**: 415-64; letter to editor of *Journal de Paris*, **12**:

JEFFERSON, THOMAS (*cont.*)
61-5; Hints to Americans Travelling in Europe, **13**: xxvi, 33n, 262, 264-76; Notes of a Tour through Holland and the Rhine Valley, **13**: 8-36; Anas, **13**: 33n; **16**: 237n; **17**: 171, 207n-8n; **18**: xxxviii; *Observations on the Whale-Fishery*, **14**: 242-56; notes on Condorcet on slavery, **14**: 494-8; notes on macaroni, **14**: 544; *Manual of Parliamentary Practice*, **14**: 691n; "Parliamentary Pocket-Book," **14**: 691n; draft charter of rights for France, **15**: 167-8; in *Gazette of the United States*, **16**: 239n-44n, 255-8n; Report on Copper Coinage, **16**: 335-49 (editorial note and documents); Report on Commerce (1793), **16**: 514; Report on Weights and Measures, **16**: 602-75 (editorial note and documents); in *National Intelligencer*, signed "A," **17**: 289n; Report on American Trade in the Mediterranean, **18**: 423-30 (*see also* Mediterranean trade); Report on American Captives in Algiers, **18**: 431-6 (*see also* Algiers, American captives in: TJ's Report on); report to President on tonnage acts, **18**: 565-70; Notes on Sheffield's *Observations on the Commerce of the American States*, **19**: 127-31; Notes on Coxe's *Commercial System for the United States*, **19**: 132-3; report on fisheries, **19**: 206-36 (*see also* fisheries: TJ's report on). *See also* Jefferson, Thomas: Continental Congress, Governor of Virginia, Secretary of State, Virginia Legislator; *Notes on the State of Virginia*
Jefferson co., Ky.: letters to county lieutenant of, **4**: 231-2, 420; divided from Kentucky co., **4**: 200n; **6**: 597n; militia, **4**: 234, 236; **5**: 310, 461, 465-6; government of, **4**: 364-5; Indian attacks on, **5**: 493; need of officials, **5**: 547-8
Jefferson-Hartley map, **6**: xxxvi, 592n-3n, 593 (illus.)
Jeffery, Patrick: letter from, to Limozin, cited, **14**: 338
Jefferys, Thomas: map of North America, **6**: 601; historical chart sent to TJ, **10**: 166, 201; *American Atlas*, **11**: 677
Jenifer, Daniel, of St. Thomas: letter

[276]

Jones, John Paul (*cont.*)
captures *Drake*, **2**: 207; commands *Ariel*, **4**: 196; **10**: 257; loses command of *Alliance*, **4**: 310; arrives at Philadelphia, **4**: 656, 670; and prize money, **7**: 420n; **8**: 277, 278, 326-7, 334, 337-8, 339, 364-5, 395-7, 439-40, 443, 448, 452-3, 603-4, 680; **9**: 10-1, 22, 44, 123, 130, 208-10, 227, 238, 261, 270-1, 378, 443, 480-1, 512; **10**: 74, 88-9, 91, 93-5, 119, 120, 128, 130, 237, 329; **11**: 159-60; **12**: 317n, 336-7, 341, 357-8, 525, 526, 531-2, 536, 564-5, 573, 659-60, 690; **13**: 102, 123, 257-8; **14**: 516; TJ recommends for command, **7**: 512; impresses British pilot, **8**: 284, 285n; TJ proposes as emissary to Barbary States, **8**: 347; sent to Brest to investigate La Pérouse expedition, **8**: 374, 593; Wuibert's service under, **9**: 78, 294; letters from cited, **9**: 162; **12**: 243; **14**: 516n, 544, 597, 604, 605, 616, 639, 672, 686; **16**: xl; bust by Houdon, **9**: 305; **13**: 585, 587; **14**: 687-8; **15**: xxxviii, 122, 376, 437, 438, 457 (illus.), 551; **16**: xl, 125, 318; proposed for naval blockade of Barbary States, **9**: 319; **18**: 381; commands *Bonhomme Richard*, **10**: 501; sails for America, **11**: 373, 619; difficulty in collecting funds, **12**: 95-6; leaves New York, **12**: 102, 105, 252, 269, 270, 283, 331, 335; medal for, **12**: 266; **13**: 585, 586; **14**: 506, 545, 555, 687; **16**: xl-xli, 34, 52 (illus.), 54n, 57n, 63n, 65n, 66n, 71, 73n-6n, 77; **17**: 413; **18**: 600; **20**: 544; letters sent by, **12**: 283, 412, 416n, 429, 432, 458, 489; Carrington praises, **12**: 337; **13**: 496; arrives at Copenhagen, **12**: 393; note due Du Bois, **12**: 393; and claim of MacCarthy, **12**: 430, 494; arrives in Paris, **12**: 438; serves in Denmark, **12**: 680; **13**: 44-5, 582; serves in Russia, **13**: 45, 126, 134-5, 209, 583-5; **14**: 506, 515, 604, 616, 672; **15**: 368; promoted to rear admiral, **13**: 45-6, 126, 135, 209, 503; packet from Dechezaulx for, **13**: 116, 582n; **14**: 555; in Black Sea naval action, **13**: 126, 134, 404, 427-9, 436, 437, 454-6, 458-9, 461, 465, 471, 483, 488-9, 491, 497, 503, 580; **14**: 29, 375; account with Staphorst, **13**: 186, 284, 301; **14**: 614, 648; letter from, to Amoureux, cited, **13**: 284,

585; sends TJ proceeds of merchandise sold, **13**: 284, 428-9, 585, 657; **14**: 686; and British press, **13**: 461, 572; Washington comments on, **13**: 555; Watson claims service under, **13**: 565; correspondence with Lafayette, **13**: 581, 582-5; correspondence with Bernstorff, **13**: 581, 582n; **19**: 589; letter to, from Framery, cited, **13**: 581, 582n; on Constitution, **13**: 583; **14**: 506; describes voyage to Russia, **13**: 583; proposes alliance of France and Russia, **13**: 584; and naval action in Netherlands, **13**: 586; sends extracts of journal to TJ, **13**: 586; **14**: 506, 515, 516n, 687; Amoureux praises, **13**: 657; in *Alliance* case, **14**: 315-7; suggests U.S. action against Algiers, **14**: 506, 516; suggests U.S. treaty with Russia, **14**: 506, 516; money for, **14**: 520; Bancroft pays, **14**: 606, 630, 692; Renaud presents account, **14**: 621; Amoureux pays, **14**: 648, 686; in Gordon's *History*, **14**: 687; and report of scandal in Russia, **15**: 130; passport issued by TJ, **15**: 485; in Warsaw, **15**: 551; letter to cited, **16**: xl; in Paris, **16**: 419; signs address on Bastille Day, **17**: 213, 214n; Bondfield's services to, **17**: 577; correspondence with Jay cited, **18**: 382n, 383, 391; letter from, to Catherine, cited, **19**: 588; letter from, to Potemkin, cited, **19**: 588; letters from, to Adams, cited, **19**: 588; letters from, to Thomson, cited, **19**: 588; letters from, to Washington, cited, **19**: 589; *Journal*, **19**: 589; letter to, from Christian VII, quoted, **19**: 589-90; letter to, from La Houze, cited, **19**: 589; meets with Crown Prince Friedrich, **19**: 590; receives medal from Catherine, **19**: 590; bust of requested by N.C., **19**: 591; interest in Algiers, **19**: 591; letter to, from Burton, cited, **19**: 591; and Littlepage's role in Russian adventure, **19**: 599-600; mentioned, **8**: 597; **9**: 107; **10**: 194, 549; **11**: 216; **12**: 327, 329, 357n, 417, 418; **14**: 568, 658; **18**: 583
Jones, Jonathan: letter to, **12**: 114; letters from, **12**: 57; **15**: 30-1
Jones, Joseph: letters to, **5**: 101; **6**: 383, 533-4; **7**: 118; **8**: 236-7; **12**: 33-5; **16**: 182; letters from, **1**: 388; **3**: 472-5; **4**: 483-4, 534, 577, 605-6, 606-7, 670-1;

Kalmia: plants requested from John Banister, **11**: 121

Kalmia angustifolia: sample to be sent to France, **10**: 227

Kalmia latifolia: sample to be sent to France, **10**: 227

Kamchatka, Russia: French ships arrive at, **11**: 217; Ledyard's expedition to, **13**: 382; **14**: 616; **15**: 492

Kames, Henry Home, Lord: *Principles of Equity*, **11**: 547; **16**: 481; **20**: 378; *Essays on the Principles of Morality and Natural Religion*, **12**: 18; **16**: 481

Kanawha river: as proposed western boundary of N.C. and Va., **1**: 572; **6**: 547, 548, 601, 602; navigation, **11**: 387; communication with, **11**: 413; price of land on, **11**: 519; Polson's landholdings on, **13**: 389; mentioned, **2**: 114; **3**: 79. *See also* Great Kanawha river

Karamanli Ali Pasha, Bey of Tripoli: letters to, from Sidi Muhammad, cited, **13**: 527n; **14**: 46

Kardt, Bernard: client of Parmentier, **13**: 470

Kare, William: signs petition, **6**: 294

Karlsruhe (Carlsruh), Germany, **13**: 25, 267

Karl Theodor, Elector of Bavaria: agreement on territorial exchange, **7**: 641; **8**: 226; illness of, **9**: 470; American medals sent to, **16**: 67

Karr, Charles. *See* Kerr

Karr, Gilbert: signs petition, **1**: 588

Karr, Samuel: signs petition, **1**: 587; signs Va. oath of allegiance, **2**: 129

Karr, William: signs Va. oath of allegiance, **2**: 129

Kaskaskia: expedition, **2**: 133n; mismanagement at reported, **2**: 442; fort at, **3**: 275; gunpowder and lead sent to, **4**: 355; Va. asks reimbursement for reducing British post at, **4**: 387, 390n; Continental money at, **5**: 386; **6**: 320; petition from, **5**: 599-600; French settlement at, **6**: 61; protection of rights of citizens at, **6**: 579; Arthur Lee's possible appointment to, **8**: 230; government, **8**: 248; land claims from, **18**: 167; St. Clair's report on, **18**: 194-6, 199; TJ's report on lands, **18**: 207-15; mentioned, **2**: 246n; **3**: 168n

Kaskaskia (Kuskuskie) Indians: enemy of the Cherokee, **2**: 74; support G. R. Clark, **2**: 258; friendly to settlers at Fort Jefferson, **3**: 522; petition Congress for protection, **8**: 79; treaties, **8**: 296; mentioned, **3**: 6; **6**: 60-4

Katchum, Mr.: inn rated by TJ, **20**: 471

Kauffmann, Angelica: Maria Cosway's patron, **16**: 551n

Kaunitz-Rietburg, Wenzel Anton, Prince: describes Penet, **3**: 359; discusses American trade, **8**: 479

Kay, John: portrait of Henry Dundas, **18**: xxxv, 268 (illus.)

Kayenlaha (Onondaga Indian): visits France, **9**: 261

Kayewla: Iroquois name for Lafayette, **7**: 447n

Kay's landing: ferry at, **2**: 456

Kean, John: letter to, **20**: 621; letter from, **20**: 608; angers Va. governor and council, **19**: 53n; seeks treasury comptrollership, **20**: 226, 230n

Kearby, John: signs Va. oath of allegiance, **2**: 129

Kearsley, George: prints *A Summary View*, **1**: 673

Keaton, James: in Albemarle co. militia, **1**: 665, 667

Keaton, William: in Albemarle co. militia, **1**: 668n

Keeble (Kibble), George: accusations against, **5**: 305, 306n

Keeble (Kibble), Walter: accusations against, **5**: 305, 306n

Keen, John: proposes decimal system of weights and measures, **16**: 617n

Keimer, Samuel: employs Franklin, **9**: 486

Keir's hydrostatical lamp, **18**: 52

Keith, George Skene: letter from, **20**: 592; "Synopsis of a System of Equalization of Weights and Measures," **16**: 604n; **20**: 592; criticizes TJ's report on coinage, **18**: 457n; letter from cited, **18**: 481n; criticizes TJ's pendulum, **18**: 481n

Keith, Sir William: interest in Franklin, **9**: 495; *History of the British Plantations in America*, **12**: 18

Kellermann, François Etienne: forwards J. P. Jones' medal, **20**: 544; introduced to TJ, **20**: 546

Kello, Richard: introduces slave importation bill, **2**: 24n

Kello, Samuel: letter from, to Short, missing, **7**: 386; Presidential elector from Va., **15**: 5

Kelly, George: signs address to TJ, **15**: 556

Kelly, James, **4**: 678

Kelly, Capt. Thaddeus: arrives from Philadelphia, **5:** 74; letter from, to James Innes, **5:** 485-6; letter from, to Fisher, quoted, **5:** 489n; letter from, to James Innes, quoted, **5:** 499n; skirmish with British, **5:** 521; mentioned, **5:** 486, 489

Kelly, Timothy, **3:** 542n

Kelly's on the Great Kanawha: militia sent to, **3:** 421, 422

Kemble, Gouverneur, & Co., **15:** 68

Kemble, Peter: administers Thomas Burke's estate, **14:** 4

Kemp, Francis Adrian van der. *See* Van der Kemp, Francis Adrian

Kemp, James: letter to, from George Muter, **4:** 3; commissioned justice of the peace, **6:** 644; commissioned for oyer and terminer for trials of slaves, **6:** 644-5; mentioned, **4:** 201, 202, 372, 378

Kemp, John: letter from, **16:** 580-1; invoice for TJ's carriage, **14:** 210n, 468, 469-72; TJ consults on weights and measures, **16:** xxxii, 580-1, 607, 614, 616n; letter from cited, **16:** 602n, 607n, 614n

Kemp, Capt. Peter, **4:** 541

Kemp (Kempe), Thomas: asks flag to Portsmouth, **5:** 625; mentioned, **5:** 163

Kemps Landing, Va., **1:** 259; **4:** 54

Kenai moose, **7:** 318

Kendrick, John (master of *Columbia*), **16:** 330n

Kennan, Mr.: and bill establishing ferries, **2:** 458

Kennebec river, Maine: settlement on, **7:** 339; expedition, **10:** 371, 375n-6n; mentioned, **1:** 269; **6:** 494

Kennedy, Capt. (master of *Sally*), **13:** 661; **14:** 52, 54-5, 182, 183; **15:** 483

Kennedy, David: and construction of barracks at Winchester, **2:** 300; and bill establishing ferries, **2:** 454; mentioned, **4:** 252; **6:** 71n

Kennedy, David J.: drawing, **17:** xxxi, 219 (illus.)

Kennedy, Dugal, **3:** 542n

Kennedy, Lieut. James, **4:** 540

Kennedy, Susannah: letter to cited, **15:** 596

Kennedy, William: letter from, **4:** 556; mission to Cherokee, **2:** 69, 82

Kenner, Rodham: signs Virginia Association, **1:** 108

Kennett, White: *Complete History of England*, **10:** 307; **16:** 481

Kennon, Mr.: trustees of, **6:** 198

Kennon, William: daughter marries, **15:** 627

Kenny, Richard: letter to, **3:** 539

Kensington, C.: letter from, to Wilson, quoted, **16:** 548n

Kent, Capt.: and outfitting of *Thetis*, **5:** 209

Kentucky: deed from Indians for, **2:** 94, 97; separation from Va., **6:** 485n, 547, 552-5, 564, 597n; **7:** 8, 219; **8:** 112, 345, 442, 483, 508, 556-7, 646, 659, 684; **9:** 75, 176, 200, 257, 479; **10:** 14; **12:** 337, 602; difficulty of government by Va., **6:** 554; elimination of TJ's "Pelisipia," **6:** 596n-7n; Indian attacks, **7:** 45, 606; **9:** 519; **10:** 294, 301, 314; TJ's name falsely linked with land speculation in, **7:** 407-8; Marbois quoted on, **7:** 568n; Le Maire's memoir on, **8:** 123-32; natural conditions in, **8:** 124-8; counties, **8:** 125; population of, **8:** 125; **12:** 426; **13:** 551; manufactures, **8:** 126; agriculture, **8:** 127; commerce, **8:** 129; separation from U.S. feared, **9:** 218; independence, **9:** 519, 556; **10:** 41, 59; **13:** 231, 248n-9n, 337, 360, 503, 506, 550-1, 620; **14:** 21n-2n; article on in *Encyclopédie Méthodique*, **10:** 5n; admission to Confederation, **10:** 28; road from Staunton, **11:** 412; purchase of land in, **11:** 528; attack on Spanish settlements reported, **13:** 93, 113, 114n; Constitutional Convention, **13:** 98, 99; **19:** 365; Constitution opposed, **13:** 494; statehood, **13:** 494-5; **15:** 154, 337; **18:** 83, 146, 594, 596; **19:** 17, 364-81; **20:** 703; reported Spanish intrigues with, **13:** 540-1; **14:** 387n-8n; toasts at banquet (July 4, 1788), **13:** 626n; lead mines, **15:** 588; proposed black settlement in, **20:** 553n-5n; postal service, **20:** 711, 712; mentioned, **6:** 11, 552; **10:** 57

Kentucky co., Va.: boundaries designated, **1:** 570, 572; representation in Va. HD, **1:** 570-1; courts, **1:** 572-3; renunciation of Henderson necessary for holding office in, **1:** 575; place of court of assize, **1:** 629-30; commissioners for, **2:** 165n; **3:** 107; senatorial district, **2:** 336; defends western frontier, **3:** 50, 51, 53, 79, 420; Indian depredations, **3:** 356; gunpowder and lead sent to, **3:** 422; militia, **3:** 422; **4:** 200,

King, Henry: signs Virginia Association, **1**: 109; killed, **5**: 96

King, John: contract with Gruel & Co., **3**: 91; and shoes for troops, **4**: 454n; money due, **4**: 481

King, Miles: letter to, **6**: 41-2; letters from, **5**: 188, 260-1, 579, 635-6; **8**: 448-9; votes against bill for religious freedom, **2**: 549n; writes letter for Gerlach, **6**: 42; on Va. H.D. committee to welcome TJ, **16**: 11n; mentioned, **9**: 523

King, Sir Richard, the Elder: commands *Astrea*, **18**: 338

King, Rufus: letter from, **8**: 425; Mass. delegate in Congress, **7**: 572; **10**: 144; recommends Stephen Sayre, **8**: 572; marries Mary Alsop, **9**: 609; Mass. delegate to Federal Convention, **11**: 219, 400; letters from cited, **12**: 395, 401; supports James Swan, **12**: 636; letter from quoted, **13**: 97n; correspondence with Gerry, **14**: 77; **19**: 490-1; criticizes Franklin, **14**: 78n; supports Jay, **14**: 80; senator from N.Y., **15**: 427; in residence bill controversy, **17**: 164, 167, 169, 170; in Senate-House conference, **17**: 219; attitude toward Britain, **18**: 227n; **20**: 337; and Smith's mission to England, **18**: 244, 245, 261; and U.S. policy toward Barbary States, **18**: 386n, 410; committee report on *Alliance* sale, **18**: 388; and tonnage acts, **18**: 517, 524, 541, 546, 547; and arrearages of soldiers' pay, **18**: 611, 616, 617n, 624, 625, 649; appointed Senate conferee on excise bill, **19**: 37; and Franklin's death, **19**: 78, 84; and TJ's report on the fisheries, **19**: 165; on committee on Vt., **19**: 374; supports Spanish treaty, **19**: 497; letter from, to Hamilton, **20**: 146-7; and speculation in U.S. foreign debt, **20**: 177n; mentioned, **14**: 82n; **16**: 329n; **20**: 567

King, Sabert: in Albemarle co. militia, **1**: 667, 668n

King, Walter: and bill establishing ferries, **2**: 457, 459; imports slaves, **15**: 654

King and Queen co., Va.: letters to county lieutenant of, **5**: 588, 612, 618; **6**: 34-5; appoints infantry officers, **1**: 580; place of court of assize, **1**: 629; militia, **2**: 131; **3**: 239, 600; **4**: 62, 63, 307; **5**: 29, 310, 588, 612, 618, 646;

senatorial district, **2**: 336; levies of soldiers, **3**: 7; tobacco loan office certificates, **3**: 516; commissioner of, **3**: 539; supply post for, **4**: 286; fails to furnish wagons, **5**: 274

King and Queen Court House, Va.: proposed meeting of school overseers at, **2**: 529; place of court of assize, **7**: 588

King Fisher (warship), **1**: 258, 260, 265

King George co., Va.: letters to county lieutenant of, **5**: 255; **6**: 34-5; militia, **1**: 160; **2**: 131; **3**: 600; **4**: 62, 63, 376-7; **5**: 255, 309n, 310, 329n, 399, 406-7, 451; appoints infantry officers, **1**: 580; place of court of assize, **1**: 629; senatorial district, **2**: 336; levies of soldiers, **3**: 7; tobacco loan office certificates, **3**: 516; supply post for, **4**: 286; Monroe's estate in, **6**: 95, 125; taxes, **6**: 565

Kingsbridge, N.Y.: battle at, **1**: 520; **10**: 383n; British at, **3**: 31; **4**: 29; American army at, **6**: 110

King's Mountain, battle of, **4**: 32n, 42, 44, 84, 86, 178, 238-9; **5**: 570n. *See also* prisoners of war, British: taken at King's Mountain

Kingston, Mme: heritage, **14**: 11

Kingston, Elizabeth Chudleigh, Countess of Bristol, Duchess of: relations with Cosways, **10**: 394; **11**: 569

Kingston, Evelyn Pierrepont, second Duke of, **10**: 506

Kingston, N.C., **4**: 583

King v. Dugard, **6**: 124

King William co., Va.: letters to county lieutenant of, **5**: 128, 416, 612, 617; **6**: 34-5; letter to members of Va. GA for, **5**: 585-6; appoints infantry officers, **1**: 580; place of court of assize, **1**: 629; militia, **2**: 131; **3**: 238, 600; **4**: 62, 63, 307; **5**: 29, 128, 141, 181, 310, 612, 617, 646; senatorial district, **2**: 336; levies of soldiers, **3**: 7; tobacco loan office certificates, **3**: 516; supply post for, **4**: 286; fails to supply wagons, **5**: 274; mentioned, **2**: 239

Kinloch, Anne Cleland: letter to, **11**: 520-1; letter from, **9**: 129; rice sent to, **11**: 517, 520; and Mrs. Adams, **11**: 573

Kinloch, Francis: letter to, **18**: 80-1; letters from, **4**: 279-80; **15**: 71-2; marries Mildred Walker, **4**: 280n; visits TJ, **9**: 129; and *Notes on Virginia*, **12**: 570; **15**: 71-2; **18**: 60; introduces Huger to

duces Haskell to TJ, **14**: 427; TJ sends musket to, **15**: 422, 437, 454-5; letters to cited, **15**: 437, 455; **16**: 317n; certificates carried under cover to, **16**: 24; correspondence with Humphreys, **16**: 53n, 61n, 62n, 63n; Humphreys consults on medals, **16**: 61n, 63n; presents swords, **16**: 62n-3n; plan for militia, **16**: 125; Bourne corresponds with, **16**: 265n; correspondence with Wayne, **16**: 408n-9n; opinion on Indian lands, **16**: 408n-9n; and war crisis of 1790, **17**: 44n, 55, 61, 79, 90, 140-2; letter from, to Harmar, quoted, **17**: 132n; correspondence with St. Clair, **17**: 132n, 133n; **19**: 439; and St. Clair's expedition against Indians, **17**: 132n-3n; letters to, from Henry Jackson, quoted, **17**: 165-6, 166n; and Indian treaties, **17**: 290n, 388n; letters to, from Burbeck, quoted, **17**: 472n-3n; letter from missing, **17**: 598n; McGillivray's nephew in care of, **18**: 6; message from, to Adams, cited, **18**: 78; sends report on Miami Indian expedition to Washington, **18**: 144n-6n; promotes employment of Sargent, **18**: 161n; and Ohio Company, **18**: 174n; as friend of Smith, **18**: 244; letter to, from Miranda, quoted, **18**: 247; Maunsell communicates with, **18**: 263-7; correspondence with Maunsell, **18**: 264n, 265, 267n, 277n, 283n; correspondence with Brett, **18**: 264n; letter to, from William Knox, cited, **18**: 265; and Lords of Trade report, **18**: 271; correspondence with W. S. Smith, **18**: 274n; and Anglo-American reunion, **18**: 529; favors standing army, **18**: 530; on Hamilton in Reynolds case, **18**: 684; letter to, from John Glover, quoted, **19**: 156n; letter to, from Barrett, quoted, **19**: 306; aids Anderson candidacy, **19**: 386; letters from, to Duer, quoted, **19**: 446, 451; letter from, to Jean (John) Holker, quoted, **19**: 447; business dealings with Duer, **19**: 452-62; letter from, to Peters, quoted, **19**: 465; reports on Ste. Marie's memorial, **19**: 505; relations with L'Enfant, **20**: 10; consults with TJ, **20**: 87, 93; attends Apr. 11, 1791, cabinet meeting, **20**: 118, 144; land speculation, **20**: 121, 123-4; proposes Pickering mission to Iroquois, **20**:

121-32, 144-5; interview with Beckwith, **20**: 133-6, 138; letter to, from Beckwith, quoted, **20**: 135n; role in speculation on U.S. foreign debt, **20**: 177, 189, 192; supports Wolcott, Jr., **20**: 224; and controversy over *Rights of Man*, **20**: 277-8; mentioned, **5**: 620; **6**: 530; **15**: 52; **16**: 446; **18**: 280n, 380, 532

Knox, James: commands battalion for western defense, **3**: 51, 52, 161, 186; mentioned, **3**: 253

Knox, Thomas Fitzhugh: education, **20**: 474

Knox, William: letters to, **17**: 423-5; **20**: 401-3; letters from, **18**: 81; **20**: 241-4; as consul at Dublin, **17**: 246, 251, 253n, 255n, 280; **18**: 81; letter sent by, **17**: 669; letter from, to Henry Knox, cited, **18**: 265; recommends William Pearce, **20**: 242, 322n; in *Rachel* case, **20**: 483, 496, 504, 519; financial difficulties, **20**: 489n; contributes to *National Gazette*, **20**: 745

Knyphausen, Gen. Wilhelm von: and prisoners of war, **2**: 270; commands British raid on N.J., **3**: 436n, 474; Clinton joins, **3**: 461; embarks from N.Y., **4**: 195; Beckwith as aide to, **17**: 39, 41

Koch, Mr., **8**: 527

Koen, Capt. Claas Arends (master of *De Jonge Bernardus*), **13**: 148, 172, 186, 420, 482n

Koenig, Amand: letters to, **13**: 182, 300, 536; **15**: 223-4, 350; letters from, **13**: 203-4, 240, 411; **15**: 260; bookshop in Strasbourg, **13**: xxviii, 17 (illus.), 204n, 267; **16**: 495; books ordered from, **13**: 300, 536; **15**: 223-4, 260, 350

Kohle, Pastor: TJ's favorable opinion of, **4**: 102; chaplain of German Convention troops, **4**: 117

Kohly, John August Leonhard: requests permission to visit Lutheran friends, **3**: 308

Kollock, Shepard: publishes *New-Jersey Journal*, **17**: 509n

Königsberg, Prussia: Laws concerning trade with, **7**: 624; **8**: 28

Koon, Mr.: finds huge tooth at Claverack, **7**: 313

Koopman, Mr.: desires to settle in Ga. or S.C., **8**: 140, 187

Koran: cited on war against unbelievers, **9**: 358; precepts of modified by Emperor of Morocco, **10**: 346

Kortright (Courtwright), Eliza: marries James Monroe, **9**: 511, 609

Kosciuszko, Col. Thaddeus: money for, **3**: 647, 659; bills against Va., **5**: 391

Koster, Janszoon. *See* Coster

Krems (Crems), Austria: giant skeleton found near, **7**: 316

Kretschmar (Kratchmar), Gen. Willem Gerrit van: letter to, from Dumas, cited, **12**: 191n

Krohn, Danckert Danckertsen, **10**: 282n

Krüdener, Bourkhard Alexis Constantin, Baron von: letter from cited, **12**: 690

Krumfoltz, Mr.: invents foot bass, **10**: 625-6

Krumfoltz, Julie de, **10**: 445

Kuhl, Henry: and Ohio Company, **18**: 174n

Kuhn, Lewis Conrad: contract with Frau Zeller, **16**: 551-2

Kullen, Mr.: seeks employment, **18**: 156-7; recommended as translator for Department of State, **20**: 728n

kuskus. *See* couscous

Kutzleben, Baron von: TJ visits in London, **9**: 363n

Kuykendall, Benjamin, **4**: 332

Kyth's (Lawn's) creek: naval officer for, **2**: 375

La Balme, Augustin Mottin de: at Kaskaskia, **4**: 442n, 443n

La Baraque, **11**: 416

La Bastille dévoilée: TJ requests, **16**: 445n

Labat, Jacques Arnaud de: in Estates General, **15**: 45

Labat, Pierre de: letter from, **13**: 664

La Becède, M. de, **15**: 236

La Blancherie, Mammès Claude Pahin de: letters to, **12**: 333-4; **13**: 111-2; letters from, **12**: 317-8, 344-5, 657, 690-1; **13**: 116-7; Adams' subscription to periodical, **12**: 99, 351, 553; **13**: 112, 116; Adams' account with, **12**: 611; *Notes on Virginia* sent to, **13**: 112, 117

labor: high cost in Va., **8**: 507; in France, **11**: 415, 419, 427, 428, 430, 435, 440, 445, 455; **13**: 27; in Germany, **13**: 18. *See also* artisans; blacks; bricklayers; carpenters; laborers; sawyers; slaves

laboratory, army: land appropriated for, **3**: 535

La Bord, M. de, **7**: 359

Laborde, Jean Benjamin de: *Voyage Pittoresque de la France*, **11**: xxxiii, 414 (illus.)

Laborde, Jean Joseph, Marquis de: banker to Louis XV, **20**: 202n

Laborde de Méréville, François Louis Jean Joseph de: and directorship of Royal Treasury, **12**: 70, 72, 75-6, 110, 162, 175, 190; letter from, to Martha Jefferson, **14**: 478; bank proposed by, **16**: 33, 43; opposes Lafayette, **16**: 474

laborers: compared with slaves, **1**: 321; scarcity for public works in Richmond, **3**: 282; pay, **4**: 548, 552; wages in Germany, **13**: 16, 23; in France, **13**: 30, 654. *See also* munition workers

La Boullaye, Gabriel Isaac Douet de: letters to, **11**: 596, 599-600, 637; **12**: 170-1, 418-20, 604; letters from, **12**: 348-9, 449-50, 687; letter to quoted, **8**: 390n-1n; and U.S.-French trade; **12**: 59, 140, 143; **13**: 52n, 194n; **14**: 392 letter from, to Barrett, cited, **12**: 210; correspondence with Lambert, **12**: 259-62, 325; sends TJ statement on tobacco purchases by farmers-general, **13**: 54n; in whale oil negotiations, **14**: 261; decision on seizure of Irish and Scottish vessels, **14**: 393n

La Bourdonnaie, Anne François Auguste, Comte de: duel, **16**: 46

Labrador. *See* Newfoundland

La Brissane, M. de: letter from, **15**: 152

La Brune, Mr.: remission of sentence against, **3**: 486

La Bruyère, Louis Sextius de Jarente de, Bishop of Orléans: Lafayette recommends Walton to, **10**: 581

La Caille, Nicolas Louis de: catalogue of fixed stars, **8**: 298

lace: purchased for Mrs. Adams, **9**: 278; **11**: 175, 573, 574; ordered for Mrs. Smith, **12**: 619

Lacépède, Bernard Germain Etienne de LaVille-sur-Illon, Comte de: letter from, **12**: 287-8; letter to cited, **14**: xxxi

Lacey, Col. Edward: at King's Mountain, **4**: 32n

La Chaleure, France, **11**: 415-6

Lachine, Que., **1**: 452

Lackington, James: letters to, **14**: 647; **15**: 406; **20**: 408; books ordered from, **10**: 362, 398, 478; **11**: 522; **13**: 178-

Lafayette, Marquis de (*cont.*)
327; Greene advises, **5:** 361; sends
weapons to Greene, **5:** 388, 429;
moves detachment southward, **5:** 477,
482, 495, 529, 598; correspondence
with Phillips, **5:** 590n-2n, 633; reinforcements, **5:** 612, 615, 616, 617,
637; **6:** 3, 24, 74, 83, 97; and Va. Executive Council, **5:** 614n; provision for
hospital facilities, **5:** 664; and Turberville's interest in command, **5:** 700,
701; warrant for, **6:** 5; fears loss of
credit, **6:** 14n; and Convention troops,
6: 20-1; opinions cited, **6:** 28; at Richmond, **6:** 32; corn for, **6:** 34; letter to,
from Weedon, quoted, **6:** 42n; at Holts
Forge, **6:** 78n; joins forces with Gen.
Wayne, **6:** 85, 92, 635; inadequacy of
forces, **6:** 90, 91, 93; Greene orders to
remain in Va., **6:** 102-3; letter from, to
La Luzerne, quoted, **6:** 112n; and Definitive Peace Treaty, **6:** 238n, 259n;
news from, **6:** 265, 568; letter from, to
Livingston, quoted, **6:** 475n; relations
with Steuben, **6:** 619n, 620n, 621n,
622n-5n, 629n, 631, 632, 633, 639;
asks assistance of De Grasse, **6:** 630n;
plan to unite forces with Pa. line, **6:**
636; letters from cited, **7:** 12, 15, 31,
41, 42; **8:** 544, 608; **13:** 117; **16:** 252;
18: 378n, 380n; postwar visit to
America (1784), **7:** 16, 42, 433, 438;
purchases silver plate for Washington,
7: 47; and Society of the Cincinnati, **7:**
88; **9:** 161, 382; **10:** 532; **12:** 522; receives copy of Mazzei's notes on U.S.-
French West Indian trade, **7:** 389; and
Martha Jefferson's admission to Pentemont, **7:** 411n; popularity in U.S., **7:**
416, 438, 573; **8:** 461; travels in U.S.,
7: 416; **8:** 73; proposes Vergennes' intervention in Mississippi trade question, **7:** 417; Madison accompanies on
trip north, **7:** 421; letter from, to Vergennes, cited, **7:** 422; addresses Indians at Fort Schuyler, **7:** 439-40, 444-
6, 449n; opposed to slavery, **7:** 446;
Madison on character of, **7:** 446,
451n-2n; **8:** 39, 414-5; Iroquois name
for (Kayewla), **7:** 447n; returns to
France, **7:** 629, 635; **8:** 39, 43; attitude toward animal magnetism, **8:** 15,
17n; and dispute with Barbary States,
8: 81; **10:** 86, 486, 561n, 566n; **18:**
370, 377-8, 380-1, 391-2, 395, 407,
409; correspondence with Madison, **8:**

114; **11:** 216n; **14:** 3, 4n; TJ invites
to dinner, **8:** 133, 257n; wants Le
Havre as free port, **8:** 142; role in supplying American whale oil to France,
8: 143, 516; **9:** 42, 73n, 88, 117, 140,
262, 359, 471; **10:** 101, 140, 294,
312; **11:** 247; **12:** 328; **19:** 214; letter
from, to Adams, quoted, **8:** 144n-5n;
attempts to purchase arms for Va., **8:**
213; **9:** 523, 524, 536-7, 540-1; and
tobacco trade, **8:** 213, 220; **9:** 502-3,
583, 585, 588n; **12:** 76n-7n; **13:** 51,
59, 62, 91n; **16:** 271n; **17:** 442; Houdon bust of, **8:** 214-5, 422; **9:** 213,
226, 518, 544, 613; **10:** 229, 407-10,
414-5, 480-1, 507; **11:** 104, 124, 151-
2, 165-6, 170-1, 171n-2n, 230, 560;
12: 348, 354, 369, 592, 593, 603,
615, 630, 661, 684; **13:** 419, 471,
533, 661; **14:** 52, 54-5, 182; **15:**
xxxviii, 46, 457 (illus.); letter to, from
Carmichael, cited, **8:** 321, 322n; correspondence with Calonne cited, **8:**
369n-70n, 592; **10:** 474; counteracts
anti-American propaganda, **8:** 461,
678n; gives letter of credit to Franks,
8: 470; letter from, to Patrick Henry,
cited, **8:** 507; aids American-French
commerce, **8:** 662; **10:** 474, 475, 484-
5, 487, 602; **11:** 171n, 268; **12:** 314,
479; **13:** 136n; **20:** 533; "Avis au
Comité," **9:** xxviii, 386 (fac.); **10:**
319n, 321n; Barrett introduced to, **9:**
74n; Geismar's meeting with, **9:** 81;
letter to, from Janet L. Montgomery,
cited, **9:** 87, 470; Ramsay's book sent
to, **9:** 90; encourages French import of
live oak timber, **9:** 167-8; letters from,
to Greene, quoted, **9:** 168n; and Va.
naturalization act, **9:** 196, 297; attempts to settle Littlepage's debts, **9:**
213; **10:** 357, 442; **11:** 83; **12:** 27;
opinions of monarchical power, **9:** 266;
16: 333; TJ urges gift of land by Va.
to, **9:** 266-7; letters to, from Boylston,
cited, **9:** 299, 308; hosts discussion on
American politics, **9:** 329-30; resumé
of speech to Comité du Commerce, **9:**
338-44; on U.S.-French trade commit-
tee, **9:** 338n; portraits of, **9:** 456; **12:**
xxxv, 60, 67 (illus.); **16:** 318, 555,
559n; **17:** 396; **18:** 32, 356, 359n,
450; **19:** 261; association with Mme
de Tessé, **10:** 158n; TJ seeks copy of
MacIntosh's *Travels* for, **10:** 166n,
172; relations with Ledyard, **10:** 170-

1, 188, 259, 548-9; **11**: 216, 218; **14**: 180; letter to, from Littlepage, quoted, **10**: 188n; receives report on Carleton's mission, **10**: 221; visits southern France, **10**: 229, 251; letter of recommendation for Mme Grégoire, **10**: 239; Congress thanks, **10**: 277; correspondence with Dumas, **10**: 468, 470, 631, 644; **11**: 12, 109; recommends Walton, **10**: 551, 581, 622; letters of introduction for Heywards asked of, **10**: 553; intelligence to be forwarded to, **10**: 558; letter from, to James McHenry, cited, **10**: 563n; correspondence with Jay, **10**: 563n; **18**: 381n, 391-2; advice on Indian warfare sought, **10**: 578; d'Auberteuil's verse in honor of, **10**: 582-3; **11**: 80; as member of Assemblée des Notables, **11**: 7, 47, 48, 199; reputation in France, **11**: 48, 207; TJ on character of, **11**: 95; absence from Paris, **11**: 129; jocular advice to TJ, **11**: 211; health of, **11**: 216, 259, 298; **18**: 511; urged to accompany TJ through southern France, **11**: 285; and dismissal of Calonne, **11**: 316, 363, 489; predicts Fourqueux' successor, **11**: 346; quoted on Archbishop of Toulouse, **11**: 382; assists Barclay, **11**: 466, 467, 535, 537n; Barlow's poem forwarded to, **11**: 473; correspondence with Gordon, **11**: 525; **13**: 105; safe conduct for Macarty, **11**: 608; accompanies TJ to conference with La Boullaye, **11**: 637; letter to, from Ledyard, cited, **11**: 638; aspires to command Dutch Republican army, **12**: 77n; correspondence with Lambert, **12**: 141-3, 318; sent reports on Federal Convention, **12**: 150n, 232n; copies of Adams' *Defence of the American Constitutions* sent to, **12**: 291; letter to, from Blackden, cited, **12**: 311; books for, **12**: 350; copying press for, **12**: 356; letter to, from Walsh-Serrant, quoted, **12**: 373n; and Quesnay's proposed academy, **12**: 498, 499; **14**: 627; account with TJ, **12**: 529; opinion on Paine's iron bridge, **12**: 610; letter to, from Swan, cited, **12**: 637; proposed as member of marine council, **12**: 683; discusses U.S. Constitution, **13**: 6n-7n; correspondence with Knox, **13**: 6n; **14**: 347n; **18**: 409n; investigates American trade, **13**: 52n, 194n, 195n;

opposes farmers-general, **13**: 55n; **17**: 414; receives memo from Cazeau, **13**: 113; asks George Washington Greene to visit Paris, **13**: 156, 157n, 172; Otchikeita as protégé of, **13**: 157n; assists Castaing, **13**: 218; Shippen's regard for, **13**: 220; submits Swan's proposal on beef contract, **13**: 313; portrait of Washington for, **13**: 317, 363, 519, 561; advises Shippen and Rutledge, **13**: 356n, 449n; and royal displeasure with nobles of Brittany, **13**: 374, 406, 440, 455, 464, 532; Gordon asks for news of, **13**: 516; letter to, from Barrett, cited, **13**: 523, 524n; correspondence with J. P. Jones, **13**: 581, 582-5; **14**: 544; medals sent to, **13**: 627; **14**: 687; **16**: 65n; out of favor with court, **14**: 3, 332; in Consular Convention, **14**: 70, 71; French in Cairo admire, **14**: 180; in whale fishery negotiations, **14**: 214, 223, 225, 234-42, 244, 261, 335; *Observations on the Whale-Fishery* sent to, **14**: 219, 269-70; praises TJ, **14**: 223; in war crisis of 1790, **14**: 225-6; **17**: 86-7, 121, 123, 126n-7n; letter from, to Necker, **14**: 225-6; in French politics, **14**: 436-7; **15**: 459; **16**: 375; **17**: 616; and declaration of rights, **14**: 437, 438-40; **15**: 230-3, 255, 271-2, 286, 387, 388, 390-1; relations with Moustier, **14**: 520, 522n; **16**: 424n; **17**: 642; **18**: 120n; Short approves conduct of, **14**: 540, 543n; Short requests permission to visit Toulon dockyard, **14**: 592, 608, 705; praised by TJ, **14**: 598; **20**: 688; Barrett asks for letter to, **14**: 618; Gordon seeks payment for books, **14**: 635, 663; TJ used as conduit to, **14**: 703; in Estates General, **14**: 704n; **15**: 51, 208; and G. Morris, **14**: 704n; **19**: 344-5, 346; **20**: 697-8; signs passport for TJ, **15**: xxxiv-v, 424 (fac.); Fraser sends seeds to, **15**: 47; TJ advises, **15**: 97-8, 118-9; and TJ's draft charter of rights, **15**: 165-7, 209n-10n; at Fourth of July dinner with TJ, **15**: 240n; in Mirabeau incident, **15**: 244, 246-9, 250, 251-2, 254, 255-6, 285; in National Assembly, **15**: 254, 255, 459; **16**: 267, 440n; **18**: 351-2; **19**: 110, 634; commands National Guard, **15**: 279, 280, 289, 290, 300, 304, 366, 459; **20**: 259-60, 350-1, 363, 474, 616; letter

d'Acre, Baron de: *Voyages dans Amé-rique Septentrionale,* 8: 411

La Houze, Mathieu de Basquiat, Baron de: Jones asks letter to, 10: 209; letter to, from Vergennes, cited, 10: 281; French minister to Denmark, 12: 680; reacts to rumors, 13: 582n; letter from, to Jones, cited, 19: 589; mentioned, 12: 97, 393

Lajart, France: TJ describes, 11: 457

Lake Champlain: visited by TJ and Madison, 20: 455-6, 464, 466

Lake George, N.Y.: plans for defense of, 1: 394; visited by TJ and Madison, 20: 454-5, 463-4, 466

Lake of the Woods: as part of U.S. boundary, 6: 458

Lalande, Joseph Jérôme Le Français de: letters to, 14: 475-6; 15: 346-7; letters from, 9: 156; 13: 152, 326-7; works sought by TJ, 6: 541; *Astronomie,* 7: 133; 8: 408; 13: 638; 14: 698, 699n; TJ recommends works by, 12: 18; at Grotto del Cane, 14: 573; payment to French officers in U.S. army, 15: 346-7; provides measures, 16: 570; sends books to TJ, 20: 346

La Lande and Fynje: and U.S. medals, 8: 157; failure, 8: 312; estate of, 8: 531, 655; claims of U.S. against, 13: 248, 249n

Lalemand, Jean Frédéric: U.S. agent at Honfleur, 20: 676

Lallemand, Jean Baptiste: drawings, 11: xxxiii, 414 (illus.)

Lally-Tollendall, Trophime Gérard, Marquis de: leaves France, 15: 535

Lalor, Lieut. (Queen's Rangers), 5: 557n

La Luzerne, Anne César, Chevalier de: letters to, 3: 577-8; 5: 327-8, 421-2; 6: 227-8; 16: 394-5; letters from, 4: 215; 5: 433-4; 6: 80-1, 237; 15: 602-3; French minister to U.S., 3: 65; intelligence reports on British, 3: 238, 243; and Arnold's defection, 4: 12; protests British deception, 4: 116; assists Va. delegates, 4: 292; asked to have French fleet in Chesapeake Bay, 4: 494-5, 567, 568; elected to American Philosophical Society, 4: 545n; and Congress' commercial policy, 4: 656; informs Joseph Jones of French expeditionary force, 5: 81; memorial from mentioned, 5: 193; receives dispatches from French Court, 6: 9, 132; correspondence with Lafayette, 6: 112n, 624n; correspondence with Ver-

gennes, 6: 114n, 419; arranges TJ's voyage to France, 6: 207, 211n; letter from, to Robert Livingston, 6: 209; letter from, to Villebrune, 6: 252; departure from America, 6: 546; 7: 105, 115, 120, 139, 308n; complains of discrimination against foreign holders of debts, 7: 67; visits Va., 7: 84; and Longchamps-Marbois affair, 7: 294-5; letter to, from G. Morris, abstracted, 7: 351-3; return to America discussed, 8: 372, 524; 9: 138; 11: 94, 100-1; recommends Castaing, 10: 81; relationship to Montmorin, 11: 169; political prospects of, 11: 491; 12: 153, 175, 190; vinegar of, 11: 563; 13: 144; Moustier succeeds, 12: 68; wine shipped to, 12: 104; favorable attitude toward U.S., 12: 330; appointed French ambassador to Britain, 12: 330; 13: 115; consulted on Quesnay's projected academy, 12: 499; treatment by British court, 12: 621n; commendation of, 13: 248n; secret marriage, 13: 441; Bancroft dines with, 13: 607; follows American customs, 14: 303; in Moustier's recall, 14: 521; on French aid to U.S., 15: 602-3; medal, 16: xli, 357n, 359n-61n, 367, 368n, 392, 394; 17: 279-80; 18: 358, 359n; 19: 583; 20: 368; Otto praises, 16: 354-6; correspondence with Washington, 16: 360n, 361n, 392n; 17: 104n-5n; 19: 3; TJ's tribute to, 16: 394-5; letter to cited, 16: 396; relations with G. Morris, 17: 96, 97, 98, 100, 102n; 20: 299; relations with Humphreys, 17: 105; 20: 475; mentioned, 3: 260; 4: 214, 436; 5: 74, 599; 6: 65, 142, 178, 203, 211n, 236, 237, 242, 246, 418, 509, 542; 7: 134, 292, 535; 8: 683; 9: 470; 10: 257, 258; 12: 111, 162, 219, 364; 14: 64n, 65n; 15: 49, 305-6; 16: 504; 17: 605, 606

La Luzerne, César Guillaume de, Bishop of Langres: and dismissal of Calonne, 11: 316; imprisonment rumored, 11: 363; in Estates General, 15: 189; expelled by National Assembly, 15: 456

La Luzerne, César Henri, Comte de: letters to, 14: 270-1, 485-6; letter from, 14: 465-6; attitude toward U.S., 12: 153, 154, 564; 13: 194n-7n; minister of marine, 12: 153, 162, 175, 190, 314, 449; 13: 282; 15: 291, 301, 334; 17: 619, 640; and arrêt, 12: 470; 13: 197-8; 14: 465-6, 485; and case of Alex-

11: 553-4; letters from, 11: 52-3, 384; recommended to TJ, 10: 515; work on penology, 10: 515; 11: 53n; compliments for TJ, 13: 216, 399-400; TJ compliments, 13: 234; Carmichael inquires about books for TJ, 13: 577; mentioned, 10: 634

Laredo, Governor of: punishment for injustices by, 9: 246

Large Islands, Ky. (?): plans for defense of, 3: 55

L'Argus Patriotique: sent to TJ, 20: 647-8

Larimier, Mr.: Cedars affair, 1: 451

Larimy, Mr.: trade with Indians, 1: 436

La'ritz, M.: letter sent by, 13: 621

La Rochefoucauld family, 11: 267; 15: 550; 17: 546

La Rochefoucauld, Duchesse de. *See* Enville, Louise Elisabeth de la Rouchefoucauld

La Rochefoucauld, Dominique de, Cardinal: letter to, from Louis XVI, quoted, 15: 222

La Rochefoucauld (-d'Enville), Louis Alexandre, Duc de la Roche-Guyon et de: letters to, 11: 111-2; 16: 296-7, 377; letters from, 9: 150; 10: 652-3; 20: 524; praised by Crèvecoeur, 7: 376; Mazzei's praise of, 7: 386; TJ's introduction to, 7: 414; communicates intelligence to TJ, 8: 89-90; friendship for TJ, 9: 292n; friendship for U.S., 9: 330; recommendation of Démeunier to, 10: 4n, 302; pine cones asked for, 10: 228; health of, 10: 531; asked to aid Paine, 11: 302; on hailstones, 13: 487; and election to Estates General, 15: 51; letter from cited, 15: 426; position in National Assembly, 15: 559; Mazzei sends message to, 15: 613; in Société de quatre-vingt neuf, 16: 133; correspondence with Montmorin, 16: 271n; letters to, from Short, cited, 16: 271n, 375; offers resolution on religion to National Assembly, 16: 373, 376n; Horry introduced to, 16: 377; family regrets TJ's departure, 16: 474, 502; supports Thouret's plan, 16: 573; letter to cited, 17: 212; Short at residence of, 17: 273; and news of Franklin's death, 19: 79, 80; political position undercut by Hamilton, 19: 94; reads Washington's letter to National Assembly, 19: 94; anticipates adjournment of National Assembly, 19: 634; supports Lafayette, 20: 351;

and U.S.-French tobacco trade, 20: 366; praises U.S. bookmaking, 20: 545; proposed governor for dauphin, 20: 576, 584; requests peaches from TJ, 20: 645; mentioned, 9: 155; 10: 5n

La Rochefoucauld-Liancourt, Duchesse de: letter from, 10: 530-1; Short's love affair with, 11: 260n

La Rochefoucauld-Liancourt, François Alexandre, Duc de: tells Louis XVI of fall of Bastille, 15: 288

La Rochelle, France: American agent at, 9: 627; 10: 196; TJ describes, 11: 458; *Clementina* seamen in, 14: 410; Delaire's request to be U.S. agent in, 19: 596-7; mentioned, 3: 201

La Rocque, Capt. Jean Baptiste: master of *La Diligence*, 8: 570; 9: 8; rudeness to the Fitzgeralds, 9: 554

La Rouërie, Mme de: death of, 10: 400

La Rouërie, Armand Charles Tuffin, Marquis de (Col. Armand): letters to, 9: 169, 224-5; 10: 73-4; 13: 614-5; letters from, 9: 125, 193, 260, 346; 10: 400-1; 13: 605-6, 617-9; 14: 390; cavalry corps, 3: 401, 433, 467, 589; 4: 112, 392, 422; 5: 480n-1n; legion, 3: 593; 4: 212, 411, 423, 609, 665, 671-3; 5: 183, 350, 366, 479; 6: 161, 175, 634; at battle of Camden, 3: 595-6, 597n; and military supplies, 4: 357, 358; claim against Congress, 9: 80, 125, 169, 193, 272, 471; asks payment of pension, 11: 337; imprisoned in Bastille, 13: 406; presents Breton noblemen's petition, 13: 463; and interest on American debt, 13: 605-6, 614-5, 617-9; 14: 390

Larreguy, Jean (John): recommended as consul at Marseilles, 16: 399-400, 554

La Sauvagère, Félix François de: *Recueil de Dissertations avec de nouvelles assertions sur la végétation spontanée des coquilles du chateau des Places*, 11: 460-1; 12: 30, 130, 136, 137, 144; 13: 275

Lasby Effendy: on Barclay's mission, 10: 139n

Laserre, Barbier de, Chevalier: letter from, 9: 523-4; introduced to TJ, 8: 448-9

Lasher, Conrad: and Hessian fly, 20: 447, 456-7; inn rated by TJ, 20: 471

Las Heras (Las Herat), Mr.: Spanish consul in Algiers, 14: 502; 15: 340, 342n

hill boundary, **16**: 98, 100n
Leak, William: in Albemarle co. militia, **1**: 665, 666, 667; signs Va. oath of allegiance, **2**: 129; signs petition, **6**: 294
leap years: bill concerning, **2**: 640
Lear, Tobias: letters to, **20**: 252n-3n, 569; letters from, **16**: 554-5; **18**: 146, 178-9, 191, 347n, 476; **19**: 108, 403-4, 408; **20**: 377-8, 612; correspondence with Hamilton, **15**: 360n; **17**: 429n; sends communications to TJ, **16**: 286, 287, 288n; **18**: 178-9, 190; **19**: 84, 86; letters from cited, **16**: 305n, 413n; **17**: 400n; drafts proclamation on Creek Indians, **17**: 388n; remarks on Washington's message, **18**: 167n; consults territorial papers, **18**: 170; letter to, from Remsen, **18**: 365; delivers French communication to John Adams, **19**: 82; letter from, to Senate, quoted, **19**: 83; letter to, from Gore, **19**: 200-4; and Anderson affair, **19**: 387, 402; letter from, to Jacquett, **19**: 397-8; and Potomac capital site, **20**: 22, 36n, 41, 43, 55; relations with L'Enfant, **20**: 70; and controversy over *Rights of Man*, **20**: 274-6, 277; mentioned, **18**: 78, 172; **20**: 420, 668, 682
Learmonth, Lieut., **5**: 699
Learmonth, Alexander: letter from, **8**: 161-2; passport issued by TJ, **15**: 483
leases: French and English compared, **11**: 284
"Leasowes": TJ describes garden, **9**: 371-2
leather: procured for army, **3**: 398-9, 506, 662; **4**: 375, 553, 609; **5**: 125, 241; shortage, **3**: 526; **4**: 11; **5**: 137, 164, 170, 223, 332; for shoes, **4**: 447, 453; **5**: 91; tanning, **5**: 296; manufacture in Conn., **7**: 335; export from S.C., **8**: 201, 202, 203; U.S. import of, **10**: 147; **12**: 411
leaves: TJ directs packing of, **9**: 253
Le Bailly, M., **10**: 616
Le Baron, Jacques Eugènes: U.S. agent at Dieppe, **20**: 676
Le Bègue de Presle, Achille Guillaume: TJ dines with, **12**: 265; mentioned, **12**: 258
Le Blanc, M.: use of interchangeable parts, **15**: 423n
Le Blanc fils: letter from cited, **15**: 477, 478n
Le Brasseur, J. A.: proposed appointment as minister of marine, **20**: 369-70
Le Brun, Mme. *See* Vigée-Lebrun

Le Brun, Charles Boromée: letter to, **10**: 496-7; letter from, **10**: 469-70; claim to brother's property, **10**: 469-70, 496-7
Le Brun de Bellecour, Jérôme Michel: murder of, **10**: 469
Lebzeltern, Mme: and king's flight to Varennes, **20**: 605
Le Camus, H., Marquis: in command of prize taken by French, **5**: 433
Le Cavelier, Pierre: U.S. agent at Caen, **20**: 676
Le Chapelier, Isaac René Gui: in *Journée des dupes*, **16**: 107; in moderate party, **16**: 437; proposals of, **16**: 440n; supports Thouret's plan, **16**: 573
Le Chardon (ship), **14**: 224
Le Chene, M., **8**: 181, 182
Le Clerc, Jean: *Bibliothèque Choisie*, **10**: 518
Le Clerc, Sebastien: *Traité de géometrie*, **20**: 647-8
Leclerc & Cie.: letter of credit for TJ, **11**: 184-5; mentioned, **11**: 463n, 464n
Le Couteulx (ship), **10**: 253, 283, 328, 602, 616; **14**: 457; **15**: 84
Le Couteulx (Coulteux), M. de: advances money for whale oil, **9**: 127; immigration to America proposed, **10**: 395; Barrett's connection with, **10**: 541; statement on postal service, **10**: 591; known in U.S., **11**: 54; receives letters from U.S. at Le Havre, **12**: 192; tobacco purchases, **12**: 226; letter from cited, **12**: 401; letter to, from Paine, missing, **13**: 592, 593n; and Paine's plan for bridge, **13**: 592; connections in U.S., **14**: 445; observations on the sale of public property, **17**: 265; and Swan's contract for provisions, **17**: 529, 562, 563; **18**: 22-3; serves as bondsman, **17**: 562; and Short's negotiations for loan, **18**: 22; introduces Osmont to Morris, **18**: 30; mentioned, **8**: 172; **11**: 326, 544; **12**: 302n, 340; **14**: 527; **15**: 401, 566; **16**: 124, 130
Le Couteulx, Laurent Vincent: G. Morris as business associate, **15**: 416n; speculates in U.S. foreign debt, **15**: 473n; **20**: 183n, 186-7
Le Couteulx, Pierre Barthélemy: U.S. agent at Rouen, **20**: 676, 701
Le Couteulx, Richard, **15**: 473n
Le Couteulx & Cie.: letters from, **11**: 10; **14**: 368; Madeira wine directed to, **10**: 290; contemplates establishing company for trade in U.S., **10**: 531-2; **11**:

Le Couteulx & Cie. (*cont.*)
385-8; Izard's opinion of, **11**: 265; requests return of excess duty on American ship, **11**: 579; N. Barrett's connection with, **11**: 596; sounded on lending money to U.S., **11**: 660; agency for S.C. products proposed, **12**: 300; spermaceti candles shipped to, **13**: 207; tobacco sales, **13**: 417; Nesbitt's transactions with, **13**: 562; **14**: 527n; R. Morris' draft on, **14**: 282; and U.S.-French postal service, **14**: 308n; letter of credit to Morgan for wheat, **14**: 426, 460; mercantile associates, **14**: 633; Loan Office certificates deposited for, **15**: 108; proposals to Tarbé, **15**: 247n; mentioned, **9**: 588; **11**: 406; **12**: 505; **15**: 543; **17**: 288

Le Croix, M.: letters sent by, **8**: 116, 417, 428, 430; **11**: 228

Leda (ship), **9**: 330, 331, 387, 392

Le Darth (French brigantine), **5**: 430

Lediard, Thomas: translates Mascov, **13**: 179

Ledoux, Claude Nicolas: architect of new city wall of Paris, **10**: xxviii, 211 (illus.)

Ledyard, John: letters to, **10**: 120, 170-1, 258; letters from, **9**: 260-1; **10**: 97-8, 258-60, 548; **11**: 216-8, 637-9; **13**: 305-6, 516-7, 594-7; **14**: 180-2; bill for, **8**: 492; TJ's account of, **9**: 261n; TJ recommends to Lafayette, **9**: 273; *Journal of Captain Cook's Last Voyage*, **10**: 171n; proposed expedition across Siberia, **10**: 188, 315n-6n, 316, 548-9; **11**: 637-9; **12**: 159-60; **13**: 382; **14**: 616; **15**: 492; letters from cited, **11**: 476-7; **14**: 597, 672; **15**: 128n, 137; letter from, to Lafayette, cited, **11**: 638; theory on races of man, **13**: 306; expedition from Ky. to Pacific proposed, **13**: 382; **14**: 616; expedition to Africa planned, **13**: 382; **14**: 182; Cathalan's relations with, **13**: 516-7; **14**: 184-5, 286; in Egypt, **13**: 516-7, 594-6; **14**: 180-1, 597, 616; on Alexandria, **13**: 517; esteem for TJ, **13**: 595; describes Nile, **13**: 595-6; ridicules historians, **14**: 181; death of, **14**: 182n; **15**: 134, 137, 146, 182, 193-4, 198, 274, 434; characterized by TJ, **14**: 286; correspondence with Banks, **14**: 455, 568; Banks asks for news of, **15**: 128n; appreciation of, **15**: 199; passport issued by TJ, **15**: 484, 485;

marks on skin for measurement of latitude, **15**: 492-3; TJ's suggestions to, **15**: 492-3, 493

Lee, Mr.: plants ordered from, **11**: 46; Paradise's debt to, **16**: 84

Lee, Arthur ("the Monitor"): letters to, **12**: 472-3, 573-4; letters from, **3**: 82-3; **6**: 164-5; **11**: 159-61; **12**: 341-3, 357-8, 395-6; **13**: 394; **15**: 598; toast to, **1**: 31; commissioner to France, **1**: 524n; **2**: 177n; **3**: 76; **13**: 430; and London edition of *A Summary View*, **1**: 674; goes to Prussian court, **2**: 30; and Israel Mauduit's handbill, **2**: 210; news from Paris, **2**: 214; and court at Spain, **2**: 217; dispute with Deane, **2**: 263n; **3**: 65, 105; and revisal of Va. laws, **2**: 324n; **20**: 303, 304; letter from, to Henry, quoted, **3**: 35; account with Va., **3**: 83, 295; William Lee's agent in France, **3**: 90-1; advises Gov. Henry, **3**: 91; letter from mentioned by R. H. Lee, **3**: 285; acts as commercial agent for Va. in France, **3**: 551; and Westover affair, **5**: 671n-3n, 685n; elected to Va. HD, **6**: 133; **8**: 113; **9**: 195; and Va.'s claim to western lands, **6**: 189, 266, 576-80, 651n, 652n, 654n; cited on fossil bones, **6**: 208; as possible secretary of foreign affairs, **6**: 276; elected to Congress, **6**: 318n; and housing for Va. delegates, **6**: 355; resolution on jurisdiction of Congress, **6**: 370n; and Definitive Peace Treaty, **6**: 426n, 462n, 545; **17**: 432; report referred to, **6**: 427n; member committee on Conn.-Pa. dispute, **6**: 481n, 482n; correspondence with B. Harrison, **6**: 510, 552-5; **7**: 44-5, 103-4, 248-50, 293-4; gossip concerning, **6**: 546; "A Concise View of the Title of Virginia to the Western Lands," **6**: 652n; Indian commissioner, **7**: 9n, 119, 149, 236, 250, 396, 444, 652; **8**: 79; member of committee to inspect Georgetown, **7**: 278; moves to advance TJ's salary, **7**: 290; letter from cited, **7**: 412; relations with Lafayette, **7**: 445, 446; commissioner to Kaskaskia, **8**: 79; commissioner of the Treasury, **8**: 79, 229-30, 369, 383, 499, 519, 521, 685; **9**: 15; **13**: 308; Lansdowne's regard for, **9**: 388; letter from, to Washington, quoted, **10**: 533n-5n, 535n; opposes Constitution, **12**: 281, 423, 425; advises T. L. Shippen, **12**: 501;

letter to, from Adams, quoted, **14:**
xxxviii; gift from French government
to, **16:** 362n, 365, 366; "Junius
Americanus" as pseudonym, **17:** 192n;
and diplomatic service, **17:** 227n; letter
from, to Otis, quoted, **17:** 435n; orders
military stores, **17:** 578; criticizes
Paine, **20:** 304; subscription to national bank, **20:** 616; mentioned, **3:**
221n, 237; **4:** 146; **6:** 140n, 391n; **10:**
221; **12:** 231n; **13:** 6n
Lee, Gen. Charles: appointed major general, **1:** 175; sent to defend New York,
1: 285; **17:** 574; cited on lack of pre-
paredness, **1:** 287; recommends Innes,
1: 289; to raise artillery company for
southern department, **1:** 290; in N.C.,
1: 296; notifies Wooster of appointment to Canadian command, **1:** 442;
ordered to Va., **1:** 443; letter from, to
Pendleton, cited, **1:** 480; news of, **1:**
481; captures one of Clinton's transports, **1:** 488; taken prisoner by British, **1:** 659; **2:** 4; exchange, **2:** 176;
letter from, to Washington, cited, **2:**
208; dismissal by Congress, **4:** 208,
282; opposes Clinton, **15:** 575; mentioned, **1:** 294, 461; **5:** 678n; **8:** 276;
13: 11
Lee, Charles (Va.): letter from, **3:** 531-2;
certification to practice in county
courts of Va., **5:** 518; slaves of, **6:** 473,
474
Lee, Fort, **1:** 659
Lee, Francis Lightfoot: letter from, **1:**
520-1; and nonimportation agreements, **1:** 47, 110; helps draft Fast-
Day Resolution, **1:** 106n; signs Virginia Association, **1:** 109; signs letter
to Va. HB, **1:** 112; signs agreement of
secrecy, **1:** 253; signs Declaration of
Independence, **1:** 432; as possible
president of Congress, **2:** 35; Va. delegate to Congress, **2:** 213; protests payment in paper money, **5:** 387n-8n;
supports Constitution, **13:** 98; Cresswell introduced to, **15:** 583; mentioned, **15:** 230
Lee, Henry, Jr. (Light-Horse Harry):
letters to, **3:** 546; **4:** 191; **15:** 415-6;
16: 385-6; letters from, **14:** 619-21;
20: 595-6; and nonimportation agreements, **1:** 30, 46, 110; signs Virginia
Association, **1:** 108; signs letter to Va.
HB, **1:** 111; Va. cavalry officer, **1:**
386; **3:** 365; **4:** 188-9, 210, 212, 291;

6: 103; recommends Dr. McClurg to
Congress, **1:** 475; as reference for
Mazzei, **2:** 28; Washington requests
aid of, **3:** 424; and TJ's conduct as
governor, **4:** 257n, 264-6, 267n; in
S.C., **4:** 323; in N.C., **5:** 23, 44, 62,
102-3, 115, 162; follows Cornwallis,
5: 182; protests payment in paper
money, **5:** 387n-8n; Va. delegate in
Congress, **9:** 191, 202, 242, 479; and
naturalization of Lafayette, **9:** 196;
member of Va. committee to prepare
resolution on Congress, **9:** 204n-8n;
attempts re-election to Congress, **10:**
577; supports Constitution, **13:** 98,
352, 620; Potomac river land of, **14:**
619-20, 621n; **15:** 79, 415, 416n,
526; **18:** 124n; letters from cited, **15:**
79, 180, 181n; on Va. committee to
welcome TJ, **16:** 11n; medal, **16:** 54n,
56n, 59n, 66n, 78; **17:** xxxii-iv, 395
(illus.); letter to, from Hamilton,
quoted, **16:** 461n; correspondence with
Madison, **17:** 166n; **19:** 12, 14; on Va.
HD committee of grievances, **17:**
660n; and site for capital, **19:** 6, 9, 11,
14, 20, 25-6, 34, 49; on land speculation, **19:** 10-1; views on Westerners,
19: 13; letter to, from Washington,
quoted, **19:** 49; dissatisfaction with national government, **19:** 54; address to
French National Assembly, **19:** 102;
interest in manufacturing, **20:** 316n;
on excise act, **20:** 560; land purchases,
20: 595-6; northern journey with
Madison, **20:** 595, 602, 617; and
Tench Coxe's proposed appointment as
treasury comptroller, **20:** 668, 707-8;
visits Philadelphia, **20:** 715; and *National Gazette*, **20:** 731, 754; mentioned, **1:** 500; **15:** 368; **17:** 660n; **20:**
667, 682
Lee, Henry (Va. justice): and trial of
slave, **5:** 641, 642
Lee, Henry, Sr.: letter to, **5:** 434; letter
from, **5:** 393-4; British prevented from
raiding estate of, **5:** 394
Lee, Maj. John: petition to be transferred to land service, **1:** 583n; dispute
over rank, **3:** 41; new commission issued to, **3:** 56n; infantry under, **3:**
312, 501, 527; **4:** 67, 68n, 69, 569;
meets Stevens, **4:** 65, 539
Lee, Ludwell: opposition to paper
money, **11:** 310
Lee, Col. Philip Ludlow, **5:** 630

Lee, Richard: signs nonimportation resolutions (1769), **1**: 31; taken prisoner by British, **4**: 311, 421

Lee, Richard Bland: letter from, **17**: 354-5; congressman from Va., **15**: 5, 74, 78; **17**: 355n; federalism of, **15**: 5; and residence bill, **17**: 166n, 182, 207, 208n; **19**: 18n, 19; and diplomatic establishment, **17**: 218; and compromise of 1790, **19**: 4n, 19; and Potomac capital site, **19**: 8, 17-8, 27; vote on excise bill, **19**: 38n

Lee, Richard E.: signs address to TJ, **15**: 556

Lee, Richard Henry: letters to, **1**: 455-6, 477-8; **2**: 194, 210-1, 255-6, 298-9; **3**: 39-40, 259-60, 642-3; **5**: 33-7, 51-2, 61-2, 76-7, 93, 105, 105-6, 114-5, 160-1, 161-2, 167-8, 182, 206-7, 472-3; **7**: 643-4; **8**: 286-8, 289-90; **9**: 397-9; **15**: 577; letters from, **1**: 471, 522-3, 589-91; **2**: 13-4, 20, 29-31, 175-6, 176-7, 177-8, 200-1, 201-2, 204-5, 208-9, 214-6, 236, 262-3, 270-1; **3**: 29-30, 65, 84, 87-8, 90, 105-6, 210, 285; **5**: 262-3, 394, 434-6, 629-31; **6**: 90-3; **8**: 153-5, 683-5; **15**: 606; signs nonimportation resolutions, **1**: 30, 46; helps draft Fast-Day Resolution, **1**: 106n; letter from, to Samuel Adams, quoted, **1**: 107n; signs Virginia Association, **1**: 108; Va. delegate in Congress, **1**: 141, 224n; **6**: 319; **9**: 202, 242, 479; **10**: 577; signs Continental Association, **1**: 153; signs Congress' second petition, **1**: 223; signs letter to Virginia Convention, **1**: 224; and Lord North's Proposal, **1**: 230n; and Va.-Pa. boundary dispute, **1**: 234; recommends Edmund Randolph to Washington, **1**: 236; signs agreement of secrecy, **1**: 253; member of committee to report on Canadian campaign, **1**: 296n; and resolution of independence, **1**: 298-9, 311, 414n; contributions to plan of government for Va., **1**: 332n, 334n, 335n, 337n; and Adams' advice on government, **1**: 333n; arrives in Williamsburg, **1**: 384n; and Indiana Company, **1**: 386n; and Declaration of Independence, **1**: 415n, 432; recommendation on promotion of officers, **1**: 461; TJ hopes to see in Congress, **1**: 483; expected in Philadelphia, **1**: 486, 506; innuendos against, **1**: 590; and faction in Va. GA, **2**: 16n-

7n; eligibility to serve in Congress, **2**: 17n; as reference for Mazzei, **2**: 28; and case of Thomas Johnson, **2**: 43n; on committee to amend smallpox act, **2**: 124n; on cession of western territory, **2**: 148n; on foreign trade, **2**: 210-1; resigns from Congress, **2**: 262; letter to, from Pendleton, quoted, **2**: 320n; votes against bill for religious freedom, **2**: 549n; intends to enter Va. GA, **3**: 285; unpopularity in Va., **4**: 192; as Speaker of Va. GA, **5**: 37n; and Steuben's plans, **5**: 262, 275n-7n; **6**: 619n; commands militia at Hollis' marsh, **5**: 529; supports state papers series, **5**: 563n; letters from, to Washington, quoted, **6**: 79n; **18**: 164-5; letter from, to Steuben, quoted, **6**: 93n; reports on petitions for pensions, **6**: 140n; member Va. HD, **6**: 164, 264; differences with P. Henry, **6**: 187n; attitude on cession of western territory, **6**: 266; as corresponding member of Va. delegation, **7**: 4; supports Steuben's claims, **7**: 101n; leadership in Va. GA, **7**: 260; proposal for constitutional convention, **7**: 360; as president of Congress, **7**: 499, 630, 643; **8**: 153, 498, 520; health of, **8**: 153-4, 683; on regulation of commerce, **8**: 382, 580; requests phosphorescent lamp, **8**: 685; TJ's lack of knowledge of, **10**: 225; failure to be elected governor of Va., **10**: 577; declines to be delegate to Federal Convention, **11**: 310, 312; copy of *Notes on Virginia* sent to, **12**: 133; letter from cited, **12**: 205; letter from, to Adams, quoted, **12**: 206; opinion on bill of rights, **12**: 231n; opposes Constitution, **12**: 254, 281, 285, 423, 425, 444, 490, 651; not elected to Va. Constitutional Convention, **13**: 98; dispatches to, **13**: 227; *Letters from the Federal Farmer*, **13**: 245n; senator from Va., **14**: 281, 302, 339, 394, 415, 458, 525, 529, 560, 591, 615; **15**: 154; **17**: 607, 621, 644; **19**: 497; **20**: 692; antifederalism of, **14**: 394, 529; favors title of honor for President, **15**: 148; with Va. militia, **15**: 606; letter to *Virginia Gazette*, **16**: 172n; Beckwith obtains information from, **17**: 44n; on assumption bill, **17**: 355n; TJ on political prospects of, **17**: 544; and Northwest Territory, **18**: 164-5; and arrearages of soldiers' pay, **18**:

legislative powers: restrained by Constitution, **7**: 293; in France, **15**: 337, 359, 365

legislative powers, Va.: right of dissolution usurped by King, **1**: 131; in TJ's proposed Constitution (1776), **1**: 340-1, 347-9, 358-9; in Mason's plan, **1**: 366, 369; in Constitution, **1**: 379; delegation to representatives, **6**: 287; in TJ's revised Va. Constitution (1783), **6**: 281n-2n, 295-8, 311

Legrand, Mr.: and bill establishing ferries, **2**: 461

Le Grand, Ferdinand. *See* Grand

Le Grand, Peter: signs Virginia Association, **1**: 108

Legrand & Molinos: TJ visits with Mrs. Cosway, **10**: 444-5

Legras, Col. J.M.P.: letter from, **3**: 328-9; payment to, **3**: 270, 271, 274, 295, 298, 309, 310, 315, 316, 320, 323, 327; **4**: 283; Congress' resolves on, **3**: 373, 418

Le Gros (Lego?), Charles, **6**: 236

Le Havre, France: plan of engraved by Martinet fils, **7**: 420 (illus.); communication with Paris, **7**: 504, 510-1; port for packets, **7**: 504, 510-1; **8**: 67, 142, 227; **10**: 635-6, 650; **11**: 163, 169; **13**: 357-8, 467; U.S. trade with, **10**: 227; **11**: 32; **13**: 207, 240; **15**: 506; **20**: 675-6; American consul at, **10**: 254; **12**: 636; **13**: 278; **14**: 60, 62n, 532, 537-8; **15**: 237, 284n, 316-7, 354, 374, 466; **20**: 240-1; rice trade, **10**: 402; **11**: 588; **14**: 633; export of arms for Va. from, **10**: 467; plants to be sent to, **12**: 29; Bordeaux compared with, **13**: 478; tobacco trade, **14**: 424; TJ's opinion of, **15**: 490; merchants complain of U.S. duties, **17**: 314; **18**: 526; mob seizes TJ's household goods, **17**: 435-6, 436n-7n; **18**: xxxiii; Independence Day celebrated in, **20**: 676

Lehoc, Louis Grégoire: proposed appointment as minister of marine, **20**: 369-70

Leicester, Lord. *See* Townshend, George, first Earl of Leicester

Leich, Mr., **15**: 577

Leiden, Netherlands: Short describes, **8**: 447

Leiden Gazette. See Gazette de Leide

Leigh, Benjamin Watkins: and TJ's proposed Va. Constitution, **1**: 355n

Leigh, William: signs Virginia Association, **1**: 109

Leigh, Rev. William: inheritance under will of Benjamin Watkins, **6**: 180

Leiper, Dr. Andrew: needed in Richmond, **4**: 619

Leiper, Thomas: letters to, **17**: 309-10; **19**: 342-3; **20**: 387, 423; letter from, **20**: 712-3; houses in Philadelphia, **17**: xxx, 237-9, 267-9 (sketch), 293, 294n, 309-10; letter from missing, **17**: 294n; letter to cited, **17**: 378n; TJ's landlord, **17**: 498; purchases TJ's tobacco, **20**: 99; payment to Madison, **20**: 560; mentioned, **17**: 596; **20**: 420, 593

Lejeans, Louis Honoré: in Estates General, **15**: 45, 128, 213; Cathalan introduces to TJ, **15**: 45-6; mentioned, **15**: 324

Le Jeune, M.: letter to, **9**: 563; letter from, **9**: 378-9; and prize money claims, **9**: 157, 303; **10**: 94, 95; letter from cited, **9**: 455

Lelarge de Lignac, Joseph Adrien: books sought by TJ, **6**: 529

Leleu, veuve & Cie.: Terrasson's contract for rice, **13**: 476n; bankers to queen, **15**: 261

Le Maine. *See* Maine

Le Maire, Col. Jacques: letters from, **5**: 639; **7**: 520-1, 610-1; **8**: 120-2; letters sent by, **3**: 90; **7**: 504, 505; **8**: 73, 75, 117, 142, 235, 342, 428, 515; **9**: 297; **10**: 161; **15**: 621, 625, 628; information for R. H. Lee, **3**: 106; TJ requests commission for, **3**: 124; mission to France for military stores, **3**: 124n; expenses, **3**: 160, 170-1, 181; requests copy of army commission, **7**: 400-1; applies for Va. land bonus, **7**: 430-1, 505, 514; **8**: 110-1, 121; introduced to Gov. Harrison, **7**: 430-1; brandy sent by, **7**: 500, 533; recommended by TJ, **7**: 500, 501, 505; trustworthiness, **7**: 508; packet sent by, **8**: 34, 110, 640; invitation to Rosewell, **8**: 118; memoir on Ky., **8**: 123-32; advances for, **8**: 462; **9**: 333, 336; Madison pays, **9**: 202; might accompany Polly on trip, **9**: 212; **15**: 624; letter from cited, **11**: 191; mentioned, **8**: 533; **15**: 618, 631

Le Maître, Olivié, **10**: 552

Le Mans, France: wax bleaching at, **12**: 436

Le Mau de L'Eccosay, M.: letter from, **12**: 290-1

Le Mesurier, Havilland: at Le Havre, **14**: 543; Cutting characterizes, **15**: 480-1

Le Mesurier, Paul, **15**: 480

Le Mesurier & Cie. (merchants in Le Havre): letter to, **12**: 158-9; letters from, **12**: 121, 236; **17**: 401-2, 435-7; letters to cited, **15**: 478n; **17**: 402n; relations with Cutting, **15**: 480, 491, 494, 512; **20**: 702; seeds to be sent to, **16**: 503; correspondence with Short, **16**: 583; **17**: 402n; payment of draft, **17**: 411; letters from cited, **18**: 34n, 35n; mentioned, **15**: 518, 531

Le Mesurier & Secretan (merchants in London), **15**: 481

Le Mire, M., **14**: 410

Le Moine, M., **13**: 486; **14**: 274

L'Enfant, Pierre Charles: letters to, **19**: 355-6; **20**: 80, 86-7; letters from, **20**: 76-8, 81, 83-4; and Ramsay, **8**: 360n; and Cincinnati badges, **9**: 160-1; **10**: 186; **11**: 388; City Hall (Federal Hall), New York, remodeling, **14**: 30, 294; **16**: xxxiii; comic advice to, **17**: 453; advises Washington, **19**: 50; John Mason urged to consult, **19**: 57; asked to be commissioner of Federal District, **19**: 68; arrives in federal district, **19**: 358-9; plan for Federal City, **20**: xxxi, 384 (illus.); role in design of federal capital, **20**: 9-72, 76-8, 80, 81, 82, 83-4, 86, 88; relations with TJ, **20**: 12-72; evolution of plan for capital, **20**: 57-69; dismissed, **20**: 69-72; relations with Francis Cabot, **20**: 701

Lenoir, Jean Charles Pierre: on U.S.-French trade committee, **9**: 338n; **10**: 311; **12**: 142, 143; **13**: 52n

Le Normand, Simon Emmanuel Julien: tobacco purchases, **12**: 226

Lenox (Lennox), Mr. (merchant in Charleston): introduced to TJ, **12**: 28-9

Lenox, Walter, **1**: 70n

Lenox, Watt, **1**: 240

lenses: double-focus, **7**: 508, 517; **8**: 73; effect of natural crystals, **10**: 317; sent to Bellini, **12**: 634

Lent: use of rice in, **10**: 491

lentils: cultivation in S.C., **10**: 84; French duty on, **12**: 469, 480

Leopard (ship): in Saint-Domingue rebellion, **17**: 305-9; Saint-Domingue dep-uties sail for France on, **17**: 327-9, 525

Leopold II, Grand Duke of Tuscany, King of Hungary, Holy Roman Emperor: TJ suggests borrowing money from, **2**: 27-8, 224-5; and U.S. treaty of amity and commerce, **8**: 104; **15**: 617; characterized by TJ, **15**: 195; heir of Joseph II, **16**: 201; offers Belgic States immunity, **16**: 221, 254, 268, 305; military activities, **16**: 305, 405; Bellini's anecdote of, **17**: 21-2; in Reichenbach conference, **17**: 395, 439; coronation, **17**: 526, 542, 594, 664; relations with Prussia, **17**: 628; **20**: 695; in Brabant crisis, **18**: 85-6, 114; accepts peace terms, **18**: 294; and revolt in Liège, **18**: 453, 609-10; relations with Russia, **18**: 607; protests action by French National Assembly, **19**: 118n; forged letter to Louis XVI, **19**: 118n, 257; **20**: 88; attitude toward French Revolution, **19**: 636-7; **20**: 683; and revolt in Austrian Netherlands, **20**: 695; character, **20**: 696

Le Paon, Capt. (master of the *Eolus*), **8**: 639

Le Peletier de Morfontaine, Louis: letters to, **10**: 407-10; **11**: 165-6; letters from, **11**: 104-5, 151-2; and bust of Lafayette, **10**: 407-10, 414-5, 470-1; **11**: 171n; TJ's conversations with, **13**: 487

Le Pommereux, M.: letter from, **12**: 53

Le Prince, M.: copypress purchased from, **17**: 360

Le Ray de Chaumont, Jacques Donatien: letter from, **13**: 286-7; and Lee-Deane feud, **3**: 65; offers advice on Italian trade with U.S., **3**: 367, 368, 414; and *Alliance* case, **6**: 398; **7**: 270; **8**: 439; **14**: 315; son of, **8**: 88; and U.S. trade, **9**: 43; Dechezaulx asks for payment from, **14**: 551; Deane's account with, **14**: 631; debt to Bondfield, **17**: 577; mentioned, **8**: 54, 55, 102, 585

Lerena. *See* López de Lerena, Don Pedro

Lerew, Abram: loan to Va., **3**: 386

Lerew, Jacob: loan to Va., **3**: 386

Lerew, Ruben: loan to Va., **3**: 386

Le Rocher, France: TJ describes, **11**: 458

Lerouge, Georges Louis: *Jardins Anglo-Chinois*, **13**: xxx

Le Roux, M.: letter to, **11**: 111-2

"Notices sur la vie de Benjamin Franklin," **9**: 495-8; **16**: 306n; **17**: 272-3; letter from quoted, **10**: 395n; letters to cited, **10**: 625; **16**: xxxii, 306n; sends wine to TJ, **11**: 62; and Franklin's Federal Convention speech, **12**: 233n, 234n; letter from cited, **18**: 87n; Franklin's autobiography ms. given to, **18**: 91n, 93n, 94n; mentioned, **9**: 466

Le Vendangeur (ship): loss of, **20**: 249; mentioned, **19**: 605

Lévesque, Pierre Charles: *Collection des moralistes anciens*, **14**: 28n

Levi, Mr., **6**: 261

Levis, Que. (Point Levy, Levi), **1**: 270, 434, 436

Levitical law: Va. bill annulling marriages prohibited by, **2**: 556-8

Lewis (galley), **3**: 530; **4**: 290; **5**: 130, 143, 144, 182

Lewis, Mr.: admitted to share in Nash's land scheme, **6**: 245; mentioned, **1**: 500

Lewis, Aaron: letter from, to Campbell, quoted, **5**: 553n

Lewis, Gen. Andrew: letter to, **5**: 640; letters from, **1**: 244-5; **3**: 78-80; commissioner to meet with Ohio Indians, **1**: 245n; sends reinforcements, **1**: 297; warrant from, **1**: 524; deposition concerning Henderson's land claims, **2**: 76-8, 110n; appointed to confer on western defense, **3**: 51, 53, 667; and Va.-Pa. boundary dispute, **3**: 289n; elected to Va. Executive Council, **3**: 349n; and inquiry into Va. Executive, **6**: 89n, 90n; mentioned, **2**: 81; **6**: 110; **15**: 577

Lewis, Becca: at Williamsburg, **16**: 27

Lewis, Benjamin, **7**: 274

Lewis, Betsy Washington: illness, **10**: 534n

Lewis, Charles: buys slave from TJ, **1**: 33n; and Rivanna river, **1**: 87; supports state papers series, **1**: 146; election of, **1**: 238; in Albemarle co. militia, **1**: 480, 667; signs petition, **1**: 587; mentioned, **1**: 41

Lewis, Col. Charles, **2**: 10; **5**: 22

Lewis, Charles, Jr.: signs petition, **1**: 587; signs Va. oath of allegiance, **2**: 129

Lewis, Charles Lilburne: letters to, **14**: 427-8; **16**: 191-2, 192n; signs petition, **1**: 587; signs Va. oath of allegiance, **2**:

129; loses election to Va. GA, **5**: 430, 431; appointed colonel of Albemarle militia, **5**: 469; commission for, **5**: 554; and estate of Jane Jefferson, **16**: 157; in estate settlement of Elizabeth Jefferson, **16**: 191-2, 194; letter from missing, **16**: 192n; letter to cited, **16**: 195n; mentioned, **15**: 634

Lewis, Edward: and Henry co. court, **1**: 594n

Lewis, Fielding: letter to, **1**: 467; letter from, **3**: 281; services to arms factory at Fredericksburg, **4**: 431; health of, **4**: 550

Lewis, Francis: letters to, **9**: 274; **10**: 210; **13**: 121; letters from, **9**: 483, 509; **14**: 325-6; **15**: 587; signs Congress' second petition, **1**: 222; signs agreement of secrecy, **1**: 252; signs Declaration of Independence, **1**: 432; TJ consults on U.S. commerce, **7**: 324n, 329; replies to TJ's queries on commerce of N.Y., **7**: 329; sends Madeira wine to TJ, **9**: 505; **10**: 205, 290; Berger introduced to, by TJ, **13**: 121; letters to cited, **15**: 370n

Lewis, Isham: in Albemarle co. militia, **1**: 667; signs Va. oath of allegiance, **2**: 129

Lewis, John: attorney for Johnson, **2**: 45n; warrant for, **4**: 586; furnishes gunpowder to Va., **4**: 586n; clothes for slaves, **5**: 11

Lewis, John, Jr.: signs nonimportation resolutions (1769), **1**: 31

Lewis, John, Sr.: signs Va. oath of allegiance, **2**: 129

Lewis, Lucy Jefferson (Mrs. Charles Lilburne Lewis, sister of TJ), **14**: 428; **15**: 93

Lewis, Lucy Walker (Mrs. Nicholas Lewis): letter from, **18**: 594; botanical knowledge, **9**: 254, 256; clock for, **9**: 256; presents from TJ, **9**: 400; **10**: 615; sends seeds to TJ, **12**: 135; **13**: 343; letters from cited, **16**: 406, 433, 492; **17**: 325n; bacon and venison hams sent by, **16**: 492; **17**: 324, 325n; glass for, **20**: 382, 415; mentioned, **10**: 616; **11**: 642; **12**: 136; **13**: 344; **14**: 363; **16**: 211, 411, 482, 600; **18**: 42, 499

Lewis, Mary: collects contributions for soldiers, **15**: 592n

Lewis, Mary Randolph (Mrs. Charles

from, **4**: 530; **5**: 125, 150-1, 177; commission as Va. Navy captain, **5**: 52n, 58; command at Hoods, **5**: 181; letter from, to James Maxwell, **6**: 6-7; mentioned, **5**: 132, 190

Lewis, Maj. William, **3**: 652; **5**: 534, 552

Lexington, Ky.: attack of Shawnee feared, **4**: 170; building of rammed-earth fort at, **5**: 463

Lexington, Mass.: battle of, **1**: 165, 196, 201, 209, 216; **10**: 370, 375n

Lexington, Va.: founding, **2**: 115

Lex Parliamentaria: TJ commends, **16**: 449

lex talionis, **2**: 230, 498, 505n

Ley, Mr.: and bill establishing ferries, **2**: 455

Leyden. *See* Leiden

Leyonankar (Lejonachen, Leijonanckar), Adm. Frederik Vilhelm: captured, **17**: 522

L'Heritier du Boutelle, Charles Louis, **14**: 278

L'Hommande, Jeudy de: letter to, **12**: 11; letter from, **11**: 391-2

L'Hommedieu, Mr. and Mrs. Ezra: and Hessian fly, **20**: 448, 459

Liancourt, Duc de. *See* La Rochefoucauld-Liancourt

libel: in common law courts, **2**: 605; in France, **16**: 45-6

Libertas Americana medal. *See* medals

Liberty (ship): ordered to join Md. vessels, **3**: 642; arrives at Yorktown, **5**: 94; captured by British, **5**: 95; mentioned, **15**: 67, 670, 672

libraries: Va. bill for establishing, **2**: 544-5; in Richmond, **8**: 345; in Philadelphia, **10**: 38

Library Company, Philadelphia: compared to TJ's view of libraries, **2**: 544n; building, **7**: 20

library steps (*échelle de bibliothèque*): TJ orders, **16**: 476

Licking creek: defense of, **3**: 54, 55, 78-9; mentioned, **3**: 560; **6**: 159

Licking river: defense of, **3**: 420, 422; **5**: 463

Liège: Trumbull describes, **10**: 440; constitutions, **15**: 357-8; **17**: 526; rebellion in, **16**: 7n; Prussians occupy, **16**: 41-2, 120-1; American medals sent to, **16**: 67; Prince de Rohan as regent, **17**: 526; **18**: 478, 608, 610; peace in, **18**: 478, 498; Imperial troops occupy,

18: 607-10; interest of Berlin and Vienna in, **19**: 117; conflict with Austria, **19**: 118

Liège, Bishop of. *See* Hoensbroech, Constantin François

lien law (Va., 1782), **6**: 429

Life and Adventures of Lazarillo de Tormes, **20**: 238

Lifford, Judge: British officers quartered at house of, **1**: 505

light: effect on plants, **13**: 379; TJ's observations and diagram of rainbow, **13**: 380

Lightfoot, John: assistant commissary of hides, **5**: 223; petition from, **5**: 349

lighthouses: superintendents of, **16**: 480

lightning bugs: in darkness of solar eclipse, **2**: 205

lightning rods: used by La Rochefoucauld, **7**: 376

lignum vitae: U.S. import from West Indies, **10**: 148

Ligon, Richard: *True and Exact History of Barbados*, **20**: 634n

Liguria: beauty of coast line, **11**: 441-2

Lille (L'Isle), France: Cathalan comments on, **11**: 358

Lillie, James: lost at sea, **11**: 656-7; **12**: 423

Lillington, John Alexander, **4**: 359

Lilly, Capt. Thomas, **1**: 469

lily of Canada: TJ requests seeds of for France, **9**: 254

lima beans, **12**: 595

lime: needed at Hoods, **5**: 126; for tanning, **5**: 296; as building material, **13**: 28; in wheat culture, **15**: 131

Limone, Italy: TJ describes, **11**: 433

Limozin, André (Andrew): letters to, **8**: 513, 533-4, 565, 584, 598; **9**: 27, 59, 66, 451-2, 599, 639, 652; **10**: 164, 197-8, 269, 273, 504, 601-2; **11**: 127, 138, 145, 546, 597, 642-3; **12**: 70, 75-6, 110-1, 162, 167, 167-8, 171, 223-4, 244-5, 294, 354, 450-1, 483-4, 492, 509, 527-9, 568, 575, 591-2, 615, 640, 693; **13**: 137-8, 172-3, 255, 298, 344, 365-6, 419, 437-8, 533, 573-4; **14**: 53-4, 327, 349-50, 457, 623-4; **15**: 46-7, 86-7; letters from, **7**: 554; **8**: 526, 541, 570-1, 583-4, 593, 625, 638-9; **9**: 51-2, 57, 67, 76, 82, 330, 471-2, 554, 591, 644, 652; **10**: 188-9, 223, 253-4, 327-8, 592, 616-7; **11**: 98, 110, 142, 166, 261, 349, 375, 604-5, 629-30, 660-1; **12**: 11, 19, 46-

Limozin, André (Andrew) (*cont.*)
7, 54, 71, 104, 156-8, 169-70, 171-2,
179-60, 185-6, 213-4, 234-5, 237,
237-8, 244, 250-1, 305, 334, 367-9,
370, 436, 436-7, 454-5, 465, 494,
496, 497, 506, 522, 532-4, 552, 577,
602-3, 630; **13**: 47, 184-5, 240, 282,
288, 301, 357-8, 388, 419-20, 425-6,
471-2, 482-3, 524, 661-2; **14**: 52, 54-
5, 182-3, 314-5, 338, 368-9, 390,
465, 595-6; **15**: 18, 57, 70-1; books
sent by, **8**: 535; **11**: 665, 667; **13**:
133n; **14**: 369; sailing of ship, **9**: 8,
25; letters to cited, **9**: 27; **10**: 269; **11**:
157; **12**: 140; **13**: 339n; letters from
cited, **9**: 123, 578; **10**: 193; **11**: 373;
13: 137; **15**: 245, 246n; packages sent
by way of, **10**: 144, 206, 211, 248;
11: 561; **12**: 638; **13**: 148, 171; plants
and trees to be sent through, **10**: 227,
228; **11**: 122; **12**: 29, 133, 137, 409,
687; **13**: 111, 483; activities in Robertson's affairs, **10**: 284, 294-5; sends
bill of lading, **10**: 632; American agent
at Le Havre, **11**: 99; **12**: 158, 244,
483; **13**: 388, 419; **14**: 60, 62n, 537;
forwards diplomatic papers, **11**: 135;
inquires about plants, **11**: 156; correspondence with Short, **11**: 361; **13**:
138, 301; aid to American seamen, **12**:
250-1; letters from quoted, **12**: 534n;
protests detention of the *Portsmouth*,
12: 684; forwards wine to Hopkinson,
13: 145; assists Montgomery family,
13: 253, 255, 282, 288; relations with
Collow Frères, **13**: 417; seeks TJ's advice, **13**: 425; letter to, from Swan,
quoted, **13**: 425n-6n; TJ's account
with, **13**: 533, 662; **15**: 46; advice to
Vanet, **13**: 641; sends boxes to Madison by mistake, **13**: 661, 662n; **14**:
189; letter from, to Madison, cited, **13**:
662n; **14**: 54; letter to, from Jeffery,
cited, **14**: 338; introduces Fraser to
TJ, **14**: 390; arrêt on whale oil sent
to, **14**: 465; TJ declines offer of lodging in his house, **15**: 86-7; death of,
15: 237, 241, 316; TJ's appreciation
of, **15**: 312; mentioned, **7**: 396; **9**:
657; **11**: 37, 326, **12**: 593; **13**: 44
Limozin, Edward: letter to, **15**: 312; letter from, **15**: 241-2
Limozin, veuve & fils: letter from, **15**:
237
Linch, Charles: signs Virginia Association, **1**: 108
Lincoln, Gen. Benjamin: letters from, **3**:

260-1; **13**: 512; **15**: 585, 586; at Fort
Stanwix, **2**: 29; defeat at Savannah, **3**:
232-3, 343; at Charleston, **3**: 343,
400, 401, 403, 426; **4**: 525; **15**: 585,
586; needs clothing for troops, **3**: 353;
moves British prisoners, **5**: 40; Indian
commissioner, **7**: 9n, 250; claim
against Congress, **7**: 554; and Shays'
Rebellion, **11**: 146, 222-3, 230, 240-1;
lieutenant governor of Mass., **13**: 337;
introduces Hays to TJ, **13**: 512; mentioned, **7**: 128
Lincoln co., Ky.: letter to county lieutenant of, **4**: 231-2; formation of, **4**: 200n;
6: 597n; militia, **4**: 234, 236; **5**: 310,
461
Linctot (Lanctot, Lintot), Daniel Maurice Godefroy de: letter to, **4**: 600; letters from, **4**: 180, 249-50, 479; **5**:
320; payment to, **3**: 270, 271, 274,
295, 298; **4**: 283; commission as Indian agent, **3**: 296; accounts of, **3**:
309, 310, 316, 320, 323, 327; **4**: 113-
5; negotiates with Indians, **5**: 320;
mentioned, **3**: 277; **4**: 429
Lind, Capt. Arthur: letter from, to Davies, quoted, **6**: 54n-5n
Lind, Dr. James: *Essay on the most effec-
tual means of preserving the health of
seamen in the Royal Navy*, **19**: 613n;
and desalination of sea water, **19**: 615,
619-20, 621-22, 623
Lindahl, Erik: *Lexicon Lapponicum*, **15**:
223
Linde, M. de. *See* Lynden van Blitter-
swyck
Lindsay, Adam: letters to, **19**: 581; **20**:
218-9; letter from, **20**: 166; books carried by, **19**: 245; letter from quoted,
19: 353n
Lindsay (Lindsey), Joseph: and western
defense, **3**: 55, 167; commission for, **3**:
72; as agent for Illinois co., **3**: 158,
159, 166, 416; goods purchased by, **3**:
520; **4**: 442, 443n; and canoes, **5**: 461;
unable to act as witness, **5**: 494
Lindsay, Reuben: letter to, **17**: 654; letter from, **5**: 554-5; orders to Capt.
Wallace, **4**: 295n; commissioner of Albemarle co., **5**: 431; TJ recommends
as Albemarle county lieutenant, **5**:
468, 469; correspondence with Davies,
5: 555n; **6**: 13n; mentioned, **4**: 295n;
6: 13n
Lindsay, Sarah Walker (Mrs. Reuben
Lindsay): death of, **16**: 25
Lindsay, William: letter to, **18**: 479-80;

letter from, **20**: 211; letter from, to Hamilton, quoted, **16**: 353n-4n; letter from quoted, **18**: 480n; ships furniture to TJ, **20**: 94-5

Lindsay and Johnson, **5**: 441

linen: requisition for, **3**: 345; price, **4**: 549; **8**: 602; scarcity, **5**: 143; manufactured in U.S., **7**: 335, 341, 345; U.S. import of, **8**: 309; **10**: 147; **12**: 301; Mrs. Adams' praise of Irish, **8**: 594; Irish purchased for TJ, **8**: 602; sent to Anna Scott Jefferson, **9**: 397; export to West Indies, **12**: 532; bleaching, **14**: 367; improved loom for weaving, **20**: 242-3

Lingan, J. M.: signs petition, **17**: 471

Lingan, Nicholas: owner of the *Brilliant*, **9**: 387

Linguet, Simon Nicolas Henri: *Mémoire au Roi*, **11**: 42

Linn, Andrew, **3**: 206

Linn, Benjamin: drafts drawn by, **3**: 158

Linn, William: letter to, **20**: 706-7; letter from, **20**: 646; *The Blessings of America*, **20**: 646, 706; biographical note, **20**: 706n-7n; *Serious Considerations on the Election of a President*, **20**: 707n

Linnaeus, Carolus: works, **8**: 111; *Systema Vegetabilium*, **9**: 228, 444; **10**: 593; **11**: 27, 228; English edition sent to Richard Cary, **10**: 226, 635; *Dissertation on the Sexes of Plants*, **10**: 384; **12**: 227; *Genera Plantarum*, **11**: 229; **12**: 18, 129; *Species Plantarum*, **11**: 229; **12**: 18, 129; *Philosophia Botanica*, **12**: 18, 129; *Mantissa Plantarum*, **12**: 129; *Systema Naturae*, **12**: 129; **20**: 429n; *Reflections on the Study of Nature*, **12**: 227; *Families of Plants*, **13**: 651; mentioned, **9**: 461

Linnet (ship): TJ's possessions carried on, **18**: 34n, 69, 74n

Linton, John (cotton manufacturer): desire to go to America, **13**: 154

Lion (French frigate): on cruise, **6**: 237‚

Lipscombe, Bernard, **4**: 542

Lipscombe, Yancey, **4**: 542

Lipsius, Justus, **12**: 16

Liquier, André: in Estates General, **15**: 45

liquor: taxed in Va., **2**: 219, 537, 540; license to sell, **2**: 447; ordered to be furnished to Cherokee, **3**: 160; for army, **3**: 529, 530, 543, 550, 609, 641; **4**: 9, 133, 217, 220, 412, 450, 474, 488-9; **5**: 459n; purchase of, for army, stopped, **3**: 643; for Albemarle garri-

son, **3**: 661; issued to wagoners, **5**: 12; no allowance for carpenters and laborers, **5**: 128n; ration for seamen, **5**: 151, 176, 178; **6**: 6; for Innes' troops, **5**: 533; duty on in Va., **11**: 146, 147n; prohibition of import into Va., **12**: 411, 444, 570

Liriodendron tulipiferum. See tulip tree

Lisbon: Pequet assists American sailors at, **6**: 400; flour trade, **7**: 454-5; U.S. consulate at, **9**: 127, 263, 273; **12**: 192-3; **19**: 247-8, 314, 317; **20**: 160, 161n, 565; Rutledge advised to visit, **13**: 358, 375, 531; Humphreys reports on, **18**: 48-50; and the fisheries, **19**: 197; U.S. trade with, **20**: 361n; U.S. vice consul in, **20**: 361n-2n

L'Isle, France. *See* Lille, France

Lisle, M. de, **10**: 509

Liston, Sir Robert: British minister at Madrid, **12**: 240, 242n, 365; **13**: 143, 144n; attempts to prejudice Spain against France, **12**: 324; Carmichael on, **12**: 361-4, 424; possible British minister to U.S., **12**: 363

"Literary Christmas Gambol," **6**: 445-6

literary style: Francis Hopkinson on, **6**: 445-6; TJ on, **8**: 637

Little Beaver creek: defense of, **3**: 55

Little Carpenter (Cherokee chief). *See* Attakullaculla

Little Kanawha (Kanhaway) river: defense of, **3**: 54, 55, 259, 420; mentioned, **8**: 125; **12**: 489

Little Meadows, **2**: 99

Little Miami river: bounty land to soldiers on, **6**: 579; mentioned, **6**: 572n

Little Miamis: defense of, **3**: 55

Littlepage, Lewis: letters to, **10**: 442; **12**: 27; **15**: 105-6; **20**: 703-4; letters from, **9**: 193; **10**: 130-1, 357; **12**: 334; **14**: 544-5; **19**: 417-9, 599-600; letters sent by, **8**: 517, 518, 640, 659; **12**: 397, 401, 484, 501, 557-8; **18**: 506; correspondence with Jay cited, **9**: 83, 193; relations with Jay, **9**: 86-7, 213, 236; **10**: 107; **11**: 328; criticized by Barclay, **9**: 210; TJ's comments on his behavior, **9**: 215, 239; debt to Livingston, **10**: 188; letter from, to Lafayette, quoted, **10**: 188n; money owed by, **10**: 442; note to signed by Lafayette, **11**: 83; debt to Va., **12**: 27; commission from King of Poland, **12**: 112, 202; Carmichael's financial arrangement with, **12**: 334, 426; **13**: 94, 230, 399; Smith's characterization of, **12**: 517;

Littlepage, Lewis (*cont.*)
disappearance reported, **13**: 239; as secret agent for Poland, **13**: 441; **14**: 544-5, 672-3; TJ on, **13**: 441; J. P. Jones sends messages by, **13**: 506, 580-1, 584, 586, 587n; **14**: 515, 544; absence of news about, **13**: 592; naval service in Black Sea, **14**: 375; in Paris, **19**: 589; role in Jones' Russian adventure, **19**: 599-600; mentioned, **12**: 660, 685, 690

Littlepage, William: letter from cited, **19**: 575

Littleton (Lyttleton), Lord George, first Baron: estate of, **9**: 375n

live oak: sale of timber in France, **8**: 205; **9**: 167-8; **10**: 227; plants asked from John Banister, **11**: 121

Livermore, Samuel: appointed House conferee on excise bill, **19**: 37

Liverpool, England: importance as port, **10**: 388; Independence Day celebration at, **20**: 621; U.S. ships seized at, **20**: 621, 704

Livesey & Co.: failure of, **13**: 210n

livestock: held in execution of judgment, **2**: 646; power of commissioners of provision law over, **3**: 486, 492; Weedon suggests driving northward from Williamsburg, **5**: 273; Conn. export to West Indies, **7**: 334; trade statistics, **7**: 349; S.C. export before Revolution, **8**: 200; U.S. export of, **10**: 147

Livingston, Eliza: letter from cited, **11**: 109

Livingston, John: taken prisoner by British, **4**: 311, 421

Livingston, Mary Stevens (Mrs. Robert R. Livingston), **17**: 326

Livingston, Peter B.: recommends John Kean, **20**: 226

Livingston, Philip: signs Congress' second petition, **1**: 222; signs Declaration of Independence, **1**: 432

Livingston, Robert R.: letters to, **6**: 206, 228-9, 238-9, 257, 260; **12**: 213; **17**: 325-6; letters from, **6**: 202, 239-40, 250-1, 259-60; **12**: 640; **17**: 294, 552-4; **18**: 146-50; **19**: 295-7; signs Congress' second petition, **1**: 222; signs agreement of secrecy, **1**: 252; member of committee on Canadian campaign, **1**: 296n; opposes resolution on independence, **1**: 309; on committee to prepare Declaration of Independence, **1**: 313, 414n; letter to, from La Lu-

zerne, **6**: 209; letter to, from Washington, quoted, **6**: 217n; letters to cited, **6**: 245, 259n; **18**: 148n, 150n; departure of, **6**: 247; resignation from Department of Foreign Affairs, **6**: 275-6, 336n; **15**: 612n; letter from, to Lafayette, quoted, **6**: 475n; ministry to Britain discussed, **7**: 570; **18**: 260; N.Y. delegate in Congress, **7**: 572; sent list of *Alliance* crew, **8**: 439, 453; Littlepage's debt to, **10**: 188; letter to, from Houdon, quoted, **13**: 319n-20n; as federalist, **13**: 414n; in N.Y. Constitutional Convention, **13**: 611n; receives votes as Vice President, **15**: 92; seeks appointment as Secretary of Foreign Affairs, **15**: 153; letter to, from Franklin, quoted, **15**: 316n; **16**: 55n; Franklin's project for medals approved, **16**: 55n, 56n; plan for weights and measures, **16**: 616; letters from cited, **16**: 616n; **18**: 148n; report on ministers to foreign courts, **17**: 228n; interest in machinery, **17**: 294, 325, 552-3; **18**: 146-50; **19**: 240-1; Report on Weights and Measures sent to, **17**: 325, 553; **19**: 295; and Barbary States, **18**: 386; "Thoughts on Coinage and the Establishment of a Mint," **19**: 295; "A Customer" letters attributed to, **20**: 301; confers with TJ and Madison, **20**: 434-5, 452; mentioned, **6**: 211n, 251n, 273; **7**: 64

Livingston, Walter: letters to, **12**: 698-700; **14**: 593-4, 656-7; **15**: 125; letters from, **9**: 80, 479-81; **11**: 159-61; **13**: 394; **14**: 581-2; deputy commissary, **1**: 451, 453; commissioner of the treasury, **7**: 159n; **8**: 79, 86, 499, 519; **9**: 15; **13**: 308; Barclay's expense account sent to, **9**: 210; correspondence with Willink & Van Staphorst, **15**: 41-2, 474-5; victim of Duer scheme, **19**: 445n

Livingston, William: letter to, **6**: 218; letters from, **4**: 241; **6**: 223-4; **7**: 304; signs Continental Association, **1**: 153; and draft of Declaration of Causes, **1**: 187n; quoted, **1**: 189n; signs Congress' second petition, **1**: 222; signs agreement of secrecy, **1**: 253; member of committee on Canadian campaign, **1**: 296n; councillor of American Philosophical Society, **4**: 545; governorship of N.J., **7**: 630; nominated minister to Netherlands, **8**: 77; declines mission to

The Hague, **8**: 293, 420; **9**: 15, 176; letter to cited, **10**: 558; member of Federal Convention, **11**: 400; death of, **17**: 77

Livy: studied by Peter Carr, **9**: 38, 201; **12**: 18; studied by Martha Jefferson, **11**: 203, 238, 251, 282, 381; Bible compared with works of, **12**: 15-6; Arabic translation of (hoax), **13**: 382, 383n; *History of Rome*, **13**: 656n; bust of, **14**: 312; *Historiarum*, **15**: 223; *Annals of the Roman People*, **20**: 634n

Lloyd, Mr., **9**: 364n

Lloyd, Richard, **7**: 131

Lloyd, Mrs. Richard, **7**: 131, 355

Lloyd, Robert: speaker of Maryland Assembly, **1**: 20n

Lloyd, T., **12**: 231n

Lloyd's List: data on British coins, **20**: 546n

Lloyd's of London: insurance of American ships, **7**: 556, 604, 629, 634-5

Loan Office, Continental: arrears of interest, **7**: 66; mentioned, **2**: 31; **3**: 492

Loan Office certificates: punishment for theft of, **2**: 501; Va. bill concerning, **2**: 507-10; interest on, **6**: 559; **7**: 94; **9**: 452; **10**: 584; **11**: 136; receipt for, **6**: 645, 668 (illus.); in payment of national debt, **7**: 67-8, 71-2, 213-4; payment, **9**: 435; settlement of, **11**: 23, 51; Grand & Cie. inquiry on, **15**: 108-9; Holker's interest on, **17**: 286, 288

loans: from Europe, **2**: 27; circular from John Jay concerning, **3**: 29; public, **3**: 104; reliance on foreign, **4**: 106; French, **4**: 144-7; **7**: 65; discrimination against foreign holders of debts, **7**: 67. *See also* France: Loan to U.S.; Netherlands: Loan to U.S.; Spain: loan to U.S.

lobster, **11**: 442

Lochabar (Lochaber), Treaty of: cedes land to Cherokees, **2**: 67, 74, 78-9, 111n

Loche, M. de: vineyard of, **11**: 422

Locke, John: TJ's notes on, **1**: 544-51; *Conduct of the Mind*, **12**: 18; *Essay concerning Human Understanding*, **12**: 18; portrait of, **14**: 467, 525n, 561 (sketch); bust of, **14**: 468, 525; *Some Thoughts concerning Education*, **15**: 406; *Treatise on Government*, **16**: 449, 481; mentioned, **20**: 662

Lockhart, Patrick: letter to, **4**: 103-4; letter from, **4**: 177-8; on committees to

divide Va. counties, **1**: 566n; **2**: 117n; guards prisoners of war, **4**: 102, 103-4, 178-9, 238

locks: Academy of Sciences report on, **20**: 371-2

Lockwood, James: supports American state papers series, **1**: 145

Lockwood, Maj. James: testifies on Canadian campaign, **1**: 447-8

Lockyer, Mr.: flees from creditors, **10**: 80

locust: seeds sought by TJ, **9**: 253, 254; **10**: 616; plants asked from John Banister, **11**: 121. *See also* honey locust

Locust Point, Va.: ferry at, **2**: 455

Lodi, Italy: TJ describes manufacture of Parmesan cheese at, **11**: 438

Loftin, John: imports slaves, **15**: 654

Logan (Shawnee Indian), **4**: 442, 546

Logan, Benjamin: votes for bill for religious freedom, **2**: 549n; ordered to raise volunteers, **19**: 465

Logan, Charles: Zane recommends to TJ, **6**: 160

Logan, George (Pa.): contributions to *National Gazette*, **20**: 734-6; *Letters Addressed to the Yeomanry of the United States* (1791), **20**: 734, 735n

Logan, George (Va.): signs nonimportation resolutions (1770), **1**: 46

Logan, James: grandson of, **6**: 160; Franklin's friendship with, **9**: 487; bequest for public library in Philadelphia, **10**: 38

Logan, William, **6**: 160

Loganian Library (Philadelphia): building, **7**: 20

Loggstown (Logstown): inhabited by Shawnee, **2**: 99; defense of, **3**: 55; mentioned, **2**: 91, 92

Loggstown, Treaty of (1752), **2**: 90, 250; **6**: 177

Logie, Charles: British consul at Algiers, **8**: 440, 525; **12**: 550; **13**: 180, 249; **15**: 181; **18**: 375; treatment of Americans taken captive by Algiers, **9**: 530-1; relations with Lamb, **9**: 550, 620, 621; hostility to U.S., **9**: 615, 618; report to Dey of slander against Lamb, **10**: 149; Carmichael's opinion of, **12**: 239; letter to Anderson on American captives, **18**: 399-400; promotes truce between Portugal and Algiers, **18**: 414; commissioned to purchase frigate for Algiers, **19**: 333

Logo graphique: sent to TJ, **20**: 347

[319]

37; battle of, **10**: 154, 381-2, 383n
Long Island, Tenn.: treaty at, **2**: 90, 92, 93, 109; identified, **4**: 201n
Long Island Sound: skirmishes on borders, **1**: 589
longitude: methods of finding, **11**: 293-4, 398-9, 403, 533, 562; Rittenhouse's calculations on, **16**: 595-6
Long Lake, Mich.: as part of U.S. boundary, **6**: 458
Longman, Thomas, **18**: 333n
Longman & Brodsip, **12**: 297
Lonpry, M. (tailor): Williamos' indebtedness to, **8**: 269, 275
loom: William Pearce's improved version of, **20**: 242-3, 313-22
Looney, John: petitions Va. HD for care of livestock, **2**: 41n-2n; claims against Va., **2**: 63
López de Gómara, Francisco: *Histoire generale des Indes Occidentales*, **11**: 554; *Historia de Mexico*, **16**: 214
López de Lerena, Don Pedro, Conde de Lerena: as Spanish minister of war, **8**: 83; **18**: 473
López de Vargas Machucha, Don Tomas: map of South America by, **10**: 212-3, 214n, 216n
Lorain (Lorin), Peleg: captured by Algerians, **14**: 395; **17**: 32; **20**: 625
Lord Cornwallis (British ship): captured by French, **4**: 659; new commander for, **4**: 678; captures Sisson, **5**: 306n
L'ordre architecture, **20**: 647-8
Lords Commissioners of Appeals: Philip Wilson petitions, **20**: 638n
Lords of the Admiralty: in Crozier case, **20**: 491-2; in *Rachel* case, **20**: 500
Lords of the Treasury: in *Rachel* case, **20**: 484, 499, 506, 509, 511-22; letter to, from Commissioners of Customs, **20**: 511-2
Lords of Trade: report on U.S commercial policy, **18**: 224-5, 228, 253, 259, 263, 267-72, 279; **19**: 166
Loreilhe, Zachariah: letters to, **9**: 599; **10**: 304, 309-10, 497, 543; **11**: 92; **12**: 7, 111, 224, 294, 587; letters from, **9**: 308; **10**: 254-3, 290-1, 331, 472, 523; **11**: 671; **12**: 168, 378-9, 565-6; letter for, from Henry Champion, **10**: 552; absent from L'Orient, **11**: 395; **12**: 498; needs safe conduct, **11**: 467; sails from Bordeaux to U.S., **11**: 499n-500n, 538; declaration on U.S. marine insurance at Amsterdam,

11: 593-4; letters from cited, **11**: 662; **12**: 5n; financial difficulties, **12**: 565-6; consul in L'Orient, **14**: 60, 62n; mentioned, **10**: 87; **11**: 112, 552, 583, 626, 627
Lorentz, Jean Daniel, **13**: xxviii
Lorenzana y Butron, Francisco Antonio: *Historia de Nueva-España*, **20**: 210
Loreto, Italy, Santa Casa: Short describes, **14**: 380
L'Orient (Lorient), France: letter from Americans in, **12**: 359; TJ desires to land at, **7**: 311; communication with Paris difficult, **7**: 504, 511; port for packets, **7**: 510-1; **10**: 650; **16**: 303; seizure of merchandise at, **8**: 181; port for American tobacco, **8**: 223; **11**: 507; **12**: 648; **13**: 58, 75-91; **14**: 283; *entrepôt* for U.S.-Irish commerce, **9**: 28; as free port, **9**: 459n; **10**: 227; **12**: 378; **16**: 280, 281n; insurance on American vessels at, **10**: 302; TJ visits, **11**: 459, 516, 571; American vessels entering harbor, **11**: 488; rice importation, **11**: 591; American agent at, **11**: 669; plants ordered sent to, **12**: 29; lack of broker service for American vessels, **12**: 359, 371-2, 377-8; and farmers-general, **12**: 650; **13**: 429; merchants in, **13**: 55n, 75, 89, 119; consul in, **14**: 60, 62n; **19**: 314, 317; Irish and Scottish vessels seized at, **14**: 391-2, 392n-3n; in Necker's speech to Estates General, **15**: 113; mentioned, **6**: 398
Lorin, Peleg. *See* Lorain, Peleg
Loring, Capt. (master of *Phoenix*), **13**: 207
Loring, Joshua: British commissary of prisoners, **3**: 86, 99, 103; requests concerning British prisoners of war, **4**: 33-4
Loring, Patrick: on crew of *Dauphin*, **19**: 333
Loriottière, France: TJ describes, **11**: 459
Lorme, M. de, **12**: 348
Lormerie, M. de: letters to, **11**: 554-5; **12**: 630-1; letters from, **11**: 528; **15**: 155, 478; **16**: 433-5; relations with Blackden, **11**: 519; **12**: 197, 601-2; **14**: 359; publication on public safety in U.S. sent to TJ, **11**: 528; papers sent to Washington, **15**: 155; land in Va., **15**: 478; letter from cited, **15**: 499n; land on Scioto river, **16**: 434n-5n; mentioned, **14**: 359

188-9, 195, 206-7, 222, 266-7, 271, 299; charter of rights, suggested, **15**: 165-7, 167-8 (TJ's draft); supports aristocratic party, **15**: 166; letter from, to Cardinal La Rochefoucauld, quoted, **15**: 222; appeals for peace, **15**: 277-80, 288; and National Assembly, **15**: 279, 280, 286, 289, 300, 334n, 548; **16**: 160, 162-3, 165n, 188, 269; **20**: 648, 650; letter from, to Lafayette, cited, **15**: 290; veto power discussed, **15**: 354, 355n, 424, 425, 426, 457; **16**: 571, 586; possibility of flight from Versailles, **15**: 458-9; effect of march on Versailles on, **15**: 511, 522, 531; **16**: 4n-5n, 278; protected by National Guard, **15**: 535; correspondence with Washington, **15**: 568; **16**: 3, 34, 310n, 314, 316, 317n, 395, 504; **19**: 108-9, 357, 425; and Declaration of Rights, **16**: 4n; **19**: 335; Van der Noot's letter to, **16**: 49, 267; reported plot against, **16**: 51, 106, 124, 134; household expenses, **16**: 86-7; Belgian congress appeals to, **16**: 220; condition of, **16**: 274; refuses Latour du Pin's resignation, **16**: 302; refuses to leave Versailles, **16**: 303; receives Lafayette's ideas on authority, **16**: 333, 375; miniature of given to TJ, **16**: 362n-3n, 366; **18**: 601, 602n; **20**: 352n; miniature of given to Franklin, **16**: 365, 367n; power to make war, **16**: 430, 431, 436, 437; at Bastille Day celebration, **16**: 507; **17**: 17, 27-8, 212; and French constitution, **16**: 507; **19**: 93; receives Duc d'Orléans, **17**: 27; removal from St. Cloud proposed, **17**: 491; proposed address to, on royal ministers, **17**: 612; letter to, from ministers, cited, **17**: 619, 640, 663; appoints Garde de Sceaux, **18**: 114; uneasy about Condé, **18**: 352; portrait presented to Congress, **18**: 547; and civil constitution of clergy, **18**: 605; form of address to U.S. discussed, **19**: 85n, 87n; and Franklin's death, **19**: 91-2; correspondence with Leopold II, **19**: 118n, 257; **20**: 88; departure of aunts, **19**: 533; reaction to scene at the Tuileries, **19**: 635; escape from Paris feared, **20**: 258-9; flight to Varennes, **20**: 311, 561-2, 573-8, 600, 604-5, 620; gives books to U.S. colleges, **20**: 433n; requested to negotiate new

treaty of commerce with U.S., **20**: 529; declaration to French people, **20**: 561; restrictions on, **20**: 575-7, 609, 650, 656; expresses support for Revolution, **20**: 660-2; dislikes Lafayette, **20**: 697

Louisa (ship): departs for Va., **10**: 352; **13**: 519

Louisa, Va.: Tarleton's cavalry observed in, **4**: 261, 265; Marks' plantation in sold, **15**: 93-4

Louisa co., Va.: letter to commissioner of provisions for, **3**: 568n; letters to county lieutenant of, **5**: 255, 601-2, 616-7; **6**: 48; letter to members of GA for, **5**: 585-6; senatorial district, **1**: 476; **2**: 336; appoints infantry officers, **1**: 580; place of court of assize, **1**: 630; boundary of, **2**: 15; militia, **2**: 131; **3**: 599; **4**: 62, 63, 383, 398, 443, 452; **5**: 255, 309n, 311, 329n, 475, 501, 561, 601-2, 616-7, 646; levies of soldiers, **3**: 8; defends western frontier, **3**: 50, 51, 53; provision law in, **3**: 486; tobacco loan office certificates, **3**: 516; commissioner of provisions for, **3**: 573; supply post for, **4**: 286; arms, **5**: 341

Louisa Court House, Va., **6**: 634

Louisa river. *See* Kentucky river

Louis Charles, Duc de Normandie, Dauphin of France (later Louis XVII): birth of, **8**: 68n; at Versailles, **15**: 222; greets National Assembly delegation, **16**: 163; governor for, **20**: 576, 584, 609; restrictions on, **20**: 609

Louise (ship): TJ receives rice by, **11**: 509n; carries whale oil from Boston, **13**: 221

Louisiana: Mrs. Trist describes, **8**: 26; exports, **8**: 412; population, **8**: 412; **10**: 57; deer native to, **9**: 520; apprehension of disturbances in, **10**: 399-400; rumors of possession transferred to France, **11**: 130n-2n; work by Hennepin cited, **11**: 666; Spanish intrigue in, **14**: 387n-8n; Estaing comments on, **16**: 556-7; in Spanish war crisis, **17**: 25, 109-11, 113-7, 124n-5n; U.S. policy on, **17**: 122; foreign settlers invited to, **20**: 98n; independence favored by Lafayette, **20**: 540-1. *See also* Mississippi river

Louis Joseph Xavier, first Dauphin of France: death of, **14**: 653, 654n; **15**: 190

5: 507-8, 621-3; signs Virginia Association, 1: 108; on committee to divide Fincastle co., 1: 566n; appointed commissioner to investigate land claims, 2: 65n; appointed commissioner for Ky., 3: 107; elected to Va. Executive Council, 6: 89n, 93; offers to raise regiment, 6: 106

McDowell Hall, St. John's College, 1: 21n

McDuffee, Col. John: information on moose, 7: 21-4

Mace, Charles: consul in Algiers, 18: 375

Mace, Samuel: sent on expedition to Va., 1: 282

Macedonians: TJ's notes on, 1: 555

Mcelhany, Capt. John, 4: 540

Macerata, Italy, 14: 380

McFingal (Trumbull): copy sent to TJ, 7: 317

McGavock, Ens. Hugh: letter from, 5: 145-6; member of court-martial, 3: 350

McGehee, Billy, 16: 309

Mcgehie, William: signs Va. oath of allegiance, 2: 129

McGill, Charles. *See* Magill

McGillivray, Alexander: knowledge of Indians, 9: 641; 11: 414; letter from cited, 11: 201; brings Creek chiefs to New York, 17: xxix, 269, 271; Hawkins describes, 17: xxx; monopoly of commerce, 17: 288-91, 389n; 19: 431n; correspondence with Houstoun, 17: 321; slaves among followers of, 17: 341n-2n; Bowles' allegations about, 17: 666n

McGinnis, Robert: death of, 14: 397n; 19: 332

M'Gleester, Neal: signs petition, 1: 588

McGra, Christopher, 3: 542n

McGregor (McGriger), Capt.: death at sea, 12: 44; owner and master of the *Charlotte*, 12: 400

McGregor, Alexander: settlement near Fort Pitt, 2: 101

McHenry, James: letters to, 6: 410-1; 19: 253-4, 628; 20: 708; letters from, 9: 516-7; 16: 413n; 18: 155-6; and Washington's resignation, 6: 404n-7n, 409-10; motion on Committee of the States, 6: 521n; member committee on Indian trade and government, 6: 584n; Md. delegate in Congress, 7: 235n, 572; originator of navigation act plan,

8: 382; and naval stores project, 9: 168n; letter from cited, 10: 204; letter to, from Lafayette, cited, 10: 563n; member of Federal Convention, 11: 400; in Md. Constitutional Convention, 13: 334; introduces Cruse to TJ, 16: 413n; letter to, from Hamilton, quoted, 18: 611; and Hamilton's challenge to Monroe, 18: 669n, 670n; letters from, to Short, quoted, 19: 253n-4n; affairs of referred to Short, 19: 425; supports Wolcott, Jr., 20: 223; recommends John H. Purviance, 20: 226; assistance received in France, 20: 529; mentioned, 10: 296

Machias (ship): carries cargo to Morocco, 18: 401; mentioned, 12: 462; 14: 578

Machiavelli, Niccolò: admired by John F. Mercer, 7: 228; mentioned, 20: 663

machinery: diminishing friction in, 17: 294, 325, 552-3; 18: 146-50. *See also* cotton manufacture; mill machinery; steam engine

Machunck creek, 2: 15

McIntire, Neil: petition of, 6: 448-52

McIntosh, John: TJ's opinion on note asked, 6: 188

McIntosh, Gen. Lachlan: provisioning of army under, 2: 241; and Detroit campaign, 2: 258, 289; petition on behalf of, 3: 651-2; 5: 35; family aided by Va., 5: 218, 542; TJ's opinion on note asked, 6: 188

McIntosh, Sarah Threadcraft (Mrs. Lachlan McIntosh): letter to, 5: 218; letter from, 5: 542

MacIntosh, William: *Travels in Europe, Asia and Africa*, 10: 166, 172, 201, 294

McIntosh, William: affidavit of, 19: 526

McIntyre (?), Donald, 5: 4n

MacKay, Capt.: impresses U.S. seamen, 20: 242

Mckay, Eneas: settlement near Fort Pitt, 2: 101

McKean, Thomas: letters to, 6: 113-4, 116-7, 123, 141; 18: 347-8; letter from, 6: 116; signs Continental Association, 1: 153; signs Congress' second petition, 1: 223; signs agreement of secrecy, 1: 253; signs Declaration of Independence, 1: 306n, 432; and Barbé de Marbois' queries, 4: 167n; councillor of American Philosophical Society, 4: 545; cited on Ohio river travel, 7: 218; defeat in 1785 election, 8: 672;

McKean, Thomas (*cont.*)
letter from, to Washington, quoted, **18**: 347n; and Wilson's papers, **18**: 347n; favors Potomac capital site, **19**: 16; mentioned, **6**: 165n; **7**: 20; **20**: 637

Mackennen (Mackinnen), William: Yale confers degree on, **10**: 386

M'Kenzie, Alexander: signs petition, **1**: 588

Mckenzie (McKinzie), Alexander: on Albemarle co. militia roll, **1**: 667, 668; signs Va. oath of allegiance, **2**: 129

Mackenzie, James: recommends Auldjo, **15**: 523; converses with Burgess, **18**: 4; letter from, to Auldjo, cited, **18**: 5n; letter to, from Aust, **18**: 25n-6n; letter from cited, **18**: 42

Mackenzie, Roderick: *Strictures on Lt. Col. Tarleton's History of the Campaigns of 1780 and 1781*, **13**: 651

MacKenzie, Maj. Thomas: assistant to André, **17**: 41

McKerdy, Capt., **4**: 310

mackerel fishery: N.H., **7**: 344, 346

Mackie, Andrew: signs nonimportation resolutions (1770), **1**: 47

Mackinac, Fort: attack by Indians rumored, **7**: 421

Mackinac island: importance of post to U.S., **7**: 280

McKinzie, Robert, **1**: 18

Mckitrick, Robert, **5**: 604

Macklinn, John, **5**: 246

McLane, Maj. Allen: and captured pirates, **5**: 283, 284n; resigns as port collector at Wilmington, **19**: 399

Maclay, Samuel: resolution quoted, **19**: 95

Maclay, William: senator from Pa., **14**: 3, 17, 275, 277, 302, 339, 385, 394, 473, 529, 539, 560, 615; federalism of, **14**: 394, 529; *Diary* quoted, **16**: 381n-2n; **19**: 34; describes TJ, **16**: 381n-2n, 445n; *Diary* cited, **16**: 409n, 513, 517; *Journal* cited, **16**: 445n, 456n-8n; **17**: 54n, 167n-70n, 172n, 217n-20n, 247n, 248n, 349n, 350n; **18**: 175, 410n, 412n, 413n, 456n, 523n, 525n, 546n, 611n, 613n, 615n, 617n, 685n; *Journal* quoted, **16**: 445n; **18**: 547-8, 611; **19**: 294n; opposes Steuben's claim, **16**: 457n; and arrearages in soldiers' pay, **16**: 458n; **18**: 611-3, 615, 617n; on commercial pol-

icy, **16**: 513, 517; in residence bill controversy, **17**: 164, 165, 167-70, 172; and diplomatic establishment, **17**: 217-9; **20**: 488n; on consular appointments, **17**: 247, 248; departs for home, **17**: 290n; and Northwest Territory, **18**: 167; and TJ's reports on Mediterranean, **18**: 410, 412, 413; fears on growing sentiment for navy, **18**: 415n; on Senate resolution on coinage, **18**: 456-7; and tonnage acts, **18**: 524-5, 546-8; and capital site, **19**: 4-5, 26, 34, 35, 36, 37; **20**: 9; criticizes Washington, **19**: 30-1, 33-4, 47-8; quoted on Va. act of cession, **19**: 31; opinion of Robert Morris, **19**: 34; life at end of congressional career, **19**: 35n; quoted on capital and excise bills, **19**: 38; censures Hamilton on patronage policy, **19**: 38n; on bank bill, **19**: 39; and Franklin's death, **19**: 78, 83n, 90, 95, 101; describes receipt of French communication, **19**: 83; attitude toward France, **19**: 88, 90, 95, 99; and authorship of address to National Assembly, **19**: 96n; opinion of Tench Coxe quoted, **19**: 124-5; on TJ's report on the fisheries, **19**: 162, 165n; mentioned, **18**: 541

McLean, Andrew: paid by Department of State, **17**: 366

McLean, Archibald: Pa. boundary line commissioner, **5**: 13n; sells *Daily Gazette*, **17**: 360, 362

McLene, James: offers resolution to congratulate National Assembly, **19**: 95-6

McLeod, Capt.: and capture of Monticello, **13**: 363

Maclin (McLin, Macklin), Frederick: and vestry bill, **2**: 113n

McMannus, Henry: in Albemarle co. militia, **1**: 667

McMannus, James: signs Va. oath of allegiance, **2**: 129

M'Mekin, Hugh: signs nonimportation resolutions (1770), **1**: 46

McMillan, Mr., **5**: 434

McMurray, William: *The United States According to the Definitive Treaty of Peace*, **6**: 595n

McNairy, John: judge in Southwest Territory, **16**: 478; **17**: 293n

McNeal, Mr., **4**: 674

McNeal, Capt. Hector: and Canadian campaign, **1**: 434-6, 444

MADISON, JAMES (*cont.*)

passage of Va. court bill, **8**: 646; commissioner on federal control of commerce, **9**: 197, 199, 206n; leader of nationalists in, **9**: 204n; and resolutions on Congress, **9**: 204n-8n; efforts against paper money emission, **10**: 133; supporters elected to, **10**: 387

House of Representatives

and proposals on funding of foreign debt, **14**: 189; **15**: 473n; activities in, **14**: 341-2, 415, 458, 529, 558, 607; **15**: 6, 22, 74, 78; **16**: 117; dispute with Monroe, **15**: 6; receives Morris' plan for American finances, **15**: 122-4; motion on executive departments, **15**: 216-7; and removals from office, **15**: 227-8; proposal of on domestic debt, **16**: 393; proposal to discriminate among public debt holders, **16**: 419; and commercial policy, **16**: 513-23; **18**: 223, 229-30, 242; **19**: 123, 124, 157; and TJ's appointment as secretary of state, **17**: 46n, 218; in war crisis of 1790, **17**: 47-51, 53, 57-9, 77, 87, 89, 107; warnings about G. Morris, **17**: 99; and residence bill, **17**: 163-6, 168, 170, 172-8, 180-3, 191n, 192n, 199-203, 206-7; consulted on consular appointments, **17**: 245; proposes consul's salary, **17**: 249n; and permanent seat of government, **17**: 454, 457, 458n, 644; **19**: 5, 6, 8n, 13-4, 16-7, 18n, 25, 27-9, 30, 31, 56; **20**: 8-9, 16, 20n, 22n, 37, 39, 42n, 61, 65, 69, 84-5; on relations with Britain, **18**: 221-3, 229-30, 238-9, 261, 271; and Washington's message to Congress (1790), **18**: 221, 229; navigation bill, **18**: 228-9, 232, 234, 237; **19**: 281n; and Algerian captives, **18**: 403, 405; and tonnage acts, **18**: 521-6, 540, 541, 544, 556; and arrearages of soldiers' pay, **18**: 614-7; on Hamilton in Reynolds case, **18**: 684; and compromise of 1790, **19**: 4n, 18; on R. Morris' role in capital site issue, **19**: 6n-8, 15-6; fears Western separation from union, **19**: 17; vote on excise bill, **19**: 38n; capital site speculation, **19**: 49; effect of titles on public opinion, **19**: 51n; on report

MADISON, JAMES (*cont.*)

on settling state accounts, **19**: 53n; on executing Residence Act, **19**: 58-61; and tribute to Franklin, **19**: 78, 79; and Tench Coxe, **19**: 123n, 125, 126n, 127; and the whale fisheries, **19**: 146, 155, 159, 160, 179; and report on navigation and commerce, **19**: 167, 168; memoranda on insurance shipping rates, **19**: 199-200; on national bank, **19**: 280n-2n; on opposition to 1784 Consular Convention, **19**: 305; Jay's recommendations referred to, **19**: 495; and L'Enfant's dismissal, **20**: 71; and Barclay's consular commission, **20**: 87; interview with Beckwith, **20**: 136-7, 145, 147-50 (text), 251-2; and appointment of treasury comptroller, **20**: 231, 233, 234; lends *Rights of Man* to TJ, **20**: 271, 296, 302; and founding of *National Gazette*, **20**: 336, 718-59 (editorial note and documents); criticizes fraudulent claims, **20**: 336-7

Opinions

on invasion of New York, **1**: 508; on navigation of Mississippi, **4**: 137; on Ebenezer Hazard, **5**: 563n; criticism of schools, **7**: 362; on Chastellux' *Travels in North America*, **7**: 580-3; on agriculture in Va., **13**: 99, 414, 626; on Congress, **15**: 5-8, 224-5, 324; on TJ's future position in government, **15**: 153, 369, 510; on TJ as Secretary of State, **15**: 510; **16**: 118n, 125, 126n, 169n-70n (editorial comment); on housing shortage in New York, **16**: 279n; on communications in government, **16**: 287; on G. Mason, **19**: 50n, 242; on the whale fisheries, **19**: 145

Other Correspondence

with Washington, **2**: 322n; **9**: 206n; **10**: 533n; **14**: xxxviii; **16**: 118n, 183n; **19**: 7, 15-6; with Mazzei, **6**: 79n; **14**: 4n; **18**: 218; letter to, from Edmund Pendleton, quoted, **6**: 137n; with E. Randolph quoted, **6**: 179n, 187n, 199n, 207n, 217n, 251n, 269n; **16**: 516; letter to, from Joseph Jones, quoted, **6**: 269n; letters to, from Chastellux, cited, **7**: 581, 585; **8**: 469; with Mrs. Trist,

MADISON, JAMES (*cont.*)

15: 436, 438, 524; medals, 15: 438; 16: xxxv, 66n, 125; favored as minister to France, 15: 558; 16: 272-3, 424; 17: 14n; 18: 32-3; health of, 16: 125, 171n, 183; 20: 297, 298, 558-9, 593, 668, 670; TJ asks help in finding lodgings, 16: 183; and A. Donald's books, 16: 406; obtains book for TJ, 16: 485; copies information on Phlegon for TJ, 16: 495n; sends Leslie's manuscript to TJ, 16: 576, 605, 607; TJ travels with to Va., 17: 417; Shippen travels with, 17: 464-5; sells horse to TJ, 17: 512n; 18: 480, 490, 491n; Ewell's papers sent to, 17: 599; TJ confers with on Harmer will, 18: 28; and TJ's expenses for moving to Philadelphia, 18: 74; TJ invites him to share house in Philadelphia, 18: 242; Mason praises, 18: 484-5; assessment of in *Maryland Journal*, 19: 545; proposed visit to Charles Thomson, 20: 244; compared to Charles James Fox, 20: 436, 573; criticism of, 20: 445, 718-23; northern journey with Lee, 20: 595, 602, 617; relations with Freneau, 20: 667

Political Theories

on need of coercive power in Confederation, 5: 471n-2n; observations on TJ's draft of a constitution for Va. (1783), 6: 308-16; on Congress, 7: 257; 12: 273-9; 13: 625; on majority, 14: 19-20; on federalism, 15: 6; and TJ's "The Earth Belongs to the Living," 15: 387-90, 392-8; 16: 146-54

Scientific Interests

in American Philosophical Society, 6: 542, 556; 8: 51; wants magnifying glass, 8: 111-2; pedometer sent to, 13: 132, 497; pamphlet on Mohegan language sent by, 13: 625, 626n; weights and measures, 16: 602-3, 607-14, 615, 617, 643n, 645n, 646n, 648n, 649-50; investigates opossum, 20: 328-9; proposed table mechanism, 20: 337-8

U.S. Senate

Crèvecoeur on opposition to, 14: 274, 415; attempts to secure election to, 14: 302, 342, 529, 607; 16: 143n

MADISON, JAMES (*cont.*)

Virginia Convention

and Mason's plan for Va. government, 1: 368n; on committee to prepare bill on disestablishment of church, 1: 527n

Writings

"Notes on Debate" quoted, 6: 238n; *Federalist* papers by, 13: 157, 158n, 498-9; 18: 397n, 414, 520; "Publius" essays attributed to, 13: 337; *Debates of the Federal Convention*, 19: 547; contributes to *National Gazette*, 20: 732

Madison, Col. James, 3: 201, 310

Madison, Rev. James: letters to, 5: 303-4, 374-5; 6: 7-8, 72, 420; 7: 231, 508; 13: 379-83; 14: xxxii; letters from, 2: 205-6; 6: 507-8; 7: 133-4; 8: 73-5; 9: 355-7; 10: 642-4; 11: 252-3; 14: 533-6; 15: 572, 605-6; signs commission, 1: 99; returns from England, 1: 487, 494; and Henley's books, 2: 198; as Va.-Pa. boundary commissioner, 3: 14, 18n, 77; 5: 478n; 6: 8; 7: 236; 8: 417; 15: 605-6; at College of William and Mary, 4: 52; 7: 302; 13: 372; elected to American Philosophical Society, 4: 545n; confers honorary degree on TJ, 6: 222; weather observations, 6: 545; Stiles on, 7: 303; books sent to, 8: 323; 9: 264; 11: 229; 12: 130; 14: 533; 16: 82n; copy of *Notes on Virginia* sent to, 12: 130; TJ discusses science with, 13: 379-82; scientific observations, 14: 534-6; 15: 611; letter from, to Paradise, cited, 14: 536; humor, 15: 593; letter to cited, 16: 82n; bishop of Va., 16: 445; 17: 21; recommends Andrew Ellicott as U.S. geographer, 20: 61n; mentioned, 2: 217; 5: 339, 373; 8: 471; 13: 152n; 17: 23n, 520

Madison, James, Sr.: spectacles, 7: 57, 228; weather observations, 16: 448; letter to, from James Madison, quoted, 16: 496n; rice seed from Capt. Bligh sent to, 16: 496n; mountain cress seed sent to TJ, 17: 512n; mentioned, 6: 144, 271

Madison, John: land grant for military service, 6: 645

Madison, John, Jr.: quoted, 4: 526n

Madison, Rowland: letter to, 4: 225-6; letter from, 4: 434; to furnish supplies

quise de: Mrs. Paradise comments on, **15**: 282

Mainville, Jacques de, fils: letter from, **11**: 655; mentioned, **12**: 58

Mainz: Trumbull describes, **10**: 439; TJ's notes on, **13**: 18-21, 48, 266

Mainz, Archbishop of (Friedrich Karl Joseph Erthal): American medals sent to, **16**: 67

Mairan, Jean Jacques Dortous de: calculation of latitude, **16**: 543, 652n

Maison Blanche: TJ describes, **11**: 418-20

Maison Carrée (Nîmes): architecture, **8**: 534-5, 537-8; as model for Va. Capitol, **8**: 535; **9**: 220-1, 267; **15**: xxvii; TJ's admiration of, **11**: 226; drawing of sent to L'Enfant, **20**: 28; mentioned, **9**: xxvii, 226 (illus.)

Maisoncelles, M. de: proposes translation of Gordon's book, **14**: 345; *Situation actuelle des finances de la France et de l'Angleterre*, **15**: 306n

Maisonneuve, France, **11**: 415-6

Maître Cuisinier, Le: sought by TJ, **6**: 541

maize: Racconigi, **11**: 434; Piedmont, **11**: 435; method of sowing in Campo Marone, **11**: 440; Languedoc, **11**: 448; Toulouse, **11**: 454. *See also* corn

Maizière(s), M.: financial difficulties, **15**: 54-5

majority, will of: TJ on, **12**: 442

Makins, Capt. Samuel, **18**: 323

Malabar: rice seed from, **14**: 707

Malaga: American consulate at, **19**: 317

Malaspína, Alejandro, Don: commands Spanish expedition, **14**: 503n

Malesherbes, Chrétien Guillaume de Lamoignon de: letter to, **14**: 636-7; letters from, **9**: 452-3; **12**: 123; **14**: 647-8; TJ visits, **8**: 683; **11**: 515; praises Lafayette, **9**: 337; speech before Assemblée des Notables, **11**: 176, 179; seeds to be sent to, **11**: 253; appointment as keeper of seals, **11**: 316, 400; interest in plants, **11**: 349, 374; TJ praises, **11**: 482, 490; relative of La Luzerne, **11**: 491; retirement expected, **13**: 455, 464, 492; dismissal of, **13**: 565, 580, 633, 634; Bancroft dines with, **13**: 607; TJ asks for rice seed, **14**: 636-7; on rice culture in France, **14**: 647-8; suicide of, **15**: 137, 141; mentioned, **14**: 528n

Mallenly, Mark: signs nonimportation resolutions (1770), **1**: 47

Mallet, Paul Henri: *Histoire de Dannemarc*, **8**: 411; *Northern Antiquities*, **12**: 18; **16**: 481

Mallett, Peter: bills against Va., **3**: 604, 605, 637; **5**: 391

Mallory (Malory), Col.: killed, **5**: 96, 294n

Mallory, Francis: letter from, **3**: 475

Malmedy, Françoise, Marquise de, **14**: 37

Malmesbury, James Harris, first Earl of: memorial to Netherlands, **9**: 119; intrigues as British minister to Netherlands, **11**: 244, 245n; arrival in London, **13**: 515; political prospects, **14**: 482; on Dr. Gem, **15**: 386; mentioned, **12**: 631

Malta: defense against Algiers, **9**: 24; attitude toward plan for concert of powers against Barbary States, **10**: 562n, 565n; climate, **11**: 119; American medals sent to, **16**: 67

Malta, ambassador from. *See* Suffren de Saint-Tropez, Pierre André

Malvern Hill, **5**: 631

mammoth: TJ asks to have teeth sent him, **6**: 139; fossils, **6**: 159, 371; **7**: 312; **8**: 300; **19**: 359-60; identity with elephant, **7**: 304-5, 312-7; **8**: 632; Stiles discusses, **7**: 364-5; Indian knowledge of, **9**: 260-1; bones found on Ohio, **13**: 568, 593; elephant confused with, **13**: 593; description of, **13**: 593-4

Mamo, Pelegrino de: letter from, **12**: 539

Mamora, Morocco: harbor, **10**: 339

man: TJ disputes theories of degeneracy of in America, **8**: 184-6; Rodney's theory on origin of, **17**: 548-51

Man, Isle of: inhabitants natural subjects of England, **6**: 435

Manakin, Va.: ferry, **5**: 525

Manchac, La.: defenses, **3**: 258

Manchester, George Montagu, fourth Duke of: recommendation of Williamos, **8**: 270n

Manchester, Va.: ferry at, **2**: 458; British at, **4**: 260; **5**: 580, 623, 626, 631; TJ lodges at, **4**: 263; camp at, **4**: 329; militia at, **4**: 379; **5**: 496n-7n, 501, 527, 549; seizure of boats at, **5**: 124; lead at, **5**: 417

Mandar, Theophile: letter to, **9**: 452; letter from, **9**: 435

Mangnall, John: in *Dover* case, **20**: 205n-7n

Mangon, La Forest & Co., **11**: 546; **12**: 637; **13**: 243

Manigault, Gabriel: marries Izard's daughter, **8**: 197; returns to S.C., **17**: 179n

Manlius, Marcus: *Astronomicon*, **11**: 610; **20**: 635n

Manly, George: in Albemarle co. militia, **1**: 666

Manly, Capt. John: ordinance stores taken by, **1**: 391

Mann, Mr., **5**: 26

Mann, David, **4**: 540

Mann, George: signs Va. oath of allegiance, **2**: 130

Mann, John: British war prisoner, **2**: 31

Mann, Robert, **3**: 606n

Mann, William, **5**: 342

Mannaturiia (Cherokee), **2**: 74

manners: European compared with American, **8**: 569

Mannheim, Germany: TJ's notes on, **13**: 24-5, 48, 266

Manning, James: letter from, **10**: 461-3

Manning & Vaughan: purchase of plantation articles from, **11**: 263; bills of exchange drawn on, **13**: 615; **14**: 11

Mann's tavern, Annapolis: dinner for Washington given at, **6**: 403n-4n

Mansfeild, George: in Albemarle co. militia, **1**: 664, 667

Mansfield, William Murray, Earl of: influence on Court of Chancery, **9**: 71; decisions cited in American courts, **13**: 649, 663

Mansiack, Fort: defense of, **3**: 55

manslaughter: punishment for, **2**: 325, 495; **10**: 47

Manson, David: endorses Pearce's loom, **20**: 243n

Mantapike, Va.: ferry at, **2**: 456

Mantel, M.: French consular secretary in U.S., **14**: 63n, 65n

Mantone. *See* Menton

manufacturers: protection in enemy countries, **7**: 267, 486, 622; **9**: 419, 426; TJ criticizes, **8**: 426

manufactures: Hogendorp's queries on, in U.S., **7**: 298; Conn., **7**: 335-6; Mass., **7**: 341; N.H., **7**: 345; U.S., **7**: 406; **8**: 581; **9**: 20; France vs. Great Britain, **7**: 511; import by U.S., **8**: 309; exchange for tobacco, **8**: 386; Va., **8**: 660; **11**: 319; TJ on, **13**: 269; **20**:

563, 565; Crèvecoeur on, **14**: 30, 416; Washington on, **14**: 546-8; in Philadelphia, **15**: 55-6; Paine recommends for America, **15**: 194; Hamilton's plan for, **18**: 123n; and fish industry, **19**: 192; Tench Coxe's plan for, **20**: 216-8. *See also* cotton manufacture; textile manufacture

manufactures, British: and Virginia Association, **1**: 44; American sale of, **7**: 527-8; restrictions on importation, **8**: 341; import by U.S., **8**: 393

manufactures, French: import by U.S., **8**: 162, 402; **9**: 29-30, 112; **11**: 617; House desires to import, **8**: 169; in Paris, **11**: 32, 123; Izard desires to import, **11**: 263-4

manuring: France, **11**: 284, 420

Manyo, pond of, **11**: 450

maple: seeds sought by TJ for France, **9**: 255, 520

maple, ash-leaved: plants asked from John Banister, **11**: 121

maple, striped: sample to be sent to France, **10**: 227

maple, sugar: seeds of, **9**: 267; **12**: 408, 412; **14**: 4; **18**: 308

maple, swamp: plant ordered from London, **11**: 46; plants sent to TJ, **11**: 90

maple sugar: TJ recommends as substitute for cane sugar, **16**: 579, 580n; export possible, **18**: 506

Map of the City of Washington in the Territory of Columbia, **20**: 40

maps: of Va., **1**: 41n; **3**: 658; **4**: 41; **6**: 169, 509; **9**: 300, 354; **10**: 212, 219-20, 225-6, 236, 243, 249, 354, 363, 393, 398, 621-2; **11**: 46, 91, 107, 183, 207-8, 213, 233, 240, 246, 268, 349, 364, 383, 468-9, 500, 519, 521-2, 576-7, 597; **12**: 163-4, 241, 484, 488, 597; of Albemarle co., Va., by TJ, **2**: xxiii, 208 (illus.); transcript made of Dr. Smith's, **3**: 664; of western Va. and Carolina, **4**: 240; of Tidewater Va., **5**: 51, 75, 92, 130, 145, 159; sought from Dr. Smith, **5**: 325; requested by TJ, **5**: 584-5; **13**: 375; of bounds of proposed colonies and states, **6**: xxxv, 588 (illus.), 590 (illus.), 591 (illus.); Jefferson-Hartley manuscript, **6**: xxxvi, 593 (illus.); of U.S., **6**: xxxvi, 605 (illus.); **7**: 284; **9**: 299-300; **10**: 417; **12**: 133, 136; of Spanish settlements in America, **9**: 105; of South America, **10**: 285, 393, 398, 411, 479;

Va., Pa., Md., bill for correction of plates, **11**: 603; charge for use of, **12**: 227; Mitchell's used by TJ and Franklin, **16**: xxxiv-v, 52 (illus.), 326; **17**: 591; **18**: 86-7, 96n; TJ sends to Randolph, **16**: 13; Randolph sends, **16**: 13, 29, 81; Donald thanks TJ for, **16**: 91; of Shadwell-Edgehill boundaries, sketch by TJ, **16**: 99; Tatham's plan for, **16**: 185-6; of Poplar Forest, sketch by TJ, **16**: 190; Churchman's interest in, **18**: 492-3; of Federal City, **20**: xxxi, 32-6, 40-2, 62, 68-9, 384

Mara, Gertrude Elisabeth: singing, **9**: 126

Marable, Matthew: signs Virginia Association, **1**: 108; mentioned, **1**: 22

Maranhão, Brazil: Portugal's importation of rice from, **8**: 200

Marans, France: TJ describes, **11**: 458

Marbeuf, Comtesse de, **10**: 332

marble: U.S. import of, **10**: 147; ordered by TJ from Genoa, **14**: 598, 667, 704; chimney piece for TJ, **16**: 349-50

Marblehead, Mass.: and the fisheries, **19**: 147, 148, 152-3, 155, 156-7, 209, 225-6

marble pedestal: presented to TJ by Mme de Tessé, **15**: 363n-4n, 506; **17**: 378n; **18**: xxxiii-iv, 35n, 37n, 268 (illus.), 306, 307n; **19**: 423

Marc (TJ's valet de chambre): engagement of, **7**: 400; estimate of wine prices, **8**: 172; dismissed from TJ's service, **10**: 213n, 214n

Marcellinus, **20**: 635n

Marchant, Henry: signs agreement of secrecy, **1**: 253; mentioned, **3**: 5n-6n

Marchesi, Luigi (singer): Cosway compliments, **13**: 115; accompanies Maria Cosway, **16**: 551n

Marchetti, Alessandro: translation of Lucretius, **6**: 173

Marck, Nephew, & Co.: fails to reply to letters, **9**: 219, 220n; funds under care of, **9**: 513-4; debts owed to, **10**: 267-8

Marck, Ulrich: further payment to stopped, **11**: 351

Maréchal, M.: drawings of the Halle aux Bleds, **10**: xxix, 434 (illus.)

Maréchal, Ambrose: letters to, from Dugnani, quoted, **14**: 356n-7n

Maréchal, Pierre Sylvain: *Antiquités d'Herculaneum*, **13**: 623

Mareil, Guichard de: letter to, **14**: 589; letters from, **14**: 576; **15**: 74-6; letter

to missing, **15**: 76n

mares: purchased in England, **9**: 119

Mareshall, Mr.: Saxon gospels of, **13**: 652

Margaretta (ship), **12**: 236

marginalia: use by TJ's contemporaries, **10**: 365n

Margrave of Baden. *See* Baden, Karl Friedrich, Margrave of

Mari, Cosimo: letter to, **9**: 164; letters from, **9**: 102-3, 123

Maria (ship): captured by Algerian pirates, **8**: 440, 555, 616-7; **14**: 395, 397n; **18**: 375, 400n; **19**: 333; enforces customs regulations, **20**: 466-7

Maria I, queen of Portugal: offers protection to vessels flying American flag, **10**: 79n, 87; **11**: 357; approval of Carmichael as minister intimated, **10**: 179; absence from capital, **11**: 66, 78; attitude toward U.S., **11**: 513n; Smith's audience with, **12**: 147; appoints Freire minister to U.S., **17**: 12, 213, 240, 394, 482; **18**: 103; **19**: 321; letter to, from Washington, cited, **18**: 572; criticism of, **20**: 327; Humphreys' audience with, **20**: 421; mentioned, **18**: 104-5, 158

Maria Luisa, queen of Spain: Carmichael describes, **14**: 500-1; **18**: 599; Humphreys describes, **18**: 473, 474

Mariana, Juan de: *Historia general de España*, **7**: 507; **12**: 18

Mariana Victoria, Princess of Portugal: marriage by proxy, **8**: 66, 69, 84, 95, 137, 321; death of, **14**: 46-7

Marianne (ship), **7**: 395; **11**: 88, 89, 98

Marie Antoinette Josèphe Jeanne de Lorraine, queen of France: fondness for Franklin, **3**: 220; Rohan affair, **8**: 47, 395; TJ observes, **8**: 164; determination to wear only French gauze, **8**: 472; TJ asked to present Bridgen's book to, **9**: 656; birth of daughter, **10**: 203; letter from, to King of Spain, cited, **10**: 537; influence over husband, **11**: 482; unpopularity of, **11**: 664; **12**: 68; **18**: 352; supports Baron de Breteuil, **12**: 72; favors alliance with Russia, **12**: 174, 190; letter from cited, **12**: 177n; in favor of war, **12**: 218; influence of Joseph II on, **12**: 314; supports Archbishop of Toulouse, **12**: 314-5; supports aristocratic party, **15**: 166, 188-9, 206; interview with Necker, **15**: 207; cheered at Versailles,

ship for Piccini, **7**: 388; *Penelope* presented, **9**: 126, 152; quoted by Lafayette, **9**: 262; *Guerre ouverte*, **10**: 459; invited to dine with TJ, **10**: 583; Mazzei sends message to, **15**: 614; mentioned, **3**: 414

Marmontel, Marie Adélaide Lerein de Montigny, Mme de: letter from, **10**: 459; Mazzei's praise of, **7**: 387; invited to dine with TJ, **10**: 583

marmot: resemblance to woodchuck, **9**: 520-1; described by Buffon, **9**: 521-2

Marne river, **13**: 28

Marnésia, Marquis de: Lormerie introduces to TJ, **16**: 433-4

marquees: for housing in Charlottesville, **6**: 20-1

Marquis de Lafayette (ship), **9**: 387, 392; **10**: 589; **13**: 297; **14**: 669, 670; **15**: 31, 63, 64n

Marr, John: imports slaves, **15**: 655

Marrakesh, Morocco: Barclay at, **10**: 72n

marriage: and conveyance of property, **2**: 406-7; Va. bill concerning, **2**: 556-8

"Marrowbone" (estate), **12**: 25

Mars (*Marrs*, Va. brig), **5**: 151, 152n, 182, 557

Mars: TJ sends statue of to Abigail Adams, **8**: 548

Marsac, Major: owner of estate at Caversham, **9**: 370

Mars Bluff, N.C., **3**: 463

Marsden, Mr.: TJ owes tobacco to, **16**: 82

Marsden, William: on rice in Sumatra, **14**: 708

Marsdon, Mr.: Richmond property, **8**: 49

Marseilles, France: and Morris' tobacco contract, **10**: 173, 197; TJ visits, **11**: 247, 516; Short asks TJ's opinion of, **11**: 269; TJ describes, **11**: 272, 281, 287, 427-9; **13**: 273-4; U.S. trade with, **11**: 338, 487, 645; **13**: 77; Raynal on trade of, **11**: 358; tobacco sales at, **12**: 131-2; **13**: 95; meteorological observations, **13**: 95; declaration on whale oil published at, **13**: 180; signs of peace or war at, **13**: 507; U.S. consul in, **14**: 59, 62n; olive trees in threatened by cold, **14**: 359, 371, 377, 409; mayor unpopular, **14**: 410; Estates General, **14**: 410; **15**: 45; in travel plans of Short and Rutledge, **14**: 614; riots, **15**: 24, 29-30, 44, 128; **16**: 421; Place de la Tour renamed, **15**: 30; Revolution in, **15**: 321-3; Chamber of Commerce to pay damages, **17**: 33; TJ reports on wheat market at, **19**: 541; as free port, **20**: 632

Marseillette, France: TJ describes, **11**: 447

Marsh, Mrs.: inn of rated by TJ, **20**: 471

Marshall, Mr.: and bill establishing ferries, **2**: 454

Marshall, Benjamin: *A Chronological Treatise upon the Seventy Weeks of Daniel*, **11**: 523

Marshall, Humphrey: Va. artillery captain, **4**: 541; *Arbustrum Americanum*, **10**: 250n

Marshall, J. (Albemarle co., Va.): signs Va. oath of allegiance, **2**: 129

Marshall, James Markham: as lieutenant in artillery, **4**: 542; defeated by Brown, **19**: 470

Marshall, John: letter to, from Dickinson, quoted, **1**: 187n-8n; *Life of George Washington*, **1**: 671; **10**: 5n, 7n; **17**: 171; member of committee to finish revision of Va. laws, **2**: 324n; Richmond councillor, **6**: 279n, 280n; Richmond property of, **8**: 344; support for as Va. attorney general, **10**: 577; opposition to paper money, **11**: 310; supports Constitution, **12**: 281, 410; **13**: 98, 352, 620; as counsel in Jones *v.* Wayles' Executors, **15**: 648; **20**: 167; thought to be U.S. district attorney, **16**: 27; opinion on treaty powers, **17**: 289n; opposes Monroe's election to senate, **17**: 607; on common law doctrine of citizenship, **18**: 311n; signs testimonial to Tatham map, **19**: 265n; mentioned, **15**: 390

Marshall, Joseph: in Albemarle co. militia, **1**: 665

Marshall, Mary Ambler (Mrs. John Marshall): insanity of, **15**: 635

Marshall, Thomas: commission, **1**: 500; commander of artillery regiment, **2**: 37n; **3**: 221, 240, 246, 247-8, 337, 377; **4**: 541; roster of officers under, **3**: 292; views on Wilkinson and Brown, **19**: 469-72

Marshall, Thomas (English artisan): immigrates to U.S., **18**: 274n; involvement in Society for Establishing Manufactures, **19**: 453n

Marshall, William: marriage of, **14**: 530; clerk of court, **15**: 647n

marshals: fees for services, **2**: 428-31

marshes. *See* swamps

510-1, 585-90; **18:** 353; **19:** 268, 604; **20:** 342; U.S. consul in, **18:** 23; **19:** 297-8; **20:** 655; Skipwith reports on, **19:** 540; open to U.S., **20:** 342

Martinsburg, Va.: Convention troops at, **4:** 672, 685

Mary (ship): arrives at Le Havre, **13:** 288; newspapers sent on, **16:** 97n; discharges cargo at Cowes, **18:** 5; captain certifies citizenship of crew, **18:** 326; mentioned, **11:** 629, 657, 662; **12:** 270

Mary, M., **5:** 430

Mary and Jane (ship): tea consignment on, **16:** 521

Mary Anne (flag of truce ship), **3:** 333

Mary Elizabeth (ship), **11:** 405n

Mary Fearon (ship), **3:** 551

Maryland (ship), **9:** 308, 391; **11:** 589

Maryland: Assembly of described by TJ (1766), **1:** 19-20; population of, **1:** 182; **10:** 34, 35, 38, 54-6; criticized by Pendleton, **1:** 297; position on independence, **1:** 311-2, 313, 314; votes for Chase's taxation plan, **1:** 323; boundaries, **1:** 388, 463, 595; **3:** 634n; **7:** 37-8, 119; companies of riflemen to be regimented, **1:** 390; trade of, **1:** 409; **3:** 565; **7:** 50; charter of, **1:** 595-6; **6:** 657; and ratification of Articles of Confederation, **2:** 205, 208, 269; **4:** 484, 534; **5:** 42, 469; **6:** 666; decisions of Congress considered unfair to, **2:** 216; offers galleys for sale to Va., **3:** 20; European attitude toward, **3:** 93; governorship of T. S. Lee, **3:** 223; and wartime cooperation with Va., **3:** 244, 426, 579, 642; **5:** 483; **6:** 64, 74n, 77; sale of flour to Va., **3:** 279-80, 303-4; aid to south, **3:** 366, 403, 433, 585, 607, 639; **4:** 103, 112; **5:** 16, 77-8, 101, 421, 453; troops at Charleston, **3:** 435; western lands of, **3:** 473, 625-30; **6:** 131, 147, 164; length of enlistment in, **3:** 490; troops of, **3:** 499, 576, 593; **4:** 91; money for military chests, **3:** 507; currency in, **3:** 528, 531; **7:** 178, 184, 200; **10:** 232; Va.'s importations from, **3:** 543; prisoners of war, **3:** 571; troops at Camden, **3:** 595; recapture of troops from British, **3:** 648; supplies from, **4:** 27; Continental requisitions of food, **4:** 107; attitude toward Convention troops, **4:** 255, 467, 656, 672; **5:** 136, 147; letter to, from Va. GA, **4:** 309; disaffection in, **5:** 21; troops at

Guilford Court House, **5:** 156, 162; and removal of public stores from Eastern Shore, **5:** 392; British depredations on Potomac shore, **5:** 529; asked to aid in protecting Delaware bay, **5:** 551; arms to be repaired and sent to, **5:** 567; gun from *Accomack* lent to, **6:** 46; land grants to, **6:** 176; method of electing state senators, **6:** 309, 312; adoption of impost, **6:** 334; and permanent seat of Congress, **6:** 345, 346n, 347n, 352, 366; **7:** 232, 235n; proposal to erect buildings for Congress with Va., **6:** 362n, 367-8; negligence toward Congress, **6:** 437; **7:** 130; **9:** 519; **10:** 286-7, 293, 313-4; question of adding Northern Neck of Va., **6:** 546; financial quota to national treasury, **7:** 5, 55, 71; **10:** 34, 35, 54-6; unrepresented in Congress, **7:** 31, 572; attitude toward Society of the Cincinnati, **7:** 110n; Maury desires students from, **7:** 112; opinions on slavery in, **7:** 118; **8:** 357; **10:** 18; increases Congress' powers, **7:** 139, 232; and Potomac river, **7:** 361, 589; **8:** 113, 154; tobacco trade, **7:** 371-2; **10:** 106; **12:** 83, 91, 321; act for road building, **8:** 3; proposal to exchange tobacco for French products, **8:** 213-4, 220-4; duties on foreign goods, **8:** 581; interest in Cuyahoga-Beaver creek canal, **9:** 151; delegates in Congress, **9:** 242; **10:** 380, 383n; exports, **10:** 38; and Federal Convention, **10:** 38; **11:** 154, 309-10, 311; and Chesapeake-Delaware canal, **10:** 230-1, 512; declines to send delegates to Annapolis convention, **10:** 232; flour mills, **10:** 262; attitude toward Mississippi navigation, **10:** 456; **11:** 309; agreement with Va., **12:** 33; Eastern Shore antiquities, **12:** 241; attitude toward Constitution, **12:** 281, 409, 425; **13:** 332, 333-6; ratification of Constitution, **12:** 490, 609; **13:** 39, 95, 100, 101, 156, 160, 164, 205, 209, 232, 292, 318, 331-8, 359, 370, 399, 413; senators elected, **14:** 302, 394, 529; election of governor (1788), **14:** 395; electoral votes (1789), **15:** 92; ratification of constitutional amendments, **18:** 595; and capital site, **19:** 9, 24, 26, 30n, 31, 33, 45, 61, 62, 63n, 64, 65, 72; **20:** 6, 73; and U.S. commercial policy, **19:** 130; trade with Ireland, **19:** 134;

Massachusetts (*cont.*)
British imports, **11**: 87; delegates to Federal Convention, **11**: 154, 219, 400; politics, **11**: 411; attitude toward Constitution, **12**: 280-1, 283, 409, 608; opposed to overseas embassies, **12**: 282; ratifies Constitution, **12**: 395, 406, 425, 490, 608; **13**: 95, 100-1, 159-60, 205, 232, 277, 315, 370, 412; refuses to contribute to Treasury, **12**: 444; and amendments to Constitution, **13**: 205, 208, 315; **14**: 385, 650, 688; **19**: 571; supreme court, **13**: 337; legislature, **13**: 402; prohibits importation of foreign fish oil, **14**: 214; and the fisheries, **14**: 227; **19**: 140n, 144, 146, 149-50, 151-2, 153, 155, 156-7, 158, 173; bridges in, **14**: 303; elects senators, **14**: 339, 394, 529; elects congressmen, **14**: 415; supports Adams as Vice President, **14**: 559; **15**: 4; electoral votes (1789), **15**: 4, 50, 92; and Americans in French West Indies, **17**: 283; General Court's relations with Létombe, **17**: 283, 283n-4n; **19**: 303; laws of sent to TJ, **17**: 530-3; **20**: 565; tonnage act, **18**: 535, 537; and sectional appointment of commissioners, **19**: 59; and new system of penmanship, **19**: 120n; exports of, **19**: 136-8, 139; state of codfishery in, **19**: 223; and European land sales, **19**: 626
Massachusetts (ship), **17**: 249n
Massachusetts Magazine: quoted, **16**: xliii
Massenberg (Marsenburg), Capt., **5**: 125
Masset, François Marie: U.S. agent at St. Vallery-sur-Somme, **20**: 676
Massey, Harris: in Albemarle co. militia, **1**: 665
Massey, Lee: recommended as commissioner of Federal District, **19**: 59
Massey, Thomas: in Albemarle co. militia, **1**: 665
Massiac, Claude Louis, Marquis de: plan for blockade of Barbary States, **9**: 319n, 542, 568, 569; **10**: 124, 177; **18**: 380, 408-9, 414
Massie, John: in Albemarle co. militia, **1**: 664; signs petition, **6**: 294
Masterman, Adam: affidavit on *Rachel* case, **20**: 515-6
masters: Va. bill concerning, **2**: 485-8; wages, **7**: 328, 329, 333, 344, 345, 347
Masterson, Richard, **5**: 494
Mastrandt: free port, **20**: 590
masts: American, supplied to French navy, **9**: 3

mastyards: Portugal's desire to import, **9**: 19
matches, phosphorescent: TJ describes, **7**: 500, 504-5, 514-5, 518; sold in Philadelphia, **8**: 16; sent to Madison, **8**: 110; treatise on, **8**: 640
match rope: lacking for ships at Hoods, **5**: 151
Matear, William: loan to Va., **3**: 386, 442
mathematics: difficulty of, **7**: 176; study of, **8**: 636; **10**: 306; **11**: 291
Mather, Cotton, **7**: 317n
Mather, Ralph: Boulton's representative in U.S. mint, **16**: 341n-2n
Mathew (TJ's servant): moves from New York to Philadelphia, **17**: 597, 598n
Mathews (Matthews), George: letters to, **3**: 101-3; **19**: 363-4; letter from, **11**: 235-6; prisoner of war, **3**: 86-7, 104, 205, 389, 390; **4**: 34, 550; exchange with Hamilton, **3**: 101, 112-3; parole, **4**: 164; warrant for expenses, **4**: 526; exchange, **4**: 644; **5**: 352, 364; mentioned, **6**: 204
Mathews, John: letter to, **3**: 584-5; letters from, **3**: 391-6, 397, 406-10, 434-6, 455-6, 502, 552-3, 554-7; **4**: 483; chairman of committee at headquarters, **4**: 132; committee on Davies dispute, **5**: 483n; signs petition, **6**: 294
Mathews (Matthews), Sampson: letters to, **4**: 239, 343, 486; letters from, **4**: 350, 420-1, 473; and defense of Va., **3**: 51, 53, 162, 182-3, 186, 239, 303; **4**: 34-5, 231, 377; **5**: 329, 350, 454n; council's advice on loss of money collected by, **3**: 442-3; and prisoners of war, **4**: 311; ordered to Fredericksburg, **4**: 343, 345, 346; forces under, **4**: 617; loses seat on Va. Executive Council, **12**: 445
Mathies, Richard: engaged to inspect and price hemp, **6**: 12, 13
Mathurins: and American captives in Algiers, **11**: 35-6, 101-2; **12**: 149, 151; **14**: 396n, 402n, 433; **15**: 538n; **18**: 24, 370n, 398-400, 404, 431-3, 501. *See also* Chauvier, Père
Matildaville, Va.: plans for, **14**: 620, 621n
Matlack, Timothy: letter to, **5**: 490-1; engrosses Declaration of Independence, **1**: 433n; secretary of American Philosophical Society, **4**: 544, 545n
Matra, Mr.: British consul general at Tangier, **14**: 577

Mattaponi Indians: vocabulary of, **6**: 431

Mattapony River: sale of land on, **1**: 59

Matthews, Gen.: West Indian expedition, **20**: 251

Matthews, Maj.: artillery regiment, **3**: 166, 338

Matthews, Mr.: Richmond property, **8**: 344

Matthews, Archy, **5**: 445

Matthews, Thomas: Speaker of Va. Assembly, **13**: 550; **14**: 596, 705; **17**: 622

Matthews, William: trial of as spy, **5**: 592n

Matthey, M., **11**: 507

Matthis, William: signs nonimportation resolutions (1769), **1**: 31

Mattingly (Mattenly, Mattinly), James: complaint of, **4**: 493; **5**: 72, 91

Mattox, Va.: ferry, **2**: 454

Maubourg, M. de. *See* Latour-Maubourg, Marie Charles César Fay, Comte de

Mauduit, Israel: circulates handbill, **2**: 210, 214

Mauduit du Plessis, Thomas Antoine, Chevalier de: purchases Ga. timberland, **9**: 178n; **10**: 514n; offers to take Izard's son to France, **12**: 339; commander at Port-au-Prince, **17**: 302, 304-6, 308, 556; massacred in Saint-Domingue, **20**: 261

Maunsell, John: mission to Pitt, **18**: xxxv, 263-7, 276, 277; Knox's communications with, **18**: 263-7; biographical note, **18**: 263n-4n; correspondence with Knox cited, **18**: 264n, 265, 267n, 277n, 283n; memorandum on Pitt's authorization, **18**: 265-6; letter from, to Pitt, cited, **18**: 267n

Maunsell, Mrs. John, **18**: 264

Maupertuis, Pierre Louis Moreau de: calculations on diameter of earth, **6**: 378; astronomical hypothesis, **9**: 355; theory regarding fixed stars, **12**: 30; *Figura telluris determinata per observationes*, **15**: 223

Maupin, M.: letter to, **10**: 120; letters from, **10**: 89-90, 156-7; **12**: 520-1; **14**: 477; pamphlets on viticulture and viniculture, **10**: 89-90, 156-7; *Manuel des vignerons*, **14**: 477n

Maupin, Cornelius (son of Daniel): in Albemarle co. militia, **1**: 665

Maupin, Cornelius (son of John): in Albemarle co. militia, **1**: 665

Maupin, Daniel (son of Gabriel): signs

petition, **1**: 588; in Albemarle co. militia, **1**: 665, 668n

Maupin, Daniel (son of John): in Albemarle co. militia, **1**: 665

Maupin, David: in Albemarle co. militia, **1**: 668n

Maupin, Gabriel: TJ seeks information on gunpowder from, **4**: 142

Maupin, Thomas: in Albemarle co. militia, **1**: 665

Maupin, William, Jr.: in Albemarle co. militia, **1**: 665

Maurice, James: letter to, **15**: 433-4; letters from, **15**: 406, 416, 462-3, 479; letters from cited, **15**: 406n, 434n

Mauritius: trade with, **14**: 599-601

Maury, Mr.: mentioned, **3**: 573; **8**: 536

Maury (Murry), Capt. Abraham, **5**: 152n, 517

Maury, James: letters to, **6**: 382, 539; **8**: 148; **10**: 628; **11**: 528-9; **12**: 354; **17**: 423-5; **18**: 342; **20**: 339-40, 401-3; letters from, **7**: 56, 111; **10**: 387-9, 588; **11**: 370-1; **12**: 288, 389; **17**: 501-2, 658-9; **18**: 52; **19**: 356-7; **20**: 567-8, 621, 704; desires to go to Charleston with flag, **5**: 559, 606; **6**: 21, 27, 42-3; deposition concerning the *Alert*, **5**: 590; letter from, to David Ross, **6**: 20-1; letters sent by, **6**: 167; **7**: 30, 44; Madison visits, **6**: 382, 541, 567; and business in England, **10**: 387; **13**: 328; desires consulship, **10**: 388; recommended to Adams, **10**: 619; needs proof of American citizenship, **12**: 288; consul at Liverpool, **17**: 246, 251, 253n, 280, 501-2, 669, 673; **20**: 246-7, 248, 493-4; tobacco shipped to, **17**: 657; **18**: 28; **19**: 263; letter from quoted, **18**: 11n; mentioned, **7**: 38; **11**: 299

Maury, Mrs. James, **6**: 379; **10**: 389, 628

Maury, Rev. James: incumbent in Fredericksville parish, **1**: 63; Short on, **14**: 380; and marriage of Martha Jefferson and Thomas Mann Randolph, Jr., **16**: 191n; letter from, to Ludwell, quoted, **19**: 441n; and marriage of Joseph Jones Monroe, **19**: 631

Maury, Jean Siffrid, Abbé: financial proposal, **16**: 43; in aristocratic party, **16**: 437

Maury, Mary Walker (mother of James), **10**: 389, 628

Maury, Matthew: signs Va. oath of allegiance, **2**: 128

Maury, Mrs. Matthew, **16**: 89

Maury, Rev. Matthew: letter to, **16**: 88-9; teaches Dabney Carr, **16**: 89; **20**: 331

Maury, Walker: letters to, **7**: 94; **8**: 409-12; letters from, **7**: 59, 112-3; **8**: 101; school of, **6**: 379, 416, 470, 537; **7**: 112-3, 233, 361, 408; **8**: 74, 96, 114, 115; **10**: 72; books borrowed from TJ, **7**: 37, 123; teaches Peter Carr, **9**: 38-9, 201; **10**: 550n; **15**: 618, 620, 627; death of, **14**: 530

Mauzey, Mr.: to make carriage wheels, **5**: 139

Maxwell, Col., **5**: 22

Maxwell, Lieut., **3**: 227, 305, 313

Maxwell, Mr. (British prisoner of war), **3**: 661; **4**: 47

Maxwell, Beza: signs petition, **1**: 588; **6**: 293

Maxwell, George: in Albemarle co. militia, **1**: 668n; signs petition, **6**: 294

Maxwell, Capt. James: letters to, **3**: 530, 544, 578-9; **4**: 64, 104-5, 198, 380, 630-1; **5**: 25, 132-3, 138, 189-90; **18**: 307-8; **19**: 592; **20**: 389; letters from, **3**: 585, 604, 649, 664; **4**: 4, 30, 43, 47, 105, 161, 186, 198, 212, 290, 640-1; **5**: 5, 64, 94-6, 344, 557-8; **20**: 94-5; reports on brig for purchase, **3**: 38; as commissioner of the Va. navy, **3**: 223, 498; **4**: 426, 569, 602; **5**: 25, 26, 135, 144, 170, 181, 195, 614, 645; letter from, to Barron, cited, **4**: 3; supports ward's discharge, **4**: 218; letters sent by, **5**: 126; capture feared, **5**: 186; letter to, from D. Ross, cited, **5**: 209; at Chickahominy shipyard, **5**: 270; letter from, to Steuben, cited, **5**: 549; letter to, from William Lewis, **6**: 6-7; at Norfolk, **16**: 387; **18**: 306; letters to cited, **18**: 479; letter from quoted, **18**: 480n; mentioned, **12**: 184

Maxwell, Maria: letter from, **3**: 313; mentioned, **3**: 305, 318, 661

Maxwell, Thomas: signs petition, **1**: 588; **6**: 293

Maxwell, William: signs petition, **6**: 294

Maxwell, Gen. William: and troop casualties, **2**: 197; opposes British in N.J., **2**: 201; on embarkation of British troops, **2**: 265

May, Charles: signs Virginia Association, **1**: 109

May, George: recommended for surveying, **4**: 200

May, John: appointed commissioner to investigate land claims, **2**: 65n

May, Richard: letter from, **4**: 202; recommended for surveying, **4**: 200

May, William: letter from, **4**: 202; recommended for surveying, **4**: 200

Maya Barbalho, José Joachim. See Maia (Vendek), José da

Maycox, Va.: ferry at, **2**: 458; boat at, **5**: 124; British march to, **6**: 19

Maye, Mr.: and bill establishing ferries, **2**: 458

Mayence. See Mainz

Mayer, Charles Joseph de: *Voyage de M. de Mayer en Suisse, en 1784*, **11**: 665; *Les Ligues Achéenne, Suisse, et Hollandoise, et Révolution des Etats Unis de l'Amérique*, **12**: 62, 64

Mayer, Mr.: *receveur* of Baron Breidbach Burrhesheim, **13**: 15

Mayer, Johann Tobias: description of zodiacal stars, **8**: 299; views Uranus, **8**: 419, 575

Mayes, Matthew, **5**: 139

Mayeux, Jacques Nicolas: letter from, **11**: 282-3

mayhem: punishment for, **2**: 498

"Maynard" letters (Oglethorpe and Sharp), **18**: 312n

Mayo, Mr.: boats taken by, **5**: 124; bridge at Richmond, **13**: 42; **14**: 303, 529; **16**: 26, 92n; TJ wants to exchange land with, **16**: 92

Mayo, John: signs nonimportation resolutions (1769), **1**: 30; candidate for Va. senate, **1**: 476; mentioned, **4**: 273

Mayo, John, Jr.: votes for bill for religious freedom, **2**: 549n

Mayo, Joseph: letter from, **7**: 434; death of, **8**: 342; emancipation of slaves, **8**: 342-3, 346n; **14**: 492, 494n

Mayo, Philip: and bill establishing ferries, **2**: 458, 459

Mazaret (Mazzarett), John: letter to, **3**: 530-1; letter from, **4**: 694; commission for, **4**: 541; payment of troops under, **3**: 529; arms for, **3**: 563

Mazet, **11**: 254

Mazzei, Marie Hautefeville "Petronilla" Martin (Mrs. Philip Mazzei): Mazzei's comment on, **7**: 388; bill in chancery, **7**: 555; Mazzei's desire to disinherit, **8**: 676-7, 679n; death of, **12**: 538; TJ's comment on, **13**: 415-6

Mazzei, Philip: letters to, **3**: 341-3, 405-6; **6**: 382; **7**: 134, 235, 357; **8**: 152; **9**:

67-72, 164; **11:** 159, 266-7, 354-5; **12:** 245; **16:** 307-8; **20:** 713-5; letters from, **3:** 201-3, 213, 217-21, 231-6, 285-6, 299-301, 305-7, 310-2, 319, 343-4, 349-50, 357-9, 360-2, 366-8, 374, 380-1, 382, 412-5, 447, 458-60, 557; **4:** 51-2, 309-10; **5:** 375-82; **6:** 114-6, 125, 162-3; **7:** 62, 273-5, 555-6; **8:** 177-8, 277-8, 675-9; **9:** 154, 256-8; **11:** 297-8; **15:** 613-5; supports American state papers series, **1:** 145; proposal for agricultural co., **1:** 156-9; settles near Monticello, **1:** 159n; rough draft of Declaration of Independence sent to, **1:** 415n; delay of vessel, **1:** 519; signs petition, **1:** 587, 589n; pledges to support clergyman, **2:** 7; introduces Shore, **2:** 27n; suggested as U.S. agent to Duke of Tuscany, **2:** 28n; agent for Va., **2:** 29n, 58n; **3:** 376; **4:** 51; **6:** 115, 162n-3n; signs Va. oath of allegiance, **2:** 129; recommended as U.S. commercial agent, **2:** 210-1, 224-5; R. H. Lee's comments on, **2:** 215, 216; travels with Page, **2:** 278; and TJ's bill on crimes, **2:** 506n; letter from, to R. H. Lee, cited, **3:** 87; want of funds, **3:** 202, 234-5, 285, 307; **11:** 297; captured by British, **3:** 319; Penet's comments on, **3:** 384; Adams' report on, **3:** 469-70; correspondence with Madison, **5:** 585; **6:** 79n, 541; **14:** 4n; correspondence with Va. governor, **6:** 116n; letters sent by, **6:** 318; **7:** 538; **8:** 34, 73, 139, 207, 219, 317, 381, 405, 409, 413, 417, 421, 428, 444, 460, 557; **9:** 445; **15:** 620; marriage of stepdaughter, **6:** 555n; enmity to Franklin, **7:** 30, 122; returns to America, **7:** 30-2, 62; letter from, to Lynch, cited, **7:** 117; plan to go to Annapolis, **7:** 121-2; reports archaeological discovery in Siberia, **7:** 123; interview with Patrick Henry, **7:** 124n; memoranda on persons and affairs in Paris, **7:** 386-91; sued by wife, **7:** 555n; visits "Rosewell," **8:** 117; TJ referred to for information, **8:** 118; letters to, from Page, cited, **8:** 430; **15:** 195; payment of expenses, **8:** 475, 510, 538; **11:** 85, 354; correspondence with Adams, **8:** 475n-6n, 678n-9n; letters to, from Bellini, cited, **8:** 568; **9:** 591; **12:** 634; will, **8:** 676-7; desire to serve Va. abroad, **8:** 677; *Recherches Historiques et Politiques sur les Etats*

Unis d'Amérique, **9:** 72n, 257, 446; **10:** 10n, 229; **11:** 43; **12:** 39, 631; **14:** 304; friendship with Mari, **9:** 102-3; Mari's letter of credit for, **9:** 123; plans to publish Madison's remonstrance, **9:** 264; allows Staphorsts to read *Notes on Virginia,* **9:** 275; Cary seeks seeds from, **9:** 444; **10:** 228; visits Netherlands, **9:** 636; letter to, from W. S. Smith, cited, **10:** 154; letter from, to Monroe, cited, **10:** 277; sends copy of Va. act for religious freedom to Celesia, **10:** 412; letter to, from Celesia, cited, **10:** 429; questions about Rymer's *Foedera,* **10:** 518; Crèvecoeur's dislike of, **10:** 583; and Duquesnay's experiments, **11:** 234; comments on Adams' book, **11:** 239; remittance promised, **11:** 249; debts to TJ, **11:** 267n; **17:** 422; **18:** 32; **20:** 691; on price of Ramsay's history, **11:** 316; observation on nightingales, **11:** 372; letter to, from Derieux, cited, **11:** 394; claim against Dohrman, **11:** 402, 601; **13:** 166, 167n, 499; **18:** 218; **20:** 335-6, 657, 667, 678, 713; handwriting, **11:** 575; criticizes Démeunier's work, **12:** 578-80, 593; Smith's opinion of, **12:** 620; quoted in *Mercure de France,* **12:** 667; founds Constitutional Society, **13:** 161; misfortunes of, **13:** 166; correspondence with King of Poland, **13:** 415, 441; translates Franklin's *Information to Those Who Would Remove to America,* **13:** 431n-2n; sale of books, **13:** 499; illness, **14:** 344, 383, 453; and portraits of Columbus, Vespucci, Cortez, and Magellan, **15:** xxxvi; memoir quoted, **15:** 210n; signs Fourth of July tribute to TJ, **15:** 240; on Dr. Gem, **15:** 385; passport issued by TJ, **15:** 484; messages to friends in France, **15:** 613-5; dislikes Jay, **15:** 614; account with Randolph, **16:** 13; recommends Piattoli, **16:** 214; debt to Bowdoin, **16:** 307; **17:** 422; sale of Va. property, **16:** 307-9; **17:** 234-6, 400-1; **18:** 308; **19:** 250; TJ's diary on affairs of, **16:** 308-9; tries TJ's patience, **17:** 22, 23n; obtains portrait of Castruccio Castracani for TJ, **17:** 422; letter from quoted, **18:** 218, 308; Polish chargé d'affaires in Paris, **20:** 657; account with Blair, **20:** 713-4; mentioned, **2:** 209; **3:** 98, 237; **6:** 531; **8:** 296, 400, 458; **9:** 8, 66, 230, 255, 301, 312,

proofs, **15**: 438; **16**: xxxv, 66n, 125; Webster purchases, **16**: xxxv; Fleury, **16**: xxxv, 54n, 55n-6n, 60n, 64n, 65n, 69n, 73n-5n; *Libertas Americana* (Declaration of Independence, Saratoga, and Yorktown), **16**: xxxv, 55n, 65n, 69n, 72-3; Washington's set of, **16**: xxxv-vi, 52 (illus.), 65n, 66, 77, 78, 288n-9n; editorial notes on, **16**: xxxv-xlii, 53n-66n; Gates (Saratoga), **16**: xxxvii, 52 (illus.), 54n, 55n, 56n, 59n-61n, 63n, 64n, 67n, 69n, 70, 73n, 75n, 76n; Howard (Cowpens), **16**: xxxvii, 52 (illus.), 54n, 56n-7n, 59n-61n, 65n, 66, 67n, 72, 74n, 77n, 289n; Stewart (Stony Point), **16**: xxxvii, 52 (illus.), 54n, 56n, 59n, 60n, 64n, 65n, 71, 73n-5n, 289n; W. A. Washington (Cowpens), **16**: xxxvii, 52 (illus.), 54n, 56n-7n, 59n-61n, 65n, 66, 67n, 71-2, 73n, 74n, 76n, 77n, 289n; Wayne (Stony Point), **16**: xxxvii, 52 (illus.), 54n, 55n-6n, 59n, 60n, 64n-6n, 70-1, 73n-6n, 289n; La Luzerne, **16**: xli, 357n, 359n-61n, 367, 368n, 392, 394; **17**: 279-80; **18**: 358, 359n; **19**: 583; Moustier, **16**: xli, 357n, 361n, 363n, 367, 368n; **17**: 280, 281n; **18**: 358, 359n; **19**: 425, 583; **20**: 533; Adams (from Netherlands), **16**: xli-ii, 55n, 366; diplomatic medal of 1790, **16**: xli-ii, 52 (illus.), 53n, 55n, 357n, 360n-1n, 367, 368n, 396; **17**: 279-80, 281n, 527; from Netherlands, **16**: xli-ii, 55n; cost of, **16**: 53n, 56n, 68; struck in France, **16**: 53n-79; capture of André, **16**: 54n, 55n; TJ's responsibility for, **16**: 54n, 55n, 60n-6n; Charles Lee, **16**: 54n, 56n, 59n, 66n, 78; **17**: xxxii-iv, 395 (illus.); made in America, **16**: 54n-5n; Short's responsibility for, **16**: 63n, 66n, 77, 78, 79n, 505; **17**: 527, 624; **18**: 358, 359n; distribution of, **16**: 64n-5n, 67, 69n, 288n-9n; boxes for, **16**: 65n, 77, 78, 203-4, 271; **17**: 392, 632; **18**: 31, 450; TJ's memoranda on, **16**: 67-9; TJ describes, **16**: 69-77, 396; TJ's notes on history of, **16**: 77-9; Berckel, **16**: 367, 368n; **19**: 583; dies kept in Philadelphia, **17**: 591

medical service: for army, **4**: 427-9; for British, **6**: 328

Medici: Stiles' comment on, **7**: 365

medicine: sent to Canada, **1**: 390; needed in Quebec campaign, **1**: 436; responsibility of physicians in smallpox cases,

2: 123; supplied to Continental army, **3**: 345, 550, 553, 576, 619, 641; **4**: 412; subject to needs of Va. troops, **3**: 529; supply for Dr. Gilmer, **3**: 538; furnished *Le Fendant*, **3**: 546; for new recruits, **3**: 587; requested by Dr. McClurg, **4**: 25-6; invoice for hospital at Fredericksburg, **4**: 242-3; for Va., **4**: 410; **5**: 395; for prisoners of war at Charleston, **4**: 482; practice of, **5**: 664; **9**: 93; **10**: 108; use of bark as, **6**: 26; sent from R.I., **6**: 53; study of, **8**: 636; praise of English physicians, **10**: 163

medicine chests: for Gates' army, **3**: 528-9; for western troops, **4**: 234

Mediterranean sea: danger from pirates, **7**: 231-2, 571; **10**: 302; tides, **11**: 427, 451; color, **11**: 441; river mouths, **11**: 450

Mediterranean trade: N.H. involvement with, **7**: 344; TJ's Report on, **18**: 230, 369-445 (editorial note and documents). *See also* Algiers, American captives in

Medlin, Lieut.: in Albemarle co. militia, **1**: 667

Médoc, France: vineyards, **11**: 455

Meek, William: captured by Indians, **5**: 256

Meersch (Vandermersche), Gen. van der: in Flemish revolt, **16**: 250, 351, 404-5

megatherium (megalonyx): Bru's work on, **14**: xxv, xxix-xxxi; Cuvier's study of, **14**: xxv, xxvii-xxxi; drawing and description sent by Carmichael, **14**: xxv-vii, xxxi-iv, 40 (illus.), 501-2, 504-5; TJ's interest in, **14**: xxvii-ix, xxx-i; engraving from *Monthly Magazine*, **14**: xxvii-xxx, 40 (illus.); Wistar on, **14**: xxviii-ix; Garriga on, **14**: xxix-xxxi; engraving from Bru's drawing, **14**: xxx-i, 41 (illus.); photograph from Museo de Ciencias Naturales, Madrid, **14**: xxxi-ii, 41 (illus.)

Megginson, William: and bill establishing ferries, **2**: 459

Mehegan, Father John: letter from, **8**: 597; intercedes for crew of the *William and Catherine*, **8**: 501, 639

Meherrin parish, Brunswick co., Va.: dissolution of vestry, **2**: 112-3

Meherrin (Maherring) river: bridge, **3**: 497, 583; mentioned, **3**: 611, 659; **5**: 614

Meibom, Johann Heinrich: *De flagrorum usu in re medica et venerea*, **13**: 290

Meier & Cie.: letter to, **13**: 433; letters from, **9**: 390-3; **13**: 119

Meigs, Mr.: maker of cylinder lamp, **8**: 599n

Meigs, Return Jonathan: sword presented to, **16**: 55n

Meilhan, M. de: prepares memoirs of Duc de Richelieu, **16**: 48

Meinadier, M., **11**: 358, 359

Melcher, Col. *See* Melchoir, Col. Isaac

Melcher, John: paid by Department of State, **17**: 369; publishes *New-Hampshire Gazette*, **17**: 509n

Melchoir, Col. Isaac, **3**: 63; **11**: 305

Melo e Castro, Martinho de: letter from, to de Pinto, **9**: 408-9; illness, **11**: 66, 78

melon: seeds sent to TJ, **15**: 296; potato-pumpkin, **18**: 98

Melton, Benjamin: in Albemarle co. militia, **1**: 665

Melton, Jesse: in Albemarle co. militia, **1**: 665, 667

Melton, Richard: signs nonimportation resolutions (1769), **1**: 31

Melville, Viscount. *See* Dundas, Henry

Mémoire pour des négocians de l'Orient. *See* Vernes, Jacob

Mémoires de l'Académie des Sciences: sought by TJ, **6**: 541

Mémoires de l'Amerique, **7**: 288

Mémoires sur les droits et impositions en Europe, **11**: 662; **12**: 137

Menacon, Va.: ferry at, **2**: 458

Menander and Philemon: *Reliquiae*, **13**: 300, 411, 536

Ménars, Château de: TJ urged to visit, **11**: 325

Mengen (Mingen), Otto Carl Anton: letter to, **4**: 517-8; willing to purchase bills of exchange, **4**: 672, 685; **5**: 485; leaves Williamsburg, **5**: 19; letter forwarded to, **5**: 71; and German Convention troops, **5**: 184

Mennonites: exempted from militia duty, **2**: 350

Meno, Capt. (master of the *L'Oiseau*), **12**: 599

Menou (Menon), Jean François Abdallah, Baron de Boussay et de: in National Assembly, **16**: 373; **17**: 18

Menton (Mantone), France: oranges grown at, **11**: 441; **13**: 271; TJ describes, **11**: 442

Mentor (ship): Wilson's claim for, **18**: 347n-8n; loss of, **20**: 638n

mercenaries: used by British against U.S., **1**: 313, 317, 378; TJ's proclamation to, **4**: 505-6

Mercer, Mr., **17**: 654

Mercer, Anna: marries Benjamin Harrison, Jr., **9**: 479

Mercer, Eleanor Dick (Mrs. James Mercer): death of, **3**: 262n

Mercer, Col. George, **1**: 38, 50

Mercer, Hugh (son of Gen. Mercer): education of, **7**: 132

Mercer, Gen. Hugh: commands flying camp in N.J., **1**: 473; recruitment of forces, **1**: 483; allowance for son's education, **7**: 132

Mercer, James: letters to, **2**: 199; **3**: 112; letters from, **3**: 112, 261-2; **5**: 446-8; signs nonimportation resolutions (1770), **1**: 46; and legal fees, **1**: 99; signs letter to Va. HB, **1**: 111; and Lord North's conciliatory proposal, **1**: 174n; signs TJ's commission, **1**: 246; elected Va. delegate to Congress, **3**: 4n; delivers commissions, **3**: 152; resigns from Congress, **3**: 261; hostility to Constitution, **12**: 281

Mercer, John, **8**: 641

Mercer, John Francis: letter from, **7**: 150; opposes bill for religious freedom, **2**: 548n, 549n; assisted by TJ, **3**: 262n; Anmours visits, **6**: 161; elected to Congress, **6**: 318n; visits Jersey shore, **6**: 319; fails to report proceedings in Congress, **6**: 345n, 469n; plans to leave Congress, **6**: 355; committee duties of, **6**: 391n; correspondence with B. Harrison, **6**: 392n; **7**: 44-5, 103-4, 248-50, 293-4; approves report on *Lusanna*, **6**: 455n; absence from Congress, **7**: 4; correspondent from Congress, **7**: 60; letter from, to Executive Council of Va., **7**: 94-5; Steuben's claims supported by, **7**: 101n; Harrison resents affront by, **7**: 103-4; TJ's appraisal of, **7**: 104n, 119, 228; intrigue in Congress, **7**: 119; letter from cited, **7**: 129; letter from, to James Monroe, **7**: 150; vote on secrecy of ministers' letters, **7**: 207n; dispute with David Howell, **7**: 291; introduces resolution on Committee of the States, **7**: 299; marries Miss Sprigg, **8**: 79, 134, 145; nominated commissioner of the Treasury, **8**: 79; opposes Va. Revised Code, **9**: 195; bill for appropriating Lord Fairfax's land, **9**: 200; failure to be elected to Va. GA, **9**: 518; member of Constitutional Convention, **11**: 400; death of sister, **12**: 104; copy of *Notes on Virginia* sent to, **12**: 136; attitude toward Constitution, **12**: 409; in Md. Constitutional Convention, **13**: 333, 336; and delay of medal, **16**: 63n; accuses Hamilton, **18**: 638, 639n; mentioned, **6**: 375, 378, 538; **7**: 41, 95, 96, 584; **10**: 167

Mercer, Joseph: and nonimportation agreements, **1**: 110

Merceres, Chevalier de. *See* Mézières, Chevalier de

merchandise: bills of rates and impositions on, **2**: 55; and Moroccan treaty, **10**: 423; export from France to U.S., **12**: 470

merchant marine: dependent on commerce, **7**: 350; as occupation for American citizens, **8**: 426

merchants: and Continental Association, **1**: 151-2; stipulations on in trade treaties, **6**: 394; protection as aliens guaranteed, **7**: 267; consulted by TJ on U.S. commerce, **7**: 324n; wartime protection advocated by TJ, **7**: 492; trade without capital, **8**: 399; lack of patriotism, **10**: 16

Merchants' Association, Philadelphia, **3**: 462n

merchant vessels: search for contraband, **7**: 472; trade treaty stipulations, **7**: 486, 622; safety from molestation advocated, **7**: 491, 492

merchant vessels, American: protected by France, **7**: 471-2; captured by Moroccan armed vessel, **7**: 549, 571, 574, 578; captured by Algerian armed vessel, **7**: 556, 634; insurance, **7**: 556, 604, 629, 634-5, 644, 651

Merci, Comte de. *See* Mercy-Argenteau, Comte de

Mercier, James: captivity of, **10**: 71; released, **10**: 207; TJ aids, **11**: 83; expenses, **11**: 347

Mercier, M., **10**: 402

Mercier, Louis Sébastien: quoted, **12**: xxxvi

Mercure de France: quoted, **8**: 265; **11**: 113-6; work by Paine in, **11**: 112; sent to John Banister, Jr., **11**: 477, 483; **12**: 608; sent to Madison, **12**: 569; quotation from Mazzei's book in, **12**: 667; extract from *Notes on Virginia* in, **12**: 668n

Mercury (ship): commanded by Capt. Stanhope, **9**: 5; mentioned, **8**: 653; **11**: 302; **15**: 63

Mercy-Argenteau, Florimund Claude, Comte de: proposition for treaty with Austria, **9**: 166, 167, 234, 238, 501, 507, 515, 564-5; American newspapers for, **10**: 642; requests passage of troops, **17**: 311; **18**: 354; and convention on Low Countries, **17**: 439; **18**: 85, 137; receives news of Low Countries, **18**: 136; negotiates with Brabant, **19**: 363; mentioned, **8**: 282, 295, 544

Meredith, Mr.: TJ's salary note, **17**: 596

Meredith, Hugh: Franklin's partnership with, **9**: 486, 495

Meredith, Reese, **1**: 54, 91

Méréville, De la Borde de. *See* Laborde de Méréville

Meriwether, Mr.: letter from, to Lewis, cited, **1**: 40

Meriwether, C.: visit to Scotland planned, **12**: 454

Meriwether, George: and Va. bill on Congressional representation, **2**: 18n; and case of Thomas Johnson, **2**: 42n, 43n, 47n; commissioner for settling land claims, **4**: 454

Meriwether, James, **2**: 9; **11**: 83

Meriwether, Nicholas: and Rivanna river, **1**: 87

Meriwether, Ens. Nicholas: letter from, **4**: 556; officer in Regiment of Guards for Convention troops, **3**: 156; member of court-martial, **3**: 350

Meriwether, Maj. Thomas: and Transylvania land claims, **2**: 65n; commission for, **3**: 56n, 77; **4**: 539; rank of, **4**: 168; appointed field quartermaster, **5**: 5

Merlet, Hardoin: and Canadian campaign, **1**: 452-3

Merlin, Joseph: combination of harpsichord and fortepiano, **7**: 57

Mérode, Charles Guillaume Ghislain, Comte de: envoy of Joseph II at The Hague, **13**: 221n

Mesmer, M.: selects olive trees for S.C., **14**: 184

Mesmer, Friedrich Anton: theories, **7**: 642; criticism of, **8**: 16; **19**: 100

Mesmerism. *See* animal magnetism

Mesnard, Capt. (master of *Betsey*), **1**: 500; **14**: 634

Messey, Mr., **5**: 446

paign, **1**: 391n, 404n; signs Declaration of Independence, **1**: 432; recounts fable of the fox, **6**: 667

Middleton, Conyers: cited by TJ, **1**: 554; *Miscellaneous Works*, **12**: 18, 688; **14**: 707n

Middleton, Henry: signs Continental Association, **1**: 154; signs petition to king, **1**: 223; cited on S.C. debts to Britain, **7**: 348

Middleton, Henry (son of Arthur): introduced to TJ, **16**: 544, 600; **17**: 511

Middletown, Conn.: in *Encyclopédie Méthodique*, **10**: 36; visited by TJ and Madison, **20**: 444, 456

Mieliqua (Cherokee Indian town), **4**: 362

Mifflin, Fort: British attack on, **2**: 38; evacuation of, **9**: 33n

Mifflin, Thomas: letters to, **16**: 281-2, 562-5; letter from, **7**: 275; signs Continental Association, **1**: 153; and Canadian campaign, **1**: 296n; as president of Congress, **6**: 348, 349, 461, 463; response to Washington's resignation, **6**: 404n; member of Congress from Pa., **7**: 7n; signs commission for negotiating treaties, **7**: 263; member of Federal Convention, **11**: 400, 626; **12**: 231n; president of Pa., **14**: 473, 529; **17**: 497; **18**: 144n, 386n-7n; encourages Humphreys, **16**: 58n; papers from Dumas transmitted to, **16**: 551-2; letter from quoted, **16**: 563n; letter from cited, **17**: 509n-10n; and Franklin's eulogy, **19**: 101n; mentioned, **6**: 355, 410n; **18**: 674

Migomry, William: signs certificate, **17**: 23n

Milan: TJ visits, **11**: 437-8, 586; agriculture, **11**: 440; import of whale oil by proposed, **11**: 516; cathedral at, **13**: 272; TJ's travel hints, **13**: 272; Verme's hospitality to TJ in, **13**: 356; Short and Rutledge in, **14**: 41-3, 53, 273, 590; American medals sent to, **16**: 67

Mildred, Mr.: case against Dorsey, **19**: 428

mile: measurement of, **7**: 174-5, 205

Miles, Benjamin: in Albemarle co. militia, **1**: 666; signs petition, **6**: 290

Miles, Richard: in Albemarle co. militia, **1**: 666

Miles, William: in Albemarle co. militia,

1: 666; signs petition, **6**: 290

Milford, Conn.: settlement of Nova Scotia whalemen at, **19**: 203n

Milford Haven, Va., **1**: 297

military commissions. *See* commissions, military

Military Department, U.S.: arrears of interest, **7**: 65

military officers. *See* army officers

military stores: for Canadian campaign, **1**: 439; inspected by De Klauman, **2**: 291; return of to Va., **3**: 38, 154; for frontier defense, **3**: 79; hidden from British, **3**: 238-9; for southern army, **3**: 426, 480, 496, 550, 553, 588; **5**: 232; need of officers to supervise, **3**: 504-5; subject to orders of commander in chief, **3**: 529; offered to Continental Board of War, **3**: 574; removal from Richmond, **4**: 258, 262, 269, 338, 381; destroyed by British, **4**: 264, 270, 271-2, 334; dispersal, **4**: 328-9; issue of, **4**: 337, 407; removal from Petersburg, **4**: 409; **5**: 465; commissary of, **4**: 417, 518, 519; account of in Va., **4**: 470; on *Courier d'Europe*, **4**: 556-7; excluded from booty, **4**: 571-3; supply of, **4**: 600; to be collected at Westham, **4**: 609; for western army, **4**: 628; needed for Va. forces, **5**: 30; delivered at Hoods, **5**: 150; transport of, **5**: 169-71; for navy, **5**: 178; removal from shipyard, **5**: 195; from Saint-Domingue, **5**: 228; storage of, **5**: 337; removal from Chesterfield, **5**: 465; removal from Prince George Court House, **5**: 480; sent from Philadelphia to Va., **5**: 550, 620; contradictory orders for delivery, **6**: 12, 13n; exposed to destruction by British, **6**: 91; Nathan's attempt to attach, **6**: 322n; Davies urges Steuben to defend, **6**: 631; Va.'s purchase of abroad, **8**: 67-8; orders for, **15**: 587, 589-92, 600-1. *See also* arms

militia: importance of, **1**: 266; **4**: 130-1, 268; captains' duties, **2**: 351-2, 356; use against Tory insurrectionists, **3**: 325; behavior at Camden criticized, **3**: 558-9, 563, 576-7; Washington's opinion of, **4**: 45-6; Innes' opinion of, **4**: 55-6; destruction caused by, **4**: 298-9; inadequacy of, **4**: 562, 611; **6**: 56-7; **15**: 607-8; Steuben's opinion of, **5**: 263n; TJ praises Steuben's training of,

militia (*cont.*)
 5: *559*; commissions for officers, 6: 641-4; formation of marine discussed, 11: 31; TJ criticizes, 15: 593; Knox's plan for, 16: 125
militia, French. *See* France: militia
mill (coin): name, 7: 159n
Millan, Capt., 3: 350
Millar, Daniel: signs Va. oath of allegiance, 2: 130
Millar, Thomas: supports American state papers series, 1: 145
mill dams. *See* dams
Millehome, François, 5: 387n, 388n
Miller, Capt., 4: 279, 280
Miller, Miss: marriage, 14: 530, 608
Miller, Mr.: ferry from property of, 2: 461; collects rice seed, 14: 673, 674; inn rated by TJ, 20: 471; mentioned, 5: 446
Miller, George: appointed British consul in Carolinas and Georgia, 13: 249n; loyalist status, 18: 254; mentioned, 17: 42, 43
Miller, Isaac: marries Polly Lewis, 16: 432, 433; subscription to *National Gazette*, 20: 759
Miller, Sir John Riggs: on weights and measures, 16: 542, 611, 623, 668n, 672n; 18: 457n; *Speeches in the House of Commons upon . . . Weights and Measures*, 16: 543, 614n
Miller, Nathan: letter from, 10: 461-3
Miller (Millar), Philip: *Gardeners Dictionary*, 10: 228; 13: 484n-5n; 20: 429n
Miller, Robert: signs nonimportation resolutions (1770), 1: 47
Miller, Capt. William (master of *Caesar*), 16: 563n
millers: exemption from militia duty, 2: 350; charges, 7: 348
Milligan, Mr., 3: 74
Milligan, James: letter to, 8: 227; letter from, 8: 87-8
millinery: U.S. import of, 10: 147
mill machinery: Barker's mill, 15: 504-5, 522; 16: 591; 17: 516; 18: 149n; Livingston's experiments with, 18: 146-50
Millot, Claude François Xavier: *Elémens de l'histoire de France*, 8: 411; 12: 18, 130; 20: 647-8; *Elémens d'histoire ancienne*, 8: 411; 10: 307; 11: 666; 12: 18, 130; 19: 337; *Elémens d'histoire moderne*, 8: 411; 12: 18, 130; 19: 337

mills. *See* grist mills
Mills, Charles: signs petition, 1: 588
Mills, David: in Albemarle co. militia, 1: 665
Mills, James: signs nonimportation resolutions (1770), 1: 46
Mills, John: in Albemarle co. militia, 1: 666
Mills, Joseph: in Albemarle co. militia, 1: 668n
Mills, Menan: in Albemarle co. militia, 1: 666
Mills, Robert: describes bust of TJ by Ceracchi, 15: 364n; 18: xxxiii-iv
Mills, Zachariah: in Albemarle co. militia, 1: 665; signs Va. oath of allegiance, 2: 129
millstones: U.S. import of, 10: 147; Cologne, 13: 15, 265, 447-8; Livingston's study of, 17: 553
Milne, Mr.: and cotton manufacture, 14: 546; 15: 476, 477n
Milton, George, 4: 322
Milton, John: cited by TJ, 1: 552; *Paradise Lost*, 8: 407; mentioned, 12: 18; 20: 662
Milton, Rev. Richard: signs nonimportation resolutions (1770), 1: 31; obtains patent, 11: 195; relations with Vaughan, 11: 277
Milton Falls, Va., 1: 88n
Mimosa arborea, 14: 42
Minas Gerais, Brazil: in favor of revolution, 11: 340
Minaudier fils, M., 11: 605
mineralogy: writings on by Fabbroni, 3: 237; Buffon's work on, 11: 43
mineral waters: TJ's interest in, 10: 581; described by Stiles, 10: 585; TJ's comments on at Aix, 11: 250
Minerva (newspaper), 18: 659
Minerva (ship): at L'Orient, 9: 387, 392; tobacco shipped on, 11: 358, 507; 20: 607n; sails for Baltimore, 14: 532; discharges cargo at Cowes, 18: 5; taken by Algerians, 19: 355n; mentioned, 20: 599, 676n
Minerva (statue), 8: 548
Minge, Mr.: and bill establishing ferries, 2: 458
Minge, George: slaves employed at Hoods, 5: 127
Mingo Indians: land claimed by, 2: 77; expedition against proposed, 3: 259, 561

Mingstown: plans for defense of, **3**: 55

Minier, M.: of Puchelberg & Co., **13**: 361, 390, 517

ministers, foreign (U.S.). *See* consular establishment; diplomatic service (U.S.); foreign ministers

ministers in passage: payment of debts required, **11**: 544-5

minks: weight, **6**: 343

Minnes (Minnis), Capt. Francis: requests command of recruits, **3**: 313-4; mentioned, **3**: 351

Minor, George: signs nonimportation resolutions (1770), **1**: 47

Minor, James: pledges to support clergyman, **2**: 7; signs Va. oath of allegiance, **2**: 129; commissioner of Albemarle co., **5**: 431; Carr papers in hands of, **16**: 205

Minor, Capt. Peter, **5**: 355, 517

Minorca: expedition from Cadiz against, **6**: 132

minority: protection of rights of, **12**: 277-9

mint, U.S.: congressional interest in, **7**: 153n; **8**: 516; **9**: 190; Dudley employed for, **7**: 154n; proposed establishment of, **7**: 163, 168; **9**: 15, 137; **11**: 30, 289; Hopkinson solicits superintendency of, **7**: 245; Monroe promises Hopkinson position with, **10**: 626; TJ negotiates on with Droz, **16**: 335n, 337n-9n, 368-9; **20**: 255, 256n; Hamilton confers with TJ on, **16**: 340n, 369n; **20**: 213; TJ plans for, **16**: 340n-2n, 348, 368-9, 483; **20**: 534, 578-9; Boulton supplies material for, **16**: 341n-2n; Hamilton's report on establishment of, **17**: 409n, 534n; Paine's Thoughts on Establishment of, **17**: 534-40; resolution on, **18**: 458; workmen for, **20**: 652

Minton, Thomas (?), **4**: 20

minutemen: criticism of, **1**: 266, 268

Minzies, Mr.: Richmond property, **8**: 49

Minzies, Mrs., **5**: 631

Minzies, Ninian: escheated property, **2**: 284n; mentioned, **1**: 86, 97, 101

Mirabeau, Honoré Gabriel Riquetti, Comte de: letter to, **10**: 283; translates Price's work, **8**: 503; introduces Sinclair to TJ, **9**: 405n; on hereditary aristocracy and Cincinnati, **10**: 50; **11**: 388; Va. act on religious freedom sent to, **10**: 283; letter from, to King of

Prussia, cited, **11**: 572; *Aux Bataves sur le Stathouderat*, **13**: 132; *Histoire secrète de la Cour de Berlin*, **14**: 348; elected to Estates General, **14**: 653; **15**: 24, 30, 45; support for in Marseilles, **15**: 24, 30; on TJ and Paris' bread shortage, **15**: 243-56 (editorial note and documents), 284-5; motion on troops, **15**: 255, 286; correspondence with Price, **15**: 329; and conspiracy for Duc d'Orléans, **15**: 366, 532-3, 541; **16**: 6n; denounces St. Priest, **15**: 533; hopes for ministry disappointed, **15**: 549; influence in National Assembly, **15**: 559; motion on flour contract, **15**: 565; opposes Necker, **15**: 567; proposes payment of American debt in flour, **16**: 7n; suggests Comte de Provence speak, **16**: 51n; in *Journée des dupes*, **16**: 107; bill against, **16**: 130; favors abolition of slave trade, **16**: 220; decree on power of king, **16**: 437-9; proposes confiscation of Condé's property, **17**: 312; revises Family Compact, **17**: 437; supports paper money scheme, **17**: 492; charges against, **17**: 555; *De la constitution monétaire*, **18**: 358, 359n; and Franklin's death, **19**: 80, 81, **19**: 90-1; political position undercut by Hamilton, **19**: 94; and tobacco monopoly, **19**: 258, 290; motion on national defense, **19**: 422; death of, **20**: 159, 168, 171, 568; on status of French ministers, **20**: 697-8; mentioned, **15**: 266; **16**: 46; **17**: 527; **19**: 79

Mirabeau, André Boniface Louis de Riquetti, Vicomte de: duel, **16**: 46

Miralles, Don Juan de, **6**: 211n, 213

Mirambeau, France: TJ describes, **11**: 457

Miranda, Francisco de: letter from, to Spanish minister, **9**: 54; friendship with Col. Smith, **9**: 55n; travels, **9**: 219n, 557n; **13**: 530; letter from, to Hamilton, cited, **18**: 247; letter from, to Knox, quoted, **18**: 247; mentioned, **17**: 605; **18**: 14

Miró, Esteban (gov. of La.): O'Fallon's correspondence with, **17**: 124n; **19**: 273n; proclamation quoted, **18**: 206n; Ste. Marie appeals to, **19**: 505, 526; mentioned, **14**: 388n

Miroménil (Miromesnil), Armand Thomas Hue, Marquis de: dismissal as

Miroménil, Armand (*cont.*)
  Garde des Sceaux, **11**: 316; speech to
  Estates General, **15**: 104-5; mentioned, **10**: 508
Miroménil (Mirosmenil), Nicolas
  Thomas Hue, Comte de: letter from,
  18: 513-4; vineyard, **11**: 456; wine ordered from, **17**: 493, 494n; **18**: 513-4;
  19: 266; letter to quoted, **17**: 494n;
  wine recommended by TJ, **20**: 405
Mirrour of Justices, The: cited on treason,
  2: 495n; cited on arson, **2**: 499n; cited
  on burglary, **2**: 500n; cited on escape,
  2: 502n
misfeasance in office: of county surveyors
  and deputy surveyors, **2**: 142
misprision of treason: and revisal of Va.
  laws, **2**: 502n; in Gloucester and York
  counties, **5**: 593
Mississippi Company, **2**: 138n
Mississippi river: Clark proposes clearing
  of British, **2**: 260; fortification of proposed near Ohio, **3**: 88, 355; extension
  of settlements on, **3**: 168; **6**: 661-2;
  site of Fort Jefferson on, **3**: 278; reduction of British posts on by Spanish,
  3: 343; **6**: 62; right of navigation on,
  4: 137, 203, 398; **6**: 243, 265, 460,
  536-7; **7**: 6, 26, 261, 309n, 403-7,
  433, 503, 510, 569-70; **8**: 114, 130-1,
  138n-9n, 250, 646; **9**: 185, 190, 218,
  556, 653; **10**: 143, 223-4, 233-4, 274-
  6, 400, 456, 575, 603; **11**: 93-4, 154,
  202, 221, 222, 224n, 309, 481; **12**:
  173; **13**: 132, 211, 494, 541n; **14**:
  436, 438n; **17**: 605; **18**: 164, 497-8;
  19: 17, 530; **20**: 95, 204-5, 364-5,
  480, 531, 532, 536-7, 652-3; TJ desires information on lands west of, **6**:
  204; U.S. claim to territory east of, **6**:
  213; British exploration west of, **6**:
  371; joint use of proposed at peace
  conference, **6**: 386, 388; as part of
  U.S. boundary, **6**: 458, 603; flooding
  of, **6**: 535-7; name, **6**: 596n; west
  boundary of proposed colony F, **6**:
  602; trade on, **7**: 280; **13**: 124; unoc-
  cupied land on, **7**: 406; west shore of,
  7: 406; Spain's restrictions on trade
  on, **7**: 416-7, 422; Spanish fortifications at Natchez, **7**: 454; mouth
  claimed by Spanish, **8**: 412; poverty of
  land on, **9**: 189; Spanish settlements
  on, **13**: 93, 113, 114n, 216; **14**: 387n-
  8n; **18**: 199-202; rumors of Spanish
  and American boats sinking on, **13**:

231, 277, 312; proposed treaty with
  Spain on, **13**: 494, 540, 624, 626n;
  Madison's report to Jay on, **13**: 541n;
  and Morgan's grant from Spain, **14**:
  530, 608; **15**: 7, 106; in war crisis of
  1790, **17**: 90-6, 111-7, 121-3, 124n;
  TJ's outline of U.S. policy on, **17**:
  113-7; negotiations with Spain on suggested, **18**: 292, 293, 299; confronta-
  tion with Spain on, **19**: 429-531 (editorial note and documents). *See also*
  Jay, John: Secretary of Foreign Affairs, negotiations with Gardoqui
Mississippi valley, **8**: 124
Missouri (ship): arrival in Bordeaux, **13**:
  416
Missouri river: mountains west of, **6**:
  208; floods in, **6**: 536; trade on, **7**: 280
Missy, M.: accounts of, **12**: 520
Mister, Stephen: escapes to Va., **3**: 525,
  551
Mistral (Mistrat), Jean Louis Roch: let-
  ter to, from La Forest, cited, **11**: 414;
  as intendant at Le Havre, **14**: 595,
  654-5; **15**: 18, 65, 70; letter to, from
  Reaupreau, cited, **14**: 596
Mitchel, Charles: in Albemarle co. militia, **1**: 666
Mitchel, David: signs petition, **4**: 20
Mitchell, Capt., **1**: 19; **5**: 281
Mitchell, Abram: letters on William Boswell cited, **5**: 226; mentioned, **5**: 60
Mitchell, Archibald: imports slaves, **15**:
  654
Mitchell, George: house endangered by
  flood, **6**: 515; mentioned, **3**: 397; **11**:
  536
Mitchell, James: Baptist enlisted in
  army, **1**: 662
Mitchell, John: *Map of the British Colonies in North America*, **6**: 601; **16**:
  xxxiv-v, 52 (illus.), 326; **17**: 591; **18**:
  86-7, 96n; **20**: 158
Mitchell, John Hinckley: correspondence
  with Tucker, **16**: 335n, 338n, 339n,
  342-5; negotiations on coinage, **16**:
  336n-41n; **18**: 139, 141n; correspondence with Boulton, **16**: 336n-45; letter
  from cited, **16**: 341n
Mitchell, Nathaniel, **5**: 5, 454n, 479
Mitchell, Reuben: letter from, **5**: 658-9;
  protests imprisonment without trial, **5**:
  658-9
Mitchell, Richard: signs nonimportation
  resolutions (1770), **1**: 46; signs Virginia Association, **1**: 108

money, Continental (*cont.*)
5: 386; lack of, 5: 428; purchase by
Virginians recommended by TJ, 7:
120; debated in Congress, 7: 232; purchase by speculators, 9: 612; compared
to Va. money, 10: 128; mentioned, 1:
255; 5: 650; 7: 123
money, copper. *See* copper coinage
money, hard: lack of, 1: 412, 474; 3:
272, 275, 317, 320; 4: 207; for prisoners in N.Y., 4: 550; acceptability to
Congress, 7: 362
money, paper: authorization of Treasury
notes by Va. Convention, 1: 254-5,
267, 271; importance of stabilizing, 2:
25, 26; as legal tender, 2: 44n, 170n;
credit support of, 2: 135n; taxation, 2:
220; punishment for theft of, 2: 501;
bill prohibiting forgery of, 2: 507-10;
calling in, 3: 506; emission stopped by
Congress, 4: 106, 367; delay in printing, 4: 512; exchange of, 4: 589; 9:
604-5; not acceptable at Frederick,
Md., 4: 698; rate of exchange, 5: 356;
8: 24; act on payment of debts in, 5:
387n; depreciation, 5: 599; 7: 213; 10:
17, 26; and Committee of the States,
6: 523-4; fear of, in U.S., 8: 369; in
Va., 8: 509, 642, 645, 659; 9: 199;
11: 84, 223, 310, 318, 402; 12: 346;
in S.C., 8: 581; Franklin's advocacy of,
9: 486, 496; discourages commerce in
U.S., 9: 504; emission by states, 9:
505, 608; 10: 187, 231-2; 12: 103,
276; in N.Y., 9: 609; redemption, 10:
17, 26, 92-3, 127-8, 509, 584; in
U.S., 10: 25-7; emission by Congress,
10: 54; demand for, 10: 133; traffic in,
10: 140; Madison's arguments against,
10: 232; discussed in Congress, 10:
575; Clavière's disapproval of, 11: 9;
as payment of British debts, 11: 16;
Paine's pamphlet on, 11: 112-6; in
Mass., 11: 146; 12: 112; circulation
ceases in Philadelphia, 11: 600-1;
value, 12: 53, 61; Mason's resolution
against in Va. GA, 13: 206; in Britain,
13: 209; TJ foresees danger of, 13:
209; in Md., 13: 333; in R.I., 15: 218,
297; in France, 16: 371; 17: 491-2,
503, 523-4, 555, 613-4, 652; 18: 111;
Howell's objection to, 16: 452, 454n
money, public: Va. bill for speedy recovery of, 2: 624-5
money bills, legislative: controversy over
right of Va. Senate to amend, 2: 40-63
(editorial note and documents)

money of account: France, 7: 179; dollar
as, 7: 189, 193-4, 197-200
money unit: instructions to Committee of
the States concerning, 6: 528-9; G.
Morris' proposal for, 7: 151n, 153n,
183-5, 189-93, 195; size of, 7: 166-7,
175, 179; tables of G. Morris, 7: 170-
1, 173n; TJ's rough draft of "Notes"
on, 7: 173-5; TJ's notes on establishment of, 7: 175-7; establishment of, 7:
182
Monfort (Montford, Montfort), M.: letter
from, 12: 658; forwards wine, 12: 648;
at Rouen, 13: 171
Mongé, Gaspard, Comte de Peluze: committee on weights and measures, 20:
353; report on unit of measure, 20:
354-60
Moniteur: sent to TJ, 20: 534
"Monitor, the." *See* Lee, Arthur
Monnet, M.: vineyard, 11: 422
Monnier, M. *See* Mounier, Jean Joseph
Monocacy River: and capital site, 19:
24n
monoceros: carried by flood, 7: 315
Monongahela river: as Va.-Pa. boundary
line, 1: 594; junction with Allegheny,
2: 98; settlement on, 2: 101; post service on, 2: 389; supplies purchased on,
4: 375; Le Maire's account of, 8: 123;
mentioned, 2: 103; 12: 489
Monongalia co., Va.: letter to county
lieutenant of, 4: 232; letter to surveyor
of, 6: 76; place of court of assize, 1:
630; grand jury in, 1: 638-9; militia,
2: 131; 4: 234; 5: 311; 6: 40; land
commissioners for, 2: 165n; senatorial
district, 2: 336; levies of soldiers from,
3: 6-7, 8; defends western frontier, 3:
50, 51, 53, 420; 4: 235; claimed by
both Va. and Pa., 3: 206, 288; purchase of flour in, 4: 147-9; unpatented
lands in, 4: 454; Duval's expenses
from, 4: 525-6; surveyor of, 6: 74;
price of land in, 11: 411; quality of
land in, 11: 519; state representative,
14: 403
Monongalia Court House, Va.: time of
holding court of assize, 1: 628; proposed meeting of school overseers at,
2: 530; place of court of assize, 7: 589
Monongalia river: ferry across, 2: 460,
461
monopoly: reciprocal agreement on between U.S. and Prussia, 7: 617; 8: 27-
8; restrictions against, 12: 440; 13:
442-3; 14 21. *See also* tobacco trade

Monreaux, Capt. Pierre (master of *Comte
d'Artois*), **9**: 33
Monro, Sir Alexander: recommended by
Carmichael, **12**: 100
Monroe, Elizabeth Kortright (Mrs.
James Monroe): returns to Va., **10**:
457; TJ's praise of country life to, **10**:
613; birth of daughter, **11**: 630; **13**:
50, 490; health of, **16**: 110, 536, 596;
20: 235, 633; cares for sick child, **16**:
432; TJ's desire to see, **16**: 538; at
N.Y., **18**: 489; mentioned, **9**: 516; **10**:
225; **17**: 25, 607; **18**: 29-30, 81
Monroe, James: letters to, **3**: 431-2, 451-
2; **5**: 655; **6**: 126-8, 184-7, 355; **7**:
279-81, 290, 294, 508-14, 562-5,
607-8, 637-41; **8**: 42-5, 88-90, 148-
50, 227-34, 259, 261-2, 288, 289-90,
444-6; **9**: 94-5, 236-7, 312, 499-503;
10: 111-5, 223-5, 611-3; **13**: 488-90;
16: 483, 536-8; **17**: 25, 334n; **18**: 29-
30, 514; **20**: 234-6, 296-8; letters
from, **3**: 464-7, 621-3; **6**: 95-6, 124-5,
178-9, 183, 192-3, 233; **7**: 251-3,
275-7, 290-2, 299-300, 379-81, 391-
2, 459-62, 572-3; **8**: 70, 75-80, 215-
20, 296-7, 381-4, 441-2; **9**: 186-91,
510-2, 652-5; **10**: 142-4, 274-9, 456-
8; **11**: 630-2; **13**: 49-50, 351-5; **14**:
557-9; **16**: 110-1, 432, 478-9, 596-7;
17: 231-3, 277, 607, 621-2; **18**: 81,
219, 509; **19**: 285, 631; **20**: 303-5,
556-7; Madison reports to on bills, **2**:
505n, 548n, 582n; asked by TJ to undertake mission, **3**: 431; observes British troop movements, **3**: 451-2; recommended to Gov. Nash, **3**: 452; letters
to cited, **3**: 501; **9**: 91; **16**: 288n; **17**:
164n, 165n, 166n; **18**: 163n, 164n,
377n, 380n, 384n, 392n, 394n, 517n;
refuses payment for services to Va., **3**:
622; thanks TJ for support, **3**: 622;
conducts *Riedesel* to Alexandria, **6**:
42n; proposed journey to France, **6**:
124; **7**: 559, 563; **8**: 233; introduced
by TJ to Franklin, Adams, and Jay, **6**:
126; TJ advises on France, **6**: 127;
elected to Va. HD, **6**: 178; **11**: 631;
appointed to Va. Executive Council, **6**:
193; letters sent to Madison, **6**: 273;
elected to Congress, **6**: 318n; favors
paying D. Franks, **6**: 462n; correspondence with B. Harrison, **6**: 510,
539-40, 552-5, 557, 564-5; **7**: 44-5,
47-9, 103-4, 293-4; on powers of
Committee of the States, **6**: 522n,
527n; bill in favor of, **6**: 543; pur-

chases land near Monticello, **6**: 550; **7**:
381; **14**: 558; **16**: 26; silence on diplomatic appointments, **6**: 570; signs land
cession, **6**: 576, 577, 579, 580; report
to governor, **7**: 4; supports Steuben's
claims, **7**: 101n; suggests TJ for
French mission, **7**: 148; letter to, from
Samuel Hardy and John F. Mercer, **7**:
150; correspondence with Madison, **7**:
234; **16**: 602-3, 610; **17**: 166; **18**:
165n; on TJ's appointment to negotiate commercial treaties, **7**: 235; books
sold to by TJ, **7**: 240-1; borrows
books from TJ, **7**: 240n-1n; TJ's account with, **7**: 241; member of committee to inspect Georgetown, **7**: 278;
western trips, **7**: 381, 391-2, 396,
440, 459-61, 508, 572; **8**: 383, 441-2,
579; **9**: 186; on trade treaties, **7**: 470n;
to settle near Monticello, **7**: 559, 565;
8: 150; **10**: 277; **13**: 490; Williamson
referred to for European news, **7**: 641;
TJ complains of lack of letters from, **8**:
134; *Notes on Virginia* sent to, **8**: 245;
12: 133; letters from cited, **8**: 336; **10**:
233; **14**: xxxviii; **16**: 111n, 171n; **18**:
163n, 165n, 613n; proposed Eastern
tour (1785), **8**: 416; attends Indian
treaty conference, **8**: 516; recommends
Stephen Sayre, **8**: 572; on control of
trade by Congress, **8**: 580; absence
from Congress, **9**: 89, 94; marriage of,
9: 178, 380, 499, 511, 609; **10**: 114-
5; W. T. Franklin praises, **9**: 178-9;
asks TJ for house plan, **9**: 190; **10**:
612; law practice, **9**: 190; **10**: 613; **11**:
630; Va. delegate in Congress, **9**: 202,
242, 479; TJ's opinion of, **9**: 466; **11**:
97; financial difficulties, **9**: 511; letters
from quoted, **9**: 512n; **18**: 685n; **20**:
5-6; fails in election to Va. GA, **9**:
518; and Jay-Gardoqui negotiations,
9: 654n; retires from Congress, **10**:
144, 225, 466, 612; plans to speculate
in land, **10**: 234-6, 457; promises
Hopkinson position with mint, **10**:
626; opposes paper money, **11**: 310;
receives copy of *Encyclopédie Méthodique*, **11**: 327; and Constitution, **13**:
50, 98, 351-5, 620; daughter of, **13**:
50, 490; **16**: 479, 536; **18**: 489; *Some
Observations on the Constitution*, **13**:
354n; favors second Constitutional
Convention, **14**: xxxviii-ix; opposes
Jay, **14**: 76, 80; election contest with
Madison, **14**: 415, 558; **15**: 6; sends
TJ address of welcome from Albe-

Montgomery, David: signs petition, **1**: 588

Montgomery, Dorcas: letters to, **10**: 282-3, 543-4; letter from, **13**: 164-6; invitation to tea with, **10**: 499; dines with TJ, **10**: 507; offers to chaperone Martha Jefferson on European tour, **10**: 543-4; relations with Pigott, **13**: 164-5, 235-6; biographical note on, **13**: 166n; passage to America, **13**: 228-9, 238, 288; Limozin's courtesy to, **13**: 253, 255, 282, 288; Shippen calls on, **13**: 253n

Montgomery, Fort: reduction by Sir Henry Clinton, **2**: 34

Montgomery, Hugh: imports slaves, **15**: 655

Montgomery, James: signs petition, **1**: 588

Montgomery, Dr. James: *Decius's Letters* attributed to, **16**: 141n

Montgomery, Lieut. James, **4**: 170

Montgomery, Janet Livingston: letter to, **9**: 470; letter from, **9**: 87

Montgomery, John: on committee for dividing Augusta and Botetourt counties, **2**: 118n; and Conn.-Pa. dispute, **6**: 482n-3n, 486n, 487n, 502n, 503n; motion on Va. land cession, **6**: 575n; member of Congress from Pa., **7**: 7n; letter from cited, **17**: 398n; letter from quoted, **20**: 669n; mentioned, **7**: 147n

Montgomery, Col. John: letter from, **4**: 319-21; joins G. R. Clark, **2**: 258, 259; conduct criticized, **4**: 442; Clark wishes arrest of, **5**: 253; arrests McCarty, **5**: 494n; drafts rejected, **5**: 503; complaints of Kaskaskia inhabitants against, **5**: 599

Montgomery, Gen. Richard: and siege of St. Johns, **1**: 251, 261; captures Montreal, **1**: 269; promoted to major general, **1**: 270; in Quebec campaign, **1**: 434, 437, 439, 444, 448-9, 453; **17**: 574; death of, **1**: 435, 437, 438; **10**: 352; appoints commissary, **1**: 453

Montgomery, Robert: letters to, **11**: 555; **12**: 115; **13**: 256; letters from, **11**: 376, 379, 620; **12**: 57-8, 242; **13**: 252-3; **17**: 397-8; **19**: 552; **20**: 640, 669, 678-9; propositions to Emperor of Morocco, **8**: 21; letters from cited, **11**: 492; **12**: 313; and consular appointment, **11**: 555; **17**: 254n, 398; **19**: 314, 317; Lamb's power of attorney to, **12**: 238-9; marriage and financial difficulties, **13**: 164-6, 235-6; pas-

sage to America, **13**: 228-9, 238; letter from, to Jay, **14**: 288-9; on Algerian situation, **14**: 288-9; **17**: 397-8; biographical note, **19**: 315n; mentioned, **11**: 21, 567; **13**: 288

Montgomery, William: candidate for Congress from Pa., **14**: 473

Montgomery co., Va.: letters to county lieutenant of, **4**: 85-6; **5**: 275-7; **6**: 24-5; boundaries, **1**: 572; **2**: 114, 118n; courts, **1**: 572-3; militia, **1**: 574; **2**: 131; **3**: 356, 421, 422, 479, 480, 533, 544, 600; **4**: 57, 63, 82-4, 362-3, 579, 614, 622, 637, 638, 641, 669; **5**: 7, 20, 36, 275-7, 311, 398, 436-8, 524; **6**: 24-5, 36; place of court of assize, **1**: 629-30; grand jury in, **1**: 638-9; collection of public dues or fees in newly formed counties, **2**: 115; parish of, **2**: 117; land commissioners for, **2**: 165n; senatorial district, **2**: 336; levies of soldiers, **3**: 8; defends western frontier, **3**: 50, 52, 53, 79; position of troops from, **3**: 55; insurrection among Tories, **3**: 325-6, 340; Indian depredations in, **3**: 356; lead mines guarded, **3**: 422; operations against southern Indians, **3**: 447-8; tobacco loan office certificates, **3**: 516; disaffection in, **3**: 648; **4**: 14, 88; **5**: 437; defense against Cherokee, **4**: 301; difficulty of raising troops in, **4**: 458; riflemen, **4**: 621; land purchased by Huron, **9**: 49; postal service, **20**: 664, 711

Montgomery Court House, Va.: court of assize in, **1**: 628-9; **7**: 589; as holding area for prisoners, **4**: 86, 98, 99; disaffection at, **4**: 108; rendezvous for western militia, **4**: 226, 230; lead sent to, **4**: 234

Montgommery, Capt. (master of *George*), **4**: 310

Monthieu, Jean Josef Carié de: arms purchased from, **12**: 13-4

Monthly Magazine: megatherium described and illustrated in, **14**: xxvii-xxx, 40 (illus.); on Dr. Gem, **15**: 384-5

Monthly Museum: Hopkinson's editorship, **11**: 289-90

Monthly Review: TJ recommends to Monroe, **6**: 127; issues sought by TJ, **10**: 166; **13**: 177; TJ subscribes to, **13**: 367, 376

Monticello: construction of (1769), **1**: 24; furnishing of, **1**: 61-2, 71-2; TJ describes, **1**: 63; TJ seeks architect

697; Vernes sends mémoire to, **13**: 55n; declaration to Russian minister, **13**: 134; correspondence with Moustier, **13**: 175n-6n, 234n, 410n-1n; **14**: 83, 84n, 86n, 88n, 388n, 400n-1n; **15**: 141; **16**: 357n; correspondence with Otto, **13**: 175n-6n; **15**: 557n; **16**: 360n; **18**: 241n, 376n, 413n, 529n-40n, 548n, 549-51, 552n-5n, 557n; **19**: 80n, 84n, 97, 429; **20**: 660-2; aid in forwarding TJ's correspondence sought, **13**: 586; in Consular Convention, **14**: 56, 71, 79, 81-3, 86-8, 91, 121-6; **18**: 23, 121-7, 311; **20**: 254; in Schweighauser & Dobrée affair, **14**: 61; **15**: 61n-2n; *Observations on the Whale-Fishery* sent to, **14**: 218, 254n, 269, 271; and whale fisheries, **14**: 225; and packet boats, **14**: 307n-10n; in *Alliance* case, **14**: 323n; and Moustier's recall, **14**: 520-1, 522n; discusses flour bounty, **14**: 622; and Dutch debt to Austria, **14**: 647n; G. Morris presented to, **14**: 704n; and Ternant's appointment as chargé d'affaires, **15**: 120; TJ consults with, **15**: 127, 431; and Estates General, **15**: 189; resigns from office (1789), **15**: 207, 273, 275, 286, 290; in Mirabeau incident, **15**: 244, 247, 248, 249, 253, 254, 285; friendship with La Luzerne, **15**: 291; reappointed to office, **15**: 300, 341-2; Lord Dorset writes to, **15**: 315n; seeks TJ's advice on constitution, **15**: 355n; concern over French West Indies, **15**: 360; asked to prevent flight of Louis XVI from Versailles, **15**: 458-9; and TJ's proposal for importing salt beef, **15**: 483n, 502, 536-7; letter from, to Duc d'Orleans, cited, **15**: 532; diplomatic receptions, **15**: 535; on French loan to U.S., **15**: 550; **20**: 176, 179, 184, 187-97, 201n; on Dutch role in U.S. debt, **16**: 7n; and Anglo-Spanish conflict, **16**: 123, 125n, 254; **18**: 24, 430; **17**: 121-3; on Flemish revolt, **16**: 267; correspondence with La Rochefoucauld d'Enville, **16**: 271n; TJ's intention to write to, **16**: 282; discussions with d'Estaing, **16**: 301, 619; *Observations*, **16**: 374, 376n; on Carmichael as TJ's successor, **16**: 423; praises TJ, **16**: 424n; Mercy applies to, **17**: 311; in National Assembly, **17**: 312-3, 612; wants Short named ambassador to France, **18**: 33, 446; and

U.S. tonnage acts, **18**: 222, 526-7, 535, 537, 551, 555; **20**: 171-2, 366, 371n; letters to, from Ternant, quoted, **18**: 278n-9n; and *droit d'aubaine*, **18**: 604; receives report on capital site bill, **19**: 18n; refuses Washington's letter, **19**: 94, 94n; letter from quoted, **19**: 108n-9n; letter from, to National Assembly, cited, **19**: 257; correspondence with Short, **19**: 259; **20**: 536-7; G. Morris meets with, **19**: 346; letter to, from G. Morris, quoted, **19**: 349n-50n; and Carmichael's instructions, **19**: 507, 528; opinion of French National Assembly, **19**: 634; and U.S. tobacco trade, **19**: 635; **20**: 365-6; circular letter to French diplomats, **20**: 260; and U.S. consuls in French West Indies, **20**: 324n-5n; relations with papacy, **20**: 385; petition from Cathalan, **20**: 477, 547; on U.S. acquisition of Fla., **20**: 530-1; on U.S. right to navigate Mississippi, **20**: 531, 532, 653; supports Carmichael, **20**: 531-2; letter from, to foreign ministers, cited, **20**: 562; and king's flight to Varennes, **20**: 575, 587; relations with foreign diplomats, **20**: 600, 609; and U.S. consuls in France, **20**: 612; report to National Assembly, **20**: 673; and U.S.-Spanish relations, **20**: 674; political survival, **20**: 697; G. Morris' observations sent to, **20**: 699; mentioned, **10**: 310; **11**: 177, 281, 346, 550; **12**: 97, 208, 373; **13**: 216, 282, 470, 579; **14**: 215, 654; **15**: 113, 139, 190, 344, 512n, 567; **16**: 133, 323, 396, 504, 586; **17**: 18, 27, 314, 556, 654, 671; **18**: 20, 75, 76, 241, 242, 262, 473, 583

Montmorin de Saint-Hérem, Comtesse de, **12**: 503n

Montour (Mentieur), Andrew: as public interpreter, **2**: 93

Montpelier, France: Short asks TJ's opinion of, **11**: 269; reputation of, **11**: 350; TJ describes, **11**: 444; **13**: 274

Montrachet, France: Short in, **13**: 635

Montreal, Que.: Montgomery's capture of, **1**: 269, 444; Arnold at, **1**: 293; role of merchants in Cedars affair, **1**: 399; prisoners sent from, **1**: 439; provisions for army at, **1**: 442; British forces in, **1**: 498

Montyon (Moutholon), Auget, Baron de: named keeper of seals, **13**: 573

Moody, Capt., **4**: 536; **5**: 500

Moody, Capt. Edward (?), **4**: 215, 541

Moody, Capt. James, **4**: 539

Moody, Philip: laborers of, **3**: 324, 398, 399; **4**: 439, 524; **15**: 600; constructs wagons, **4**: 8, 601; **5**: 184; tools for shop of, **4**: 315, 480; shop destroyed by British, **4**: 553

moon: Euler's tables of, **8**: 299; volcano on, **13**: 379; Laplace's study of motion of, **13**: 381

Moon, Jacob: signs petition, **6**: 293

Moon, Littlebury: in Albemarle co. militia, **1**: 668n

Moon, Richard: in Albemarle co. militia, **1**: 668n

Moon, William: in Albemarle co. militia, **1**: 666

Moor (Moore), Peter: appointed ensign in western battalion, **3**: 51, 52; to head company of riflemen, **4**: 629

Moor, Stephen: signs petition, **6**: 293

Moore, Col.: TJ visits, **1**: 21

Moore, Mr. (N.Y.): and Hessian fly, **20**: 458; inn rated by TJ, **20**: 471

Moore, Mr. (Va.): recommended by TJ, **1**: 604; and bill establishing ferries, **2**: 456; illness of, **15**: 571; mentioned, **5**: 485

Moore, Alexander: letters to, **7**: 384; **8**: 45, 83; letters from, **7**: 429-30; **8**: 17-8; TJ's letter of introduction delayed, **8**: 168; loyalism of, **8**: 398; on crew of *Indien*, **11**: 301n; mentioned, **7**: 383, 386, 422, 568

Moore, Andrew: votes for bill for religious freedom, **2**: 549n; reports on disaffection in Va., **6**: 23; counsellor in Va., **13**: 621; congressman from Va., **15**: 5, 74; federalism of, **15**: 5

Moore, Bernard: letter to, **6**: 431; and sale of property, **1**: 59, 64-5; and Dabney Carr's books, **11**: 623; **15**: 627, 639

Moore, E.: signs Va. oath of allegiance, **2**: 129

Moore, Edward: *Fables for the Female Sex*, **11**: 523

Moore, Elizabeth (Betsy): engagement to John Walker, **1**: 15

Moore, J.: letter from, to J. Holker, cited, **7**: 587

Moore, Gen. James, **1**: 296

Moore, Capt. James Francis: letter to, **4**: 239-40; letter from, **4**: 134-5; authorized to purchase flour, **3**: 670-1; **4**: 148; ordered to supply western posts, **4**: 31, 172, 235; recommended for sur-

veying, **4**: 200; orders to purchase provisions in west, **4**: 385; accused of misconduct, **4**: 391-2, 654n; **5**: 439, 494; **6**: 11; warrant for, **5**: 402; mentioned, **4**: 149, 162; **5**: 452n

Moore, John: letter to, **6**: 531; in Albemarle co. militia, **1**: 664; petition from, **2**: 15n; **5**: 349; on committee to bring in land office bill, **2**: 136n

Moore, Lewis: clock sent by, **14**: 182, 369; passport issued by TJ, **15**: 486

Moore, Peter, **5**: 145

Moore, Philip: owns *Congress* with B. McClenachan, **9**: 387

Moore, Richard: pledges to support clergyman, **2**: 7

Moore, Stephen: in Albemarle co. militia, **1**: 666

Moore, Thomas: votes for bill for religious freedom, **2**: 549n

Moore, William: daughter of marries Marbois, **7**: 308n; clock for, **14**: 53-4, 182; **15**: 46

Moorey, John: death of, **6**: 272

Moorman, Edward: and bill establishing ferries, **2**: 459

"Moor-Park": garden described by TJ, **9**: 373

Moors: expulsion from Spain, **10**: 346

moose: McDuffee's information on, **7**: 21-4; Whipple's information on, **7**: 28-30; Sullivan's information on, **7**: 132, 317-20; Sullivan asked to send to France, **9**: 160; Whipple asked to send to France, **9**: 161; hide and skeleton sent TJ, **11**: 68, 295-6, 359, 384; **12**: 41, 208; **13**: 567, 593; value of meat, **11**: 296; cost of sending skeleton to France, **11**: 320-1, 384; skin and skeleton sent to Buffon, **12**: 194-5; Buffon unaware of, **13**: 567, 593; Rutledge requests information on, **13**: 567-8; description of, **13**: 593-4

Moose Island: dispute over taxes in, **20**: 87, 90

Moracin, M.: purchases tobacco, **8**: 303

morality: TJ on, **12**: 15

moral philosophy: TJ advises against study of, **12**: 14-5

Moran, Joshua: in Albemarle co. militia, **1**: 668n

Morans, William: signs petition, **6**: 293

Moravian Indians: expedition against in Ohio, **6**: 40

More, Hamilton: *Practical Navigator*, **20**: 560, 567, 582

More, Thomas: *Utopia* cited, **2**: 495n;

History of King Richard III, **12**: 18
More, William: signs petition, **1**: 588
Morecock, Mrs.: British landing at estate of, **5**: 519
Morell, David: receives news from Va., **13**: 477
Morellet (Morelet, Morloix), André, Abbé: letters to, **10**: 225-6; **11**: 56, 529-31; **12**: 286-7; letters from, **9**: 133-4; **10**: 181-2, 219-20, 236, 333-4, 350-1; **11**: 37-8, 542-3, 661-2; **12**: 262, 484, 641-2; Mazzei praises, **7**: 387; translates *Notes on Virginia*, **8**: 270n; **9**: 244, 265, 279, 299, 384; **11**: 37; **12**: 426, 484; **16**: 319; **17**: 506; map printed for, **9**: 363, 384; **11**: 240, 268, 275; **18**: 32; Short visits, **11**: 208; Tench's account of Botany Bay sent to, **15**: 182; friendship with Gem, **15**: 384; TJ referred to, **15**: 614; and commercial policy, **19**: 123; mentioned, **11**: 374; **15**: 537; **20**: 691
Morelli, Jacopo: dictionary, **12**: 678, 688; **14**: 491; *Bibliotheca Maphaei Pinellii*, **15**: 83n
Morèri, Louis: *Le Grand Dictionnaire historique*, **7**: 506; works, **8**: 111
Moreton, Sir William: land grant to, **6**: 658
Morgan, Daniel: letters to, **3**: 514; **6**: 70-2; letters from, **4**: 80, 495-6; **5**: 218-9; to join southern army, **3**: 457n, 643; to command volunteers for southern army, **3**: 654; to form camp at Yadkin Ford, **4**: 5; drives British back in S.C., **4**: 32; to command western Va. militia, **4**: 40; letter from cited, **4**: 129; forces on Catawba river, **4**: 217, 251, 253; strategy in S.C., **4**: 322-3; victory at Cowpens, **4**: 437, 440-1, 525, 575-6, 577, 610; troops under, **4**: 441; health of, **4**: 496; retreats before Cornwallis, **4**: 562-3; reinforcements for, **4**: 620; sale of horse, **5**: 53; asks Va. GA for money and clothing, **5**: 218-9; asked to raise volunteers for Va. defense, **6**: 70; payment of, **6**: 138; called into action, **6**: 619n; medal, **14**: 545, 555; **16**: 52 (illus.), 54n, 56n-7n, 59n-61n, 63n, 65n, 66, 67n, 71, 73n, 74n, 76n, 288n; in Quebec campaign, **17**: 574; mentioned, **3**: 668; **4**: 108, 178, 561; **5**: 507; **6**: 103
Morgan, George: agent for Indiana Company, **2**: 97, 98; **6**: 652n; takes deposition, **2**: 100-3; promises to supply wine to members of Congress, **6**:

339n; petitions Congress, **6**: 597n; **7**: 6n; land grant from Spain on Mississippi with monopoly of navigation, **14**: 530, 608; **15**: 7, 106; and land speculation, **18**: 168; and Hessian fly, **20**: 446, 447; biographical note, **20**: 447n; contributions to *National Gazette*, **20**: 745n
Morgan, George C.: letters from, **15**: 266; **20**: 421-3; letter sent by, **15**: 329; mentioned, **15**: 272, 279, 321, 330
Morgan, Haynes: on Va. HD committee to inquire into conduct of Executive, **6**: 134
Morgan, John: George Gilmer introduces to TJ, **1**: 18; encourages balloon experiments, **7**: 247n; mentioned, **8**: 51
Morgan, Mrs. John: death of, **8**: 51
Morgan, père et fils: letter to, **14**: 460-1; letter from, **14**: 425-6
Morgan, Thomas: signs Va. oath of allegiance, **2**: 129
Morgan, William: letter from, **4**: 452
Morgan, Zachel: settlement on Indiana claim, **2**: 102-3
Morichie, N.Y.: visited by TJ and Madison, **20**: 460
Morini, Mr., **12**: 620, 621
Morning Chronicle, **8**: 366
Morning Star (ship): captured by Barbary pirates, **7**: 634; mentioned, **5**: 152n, 557
Morocco: U.S. treaty of amity and commerce with, **6**: 389, 396; **7**: 203, 263, 269, 496; **8**: 19, 46; **10**: 76, 141, 207, 224, 241, 246, 248, 251, 265, 294, 300, 302, 304, 349, 389-92, 418, 419-27 (text), 480, 488, 542, 557, 573, 618, 624, 629, 631, 637, 649; **11**: 22, 29-30, 36-7, 101, 125, 130, 135, 136, 163, 164, 236, 619, 626; **12**: 121-2, 150-1, 175, 186, 240, 266, 324, 364, 365, 644; **14**: 46, 72; **18**: 401, 412, 413, 445n; **20**: 377, 397-401, 406; attitude toward U.S., **7**: 269; captures American ships, **7**: 549, 571, 574, 577-8; **8**: 43, 61, 65, 80, 83, 254, 255, 555, 559; **9**: 92, 93; **15**: 342n, 360; naval force, **7**: 639; **8**: 95, 138, 254, 419; **10**: 342-3; U.S. negotiations with, **8**: 21; **9**: 352, 515-6, 590, 621; **11**: 54; **19**: 535, 536; U.S. consul to recommended by Vergennes, **8**: 47; U.S. relations with, **8**: 61-2, 69, 150, 567; **13**: 200; tribute paid to, **8**:

with L'Enfant, **20**: 10; supports Wolcott, Jr., **20**: 224, 225n; owner of *Nancy*, **20**: 238n; letter to, from Godin, **20**: 581-2; criticizes national bank, **20**: 602-3; owns *Minerva*, **20**: 607n; letter to, from Franchi, **20**: 628-9; and case of William Duncan, **20**: 677; notes on commerce, **20**: 710; mentioned, **6**: 132, 261, 273, 373; **7**: 111, 115, 243, 247n, 572; **8**: 507; **9**: 57, 164, 171, 229; **10**: 108; **12**: 325n, 643; **13**: 40n, 287; **14**: 527n; **15**: 64n; **16**: 97n; **17**: 58n, 60, 453n; **18**: 266, 271, 275, 415, 634

Morris, Robert Hunter: Franklin's disputes with, **9**: 487

Morris, Col. Staats Long: purchases land from Indians, **8**: 85; describes New York convention, **14**: 519

Morris, Thomas, **15**: 71n; **16**: 97n

Morris, William: reported death of, **2**: 256; as Clark's aide, **2**: 258

Morris, Willing & Swanwick: financial losses, **20**: 417

Morris, Zachariah: accused of selling damaged tobacco, **2**: 233-4

Morrisania, N.Y.: attacked by Americans, **4**: 534; Washington visits, **17**: 49

Morris brothers (sons of Robert Morris): letter of recommendation to Dumas, **10**: 295-6, 297; visit Le Havre, Dumas, **10**: 328; letters sent by, **10**: 404; passports issued by TJ, **15**: 485

Morrison (Morris), Capt. John: tents for company of, **4**: 531; accounts with Board of War, **4**: 645

Morriss, Jesse: signs petition, **6**: 294

Morristown, N.J.: mutiny of Pa. troops at, **4**: 325

Morrow, Charles: letter to, from Rumsey, quoted, **15**: 81n-2n

Morrow, Col. John: letter from, **4**: 452; as Berkeley co. lieutenant, **6**: 71n

Morse, Henry: signs nonimportation resolutions (1770), **1**: 46

Morse, Jedidiah: quoted on Leptoglottis, **9**: 94n; letter from, to Wolcott, quoted, **18**: 684n-5n

Mort, Joseph: involvement in Society for Establishing Useful Manufactures, **19**: 453n

mortar: mixture of fine gravel in, **9**: 222

mortars: for Portsmouth expedition, **5**: 89

Morten, Mr. *See* Morton, Perez

Mortimer, Mr. (son of Charles): intro-

duced to TJ, **11**: 298; recommended for position, **17**: 418n-9n; **18**: 219, 509, 514; makes fowling piece, **20**: 509

Mortimer, Dr. Charles: letter from, **4**: 242-3; **18**: 219n; biographical note, **4**: 243n

mortmain: Va. bill of, **2**: 414

Morton, Edward, **1**: 663

Morton, Capt. James, **5**: 571

Morton, John: signs Continental Association, **1**: 153; signs Declaration of Independence, **1**: 432

Morton, Col. Josiah, **5**: 571

Morton, Perez, **8**: 654; **9**: 5, 16

Morton (Mortins), Thomas, **5**: 450

Morton, William: *Morning Post* purchased from, **17**: 360, 362

Morton, Capt. William, **5**: 571

Morveau, M. *See* Guyton de Morveau

Mosa, Mme, **11**: 150

Mosby, Littleberry: letter to, **5**: 412; letters from, **4**: 700; **5**: 491, 508-9, 509; Fleming visits, **4**: 407; raises cavalry, **5**: 501, 525

Mosby, Littleberry H.: letter from, **5**: 183

Mosby, William, **4**: 354

Mosby, Maj. William, **3**: 495

Mosebey, Lieut.: gallantry at battle of Camden, **3**: 637

Moseby, Richard: and bill establishing ferries, **2**: 458

Moseley, Mr.: and bill establishing ferries, **2**: 458; TJ's opinion on note asked, **6**: 188

Moseley, Edward H.: contract to build ship, **3**: 223

Moseley, Edward Hack, Jr.: signs nonimportation resolutions, **1**: 31, 46

Moselle river, **13**: 16, 28

Mosheim, Johann Lorenz: *Ecclesiastical History*, **12**: 18

Mosquito Coast: disputes between Britain and Spain concerning, **8**: 252; **10**: 179, 266; effect on Spanish relations with U.S., **8**: 401

Moss, Mr.: proposals for chartering vessel, **4**: 30

Moss, John: Va. purchasing agent, **3**: 167, 205, 326, 332, 348

Mossom, Mr., **2**: 5

Mossop, William: receipt, **20**: 243n

most-favored-nation principle: TJ's notes on treaties with France, Netherlands, and Sweden, **7**: 471; trade treaty stip-

most-favored-nation principle (*cont.*) ulations, **7**: 474, 487-8, 562-3, 623-4, 651-2; **8**: 26-7; TJ's draft of treaty with Denmark, **7**: 480; treaty with Prussia, **7**: 616-7, 624; **8**: 26-7; treaty with Tuscany, **8**: 188-94; attitude of Congress, **8**: 217; Jay's attitude on, **8**: 220n; Adams' objection to, **8**: 310; Barbary treaty, **8**: 350, 400; Monroe's opinion, **8**: 382; treaty with France, **8**: 497-8; **11**: 616; TJ's dislike of, **9**: 51; TJ desires discussion with Vergennes on, **9**: 145; treaty with Portugal, **9**: 448; Moroccan treaty, **10**: 422; U.S. in France, **12**: 470, 481; mentioned, **8**: 105, 188; **9**: 412, 413, 421, 424, 429; **11**: 101

Mother-Bank, **20**: 507n

motion: attraction as first natural cause of, **10**: 97

Motte, Fort: surrenders to Gen. Greene, **6**: 52

Motte (Hobbe), Isaac: letter from, **4**: 483; letter from, to Huger, cited, **5**: 86

Motture, M.: letter to, **13**: 252; letter from, **11**: 468

Motz, Henry: letter from, to Dorcester, cited, **17**: 71n; letter from, to Beckwith, quoted, **17**: 78n; letters sent by, **20**: 109

Mouchy, Philippe, Comte de Noailles, Maréchal de: Lafayette's visit to, **12**: 141

moulding house: rebuilding at Westham, **4**: 426, 438-9

Moullin et Kroux, veuve, **14**: 648

Moulston, John: recommended for consular post at Dunkirk, **8**: 441

Moulton, Capt.: master of *Mary*, **16**: 97n

Moultrie, Fort: attack on, **10**: 382n

Moultrie, William: success at Charleston, **1**: 481; elected governor of S.C., **8**: 134; seeks auditorship of treasury, **20**: 230n

mounds: plan of at Muskinghum river mouth, **9**: xxix, 419 (fac.)

Mounier, Jean Joseph: brochures of, **15**: 210; discusses royal veto, **15**: 355n; on declaration of rights, **15**: 390-1; retires to Dauphiné, **15**: 534-5, 547-8; **16**: 6n, 7n; *Exposé de ma conduite dans l'assemblée nationale*, **15**: 548, 551n; in *Journée des dupes*, **16**: 107; revolutionary opinions, **16**: 107; work of, **16**: 423; in Switzerland, **17**: 9

mountain cress: seed sent to TJ, **17**: 512n

Mount Holly, N.J.: Hessians at, **2**: 3

Mountjoy, George: petition from, **5**: 405; reply to, **5**: 405n

Mount Vernon: British near, **5**: 448n; TJ invited to, **7**: 7-8; Lafayette's visit to, **7**: 416; meeting of Md.-Va. commissioners at, **9**: 208n; visit of West to, **13**: 644; Moustier entertained at, **14**: 23, 24n, 294, 303, 341, 399; Madison visits, **14**: 415; Washington at (in 1790), **17**: 25, 26, 473

Mouron, M., **8**: 366, 423

Mousley, Walter: TJ's overseer, **2**: 233-4

Moustier, Elénore François Elie, Comte de: letters to, **11**: 621; **12**: 74-5, 224-5, 294; **13**: 173-6, 491-2; **14**: 652-4; **15**: 141-2; **18**: 118-20; **19**: 357; letters from, **11**: 622; **12**: 192, 225, 247, 306, 319, 589-91, 662-5; **13**: 504-6; **14**: 22-4, 293-5, 399-401; **15**: 210-2; **16**: 100-2, 422-4; **18**: 12-3; **20**: 263-5; voyage to U.S., **10**: 453; **12**: 139, 190, 207, 293, 294, 306, 330, 589, 613, 629, 635, 639, 662, 692, 696; **13**: 42; TJ's characterization of, **11**: 94, 101; **12**: 66; as minister plenipotentiary to U.S., **12**: 68, 153, 157, 162, 175; **13**: 53n, 175n-6n, 409n-11n; **14**: 400n-1n; TJ invited to meet, **12**: 120; Madison's watch sent by, **12**: 137; letters sent by, **12**: 199, 310, 438, 530, 563, 607, 608; **13**: 252n, 261; **16**: 3; patron of Victor Dupont, **12**: 213; introduction to Jay, **12**: 217; introduction to Madison, **12**: 218-9; wine ordered for, **12**: 352, 353, 385, 648; **13**: 96, 110-1, 175, 297; tea vase described by TJ, **12**: 540; **13**: 214; TJ visits residence of, **13**: 16, 34n; death falsely reported, **13**: 173; in Consular Convention, **13**: 175n; **14**: 75, 83-7, 88n; letters from, to Montmorin, quoted, **13**: 175n-6n, 234n, 410n-1n; **14**: 400n-1n; reception by Congress, **13**: 175n-6n, 248n; letters to cited, **13**: 207; **15**: 140; **17**: 281n; **19**: 425; describes riot in New York, **13**: 234n, 408n; on American government, **13**: 504-5; **15**: 211-2; **18**: 518; questions Washington, **13**: 557; entertained at Mount Vernon, **14**: 23, 24n, 294, 330, 341, 399; letter from, to Crèvecoeur, cited, **14**: 28; on French consuls in U.S., **14**: 63n-6n; **19**: 302; letters from, to Montmorin, cited, **14**: 83, 84n, 86n, 88n, 388n; **16**: 357n; "Observations sur le délai de la signature

Murdock, Mr., **16**: 428

Murphy, Charles: public interpreter, **2**: 93

Murphy, James: letter from, to auditors, **5**: 515

Murphy, Teresa: letters to, **12**: 197-8; **13**: 313; letters from, **9**: 271-2, 578, 596

Murray, Mr. (?): map of U.S., **7**: 284; mentioned, **7**: 47; **9**: 363n

Murray, Rev. John, **13**: 308n

Murray, Gen. Joseph: in Flanders, **16**: 249

Murray, Maj. Patrick: commandant at Detroit, **17**: 133n, 134n

Murray, William: letter to, **19**: 598; letter from, **20**: 395-7; and Mazzei's agricultural co., **1**: 158; slaves employed at Hoods, **5**: 127; imports slaves, **15**: 655

Murray, William (Eng.). *See* Mansfield, William Murray, Earl of

Murrell, George: signs petition, **6**: 293

Murrell, Samuel: signs petition, **6**: 293

Murril, George: in Albemarle co. militia, **1**: 666

Murril, Samuel: in Albemarle co. militia, **1**: 666

Murry, William (Ky.): appointed federal attorney, **18**: 346n; **19**: 404

muscat grapes, **11**: 444

music: TJ's interest in, **2**: 196, 206; **8**: 569; Hopkinson's comments on, **7**: 19

Musick, Thomas: signs Va. oath of allegiance, **2**: 129

muskets: imported into Va., **3**: 78; purchased in France, **3**: 91; in contract with Penet, Windel & Co., **3**: 132; prices, **3**: 135; supplied to Gen. Gates' army, **3**: 530; for Va. militia, **3**: 576; **4**: 40, 126; manufacture of, **4**: 666; for Va. defense, **5**: 68, 586, 621; to be supplied to Steuben, **6**: 49

muskets with interchangeable parts: sent to Knox, **15**: 422; TJ's interest in, **16**: 316, 317n; TJ orders, **17**: 412, 527; locks delivered by Saint Trys, **17**: 642; improvements in, **18**: 69; mentioned, **8**: 455; **9**: 214; **15**: 423n, 437, 454-5; **17**: 317

Muskingum lands (Ohio): Barlow promotes sale of, **13**: 609, 612n-3n; **16**: 159; **18**: 160-2, 173-6; prospects for, **14**: 303. *See also* Scioto Company

Muskinghum (Muskingham, Muskingum) river: plans for defense of, **3**: 55; attempted settlement on, **6**: 584n; plan of mounds at mouth of, **9**: xxix, xxxi,

419 (fac.), 476, 478; prehistoric remains on, **10**: 584-5; **11**: 290; source, **12**: 489

Muskinghum, Treaty of: provisions of, **19**: 585

muskmelons: inferiority of French, **10**: 228

Musschenbroek (Musschenbroeck), Pieter Van: *Cours de physique experimentale et mathematique*, **6**: 550; **8**: 408; **12**: 18

Muter, George: letters to, **3**: 301-2, 398-9, 487, 488, 514-5, 570, 617, 644-5; **4**: 90-1, 142, 149-50, 202, 280, 306, 313-4, 343, 474, 488-9, 489-90, 519-20, 524, 530, 535, 552-3, 581, 609, 619, 677; **5**: 17, 27, 46, 52-3, 80, 81, 140, 169, 183-4; **15**: 600-1; **19**: 380; letters from, **3**: 504-5, 533, 583, 616-7; **4**: 47-8, 119, 161, 165, 173-4, 179, 201-2, 216, 217-8, 218, 224, 243, 243-4, 314-5, 315-6, 354, 408-10, 416-7, 417-8, 418, 425, 426, 434-5, 438-40, 449, 455-6, 474, 474-5, 479-80, 480-1, 489, 496-7, 518-9, 519, 530, 531, 535, 535-6, 536, 553, 571, 577-8, 578, 581, 582, 591, 601, 601-2, 610, 619, 658, 694; **5**: 12, 13, 26, 26-7, 37-8, 38, 45, 45-6, 52, 53, 65, 78-80, 80, 87, 96-7, 106, 133-4, 139, 139-40, 140, 169, 190-1, 257-8, 315, 605; comments on Josiah Philips, **2**: 192n; regiment, **3**: 377; instructions to, **3**: 439-40; **4**: 348, 420-1, 537; **5**: 147-8; list of prisoners, **3**: 541n; repairs prison, **3**: 614; letter from, to James Kemp, **4**: 3; letter from, to Charles Magill, **4**: 187; repairs cupola, **4**: 202n; letter from, to J.P.G. Muhlenberg and others, **4**: 243-4; correspondence with Rose, **4**: 295n; **6**: 119n; correspondence with William Davies, **4**: 296-7; **5**: 342; equips militia, **4**: 345; letter to, from James Cocke, **4**: 395-6; letter from, to auditors, **4**: 397; letters to, from William Spiller, **4**: 409, 409-10; and Thomas Reynolds' case, **4**: 435; asks payment of salary, **4**: 481; letter from, to Levin Walker, **4**: 490; notes to, **5**: 38, 87, 139-40; asks for inquiry into conduct, **5**: 45-6; states employment conditions, **5**: 127n; defense against Steuben's charges, **5**: 133-4; correspondence with John (Jack) Walker, **5**: 133-4; inventory by (?), **5**: 140n; resignation of, **5**: 204-5, 207-8, 233; letter from,

Muter, George (*cont.*)
to Alexander Dick, cited, **5**: 397; Ky.
chief judge, **8**: 345; commissioner from
Ky., **8**: 659; letter from, to Washington, cited, **19**: 380; uses letter against
Brown, **19**: 471n; mentioned, **3**: 166,
167, 338n, 406, 515; **4**: 9, 26, 47n,
153, 318, 354, 378, 448, 539, 620; **5**:
27n, 208-9, 293n, 607
mutiny: punishment for suggested by
TJ, **5**: 566; against Congress, **6**: 318,
466
mutton: sale to army, **5**: 192
Muy, Chevalier de: letter sent by, **10**:
644
Muy, France: TJ describes, **11**: 431
Myers, Mr.: estate of, **20**: 588
Myers, Moses: letter to, from Plunket,
cited, **16**: 354n
myrtle: wax exported from Va., **7**: 373;
effort to secure berries, **11**: 256; seeds
requested by TJ, **15**: 621, 632

Nagapatnam: kept by Britain, **6**: 387
Nahuys, P. G. (notary), **15**: 258
nailmakers: wages in R.I., **7**: 339
nail rods: scarcity, **4**: 201, 202; need for,
4: 479, 493; purchase, **5**: 281
nails: manufacture, **4**: 224, 566; need for,
4: 479, 493; manufacture in France
suggested, **13**: 393; manufactory in
Waterford, **20**: 441
Nairac (Neriac, Nérac), Edouard, **11**:
457
Nairac, Paul: as deputy for Bordeaux,
15: 293, 296n
Nairne, Edouard: makes magnets for
Franklin, **10**: 646; makes hygrometer,
11: 73; **13**: 396, 459; TJ desires to
meet, **13**: 398; uses air pump, **13**: 460
Nairne & Blunt: hygrometer, **11**: 74, 75,
162; **13**: 37; magnets, **11**: 532; **13**:
395
Naked creek, **2**: 113
Nalle (Nall), Col. William, **6**: 119
name, change of: imprisonment for, **9**:
574, 639, 658-9
Namur: capture of (1695), **3**: 48; mentioned, **18**: 114
Nancarrow (Nancarro), John, **6**: 348
Nancrède, Joseph: professor of French,
12: 492n
Nancy (ship): detention of, **7**: 271, 377n-
8n; seizure of, **11**: 69n; **17**: 420, 421n;
departs Bordeaux, **16**: 95; mentioned,

12: 437, 464; **15**: 494; **20**: 237, 238n
Nancy (slave): taken by British, **6**: 224
Nancy, Aunt. *See* Marks, Anna Scott
Jefferson
Nancy, France: TJ visits, **13**: 26, 28;
mutiny of garrison, **17**: 489-90, 524,
594
Nanjamy creek: ferry, **2**: 454
nankeen cloth: seizure of, **8**: 181-2, 205,
207, 238-9, 242-3
Nanny (slave): taken by British, **6**: 224
Nansemond, Va.: ferry at, **2**: 457
Nansemond co., Va.: letter to county
lieutenant of, **5**: 32; appoints infantry
officers, **1**: 580; place of court of assize,
1: 629; grand jury in, **1**: 638-9; militia, **2**: 131; **3**: 239, 601; **4**: 61, 63; **5**:
29, 47, 181, 311; senatorial district, **2**:
336; levies of soldiers, **3**: 8; speculation
in pork, **3**: 299; tobacco loan office
certificates, **3**: 515; appointment of cattle commissioner for, **3**: 612; supply
post for, **4**: 286
Nansemond Court House, Va.: time of
holding court of assize, **1**: 628; proposed meeting of school overseers at,
2: 529
Nansemond river, **4**: 78, 92; **5**: 12
Nantes, France: Va. arms at, **3**: 106; arrival of Penet at, **3**: 382; Thomas Barclay at, **6**: 421; imports from S.C., **8**:
203; TJ visits, **11**: 458, 516; harbor,
11: 459; American vessels enter, **11**:
488; American agent at, **11**: 669; TJ's
travel hints, **13**: 275; consul in, **14**:
59; information on shipping, **14**: 528;
Spanish ships detained in, **20**: 609
Nantucket, Mass.: and whale fishery, **7**:
342-3; **12**: 398, 404; **19**: 146-7, 152,
155, 156-7, 173n; **20**: 601, 651-2;
whale oil production, **9**: 82; desire for
independence, **9**: 176; emigration
from, **19**: 160-1, 163, 164; discontent
in, **19**: 200-4
Nantucket Road: damage to d'Estaing's
ships in, **2**: 213
Nantucket whalers at Dunkirk ("Les
Nantucois"): and American trade, **13**:
66-7, 196n; British policy toward, **13**:
291; **19**: 201; and the whale fishery,
14: 218, 220-5, 386; examined before
House of Commons, **14**: 227-8; Lafayette's inquiries of Rotch, **14**: 235-6;
TJ's *Observations* on, **14**: 243-4, 250;
18: 545; French observations on, **14**:
257-67; Boston criticism of, **16**: 397-8;

Nelson, John (of York) (*cont.*)
142, 422, 461, 472, 485; **5**: 259, 369;
6: 18, 41; clothing for troops, **3**: 100,
616; **4**: 206; officers in corps of, **3**:
224; corps ordered to York, **3**: 238;
forces under, **3**: 365; **5**: 350, 366;
horses for troops, **3**: 616; **5**: 581;
wishes to join Continental line, **3**: 617;
defense of James river, **4**: 423; mentioned, **2**: 45n
Nelson, Lucy Chiswell (Mrs. William
Nelson): letter to, **2**: 36-7; letter from,
2: 33-4
Nelson, Lucy Grymes (Mrs. Thomas
Nelson, Jr.), **1**: 286, 292; **2**: 33n
Nelson, Thomas: bears documents for
TJ, **19**: 243
Nelson, Thomas, Jr.: letters to, **1**: 292-3,
330n; **4**: 297, 344, 371-2, 372, 382,
419, 449-51, 578-9, 602, 631, 677-8,
687; **5**: 208, 357; **9**: 593; letters from,
1: 37, 285-6; **2**: 3-4; **4**: 54-5, 142,
307, 307-8, 321, 351, 373, 382-3,
426-7, 456, 520-1, 553-4, 650-1, 658-
9; **5**: 631; **15**: 601, 607; signs nonimportation resolutions, **1**: 30, 47; signs
Virginia Association, **1**: 109; and nonimportation agreements, **1**: 110; signs
letter to Va. HB, **1**: 112; supports
American state papers series, **1**: 146;
and Mazzei's agricultural co., **1**: 157-8;
signs agreement of secrecy, **1**: 253; letter to, from Page, **1**: 256; signs Declaration of Independence, **1**: 432; and
Johnson case, **2**: 47n; on committee to
amend inoculation act, **2**: 124n; on
committee on sale of unappropriated
lands, **2**: 135n; votes for as Va. governor in 1779, **2**: 278n; and bill establishing ferries, **2**: 457n; letter to, from
Francy, cited, **3**: 14; plans for battle at
Cape Henry, **4**: 38n; called to command troops on Va. coast, **4**: 58, 60,
61; position of forces under, **4**: 111;
letters from cited, **4**: 150, 151, 398;
defensive measures against British, **4**:
254, 262; militia under, **4**: 260, 263;
5: 638; succeeds TJ as governor, **4**:
260-1, 277; **5**: 686n; **6**: 89n, 96;
warns of British invasion, **4**: 269; commands force opposing invaders, **4**: 274,
275; **5**: 36; letters to, from Wray,
cited, **4**: 289n, 290n, 377; ammunition
for, **4**: 313-4, 315, 318, 319n; letter
from, to Dick, quoted, **4**: 321n; artillery for, **4**: 326; reinforcements for, **4**:

332, 335, 336; **5**: 154-5; sent to repel
British invaders, **4**: 333; letters to
cited, **4**: 338, 339; authorized to call
out militia for defense, **4**: 352; asked to
procure boats, **4**: 384; rum for troops
of, **4**: 413, 416; against attack on British at Portsmouth, **4**: 422; defense of
James river, **4**: 423; letter from, to
Syme, cited, **4**: 458; prevents Capt.
Joel from using *Dragon*, **4**: 569-70,
608-9; and British prisoners, **4**: 594;
correspondence with Steuben, **4**: 651n;
5: 687-8; **6**: 620n; illness of, **4**: 661n,
675, 678; **5**: 107n; letter to, from
Sans, **4**: 678-9; meets with Va. legislature, **5**: 15; called to oppose invasion
of Va., **5**: 35; obtains laborers for
York, **5**: 89; Steuben's plan for operations of, **5**: 479-80; offers pardons, **5**:
515n; suggests removing horses from
path of British, **5**: 656n; note from, to
Davies, **5**: 662n; transmits Hare papers
to TJ, **5**: 680n; letter to, from Mrs.
Byrd, **5**: 703-4; directs impressment of
horses, **6**: 52; letter to, from Gen.
Morgan, quoted, **6**: 71n-2n; evaluation
of governorship, **6**: 78n; letter from, to
G. R. Clark, quoted, **6**: 86n; asked to
assemble county lieutenants, **6**: 107-8;
Nicholas' query about, **6**: 108; resigns
as governor of Va., **6**: 137n; and evacuation of College of William and Mary,
6: 144; and new colony on Ohio, **6**:
176; on cession of western territory, **6**:
266; gives pass to Turpin, **6**: 326; declines appointment as commissioner on
Conn.-Pa. dispute, **6**: 478n; letter to,
from Lafayette, cited, **6**: 623n; marriages of son and brother, **9**: 66;
elected to Va. GA, **9**: 518; appointment as Va. delegate to Federal Convention, **11**: 219, 310, 312; copy of
Notes on Virginia sent to, **12**: 130; opposes Constitution, **12**: 284, 410, 423,
425; death of, **15**: 78, 85, 106; discharge of TJ's debt to, **18**: 493; mentioned, **1**: 15, 16, 18, 256, 261, 270,
291n, 294, 455, 469, 485; **2**: 33n; **3**:
247-8, 475, 668; **4**: 10, 62, 78, 125,
163, 312, 316, 317, 322, 331, 337,
347, 357, 385, 399, 412, 429n, 452,
498, 504, 508, 624, 631n, 640, 660,
669, 670, 691, 699; **5**: 267, 282, 637,
658-9, 681n, 695; **6**: 77n, 124, 330n,
331n, 387n, 634; **15**: 611
Nelson, Thomas, Sr. (the Secretary): let-

ter from, **1**: 37; letter sent by, **1**: 14; marriage of son, **2**: 34n

Nelson, W.: price of seal paid to, **16**: 308; books received from, **19**: 581

Nelson, William (brother of Thomas Nelson): letters from, **3**: 85, 166-7, 171, 173, 174, 175, 182-3, 187-90, 191, 195, 199, 209-10, 215, 221, 223, 224, 229, 236, 238-40; appointed commander of Va. artillery regiment, **2**: 33, 36-7; marries Lucy Chiswell, **2**: 34n; appointed to Va. Board of War, **3**: 58n; report on magazines, **3**: 174; on cession of western territory, **6**: 266; letter from, to Lord Hillsborough, cited, **6**: 647n, 648n-9n, 664; retires from Va. Executive Council, **8**: 345; correspondence with Short quoted, **10**: 3n, 245n; **11**: 171n-2n; **20**: 266n-7n; letter to quoted, **10**: 416n; opposes Constitution, **12**: 284; mentioned, **7**: 273. *See also* Virginia: Board of War

Nelson, William, Jr. (son of Thomas Nelson): letter to, **19**: 631-2; letter from, **18**: 56-60; on committee to revise Va. laws, **2**: 324n; **20**: 303; Heth's probable consultation with, **16**: 565; Va. laws on British subjects sent by, **18**: 56-60; signs testimonial to Tatham map, **19**: 265n

Nelson's Ferry, **5**: 116

Nemers, M. (gardener). *See* Nesmer, M.

Nemo, David: signs Va. oath of allegiance, **2**: 129

Nenoctuckie co., Va: Tatham's map of, **19**: 265n

neo-classicism: in architecture, **15**: xxvii; in silver, **15**: xxix

Nepean, Evan: Vaughan sends TJ's letter to, **16**: 580n

Neptune (ship): seized at Port-au-Prince, **11**: 192n; mentioned, **15**: 263, 666

Nérac, M. (wine merchant). *See* Nairac, Edouard

Nérac, Paul. *See* Nairac, Paul

Neronha, Diego, Conde de: recommended for membership in American Philosophical Society, **20**: 476

Nervi, Italy: oranges grown at, **11**: 441; Short visits, **11**: 441; **14**: 705; TJ's travel hints, **13**: 270

Nesbitt, Jonathan: letters to, **14**: 527-8, 637; letters from, **13**: 561-2; **14**: 577; in tobacco trade, **13**: 562; letters carried by, **14**: 288, 527, 536-7, 644; let-

ter from sent to TJ by Le Couteulx & Cie., **14**: 368; letter to, from Amoureux, cited, **14**: 520; appeal to Villedeuil, **14**: 527, 536-7, 575; arrested in France, **14**: 527n-8n, 637n; Morris' efforts to obtain release, **14**: 527n-8n, 637n; Fourth of July tribute to TJ not signed by, **14**: 532n; **15**: 240n; creditors, **14**: 555n; safe conduct for, **14**: 577, 584, 648-9; remains in Paris, **14**: 658

Nesmer (Nemer, Nesmes), M. (gardener): olives for S.C. sent by, **13**: 249; **15**: 43; letter sent by, **14**: 635

Netherlands: revolt against Spain, **1**: 312; attitude toward American Revolution, **1**: 498; **3**: 76, 118-9, 202; loan to U.S., **2**: 27; **3**: 92; **6**: 128, 212n; **7**: 63, 65, 227, 496-7; **8**: 541, 630; **9**: 359, 635-6; **10**: 24; **11**: 5, 575, 631, 633-4, 663-4; **12**: 55, 154, 341-2, 396, 413, 456-8, 543-9, 566, 581-2, 611, 623-4, 637, 661, 671-2, 698-9; **13**: 102, 126-31, 133-4, 136n-7n, 168, 192, 230, 302, 569, 575, 612n-4n, 630, 631n, 633, 657; **14**: 5, 12, 56, 191, 215, 284-5, 433n, 464, 475-6, 581-2, 586-7, 609-11, 644-5, 656-7, 680-1; **15**: 125; **20**: 119-21, 144, 343, 349-50, 557, 619; relations with Britain, **3**: 30, 374; **5**: 551; **6**: 338; **7**: 350; **8**: 167; **11**: 245n; **12**: 681; **13**: 125, 191, 298, 455, 458; **17**: 594; **18**: 293, 477, 502-3; **19**: 637; as market for tobacco, **3**: 92; **7**: 369, 370; joins League of Armed Neutrality, **4**: 161, 222; merchant ships, **5**: 125, 170; war against British, **5**: 176, 177, 193; States General of, **5**: 266; Mazzei comments on, **5**: 375-8; defeat in West Indies, **5**: 376-7; U.S. treaty of amity and commerce, **6**: 227; **7**: 305, 308-9, 473-5, 495-6, 638; **8**: 521, 605, 608; **9**: 188; relations with France, **6**: 275; **9**: 92, 95, 235, 436n-7n; **11**: 13n, 245n, 660; **12**: 310, 315, 362, 482, 564, 675-6; **13**: 125, 465; **14**: 565, 646, 653, 662, 672; **15**: 366; relations with U.S., **6**: 334, 396; **12**: 189, 257; pressure of citizens for constitutional rights, **6**: 431-2, 433, 438; disorder in, **6**: 438; settlements in North America, **6**: 489-90, 491, 496; rejects U.S. bills, **7**: 53; relations with Austria, **7**: 60, 501, 506, 609; **8**: 79, 119, 149, 206, 226, 228, 236, 261, 280, 287, 300,

New Hampshire (*cont.*)
6: 131, 147; 7: 4-5; vote on permanent seat for Congress, 6: 365; remonstrance of legislature in case of *Lusanna*, 6: 447; Court of Judicature, 6: 449; sovereignty, 6: 450, 454n; claim to Vt., 6: 505; financial quota to national treasury, 7: 5, 55, 71; 10: 34, 35, 54-6; attitude on Society of the Cincinnati, 7: 109n; value of pound, 7: 178; government, 7: 343; 10: 314; commerce, 7: 343-7, 349; replies to TJ's queries, 7: 343-7; information on promised Hogendorp, 7: 545; delegates in Congress, 7: 572; 9: 504; navigation act, 9: 15, 43, 110, 143, 182, 314; 10: 178, 293, 301; economic conditions, 9: 314; votes power over commerce to Congress, 9: 666; constitution, 10: 12; public debt, 10: 12; area, 10: 34; does not emit paper money, 10: 232; sends delegates to Annapolis convention, 10: 232; popular disturbances in, 10: 633; Démeunier's interest in, 11: 24; delegates to Federal Convention, 11: 154, 219, 401; attitude on Mississippi navigation, 11: 309; ratification of Constitution, 12: 280, 409, 609; 13: 39, 50, 100-1, 156, 160, 205, 209, 232, 239, 248, 354n, 359, 370, 401, 413, 434, 436, 438, 440, 506, 542; whale fishery, 14: 227; elects senators, 14: 339, 394, 525, 529; 15: 418; electoral votes for Adams, 14: 559; 15: 92; electoral votes for Washington, 15: 92; laws sent to TJ, 17: 607-8; 19: 632; tonnage act, 18: 535, 537; ratification of constitutional amendments, 18: 595; exports, 19: 136-8, 139
New-Hampshire Gazette, 17: 509n
New Haven, Conn.: plundered by British, 3: 31, 33, 34; and fisheries, 7: 334; in *Encyclopédie Méthodique*, 10: 36; honorary citizenship for friends of Crèvecoeur, 13: 547n
New Haven colony: union with Conn., 6: 489
New Haven Gazette: criticizes Adams, 20: 307n-8n
New Holland: French wish to colonize, 8: 588, 593
New Jersey: population of, 1: 182; 10: 34, 35, 54-6; and independence, 1: 310, 313, 314; votes against Chase's

taxation plan, 1: 323; constitution of, 1: 333n; quota of troops, 1: 467-8; military operations in, 1: 659; 2: 201; 3: 424-5, 437; 441, 461, 474, 490; war effort in, 2: 3; Loyalists in, 2: 13; delay in ratifying Articles of Confederation, 2: 205, 208; approves act of Congress emitting new currency, 3: 528, 531; militia, 4: 55; and Continental requisitions of food, 4: 107; acts of assembly sent to Va., 4: 241; quota for army pay, 4: 369; troops mutiny, 4: 484; asked to aid in protecting Delaware bay, 5: 551; and revaluation of Continental currency, 5: 608-9; delegates in Congress, 6: 3, 461n; 7: 572; and western lands, 6: 131, 147, 575n; 7: 4-5; adoption of impost, 6: 334; and permanent seat for Congress, 7: 347n, 352, 366; financial quota to national treasury, 7: 5, 55, 70-1; 10: 34, 35, 54-6; and Society of the Cincinnati, 7: 109n; vote on meeting place of Congress, 7: 118; vote on slavery in western territory, 7: 118; hires horse teams, 7: 126, 127, 128, 138; value of pound, 7: 178; currency, 7: 200; troops for western posts, 7: 412; duties on foreign goods, 8: 581; free ports, 9: 334; votes power over commerce to Congress, 9: 666; geography of, 10: 37; and paper money, 10: 231; sends delegates to Annapolis convention, 10: 232; flour mills, 10: 262; wheels with single-piece circumference made by farmers in, 11: 43-4; attitude toward Mississippi navigation, 11: 154, 202, 221; delegates to Federal Convention, 11: 154, 400; ratification of Constitution, 12: 281, 409, 425, 443, 490, 608; 13: 100-1, 205, 370; elects senators, 14: 339, 394, 529; electoral votes (1789), 15: 92; laws sent to TJ, 18: 151; legislative act on Sandy Hook, 18: 476; ratification of constitutional amendments, 18: 595; exports, 19: 136-8, 139
New Jersey, College of: president of, 2: 249n; solicits funds in Europe, 7: 399n; honorary degree given to Shippen, 14: 473-4; J. Brown student at, 19: xxxiv
New-Jersey Journal, 17: 509n
New Kent co., Va.: letter to commissioner of provisions for, 3: 569; letters

of, **3**: 659; **4**: 383; letter to Assembly of, **5**: 53-4; letter from Board of War of, **4**: 322; letter from Assembly of, **4**: 610-1; population of, **1**: 182; **10**: 34, 35, 39, 54-6; affirmative vote for independence, **1**: 314; votes for Chase's taxation plan, **1**: 323; John Adams' advice on constitution, **1**: 333n; supplies for Continental army, **1**: 462; **4**: 184, 323; boundary with Va., **3**: 13-4, 20, 488, 490; **6**: 662, 666; European attitude toward, **3**: 93; relations with Cherokees, **3**: 175, 179-80; **5**: 234, 236; cooperation with Va. for defense, **3**: 239, 240; sends troops to S.C., **3**: 343; British propaganda in, **3**: 397; militia, **3**: 401, 563, 593; **5**: 138, 156, 298, 595-6; British invasion of feared, **3**: 403, 437; military supplies for, **3**: 426, 433, 524-5, 589; troops sent south, **3**: 433; ravaged by British, **3**: 462; **4**: 579; defenses, **3**: 463; powers of governor, **3**: 466; disaffection in, **3**: 585; **4**: 503, 582, 590; **5**: 111; reinforcements for, **3**: 589; quota of troops and provisions, **3**: 640n; Continental requisitions of food, **4**: 107; distress of inhabitants, **4**: 132; military situation, **4**: 150; called upon for Convention army provisions, **4**: 370; aid from Va., **4**: 470; **5**: 398, 421; and southern army, **5**: 77; danger to Va. from subjugation of, **5**: 541; recovery from British, **6**: 118; land office in, **6**: 245; constitution, **6**: 310; and presidency of Congress, **6**: 348, 349; vote on permanent seat for Congress, **6**: 366; cession of western territory, **6**: 547, 591n, 593n; **7**: 273, 630; **8**: 218, 483, 508; **17**: 292n-3n; **19**: 605-6; **20**: 639, 681; boundary with proposed northwest colonies, **6**: 601; founding, **6**: 658; financial quota to national treasury, **7**: 5, 55, 71, 114; **10**: 34, 35, 54-6; eastern land, **7**: 46; attitude toward Society of the Cincinnati, **7**: 110n; vote on slavery in western territory, **7**: 118; value of pound, **7**: 178; value of dollar in relation to pound, **7**: 184; currency, **7**: 200; and impost, **7**: 226, 232, 273; credentials of delegates in Congress, **7**: 272-3; exports, **7**: 372; **10**: 39; **11**: 541; **19**: 136-8; speculation in western lands, **7**: 503-4; Va. asks concurrence in building canal, **8**: 3; land south of the Ohio, **8**: 124; Congress contem-

plates sending committee to, **8**: 219; and state of Franklin, **8**: 280, 659; **9**: 186; boundaries, **8**: 520; **10**: 39; commercial rivalry with Va., **8**: 556; and abolition of slavery, **8**: 667; **10**: 18; article on in *Encyclopédie Méthodique*, **9**: 155; **10**: 39; negotiations on Dismal Swamp canal, **9**: 201; law concerning foreign debts, **9**: 504-5; protests Congress' interference in Indian affairs, **9**: 641; Indian tribes, **9**: 641-2; paper money, **10**: 26, 231; attitude toward Annapolis convention, **10**: 233; calls for constitutional convention, **11**: 201; delegates to Federal Convention, **11**: 154, 241, 401; attitude toward Mississippi navigation, **11**: 202, 221; ratification of Constitution, **12**: 254, 281, 412, 443-4, 609; **13**: 101, 160, 205, 209, 248, 331, 359, 370, 413, 436n, 495, 496, 498, 502, 506, 523, 609, 642, 644-5, 659-61; **14**: 48, 301, 385, 525, 615, 688; **15**: 17, 105-6; **16**: 26; refuses to vote on location of Congress, **13**: 540; and amendments to Constitution, **14**: 48; **18**: 595; duties on imports and exports, **15**: 276; recommendations for federal offices, **16**: 476-8; and treaty of Hopewell, **17**: 430-1; laws of sent to TJ, **18**: 137-9; and U.S. commercial policy, **19**: 129, 130; requests bust of Jones, **19**: 591; laws of sought by TJ, **20**: 92

northern lights. *See* aurora borealis

Northern Neck, Va.: titles to lands in, **2**: 657; question of adding to Md., **6**: 546; grant of, **6**: 658-9; jurisdiction over, **7**: 36; act to extend operation of escheat law to, **9**: 200; disposal of waste land, **9**: 201

North Fork of the James river, **6**: 634

North Hampton (vessel): compromise with recaptors of, **3**: 517n

North Hero Island: blockhouse on, **20**: 466

North Holston river: prehistoric bones found on, **7**: 305

North Mountain, Va.: post service to, **2**: 389; mentioned, **2**: 113, 114

North river. *See* Hudson river

North river, Va., **2**: 113; **6**: 48

North Sea: discomforts of crossing, **8**: 435

Northumberland co., Va.: letter to county lieutenant of, **6**: 34-5; place of

Northumberland co., Va. (*cont.*)
court of assize, **1:** 629; militia, **2:** 131;
3: 600; **4:** 63, 376-7; **5:** 311; senatorial
district, **2:** 336; British raid on, **3:** 5;
levies of soldiers, **3:** 7; tobacco loan office certificates, **3:** 516; small quantity
of grain in, **3:** 566; supply post for, **4:**
286; draft riots in, **4:** 693; discontent
in, **5:** 165; draft, **5:** 430; mentioned, **5:**
434
Northumberland Court House, Va.: place
of court of assize, **7:** 588
North West Bridge: arms for militia at,
4: 570, 643
northwest colonies: proposed bounds of,
6: 600-2
North West Landing, Va.: defense of, **3:**
239
Northwest Ordinance of 1784, **6:** 581-
617; **18:** 162-5
Northwest Ordinance of 1787: territory
covered, **6:** 582n; discussed, **18:** 162-6
Northwest Territory: importance of Vincennes expedition, **2:** 246; size of states
in, **6:** 578; application of Ordinance of
1784 to, **6:** 582n; boundaries according to TJ's plan, **6:** xxxv, 582n, 588
(illus.), 590 (illus.); committee to draw
plans for Indian trade and government
in, **6:** 584n-5n; and act on Southwest
Territory, **17:** 292n; and Hamtramck's
report on navigability of rivers, **17:**
448-9; promotion of settlement in, **18:**
159-62; editorial note and documents,
18: 159-218; French emigrants in, **18:**
162, 173-4, 176, 204, 206n; trade and
trade routes, **18:** 199-201; population
of (1790), **18:** 217-8
Norton, Mr.: debt to John Paradise, **13:**
544; **15:** 10; **16:** 84
Norton, Mrs.: death of, **16:** 25
Norton, John H.: signs nonimportation
resolutions (1770), **1:** 47; mentioned,
6: 121n
Norval, Thomas: signs petition, **1:** 588
Norvell, William: votes for bill for religious freedom, **2:** 549n
Norvil, Spencer: signs Va. oath of allegiance, **2:** 129
Norvill, George: signs Va. oath of allegiance, **2:** 128
Norwalk, Conn.: burned by British, **3:**
31
Norway: tobacco imports from Va., **7:**
370; American medals sent to, **16:** 67;

and the fisheries, **19:** 180. *See also*
Denmark
Nostra Senhora de Carmo è Santo Antonio
(Portuguese vessel): captured by
American privateer, **3:** 57, 184-6, 197-
8, 249
"Notes on Coinage": date, **7:** 157n; text,
7: 175-85
Notes on the State of Virginia: account of
revisal of Va. laws, **2:** 307n, 314n-5n,
321n; genesis of, **5:** 58-9; printing of,
7: 282, 563; **8:** 147, 295; **10:** 323n,
325; **11:** 38-9, 45, 107-8, 143, 183,
577, 588; **12:** 73; Hopkinson's copy,
7: 535; **8:** 263, 562, 566; **12:** 144;
Hogendorp's copy, **7:** 546; **8:** 324,
502; inscription in Price's copy, **8:**
xxviii, 246 (fac.); Monroe's copy, **8:**
147, 229, 245; Madison's copy, **8:**
147; **12:** 136; TJ invites comments
on, **8:** 147-8, 462; Adams' opinion on,
8: 160, 164; Fabbroni's copy, **8:** 161;
Otto's comments on, **8:** 169-70; ex-
tracted in *Journal de Physique*, **8:** 174,
184; Chastellux' comments on, **8:** 174-
5; Buffon's copy, **8:** 184; Daubenton's
copy, **8:** 184; Thomson's copy, **8:** 229,
245, 295; **9:** 9; Price's copy, **8:** 258;
compared to Bacon's work, **8:** 260;
Rittenhouse's copy, **8:** 263, 562, 566;
9: 216; **12:** 144; French translation of,
8: 270n; **9:** 133, 244, 264-5, 299,
444; **10:** 181-2, 243, 350, 570-1; **12:**
426, 641; praised by Rochambeau, **8:**
358; Hogendorp's comments on, **8:**
502-3, 631-2; **10:** 190; for students of
William and Mary, **9:** 38, 194; **10:**
644; **11:** 657; Madison's comments on,
9: 38, 517; Hopkinson's comments on,
9: 132; Wythe's copy, **9:** 165, 277;
Monroe's comment on, **9:** 190; Dumas'
copy, **9:** 230, 384; Dumas' comments
on, **9:** 243-4, 279; **10:** 504-5; **12:** 326;
Williamos' copy, **9:** 265, 267n; Staphorsts' copy, **9:** 275, 312, 635; Jodrell's copy, **9:** 277; **10:** 243; **11:** 186;
Favi's copy, **9:** 280; map for, **9:** 299-
300, 363; **10:** 226; **11:** 364; **12:** 175;
17: 445n; unauthorized publication, **9:**
299; Hopkinson requests copies for
Philosophical Society and Philadelphia
library, **9:** 320; Rev. James Madison's
comments on, **9:** 357; **14:** 534; Ramsay's comments on, **9:** 441; Page's
copy, **9:** 444-5; **12:** 650; copy re-

quested by de Riario, **9**: 645; used for article in *Encyclopédie Méthodique*, **10**: 9n, 11n; Currie's copy, **10**: 108; Pinto's copy, **10**: 129-30, 140; possibly sent to Mme de Tott, **10**: 160n; copy promised to Philosophical Society, **10**: 249, 250n; Lafayette's comments on, **10**: 312; Carmichael's copy, **10**: 429, 633; **12**: 187n, 240; Rutledge's comments on, **10**: 464; **12**: 264; Brissot de Warville's comments on, **10**: 515; Stockdale wishes to publish, **10**: 545; Crèvecoeur's copy, **10**: 591; **11**: 294, 350; Wythe's praise of, **10**: 593; Campomane's copy, **10**: 633; **12**: 187n, 365; demand for, **10**: 634n-5n; section on shells cited, **10**: 643; TJ's errata for Morellet's translation, **11**: 37; Vaughan's comments on, **11**: 69-72; Maria Cosway's comments on, **11**: 149; extract in *American Museum*, **11**: 290; ordered in London by Richard Claiborne, **11**: 468; publication of in American newspapers, **11**: 473; reviewed in *Mercure de France*, **11**: 509; copy sent to Edinburgh Society for Encouragement of Natural History, **11**: 558; Cathalan's copy, **11**: 606; Moustier requests copy, **11**: 622; copies for College of Philadelphia, **11**: 657; Rev. James Madison's copy, **12**: 31; copies sent to U.S., **12**: 35, 115-6; Clerici's copy, **12**: 39, 555; Verme's copy, **12**: 42, 588; Paine's copy, **12**: 45; sent to Boutin, **12**: 120; copies sent to Va., **12**: 130; copies sent to Donald for distribution, **12**: 133; copies sent by Stockdale, **12**: 227; Warner Lewis' copy, **12**: 427; American edition, **12**: 428, 595; inquiry as to sales in England, **12**: 488; Kinloch's copy, **12**: 570; extract printed in *Mercure de France*, **12**: 668n; La Blancherie's copy, **12**: 690; **13**: 112, 116, 117; Price praises, **13**: 120; sale in Paris prohibited, **13**: 367; Stockdale on sales of, **13**: 518; describes mammoth and moose, **13**: 594; sent to Cayla, **13**: 628, 643; *Encyclopaedia Britannica* quotes, **14**: 412n; Rutledge praises, **15**: 11; Kinloch's comments on, **15**: 71-2; **18**: 80; sent to Bayard de La Vingtrie, **15**: 514; Lormerie praises, **16**: 434; on weights and measures, **16**: 610n, 618-4; plan for distribution of,

16: 616; on lead mines, **17**: 24n; Churchman cites, **18**: 61; Webster's use of, **18**: 133n-4n; TJ corrects on Natural Bridge, **19**: xxxi; remarks on capital area, **19**: 58; interest in preserving state papers, **19**: 288n; Morgan's comments on, **20**: 422; Carey's comments on, **20**: 596; mentioned, **8**: 16; **13**: 363; **16**: 187n, 323; **18**: 384n

Notice sur la vie de M. le Poivre, **14**: 708

Notre Dame, Cathedral of: Te deum at, **8**: 68

Notre Dame d'Aspoets: TJ comments on, **11**: 451

Notre Dame de la Garde, Chateau de: TJ visits, **11**: 429

Notten, Peter and Charles van, & Co.: bill of exchange on, **10**: 185

Nottingham, Heneage Finch, Earl of: as Chancellor of England, **9**: 69

Nottoway Indians: vocabulary of, **6**: 431

Nottoway river: post service on, **2**: 389; ferries across, **2**: 460; mentioned, **5**: 614

Nourse, Joseph: letters to, **9**: 272; **18**: 150-1; debt to Barbé de Marbois, **14**: 37; letter to, from Peters, cited, **16**: 538, 540; and Ohio Company, **18**: 174n; in Glaubeck case, **18**: 686n-7n; abstract of British fishery imports, **19**: 225; mentioned, **9**: 225, 471; **16**: 494n

Nouvelles de la République des Lettres et des Arts: Adams ends subscription to, **12**: 99

Novara, Italy: TJ describes, **11**: 436; rice culture, **14**: 42-3

Nova Scotia: and Articles of Confederation, **1**: 179; **6**: 121; **10**: 27-8; danger from continued warfare, **2**: 215; negotiations regarding boundaries, **6**: 169, 457, 458; slaves sent to, **6**: 430n-1; fisheries, **6**: 459; **7**: 344; **19**: 174, 193; encroachments on Mass., **6**: 511; **19**: 128-9; export carriage, **7**: 468n; U.S. relations with, **9**: 44; Franklin's land grant in, **9**: 488; inhabitants correctly called Anglo-Americans, **10**: 262; possible settlement of Nantucket whale fishermen on, **12**: 398, 404; famine threatened, **15**: 104

Novi: TJ visits, **11**: 440

Nugent, Thomas, **3**: 542n

Nukeham, John: signs Va. oath of allegiance, **2**: 129

Odds, Capt. (master of *Young Mary*), **15:** 547

Odell, Rev. Jonathan: uses pseudonym "Osborne," **17:** 41

Oder river: Spain's attitude toward navigation on, **7:** 404; trade on, **7:** 405

Odin (slave), **7:** 356

Odiot, Jean Baptiste Claude: makes silver coffee urn from TJ's design, **15:** xxvii-ix, 280 (illus.); makes silver goblets from TJ's design, **15:** xxxiv, 281 (illus.)

odometer: pendulum, **11:** 437; triangular, **12:** 597; ordered for TJ, **12:** 629; TJ finds too expensive, **13:** 178; TJ's inquiry about, with drawing, **13:** 398; Vaughan on, **13:** 460

O'Fallon, James: letter from, to Miró, quoted, **17:** 124n; agent for S.C. Yazoo Company, **17:** 124n-5n; proclamation by President against, **19:** xxxiii, 348 (illus.); intrigues against Spain, **19:** xxxiii, 273n-4n, 484, 514n, 598; decision not to prosecute, **20:** 395-7; plan for black settlement in Ky., **20:** 554n-5n

officials, public: TJ's notes on right of removal, **4:** 281-2; disadvantages suffered by, **9:** 215, 239, 450; TJ's objections to life tenure, **12:** 356

Ogden, James: trial and execution, **11:** 493n

Ogden (Ogdon), Samuel: proposal on contract for salt beef, **15:** 362; agent for Robert Morris, **20:** 126

Ogilby, John: *America*, **6:** 489; **13:** 179

Ogilvie (Ogilvy), James: letter to, **1:** 62-4; letters from, **1:** 38, 67-8; TJ recommends for ordination, **1:** 48-51, 61-2,; TJ's kindness to, **1:** 75; TJ offers to pay debt of, **2:** 199; letter from cited, **11:** 209; seeds to be sent by, **11:** 233, 246; plants forwarded by, **11:** 268

Ogilvie, John: letter from, **1:** 75-6

Ogle, William: *Accounts of William Ogle, Esq., Superintendent of the Newry Canals*, **20:** 474

Oglesby, Jacob: signs Va. oath of allegiance, **2:** 129

Oglethorpe, Elizabeth Wright (Mrs. James Edward Oglethorpe): right to inheritance of husband's estate, **9:** 108-10

Oglethorpe, Gen. James Edward: TJ's opinion on inheritance of, **9:** 108-10,

120-2, 127, 143, 144; estate of, **9:** 120-2, 181; **10:** 280-1, 640, 641n; **11:** 236; ownership of Ga. land questioned, **9:** 259; journey to America, **12:** 402; "Maynard" letters, **18:** 312n

Ogny, Claude François Marie Rigoley, Baron d': letter to, **11:** 334-5; letters from cited, **11:** 492; **16:** 305n; letters to, from Moustier, cited, **13:** 504; plans for packet boats, **14:** 309n-10n; **16:** 304; letter to cited, **16:** 305n

O'Hara, Charles: at Guilford Court House, **5:** 183; fortifies Gibraltar, **17:** 25

O'Hara, Capt. James: infantry company under, **3:** 154; drafts drawn by, **3:** 158, 159; Continental troops under, **3:** 204, 244

Ohio co., Va.: letter to county lieutenant of, **4:** 232; place of court of assize, **1:** 630; militia, **2:** 131; **3:** 420; **4:** 234, 235; **5:** 311; **6:** 40; land commissioners for, **2:** 165n; senatorial district, **2:** 336; recruits from, **3:** 3-4; levies of soldiers from, **3:** 6-7, 8; defends western frontier, **3:** 50, 51, 53; claimed by both Va. and Pa., **3:** 206, 288; unpatented land in, **4:** 454; land in purchased by J. B. Huron, **9:** 49

Ohio Company: George Mason a member of, **2:** 64n; and Transylvania land claims, **2:** 65n, 66n; right to western land, **6:** 647n; petition for land grant, **6:** 661; description of, **18:** 165; shareholders in government office, **18:** 174n; mentioned, **2:** 136n, 138n; **18:** 173, 176; **20:** 128. *See also* Scioto Company

Ohio Indians: aid to Cherokees, **1:** 508; lands of, **2:** 76

Ohio river: forts and garrisons on, **1:** 461, 467n; **4:** 31; Shawnee lands on east side of, **2:** 81; southeast side of, **2:** 91; settlements on or near, **2:** 102; as Va. boundary, **2:** 142, 148n; **6:** 578, 601; land to northwest of, **2:** 150n; plan for regimenting and stationing western battalion on, **3:** 54; defense of settlements on, **3:** 447-9; counties on, **3:** 665; land on ceded by Va., **4:** 387; fossil bones found near, **6:** 208; **7:** 312, 317; **9:** 476-8; floods, **6:** 536; navigation of, **6:** 548; **7:** 16, 26, 49-50, 558; **8:** 130; **14:** 547; proposed tax to open, **6:** 567; TJ's scheme for six states on,

mentioned, **1**: 35; **2**: 278, 279; **7**: 515; **8**: 419; **9**: 446

Page, John: letters to, **1**: 3-12, 13-4, 14-5, 17-8, 18-21, 34-7, 250-1, 270-1, 293-4, 482-4, 485-7, 497-501; **2**: 279; **3**: 485-6; **5**: 491-2; **7**: 514-5; **8**: 417-9; **9**: 444-6, 593; **15**: 593-4; letters from, **1**: 38, 41, 256-9, 264-6, 287, 288-90, 454-5, 461-2, 468-70; **2**: 210, 278; **3**: 66, 309, 349, 575-6, 655-6; **4**: 52-3, 191-3, 497; **5**: 436; **8**: 34, 116-20, 428-31; **12**: 650-4; portrait of by John Wollaston, **1**: lvii, 119 (illus.); courtship of Frances Burwell, **1**: 16; signs nonimportation resolutions (1770), **1**: 47; and Mazzei's agricultural co., **1**: 157-8; letter from cited, **1**: 292; rough draft of Declaration of Independence probably sent to, **1**: 415n; elected to Va. Executive Council, **1**: 455n; health of, **1**: 604; and bill pardoning Loyalists, **2**: 179n; and special revenue bill, **2**: 188n; observations of solar eclipse, **2**: 205, 210; votes for as governor of Va., **2**: 278n; member of committee on sale of alien property, **2**: 283n; votes against bill for religious freedom, **2**: 549n; replies to Board of War, **3**: 58, 308n; letter from, to Va. Board of Trade, quoted, **3**: 307n; resigns from Va. Executive Council, **3**: 349; declines to consider Va. governorship, **3**: 656; **4**: 53; commissioner to determine Va.-Pa. boundary, **7**: 236; **8**: 117; letter from, to Bancroft, quoted, **8**: 93; delegate to Episcopal convention, **8**: 343, 428; books sent to, **8**: 575; **12**: 130; marriage of daughter, **9**: 66; fails in election to Va. GA, **11**: 631; copy of *Notes on Virginia* sent to, **12**: 130; supports Constitution, **12**: 410, 650-2; **13**: 98; congressman from Va., **15**: 5, 74, 78; federalism of, **15**: 5; letter from, to Mazzei, cited, **15**: 195; death of wife, **15**: 635; remarriage, **16**: 319, 351; **17**: 547; in residence bill controversy, **17**: 173, 175-8, 182, 200-1; letter to, from Upshaw, cited, **17**: 291; mentioned, **1**: 21; **3**: 201; **4**: 426; **5**: 605; **6**: 387n; **11**: 193

Page, John, Sr.: involved in scheme to purchase land from Cherokees, **2**: 69, 82

Page, Lewis Little. *See* Littlepage, Lewis

Page, Mann: letter to, **6**: 358; letters from, **5**: 321, 640-3; **15**: 604-5; and Mazzei's agricultural co., **1**: 158; letter to, from James Innes, **3**: 121-3; letter from, to Muter, quoted, **5**: 134n; opposes motion to appoint Va. dictator, **6**: 85n; on cession of western territory, **6**: 266; estate of, **8**: 34; elected to Va. GA, **9**: 518; supports Constitution, **12**: 281; **13**: 98; horse appropriated by Gen. Greene, **15**: 604; nominated for U.S. senator, **17**: 607; letter from, to Monroe, cited, **18**: 219; letter from quoted, **18**: 219n; letters from cited, **18**: 509; mentioned, **4**: 52; **6**: 387n; **18**: 514

Page, Mann, Jr.: signs Virginia Association, **1**: 108; signs nonimportation agreements, **1**: 110; signs letter to HB, **1**: 111; signs agreement of secrecy, **1**: 253

Pagès, Pierre François Marie, Vicomte de: *Voyages autour du Monde*, **8**: 411

Page, Robert: signs petition, **6**: 294

Page, Maj. Robert Carter: Weedon asks commission for, **5**: 108, 122

Page-Turner, Sir Gregory: letter from cited, **18**: 227n

Paimboeuf (Point Boeuf), France: vessels of eight foot draught at, **11**: 459

Paine, Ephraim: member of committee to report on letters of commissioners in Europe, **6**: 401n

Paine, Robert Treat: signs Continental Association, **1**: 153; signs Congress' second petition, **1**: 222; signs agreement of secrecy, **1**: 253; debate in Congress on taxation, **1**: 322; on committee respecting Canada, **1**: 391n, 404n; signs Declaration of Independence, **1**: 432; on committee to draw up rules for Congress, **1**: 457n; on committee on treaties, **7**: 204n

Paine, Thomas: letters to, **13**: 307; **14**: 372-7, 671-3; **15**: 136-7, 266-70, 273, 279, 302, 522; **20**: 308-10, 312-3; letters from, **12**: 45, 610; **13**: 4-8, 222-8, 254, 587-93; **14**: 363-4, 453-5, 561-9; **15**: 193-4, 197-9, 274-5, 429-30, 449; **17**: 533-4; *Common Sense*, **1**: 284n, 286n; **20**: 277n; *Public Good*, **6**: 572n, 652n, 667n; remuneration for, **7**: 289, 361, 558; pamphlet on paper money cited, **11**: 112-6; packet sent by, **11**: 294; and iron bridge, **11**: 302, 533, 657; **12**: 45, 610; **13**: 254, 487, 588-

Paine, Thomas (*cont.*)
9, 591-2; **14**: 353n, 363, 373-4, 454,
561-4, 566, 698; **15**: 137, 193-4, 274,
427, 429-30, 449; **16**: 428, 532n; **17**:
516; letters sent by, **11**: 407; **12**: 65,
69n; relations with Moustier, **11**: 621,
622; miniature by Trumbull, **12**: 45,
207, 307, 405; **14**: xxxvi-viii, 328 (illus.), 364, 365n, 440; *Prospects on the
Rubicon*, **12**: 392n; on natural and civil
rights, **13**: 4-5; *Rights of Man*, **13**: 7n;
20: xxxi, 158, 266, 268-313 (editorial
note and documents on controversy
over), 304, 384 (illus.), 391, 410,
422, 425, 443, 478, 556, 567, 692,
703; *Age of Reason*, **13**: 157n; on attraction of cohesion, **13**: 222-4; problem of fountains and trees, **13**: 225-6;
criticizes Silas Deane, **13**: 227-8; air
pump given to, **13**: 398, 592; gives
TJ Hopkinson's description of Independence Day celebration, **13**: 551,
589, 593n; **14**: 363; inquiries on map,
13: 592; attends Society for Political
Enquiries, **14**: 50n; letters from cited,
14: 468, 469n; **15**: 80n, 128n, 274; on
French Revolution, **14**: 564-5; **16**:
532n; on British politics, **14**: 565-9;
and Hessian fly, **14**: 567; **20**: 446; on
U.S. debt, **14**: 567-8; extracts of letters sent to Washington, **14**: 569n; **15**:
118, 119n; letters to, from Banks,
quoted, **15**: 193-4, 197-8; on geomet-
rical wheelbarrow, **15**: 194; on U.S.
minister to Britain, **15**: 194; recommends manufactures for America, **15**:
194; letters to cited, **15**: 199n, 272n;
shows Burke TJ's letters on French
Revolution, **15**: 269n-70n; funds in
U.S., **15**: 274-5; wants to return to
America, **15**: 430; passport issued by
TJ, **15**: 486; transmits key of Bastille
to Washington, **16**: 531n-2n;
"Thoughts on the Establishment of a
Mint in the United States," **17**: 534-
40; **20**: 738; in London, **18**: 287; in-
dicted for seditious libel in Britain, **20**:
270; criticism of, **20**: 270, 277n, 280-
3, 304; recommended as postmaster
general, **20**: 288, 616, 657, 667; on
copper coinage, **20**: 308-9; criticizes
Adams, **20**: 309n; and case of William
Green, **20**: 522n; letter from, to
Siéyès, cited, **20**: 645; contributions to
National Gazette, **20**: 738; mentioned,
11: 289, 291; **12**: 291, 505, 557, 558;

15: 400, 441, 465, 504, 523; **18**:
667n; **20**: 662
Paines Hill: visited by the Adams family,
10: 68
paintings: varnishing, **7**: 295; blanching,
7: 296; TJ's enjoyment of in France,
8: 569; Garreau's collection offered
TJ, **9**: 106, 121; reproduction, **10**:
317, 320n-1n; **12**: 358; sold by
weight, **10**: 506
paints: U.S. import of, **10**: 147
Paissonnier, Dr.: and desalination of sea
water, **19**: 620
Palais Royal: destruction, **12**: 32
Palatinate: immigration from, **13**: 10, 48
Palavas, pond of, **11**: 450
paleontology. *See* fossils
Palfrey, William, **5**: 391
Palisier, Mr. *See* Pelissier, Christophe
Palladio, Andrea: Short admires architecture in Vincenza, **14**: 311; Short considers buying works of, **14**: 311
Pallard, Lullin, Charton & Cie., **14**: 424,
425
Pallas (ship): prizes, **8**: 680; **9**: 22, 392;
10: 94
Pallas, Dr. Peter Simon: Ledyard's account of, **11**: 218, 638
palm: growth of, **11**: 433; effect of altitude on, **11**: 650
Palmer, Capt. (master of the *Clementina*), **9**: 646; **10**: 68
Palyart, Ignatius: letter from, **17**: 571;
Portuguese consul general to U.S., **17**:
571; letter from cited, **17**: 598n; comments on Bulkeley, **19**: 314; issues
vice consular commissions, **20**: 262
Pamphili, Prince Doria (papal nuncio):
letter from, **11**: 266; instructions to
Franklin regarding, **6**: 398; **7**: 269;
correspondence with American Commissioners, **7**: 424n, 575-6; letters
from cited, **8**: 36; **11**: 276; letters sent
by Short to Jay, **16**: 123-4, 125n
Pamunkey ferry, Va., **2**: 454; **3**: 497
Pamunkey Indians: vocabulary of, **6**: 431
Pamunkey Neck: land granted to College
of William and Mary, **2**: 536
Pamunkey River: TJ's accident at ford,
1: 19; sale of land on, **1**: 60, 64-5; post
service on, **2**: 389; Ruffin's ferry on, **5**:
538n; Innes' crossing of, **5**: 540, 549;
collection of boats on, **6**: 4
Panama, isthmus of: proposed canal
across, **10**: 529; **12**: 426-7; **13**: 93-4,
230-1, 235n, 399, 577; **14**: 499,

Paradise (Paradies), John (*cont.*)
200-1, 229, 270, 292, 350, 352, 379;
16: 197; TJ advises Bancroft on family
problems of, **14**: 493-4, 602-3, 657-8;
15: 8-9; letter to, from Rev. J. Madison, cited, **14**: 536; trustees for, **14**:
603, 630, 658; **15**: 73; may go to
America, **14**: 657, 658n, 694; **15**: 3,
34; letters to cited, **15**: 4; **16**: 559-60;
drinking problem, **15**: 95-6, 131, 165,
379, 403, 508; **16**: 137; and Fourth of
July tribute to TJ, **15**: 240-2; letters
sent to England by, **15**: 269, 273;
pays TJ through Bancroft, **15**: 270,
328, 332-3; **16**: 109, 197; in London,
15: 270, 275, 281, 292, 352-3; **16**:
197, 198n, 294n; **17**: 482-3; letter
from, to Wilkinson, quoted, **15**: 270n;
bill on Bancroft, **15**: 328, 332-3; passport issued by TJ, **15**: 486; wife suggests appointment as minister to England, **16**: 137-8, 197; introduces
Andriani to TJ, **16**: 294; father of, **16**:
446, 447n; mentioned, **9**: 299, 302,
330, 363n, 655; **10**: 117, 362, 539;
12: 128, 377; **13**: 211, 234n, 242,
277, 650; **14**: 43, 52, 273, 382, 413,
417, 453, 516-7, 519, 543; **15**: 119,
130, 151, 163, 173, 230, 412, 476,
504; **16**: 138, 560; **17**: 240-1, 520,
606
Paradise, Lucy: TJ advises taking her to
America, **9**: 592; marriage to Count
Barziza, **11**: 242; mentioned, **9**: 447;
10: 75, 121, 199. *See also* Barziza,
Countess
Paradise, Lucy Ludwell (Mrs. John Paradise): letters to, **9**: 592; **10**: 121, 304-5; **13**: 537, 566-7, 599-600; **14**: 418-20, 461-2, 694; **15**: 34-5, 82-3, 162-3,
275, 412; **16**: 559-60; letters from, **9**:
454-5; **10**: 69, 255-6; **11**: 501; **12**:
377; **13**: 457-8, 522-3, 533-4, 599,
601-3; **14**: 9, 52-3, 413-4, 455-7, 466-7, 512-3, 516-7, 594; **15**: 10, 51-3,
94-6, 130-1, 151, 164-5, 229-30, 281-2, 350, 379, 402-3, 508; **16**: 137-8,
196-8, 446-7; **17**: 240-1, 482-3, 519-20; **19**: 354; marriage, **9**: 40; U.S. citizenship, **10**: 199; relations with husband, **11**: 242; **13**: 457, 599; **14**: 414,
483, 494, 567; **15**: 52, 95-6, 131,
151, 164-5; departs for Va., **11**: 573;
affidavit on by TJ, **13**: 309-11; reception in Va., **13**: 314-5; asks TJ's help

with financial problems, **13**: 457-8,
522-3, 602-3; **14**: 467; **15**: 165; **16**:
446; payments to, **13**: 472, 544, 566;
15: 270; asks TJ to help Fondate, **13**:
534; thanks TJ for help, **13**: 534, 601;
14: 512-3, 594; **15**: 165, 229, 281,
350; **16**: 446; TJ's advice to on debts,
13: 537, 599-600, 603-4; **14**: 418-9,
461-2; travels to Italy, **13**: 544, 634-6,
653; **14**: 26, 43, 52-3, 298-9, 312-3;
provision for support of, **13**: 566, 599;
14: 456, 603; **15**: 8-9; **16**: 446; marriage settlement, **13**: 570-1; **14**: 419;
Short invited to travel with, **13**: 601-2;
invited to dine with TJ, **13**: 604; **14**:
516; characterized by Short, **13**: 634-5; Short visits in Italy, **14**: 52-3, 272;
returns to Paris, **14**: 52-3, 273, 277,
299, 313, 384; letters from cited, **14**:
275, 277, 278n; **15**: xxvii, 160; **16**:
198n, 551n; complaints of daughter
against, **14**: 298-9, 611-2; family quarrel described by Short, **14**: 312-3; disapproves of Barziza's financial arrangement with her husband, **14**: 384; plans
for future, **14**: 413-4, 455-6, 467, 483,
493, 512-3; TJ's advice to on personal
problems, **14**: 418-9; offers to care for
Mary Jefferson, **14**: 456-7, 461; letter
to Jay conveyed by, **14**: 521n, 524n;
in London, **14**: 531, 580; buys books
for TJ, **14**: 658, 663; **15**: 3, 10n, 35,
38, 51-2, 82-3, 94-6, 130, 144, 151,
163; letter to, from Martha Washington, cited, **15**: 35n, 95; letters to cited,
15: 73; **16**: 86n; Va. estate, **15**: 165,
229, 275, 292; **16**: 197-8; interest in
Portugal, **15**: 350; sympathy with
French Revolution, **15**: 350, 379; Jodrell writes to, **15**: 478; passport issued
by TJ, **15**: 486; letter from, to Washington, cited, **16**: 198n; letter from
quoted, **16**: 294n; TJ obtains information on diplomatic establishments
from, **17**: xxxi, 221; moves to Bath,
17: 250; wants to return to America,
17: 483; would mourn for Washington, **17**: 520; mentioned, **9**: 447; **10**:
174, 199, 516, 539; **11**: 351; **13**: 277;
14: 343, 417, 519, 543; **15**: 3, 70,
434, 479; **16**: 85, 86
Paradise, Peter (father of John Paradise),
16: 446, 447n
Paradise family, **9**: 570, 580
Paragon (ship), **9**: 392

Paramus, N.J.: Washington's army at, **2**: 207

pardoning power: TJ's opinions on, **1**: 331n; denied executive in TJ's drafts of Va. Constitution of 1776, **1**: 342; Va. act of 1780, **5**: 354n; given Va. Executive for one year, **9**: 197; mentioned, **2**: 178-9, 194, 326, 503; **5**: 642n; **6**: 298, 311-2

Parent (Parant), M.: letters to, **11**: 211-3, 472-3, 608-9; **12**: 431, 465-6, 612; **14**: 480-1, 638; **15**: 102; letters from, **11**: 484-5, 546, 654; **12**: 455-6, 516, 560, 642; **14**: 570, 679-80; **15**: 155; TJ plans to visit, **11**: 463n; wine ordered from, **12**: 226-7; **14**: 480-1; account of, **12**: 658; Short visits, **13**: 635-6; wine sent by, **14**: 570, 638; son of, **15**: 155

Paret, M.: assists American captives in Algiers, **20**: 476, 547, 601n

Paris: recommended as residence for Monroe, **6**: 127; Mazzei's notes on etiquette in, **7**: 388-9; TJ's comments on, **7**: 519; **9**: 445; **11**: 122-3; climate, **7**: 636; **8**: 43, 186; **9**: 478; water supply, **8**: 574-5; maps, **9**: xxvii, 227 (illus.); **11**: 414 (fac.); plan of, **10**: xxviii, 211 (illus.); **12**: 32, 33n; manufactures in encouraged, **11**: 32; social life, **11**: 393; rice consumption, **11**: 644; bridges, **12**: xxxiv, 32, 34 (illus.); improvements in, **12**: 32; **14**: 655-6; etymological inquiry by Vieyra, **12**: 44; street lighting, **12**: 401; women of compared with Americans, **13**: 151-2; riot after appointment of Necker, **13**: 564-5; Swan and Blackden's proposals for supplying flour and wheat, **13**: 659; **15**: 245-7, 249; opera, **14**: 655; Seine frozen, **14**: 656; riot in May 1789, **15**: 104, 110-1, 121; riot in November 1790, **18**: 84; duties abolished, **20**: 363-4. *See also* Jefferson, Thomas: Residences; Parlement of Paris; French Revolution

Paris, Prévôt des Marchands et Echevins. *See* Le Peletier de Morfontaine, Louis

Paris, Richard: and Indian land claims, **2**: 86, 97

Paris, Treaty of (1763): British navigation of Mississippi under, **7**: 407. mentioned, **3**: 629; **6**: 664 *See also* Peace Treaty, Definitive

Paris Commune: and death of Franklin, **19**: 107

Pariseau, M.: Martha's study with, **11**: 203

Parish, Mr. and Mrs., **15**: 130

Parish, John: letter to, **17**: 423-5; letter from, **18**: 344-5; vice consul at Hamburg, **17**: 246, 247, 250, 253n, 254n, 280

Parish & Thomson: letter from, **12**: 667; send salt beef, **13**: 138

parishes: alterations in boundaries in Va., **2**: 554

Park, Mr.: death of, **5**: 296

Park, Catherine: letter from, **5**: 296

Parke, Mr.: speculation in American paper, **12**: 581

Parker, Col.: antifederalism of, **15**: 6

Parker, Ens., **4**: 443

Parker, Benjamin: introduced to TJ, **12**: 148; passport issued by TJ, **15**: 486

Parker, Daniel: letters to, **14**: 347; **15**: 526; letter from, **14**: 324; and tobacco for American prisoners, **5**: 435; speculation in U.S. debt, **8**: 312, 331-2, 531-2, 630; **9**: 123-4; **13**: 322n-3n; **14**: 191, 193-4, 531n; **15**: 473n, 566-7; **20**: 177, 178, 179; land claims, **8**: 655; introduction to TJ, **12**: 289-90, 291, 321-2; letters and merchandise sent by, **12**: 307, 474, 476, 633; **13**: 178, 280, 288, 291, 292, 301, 304, 337, 551, 570, 609, 657; **14**: 5, 25, 365, 412n, 454, 473, 513n, 514, 590, 640, 668; letter to, from Duer, cited, **13**: 109; proposal to transport mail, **13**: 237n; **14**: 308n; and Swan's contract for beef, **13**: 243, 278, 313; **15**: 362; correspondence with Craigie, **13**: 322n; **14**: 193-4; departs for Paris, **13**: 345; health of, **13**: 463; **15**: 515; reports Va. adoption of Constitution, **13**: 511; letter to, from Barrett, cited, **13**: 523, 524n; delivers carriage for TJ, **13**: 545; **14**: 45, 293, 468, 511n, 514; departs London, **13**: 572; on travel to America, **14**: 217n; and whale fishery, **14**: 218-9; proposal on packets from Le Havre to Boston, **14**: 307-10; and whale-oil trade, **14**: 308n, 352; delivers thermometer, **14**: 346, 347; orders portraits of Columbus, Vespucci, Cortez, and Magellan in Florence, **15**: xxxvi; does not sign Fourth of July tribute to TJ, **15**: 240n; offers flour

Patterson, John: inquisition against, **4:** 186

Patterson, Capt. Joseph, **4:** 313

Patterson, Robert: letter from, **18:** 343-4; and American Philosophical Society *Transactions,* **8:** 51; letters to cited, **15:** 82n; **16:** 610n, 617n; views on weights and measures, **16:** 589; letter from cited, **16:** 602n; on calendar reform, **18:** 343-4; recommends Andrew Ellicott as U.S. geographer, **19:** 40n; **20:** 61n

Patterson, William. *See* Patterson, James

Patteson, Samuel: correspondence with Davies, **6:** 13n, 22-4; mentioned, **6:** 48

Patton, Mr. (Va. commissary at Baltimore): letter to, **3:** 646

Patton, James: right to western land, **6:** 647n

Patton & Buchannan, **6:** 158, 159

Patty (slave): taken by British, **6:** 224

Patuxent, Va., **5:** 161

Patuxent river, Md., **5:** 142, 177

Paul, Audley, **2:** 114

Paul, F. of Venice. *See* Sarpi, Paolo

Paul, John, **5:** 294n

Paul, St.: cited by TJ on marriage, **1:** 16; cited by TJ on episcopacy, **1:** 551-2

Paulding, John: and capture of André, **4:** 487; **16:** 54n

Paulett (Paulet), Ens. Jesse: letter from, **4:** 556; officer in Regiment of Guards for Convention troops, **3:** 121, 156

Paulett, Lieut. Richard: letter from, **4:** 556n; officer in Regiment of Guards for Convention troops, **3:** 121, 156

Pauly, Mr.: letter to cited, **12:** 105; TJ's efforts to find, **12:** 312

Paulze, Jacques: on U.S.-French trade committee, **9:** 338n; **13:** 59

Pausanias: works, **13:** 317

Pauw (Paw, Paaw), Cornelius de: theory on inferiority of Indian disputed by TJ, **8:** 185; *Recherches philosophiques sur les Américains,* **8:** 502; **11:** 71; Hogendorp's ridicule of, **8:** 502; opinions on degeneracy of Americans controverted, **12:** 240-1; "lies" of, **13:** 397, 398n

Pavia, Italy, **11:** 440

Paw, M. *See* Pauw

Pawnee Indians: vocabulary compiled by Lewis, **20:** 451n

Paxton murders, **9:** 487

Payen Brothers, **9:** 67

paymasters, army: irregularities, **5:** 269

Payne, Mr.: describes Emperor of Morocco, **9:** 96; at Dover, **11:** 168

Payne, Annias: signs nonimportation resolutions (1770), **1:** 47

Payne, Edward, **7:** 376

Payne, Jacob: signs nonimportation resolutions (1770), **1:** 47

Payne, John: signs nonimportation resolutions (1770), **1:** 47

Payne, Joseph: as prisoner of war, **3:** 390

Payne, Josias, Jr.: signs nonimportation resolutions (1769), **1:** 30

Payne, Nicholas: letter to, **5:** 440-1

Payne, Thomas: prisoner of war, **3:** 390

Payne, Thomas (bookseller): letters to, **13:** 650-2; **14:** 511-2; **15:** 31; Trumbull recommends, **13:** 434, 520, 650; letters to cited, **13:** 656; **14:** 44, 440, 663; books ordered from, **14:** 25, 52, 209; **13:** 650-2, 656; **14:** 364, 468, 469n, 512; **15:** 38

"Paynshill": garden described by TJ, **9:** 370

Peabody, Joseph: signs petition, **11:** 336

Peabody, Nathaniel: letters to, **3:** 476, 500; letters from, **3:** 391-6, 397, 406-10, 434-6, 455-6, 502

Peace, Mrs. L., **8:** 147

peace, perpetual: treaties of amity and commerce, **7:** 471; **8:** 217; Denmark and U.S., **7:** 479-80; Prussia and U.S., **7:** 616; Gargaz' brochure on, **9:** 99-100, 175; U.S. and Portugal, **9:** 421, 424

peace commissioners, American: letter from, **6:** 384-5; powers, **6:** 275, 393-402; letters to Congress cited, **6:** 388

Peace Treaty, Definitive (1783): proclamation announcing ratification, **6:** xxxvi, 462-5, 604 (illus.); commercial stipulations, **6:** 212, 338; signing of, **6:** 275, 318, 334, 350; provision against punishment of Loyalists, **6:** 329-30; received by Congress, **6:** 371, 381, 385-6; Gov. Harrison desires copy of, **6:** 372; report in Congress on, **6:** 384-5; ratification of, **6:** 387, 388, 423, 424-6, 433, 437, 438, 439-42, 456-62, 512, 545; **7:** 32, 227, 250; dispatch to Europe, **6:** 461n, 468, 470, 545, 567; **7:** 3, 5, 8; celebrations of ratification, **6:** 464n; compliance with, **6:** 564; infractions, **7:** 522, 524n; **11:** 221, 308, 313; **14:** 79-80; **17:** 334n, 335-6, 339n-40n; **20:** 478-9; prohibi-

pedestal. *See* marble pedestal

Pedin, James: parole of, **5**: 148

pedometer: ordered for Madison, **9**: 265, 518; **11**: 483, 664; **12**: 569; **13**: 132, 497; mentioned, **11**: 477

Pedrick, Knott: signs petition, **19**: 226

Pedrick, Richard: signs petition, **19**: 226

Pedro III, king of Portugal: income from Brazilian mines, **16**: 340

Peeble, Mr.: inn rated by TJ, **20**: 471

Pee Dee river, N.C.: means of transportation of army supplies, **4**: 251; mentioned, **3**: 462, 465; **5**: 215. *See also* Yadkin river, N.C.

Peers, James: letter from, to Joshua Johnson, **20**: 515; in *Rachel* case, **20**: 515

Peery, William: proposed judicial appointment, **19**: 284, 354, 384, 385, 404

Peggy (ship), **9**: 392; **14**: 259; **20**: 327

Pegli, Italy: oranges grown at, **11**: 441

Peinier, Comte de: governor general of Saint-Domingue, **17**: 300-2, 304-8, 327-8, 556; La Luzerne's correspondence with, **17**: 304, 305

Peirce, Maj. William. *See* Pierce

Pelcerf, François: estate, **10**: 92-3, 127-8; mentioned, **10**: 509

Pelham, Charles, **3**: 652

Pelham, Lady Francis: garden described by TJ, **9**: 370

Pelham, Peter: as keeper of public jail, **3**: 58; **5**: 235-6

Pelham, William (?): letter to cited, **6**: 193; mentioned, **6**: 186, 187n

"Pelisipia" (TJ's name for new state), **6**: 587n, 596n-7n, 598n, 605

Pelisipi river. *See* Clinch river; Ohio river

Pelissier, Christophe: testimony on Canadian campaign, **1**: 439, 450-1

Pellegrini. *See* Tibaldi, Pellegrino

Pellegrino: employee of Mazzei, **3**: 342; Short asked to deliver letter from, **14**: 344

Pellet, M., **12**: 258

Pelloutier, Simon: *Histoire des Celtes*, **1**: 294n; **8**: 12, 411

Pelosi, Vincent M.: paid by Department of State, **17**: 369

pelts. *See* fur

Pemaquid, Me., **6**: 494

Pemberton, Henry, **9**: 486

Pemberton, John: letter from, **20**: 633-6; letter from, to Zane, quoted, **20**: 634n

pencils: bought for Hopkinson, **9**: 132, 224, 482

Pendergast, William: bills against Va., **5**: 391

Pendleton, Edmund: letters to, **1**: 408, 491-4, 503-7; **6**: 253-4, 385-8, 470-2, 567-9; **7**: 60-1, 134, 292-3; **9**: 593; **20**: 669-70; letters from, **1**: 260-1, 296-7, 297-8, 388, 462-5, 471-2, 479-80, 484-5, 488-91, 507-8; **2**: 266-7; **5**: 87-9; **7**: 44, 111, 271; **20**: 625; signs nonimportation resolutions (1770), **1**: 46; and legal fees, **1**: 99; and Fast-Day resolution, **1**: 106n; signs Virginia Association, **1**: 108; and nonimportation agreements, **1**: 110; signs letter to Va. HB, **1**: 111; appointed to Continental Congress, **1**: 141; signs Continental Association, **1**: 153; on committee to investigate land grants, **1**: 162n; signs Congress' second petition, **1**: 223; letter from, to Peyton Randolph, **1**: 223-4; signs TJ's commission, **1**: 246; signs Va. resolution calling for independence, **1**: 291; signs Declaration of Independence, **1**: 308n; and Va. Constitution, **1**: 331n, 364n, 384n, 489-90, 503-7; as president of Va. Convention, **1**: 407; sent rough draft of Declaration of Independence, **1**: 415n; and bill for naturalization of foreigners in Va., **1**: 559n; opposes TJ's revision of entail, **1**: 561n-2n; and revisal of Va. laws, **1**: 563n, 603; **2**: 302, 305n, 308n, 312n, 313n, 314n, 316n, 319n, 320n, 323n, 324n, 328, 488n, 534n, 542n, 663n; **10**: 576; **20**: 557; opposes disestablishment of Church of England, **1**: 589n; elected speaker of Va. HD, **1**: 598n; and case of Thomas Johnson, **2**: 42n, 47n-8n, 63n; on committee to amend 1769 inoculation act, **2**: 124n; letters to cited, **2**: 134n; on committee on sale of unappropriated lands, **2**: 135n; on committee to adjust titles to unpatented lands, **2**: 138n; correspondence with TJ on land policy, **2**: 147n; and payment of British debts, **2**: 171n; and bill locating Va. courts, **2**: 173n; endorsement on supply bill, **2**: 222n; and TJ's plan for public education, **2**: 249n; letter from, to R. H. Lee, quoted, **2**: 320n; desires to preserve primogeniture, **2**: 393n; and bill for care of poor, **2**: 423n; and jury trial in equity, **2**: 598n; and Nathan case, **5**: 87-9, 152; **6**: 320, 323n; on powers of Congress, **5**: 471n-2n; letter from, to Madison, quoted, **6**: 137n; and Va.'s territorial claims, **6**: 148; draft of bill establishing courts of assize, **7**: 588; Richmond property, **8**: 344; bills drawn by, **8**: 646; member committee to amend unpassed Va. bills, **11**: 153; supports Constitution, **12**: 281, 410; **13**: 98; in Va. Constitutional Convention, **13**: 351, 402, 436n, 440, 620; debts, **15**: 644; refuses appointment as judge of district court of Va., **16**: 27; letter from, to Washington, quoted, **18**: 686; proposed arbitrator in Edgehill boundary dispute, **20**: 165; recommends nephew for supreme court appointment, **20**: 625, 668, 669-70; letter from cited, **20**: 682; mentioned, **1**: 251; **6**: 188, 264; **14**: 659

Pendleton, Edmund, Jr.: letter from, **5**: 191

Pendleton, Henry: signs Virginia Association, **1**: 108

Pendleton, John: attests revisal report, **2**: 312n; mentioned, **9**: 183

Pendleton, Nathaniel, Jr.: prisoner of war, **3**: 389, 390; aide-de-camp to Greene, **5**: 86, 277n; member of Constitutional Convention, **11**: 401; seeks supreme court appointment, **20**: 625, 668, 669-70; mentioned, **3**: 501; **6**: 22

Pendleton, Col. Philip: letter from, **4**: 452

Pendleton, Sarah Pollard (Mrs. Edmund Pendleton), **1**: 507; **6**: 254

Pendleton, Spice: claim to Robert Williams' estate, **6**: 152n

pendulum: Rittenhouse's improvement in, **9**: 321; vibrating half seconds, **16**: xxxiii, 320; in calculation of weights and measures, **16**: 485, 510, 542-3, 547, 567-9, 576, 588, 602, 606; 20: 353-60; Newton's calculation, **16**: 485, 510, 542-3, 547, 567-9, 602, 606, 645n, 652n-3n, 669n-70n; Whitehurst's, **16**: 618-9; Webster's "A Pendulum without a Bob," **18**: 480-2; Rittenhouse disagrees with TJ on, **18**: 481n

Penelope (opera): presented in Paris, **9**: 126, 152

Penelvere, Ignasio, **6**: 356

Penet, d'Acosta Frères & Cie.: contract with, **3**: 91, 551; **4**: 467, 556; drafts

drawn on, **3**: 158, 159, 160; **6**: 356; bills of exchange on, **3**: 270, 309, 311, 315, 322; **6**: 115; vessel captured, **4**: 143-4, 155; letter from, to the Board of Trade, **4**: 155; bills protested, **6**: 125; mentioned, **3**: 124n, 235, 341n, 383, 385n; **6**: 324n

Penet, Peter: letters from, **3**: 70, 315, 382-5; **4**: 144-7; Va. agent, **3**: 36, 357; letter from cited, **3**: 125; letter to cited, **3**: 202; honesty questioned, **3**: 299-301; owner of *Johnston Smith*, **3**: 319; characterized by Mazzei, **3**: 357-9; bankruptcy, **4**: 147n; mentioned, **3**: 101, 201, 306, 307, 311

Penet, Windel & Company: contract with Va. to manufacture arms and cannon, **2**: 284n; **3**: 49, 70, 125, 130n, 131-46, 385n

Penguin island, **1**: 278

Penhallow, John: petition of, **6**: 448-52; part owner of the *McClary*, **6**: 453, 454

Penn, Abraham: letter to, **5**: 598-9; problems of militia in Henry co., **5**: 584n

Penn, Gabriel, **6**: 119

Penn, John: and Va.-Pa. boundary dispute, **1**: 235n; signs agreement of secrecy, **1**: 253; advised by Adams, **1**: 333n; signs Declaration of Independence, **1**: 432; death of, **14**: 296, 386

Penn, Gov. John: TJ's architectural drawings for, **1**: 421n-2n; Franklin's conduct toward, **9**: 487

Penn, Richard: impact of return to America discussed, **12**: 221; mentioned, **9**: 363n

Penn, Thomas: boundary agreement with Lord Baltimore, **1**: 463, 595

Penn, William: land grant to, **6**: 490-1, 499, 657; purchase of land from Indians, **6**: 491

Penn, Adm. William: services to King, **6**: 490

Pennamite war (1784), **6**: 484n

Pennant, Thomas: and Society for Study of Natural History, **11**: 293; works by, **19**: 211

pennants: for ships, **12**: 56

Pennock, William: Richmond property, **8**: 344; elected mayor of Richmond, **10**: 110

Pennsylvania: population of, **1**: 182; **10**: 34, 35, 37, 54-6; boundary dispute with Va., **1**: 234-6, 244-5, 387-8,

Pennsylvania (*cont.*)

389n, 462-6, 490, 505, 594-5; **3:** 77-8, 200, 206-8, 216, 248-9, 263, 281, 286-9; **4:** 30-1, 32-3; **5:** 13, 303-4, 339, 478, 611, 650; **6:** 7-8, 72, 74, 76, 600, 666; **7:** 93, 133, 140, 236; **8:** 74, 117, 124, 417; **9:** 215-6; boundary dispute with Conn., **1:** 248; **6:** 474-507; **7:** 432, 439; **9:** 652-3; instructions to delegates on independence, **1:** 311-2; votes against Chase's taxation plan, **1:** 323; boundary dispute with Md., **1:** 463, 595; letter to Convention of from Va. delegates in Congress, **1:** 465-6; boundaries, **1:** 595; **3:** 586, 634n; **8:** 565-6; **9:** 445; **10:** 37, 73, 249-50; criticized by Harvie, **2:** 34, 125-6; Land Office, **2:** 102; surveys made under warrants of, **2:** 103; relations with Va., **3:** 353-4; **5:** 264; gives dictatorial authority to governor, **3:** 412; contribution to good of nation, **3:** 454; approves act of Congress emitting new currency, **3:** 528; Continental requisitions of food, **4:** 107; quota for army pay, **4:** 369; objects to removing Convention troops from Va., **4:** 656; transfer of Convention troops to, **5:** 56, 168; repeals embargo legislation, **5:** 251, 483n; asked to aid in protecting Delaware bay, **5:** 551; revaluation of Continental currency, **5:** 608-9; represented on western lands committee of Congress, **6:** 131, 147; attitude toward Congress, **6:** 334; and presidency of Congress, **6:** 348, 349; vote on permanent seat for Congress, **6:** 352, 366; charter (1681), **6:** 490, 657; extension of settlements, **6:** 491; appropriates proprietary lands, **6:** 492; western commerce, **6:** 548; **7:** 35; vote on Va. land cession, **6:** 575n; **7:** 4-5; as boundary of new states, **6:** 602, 603, 607, 614; financial quota to national treasury, **7:** 5, 55, 71; **8:** 215, 325; **9:** 480; **10:** 34, 35, 54-6; **11:** 5, 470; politics, **7:** 19-20; **8:** 99, 562, 671-2; **9:** 3, 10, 320-1, 466; **10:** 18; vote on meeting place of Congress, **7:** 118; vote on slavery in western territory, **7:** 118; increases Congress' powers, **7:** 139, 232; value of pound, **7:** 178; currency, **7:** 199-200; laws on international offenses, **7:** 307n; commerce, **7:** 347, 348, 349; delegates in Congress, **7:** 572; leave to clear road asked, **7:** 590-1; **8:**

3; land south of the Ohio, **8:** 124; public debt, **8:** 218; proposal to suppress Bank of North America, **8:** 248; presidency of Executive Council, **8:** 420, 562, 581; characteristics of inhabitants, **8:** 468; duties on foreign goods, **8:** 580; interest in Cuyahoga-Beaver creek canal, **9:** 151; grants commercial powers to Congress, **9:** 235; revises Test Act, **9:** 320-1; commercial discrimination against Portugal, **9:** 408; and impost, **9:** 510, 608; **11:** 161, 470; constitution, **10:** 18; **15:** 16; **17:** 497; Démeunier's errors on corrected, **10:** 37; myth of pacificity of, **10:** 37; condemns the Cincinnati, **10:** 50; paper money, **10:** 231; sends delegates to Annapolis convention, **10:** 232; flour mills, **10:** 262; reformation of criminal law, **10:** 288; removes charter from Bank of North America, **10:** 314; attitude toward Mississippi navigation, **10:** 456; **11:** 154, 221; appoints commissioners for Chesapeake-Delaware canal, **10:** 519; cost of land in, **11:** 50; delegates to Federal Convention, **11:** 154, 241, 310, 400; **12:** 229, 231n; ratification of constitution, **12:** 230, 253-4, 281, 409, 423, 425, 443, 490, 608; **13:** 100-1, 156, 205, 370; opposes federal government, **13:** 39; election laws, **14:** 3; elects senators, **14:** 3, 17, 275, 277, 302, 339, 344, 385, 394, 473, 529; elects representatives in Congress, **14:** 340, 352, 395, 473; electoral votes (1789), **15:** 92; laws sent to TJ by Lewis, **18:** 73n, 461-71; ratification of constitutional amendments, **18:** 595; and capital site, **19:** 9; defects from Va. alliance, **19:** 36; and Franklin's death, **19:** 95, 96-97, 102, 105; exports, **19:** 136-8, 139; and the fisheries, **19:** 191; murder of Indians in, **19:** 628; laws sought by TJ, **20:** 90

Pennsylvania (ship), **19:** 605; **20:** 249

Pennsylvania, University of: attempt of Constitutionalists to control, **8:** 562

Pennsylvania Gazette: Franklin's connection with, **9:** 486, 495

Pennsylvania Journal: quoted, **19:** 299n

Pennsylvania Packet: satire by Hopkinson, **10:** 512; mentioned, **6:** 594n, 596n; **14:** 67n

Pennsylvania Packet (ship): sails for Philadelphia, **19:** 588

Peter, Robert (*cont.*)
22n; proposes wharves for Federal
City, **20**: 35n, 38; signs landholders
agreement, **20**: 85n
Peter, St.: cited by TJ, **1**: 552
Peter, Walter: signs nonimportation resolutions (1770), **1**: 47; to hire laborers
for work at Hoods, **3**: 616
Peters, Lord: owner of estate at Woburn,
9: 370
Peters, Richard: letters to, **6**: 124; **11**:
182-3; **16**: 494; **20**: 590-1; letters
from, **5**: 239-40; **10**: 416-7; **16**: 538-
40; **20**: 573; to provide TJ with song
or receipt, **2**: 236, 263n; and parole of
Geismar, **2**: 270; member Board of
War, **4**: 182; letter from, to James
Wood, **5**: 240; dinner at Dolly's Chop
House, **9**: 351n; Speaker of Pa. Assembly, **14**: 473, 529; letter from
quoted, **17**: 167; certificate to Bondfield for clothing, **17**: 578-9; letter to,
from Knox, quoted, **19**: 465; mentioned, **10**: 583; **18**: 515
Peters, Sarah Robinson (Mrs. Richard
Peters), **11**: 193
Peters, Walter: British parole, **4**: 489-90
Petersburg, Va.: rendezvous for troops,
3: 7, 8, 432, 439; **4**: 294, 339; **5**:
496n-7n, 501, 520-1, 546; appointed
as recruiting station, **3**: 181; Bermu-
dian vessels to land salt at, **3**: 238; review of recruits at, **3**: 283; supply
post, **3**: 537; **4**: 285, 286, 288; place
of collection under provision law, **4**: 7,
8; supposed British objective, **4**: 269,
307, 312, 334, 579, 659; **5**: 486n;
captured by British, **4**: 287n; removal
of military stores from, **4**: 296, 409; **5**:
453n, 465n, 480n; arms needed at, **4**:
317, 318; defense, **4**: 318; provisions
for army at, **4**: 324; store of clothing
at, **4**: 453; supply of arms at, **4**: 696;
5: 7, 8; forage magazine at, **5**: 319;
possible British juncture at, **5**: 384;
rendezvous for volunteer cavalry, **5**:
412; public workmen at, **5**: 442; removal of inhabitants from, **5**: 503n;
militia at, **5**: 527; battle of, **5**: 550n,
556, 559n, 571n, 580, 623, 624n-5n,
660; British cavalry at, **5**: 631; loss of
goods at, **5**: 660-1; **6**: 13, 626n, 631;
arrival of British at, **5**: 662; evacuated
by British, **6**: 19, 32; competition with
Norfolk for trade, **7**: 215; place of
court of assize, **7**: 588; memorial by

merchants on payment of British
debts, **7**: 595; mentioned, **3**: 371; **4**:
50
Petersburgh ferry, **3**: 497
Peter's mountain, **2**: 114
Petit, Adrien: letters to, **11**: 214, 243;
19: 76-7; letters from, **11**: 216, 261,
278, 291; **17**: 297-8; estimate of wine
prices, **8**: 172; bill for wine, **8**: 317;
purchases for Mrs. Adams and Mrs.
Smith, **10**: 211; **11**: 175; **12**: 112,
394; promotion, **10**: 213n; report on
TJ's horse, **11**: 209; orders for receiv-
ing wine, **11**: 212; to oversee removal
of former servants, **11**: 350; exercises
TJ's horses, **11**: 362; sent to accompany Mary Jefferson to France, **11**:
514, 515, 551, 572; books to be
brought by, **11**: 522; TJ's instructions
to, **11**: 531-2, 592; payment to Mrs.
Adams, **12**: 65; bill for baggage, **15**:
377n; passport issued by TJ, **15**: 485;
payment to, **15**: 521, 526; **17**: 411,
506; considers going to America, **16**:
229, 319, 500-1; **17**: 11, 545-6; **18**:
600-1; prepares TJ's furnishings for
shipment to America, **16**: 229-30,
320-3, 500, 583; **17**: 11, 212, 258;
sells part of TJ's furniture, **17**: 315-6,
632; plans for future, **17**: 316; bill for
articles bought for TJ, **17**: 392; **18**:
34n, 35n; letter to cited, **18**: 600; letter from cited, **19**: 291; letter to, from
Short, cited, **19**: 291; returns to TJ's
service, **20**: 265, 345, 382, 670, 691,
706; letter sent by, **20**: 346, 541, 544,
642; orders vanilla, **20**: 693; mentioned, **8**: 166, 173n, 184, 297; **10**:
154, 162, 203, 573; **11**: 208, 210,
234, 235, 253, 269, 276, 298, 337,
362, 373, 383, 551, 552, 573; **12**:
193, 559, 603, 619, 638, 658; **13**:
146n; **14**: 426; **15**: 510; **16**: 203, 272,
363, 444; **17**: 282, 412, 632; **18**: 358,
449, 450
Petit Grandison: TJ orders from Stockdale, **12**: 115
petit juries. *See* juries, petit
petit treason. *See* treason, petty
Petrarch: love for Laura, **11**: 358; chateau, **11**: 369, 372; **13**: 23, 104, 267,
273
Petre, Mr., **17**: 606
Petree, Mr.: cited on trade negotiations
between Britain and American Commissioners, **8**: 57n

petrified plants, **10**: 604

Petronius, Gaius, **20**: 634n

Petry, M. (of Paris): financial transactions with TJ, **12**: 676; **13**: 368; **15**: 559; **16**: 318-9; **17**: 506

Petry, Jean Baptiste: letter to, **13**: 535; letter from, **16**: 52; and olive culture in S.C., **12**: 676; letter from, to Cambray, cited, **13**: 244; Cambray's papers sent to, **13**: 535, 662; **15**: 347-8, 407-8; **16**: 52; French vice consul in Charleston, **14**: 65n; **16**: 332, 333n

Pettijohn, William: votes for bill for religious freedom, **2**: 549n

Pettit, Charles: as assistant quartermaster general, **3**: 494; **4**: 514n, 521; letter to, from Richard Claiborne, **4**: 510-4; letter from, to Carrington, cited, **5**: 575; candidate for Congress from Pa., **14**: 473; mentioned, **8**: 100n

Pettus, Charles: in Albemarle co. militia, **1**: 666

Pettus, Lieut. Samuel O.: letter from, **4**: 556; officer in Regiment of Guards for Convention troops, **3**: 156; mentioned, **3**: 121

Pettus, Thomas: signs nonimportation resolutions (1770), **1**: 46; signs Virginia Association, **1**: 108

Petty, Sir William: *Several Essays in Political Arithmetick*, **11**: 523

petty treason. *See* treason, petty

Peuchen, Jean Jacques: letters to, **13**: 43, 537-8; letter from, **13**: 107-8; Damen recommends TJ to, **13**: 15; payments to, **13**: 148, 167, 336; mentioned, **13**: 186

pewter: manufacture in Conn., **7**: 336; U.S. import of, **10**: 147

Peyrinault, Cabarrus & Cie., **12**: 58

Peyronet, M.: death, **10**: 624; **11**: 302

Peyrouse, Capt. *See* La Pérouse, Jean François de Galaup, Comte de

Peyrouse, Mme la veuve: vineyards, **11**: 421

Peyton, Craven: Shadwell leased to, **17**: 325n

Peyton, Francis: signs nonimportation resolutions, **1**: 30, 46; signs Virginia Association, **1**: 108; on committee to bring in land office bill, **2**: 136n; votes for bill for religious freedom, **2**: 549n; commissioner for settling land claims, **4**: 454; commander of Loudon co. militia, **15**: 602

Peyton, Capt. John: letter to, **5**: 200-1;

as Va. clothier-general, **3**: 167, 172; **4**: 493, 514; **5**: 173, 175; **6**: 17; letter from, to Davies, quoted, **6**: 21n

Peyton, Sir John: letter to, **5**: 605-6; letters from, **5**: 282-3, 596; as county lieutenant of Gloucester co., **4**: 426, 651n; purchases arms, **5**: 210, 451

Peyton, Adm. Joseph: capture reported, **16**: 427; arrival in Lisbon, **18**: 49

Pfeffel, Chrétien Frédéric: books sought by TJ, **6**: 529; *Nouvelle abrégé chronologique de l'histoire et du droit publique d'Allemagne*, **11**: 666

Pfeiffer, George: as clerk in Dept. of State, **17**: 356n-8n

Phaedrus: Stirling's edition of, **11**: 523; *Fabularum Aesopiarum*, **12**: 688; **20**: 634n

phaeton: sent to TJ, **16**: 491. *See also* cabriolet and phaeton

Phalsbourg, France, **13**: 26

pheasants: TJ's efforts to send to Va., **8**: 17, 560; **9**: 158; for Louis XVI's natural history museum, **9**: 148-9; promised TJ by Hopkinson, **10**: 512; at Karlsruhe, **13**: 25

Phelon, Capt. Patrick, **18**: 135

Phelps, Oliver: land speculation, **20**: 124, 125-32, 582

Phelps, Samuel: imports slaves, **15**: 654

Philadelphia: letter to mayor of, **20**: 414; map and view of State House by Nicholas Scull and George Heap, **1**: lvii, 358 (illus.); strategic importance, **1**: 659; crime in, **2**: 4; TJ desires workmen from, **2**: 35; British army in, **2**: 176-7, 178; abandonment by British, **2**: 201, 202; high cost of living in, **2**: 264; subscription of merchants for benefit of army, **3**: 454, 461, 462n; merchants of and Va. tobacco, **5**: 265; currency depreciation in, **5**: 608, 609n, 620; library, **6**: 169; **9**: 486; **10**: 38; Madison hopes TJ will return to, **6**: 252; discontent with as capital, **6**: 319; as permanent seat of Congress, **6**: 352, 365, 547; **7**: 35; **8**: 78; considered for temporary seat of Congress, **6**: 363; **7**: 118; comparative table of distance from various states, **6**: 366-7; meeting of army in, **6**: 381; removal of Congress from, **6**: 386, 466; **7**: 272; **10**: 41; trial of *Lusanna* case at, **6**: 449; public buildings, **7**: 20; Committee of States meets in, **7**: 21; attitude toward Congress, **7**: 130; business failures in,

Pio, Chevalier de (*cont.*)
  11: 248, 255, 372, 382; 13: 637; 14: 465n
pioneers, company of: recommended by Senf, 5: 249
pipe staves: production in S.C., 8: 198
piquette, 11: 427
piracy: Va. bill to prevent losses by, 2: 437-8; proposed punishment for, 4: 198; prisoners arrested for, 5: 283; Congress establishes courts for trial of, 5: 497-9, 626; and Committee of the States, 6: 523-4; and trade treaty stipulations, 7: 472, 475; 8: 108, 192; punishment by death in U.S., 12: 4. *See also* Barbary States: privateering
Piranesi, Giovanni Battista: drawings of Pantheon, 19: 578; *Varie vedute di Roma antica e moderna*, 20: 544, 648
Pirkman, John: bill of, 7: 251, 356
Pisa, Italy: educational advantages, 8: 636
Piscataqua, N.H., 6: 448, 453
Piscataway creek, Va.: ferry at, 2: 455
pisé (rammed-earth construction): and fort at Lexington, Ky., 5: 463n; Cointereaux' use of, 15: 184-5, 185n-6n, 379-80; TJ doubts value of, 15: 185n; Cocke's buildings, 15: 185n-6n
Pissot, M.: publishes *General Advertiser*, 13: 247n, 309n; publishes English books in Paris, 13: 309; 14: 32-3; Franklin promotes sale of books in America, 14: 36
pistachio nuts: cultivation of in southern France, 11: 266, 428; TJ recommends study of, 13: 263, 369, 375; plants ordered for S.C., 13: 508; 14: 183
pistols: patterns specified in contract with Penet, Windel & Co., 3: 132; prices, 3: 135
Pitcairn, Mr.: supercargo of *Cato*, 15: 524
Pitcairn, Maj. John: killed at Bunker Hill, 1: 184, 185; signal to fire at Lexington, 10: 375n
pitch: Va. bill concerning, 2: 444-7; exported from S.C., 8: 201, 202, 203; Portugal's desire to import, 9: 19; French duty on, 11: 516, 541; 12: 163, 165, 167, 172, 469, 480-1
Pitcher, Mason: petition from, 5: 405; reply to, 5: 405n
Pitt, Fort: meeting of Indians with Va. commissioners at, 1: 244; garrison at, 1: 463; importance of to Va. and Pa.,

1: 469; report from commissioners at, 1: 493; distance to mouth of Shawnee river, 2: 85; establishment, 2: 99; Hamilton's proposed expedition against, 2: 256; post service to, 2: 389; Col. Gibson's regiment at, 3: 154; Va. troops at, 3: 186, 246, 364; 4: 349-50; purchase of cattle for, 3: 353; 5: 264, 492; Indian depredations at, 3: 356; Brodhead commandeers house at, 3: 362; supplies for, 3: 586; 4: 30, 489; clothing for soldiers, 4: 31; base of proposed Detroit expedition, 4: 205; provisions for western posts at, 4: 235; 6: 69; provisions for, 4: 239, 246, 595; gunpowder sent to, 4: 467, 599, 655; forces at, 4: 603; dispute between Va. and Pa. over, 5: 304, 374; 6: 666; TJ asks to have mammoth teeth kept at, 6: 139; center of Indian trade, 7: 280; Indians killed at, 20: 90; mentioned, 1: 235n; 2: 81, 101, 102; 4: 451; 5: 504, 548; 6: 584n; 8: 128
Pitt, John, Lord, 1: 270
Pitt, William the Elder. *See* Chatham, William Pitt, Earl of
Pitt, William the Younger: rumored to become prime minister, 6: 568; ministry, 7: 6, 8, 12, 16, 31, 41, 59, 60, 90, 93, 114, 115, 121, 134, 136, 139, 289, 293; 12: 517-8; 18: 106; resignation, 7: 58, 59, 60, 83, 114; popularity in London, 7: 60, 90, 121, 136, 139; attitude toward U.S., 7: 102; supported by George III, 7: 121; and U.S. trade, 7: 510; 8: 59n; 9: 184, 281; intimacy with Price, 8: 89; conference with Adams, 8: 179, 249; on tobacco duty, 8: 392n; policy toward France, 9: 635; praises Sheridan's speech against Hastings, 11: 149; secrecy of war preparations, 12: 292; alleged plan to recover U.S., 12: 311; and British minister to U.S., 12: 363; 18: 223, 227, 276; governmental appointments, 13: 462; maintains peace by preparation for war, 13: 510; 17: 415; and British interference in Netherlands, 13: 589-90; standing in Parliament, 14: 448; and regency bill, 14: 519, 580, 664; Paine criticizes, 14: 565; influence over Dundas, 15: 175; and creation of peers, 15: 441; letter to, from Trumbull, 15: 517-8; Brissot de Warville suspected of association with, 16: 46; praises Burke's speech,

16: 252; and Nootka Sound incident, 16: 413-4; 17: 35-6; 18: 25; G. Morris confers with, 17: 64-5, 96; 18: 288-92; Short's comments on, 17: 525-6, 614; Vaughan's comments on, 17: 620; public attitude toward, 17: 650; Maunsell's mission to, 18: xxxv, 263-7; letter to, from Maunsell, cited, 18: 267n; G. Morris' comments on, 18: 299; Spanish policy criticized, 18: 309n; and Purdie's impressment, 18: 318, 321, 334; and British commercial policy, 19: 133; caricature of, 20: xxxi, 384 (illus.); Dundas' report to, 20: 140; reportedly dominated by Grenville, 20: 168, 478; unpopularity, 20: 249; criticizes Paine, 20: 270; criticizes Washington, 20: 299; opposition to, 20: 535; map of South America, 20: 593; and case of *Mentor*, 20: 638n; mentioned, 9: 403, 406; 15: 554; 16: 254; 17: 489; 18: 229, 246, 249, 251, 478, 607

Pitt Packet (ship), 18: 312n

Pittsburg, Va.: ferry at, 2: 460; removal of militia to, 5: 565

Pittsburgh, Pa.: and Va.-Pa. boundary dispute, 1: 235n; 6: 7; rendezvous for western militia, 3: 8; 4: 230, 232; plans for defense of, 3: 55; lack of extra provisions, 3: 89; appointed as recruiting station, 3: 181; military post at, 3: 259; headquarters for western troops, 4: 235; Mrs. Trist's projected journey to, 6: 376; described by Mrs. Trist, 7: 86-7; distance from western boundary of Va., 9: 216; proposed as site of capital, 19: 6. *See also* Pitt, Fort

Pittsburgh Gazette, 17: 509n

Pittsfield, Mass.: visited by TJ and Madison, 20: 458

Pittsylvania co., Va.: letters to county lieutenant of, 3: 603-4; 5: 275-7, 617; appoints infantry officers, 1: 580; bill to establish places of holding courts, 1: 592-4; place of court of assize, 1: 629; militia, 2: 131; 3: 599; 4: 63, 614, 622, 637, 638, 641, 669; 5: 7, 36, 275-7, 311, 617, 646; 6: 93; senatorial district, 2: 336; levies of soldiers, 3: 8; defends western frontier, 3: 50, 52, 53, 79; tobacco loan office certificates, 3: 516; insurrection in prevented, 4: 77; supply post for, 4: 286; riflemen, 4: 621

Pittsylvania Court House, Va.: proposed

meeting of school overseers at, 2: 529; probable storage place for arms, 4: 563; arms stored at, 4: 648

Pius IV Pope: pamphlet about, 20: 656-7

Pius VI Pope: sent copy of Va. act for religious freedom, 10: 412; controversy with King of Naples, 13: 428, 465-6; mass in St. Peter's, 14: 405; as art collector, 14: 406, 449; improves roads, 14: 541; performs Lenten ceremony, 14: 591; and French clergy, 18: 503, 605; and forged bull, 19: 117; 20: 88; and conflict with France, 19: 634-5; 20: 368, 385, 539, 556

Pizay, M. de: hospitality to TJ, 11: 287, 463n

plague: quarantine for, 2: 524, 525; in Algiers, 9: 551; 11: 369, 512; 12: 58, 184; in Constantina, 11: 21-2; in Spain, 11: 334; among American captives on Minorca, 11: 376

Plains of Abraham, Que., 1: 447

planetarium: of Rittenhouse, 2: 202, 203n; proposed for use of College of William and Mary, 2: 541; Rittenhouse asked to make for Louis XVI, 6: 418; 9: 149n; 10: 250, 587; Jones describes, 14: 411, 412n; mentioned, 16: 481

planks: purchase for boatmaking, 4: 332; for repairing buildings, 4: 373

Plan of the City of Washington in the Territory of Columbia, 20: 17n

Planta family, 15: 130

plantation system: management in, 17: 345-6

Planter (ship): presumed loss of, 15: 649, 651; Paradise sends produce by, 16: 84

planting of crops: delayed by militia duty, 5: 441, 444, 449-50, 464-5, 507-8, 539, 583, 587; 6: 3

plants: imported by W. T. Franklin, 9: 180; requested by TJ of John Bartram, 9: 229-30; catalogue of Va. flora sent Mme de Tessé, 10: 157; forwarded by Thomson, 10: 176; exchanged with Cary, 10: 226-5; methods of packing, 10: 227; 11: 122; sent from S.C. to France, 11: 92, 112, 138, 142, 156-7, 173, 187, 206, 323, 324; sent to Buffon from N.C., 11: 413-4; ecology in southern France and northern Italy, 11: 649-50; sent to France, 12: 29; sent to TJ, 12: 75, 140, 159,

plants (*cont.*)
528, 533, 568, 569; **13**: 111, 123,
137-8, 151, 172; for French gardens,
13: xxx; **14**: 42; French imports of, **13**:
69; sent to Mme de Tessé, **13**: 110,
138, 187, 188n, 476-7, 483; **14**: 629;
16: 222, 223n, 227, 237, 308n; effects
of light on, **13**: 379; electrical fluid
and growth of, **13**: 379; lists, **13**: 476-
7, 484, 485n; **16**: 227; ordered for
S.C., **13**: 508; shipped from France by
TJ, **14**: 45; **15**: 376-7; ordered by TJ
from France, **16**: 322. *See also* seeds;
names of individual plants
plaster: for interior of Va. Capitol, **8**: 367
plate: taxation in Va., **2**: 218, 220
plateaux. *See* dessert plates
Plater, George, **3**: 628
Platière. *See* La Platière
platinum: use in telescopes, **9**: 148, 216,
232, 240; **10**: 317
Plato: *Dialogues*, **8**: 407; TJ seeks information on best Italian translation, **11**:
159; *Opera*, **13**: 300, 411, 536; TJ
possesses works of, **13**: 391
Platt, Richard: letter from, **16**: 24; and
Scioto Company, **18**: 172-3, 174n,
175n, 176, 177; letter from, to Hamilton, quoted, **18**: 260
Plautus, Titus Maccius: TJ seeks information on best Italian translation, **11**:
159; *Comœdiæ*, **15**: 406; **20**: 634n
Plaw, John: *Ferme ornée*, **15**: 186n
Playfair, John: teaches mathematics, **15**:
205n
Playfair, William: letters from, **14**: 654;
19: 592, 592-6; *Tableaux d'arithmé-
tique linéaire*, **14**: 635n, 654; and
Scioto Company, **18**: 160; **20**: 352;
and the fisheries, **19**: 189; letter from,
to Hamilton, quoted, **19**: 595n-6n
Pleasant, Matthew, **4**: 354
Pleasant, Philip, **4**: 354
Pleasants, Col.: letter to, **5**: 412
Pleasants, Mr., **6**: 7
Pleasants, Isaac, **5**: 353
Pleasants, James B.: letters from, **16**:
412-3; **17**: 320; and Cruse's applica-
tion for steam engine patent, **16**: xlii-
iii, 53n, 412-3; **17**: 320
Pleasants, John, **4**: 353, 354
Pleasants, Nancy Parsons (Mrs. Thomas
Pleasants, Jr.), **9**: 473
Pleasants, Robert: and Mazzei's agricul-
tural co., **1**: 158
Pleasants, Samuel: supports Thompson's

consular appointment, **19**: 314; **20**:
161n; recommended by TJ, **20**: 238-9
Pleasants, Samuel, Jr., **4**: 353
Pleasants, T.: recommends Thompson,
19: 314
Pleasants, Thomas: letter to, **3**: 638; and
Mazzei's agricultural co., **1**: 158; interest in trading in Europe, **2**: 26n; laborers, **4**: 354; letter from cited, **15**:
353
Pleasants, Thomas, Jr.: letter to, **9**: 472-
3; letters from, **8**: 650-3, 666-7; proposal for selling tobacco to French
farmers-general, **8**: 646; **9**: 214; letters
to cited, **11**: 328; mentioned, **7**: 20
Pleasants family, **6**: 160
plebiscite: recommended for approval of
Va. Constitution, **6**: 286
Pliny: *Epistolae*, **12**: 678; **14**: 491; *Natural History*, **20**: 634n
plow, moldboard: preliminary sketches
for, **13**: xxv-vi, 16 (illus.), 27; improvement of, **13**: 27, 34n; Randolph's
interest in, **16**: 370, 371n, 416, 450;
models and blocks, **16**: 371n; model
sent to Randolph, **17**: 327
Plowden, Edmund: cited on treason, **2**:
495n
Plowden, Francis: defends Mezières'
claim, **9**: 113n-4n
Plowed Hill, Mass.: held by Continental
army, **1**: 243
Plowman, Capt. (master of *Herald*), **15**:
495, 496, 498
plows: windlass operation, **8**: 553; Monte-
limart, **11**: 422 (TJ's drawing); Piedmont, **11**: 435
Plumard de Bellanger, Mme: letters to,
12: 155-6; **16**: 298-9; letters from,
12: 124-5; **15**: 318; **17**: 263-5; TJ's praise
of, **12**: 125; correspondence with Derieux, **12**: 125; **16**: 299n; **17**: 265n;
19: 249; relations with Derieux, **12**:
126, 134-5, 537; letters to cited, **12**:
538; **16**: 192n; **18**: 46-7; **19**: 602; **20**:
253, 379; letter from cited, **20**: 671n;
mentioned, **11**: 394; **12**: 308; **17**: 234-6
Plume *v.* Portlock, **1**: 72, 81-3
plums: French and American compared,
8: 683; wild seeds requested by TJ for
France, **9**: 254; at Monticello, **9**: 623;
in Brignolles, **11**: 443; planting, **16**:
194
Plunket, David: letter from, to Myers,
cited, **16**: 354n
Plutarch: TJ seeks information on best

Polish Order of Knights (*cont.*)
dence: American membership in rejected by Congress, **7**: 108n-9n

Polk, Col. Thomas: payment to, **3**: 604, 637; **4**: 53; as commissary at Charlotte, **4**: 5, 37, 103

Polk, William: letter to, **19**: 363-4

pollack: fishing for, in N.H., **7**: 346

Pollard, Mr.: cotton manufacturing project, **16**: 582

Pollard, Absolem: letter from, **5**: 322

Pollard, Benjamin: offers sugar for sale, **3**: 238; presents bills for payment, **3**: 614; signs address to TJ, **15**: 556

Pollet, Ens.: member of court-martial, **3**: 350

Pöllnitz, Baroness de, **8**: 525

Pöllnitz (Pelnitz), Julius Ludwig August, von: permit to accompany Riedesel to medicinal springs, **3**: 60n; pass for, **3**: 73; introduction to TJ, **8**: 525; visits TJ, **9**: 90-1; letters sent by, **9**: 115

Pollock, Mr.: TJ's opinion on note asked, **6**: 188; mentioned, **11**: 363

Pollock, Matt: petition from, **5**: 349

Pollock, Oliver: letter to, **6**: 511; letter from, **6**: 356-7; bills on, **2**: 259; **6**: 320; reimbursed for payments to Ill. officers, **3**: 158, 159, 160; draft on Penet, d'Acosta Frères, **3**: 160; needs remittances, **3**: 168-9; given drafts on France, **3**: 274; drafts drawn on, **3**: 320; draws bill of exchange, **3**: 323n; assistance to Fort Jefferson, **4**: 320; claims against Va., **5**: 586-7; **6**: 321n, 511, 551; **9**: 513; deposition on payment of bills, **6**: 323n; account with Va., **6**: 356-7; letter from, to Va. delegates in Congress, cited, **6**: 510; account of Cuba, **20**: 564n; mentioned, **3**: 317; **4**: 170, 283; **5**: 462; **6**: 324n

Pollon, Chevalier de, **9**: 363n

poll tax: Va., **2**: 218

Pollux, Julius: *Onomasticum Graece & Latine*, **12**: 137

Polly (ship): captured by Moors, **15**: 342n, 405n; detained in Port-au-Prince, **16**: 353n-4n; **17**: 417

Polly and Sally (ship), **12**: 436, 534n

Polnitz, Baron. *See* Pöllnitz

Polson, John: letter to, **13**: 433-4; letters from, **8**: 152, 258; **13**: 388-9; land claim against Va., **8**: 152, 237, 258; **13**: 388-9, 433; letter from, to Washington, cited, **13**: 389n

Polson, William: land allotted to, **13**: 388-9

Polybius: TJ seeks information on best Italian translation, **11**: 159; TJ recommends works of to Peter Carr, **12**: 18, 129; copy sent to Wythe, **12**: 127-8; Madison comments on, **12**: 274; *Historiarum*, **12**: 688; *The General History*, **13**: 179; TJ seeks copy of works of, **14**: 491, 707n

polychrest machine, **7**: 645

polygamy: punishment for, **2**: 497

polygraphic. *See* Polyplasiosmos

Polygraphic Society: receipt for picture purchased by Trumbull for TJ, **12**: xxxvi-vii, 483 (fac.)

Polyplasiosmos: description, **12**: 358n; sent to TJ, **12**: 405, 597, 647; purchased by Trumbull, **12**: 622; **13**: 280; acquired by TJ, **13**: 178, 199, 519

"Polypotamia" (TJ's name for new state): part of territory within area claimed but not ceded by Va., **6**: 587n; mentioned, **6**: 595n, 605

polytype printing: specimen pages, **10**: xxviii, 210 (fac.); TJ describes, **10**: 317; mentioned, **10**: 318-26; **13**: 37n-8n

pomegranate: growth of, **11**: 433; Milan, **11**: 437; effect of altitude on, **11**: 650

Pomeroy, Ralph: hires ox-teams, **7**: 126, 127, 128

Pomey, François Antoine: Sterling's edition of *Pantheon*, **11**: 523

Pommard: wine, **11**: 417

Pompadour, Jeanne Antoinette, Marquise de: Latude's verses on, **10**: 423; owner of the Château de Ménars, **11**: 325

Pompeii, **14**: 574

Pompey (slave), **4**: 440

Pompignan, Jean Georges Le Franc de, Archbishop of Vienne: in ministry, **15**: 333

Pompus Sextus, **20**: 635n

Ponçins, Marquis de: letter to, **8**: 514; letter from, **8**: 449-50; *Le Grand œuvre de l'agriculture*, **8**: 514

Pondicherry: French permit U.S. to use, **13**: 3; French troops withdrawn from, **16**: 573

Poniatowski. *See* Stanislas II Augustus, King of Poland

Pons, France: TJ describes, **11**: 457

33; **18**: 408, 414; need of American consul in, **8**: 600; relations with U.S., **9**: 21-2, 182-3, 466; **11**: 341, 566; **19**: 293, 421; resents commercial discrimination by Pa., **9**: 408; relations with Spain, **9**: 527; relations with Morocco, **9**: 547; **10**: 358; colonies, **9**: 631-2; **10**: 546-7; **11**: 339-41; protects American vessels in Straits of Gibraltar, **10**: 79, 302; and proposed concert of powers against Barbary pirates, **10**: 124, 486, 562n, 565; **18**: 408, 409, 412; Smith's mission to, **12**: 146, 173; travel in recommended, **13**: 358, 375, 531; Rutledge plans to visit, **14**: 614; **15**: 72-3; Lucy Paradise's interest in, **15**: 350; **16**: 197; American medals sent to, **16**: 67; ministers to European courts, **16**: 197, 198n; fleet in Mediterranean, **17**: 398; Humphreys reports from, **18**: 48-50, 102-6; **19**: 254-6, 270-1, 421-3, 643-4; **20**: 168-9, 327, 361-2, 421, 474-6, 538-9, 556, 592, 604-5, 620, 656-7, 677; British trade with, **18**: 49; American merchants in, **18**: 157-8; navigation bill sent to, **18**: 241-2; and the fisheries, **19**: 185, 186; Humphreys appointed minister to, **19**: 536; U.S. consular officials appointed, **20**: 262; trade regulations, **20**: 589
Portugal, ambassador to France. *See* Sousa de Coutinho, Conde de
Portugal, envoy extraordinary and minister plenipotentiary. *See* Pinto de Sousa Coutinho, Chevalier de
Portugal, King of. *See* Pedro III
Portugal, Princess of. *See* Mariana Victoria
Portugal, Queen of. *See* Maria I
Posey, Mr.: and bill establishing ferries, **2**: 454
Posey, John Price: removal from office, **6**: 280n
Posey, Thomas: letter from, to Steuben, cited, **4**: 350; letter from, to Davies, quoted, **5**: 605n; arrearages, **18**: 616
Posilipo, Italy: Short describes, **14**: 572-3
postage rates: changing excluded from powers of Committee of the States, **6**: 526; France, **8**: 553, 555
postal conventions: proposed between U.S. and Europe, **7**: 564; **8**: 454; **12**: 267
postal service: Va. bill for establishing cross posts, **2**: 388-91; cost, **2**: 390; **9**:

104; loss of official letters, **7**: 94; delays, **7**: 129; between France and U.S., **7**: 564; **8**: 286, 337, 558; **9**: 75, 136-7; **10**: 591; **11**: 189, 274, 276, 285, 335, 492, 643, 661; **12**: 74-5, 530, 683; between U.S. and Europe, **7**: 636; between England and France, **8**: 394; **10**: 555; Europe, **8**: 515, 520; U.S., **8**: 516, 684-5; France, **8**: 539, 552-3; Britain, **8**: 552-3; Va., **8**: 584; **20**: 618, 641, 664-5, 711-2; use of stages, **9**: 15; franking privilege for U.S. diplomats, **12**: 40; TJ criticizes, **19**: 328; poor quality of, **19**: 555-6; Boston to Richmond, **20**: 666
Postlethwayt, Malachy: *Universal Dictionary of Trade and Commerce*, **1**: 237
postilions: German, **13**: 48
postmaster general (Va.), **2**: 389, 390
postmasters (Va.): exemption from militia duty, **2**: 350
post office (U.S.): delay in regulating, **2**: 19; difficulties in organization, **2**: 21, 22n; regulation within powers of Committee of the States, **6**: 523-4
post roads: Va., **2**: 391; TJ proposes change in, **3**: 427
potash: export from Conn., **7**: 334, 336; export from R.I., **7**: 338; export from Mass., **7**: 339-40; export from N.H., **7**: 345; trade statistics, **7**: 349; export from New England, **7**: 374; export from U.S., **8**: 309; **10**: 147; Portugal's desire to import, **9**: 19; export to France, **9**: 112, 141; **11**: 617; duty on in France, **10**: 289; **11**: 541; **12**: 156, 163, 165, 167, 172, 349, 469, 480; French import of, **10**: 475; **11**: 459; **13**: 68-9, 72; export to Sardinia desirable, **11**: 353; in soap manufacture, **14**: 279-80, 354-5, 508-9; manufacture of, **20**: 580
potatoes: bill empowering governor of Va. to prohibit exportation of, **2**: 348; distillation of brandy from, **6**: 509; **7**: 113; crop at Dijon, **11**: 416; French inferior to American, **13**: 635; Duchesse d'Enville orders seed of, **17**: 558
potato-pumpkin (melon species), **18**: 98
Potawatomi Indians: sell blacks, **17**: 132n
Potclay (Cherokee chief): badge worn by, **4**: 36n, 52
Potemkin, Prince Grigorii Aleksandrovich: in Russo-Turkish war, **13**: 427,

press, freedom of (*cont.*)
9: 450; not secured by Constitution,
12: 425; in France, 14: 370, 375, 376,
386, 423, 432, 443, 482, 677, 689;
16: 45; mentioned, 12: 440, 558, 571,
583
Preston, Jonas: passport issued by TJ,
15: 484
Preston, Robert: letters sent by, 8: 602,
669; 9: 10, 41, 47, 54; arrival at London, 8: 663; mentioned, 8: 423
Preston, William: letters to, 1: 23; 3: 62-
3, 107, 111, 325-6, 447-9, 469, 480-
1; 4: 85-6; 5: 236-7, 524; 15: 589; letters from, 3: 340, 533-4; 4: 579; 5:
398-9, 436-9; present at Long Island
treaty, 2: 92; letter sent by, 3: 113;
and loyalist uprising, 3: 479; proposes
to raise body of volunteers, 3: 653; letter to, from Gates, quoted, 4: 87n; letter from cited, 4: 91, 108; joins
Greene, 4: 683; 5: 44; at Guilford
Court House, 5: 115; and negotiations
with Cherokees, 5: 234, 236, 396n;
defense against criticism, 5: 438; and
Cherokee archives, 6: 141n; opinion of
fossil tooth, 6: 208; mentioned 4: 57,
86; 6: 80; 12: 133
Preudhomme de Borre, Philippe Hubert,
Chevalier de: statement on Champagne
case, 10: 255
Prévost, M.: bookseller, 13: 203-4
Prevost, Gen. Augustine: besieged at Savannah, 3: 233; reinforces Cornwallis,
4: 555, 559
Prevost, L. N.: payment to for books
from Koenig, 13: 300, 411; 15: 260,
350
Prévôt des Marchands. *See* Flesselles
Prévôt des Marchands et Echevins de
Paris: letter to, 11: 165-6
Price, Mr., 4: 480
Price, Ben (?), 5: 535
Price, Daniel: imports slaves, 15: 654
Price, James: supplies hard money to
Continental army, 1: 438; commissary
for American army in Canada, 1: 440,
441; 17: 574; testimony on Canadian
campaign, 1: 448-50
Price, John: enters land caveats, 1: 94
Price, Joseph, 16: 308
Price, Richard: letters to, 7: 630-1; 8:
356-7; 13: 344-5; 14: 420-4; 15: 137-
9, 271-2, 279-80, 425; letters from, 8:
52-4, 258-9, 667-9; 13: 119-20; 14:
38-40; 15: 90-1, 329-31; *Observations
on the Nature of Civil Liberty*, 1: 471,

477, 488; *Observations on the Importance of the American Revolution*, 2:
236, 262; 7: 630; 8: 54, 258-9, 356-7,
503; 10: 201; 12: 586; and TJ's Statute for Religious Freedom, 2: 552n;
praised by Fabbroni, 3: 148, 149; inscription in copy of *Notes on Virginia*,
8: xxviii, 246, 258; friendship for
U.S., 8: 59n; 9: 398, 403, 467; letter
from quoted, 8: 88-9; arranges for insurance on Houdon, 8: 340, 424, 577,
653, 664n; and articles on America in
Encyclopédie Méthodique, 10: 8n; Mrs.
Paradise asks to urge her husband to
go to Va., 10: 69; introduces Ashburnham to TJ, 13: 119-20; *Review of
the Principal Questions in Morals*, 13:
120n; Barlow introduced to, by TJ,
13: 344; TJ's esteem for, 13: 398; 20:
392; letters to cited, 14: 440; TJ tries
to interest in slavery question, 14:
498n; on French Revolution, 15: 90,
266, 329-30; Priestley disagrees with,
15: 330; *Sermons on the Christian Doctrine*, 15: 331n; *Two Schemes of a
Trinity considered*, 15: 331n; letter
from, to Adams, cited, 16: 294n; and
TJ's Report on Weights and Measures, 17: 620; letter to, from Rush,
quoted, 19: 80n; death of, 20: 159,
278, 421-2; sermon satirized, 20:
292n; mentioned, 9: 45, 570; 12:
504n, 517; 15: 321
Price, Thomas (Cherokee interpreter):
deposition concerning Henderson's
land claims, 2: 71-6, 110n; chosen to
report on Sycamore Shoals conference,
2: 72; and Indian land claims, 2: 97
Price, Rev. Thomas: as chaplain of Va.
HB, 1: 23; appointed to give Fast-Day
prayers, 1: 106, 107n; signs Virginia
Association, 1: 109; death of, 9: 65
prices: Congress recommends laws for
general limitation of, 3: 197; of army
supplies, 4: 547-8; Hogendorp's queries on in U.S., 7: 297; N.Y., 7: 330;
Va., 7: 402; 13: 99; 14: 458; crops, 8:
115; 9: 202; Morocco, 10: 347-8;
Marseilles, 11: 272; Germany, 13: 23;
British affected by possible war with
Spain, 17: 663-4. *See also* individual
commodities
Prichett, Jacob: settlement on Indiana
claim, 2: 103
Priddy, Robert: in Albemarle co. militia,
1: 667
Pride, Mr.: antifederalism of, 15: 5;

Princeton, N.J. (*cont.*)
advantages as seat for Congress, **6:**
319, 337; living accommodations in, **6:**
339, 341; discussed as permanent seat
of Congress, **6:** 345; Washington's Farewell Orders to Army at, **6:** 402n-3n
Princeton College. *See* New Jersey, College of
Prince William co., Va.: letters to county
lieutenant of, **4:** 636-7; **6:** 34-5; letter
to tax commissioners of, **5:** 323; appoints infantry officers, **1:** 581; place of
court of assize, **1:** 630; militia, **2:** 131;
3: 598, 600; **4:** 63, 377, 636-7, 687;
5: 109, 181, 271, 309n, 311, 329n,
332-3, 410, 411n, 484; senatorial district, **2:** 336; levies of soldiers, **3:** 7;
defends western frontier, **3:** 50, 51, 53;
tobacco loan office certificates, **3:** 516;
supply post for, **4:** 286
Pringe, Martin: commands expedition to
Va., **1:** 282-3
Pringle, Mr.: selected as arbiter, **6:** 236
Pringle, Capt. James (master of the *Pallas*), **9:** 392
Pringle, John: part owner of *Canton*, **13:**
4n
Pringle, Mark, **7:** 241
printer, public: to be temporary postmaster general of Va., **2:** 390; need for in
Va., **3:** 492; Va. engages John Dunlap
as, **3:** 579-80
printers: to be liable only for anonymous
writings, **6:** 288
printing: invoice of Dixon & Nicolson, **5:**
211-2; of Va. laws, **5:** 243n; and movable type, **8:** 447; costs, **8:** 480; TJ's
interest in, **10:** 318n; polytype, **13:**
37n-8n; English books printed in
France, **13:** 309. *See also* polytype
printing
printing apparatus: captured by British,
3: 580n; transportation to Va., **5:** 157-
8
printing press: for Va., **4:** 396, 421-2; **5:**
193, 386n; paper for, **4:** 431-2; destruction by British, **4:** 433; R. H. Lee
erroneously comments on lack of, **6:**
92
prisoners: support of, **2:** 372; escape of,
2: 502, 586-7; guard for, **4:** 187; exchange of, **5:** 94n; arrested for piracy,
5: 283; in Barbary States, **8:** 621; redemption, **12:** 149, 151. *See also* Algiers, American captives in; convict labor

prisoners, French: supplies for, in America, **11:** 643
prisoners of war: Washington asked to
retain hostages for security of, **1:** 267;
exchanges, **1:** 390, 398-9, 400; **2:** 255,
270; **3:** 222-3, 363, 374, 605; **4:** 88,
154, 174, 199, 311, 419, 462, 517,
566-7, 622, 623, 644; **5:** 116, 324,
329-31, 352, 364-5, 383-5, 401-2,
456-8, 555-6; **6:** 26; attitudes of, **1:**
407; treatment of, **2:** 294; **3:** 44-9,
102, 104, 198-9, 205; and international law, **3:** 41, 47, 61, 98; **5:** 227-8;
Va. laws concerning, **5:** 148-50; negotiations on with Britain, **7:** 458; trade
treaty stipulations, **7:** 478, 486-7, 622;
subsistence of, **7:** 487, 623; and treaty
with Portugal, **9:** 419-20; and Moroccan treaty, **10:** 390, 423. *See also* army
officers
prisoners of war, American: British treatment of, **1:** 276-7, 403; **4:** 324; advice
of Va. Council concerning, **3:** 103-4;
memorial of officers of Va. line to TJ,
3: 388-91, 458, 481; provisions for, **3:**
389, 458; **4:** 550, 656; clothing for, **3:**
638; in N.Y., **3:** 639; **4:** 33; in
Charleston, **3:** 651-2; **4:** 471; **5:** 38-9,
141, 460, 509-10, 588, 632-3; **6:** 20-
1, 27; on Long Island, **4:** 164; money
for, **4:** 324, 516-7, 698; supplies for,
4: 481, 507; petition in favor of Gen.
McIntosh, **5:** 35; tobacco for, **5:** 243,
307, 559, 606; Continental commissary of, **5:** 402; Pecquet's aid to at Lisbon, **8:** 208-9, 235, 238; return from
East Indies, **9:** 173; starvation at Philadelphia, **10:** 61; forced to fight
against Americans, **10:** 62; death on
prison ship *Jersey*, **10:** 269
prisoners of war, British: taken at Trenton, **2:** 3; Va.'s policy toward, **2:** 5; list
of, in Albemarle co., **2:** 31-2; account
of guard for, **2:** 32-3; skilled workmen
among, **2:** 127; taken at Vincennes, **2:**
258, 298, 301; Gen. Phillips' plea for,
3: 65; irons removed, **3:** 97; removed
from Williamsburg to prison ship, **3:**
194; regulations of Congress on, **3:**
263-4; transferred to Congress by Va.,
3: 333, 488; censorship of letters, **3:**
339; held at Winchester, **3:** 538-9,
541-2, 624, 664, 665; **4:** 119-20; **6:**
51; in public prison, **3:** 614; provisioning, **4:** 33-4; **5:** 26, 27; taken at King's
Mountain, **4:** 84, 86, 98-9, 102, 103-

Protestant Episcopal Church (*cont.*)
attitude toward dissenters, **7**: 558; jealousy of other sects, **8**: 343; Richmond convention, **8**: 343, 641; liberalism of, **8**: 428; Philadelphia convention, **9**: 296; **10**: 78, 110. *See also* Church of England

Protestants, French: laws regarding, **12**: 557, 564; eligibility for election, **16**: 44-5

Provence: climate, **11**: 199, 247, 351, 427-8; TJ's comment on language of, **11**: 254; olive groves, **11**: 648; Bernard's work on natural history of, **12**: 634-5

Provence, Louis Xavier Stanislas, Comte de (later Louis XVIII): Gargaz' brochure given to, **9**: 100; Démeunier secretary to, **10**: 4n; and Assembly of Notables, **11**: 203; popularity, **12**: 68; in Estates General, **14**: 376, 431; suspected of conspiracy, **16**: 50, 106, 116n; speech by, **16**: 50-1, 106, 109n; French public trusts, **16**: 95; flees Paris, **20**: 561, 574, 651; financial perquisites suspended, **20**: 610

Provence, Louise Marie Josèphe de Savoie, Comtesse de: flees Paris, **20**: 574, 651; mentioned, **7**: 387

Providence (American sloop), **5**: 40

Providence, College at. *See* Brown College

Providence channel: reduction of, **10**: 559

Providence Gazette and Country Journal: quoted, **7**: 157n; TJ's notes on coinage published in, **7**: 164 (fac.); mentioned, **16**: 452; **17**: 509n, 516-7

Providence, R.I.: Démeunier's errors on corrected, **10**: 36

Province, John Williams. *See* Williams, John

Province Island, **2**: 38

provision law (Va.): TJ's notes on, **3**: 486, 487; Barron appointed commissioner for islands in Chesapeake Bay, **3**: 672; places of collection, **4**: 7-9; enforcement of, **5**: 3; local ignorance of, **5**: 71

provision law (Va.), commissioners of: letters to, **3**: 568, 569, 609-10; limited to three per county, **3**: 485; TJ's notes on, **3**: 492; instructions regarding, **3**: 537, 538; required to seize corn being held, **3**: 562; duties and powers, **3**: 610n; appointment, **4**: 22; accounts of, **4**: 552

provisions: in Canadian campaign, **1**: 390, 436, 437, 439, 441; subject to orders of commander in chief, **3**: 529; storage posts for, **3**: 537, 538; for Continental army, **3**: 588; **4**: 105-8, 133, 472; **5**: 34; difficulty in transporting, **3**: 607; impressment of, **4**: 59, 62; **5**: 194-5; magazines of, **4**: 184; **5**: 533; Va. act for supplying to army, **4**: 415; for Portsmouth expedition, **5**: 50, 75, 130; Va. superintendent of, **5**: 94; for Lafayette's forces, **5**: 145, 232, 522; restrictions on sale of, **5**: 263-4; sent from Port-au-Prince, **5**: 430

Provost, Rev. Samuel: letter sent by, **10**: 489

provost marshal: salary of, **3**: 570

Prudentius, Clemens Aurelius: *Opera*, **13**: 290; mentioned, **20**: 635n

Prunty, John: and bill for religious freedom, **2**: 549n

Prus, Thomas, **3**: 542n

Prussia: refuses to receive minister from U.S., **2**: 215; as market for tobacco, **3**: 92; attitude toward American Revolution, **3**: 118-9; commerce with Va. proposed by Arendt, **4**: 456; U.S. treaty of amity and commerce, **6**: 393; **7**: 48, 263, 267, 421, 436-7, 466n, 490-2, 494, 565-6, 574, 611-2, 616-28, 646, 649-50; **8**: 8-10, 14-5, 26-33, 37, 134-5, 141, 143, 165, 173, 234, 265-6, 301-2, 305-6, 310, 312-20, 323-4, 375, 431-6, 459, 478-9, 505-6, 515, 516, 544, 566 (fac. of signatures), 585, 603, 606, 608, 625, 639, 664; **9**: 136, 349, 466, 511, 666; **10**: 61, 106, 140, 176, 196, 285, 286, 313, 317, 348, 403, 462, 473, 479, 556; **12**: 359; **14**: 72, 76-7; probable status in European war, **6**: 471; influence on Russo-Turkish relations, **7**: 5; freedom of trade on rivers, **7**: 405; relations with Netherlands, **7**: 501, 506; **9**: 151, 436n-7n; **12**: 27, 31, 33, 34, 37, 152, 681; relations with Danzig, **7**: 506, 515, 649; **19**: 534; and war between Austria and Netherlands, **7**: 509, 514, 517, 518, 566, 571, 577, 609; provinces, **7**: 624; relations with Austria, **8**: 196, 592; **10**: 605, 624, 629, 634; **20**: 649; relations with Russia, **8**: 196; **12**: 309-10; **19**: 531; **20**: 166, 410; relations with Hanover, **8**: 302, 316, 373, 418; relations with Britain, **8**: 373; **12**: 309-10; **13**: 191, 295, 298, 408n, 455, 458, 556, 589;

Pultenay, William (*cont.*)
  mission to England, **18**: xxxiv, 246, 249-51, 259; letter to, from Smith, quoted, **18**: 249-50; letter to, from Grenville, cited, **18**: 250n; letter to, from Grenville, quoted, **18**: 251; and Hawkesbury's report, **18**: 267
Pulteney Associates, **18**: 246, 274n; **20**: 127, 140n
Pulvar, Mr.: and Hessian fly, **20**: 457-8; inn rated by TJ, **20**: 471
pulvis fulminens (chemical compound): explosive power of, **13**: 381
puma: size, **6**: 342; **9**: 131; hide sent to Buffon, **9**: 130; new to Buffon, **10**: 625
pumice: produced at Sète, **11**: 446
pumps: machinery, **10**: 102; worked by one horse, TJ's drawing, **11**: 462
Punic War, Third: compared to Steuben's plan, **5**: 262
punishment. *See* crimes and punishment
Purchas, Samuel: *Purchas his Pilgrimage*, **6**: 169, 488, 489; influences TJ's spelling, **6**: 606n; accounts of giants, **7**: 316
Purdie, Alexander: letter from, **2**: 207-8; publishes newspaper, **1**: 265; packs TJ's books, **1**: 406; prints TJ's bill for diffusion of knowledge, **2**: 249n; prints TJ's education bill, **2**: 266; son's impressment, **18**: 313, 317; Va. postmaster, **18**: 333
Purdie, George: signs nonimportation resolutions (1770), **1**: 47; articles purchased from, **3**: 152
Purdie, Hugh: impressment of, **18**: 310-42 (editorial note and documents); letter from, to Adams, **18**: 317; correspondence with Cutting, **18**: 318-9, 334-6; affidavit of, **18**: 337-41; threats against Cutting, **19**: 624
Purdie & Dixon: sign nonimportation resolutions (1770), **1**: 46; and Fast-Day resolution, **1**: 106n
Pursell, H. D.: engraves map of U.S., **6**: 605 (illus.)
Purviance, John H.: seeks treasury comptrollership, **20**: 226
Purvis, Capt. James: officer in Regiment of Guards for Convention troops, **3**: 121, 155-6; **5**: 428, 661; member of court-martial, **3**: 350
Purvis, John: cited on English statutes, **1**: 555, 596
Putnam, Benjamin: letter to, **12**: 7-8; let-

ter from, **10**: 351-2; claim against Comte d'Arbaud for loss of sloop, **10**: 351; **12**: 7-8
Putnam, Gen. Israel: in command on Hudson, **2**: 29; interview with Wheeler, **11**: 241
Putnam, Rufus: Sargent's comment on, **18**: 175n; trip to west, **20**: 87, 93
Puymarin, M.: uses spathic acid as engraving agent, **13**: 381
Puységur, Pierre Louis de Chastenet, Comte de: succeeds Brienne, **14**: 343; and Estates General, **15**: 189; dismissed from office, **15**: 286; supports aristocratic party, **15**: 286; seeks to justify conduct, **15**: 555; denounced by commons of Paris, **16**: 47; released from prosecution, **16**: 124
Pyrenees, **11**: 446

Quadruple Alliance, **14**: 569
Quakers. *See* Friends, Society of
Quantico, Va.: rendezvous of militia, **5**: 394
Quantico creek, Va.: ferry, **2**: 454; warehouses on, **5**: 393
quarantine: for smallpox, **2**: 122-3; Va. bill concerning vessels and persons coming from infected places, **2**: 524-6; Algiers, **9**: 551, 566; Spain, **10**: 220; Barclay permitted to evade, **10**: 392
Quarles, James: signs Va. oath of allegiance, **2**: 128; correspondence with Lafayette, **5**: 274n; certifies election return, **6**: 174-5
Quarles, Maj. James: compensation for services, **3**: 344-5; instructions from Va. Council, **3**: 439
Quarles, John, **4**: 542
Quarles, Thomas, **4**: 540
Quarles, Wharton, **4**: 541
quarter dollar: adopted by Congress, **7**: 159n
quartermaster general (U.S.): ordered to supply army in Canada, **1**: 394; Pickering appointed to office, **3**: 559. *See also* Virginia: Quartermaster's Department
quartermasters (U.S.): ordered to make weekly reports, **1**: 393; appointment of deputies, **3**: 608; **5**: 59; rule for invaded states, **4**: 327, 337-8, 351-2
Quatres saisons littéraires, Les: TJ quotes verse from, **8**: 240-1; review in *Journal de Paris*, **8**: 242n

Raleigh, Sir Walter (*cont.*)
  of England attributed to, **13**: 651; *History of the World*, **13**: 656; mentioned, **1**: 278, 340; **6**: 111n
Ralliter, Peter: settlement on Monongahela river, **2**: 101
Ralph, James, **9**: 486
Ramadan: strictness of fast, **10**: 335
Rambler (ship): arrival in Le Havre, **18**: 55
Rameau, veuve et fils: bankers at Dijon, **13**: 456; letter of credit on, **13**: 480
rammed-earth construction. *See* pisé
Ramond (Raymond) de Carbonnières, Louis François Elisabeth: assistant to Short in Paris, **18**: 352, 355n; meets with Americans on U.S. trade, **19**: 345; letter to cited, **20**: 257
Ramsay (Ramsey), Alexander: signs petition, **1**: 588; **6**: 294
Ramsay (Ramsey), Capt. Andrew: letter to, **15**: 637-8; letter from, **11**: 556; master of the *Robert*, **11**: 327; **15**: 636; Mary Jefferson put under care of, **11**: 351, 524; packet sent by, **11**: 352; bears letter, **11**: 360; Mary Jefferson's attachment to, **11**: 501, 612, 634; letters sent by, **11**: 502; offers to escort Mary Jefferson to Paris, **11**: 551, 556; TJ thanks for care of Mary Jefferson, **15**: 637-8
Ramsay, David: letters to, **8**: 457-8, 629; **9**: 228, 238; **10**: 122, 490-2; **12**: 8-9; **13**: 138-40; **15**: 199, 450; **16**: 577; letters from, **8**: 210-1, 293-4, 359-61; **9**: 89-90, 440-1; **11**: 279-80, 294, 295; **12**: 654-5; **14**: 5; **15**: 37-8; **16**: 332-3; *History of the Revolution in South Carolina*, **8**: 210-1, 293, 359-61, 457, 481, 596, 628-9; **9**: 89-90, 228, 357, 440; **10**: 117, 122, 153, 250, 291n, 362, 398, 513; **11**: 279, 316, 350, 525, 622; **12**: 42, 555, 588, 654-5; **13**: 317, 362; **14**: 5, 278; **16**: 332, 577; letter to, from Marbois, quoted, **8**: 360n; letters from cited, **8**: 472; **10**: 178; **15**: 160; chairman of Congress, **9**: 179, 504; **10**: 144n; books ordered for, **9**: 223; **13**: 132; *History of the American Revolution*, **10**: 513; **14**: 304; plants sent by, **11**: 92; and publication of TJ's letter on rice, **11**: 286; copy of *Notes on Virginia* sent to, **12**: 73; rice specimens sent to, **12**: 381; praised by Clerici, **12**: 555-6; TJ's assistance to, **13**: 105, 515; account with

Frouillé, **13**: 138-9; Cutting introduced to, **13**: 538, 542; **15**: 37; Madison pays, **14**: 5, 341, 427; in S.C. congressional election, **14**: 394; rice trade statistics sent to, **15**: 446n, 450; letters to cited, **15**: 469; **16**: 333n; contests election of William Loughton Smith, **17**: 179, 191n; mentioned, **13**: 511, 518; **15**: 241n
Ramsay, John: letter to, **14**: 427; letter from, **14**: 278; European trip, **12**: 654
Ramsay, Nathaniel: Md. delegate in Congress, **9**: 242
Ramsay, Patrick: signs nonimportation resolutions (1770), **1**: 47
Ramsay, Simon: in Albemarle co. militia, **1**: 665
Ramsay (Ramsey), William: signs petition, **1**: 588; in Albemarle co. militia, **1**: 665; signs Va. oath of allegiance, **2**: 129
Ramsbotham, Mr.: application from, **16**: 82
Ramsden, Jesse: makes scientific instruments, **15**: 257; biographical note, **15**: 257n
Ramsey, Andrew: loan to state, **3**: 386; mentioned, **3**: 442
Ramsey, John: loan to state, **3**: 386
Rand, R., **6**: 470
Randall, Abel: letter from, to Va. Auditors, **5**: 515
Randall (Randolph), Paul R.: letters to, **9**: 667-8; **18**: 73; letters from, **9**: 547-8; **16**: 226; letters sent by, **8**: 33, 54, 86; **10**: 99, 121n, 122n, 151, 649; mission to Algiers, **8**: 544, 572-3, 605; **9**: 14, 187, 223, 247-8, 376-7, 383, 506-7, 526, 536, 547, 549, 564, 610, 615, 619, 621, 646, 667; **10**: 139; **12**: 181, 239; arrival in Paris, **8**: 603; **10**: 105; Spanish passport asked for, **8**: 657-8, 670; **9**: 25; bills drawn by, **8**: 658; description of, **9**: 105; stay in Spain, **9**: 246, 248; letters from, to American Commissioners, **9**: 284-5, 525-6; letters from cited, **9**: 359, 565; **16**: 226n; return to France, **9**: 364, 365, 516, 533, 536, 539; **10**: 96-7; letter from, to father, **9**: 526-36; letter from quoted, **9**: 565n; personal report to Congress urged, **9**: 594, 611, 668; **10**: 105; salary, **9**: 610; departure from Madrid, **9**: 647; letters to cited, **9**: 665; **10**: 65, 79, 137; arrival in London, **10**: 140; map sent by, **9**: 649; **10**:

erations on the Present State of Virginia, **1**: 106n; mentioned, **1**: 20, 39, 40n

Randolph, Col. John: in Wayles estate debt, **13**: 327; **15**: 646-8, 649n, 672, 675; **16**: 447, 672

Randolph, Mrs. John, **1**: 270

Randolph, Judy, **7**: 3; **10**: 107

Randolph, Lucy: marriage, **15**: 637

Randolph, Lucy Bolling (Mrs. Peter Randolph), **1**: 250

Randolph, Martha Jefferson (Mrs. Thomas Mann Randolph, Jr., daughter of TJ): letters to, **16**: 300, 386-7, 429, 474-5, 577-8; **17**: 214-6, 326-7, 402-3; **18**: 110-1, 350, 579-80; **19**: 239, 264, 358, 604; **20**: 236-7, 381-2, 463-4, 568-9, 618, 670-1; letters from, **16**: 384-5; **18**: 499-500; **19**: 598-9; **20**: 477; recollections of mother's illness, **6**: 196n; bequeaths silver askos to family, **15**: xxxi-ii; marriage, **16**: 135, 154-5, 161, 171n, 182, 183n, 191n, 228, 297, 474, 560; **17**: 240, 264, 265n, 399; **18**: 80; **20**: 241, 250; letters to cited, **16**: 135n, 279n, 351, 352n, 389n, 436, 541, 606n; **17**: 24n, 271n; marriage settlement, with map by TJ, **16**: 154-5, 189-91; describes TJ's welcome at Monticello (1789), **16**: 167n-8n; letter to, from Nathaniel Cutting, **16**: 207n; letter to quoted, **16**: 241n; *Gazette of the United States* sent to, **16**: 241n, 386, 387n, 429n; TJ sends regards for, **16**: 278, 331, 352, 405, 419; **17**: 26, 299, 520; TJ's advice to, **16**: 300, 386; **17**: 215; visits Carr, **16**: 370, 393; health of, **16**: 406, 560; **17**: 3; **19**: 271; **20**: 157; letters from cited, **16**: 416, 475n; **18**: 594n; **20**: 382n; plans for moving to Varina, **16**: 441, 474, 475n; writing habits, **17**: 560; **18**: 579; Eppes sends compliments to, **17**: 592; TJ's deed of gift of slaves for, **18**: 12; at Monticello, **18**: 29, 499-500; TJ's plan for writing to, **18**: 39n, 65, 110, 141, 142n, 488-9; cypress vine seeds sent to, **18**: 308; seeds sent to, **18**: 308, 500; birth of daughter, **18**: 350n, 594; **19**: 239-40, 264, 337; exchanges Christmas presents with sister, **18**: 594n; receives copy of Gregory's *Comparative View*, **19**: 282-3n; letter to, from Mlle Bruny, cited, **20**: 377; books for, **20**:

381, 417; need for sister, **20**: 413; mentioned, **16**: 446, 549, 593; **17**: 260, 332, 657, 658; **18**: 509. *See also* Jefferson, Martha

Randolph, Nancy Cary (Mrs. Thomas Mann Randolph, Sr.): health of, **8**: 687; visits Boston, **9**: 60; mentioned, **8**: 560; **12**: 22

Randolph, Nathaniel: letters from, **4**: 147-9, 162; authorized to purchase flour, **4**: 135; appointed as purchasing agent, **4**: 375; mentioned, **4**: 574

Randolph, Paul R. *See* Randall, Paul R.

Randolph, Peter: advice on TJ's education, **1**: 3; relationship to TJ, **1**: 3; and Mazzei's agricultural co., **1**: 158; marriage, **16**: 25; madness, **20**: 293

Randolph, Peyton (1721?-1775): letters to, **1**: 49-51, 223-4; appointed moderator of Association of former Va. burgesses, **1**: 27; signs nonimportation resolutions, **1**: 30, 46; toast to as late Speaker of Va. HB, **1**: 31; member of Committee of Correspondence, **1**: 106n; signs Virginia Association, **1**: 108; chairs meeting of Virginia Association, **1**: 109; and nonimportation agreements, **1**: 110; writes letter to Va. HB, **1**: 111-2; copy of *A Summary View* sent to, **1**: 135n, 670; appointed to Continental Congress, **1**: 141; signs Continental Association, **1**: 153; and Mazzei's agricultural co., **1**: 157-8; presides over Va. HB, **1**: 169n; and Lord North's conciliatory proposal, **1**: 174n; death of, **1**: 249, 254, 268; son sent to Europe, **9**: 465; horses owned by, **17**: 243n; mentioned, **1**: 250, 267; **2**: 39n

Randolph, Peyton (1738-1794): quarrel with Lewis Burwell, **1**: 250; mentioned, **4**: 274; **17**: 570n

Randolph, Peyton (of Wilton): death of, **8**: 345; **9**: 65

Randolph, Rayland: and Mazzei's agricultural co., **1**: 158

Randolph, Richard: signs nonimportation resolutions (1770), **1**: 46; and sale of slaves, **1**: 96n; and Mazzei's agricultural co., **1**: 158; slaves for hiring out, **4**: 583; slaves employed at Hoods, **4**: 127; in Wayles estate debt, **6**: 416; **13**: 326, 328; **15**: 644, 650, 653, 655-7, 660, 662-70, 672-4, 676, 677n; **20**: 166-8, 374-6; death of, **10**: 109; letters to, from Farrell & Jones, **15**: 651-2,

Randolph, Richard (*cont.*)
656, 662-70; letter to, from William
Jones, **15**: 672-4
Randolph, Robert: prisoner of war, **3**:
390
Randolph, Ryland (Reyland): slaves employed at Hoods, **4**: 626; **5**: 127; design of Va. Capitol, **7**: 385; death of,
8: 116; **9**: 65
Randolph, Thomas (uncle of TJ): resi-
dent of Dungeness, **1**: 410n; slaves
employed at Hoods, **5**: 127; Peter Carr
lives with, **15**: 156; health of, **15**: 634,
640; mentioned, **1**: 16
Randolph, Thomas, Sr., **16**: 90
Randolph, Thomas Eston, **1**: 410n
Randolph, Thomas Jefferson: on TJ's
educational opinions, **8**: 412n; letter
from cited, **16**: 66n; drawing of pedestal attributed to, **18**: xxxiii
Randolph, Thomas (of Tuckahoe), **4**:
276
Randolph, Thomas Mann, Jr. (son-in-
law of TJ): letters to, **9**: 59-60; **10**:
305-9; **11**: 556-9; **12**: 631-2; **16**: 214,
277-9, 351-2, 416, 436, 448-50, 540-
1; **17**: 26, 274, 298-9, 390-1, 402n-
3n, 473-4, 622; **18**: 44-5, 64-5, 308,
488-9; **19**: 328-31, 582; **20**: 160-1,
295-6, 341-2, 414-6, 464-6, 640-1;
letters from, **10**: 260-1; **11**: 291-3; **12**:
685; **16**: 370-1, 441-2; **18**: 42-3; **19**:
239-40, 259, 323, 420, 555-6; **20**:
327-30, 605-7; character, **8**: 687;
health of, **9**: 58, 59; **16**: 406; **20**: 477;
education, **9**: 58-9, 60; **10**: 260-1,
305-9; **11**: 291-3, 556-9; **12**: 21-3,
370-1, 632; **15**: 639; TJ proposes trip
to southern France, **11**: 372; Short's
comments on as possible traveling
companion, **11**: 382; map of Va. sent
to, **11**: 598; letters to cited, **14**: 367n;
16: 209n, 279n, 352n, 371n, 386,
429, 509, 577; **17**: 130n, 165n, 166n;
returns to America, **14**: 367-8n; letters
from cited, **14**: 367n-8n; **16**: 279n,
352n, 406n, 416, 475; **17**: 299n; **18**:
141, 142n; **20**: 758; romance with
Martha Jefferson, **14**: 367n-8n; **16**:
290; letter from, to Anne Cary Randolph, cited, **14**: 368n; letter to, from
Leslie, cited, **14**: 368n; TJ's opinion
of, **14**: 368n; in Wayles estate debt,
15: 646, 676; marries Martha Jefferson, **16**: 135, 154, 182, 183n, 191n,
297; marriage settlement, **16**: 189,
387; prudence of, **16**: 300; interest in

moldboard plow, **16**: 370, 371n, 416,
450; **17**: 327; wife's love for, **16**: 385;
TJ's plan for writing to, **16**: 386; **18**:
39n, 65, 110, 141, 142n; visits Carr,
16: 393; weather observations, **16**:
409-10; **20**: 329-30, 607; wants to live
near Monticello, **16**: 441, 449, 540;
plans for moving to Varina, **16**: 441,
474, 475n; TJ's advice on law studies,
16: 449; Tarquin given to, **17**: 243n;
Report on Weights and Measures sent
to, **17**: 298-9; and purchase of horse
for TJ, **17**: 402n-3n, 512; wants to
buy Carter's land, **17**: 656, 657; TJ's
deed of gift of slaves for, **18**: 12; TJ's
memorandum to Lewis on arrange-
ments at Monticello for, **18**: 29; and
navigation of Rivanna, **18**: 40n; TJ
sends pamphlet to, **18**: 350; recommends Thompson as consul, **19**: 420;
maintains diary, **19**: 556; scientific observations, **19**: 556; investigates opossum, **20**: 160, 328, 330n, 382-3; buys
horse, **20**: 335; books for, **20**: 381,
417; and Hessian fly, **20**: 448; teaches
Mary Jefferson, **20**: 479-80; mentioned, **13**: 141n; **16**: 276, 331, 384,
405, 475, 593; **17**: 3, 402, 592, 656,
657; **18**: 111, 500, 509, 580; **20**: 675.
See also Edgehill; Randolph, Martha
Jefferson; Varina
Randolph, Thomas Mann, Sr.: letters to,
6: 533; **7**: 3, 115, 241; **9**: 261, 593;
12: 20-3; **16**: 154-5; **17**: 274-6, 623-4;
20: 340-1, 409; letters from, **1**: 70-1;
12: 370-1; **16**: 135; signs nonimportation resolutions (1770), **1**: 46; supports American state papers series, **1**:
145; and Mazzei's agricultural co., **1**:
158; illness of, **1**: 250; nickname, **1**:
406n-7n; candidate for Va. senate, **1**:
476; and money from Gen. Phillips, **3**:
75; lighter of, **5**: 517; money provided
for, **6**: 531; sons at University of Edinburgh, **8**: 687; indebtedness to Wayles
estate, **9**: 396; loss from flood, **10**:
108; mentioned as trustee in George
Harmer's will, **11**: 28; endorsement of
bills, **11**: 651; letters from cited, **14**:
367n; **16**: 155n; tobacco shipments,
15: 653, 667; imports slaves, **15**: 654;
Edgehill plantation, **16**: 93, 97, 98,
136, 540; son's marriage to Martha
Jefferson, **16**: 135, 154, 182, 183n,
189; letters to cited, **16**: 155n, 191n;
subscription for clearing Rivanna river,
16: 510-1, 578; marries Gabriella Har-

178, 197; form of commission, **3**: 203-4; and reviewing, **3**: 283; problems with, **3**: 393; places of rendezvous for, **3**: 619; Steuben's instructions for, **4**: 193-5, 197, 244-5; bounty money for, **4**: 601-2, 604; fraudulent practices, **5**: 174; John Nelson offers his services for, **5**: 363; outfitting for, **6**: 15

recruiting officers: appointed for each Va. county, **2**: 379; **3**: 508; funds for, **3**: 39; commission for, **6**: 641-2

Recueil alphabetique des droits de traites uniformes: sought by TJ, **11**: 373

Red Bank, N.J.: British attack on, **2**: 38

red birds. *See* cardinals

redbud: plants requested from John Banister, **11**: 121

Redd, Samuel, **1**: 64

Reddy, Richard: passport issued by TJ, **15**: 485

redemptioners. *See* servants, indentured

Redman, Dr., **2**: 39

Redman, Vincent, **3**: 7

Redmayne, Mr., **9**: 486

Reed, Col.: commanding officer at Fort Pitt, **2**: 101

Reed, Mr. *See* Ramsay, David

Reed, Edmund. *See* Read, Capt. Edmund

Reed, Esther DeBerdt (Mrs. Joseph Reed): death of, **5**: 611n; mentioned, **3**: 532n

Reed (Reid), Joseph: letters to, **3**: 211-2, 353-4, 489; **5**: 478-9, 492-3; **6**: 8, 74; letters from, **3**: 200, 262-3; **5**: 13, 263-4, 611, 650; **6**: 350-1; and Va.-Pa. boundary dispute, **3**: 200, 216, 262-3, 286, 288, 489; **5**: 13, 303, 304, 306-7, 339, 373, 374, 478-9, 611; **6**: 7, 8, 72, 74, 76; letter to, from Thomas Scott, **3**: 206-8; marches to N.Y., **4**: 55; orders restrictions removed on purchases at Fort Pitt, **5**: 504; arbiter in Nathan case, **6**: 323n; *Remarks on a Late Address*, **6**: 350-1; and orrery for Louis XVI, **6**: 418; Pa. commissioner in dispute with Conn., **6**: 476n; proposed trip to Europe, **7**: 98; Pa. delegate in Congress, **7**: 572; death of, **8**: 116, 134; mentioned, **7**: 41

Reed Island, Va., **1**: 263

reeds: export from S.C., **8**: 203

Reeveley (Reveley), John: partner of Ballendine, **3**: 126-7; money lent to by state, **3**: 138-9; manager of Westham

foundry, **3**: 147n, 188, 189, 387; estimate of ordnance and surplus from Westham foundry, **3**: 189; warrants to, **4**: 444

Reeves, Capt.: information against, **5**: 369-70; mentioned, **5**: 233

Reeves, Richard: petition to Va. HD, **2**: 42n; resolution in Va. HD respecting claim of, **2**: 63

refugees. *See* Loyalists: Va. policy toward

Regibus, Abbé de, **11**: 464n

regimental officers: commission for, **6**: 643

Regiment of Guards for Convention troops: letter from subaltern officers, **4**: 556; enlistment in Continental army, **4**: 353; troops, **4**: 366; grievances, **4**: 556, 565; discharge, **4**: 565, 573-4; **5**: 71, 100, 147, 408-9, 426-8, 607, 661-2; **6**: 21-2, 66-7; provisioning, **4**: 574; reorganization, **4**: 603; reenlistment, **4**: 604, 607; lack of money, **5**: 64; needed at Winchester, **5**: 432-3

register of U.S. Land Office, **7**: 141-6

register of Va. Land Office: letter to, **5**: 502-3; appointed by Va. GA, **6**: 298; mentioned, **2**: 137n, 139, 145-6, 161-2

Registry Act (1792): terms, **20**: 503-4

Regny, Aimé, père et fils, **11**: 464n

regrating: Va. bill to prevent, **2**: 561-6

Regulators: Shays' Rebellion compared to, **11**: 230

rei (Portuguese coin), **7**: 189, 190

Reichenbach: conference at, **17**: 395, 439, 651; **18**: 354; **20**: 168, 169, 695

Reid, Mr., **7**: 59

Reid, Edmund. *See* Read, Capt. Edmund

Reid, James: signs Va. oath of allegiance, **2**: 128; signs petition, **6**: 294

Reid, James Randolph, **7**: 280

Reid (Read), John: signs petition, **1**: 587; **6**: 294; deposition concerning Henderson's land claims, **2**: 85-7; and Indian land sales, **2**: 90; signs Va. oath of allegiance, **2**: 128; and bill establishing ferries, **2**: 457

Reid, Nathan: letter from, to William Davies, **5**: 643

Reid, Nelson: signs nonimportation resolutions (1770), **1**: 47

Reid, P., **6**: 667

Reid, Dr. Thomas, **13**: 242

Reid & Barret: payment to, **16**: 211

Reid v. Snaip, **1**: 69, 70n

Reims, France, **13**: 48

reindeer: compared to caribou, **7**: 29; Buffon confuses with moose, **13**: 593

Reine de France (ship), **7**: 628

religion: TJ's list of laws concerning, **1**: 539-44; TJ's miscellaneous notes on, **1**: 555-8; Robert Carter's comments on, **2**: 206-7; probable sectarian rivalry in control of public education, **2**: 247-8, 254; union of sects proposed, **2**: 248, 253; proposed support of in Va., **7**: 519; **8**: 113, 154, 428-9, 509; **9**: 195-6, 264; Madison's remonstrance against general assessment for, **8**: 415, 416n-7n; TJ's advice on to Peter Carr, **12**: 15-7; Madison's remarks on, **12**: 278-9; Price's opinions on, **14**: 39, 420; Dalzan's opinions on, **15**: 233-7; TJ's opinions on, *see* Jefferson, Thomas: Religion

religion, freedom of: provisions for in TJ's drafts of Va. Constitution (1776), **1**: 344, 353, 363; TJ's draft of resolutions repealing Va. laws interfering with, **1**: 530-1; TJ's outline of argument in support of, **1**: 535-9; TJ's notes on Locke and Shaftesbury, **1**: 544-51; Samuel S. Smith's remarks on, **2**: 253-4; Va. act establishing, **2**: 305 (illus.), 308n, 309n, 310n, 545-53; **3**: 68-9; **6**: 279n; **9**: 195-6; **10**: 11n, 65, 159n, 171-2, 186n, 200, 244, 283, 288, 333, 350, 412, 603-4; **11**: 6; **15**: 387-8, 536; and TJ's proposed revision of Va. Constitution (1783), **6**: 288-9, 293, 298, 311; trade treaty stipulations, **7**: 482, 618-9; **9**: 415, 425, 432; for aliens, **8**: 319; St. Lambert's comments on, **10**: 170-1; in France, **11**: 32; **16**: 373, 376n, 401; **20**: 384, 426-7; TJ on need for constitutional guarantee of, **12**: 440, 558, 571, 583; Buissel's comments on, **12**: 686; in Bill of Rights, **13**: 442; **14**: 18-9; in Fla., **20**: 98n; in La., **20**: 98n

religious worship: Va. bill for punishing disturbers of, **2**: 555-6

Remagen, Germany: vineyards at, **13**: 447

Remarks on Chastellux's Travels, **11**: 522

Remarks on the Manufacture of Maple Sugar, **20**: 344n

Remarks on the Taxation of Free States, **12**: 73, 115

Remoulins, France: TJ describes, **11**: 423, 443

Remsen, Henry, Jr.: letters to, **16**: 310;

17: 329-30, 498, 554-5; **20**: 462; letters from, **12**: 418, 612; **17**: 495-6, 502, 518-9, 595-8; **20**: 555-6; witnesses cession, **6**: 580; letters from cited, **12**: 563; **13**: 133, 569, 631n; **14**: 211; **16**: 8n; **17**: 644; **18**: 41n; state papers in care of, **15**: 520; and Short's letters, **16**: 310; memoranda for TJ, **16**: 317n; **17**: 339n; memorandum on costs of removal of offices to Philadelphia, **17**: 330n; clerk in Department of State, **17**: 347, 349n, 350n, 358n; **20**: 737; TJ's friendship with, **17**: 352n, 353n, 358n; translations by, **17**: 352n, 361; **18**: 407; letters to cited, **17**: 358n; **18**: 41n; paid by Department of State, **17**: 368, 369; **20**: 730; memoranda on Department of State personnel and services, **17**: 379-87; TJ's confidence in, **17**: 474; letter from quoted, **17**: 498n; correspondence with printers, **17**: 509n; **18**: 65-6, 78n, 112, 135n, 307n, 486; statement of TJ's expenses for moving to Philadelphia, **18**: 73-4; letter from, to Lear, **18**: 365; transcription by, **18**: 422n; letter from, to Bradford, cited, **18**: 490; on desalination of sea water, **19**: 610-1; and Potter's bill, **20**: 411-2, 420; instructions from TJ, **20**: 419-20; trip to N.Y., **20**: 558; engages lawyer, **20**: 613; letter to, from Bourne, **20**: 627; mentioned, **17**: 89n, 248, 355, 422; **18**: 268, 595; **20**: 659, 692

Renaud, Mlle: singing praised, **9**: 126, 152

Renaud, Jean Martin: letter from, **14**: 621; medal for J. P. Jones, **13**: 587n; **14**: 687; **16**: xl

Renaudin, M.: instrument for determining musical tempo, **9**: 146-7

Render, John: complaint against *L'Aigrette*, **14**: 84-5

Rendon, Francisco: Spanish representative in U.S., **7**: 433, 433n

Reni, Guido: paintings, **13**: 444

Rennes, France: TJ describes, **11**: 459; Parlement at protests against suppression, **16**: 103, 106, 116, 130

Rennie, John: work on steam mill, **9**: 401n

Renown (ship), **4**: 530n; **5**: 57n, 151, 182, 557

Rentfro, John: votes for bill for religious freedom, **2**: 549n

rents: effect of currency depreciation on,

Revolution, American (*cont.*)
  precedent for Brazilian revolution, **11**:
  340; effect on European thought, **12**:
  490; Bondfield's summary of his services in, **17**: 574-80. *See also* Canadian
  campaign; Carolina campaign; Continental army; French Army (Navy; officers) in American Revolution; German
  prisoners in American Revolution; Indians: activities in American Revolution; medals; militia; Peace Treaty,
  Definitive; southern army; and under
  names of battles
Rey & Brandebourg, **3**: 92
Reymond de St. Maurice, Abbé de: letter
  from, **11**: 622-3
Reynald, Abbé. *See* Raynal
Reynaud de Villeverd, François: letter to,
  5: 228-9
Reynder, Thorp: petition of, **5**: 148-9
Reyneval, M. *See* Gérard de Rayneval
Reynolds, Mr., **4**: 651n
Reynolds, Daniel: signs Va. oath of allegiance, **2**: 129
Reynolds, David: son's claims, **18**: 626;
  Wadsworth's orders to, **18**: 628
Reynolds, James: speculates in arrearages
  of soldiers' pay, **18**: xxxv-viii, 614,
  626-37; TJ's record of, **18**: xxxviii,
  268 (illus.), 649; Hamilton's connection with, **18**: 626-7, 643-59, 676,
  678-82; petition to Washington, **18**:
  627; imprisonment and prosecution,
  18: 630-5; investigation of case by
  Monroe and others, **18**: 630n, 631n,
  634-42; correspondence with Clingman, **18**: 640-1, 681; disappearance of,
  18: 642-3, 656, 658; Commonwealth
  v. Reynolds and Clingman, **18**: 655-6;
  Hamilton's documents on, **18**: 658-65;
  letters to Hamilton analyzed, **18**: 679-
  84; and case of William Duncan, **20**:
  677n-8n
Reynolds, Sir Joshua: blanching of pictures, **7**: 296
Reynolds, Maria Lewis (Mrs. James
  Reynolds): Hamilton's connection
  with, **18**: 627n, 628-31, 640, 643n,
  644, 647-51, 657, 660-1, 670, 673-
  85; character, **18**: 628-9; married to
  Clingman, **18**: 629n, 675, 676, 677n,
  683; and prosecution of husband, **18**:
  630-3, 641; accuses Hamilton of forgery, **18**: 666, 667, 673-8, 682-3; letters from, to Hamilton, analyzed, **18**:
  679-84

Reynolds, S. W.: portrait of George
  Beckwith, **20**: xxxii, 384 (illus.)
Reynolds, Simeon: dismissed from Treasury department, **18**: 656-7
Reynolds, Thaddeus: signs Va. oath of
  allegiance, **2**: 129
Reynolds, Thomas: paroled by British, **4**:
  435, 480
Reynolds, William: in Albemarle co. mi-
  litia, **1**: 668n; signs Va. oath of alle-
  giance, **2**: 129; recommended as clerk
  to TJ, **16**: 166, 352; **17**: 546-7
Reynst (Rhynst), Vice Admiral: forces
  Jones from Texel, **13**: 586
Rhea, Thomas: criticized by Beckwith,
  20: 138
rhetoric: importance to Americans, **11**:
  557, 558
Rhind, David, **12**: 402
Rhine river: Spain's attitude toward navigation on, **7**: 404; trade on, **7**: 405;
  Trumbull describes, **13**: xxviii-ix;
  Trumbull's sketches of near Mainz,
  13: xxviii-ix, 448 (illus.); TJ's notes
  on, **13**: 12-4, 16, 18, 19, 22; bridges,
  13: 18, 22, 26; Shippen and Rutledge
  travel on, **13**: 448, 454
Rhine valley: Trumbull describes, **10**:
  439; TJ's tour in, **13**: 13-26, 33n-6n;
  Shippen and Rutledge travel in, **13**:
  146
rhinoceros: possible bones of found in
  Siberia, **11**: 638
Rhode Island: letter to delegates in Congress, **11**: 609-10; letter from delegates
  in Congress, **10**: 461-3; population of,
  1: 182; **10**: 34, 35, 54-6; affirmative
  vote for independence, **1**: 314; votes
  against Chase's taxation plan, **1**: 323;
  sea battle at expected, **2**: 209; evacuation by British, **3**: 342; and act of
  Congress emitting new currency, **3**:
  528; Continental requisitions of food
  on, **4**: 107; represented at Hartford
  Convention, **4**: 138; quota for army
  pay, **4**: 369; charter, **5**: 603; **10**: 33;
  arrival of arms from, **6**: 32; medicine
  from, **6**: 53; represented on western
  lands committee of Congress, **6**: 131,
  147; extreme states rights position, **6**:
  263n-5; entitled to offer candidate for
  presidency of Congress, **6**: 348, 349;
  vote on permanent seat for Congress,
  6: 365; delegates from expected in Annapolis, **6**: 381; vote on land cession
  by Va., **6**: 575n; **7**: 4-5; financial quota

rice (cont.)
660; **12:** 321; **13:** 68; **14:** 252, 331, 633; **15:** 99-100, 104, 414, 544; Boutin's experiments with, **12:** 120; machine for cleansing, **12:** 187; Bérard's proposals for trade in, **12:** 250; lost in transit to S.C., **12:** 270-1; cooking, **12:** 338; shipped to L'Orient, **12:** 461, 505; seeds sent to U.S., **12:** 466; culture in Europe, **13:** 263, 369, 375; **14:** 42-3, 647-8; sent to TJ, **13:** 367-8, 533n; **14:** 707-8; **15:** 133, 425; **16:** 274, 276n; **17:** 4-5, 564-5; **18:** 65, 79; sent to Drayton, **13:** 368; Egyptian, **13:** 372; shipments to Bérard & Cie., **13:** 377; **14:** 633; **15:** 12; Terrasson's contract for, **13:** 476n; British demand for, **14:** 633; **16:** 390; from Cochin China, **14:** 636-7, 641, 647; dry culture, **14:** 640-1, 673-4, 707-8; **15:** 133; **16:** 274, 276n; **17:** 564-5; **18:** 65, 79, 97-8; culture in West Indies, **14:** 673-4, 707-8; **17:** 565n; shipments to Turkey advised, **15:** 13, 22, 37-8, 372, 408-9, 444, 450, 451; African, **15:** 146; **17:** 4-5; **18:** 97; **20:** 332, 602; seed brought from Timor by Bligh, **16:** 274, 276n, 492, 495, 496n, 578; **17:** 564-5; **18:** 97; **20:** 391; in Va., **20:** 605-6; export to Spain, **20:** 710

Rice, Capt.: certificate of, **19:** 322

rice, Carolina: production, **8:** 197; exportation, **8:** 198, 200, 202, 203; compared with Mediterranean rice, **9:** 585-6; **10:** 463-4; **11:** 264; French market, **10:** 475, 490-1, 541, 590-2; **11:** 98; **12:** 263, 287, 295-6, 298-9, 338; inferior to rice from Levant, **10:** 490-1; price, **10:** 491; compared to Piedmont rice, **11:** 338-9, 516, 587, 644-6, 659; **12:** 338; **13:** 372; **15:** 447-8; preferred for slave trade, **11:** 459; sold at Marseilles, **11:** 507; used to pay debts, **16:** 332

Rice, Charles: TJ's accounts with, **10:** 614

rice, Cochinchina, **11:** 646; **12:** 508

Rice, David: petition on organization of military service, **6:** 55-60

rice, Egyptian: exported to S.C., **12:** 437, 464, 507, 509, 522, 528, 534, 567; sent to Drayton, **12:** 500

Rice, George: letters from, **4:** 611-2; **5:** 223, 237, 346-9; mentioned, **4:** 287n; **5:** 288n

rice, Levant: compared to S.C. rice, **10:** 490-1; price, **11:** 358

rice, Lombardy: sent to S.C., **12:** 380-1

rice, Mediterranean: process of preparation requested by Rutledge, **10:** 463-4

Rice, Lieut. Nathaniel, **4:** 542, 694

rice, Piedmont: import by France, **10:** 491; TJ's interest in, **11:** 267; compared to Carolina rice, **11:** 338-9, 516, 587, 644-6, 659; **12:** 338; price, **11:** 358; processing, **11:** 436; sent to Drayton, **11:** 520; **12:** 148; smuggled from Italy by TJ, **11:** 587, 645, 659; sent to S.C., **12:** 508

Rice, Tandy: TJ's accounts with, **10:** 614

rice-beater: TJ describes at Casino, **11:** 437-8

rice pudding: recipe sent to TJ, **12:** 381

Richard, John: letter from, **10:** 289; financial difficulties, **9:** 293; mentioned, **9:** 524, 581

Richardson, Col., **3:** 577

Richardson, Mr.: books for TJ ordered from, **12:** 73, 164

Richardson, George: prisoner of war, **5:** 432

Richardson, John: signs petition, **6:** 293; passport issued by TJ, **15:** 484; land grant from Cayugas, **20:** 130

Richelieu, Louis François du Plessis, Duc de: death of, **13:** 492, 497; **20:** 568; memoirs, **16:** 48

Richelieu falls, Que., **1:** 442, 446

Richeson, Capt. James, **4:** 675, 686

Richmond (ship): captured by the *Holker*, **7:** 435

Richmond, C.: bills against Va., **5:** 391

Richmond, Charles Lennox, third Duke of: supports king on Netherlands policy, **11:** 697

Richmond, Christopher: seeks treasury comptrollership, **20:** 225, 230n

Richmond, N.Y.: visited by TJ and Madison, **20:** 460

Richmond, Va.: removal of seat of government to, **2:** 271, 288; **3:** 284, 297-8, 330, 332, 333-4, 342, 427; **7:** 361; escheated real estate in, **2:** 283, 284n; ferry at, **2:** 458; bill for establishing public library at, **2:** 544; rendezvous of recruits, **3:** 8; **4:** 295, 339; **5:** 496n-7n, 501, 520-1, 546, 616-7, 645, 646; public buildings, **3:** 18, 230; **7:** 361, 385; **8:** 257, 343-4, 462, 534-5, 537-8; **9:** 221-2; power of state to survey

Ridley, Matthew (*cont.*)
nam's affairs in hands of, **10**: 351-2;
mentioned, **12**: 8
Ridley, Thomas: praised by Gen. Stevens, **4**: 125
Ridley & Pringle: Garvey's claim against, **12**: 379, 384
Ridout, Mr.: desires writ of surseance, **9**: 656-7
Riedesel (ship). *See General Riedesel* (ship)
Riedesel, Frederika, Baroness von: birth of daughter, **3**: 338, 368; borrows books from Mazzei, **3**: 342; sends message to Mrs. Jefferson, **5**: 184; mentioned, **3**: 15, 24, 99, 212, 291
Riedesel, Friederich Adolphus, Baron von: letters to, **3**: 24-5, 59-60, 368-9; letters from, **3**: 212-3, 291, 338, 440; **4**: 4; **5**: 184-5; garden of, **2**: 242; TJ invited to meet, **2**: 252; permit from TJ to visit medicinal springs, **3**: 59-60; parole, **3**: 86n, 341; TJ asks Washington to forward letter to, **3**: 227; letter from quoted, **4**: 174; sends flag-of-truce ship, **5**: 257; mentioned, **3**: 3, 15, 73, 99, 235, 294, 306, 561, 581; **5**: 259
Rieger, Baron (minister of Württemberg): letter from, **13**: 100; mentioned, **16**: 49
Riemersma, Capt. (of Rotterdam): attack on, **13**: 408n
Rieux, de. *See* Derieux
Rieux, Justin Plumard de. *See* Derieux
Rieux, Peter de: signs address, **16**: 178
riflemen: for southern army, **4**: 629; discontented with use in southern army, **5**: 115; expected from certain counties, **5**: 644; need of Lafayette for, **6**: 18, 36, 93
rifles: recommended for western service, **3**: 79; for Va. militia, **4**: 40
Right, James, Jr.: signs petition, **1**: 588
right of soil, private: within powers of Committee of the States, **6**: 523-4; mentioned, **6**: 478n, 481n, 483n, 485n, 486n, 501, 502n, 504, 505, 520n
Rights, Bill of. *See* Bill of Rights
rights, charter of (French). *See* charter of rights
rights, civil: declaration of lacking in Constitution, **12**: 276, 425; protected by government, **12**: 278-9; Paine on,

13: 4-5; Paine and TJ discuss, **13**: 6n-7n; French National Assembly statement on, **15**: 268-9; state constitutions and, **18**: 132-3
Rights, Declaration of (French). *See* Declaration of Rights
rights, natural: cited by Albemarle freeholders, **1**: 117; discussed in Declaration of Rights (1774), **1**: 119; discussed in *Summary View*, **1**: 121; and free trade, **1**: 123; slavery a violation of, **1**: 129-30, 317-8; **10**: 58; to ownership and distribution of land, **1**: 133; discussed in Declaration of Independence, **1**: 315-8; discussed in Va. Constitution, **1**: 337-9; discussed in drafts of Va. Constitution, **1**: 356-7; violated by King, **1**: 377-9; to purchase land, **2**: 67; to unappropriated lands, **2**: 139-40; of widows, **2**: 415; to citizenship, **2**: 477; to expatriation, **2**: 477; **18**: 311-2; to trial by jury, **2**: 480; preservation through education, **2**: 526; to religious freedom, **2**: 545-7; **6**: 279n, 289; TJ on, **5**: 356; **16**: 179, 450; **17**: 195; **18**: 311; curtailed by military needs, **5**: 568; to restitution to family of escheated property, **6**: 157; need of understanding by citizens, **6**: 286; to voting, **6**: 286; to government by consent, **6**: 286; **17**: 195; of approving or disapproving laws, **6**: 287; to freedom of the press, **6**: 288; subjection to property rights, **6**: 310; treatment of Indians an invasion of, **6**: 656; to freedom of opinion, **8**: 260; to employment on land, **8**: 682; as basis of good government, **12**: 326; Paine on, **13**: 4-5; Paine and TJ discuss, **13**: 6n-7n; in Lafayette's declaration, **14**: 438-9; **15**: 232n. *See also* conscience, liberty of; press, freedom of; religion, freedom of
Rigoley de Juvigny, Jean Antoine: *De la decadance des lettres et des moeurs*, **11**: 666
Rigoley d'Ogny, Baron: letter from, **11**: 274; letter from cited, **11**: 276
Rilliet & Cie., **14**: 507
Rimini, Italy: Short describes antiquities in, **14**: 380
Rind, Clementina: and Fast-Day resolution, **1**: 106n; and Virginia Association, **1**: 109n; printer, **1**: 672n
Rind, James: libel on Charlottesville inhabitants, **18**: 26, 43-4; TJ's uneasiness towards, **19**: 252

Rind, William: signs nonimportation resolutions (1770), **1**: 47

ring dial: invention, **11**: 293; application of, **11**: 562

Rio de Janeiro: in favor of revolution, **11**: 340; port, **11**: 341

Rioms, Albert de. *See* Albert de Rions, François Hector, Comte de

riots: Va. bill concerning, **2**: 517-9; punishment for, **6**: 420

Rippert, Françoise: claim to prize money, **9**: 130, 153, 156-7, 162-3

Rippetoe, James: in Albemarle co. militia, **1**: 665

Rising Sun (ship), **12**: 71, 180; **13**: 371n

Ritchie, Capt. (master of the *Peggy*), **9**: 392

Ritchie, Archibald: signs nonimportation resolutions (1770), **1**: 46; and bill establishing ferries, **2**: 455

Ritherford, Mr., **5**: 446

Rittenhouse, Miss: TJ sees, **16**: 300; TJ carries fan to, **18**: 111

Rittenhouse, Benjamin: and scientific instruments, **19**: 41n-2n

Rittenhouse, David: letters to, **2**: 202-4; **7**: 516-7; **9**: 215-7; **12**: 144-5; **16**: 484-5, 509-10, 542-3, 574; **17**: 295; **19**: 323, 584, 596; **20**: 382-3; letters from, **8**: 565-6; **10**: 73; **11**: 293-4; **14**: 51; **16**: 545-7, 567-70, 594-6; **18**: 476; **20**: 383; appointed to confer with Va. delegates, **1**: 466n; government use of talents of, **2**: 203; observation of solar eclipse, **2**: 206; draft of letter to, **2**: 208 (illus.); fair copy of letter to, **2**: 209 (illus.); planetarium of, **2**: 541; **6**: 418-9; Pa. boundary commissioner, **3**: 77; **8**: 74; vice president of American Philosophical Society, **4**: 544; orrery, **6**: 418, 420, 508; TJ praises family, **6**: 465; astronomer to Pa., **6**: 556; **7**: 41; pension, **7**: 20; consulted on coin design, **7**: 154n; TJ provides information for, **7**: 602; judges harpsichord experiment, **8**: 50; astronomical observations, **8**: 117; Page's admiration of, **8**: 117-8; literary interests, **8**: 118; copy of *Notes on Virginia* for, **8**: 263; **12**: 136; survey of Va.-Pa. boundary, **8**: 310; proposed as faculty member of College of William and Mary, **8**: 417; TJ hopes for chart of Va.-Pa. boundary from, **8**: 417; scientific research, **8**: 562-3, 565-6; experiments, **9**: 132; message to on platinum, **9**: 148; improvement in pendulum, **9**: 321; guest of Franklin, **9**: 322, 440; *Oration . . . into the Influence of Physical Causes upon the Moral Faculty*, **10**: 141n; TJ's queries of, **10**: 250; commissioner for Chesapeake-Delaware canal, **10**: 512; health of, **10**: 512, 587; **11**: 563; **13**: 370; **14**: 33, 51, 325; **15**: 17; and hygrometer, **10**: 647; **11**: 75; books for, **12**: 136, 423; **13**: 38; **14**: 369; antifederalism of, **13**: 40; letters to cited, **14**: xxvi; **15**: 82n; **16**: 605n, 607n, 614n, 616n, 668n, 669n, 671n-3n; **17**: 350n; TJ's discussion of prehistoric animals with, **14**: xxvi-ix; and Fitch's steamboat, **15**: 642; and Report on Weights and Measures, **16**: 484-5, 509-10, 542-3, 545-7, 567-70, 574, 587-8, 594-6, 607-8, 614, 643n, 645n, 668n, 669n, 672n; **17**: 295; **18**: 457; letters from cited, **16**: 604n, 668n, 669n, 671n, 672n; **17**: 295n, 445n; **18**: 457n; letter from quoted, **17**: 350n; recommends Barton to TJ, **17**: 350n; notes on boundaries of Pa., **17**: 445n; disagrees with TJ on pendulum, **18**: 481n; recommends Andrew Ellicott as U.S. geographer, **19**: 40n; **20**: 61n; and eulogy of Franklin, **19**: 98, 99, 101; views on opossum, **19**: 330; **20**: 160, 328, 382-3; and desalination of sea water, **19**: 612, 614, 616; unable to travel with TJ and Madison, **20**: 293; weather observations, **20**: 383; contributions to *National Gazette*, **20**: 733; mentioned, **3**: 664; **6**: 444, 543; **7**: 111, 518; **8**: 100, 264; **9**: 149; **10**: 140, 350, 452; **11**: 657; **13**: 152n; **14**: 370, 651; **15**: 80n; **16**: 617

Rittenhouse, Elizabeth: marries J. D. Serjeant, **15**: 17

Rittenhouse, Esther (Hetty). *See* Waters, Esther Rittenhouse

Rittenhouse, Hannah Jacobs (Mrs. David Rittenhouse), **6**: 465, 543; **7**: 517; **8**: 438, 566; **9**: 149, 217; **12**: 145

Rittenhouse family, **9**: 322; **11**: 290

Rivanna canal, **1**: 88n; **16**: 140n

Rivanna river: TJ's plans for, **1**: 87; clearing of, **1**: 88n; **16**: 510-1, 578; **18**: 39-41; post service on, **2**: 389; ferries across, **2**: 458, 459; plans for fortifications on, **5**: 249

Riverhead, N.Y.: visited by TJ and Madison, **20**: 460

Va., **5**: 196n, 459; certificate of, **19**: 322

Robertson, Robert: letter to, **10**: 294-5; letter from, **10**: 283-4; debt for mourning suit, **10**: 253-4, 273; complaints of Ruellan's behavior, **10**: 328

Robertson, William: captain of frigate for S.C., **11**: 301n

Robertson, William (of London): letter to, **13**: 648; letter from, **13**: 640

Robertson, Dr. William: *History of America*, **8**: 175, 185; **12**: 18; **13**: 651; **16**: 384, 436, 481; TJ criticizes, **8**: 185; **13**: 397; errors in writings on America, **11**: 71; **14**: 698; cited on Mexico, **11**: 324; **12**: 159; Ramsay comments on, **9**: 441; *History of Charles V*, **12**: 18; *History of Scotland*, **12**: 18; **13**: 651

Robeson, Capt., **9**: 8

Robeson, William: letters to, **8**: 446; **9**: 118; letters from, **8**: 441; **9**: 107; loan from TJ, **9**: 107, 118

Robin, Claude C., Abbé: *New Travels through North America*, **12**: 62

Robindar, Mr., **15**: 181

Robins, Capt., **3**: 91

Robins, John: prisoner of war, **3**: 391

Robinson, Capt.: probable loss at sea, **12**: 423

Robinson, Mr.: and bill establishing ferries, **2**: 455

Robinson, Arthur (midshipman in the *Alliance*), **9**: 156, 163

Robinson, Col. Beverley: regiment of loyal provincials, **5**: 74; aids spies, **17**: 41

Robinson, Gov. Beverley, **17**: 124n

Robinson, David: replaced by H. Innes, **15**: 583

Robinson, Edward: clerk in Dept. of State, **17**: 357n

Robinson, Rev. Henry: introduction to TJ, **8**: 17

Robinson, Isaac, **11**: 657

Robinson, J., **12**: 518

Robinson, James: signs nonimportation resolutions (1770), **1**: 46; in Albemarle co. militia, **1**: 666, 667

Robinson, John: lead mines of, **2**: 388n; debts to, **6**: 472n; on crew of *Dauphin*, **19**: 333

Robinson, Joseph: in *Rachel* case, **20**: 516

Robinson, Moses: recommended for office, **19**: 378-9; hospitality to TJ and

Madison, **20**: 440, 440n, 444; and Hessian fly, **20**: 447, 458; trees of, **20**: 560

Robinson, S.: share of prize money claimed by François Rippert, **9**: 130, 153, 156-7, 162-3

Robinson, William (of Conn.): and Hessian fly, **20**: 448

Robinson, William (of Va.): signs nonimportation resolutions (1770), **1**: 46; prisoner of war, **3**: 390; imports slaves, **15**: 655

Robinson v. Fauntleroy, **10**: 29

Robison, Capt., **4**: 320

Robison, Prof. John: illness of, **13**: 242; teaches physics, **15**: 205n

Robson, James: buys books for TJ, **15**: 51-2, 83n, 94, 96, 130

Rochambeau, Mme de: health of, **13**: 152

Rochambeau, Donatien Marie Joseph de Vimeur, Vicomte de: son born to, **11**: 89

Rochambeau, Jean Baptiste Donatien de Vimeur, Comte de: letters from, **11**: 89; **15**: 416-7; commands French troops, **3**: 374; Mazzei sends naval plan to, **3**: 382; letter from, to Congress, cited, **4**: 567; correspondence with Washington, **4**: 660; **16**: 237n, 375, 376n; plans for aid to Va., **5**: 81; Washington confers with, **5**: 663; **6**: 9, 82; and evacuation of College of William and Mary, **6**: 144; intends to visit Monticello, **6**: 150; asked to forward letters to Philadelphia, **6**: 165; TJ hopes to call on, **6**: 203; departure from U.S., **6**: 216-7, 246; praises *Notes on Virginia*, **8**: 358; respect for American law, **9**: 6-7; **15**: 338; reports non-payment for Cincinnati badges, **9**: 160-1; TJ urges Va. gift of land to, **9**: 266; bust of for Va. Capitol suggested, **9**: 267; Trumbull to paint portrait of, **9**: 456; statue of proposed, **9**: 518; commands camp near Brabant, **11**: 517; portrait in Trumbull's "Surrender of Lord Cornwallis at Yorktown," **12**: xxxv, 60, 67 (illus.); medal presented to, **12**: 106n; **14**: 687; **16**: 65n, 67; member of Society of Cincinnati, **12**: 522; letter to, from Coxe, quoted, **15**: 417n; orders measurement of Natural Bridge, **19**: 300n; supports French Revolution, **20**: 673; mentioned, **3**: 382; **4**: 190; **6**: 191n, 243; **8**: 585

Roche, Chevalier: commander of *l'Union*, **13**: 286

Rocheblave, Phillippe de Rastel de: described, **3**: 333; breaks parole, **3**: 665

Rochefort (Rochfort), France: American agent at, **9**: 599, 627; **10**: 196; TJ describes, **11**: 457; consular agent recommended, **14**: 61; mentioned, **13**: 275

Rochefoucauld. *See* La Rochefoucauld

Rochegude, Daqueria: makes wine resembling port, **11**: 443; wine ordered from, **15**: 66, 67n; killed in riot, **16**: 572

Rochelle, France. *See* La Rochelle

Rochet, M. de, **1**: 399

Rochon, Alexis Marie de, Abbé: discovery in optics, **7**: 508, 517; **8**: 73, 75; **9**: 216, 232, 240; and use of crystal, **8**: 575; friendship with Franklin, **9**: 106; experiments in using platinum in telescopes, **9**: 148; **10**: 317; report on polytype printing, **10**: 319n; method of engraving, **10**: 324n, 325-6, 356; comments on Franklin and TJ, **15**: 82n

Rockbridge, parish of, Va.: election of vestry, **2**: 117

Rockbridge co., Va.: letter to county lieutenant of, **5**: 275-7; letter from county lieutenant of, **6**: 72; formation of, **2**: 114; administration of justice in, **2**: 114-5; public dues or fees, **2**: 115; election district for Va. senators, **2**: 115, 336; lawsuits in, **2**: 116; levies of soldiers from, **3**: 8; defends western frontier, **3**: 50, 51, 53, 79; militia, **3**: 356, 420, 422, 598, 600, 643; **4**: 63, 296n, 346, 350, 352, 364, 371, 477, 621, 624; **5**: 29, 35, 183, 275n, 311, 315, 507-8, 541-2, 598; **6**: 36, 93; requests dissolution of vestries, **3**: 467n; tobacco loan office certificates, **3**: 516; supply post for, **4**: 288n; insurrection in, **5**: 605n; **6**: 23; draft rioting, **5**: 621-2

Rock creek, Va.: ferry, **2**: 454

Rockets, Va., **6**: 512, 515

Rockfish gap, Va.: route of Convention troops, **3**: 424; **4**: 160; military stores removed to, **6**: 49, 50

Rockfish river: ferry across, **2**: 459; mentioned, **6**: 48

Rockingham, Charles Watson-Wentworth, second Marquis of, **7**: 318

Rockingham, parish of, Va.: election of vestry, **2**: 117

Rockingham co., Va.: letter to commissioner of provisions for, **3**: 568; letter to county lieutenant of, **5**: 416; letter from county lieutenant of, **6**: 72; formed from part of Augusta co., **2**: 114; administration of justice in, **2**: 114-5; public dues or fees, **2**: 115; election district for Va. senators, **2**: 115, 336; lawsuits in, **2**: 116; levies of soldiers from, **3**: 6-7, 8; defends western frontier, **3**: 50, 51, 53; militia, **3**: 420, 422, 598, 599, 643; **4**: 63, 296n, 346, 350, 352, 364, 371, 477, 621, 624; **5**: 29, 35, 311, 315; **6**: 36, 93; tobacco loan office certificates, **3**: 516; commissioner of provisions for, **3**: 573; supply post for, **4**: 288n

Rocky Hill, N.J., **6**: 584n

Rocky mountains: visited by Stanley, Indian captive, **6**: 208

Rocky Ridge, Va.: land lottery drawing at, **1**: 22; as place for rendezvous of recruits, **3**: 360, 363

Rocounier, M.: repairs chariot, **15**: 506

rod (standard of measurement): vibrating, **16**: 485, 546, 576, 589, 606, 607, 618-9, 623, 651; variation in, **16**: 542; Rittenhouse's views on, **16**: 545-6; TJ prefers to pendulum, **16**: 576, 588, 606

Rodgers, Dr., **9**: 47

Rodney, Caesar: signs Continental Association, **1**: 153; signs Congress' second petition, **1**: 223; signs agreement of secrecy, **1**: 253; signs Declaration of Independence, **1**: 308n, 432; mentioned, **5**: 101

Rodney, Adm. George Brydges: captures Spanish merchantmen, **3**: 285; escapes from Spanish fleet, **3**: 306; defeat in West Indies, **3**: 414-5; engagement with Guichen's fleet, **3**: 474; arrives at N.Y., **3**: 654; **4**: 10, 15; departs from N.Y., **4**: 122n, 158, 159; at St. Eustatius, **5**: 176, 177; **6**: 74n; victory in West Indies, **5**: 376, 382; fleet intercepted by Spanish, **5**: 551; sails for West Indies, **6**: 164; victory over De Grasse, **6**: 191, 192n; suit against by St. Eustatius merchants, **8**: 161-2

Rodney, Capt. John, **4**: 57n, 78

Rodney, Thomas: letter from, **17**: 547-51; theory on origin of man, **17**: 548-51

roebuck: horns sent to TJ, **11**: 326; horns sent to Buffon, **12**: 194

Roebuck (British ship), **2**: 3; **5**: 283, 552
roedeer: Madison queries finding in America, **9**: 520
Roederer, Pierre Louis, Comte de: opposes tobacco monopoly, **9**: 292n; admires Condorcet's style, **9**: 345n; possible authorship of speech before Comité du Commerce, **9**: 345n; in committee on taxes, **16**: 271n; on farmers general, **17**: 396; opposes Lafayette, **20**: 351
Rogers, Capt., **4**: 355
Rogers, Col., **15**: 417n
Rogers, Achilles: in Albemarle co. militia, **1**: 665
Rogers, Bayard: passport issued by TJ, **15**: 484
Rogers, Daniel Denton: letter from quoted, **17**: 248; recommends Bromfield as consul, **17**: 248
Rogers, Col. David: G. R. Clark to supply, **2**: 259; leaves New Orleans, **3**: 71, 72, 167, 169
Rogers, Edward: and Indian land claims, **2**: 97
Rogers, John (Md.): signs agreement of secrecy, **1**: 253; Creswell introduced to, **15**: 583
Rogers, John (Va.): signs petition, **1**: 588
Rogers, Capt. John: commissioned to raise cavalry troop for Ill., **3**: 268; cavalry troop under, **3**: 277
Rogers, Col. John: letter from, **5**: 574; complaints of Kaskaskia inhabitants against, **5**: 599
Rogers (Rodgers), Dr. John, **8**: 664, 667
Rogers, Dr. John, Jr.: letters sent by, **8**: 664, 669; introduced to TJ, **8**: 667
Rogers, Joseph: prisoner of war, **3**: 390
Rogers, Maj. Robert: suspected of role in Hickey Plot, **1**: 412; escapes from Indians, **20**: 453-6
Rohan (Rouen), Louis René Edouard de, Cardinal: imprisonment, **8**: 395, 421, 450, 472; **9**: 447, 470; expected sentence, **9**: 152; memoir published, **9**: 580; acquittal, **9**: 605-6, 634; flight of, **17**: 312. *See also* diamond necklace, affair of
Rohan family: Puisaye a member of, **11**: 105
Rohan-Guemené, Ferdinand Maximilien Meriadec, Prince de (Archbishop of Cambray): regent at Liège, **17**: 526; **18**: 478, 608, 610

Roland, M.: work on chemistry, **8**: 559; painting of crucifixion, **12**: 69
Rolands, John: and Henry co. court bill, **1**: 593
Rollin, M.: dismissed as censor, **12**: 667
Rollings, John: signs nonimportation resolutions (1770), **1**: 47
Rollings, Robert, **5**: 190
Roma Casa, Milan, **11**: 437
Romain, Pierre Ange: killed in balloon ascension, **8**: 245
Roman Catholics: laws on in colonies, **1**: 557; in U.S., **7**: 575
Roman Eagle (ship), **20**: 612n
Roman Empire: Stiles reports on debt of, **17**: 442-3
Roman law: and Va. Court of Admiralty, **2**: 572; basis of equity law, **9**: 68
Roman remains: France, **11**: 226; razed for road building, **11**: 226; TJ's description praised, **11**: 258; Orange, **11**: 423; Arles, **11**: 425; Bordeaux, **11**: 454; Short admires, **13**: 655-6; **14**: 380-2, 405-6, 448-52
Romans, king of: supported by Elector of Hanover, **14**: 565
Rombourg & Sons, **12**: 384
Rome: U.S. treaty of amity and commerce, **6**: 393; **7**: 48; educational opportunities in, **8**: 635-6; **9**: 58, 60; history of, **10**: 307; inclusion in proposed concert of powers against Barbary pirates, **10**: 486; TJ's reason for not visiting, **11**: 519, 532; Short plans to visit, **13**: 655-6; **14**: 273; Pantheon, **14**: 381-2; Short describes, **14**: 381-2, 405-6, 448-52; Rutledge describes, **14**: 404; English travelers in, **14**: 448; Forum, **14**: 449, 453n; catacombs, **14**: 450; Coliseum, **14**: 450; climate of, **14**: 464; American medals sent to, **16**: 67; Ségur appointed French ambassador to, **19**: 637. *See also* Vatican
Romilly, Samuel: letter sent by, **13**: 460; biographical note on, **13**: 461n; book carried by, **13**: 623; visits TJ, **15**: 426
Roms, Pierre Joseph, **15**: 42
Romulus (British ship): taken by French, **5**: 50, 72, 651; TJ offered passage in, **6**: 211n; delay in sailing, **6**: 229, 230, 232, 236n, 237, 242, 246, 253; mentioned, **4**: 90, 92; **5**: 651; **14**: 578
Ronald, Andrew: opinion in Wayles estate debt, **20**: 167, 167n-8n; mentioned, **10**: 109
Ronald, William: letter to, **17**: 512-3;

Ronald, William (*cont.*)
  and plan for federal control of commerce, **9**: 199, 204n-8n; opposes Constitution, **13**: 98; purchases Elk Hill, **17**: 512-3, 569-71, 581; **20**: 388, 415-6; buys Cumberland property, **17**: 581, 592; **20**: 153; legal opinion for, **17**: 673; bonds, **20**: 326
Ronaldson, Patrick: solicits flag to go to Bermuda, **5**: 425n
Rondette, M. (wine merchant): purchases Frontignan wine, **11**: 445
Roosevelt, John, **17**: 601
Roosevelt, Nicholas, **17**: 601
Root, Jesse: Conn. commissioner in dispute with Pa., **6**: 476n, 477n, 478n, 481n; nominated as Conn. representative, **14**: 525
Rootes, George, **6**: 71n
ropemakers: wages in N.Y., **7**: 327; wages in Conn., **7**: 333; wages in R.I., **7**: 339; wages in Mass., **7**: 342; wages in N.H., **7**: 343
Rosamond (ship), **7**: 429
Rosaubo, M.: letter from, **11**: 90
Roscoff, France: landing of *William and Catherine* near, **8**: 477, 493
Rose (British frigate), **18**: 312n
Rose, D.: death of, **9**: 185
Rose, Duncan: letter to, **6**: 137-8; letters from, **3**: 32, 35, 38, 85, 86, 100, 101, 108-9, 123, 152-3, 158-9, 160, 170, 180, 181, 200-1, 209, 213, 282-3, 295, 326, 329, 332, 337, 344, 345; **4**: 383; **5**: 53, 307-8; **14**: 592-3; member Va. Board of Trade, **3**: 17n, 19n, 316n; memorandum for TJ, **3**: 583; desires payment of warrant, **4**: 591; denies payment of certificates for wagon hire, **4**: 632, 642, 643; executor of Banister estate, **14**: 592-3; **16**: 22; mentioned, **4**: 413, 439, 453, 489, 582; **5**: 432; **6**: 270
Rose, Duncan, & Co.: imports slaves, **15**: 655
Rose, Hugh: letter from, **6**: 118-20; letter from, to Muter, quoted, **4**: 295n; mentioned, **4**: 261
Rose, Mrs. Hugh, **6**: 118
Rose, John: debt to McCaul, **13**: 513
Rose, William: letter to, **3**: 541; letter from, **5**: 17-8; letter from cited, **4**: 315; return of tents, **4**: 531-2; provision of clothes to, **5**: 97n; mentioned, **5**: 26, 96
roselet. *See* ermine

Rosencrone, Marcus Gerhard, Baron: instructions to Walterstorff concerning Franklin, **7**: 466n
Rosette, Carlo, Count: describes Ledyard's death, **15**: 198
Rosewell (Page estate): Mazzei's visit to, **7**: 62, 273; mentioned, **1**: 35, 36n
Rosicrucians, **7**: 365
Rosier, Jean François de, Abbé: letter to, **11**: 111-2
Ross, Capt.: commands captured British vessel, **5**: 283, 284n; commander of the *Surprise*, **5**: 424; mentioned, **5**: 338
Ross, Mr. (servant): applies for job in Department of State, **17**: 519
Ross, Archibald: fraudulent account of capture of the *Julius Caesar*, **16**: 563n, 564-5; **18**: 643n
Ross, David: letters to, **4**: 475, 506-7; **5**: 141, 171, 191-2, 266, 296-7, 308; **6**: 6, 17-8, 21; **7**: 25, 244; **9**: 473-5; **17**: 630-1; **18**: 489-90; **20**: 373; letters from, **4**: 226-8, 354-5, 554-5, 582-3, 591-2, 659-60; **5**: 169-71, 208-9, 264-5, 372, 458-9, 600-1, 606-7, 660-1; **6**: 12-4, 19-21, 27-8, 540; **7**: 17; **8**: 650-3, 659-61; contract for iron for Westham foundry, **3**: 188, 189; purchase of iron from, **3**: 214; **4**: 354; **5**: 281, 321; draft for, **3**: 592; health of, **3**: 638; **5**: 358; supplies clothing to army, **4**: 358, 445, 453, 679; **5**: 139; **6**: 16; warrants to, **4**: 444; Va. commercial agent, **4**: 445n, 475n, 503, 506-7, 590; **5**: 168, 228-9, 368, 430, 586; **6**: 220; with Senf, **4**: 602; report on clothing for army, **4**: 668; memorandum concerning supplies, **5**: 30; superintendent of lead mines, **5**: 191, 417; appointed to Va. Board of Trade, **5**: 263; purchases for army, **5**: 359n-60n, 523n; **6**: 25, 50; funds for, **5**: 482; letter from, to Steuben, quoted, **5**: 559n; plan for building Anderson's shop, **5**: 580; authorized to purchase and exchange flour, **6**: 9; letter from, to Davies, quoted, **6**: 23n; funds for Short, **7**: 253; property in Richmond, **7**: 605-6; shares in James River Company, **8**: 343; consulted on purchase of building lots, **8**: 344; loss of credit in London, **8**: 358; purchases coal mine, **8**: 643; proposal for selling tobacco to French farmers-general, **8**: 646, 666; **9**: 214; letters from quoted, **8**: 651n-2n; com-

letter from, to Morrow, quoted, **15:** 81n-2n; TJ's interview with, **15:** 81n-2n; investigation of tooth drawers, **15:** 145, 172, 404; on patents, **15:** 171; improvement on Barker's mill, **15:** 504-5, 522; **16:** 591; **17:** 516; mentioned, **15:** 523

runaways: Va. bill concerning, **2:** 475-6

Rush, Benjamin: letters from, **6:** 223; **8:** 220; **16:** 411-2; **17:** 391-2; signs agreement of secrecy, **1:** 253; debates Congressional representation, **1:** 326; signs Declaration of Independence, **1:** 432; newspaper quarrel with Ewing, **8:** 52; introduces Samuel Fox, **8:** 653; oration before American Philosophical Society, **10:** 140; and Society for Political Enquiries, **14:** 50n; letter from cited, **16:** 240n; introduces Coxe to TJ, **16:** 411; **19:** 123; recommends Andrew Brown to TJ, **17:** 391; **18:** 66n; **19:** 252n; *An eulogium in honor of the late Dr. William Cullen*, **17:** 391n; on sea power, **18:** 516n; favors Potomac capital site, **19:** 16; and Franklin's death, **19:** 80n; letter from, to Richard Price, quoted, **19:** 80n; opinion of Rev. William Smith, **19:** 99n; on new system of penmanship, **19:** 121n; criticizes Adams, **20:** 279-80; encourages maple sugar production, **20:** 344n; educational fees, **20:** 474

Rush, Mathias, **5:** 84

Rushworth, John: *Historical Collections*, **1:** 106n

Russel (ship), **15:** 57

Russel, Capt. (master of *Les Trois Frères*), **15:** 65

Russel, Mr.: wine sales, **19:** 600

Russel, Lieut. John, **4:** 540

Russel, Thomas: impresses boats, **4:** 81n; recommends John Bulkeley, **20:** 362n

Russell (ship): Purdie on, **18:** 337

Russell, Gen.: finds prehistoric bones, **9:** 202

Russell, Mr.: and bill establishing ferries, **2:** 455; introduced to Short, **20:** 409-10

Russell, Benjamin: letter to, **18:** 65-6; letter from, **18:** 135; paid by Department of State, **17:** 363, 366, 368, 371, 372; publishes *Columbian Centinel*, **17:** 509n; prints U.S. laws, **18:** 135; prints "Publicola" letters, **20:** 280-3

Russell (Russel), Capt. Charles: superintends supplies, **4:** 287n; **5:** 288n; **6:** 21n; letter to, from Claiborne, quoted, **6:** 10n

Russell, Lieut. Charles, **4:** 540

Russell, Hinde: signs Virginia Association, **1:** 109

Russell, John (master of *Nancy*), **17:** 421n

Russell, Thomas: letter to, **16:** 494-5; warrant to impress boats, **4:** 80-1; TJ recommended to, **7:** 298; TJ's business dealings with, **7:** 362; father of Thomas Russell-Greaves, **12:** 408; **13:** 617n; **14:** 462, 463; William Pearce recommended to, **20:** 316n; mentioned, **7:** 578; **8:** 399; **12:** 319; **18:** 399

Russell, William: signs nonimportation resolutions (1770), **1:** 47; appointed commissioner to investigate land claims, **2:** 65n; signs petition, **11:** 336

Russell, Col. William: commands troops against southern Indians, **1:** 386; paid money for Gen. McIntosh's family, **5:** 218, 542; mentioned, **3:** 652

Russell-Greaves, Thomas: letters to, **14:** 464-5, 595; letters from, **13:** 616-7; **14:** 350-1, 413; introduced to TJ, **12:** 408; biographical note, **13:** 617n; in Nîmes, **14:** 350; on olive culture in S.C., **14:** 350-1; introduced to Cathalan by TJ, **14:** 462, 463, 464; in Marseilles, **15:** 44

Russia: attitude toward American Revolution, **3:** 118-9, 202, 236, 336, 349, 413; relations with Britain, **3:** 374; **9:** 366; **11:** 218; **12:** 692; **19:** 607; **20:** 159, 410, 535, 658; maritime strength, **5:** 377; offers to mediate between Britain and U.S., **6:** 65, 94, 96, 99-100, 210n, 334; commerce, **6:** 213; relations with Austria, **6:** 389, 437; **8:** 196; **12:** 189-90; **19:** 336; treaty of amity and commerce, **6:** 393; **7:** 48, 267, 424n; relations with Turkey, **6:** 469, 471, 540, 567, 568; **7:** 3, 5, 16, 31, 41; **10:** 405, 605, 613, 624, 629, 634, 650; **11:** 476, 490; **12:** 108, 109, 110, 111, 113, 128, 132, 134, 145, 152, 157, 160-1, 166, 174, 292, 307, 320, 361, 446, 448, 490, 564; **13:** 103; tobacco culture, **7:** 371; rivers, **7:** 405; and war between Austria and Netherlands, **7:** 509, 514, 518, 566,

Russia (*cont.*)
571, 577; coinage, **8**: 90; relations with Prussia, **8**: 196; **12**: 309-10; **14**: 429, 482-3, 531; **19**: 531; **20**: 410; relations with Venice, **8**: 373, 418; relations with Denmark, **9**: 366; **14**: 54, 186, 287, 333, 362-3, 672; **15**: 110, 116; relations with Algiers, **9**: 532; **10**: 150, 224; **12**: 242, 313; **15**: 341; relations with Spain, **9**: 648-9; **12**: 673; **13**: 114n, 134, 216, 217n; ambassador to Spain, **10**: 150; foreign relations, **10**: 251; **12**: 446, 482; relations with France, **11**: 102, 118; **12**: 174, 189-90, 309-10, 350; **13**: 496-7, 584; **14**: 603, 604n-5n; war with Turkey, **12**: 209, 682; **13**: 124-6, 134, 139, 145, 212, 215-6, 388, 404-5, 455, 456, 458, 465, 471, 475, 483, 491, 496-7, 501, 506, 510, 531, 538, 565, 572, 633, 650; **14**: 186, 211-2, 305, 328, 333, 366, 370, 375, 387, 429, 443, 448, 482, 506, 516, 531, 597; **18**: 86, 354, 452-3, 477-8, 479, 504, 593, 606-7; **19**: 418, 552; **20**: 169, 303, 327, 369, 410, 535, 658; Liston's desire for mission to, **12**: 363; Mediterranean fleet, **12**: 673, 692; **13**: 113, 114n, 191; Black Sea naval action in war with Turkey, **13**: 126, 134, 404, 427-8, 436-8, 454-6, 458-9, 461, 465, 471, 483, 488-9, 491, 497, 503, 529, 580, 632-3, 650; **17**: 593, 627-8; war with Sweden, **13**: 295, 298, 316, 344, 360, 365, 373, 378, 404-5, 483, 489, 491, 496, 503, 579; **14**: 645; **15**: 357, 513n; **17**: 209, 313-4, 522; trade with U.S., **13**: 583; **19**: 128-30; alliance with France proposed by J. P. Jones, **13**: 584; British attitude toward, **13**: 590; peace with Sweden, **14**: 54, 186, 287, 333, 362-3, 672; **15**: 110, 116, 121, 187, 195; **17**: 500, 501n, 503, 526, 542, 593, 628; **18**: 64, 296; **20**: 695; timber trade with Britain, **14**: 252; relations with Poland, **14**: 329, 366, 370, 375, 387, 429, 482-3, 531, 603, 604n-5n; **16**: 119-20, 304; Spanish territories approached by, **14**: 501, 503n; Alaskan settlements, **14**: 503n; treaty with U.S. suggested by J. P. Jones, **14**: 506, 516; peace with Turkey, **14**: 645, 652-3, 661, 672; **15**: 110, 187, 195; **16**: 254-5; **18**: 452-3, 606-7; **20**: 582-

3, 704; military action in Hungary, **16**: 41; minister released from Constantinople, **16**: 41; American medals sent to, **16**: 67; alliance of European powers against, **16**: 538, 541; **20**: 261; and proposed Barbary States blockade, **18**: 408, 409, 412; and the fisheries, **19**: 178; ambassador to France, *see* Simolin

Ruth, Thomas: British war prisoner, **2**: 31

Rutherford, Mr.: work cited, **6**: 490

Rutherford, Gen. Griffith: forces in N.C., **3**: 463, 466; taken prisoner at battle of Camden, **3**: 596

Rutherford, John: letters to cited, **16**: 610n, 616n; **18**: 457n

Rutherford, Robert: signs nonimportation resolutions, **1**: 30, 46; signs Virginia Association, **1**: 108; and nonimportation agreements, **1**: 110; signs letter to Va. HB, **1**: 112; land grant for military service, **6**: 645

Rutherfords Ordinary, Goochland, Va., **3**: 429

Rutledge, Mr., **3**: 345

Rutledge, Edward: letters to, **11**: 587-9; **12**: 225-6; **13**: 377-9; **15**: 451-3; **16**: 600-1; **18**: 228n; letters from, **2**: 234-5; **10**: 463-5; **12**: 263-4; **15**: 11-6; **16**: 389-90, 544-5; signs Continental Association, **1**: 154; signs Congress' second petition, **1**: 223; signs agreement of secrecy, **1**: 253; member of committee to report on Canadian campaign, **1**: 296n; and debates on Declaration of Independence, **1**: 309, 314; signs Declaration of Independence, **1**: 432; on committee to draw up rules for Congress, **1**: 457n; and Howe's peace proposal, **1**: 520-1; opinion on Mezières case, **9**: 182; and production of rice, **10**: 463-4; **11**: 645; and *Notes on Virginia*, **10**: 464; **12**: 136; ships rice to France, **12**: 461; **13**: 377; **15**: 12; letters from cited, **12**: 505; **13**: 511, 643n; **15**: 160; **18**: 228n; bill of exchange, **12**: 626; letters to cited, **13**: 415; **15**: 469; Presidential elector from S.C., **14**: 666; **15**: 51; rice trade statistics sent to, **15**: 446n, 451-2; criticizes Esek Hopkins, **15**: 582n; introduces Middleton to TJ, **16**: 544, 600; and TJ's commercial policy, **18**: 228-9; mentioned, **11**: 406; **13**: 338

Rutledge, Elizabeth Grimké (Mrs. John Rutledge, Sr.): sends regards to TJ, **17**: 522

Rutledge, Henrietta Middleton (Mrs. Edward Rutledge), **11**: 589

Rutledge, John, Jr.: letters to, **12**: 349, 556-7, 631; **13**: 124, 262-4, 358-9, 506, 593-4, 615; **14**: 481, 701-2; **15**: 63; **19**: 297; letters from, **12**: 340-1, 492, 605-7; **13**: 138, 282-3, 318, 454, 530-2, 551-2, 567-8, 631; **14**: 404-5, 538, 613-4; **15**: 24, 72-3; **16**: 266-7, 413-5, 426-8; **17**: 521-3; **18**: 52-4; **20**: 549; letters sent by, **11**: 410; **16**: 446; **20**: 662; funds for, **12**: 343, 349, 626, 676; **13**: 368; **14**: 11; **16**: 318-9; introduced to John Adams, **12**: 349; stay in Paris, **12**: 461, 676; **15**: 173; travels in Europe, **12**: 504n; **13**: 146, 221n, 318, 358, 374-5, 448, 449n, 454, 530-1, 551-2, 605, 654; **14**: 25-6, 286, 401, 627, 636; **15**: 74, 85, 91, 125n, 147; package sent by, **12**: 647; travel hints from TJ, **13**: xxvi, 33n, 262, 264-76, 318, 449n; letters from cited, **13**: 149, 374; **14**: 418n; **15**: 50, 87; **17**: 36n, 523n; TJ asks to observe agriculture, **13**: 263, 375; letter to, from Dumas, cited, **13**: 312; letters to, from John Rutledge, Sr., cited, **13**: 318, 426, 615; **14**: 276, 278, 481; introduced to Verme and others, **13**: 356, 359n, 360; **14**: 41; assumes military rank, **13**: 356n, 449n; introduced to Geismar, **13**: 356-7, 527-8; **14**: 583n; **15**: 49; letters to cited, **13**: 374, 663; TJ praises, **13**: 375; **16**: 601; Berckel's comments to, **13**: 408n; on moose, **13**: 567-8, 593-4; travels in Italy with Short, **14**: 41, 43, 53, 273, 310-2, 377-8, 404, 417, 453, 464, 519, 539, 574, 590-1, 608, 614; letters for sent to TJ, **14**: 276; **15**: 144-5; health of, **14**: 296; on olive culture, **14**: 404; studies architecture, **14**: 452; letters for forwarded by TJ, **14**: 481, 483, 531, 538, 598; **15**: 51; letters to, from Cutting, cited, **14**: 481n; plans for travel in Spain, **14**: 538, 613-4, 666, 705; **15**: 66, 72-3, 77; bills of exchange for, **14**: 577; **15**: 9, 559; permitted to visit Toulon dock yards, **14**: 649, 667; **15**: 29; letters from, to Shippen, cited, **14**: 666; introduced to Aranda, **14**: 700; introduced to Fab-

broni, **14**: 701; in Marseilles, **15**: 43; Fabbroni entertains, **15**: 149-50; passport issued by TJ, **15**: 485, 486, 487; voyage from Ireland to England, **15**: 530; letter from, to Short, quoted, **16**: 162n; leaves Paris, **16**: 230; plans return to America, **16**: 251-2, 415, 428, 601; letter from, to Cutting, cited, **16**: 263; introduces Andriani to TJ, **16**: 266; at ratification of treaty with Creek Indians, **17**: 341n; sends London paper to TJ, **17**: 402; gives lamp to TJ, **18**: 52; on liberty and revolution, **18**: 53; mentioned, **11**: 589; **12**: 629, 656; **13**: 141n, 277, 338, 360, 621, 642; **15**: 414, 441

Rutledge, John, Sr.: letters to, **3**: 179-80; **7**: 283; **13**: 374-5; letters from, **3**: 415; **11**: 405-6; **12**: 287, 461-2; **13**: 41, 426, 492, 542, 594; **14**: 278, 577; signs Continental Association, **1**: 154; and draft of Declaration of Causes, **1**: 187n; signs Congress' second petition, **1**: 223; letters to cited, **3**: 176; **10**: 558; **12**: 380; **13**: 415, 627; letters from cited, **3**: 333, 434; **12**: 505; **13**: 283n, 358, 375n, 642, 643n; defensive measures against British, **3**: 400-1; member of committee on public debt, **6**: 263n-5; appointed commissioner in Conn.-Pa. dispute, **6**: 477n, 478n; member committee on coinage, **7**: 153n; appointed minister to Netherlands, **8**: 77, 293, 369, 420, 447, 499, 583; declines appointment as minister to Netherlands, **8**: 519, 654, 664; **9**: 15, 176; S.C. delegate to Federal Convention, **11**: 219, 401; son introduced to TJ, **11**: 405-6; bill of exchange sent by, **12**: 631; letters from, to John Rutledge, Jr., cited, **13**: 318, 426, 615; **14**: 276, 278, 481; as possible candidate for vice president, **13**: 502; **14**: 17; sends money to son, **14**: 11; **16**: 318-9; TJ praises, **14**: 700; justice of Supreme Court, **16**: 27; on Washington's attitude toward bank bill, **19**: 39; resigns from Supreme Court, **20**: 625; mentioned, **3**: 397, 451, 470, 664; **12**: 402, 433, 492; **14**: 481; **17**: 522

Rutlege, Capt., **5**: 232

Ryan, Rev. Thomas: educates Carter's son, **20**: 474

Ryberg & Co., Copenhagen, **15**: 525

against Miami Indians, **17**: 131, 132n-4n; **18**: 82, 144n-6n, 308, 596; **20**: 107; correspondence with Knox, **17**: 132n, 133n; candidate for governor of Pa., **17**: 497; correspondence with Washington, **18**: 169, 170-1; report on Northwest Territory, **18**: 194-207; memorials to, **18**: 209-12, 213-4; letter from, to inhabitants of Prairie du Rocher, **18**: 212-3; letter from, to Hamtramck, **18**: 213; and new system of penmanship, **19**: 121n; charges raised against, **19**: 467-9; and papers on the western territory, **19**: 630n; orders from Knox, **20**: 138

St. Clair, Lake: on boundary of Old Northwest, **6**: 583n

St. Clair, William Boulton, **3**: 541n

St. Cloud, France: TJ visits with Mrs. Cosway, **10**: 445; Louis XVI's move to, **16**: 507

St. Croix, W.I., **5**: 177

Saint Croix river: as part of U.S. boundary, **6**: 457, 458; in boundary dispute, **9**: 8; **16**: xxxiv, 283, 284n, 326; Franklin's map, **16**: xxxiv-v, 52 (illus.); **18**: 86-7, 96n

St. Denis, France: TJ visits with the Cosways, **10**: 441

St. Dizier, France, **13**: 28

Saint-Domingue (Hispaniola), W.I.: letter to governor of, **5**: 228-9; Drake's expedition against, **1**: 280, 282; trade with Va., **5**: 209, 228-9, 430, 546-7; deputies sent to Estates General, **15**: 190, 221, 380n, 536; interest in pisé construction, **15**: 379, 380n; U.S. trade with, **15**: 456; **17**: 609-10; **18**: 538; **19**: 238; **20**: 240; mulattoes petition for rights, **15**: 536; relations with National Assembly, **16**: 87, 201; **17**: 608; **20**: 240, 261; Cutting reports on events in, **17**: 5-7, 299-309, 327-9; **18**: 79; **20**: 240; celebration of Bastille Day, **17**: 299-300; rebellion in, **17**: 300-9, 608-9; **18**: 504; **19**: 87n, 604; restrictions on American vessels, **17**: 301-2; General Assembly, **17**: 301-9, 327-9, 525, 556, 608-9; population, **20**: 240; slaves, **20**: 240; trade, **20**: 240; French regiment in massacred, **20**: 261

St. Elizabeth, Hospital of: history, **11**: 297

Saintes, France: TJ describes, **11**: 457

St. Esprit, France: farmers-general at, **13**: 119

St. Etienne. *See* Rabaut de St. Etienne

St. Eustache, Curé of: takes oath to Constitution, **18**: 605

St. Eustatius, Dutch West Indies: taken by British, **5**: 176, 177, 193, 208; Rodney at, **6**: 74n; tobacco exports, **7**: 369, 370; destitution of merchants, **8**: 161-2; use for carrying on contraband trade, **9**: 631-2; U.S. consul at, **20**: 581-2; mentioned, **1**: 498

St. Feriol, France: TJ describes, **11**: 448

St. Fond, Barthélemy Faujas de: *Description des expériences de la machine aérostatique de MM. Montgolfier*, **7**: 135, 137n; mentioned, **7**: 123

St. Fulgent, France: TJ describes, **11**: 458

St. Genis, France: TJ describes, **11**: 457

St. George, France: TJ describes, **11**: 418-20, 459

St. George Island, Md., **1**: 471

St. Germain, France: TJ visits with Mrs. Cosway, **10**: 445, 446

St. Germain, J. J. de: *Manuel des Végétaux*, **20**: 429n

St. Gervasy, France: TJ describes, **11**: 423

St. Gilles, France: no longer a seaport, **11**: 451

St. Helens, Alleyne Fitzherbert, Baron: on U.S.-British relations, **20**: 96; relations with Humphreys, **20**: 475; British ambassador to Spain, **20**: 594, 677

St. Hermines, France: TJ describes, **11**: 458

St. Hillaire, Antoine Félix de: consul in Va., **15**: 583

Saint James, Boudard de: bankruptcy of, **11**: 123; death of, **11**: 572

St. James', Cumberland co., Va., **1**: 103

St. James' Mountain Club (agriculture society, Jamaica), **17**: 565

St. Jean, France, **13**: 32

Saint-Jean-de-Luz, France: merchants demand duty for import of foreign fish, **10**: 126

St. John, Mr.: news from, **8**: 90; efforts to import live oak timber, **9**: 167-8; description of system of nature, **12**: 610

St. John, Hector. *See* Crèvecoeur

St. John's, Antigua: port, **7**: 338, 348; mentioned, **1**: 282

St. Johns, Newfoundland: and Articles of

St. Victour & Bettinger: letters to, **9**: 523; **11**: 355; letters from, **9**: 381, 524, 536-7, 593; **10**: 81-2, 292; **11**: 62; mentioned, **11**: 47

St. Vincent, W.I.: rice in, **14**: 673-4, 707-8

St. Vrain, Mr., **2**: 246

Sakuntala (Sacontolae), **17**: 515; **20**: 381, 391, 392n, 417

Salaberri, M. le President de: recommends Abbé André, **10**: 402

salaries of Va. public servants: bills for ascertaining, **2**: 231-2, 274-5, 424-34

Sale, Mr.: *Second Voyage to America*, **20**: 635n

Salé, Morocco: harbor, **10**: 338-9

Salih, Bey of Constantine: Spanish tribute to, **10**: 329

Salina, Washington co., Va.: tooth of prehistoric animal found at, **6**: 201

Salisbury (Salsbury), Lieut.: killed at Racepaths, **5**: 96, 294n

Salisbury, N.C.: British prisoners at, **4**: 561; militia sent to, **5**: 657; mentioned, **3**: 466, 621; **5**: 182

Salkeld, William: *Reports of Cases Adjudged in the Court of King's Bench*, **11**: 548; **16**: 277, 481

Sallust: TJ seeks information on best Italian translation, **11**: 159; mentioned, **12**: 18; **20**: 634n

Sally (ship): taken by British, **6**: 224; arms shipped by, **11**: 255; madness of carpenter of, **11**: 508, 606; duty on cargo of oil, **11**: 579; leaves Annapolis, **12**: 552; arrival at Le Havre, **13**: 214, 661; information on, **13**: 228; departs Le Havre, **13**: 238, 255; carries goods for TJ, **14**: 52, 54-5, 182, 183, 273; mentioned, **4**: 310; **12**: 402, 448; **15**: 483

Salm-Kyrbourg, Frederic Othon, Prince: carries letters from Dumas, **9**: 279; **11**: 210; recommended to TJ, **9**: 301, 462; interest in Dumas, **9**: 503; supports Patriot party, **9**: 561; departs for Paris, **11**: 197; commands Dutch Republican army, **12**: 77n; **14**: 521; evacuates Utrecht, **12**: 166, 167, 215; in National Guard, **15**: 535; mentioned, **10**: 540

Salmon, Juan Manuel: on Barclay's mission, **10**: 138n

Salmon, Thomas: *Geographical Grammar*, **4**: 118; *Modern Gazeteer*, **7**: 405;

Nouvelle abregé chronologique de l'histoire d'Angleterre, **11**: 666

Salmour, M.: letter from, **12**: 305

Salon (1787), **12**: xxxiv-v, 35 (illus.), 69

salt: lack of, **1**: 255, 259, 288, 294; **3**: 382; **4**: 9; congressional committee to study manufacture of, **1**: 275; for Canadian campaign, **1**: 439, 440; resolution of Va. Convention on, **1**: 461; for Transylvania settlers, **2**: 83, 109; extraction from sea water, **2**: 174-5; **19**: 608-24; storage, **2**: 469; import from Bermuda, **3**: 13, 238, 307, 326; **4**: 376, 466; **5**: 171n; purchases of, **3**: 85, 268; **4**: 375; supplies of, **3**: 200; **4**: 199; **5**: 468; for Va. troops, **3**: 329; **4**: 577; for Continental army, **3**: 335, 409; **4**: 502, 503; notice to commissioners of the provision law on, **3**: 609; for gun factory at Fredericksburg, **3**: 617; for Convention troops, **4**: 182; seizure of, **4**: 240; mismanagement in making, **4**: 355; to be sent to Va., **4**: 416; taken off *Le Comité*, **4**: 467; for Detroit expedition, **4**: 534; for curing fish, **5**: 234; British vessel with taken, **5**: 283; on Eastern Shore, **5**: 619; import by S.C., **8**: 201; U.S. import of, **9**: 19-20, 62; **10**: 147, 148; **11**: 41; trade in, **13**: 77; for curing beef, **13**: 472; memoirs on by farmers-general, **15**: 488-90; **16**: 17-20; obtained in France for American vessels, **15**: 491, 502-3; **16**: 17-20, 374; prices, **15**: 502; **19**: 190

salt foods: project for selling at L'Orient, **12**: 667

salt mines: prehistoric fossils found in, **6**: 201

Saltonstall, Capt. Dudley: charges against, **15**: 581n

saltpetre: production promised by Charles Lynch, **1**: 261-4; found in southwestern Va., **1**: 262-4; supplies received, **1**: 285; need for, **1**: 288; **4**: 463; recommended for cooling Congress' meeting place, **20**: 596-7

Salt river, **2**: 82

salt springs, Ky., **6**: 553

Saluces, Comtesse de: wine ordered from, **19**: 266

Saluces, Marquis de: sends wine to TJ, **14**: 45

Sam (slave): taken by British, **6**: 224

Samatan, Basile: in tobacco trade, **14**: 425

237, 259; **3**: 47; **4**: 93, 95, 160. *See also* Convention troops

Saratoga, N.Y.: mineral springs described by Stiles, **10**: 585-6; visited by TJ and Madison, **20**: 453-6, 458, 465, 466

sardines, **11**: 442

Sardinia: U.S. treaty of amity and commerce, **6**: 389, 393; **7**: 48, 263, 267, 424n, 425, 632-3; relations with Algiers, **10**: 266; U.S. trade with, **11**: 352-3; **20**: 322-3, 334, 372, 685

Sardinia, King of. *See* Victor Amédée Marie

Sargeant, William H.: letter to, **10**: 101-2; letter from, **9**: 645

Sargent, Fitzwilliam (master of *Marietta*), **18**: 328

Sargent, Winthrop: appointed temporary secretary of western territory, **12**: 256; correspondence published, **18**: 159n; recommended by Knox, **18**: 161n; address of citizens of Vincennes to, **18**: 166, 185; sends Northwest Territory documents to TJ, **18**: 166-7, 179-86; and Vincennes land claims, **18**: 167; secretary of Northwest Territory, **18**: 171-8; letters from, to Washington, cited, **18**: 172, 177, 178n, 191n; TJ compared with, **18**: 172; in Scioto Company, **18**: 172-7, 530; **19**: 630; letter from, to inhabitants of Gallipolis, quoted, **18**: 174n-5n; TJ's interview with, **18**: 177-8; and Executive Proceedings of Northwest Territory, **18**: 188-90; memorial to, from Ste. Marie, **19**: 505, 524-7 (text); and papers on the western territory, **19**: 630n; confers with Hamilton, **20**: 107

Sarly, Jacob: letter from, **16**: 39-40; master of *America*, **16**: 40n; letter from cited, **17**: 246n, 252, 255n

Sarmento, Francisco: applies for vice consulship at Tenerife, **17**: 247, 250, 255n; **19**: 313

Sarmiento, Marqués de, **8**: 570

Sarpi, Paolo: Stiles' comment on, **7**: 365

sarsaparilla: U.S. import from West Indies, **10**: 148

Sarsfield, Guy Claude, Comte de: letter to, **15**: 25-7; letters from, **10**: 289-90; **12**: 530-1, 531; **13**: 211; **15**: 18-9, 35-7, 72; note to Humphreys, **9**: 329; departure for London, **11**: 515; publication sent by, **11**: 532; on British pol-

icy, **12**: 205; letter to cited, **12**: 432; payment to, **12**: 554; letter from, to Mrs. Izard, cited, **13**: 373; sends prospectus to TJ, **13**: 374n; inquires about currency standards, **15**: 18-9, 35-7; asks Adams to import mirrors, **17**: 437n

Sarsnet, Marquis de. *See* Sassenay

Sartine, Antoine Raymond Jean Gualbert Gabriel de, Comte d'Alby: and Mazzei, **3**: 233; and *Alliance* case, **7**: 270; **8**: 439; **14**: 315; letter from, to Vergennes, cited, **8**: 61; and Schweighauser case, **11**: 135; on *droit d'aubaine* in colonies, **17**: 435n

Sartorius, Lieut., **3**: 304

Sartorious, M.: bill in favor of, **12**: 238; TJ makes payment to, **13**: 533n; **15**: 46, 310, 324

Sartorius & Co., **14**: 52; **15**: 47n, 372

sassafras: seeds asked by TJ for France, **9**: 255; plants asked from John Banister, **11**: 121; sent to Mme de Tessé, **13**: 187

Sassenay (Sarsnet), Marquis de: vineyards, **11**: 418

Sasserno, André de: letter from, **14**: 401; hospitality to TJ, **11**: 288, 463n, 464n; TJ recommends visit to, **13**: 271, 277; letter to quoted, **13**: 356n

saticide: punishment for, **2**: 325

Sattoga (Sattoogo). *See* Chatuga

Saturn (planet): Herschel's studies of, **17**: 515

Saugrain, Dr.: introduced to G. R. Clark, **11**: 487

Sauk Indians: support G. R. Clark, **2**: 258

Saulger, J. N.: address to Washington, **20**: 551-5

Saulx, Duc de: not recalled, **16**: 47

Saunders, Capt. Daniel (master of *The Three Sisters*), **13**: 119

Saunders, Lieut. Joseph, **5**: 494; **6**: 55

Saunders, William: appointed commander of *Tartar*, **3**: 315n

Saunderson, George: letter from cited, **20**: 588

Saussure, Horace Bénedict de: *Voyages dans les Alpes*, **11**: 665; designs hygrometer, **13**: 37, 396-7; Rutledge describes moose to, **13**: 567; TJ praises, **13**: 594

Sauterne wine: Bondfield as agent for, **12**: 24, **14**: 45, 353; ordered by TJ, **12**: 434, 435

Scioto, Ohio: proposed as site of capital, **19**: 6

Scioto Company: receives land grant from Congress, **12**: 256, 283; Muskingum lands, **13**: 609, 612n-3n; **14**: 303; **16**: 159; **18**: 160-2, 173-6; criticism of, **16**: 159-60, 162n; affairs in England, **17**: 88n; promotion of in France, **18**: 160-2, 364-5; French emigrants in, **18**: 162, 173-4, 176, 204, 206n; **19**: 592-6; Sargent in, **18**: 172-7; Morris disapproves of, **18**: 364-5; Otto and, **18**: 530-1

Scioto river, Ohio: plans for defense of, **3**: 54, 55; military post at, **3**: 259; bounty land to soldiers on, **6**: 572n, 574n, 579; Weedon desires land on, **6**: 573n; Lormerie's land on, **16**: 434n-5n; French settlement on, **17**: 410; mentioned, **2**: 76, 77, 81, 84, 99; **6**: 572n

Scipio Aemilianus Africanus Numantinus, **5**: 262

Scipio Africanus: tomb discovered, **14**: 406, 449

Scittigo. See Settico

Scot, Robert: letter to, **6**: 43; invoice for executing Indian medal, **4**: 35-7; biographical note, **4**: 36n-7n; executes Indian medal for Va., **4**: 106 (illus.)

Scot, Samuel: signs petition, **1**: 588

Scot Highlanders: captured, **1**: 407, 412, 454

Scotland: engagement of tutor from, **6**: 433; British difficulties with, **7**: 638; vessels seized by French, **14**: 391-2, 392n-3n; and the fisheries, **19**: 177

Scots: in S.C., **12**: 299

Scots-Irish: emigration to the Ohio Valley, **19**: 19

Scott, Capt., **1**: 453

Scott, Mr.: petition, **1**: 103; in charge of military stores, **4**: 337

Scott, Charles: letter to, **3**: 7-9; letters from, **4**: 278, 481-2, 507; **5**: 38-9; commands Va. volunteers, **1**: 237; forces under, **3**: 204, 244, 364; commands troops sent to S.C., **3**: 343; to receive tobacco for prisoners at Charleston, **5**: 141, 400; testimonial in favor of Philip Turpin, **6**: 330n; expedition against Indians, **19**: 465, 466; **20**: 295, 303, 309, 480-1, 563, 566, 614, 616, 657, 667, 670, 680, 682, 690, 703; and settlement of Ky., **20**: 553n; mentioned, **3**: 154, 180, 253,

263, 294, 296, 378, 433, 652; **4**: 337, 471; **5**: 307, 559n, 632

Scott, David: votes for bill for religious freedom, **2**: 549n

Scott, Maj. George: letter from, **4**: 452; mentioned, **6**: 71n

Scott, Gustavus: and legal fees, **1**: 99

Scott, James: signs Virginia Association, **1**: 108

Scott, James, Jr.: signs nonimportation resolutions (1769), **1**: 30

Scott, John: and bill establishing ferries, **2**: 459; commission for, **4**: 542

Scott, Joseph: and Mazzei's agricultural co., **1**: 158; prisoner of war, **3**: 390

Scott, Richard: signs Va. oath of allegiance, **2**: 129

Scott, Thomas (Pa.): on Va. Land Office, **2**: 138n; letters from, to Joseph Reed, **3**: 206-8, 248, 286; congressman from Pa., **14**: 395, 473; federalism of, **14**: 395; Beckwith obtains information from, **17**: 44n, 90n; resolution on site for capital, **19**: 8

Scott, Thomas (Va.): signs nonimportation resolutions (1770), **1**: 30, 46; loan to state, **3**: 386, 442

Scott, Walter, **4**: 542

Scott, Sir William: king's Advocate-General, **18**: 347n-8n; on status of British seamen, **20**: 499, 499n-500n

Scotts ferry, Va., **2**: 15

scows: for transportation of cannon, **5**: 50, 89, 92

screw propulsion. See boats: screw propulsion

Scull, John: paid by Department of State, **17**: 372; publishes *Pittsburgh Gazette*, **17**: 509n

Scull, Nicholas: map and view of State House of Philadelphia by, **1**: 358 (illus.); map of Pa., **9**: 300; **10**: 213; **11**: 519

sculpture: TJ's enjoyment of in France, **8**: 569

scurvy: causes of, **15**: 482

scythes: manufacture in Conn., **7**: 335

Seabrook, Nicholas B.: letter to, **16**: 82

Seading, Jacob: British war prisoner, **2**: 31, 32

Seagrove, James: serves as emissary, **19**: 432; confers with Quesada, **19**: 518; letter to, from Washington, **19**: 520

sealing wax, **14**: 442

seal of the United States: Franklin's proposal, **1**: 494; TJ's proposal, **1**: 495;

Du Simitère's proposal, **1**: 495-6; report of committee on, **1**: 496-7; Adams' proposal, **1**: 497n; design for by Du Simitière, **1**: 550 (illus.); and Definitive Peace Treaty, **6**: 426n; in TJ's custody, **16**: xlii; on medal, **16**: xlii, 52 (illus.)

seal of Jefferson: described, **16**: xxxii, 52 (illus.); affixed to correspondence, **16**: 298n

seal of Va. High Court of Chancery: design of, **19**: 556-7

seal of Virginia: use of, **5**: 636

seals: used by TJ, **10**: 629n; use of Congress', **11**: 280, 281n

seamen: lack of, **1**: 590; Va. bills concerning, **2**: 378-81, 382-8; wages, **2**: 385; **7**: 347; **10**: 257, 258; **17**: 670; desertion, **2**: 386; mutiny, **2**: 387; treatment of, **2**: 387; wills of, **2**: 395; enlistment, **3**: 171; for navigating boats on the Chickahominy, **5**: 135; need liquor, **5**: 151; clothing, **5**: 172; conditions compared with slavery, **5**: 172; for armed vessels, **5**: 270; victualling, **7**: 328, 329, 344, 347; number needed, **7**: 328, 341; Great Britain, **7**: 350; West Indies, **7**: 351; usefulness, **8**: 426; treatment at Le Havre, **10**: 328; return passage to America, **11**: 99; stranded in France, **13**: 297; **14**: 483-4, 549, 622; TJ on importance of, **14**: 219; **19**: 186-7, 219; in U.S.-French trade, **14**: 331; of *Clementina* in La Rochelle, **14**: 410; protection of as American citizens, **17**: 670; consuls settle disputes of, **18**: 107; consular jurisdiction over, **20**: 403n. *See also* Algiers, American captives in

seamen, impressment of: in Va., **5**: 189; Alexander Gross, **10**: 80; in England, **12**: 185, 213, 237, 244, 250; **16**: 413, 415n, 418, 419, 518; **17**: 629-30; **20**: 102, 241-3; in France, **12**: 226; Rutledge comments on, **16**: 426-8; Cutting and, **17**: 19, 489, 583, 594, 630; **18**: 313-22, 326-9, 364; Johnson and, **17**: 120, 670; **18**: 11; Morris confers on with Leeds and Pitt, **18**: 287-9, 313n; Purdie and others, **18**: 310-42 (editorial note and documents); in colonial period, **18**: 310n, 312n; Morris refuses loan for, **18**: 364

seaports. *See* ports

search, right of: trade treaty stipulations,

7: 473, 477, 478, 481, 617-8; reciprocal agreement between U.S. and Tuscany, **8**: 106-7, 189-90; and proposed treaty with Britain, **8**: 274; and proposed treaty with Portugal, **9**: 413; Moroccan treaty, **10**: 421. *See also* contraband

Sears, Daniel: passport issued by TJ, **15**: 486

Sears, Col. Isaac: death of, **11**: 306

seat of U.S. government on Potomac (Georgetown): proposed, **16**: 224n, 491, 493, 537, 541, 575, 577, 597; **17**: 164; **19**: xxxi, 348 (illus.); discussion in Congress, **16**: 475, 491, 493, 536-8, 540-1, 575, 577; Monroe's comment on, **17**: 232-3; "Fixing the Seat of Government on the Potomac," **17**: 452-71 (editorial note and documents); building program recommended by TJ and Madison, **17**: 644; Mason's concern for location of Federal District, **18**: 485n-6n; proclamation on, **18**: 596; "Locating the Federal District," **19**: 3-73 (editorial note and documents); L'Enfant's plan of, **20**: xxxi; "Fixing the Seat of Government," **20**: 3-88 (editorial note and documents). *See also* Georgetown, Md.; L'Enfant, Pierre Charles; Residence Act

Seaton, Mr.: and bill establishing ferries, **2**: 456

Seaward, Capt.: moose skeleton sent by, **11**: 359

sea water: freshening, **12**: 145; desalination, **19**: 608-24

Seawell, Mr.: executor to Col. Whiting, **7**: 273, 274n

Seawell, Joseph: commissioner of provisions, **3**: 485, 575

Sebastian, Benjamin: letter to, from governor of New Orleans, cited, **17**: 124n; impeachment proceedings against, **19**: 470n

Seckel, David: paid by Department of State, **17**: 372

Seckel, Henry, **18**: 627n

Secotan, **1**: 279

secretary of legation: status, **11**: 246

securities (U.S.). *See* United States: Public Finance, securities

Security of Englishmen's Lives, **15**: 282

securityship: bill for lessening evils of, **2**: 275-7

Sedgwick, Theodore: motion to establish public record office, **15**: 428n; motion

Sedgwick, Theodore (*cont.*)
on TJ's Report on Weights and Measures, **16**: 615; visited by Smith, **17**: 183n; recommends Chipman, **19**: 378; mentioned, **16**: 516; **17**: 218; **18**: 649, 659

seeds: TJ takes to France, **7**: 376; requested by TJ from John Bartram, **9**: 229-30; **10**: 593; **11**: 563; sent to France, **9**: 253-5, 256, 669; **10**: 176, 197; exchanged with Cary, **10**: 226-8; **11**: 229; sent to Mrs. Eppes, **10**: 594; sent to Monticello, **10**: 616; **18**: 308; imported from England, **10**: 641; for Mme de Tessé, **11**: 253, 349, 362; **12**: 245-6, 247; sent from France, **11**: 304; sent from S.C., **11**: 323, 324; sent to TJ, **11**: 545, 546; **12**: 71, 75, 486; **13**: 47, 111, 343; **14**: 278; **15**: 47-8, 296, 632; sent from Va., **11**: 587, 642; sent to Limozin, **12**: 11; French imports of, **13**: 69; **14**: 674; sent to Drayton, **13**: 368-9; for Washington, **13**: 413; sent to Madison, **13**: 413, 533n; sent to Bernard, **13**: 502, 508; sent to Francis Eppes, **15**: 621, 624, 631; requested by TJ from Francis Eppes, **15**: 621, 632; Duchesse d'Enville orders, **16**: 503, 504n; **17**: 558; Barbancon orders, **17**: 558; sent to Martha J. Randolph, **18**: 308, 500

Segond de Sederon, Jacques Marie Blaise, Chevalier de: letter to, **11**: 82-3; letters from, **11**: 53; **12**: 623; biographical note, **11**: 53n

Séguier, Jean François: collection at Nîmes, **15**: xxx

Ségur, Louis Philippe, Comte de: J. P. Jones sends messages by, **13**: 586; wants position in ministry, **17**: 640; reported death of, **18**: 474; letter from, to Washington, cited, **19**: 588; ambassador to Rome, **19**: 637; **20**: 368, 385; mentioned, **11**: 218, 638

Ségur, Philippe Henri, Marquis, Maréchal de: retirement, **12**: 68, 70; replaced as minister of war, **12**: 153; opposes Prussian invasion of Netherlands, **12**: 174; libel against, **16**: 333; mentioned, **7**: 376-7

seigneur: duties of, **11**: 419

Seine river: navigability of, **10**: 625

Seine valley: TJ describes, **7**: 508

Seixas, Gershom M.: biographical note, **19**: 610n

Seixas, Moses: and desalination of sea water, **19**: 610; biographical note, **19**: 610n

Selden, Capt.: troops under command of, **4**: 322

Selden, John: *Mare Clausum,* **12**: 688; **13**: 290; edits Eadmer's history, **15**: 406

Selden, Miles: payment to, **3**: 486, 494, 495; to be furnished with cavalry equipment, **4**: 343, 344; Va. councillor, **7**: 597; **8**: 345; loses seat on Va. Executive Council, **12**: 445

Selden, Rev. Miles: death of, **8**: 345

Seldon, Col., **5**: 95

Seldon, Mr.: and bill establishing ferries, **2**: 461

Selim III, Sultan of Ottoman Empire: prosecutes war against Russia, **19**: 418

Selkirk, Dunbar Douglas, fourth Earl of: silverplate taken by Jones' sailors, **2**: 207

Semoulin, M. de. *See* Simolin

Senaca creek, **2**: 113

Senac de Meilhan, Gabriel: *Considérations sur l'esprit et les moeurs,* **13**: 132

Senate (U.S.). *See* United States: Senate

Seneca, Lucius Annaeus: TJ seeks information on best Italian translation, **11**: 159; *Philosophi opera,* **12**: 678; **13**: 391, 420

Seneca Falls, N.Y., **12**: 445

Seneca Indians: and Cedars Affair, **1**: 400; plans for war, **1**: 494; land claimed by, **2**: 77; in French and Indian Wars, **2**: 99, 100, 102, 104; Brodhead's expedition against, **3**: 42; treaty with, **9**: 504; land grants, **20**: 131

Senegal: trade with France, **12**: 436

Senegal Company, **12**: 437, 451, 465, 494, 533

Seney, Joshua: votes for capital bill, **19**: 36n

Senf, John Christian: letters to, **4**: 375, 679; **7**: 115, 462; letters from, **4**: 421, 475-6, 602, 620; **5**: 13-4, 248-50, 425-6, 499-500; **7**: 427-8; **9**: 7-8; praised by Gates, **3**: 662, 668; arrival at Richmond, **4**: 10; career, **4**: 11n; letter to, from Gates, cited, **4**: 37, 77; orders from Gates, **4**: 37n-8n; observations on Va. defense, **4**: 38n, 169; scheme of fortifications, **4**: 209; orders from Steuben, **4**: 255n, 701-2; and rebuilding of Westham works, **4**: 356; plan for fortifying Hoods, **4**: 358, 584, 593, 596-7, 625-6; **5**: 127; **15**: 600-1; opposes attack on British at Portsmouth, **4**: 422; plans for fortification of Yorktown, **4**: 631; letters sent by, **4**: 659; **5**: 483; **6**: 5, 13, 54; **10**: 102; appointed Va. state engineer, **4**: 679; declines appointment as Va. state engineer, **5**: 13-4; engineer for S.C., **5**: 14; requests entrenching tools, **5**: 87; maps of, **5**: 145n; to plan battery at Alexandria, **5**: 420, 612, 613; reply to, **5**: 426; letter from, to Steuben, **5**: 510-1; sent to destroy boats and bridges, **5**: 614; TJ suggests engaging as Va. state engineer, **5**: 627-8; Mrs. Byrd desires to see, **5**: 694; letter to cited, **7**: 539; package sent by, **8**: 598; returns to America, **8**: 598-9; lamp sent to Thomson by, **9**: 379; designs Santee canal, **13**: 117n; passport issued by TJ, **15**: 484; mentioned, **4**: 438; **5**: 126, 144n, 169, 270, 417, 545; **7**: 552; **8**: 583

Sennar, Sudan: Ledyard plans to visit, **13**: 596

Sennecy, France: TJ describes, **11**: 418

Senneville (Sainneville), Chevalier de: and French treaty with Algiers, **16**: 573

Sens, Archbishop of. *See* Loménie de Brienne, Etienne Charles

Senter, Isaac: letter to, **19**: 618-9; letter from, **19**: 619-21; and desalination of sea water, **19**: 609, 610n, 613, 613n, 618-21

Senter, Jacob: letter to, **19**: 621-2

Seonville, Capt. (master of the *Courier de l'Europe*), **11**: 112

separation of powers: TJ on, **6**: 279n, 280n; **11**: 480; **12**: 28, 34, 36, 43, 189, 439; in Va. government, **6**: 295; Jay on, **10**: 272, 598; **11**: 129; Madison on, **12**: 273, 275. *See also* Constitution of the United States; Virginia: Constitution

sequestration of property: Va. bills for, **2**: 168-71, 435-7; certificates of, **5**: 628

Sequeville, M. de: gift to, **16**: 318, 356n, 358n, 362n, 365, 501, 584-5; **17**: 544; **18**: 357, 601, 602n; **20**: 346; payment to, **20**: 645n

Serapis (ship): Jones' service on, **10**: 88; **13**: 45, 126, 135, 209; on medal, **13**:

586; **16**: xl, 52 (illus.), 55n

serfdom: abolished in France, **15**: 334n

Sergeant (Serjeant), Jonathan Dickinson: signs agreement of secrecy, **1**: 253; advised by Adams, **1**: 333; consulted by Mr. Nathan, **5**: 152; and Conn.-Pa. dispute, **6**: 476; marries Miss Rittenhouse, **15**: 17; and Pa. politics, **7**: 20

Serrant, Col. *See* Walsh-Serrant, Vicomte de

Serravalle, Italy, **14**: 381

Servan, Antoine Joseph Michel: *Addresse aux amis de la paix*, **16**: 116

servants: bill concerning runaways, **2**: 475-6; complaints of, **2**: 488; wages, **7**: 297, 330, 348; French ordinance against arming of, **8**: 164; for TJ's journey to southern France, **11**: 215, 248; dismissal, **11**: 362

servants, indentured: boys as seamen, **2**: 383; Va. bill concerning, **2**: 473-4; in American colonies, **10**: 8n, 30-2. *See also* runaways

Service, Capt. (master of *Hope*), **14**: 296, 474n

Sestri, Italy: oranges grown at, **11**: 441

Sète (Cette), France: TJ describes, **11**: 446; canal to sea, **11**: 450; no American vessels in harbor, **11**: 487; vessels sent to America from, **12**: 321; tobacco trade, **13**: 95, 250; **14**: 185; **15**: 45; TJ's travel hints, **13**: 274; consul in, **14**: 60, 62n; Short and Rutledge unable to visit, **15**: 66

Seton, Mr.: in Italy, **14**: 574-5

Seton, Capt. Peter: master of *Cato*, **15**: 438n, 494, 524; master of *Nancy*, **20**: 237, 238n

Seton, William: letter from, to Randolph, quoted, **19**: 355n; relations with William Pearce, **20**: 314, 316n, 318n, 320n-1n, 623; letter to, from William Pearce, quoted, **20**: 623n; mentioned, **7**: 284; **20**: 146

Settico, **4**: 362

Sevenne fils, **13**: 119

Severn Hall (Lewis estate), **1**: 35, 36n

Severn river, England: plan of iron bridge over, **9**: 241

Severn river, Va.: British ships at mouth of, **5**: 150, 169

Severus, Sulpitius: works by, **13**: 290

Sevier (Sevear, Seveir, Severe), John: letter from, **18**: 509; testimony in case tried by TJ, **1**: 25-6; at King's Moun-

hulls, **13**: 69; in U.S., **14**: 417; **19**: 183

ship carpenters: wages in N.Y., **7**: 327; wages in Conn., **7**: 333; wages in R.I., **7**: 338; wages in Mass., **7**: 342; wages in N.H., **7**: 343; wages in Pa., **7**: 347; wages in Va., **7**: 348

ship chandlery: U.S. import of, **10**: 147

Shipley, Jonathan. *See* Saint Asaph, Jonathan Shipley, Bishop of

Shippen, Alice Lee (Mrs. William Shippen), **2**: 263; **13**: 146

Shippen, Edward, **5**: 677n

Shippen, Joseph, **5**: 671n

Shippen, Margaret (Peggy). *See* Arnold, Margaret Shippen

Shippen, Thomas Lee: letters to, **13**: 276-7, 359-60, 642-3; **14**: 417-8, 638-40; letters from, **13**: 218-20, 311-2, 355, 444-9, 514, 627-9; **14**: 295-7, 472-4, 517-9, 663-7; **17**: 509-10; introduced to TJ, **12**: 186, 501; **13**: 6n; letter to, from William Lewis, **12**: 228-34; biographical note, **12**: 231n; TJ's aid to, **12**: 233n, 395; **13**: xxvi, 33n, 262, 264-76, 311, 449n; characterized by W. S. Smith, **12**: 501; letters from quoted, **12**: 502n-4n; correspondence with Dr. William Shippen, **13**: 6n, 7n, 120n, 147n, 253n, 449n, 355, 454n, 514n, 535, 546, 564, 627, 629; **17**: 456, 464-6; brings papers on Constitution to Paris, **13**: 6n-7n; letters to cited, **13**: 33n, 663; **14**: 440; TJ praises, **13**: 146; travels in Europe, **13**: 146, 218-20, 221n, 311-2, 375, 444-9, 605, 627-8, 643, 654; **14**: 25-6, 41, 185, 187-8, 276, 286, 295-7, 401, 664, 701; describes arrest of de Premini and de Boulonnais, **13**: 147n; describes TJ, **13**: 164n; introduced to Geismar, **13**: 266, 267, 318, 356-7, 449n, 454, 527-8; **14**: 583n; **15**: 49; letter from, to Short, cited, **13**: 311; introduced to Verme and others, **13**: 356, 359n, 360; assumes military rank, **13**: 356n, 449n; letters from cited, **13**: 454n; diary cited, **13**: 571n; TJ sends news to, **13**: 594; praises Geismar, **13**: 628-9; letters sent by, **14**: 187-8, 217n; honorary M.A. degree from College of New Jersey, **14**: 473-4; repays loan from TJ, **14**: 473, 474; describes Parliamentary debates, **14**: 474, 518; on French struggle for liberty, **14**: 517; on American govern-

ment, **14**: 517-8; information from, **14**: 591; introduced to Lord Lansdowne, **14**: 664; on British politics, **14**: 664-6; letters to, from Rutledge, cited, **14**: 666; passport issued by TJ, **15**: 486; at ratification of treaty with Creek Indians, **17**: 341n; at Georgetown with TJ and Madison, **17**: 464-5; mentioned, **12**: 517, 530, 531, 621n; **13**: 141n, 262, 270, 359, 408n, 506, 621; **14**: 403, 514, 634

Shippen, Dr. William: letter to, **13**: 146-7; letters from, **12**: 395; **13**: 100; inoculates TJ, **1**: 18n; friend of William Lewis, **12**: 231n; opinion on bill of rights, **12**: 231n; letters from cited, **13**: 6n; correspondence with Thomas Lee Shippen, **13**: 6n, 7n, 120n, 147n, 253n, 355, 449n, 454n, 514n, 535, 546, 564, 627, 629; **17**: 464-6; on constitution, **13**: 292; regard for TJ, **14**: 473; educational fees, **20**: 474; mentioned, **6**: 274; **12**: 186

shipping: danger to from British, **6**: 230, 237, 261; held in American ports, **6**: 246; rights of, **6**: 268; **7**: 267; stipulations in trade treaties, **6**: 393-4, 395; N.Y., **7**: 329; Conn., **7**: 333-4; R.I., **7**: 338; Mass., **7**: 341; N.H., **7**: 344; Pa., **7**: 347; statistics on, **7**: 349; U.S., **7**: 353; Va., **7**: 367; S.C., **8**: 201. *See also* freight carriage

ship planks: Conn. export to West Indies, **7**: 334

ships: lack of, **1**: 590; export permits, **2**: 376; theft of, **2**: 499; quarantine, **2**: 524-6; victualling, **7**: 340; number of seamen, **7**: 348; Hopkinson's inventions for, **9**: 321, 440; purchase by Emperor of Morocco uncertain, **10**: 335; remission of duty on, **10**: 476; lightering at Amsterdam, **13**: 9; right of arrest in Consular Convention, **14**: 74; to America from France, **15**: 42, 47, 57-8, 63, 70; question of citizenship in sea letters, **16**: 284. *See also* packet boats; steamboat; vessels

ships, American: export of, **7**: 339-40; **9**: 112; **10**: 147; **11**: 353; sold in France, **13**: 69, 191, 196n; in trade with France, **13**: 526; searched by Dutch, **15**: 21n; Spanish ports exclude, **16**: 329-30; detained in French West Indies, **16**: 353, 354n

ships, British: confiscation of, **1**: 390; seized by French, **14**: 391-2

SHORT, WILLIAM (*cont.*)

dled by Remsen, **16**: 310; and miniature of Louis XVI for TJ, **16**: 362n-3n; hopes to be minister to France, **16**: 497-9; **17**: 12-3, 28-9, 51, 231n, 394, 413, 507, 633-4; **18**: 32-3, 356-7, 445, 510; hopes for other diplomatic appointment, **16**: 499-500; **17**: 214, 528-9, 559-60; **20**: 347-8, 542-4, 643-4; in Amsterdam for financial negotiations, **17**: 126n, 427n-9n, 477-8, 632-5, 643, 654, 655; **18**: 22-3, 75, 84-6, 115n, 355; describes Bastille Day celebration, **17**: 212-3; appointment of successor in Paris delayed, **17**: 330; papers sent to, **17**: 385, 387n; **19**: 265; correspondence with Le Mesurier & Cie., **17**: 402n, 436n; and Willink, Van Staphorst & Hubbard's loan to U.S., **17**: 427n-9n, 433-4; Report on Weights and Measures sent to, **17**: 528; Swan tells of contract, **17**: 563; account with Congress, **17**: 632; **18**: 447-50; Tatham's map sent to, **17**: 659; holds commission for Fenwick, **18**: 11; on French trade with U.S., **18**: 15-22; **19**: 161; and French loan to U.S., **18**: 76-7; **20**: 180, 182-4, 187-97, 199-203; U.S. navigation bill sent to, **18**: 241; aids impressed seamen, **18**: 313, 318, 320, 333; corrects document, **18**: 422n; sends *Gazette Nationale*, **18**: 454; on French reaction to tonnage acts, **18**: 526, 527, 544-5, 551, 555; time of passage of letters to America, **18**: 595; TJ recommends for appointments, **18**: 602; letters from sent to Washington, **18**: 610n; and French reaction to Franklin's death, **19**: 81; delivers Washington's letter to Montmorin, **19**: 94; TJ sends extracts of letters of to Congress, **19**: 206; ignorance about Duer's schemes, **19**: 457; TJ's confidence in, **19**: 558; advises J. P. Jones on Danish offer, **19**: 590; irregular communication with Hamilton, **19**: 637; **20**: 349; and foreign loan, **19**: 637-8; **20**: 185; authorized to negotiate Dutch loan, **20**: 119-21, 144, 557; diplomatic reporting ability assessed, **20**: 169n; and U.S. foreign debt, **20**: 178; and British navigation act, **20**: 204, 209; and U.S.

SHORT, WILLIAM (*cont.*)

right to navigate Mississippi, **20**: 204, 364-5, 531, 532, 536-7, 652-3; letter sent by, **20**: 253; and controversy over *Rights of Man*, **20**: 309n; wishes to leave France, **20**: 347; expenses, **20**: 348-9, 692; conversations with Fernán-Nuñez, **20**: 364-5; lack of communication with Carmichael, **20**: 365, 587; protests French duties on U.S. tobacco, **20**: 371n; conversations with Blome, **20**: 386; salary, **20**: 394; irregularity of letters to TJ, **20**: 416; lack of letters from TJ, **20**: 541-2; lack of communication with Cathalan, **20**: 600; reimburses La Motte, **20**: 675

Journeys

leaves Richmond, **6**: 165, 178; to France, **7**: 148-9, 229, 254, 258, 279, 416, 418, 462, 503, 521, 534, 636; to The Hague, **8**: 316, 400, 420; arrives in London, **8**: 340; returns to Paris, **8**: 544, 547, 554; **14**: 590-1, 667; proposed journey through France and Italy, **11**: 381-2; with Shippen and Rutledge, **13**: 449n, 506, 627, 628, 654; **14**: 25-6; with Paradise family, **13**: 601-2, 634-6, 653; **14**: 9, 52-3, 299, 312-3, 612; in Italy, **13**: 615, 656; **14**: 27, 41-3, 272-3, 310-4, 377-83, 405-6, 448-52, 519, 524, 538, 541-3, 571-4, 590-2, 608, 666, 701, 704; **15**: 149-50; arrives in Geneva, **13**: 631; in France, **13**: 634-6, 652-6; **15**: 63; in Switzerland, **14**: 25-8; expenses, **14**: 25; with Rutledge, **14**: 41, 43, 53, 286, 310-2, 377-8, 404, 417, 464, 590-1, 608, 614; **15**: 73, 74; in Rome, **14**: 381-2, 405-6, 448-52; in Naples, **14**: 571-2; to Toulon dock yards, **14**: 592, 608, 649, 667, 705; **15**: 29; in Marseilles, **15**: 27-30, 43; to Amsterdam, **17**: 126n, 427n-9n, 477-8, 632-5, 643, 654, 655; **18**: 22-3, 75, 84-6, 115n, 355; **20**: 602

Other Correspondence

with C.W.F. Dumas, **9**: 463-4; **11**: 195-7, 197, 243-5; **15**: 201; with W. S. Smith, **10**: 213n-4n; **12**: 618, 621n; with Carrington, **11**: 50n; with Nelson, **11**: 171n-2n; **20**: 266n-7n; with Madison quoted, **11**:

SHORT, WILLIAM (*cont.*)

216n; with E. Randolph, **11**: 230-1; with John Jay, **11**: 231, 345-7, 549-50, 619; **12**: 154n-5n, 487-8, 681-4; **13**: 195; **15**: 512, 563, 568; **16**: 3, 8n, 28n, 63n, 87n, 361n; with John Stockdale, **11**: 364; with Crèvecoeur, **12**: 332n-3n; **16**: 238n, 279n; **17**: 14n, 412, 413n; with Donald, **14**: 186n-7n; **15**: 512, 537; **16**: 91n-2n, 230n; **18**: 477; **19**: 541; with Trumbull, **14**: 365n; with Grand, **14**: 382; with Mme de Tessé, **14**: 406n, 575n, 667; **15**: 78; with Skipwith, **14**: 517; **16**: 91n; **19**: 540; with Lafayette, **14**: 592; **15**: 537n; with Carmichael, **15**: 338n, 551n; **16**: 273, 403-4, 425, 440, 585; **18**: 506-7; with Willink, Van Staphorst & Hubbard, **15**: 473n; **16**: 205n; with N. Cutting, **15**: 512n, 525n; with J. B. Cutting, **15**: 529-30, 551n, 558; **16**: 188n, 205n, 252, 255n, 258-60, 415n, 440n-1n, 507n-8n, 509n; **18**: 314n, 318, 333; with O'Bryen, **15**: 537n-8n; **16**: 6n, 334n; **18**: 441n-2n; with Hamilton cited, **15**: 563, 566-7; **16**: 273-4, 305n; **17**: 126n, 427n, 428n, 615, 639, 654, 656n, 672; **18**: 86, 114, 115n, 351n, 451, 500, 526, 603, 610n; **19**: 361, 539; official dispatches to Jay, **16**: 3-8, 32-4, 40-3, 49-51, 79-80, 86-7, 103-5, 119-25, 162-5, 199-202, 219-22, 234-6, 267-71, 279-81, 301-5, 333-4, 371-6, 400-5, 419-21, 425-6, 430-2, 436-41; with Vernes, **16**: 97n; with Rutledge, **16**: 162n; with La Rochefoucauld d'Enville, **16**: 271n; with Chauvier, **16**: 507; with Humphreys, **17**: 126n; with Parker, **17**: 412-3; with Morris, **17**: 528; with M. Smith, **17**: 672n; with Cathalan, **18**: 24, 25n; with Fenwick, **18**: 143; with Vernon, **19**: 247; with McHenry, **19**: 253n-4n; with Montmorin, **19**: 259; **20**: 536-7; with Petit, **19**: 291; with secretary, **19**: 539-40; with La Motte, **20**: 676n

Personal Affairs

licensed to practice law in Va., **5**: 518n; certified by TJ as an attorney, **6**: 122; introduced by TJ to Madison, **6**: 122-3; introduced by TJ to

SHORT, WILLIAM (*cont.*)

Robert Morris, **6**: 123; introduced by TJ to Thomas McKean, **6**: 123; introduced by TJ to Richard Peters, **6**: 124; letters sent by, **6**: 183; **7**: 301, 359, 362, 379, 391, 401, 431, 509, 557, 562, 599; **8**: 75, 316, 472, 501; **13**: 523; purchase of land near Monticello, **6**: 550; health, **7**: 18; **9**: 77, 92, 96, 116, 126, 159; **14**: 52-3, 272-3, 275, 296; Peter Carr recommended to, **7**: 233; TJ's attitude toward, **7**: 247; **8**: 150; **13**: 490; **14**: 695, 697; **15**: 163-4; financial affairs, **7**: 253, 384; **20**: 545-6, 644; and Mazzei, **7**: 390, 391n; **8**: 277; decides to settle near Monticello, **7**: 559, 565; **10**: 612; and Richmond real estate, **7**: 604; Adams' opinion of, **8**: 311n; knowledge of French, **8**: 451; **10**: 414; **12**: 214; **15**: 620, 622; visits Hogendorp, **8**: 502; views on the *Encyclopédie Méthodique*, **10**: 3n; friendship of Va. delegates to Congress toward, **10**: 458; Mme de Tessé's comments on, **11**: 61, 206; **13**: 187; **17**: 9; love affair with Duchesse de La Rochefoucauld, **11**: 260n; and Greene's education, **13**: 348; Shippen corresponds with, **13**: 448; Trumbull sends books on Italy to, **13**: 564, 570, 597; J. P. Jones orders copies of bust for friends, **13**: 585, 587; **14**: 688; introduced to Verme, **13**: 605; **14**: 41; on wines and grapes, **13**: 635-6; suggests Trumbull's miniature of TJ be sent to Martha Jefferson, **14**: xxxvi, 365n; Skipwith's papers left with, **14**: 11; on life in Europe or America, **14**: 43-4, 276-7, 591, 607-8, 695-6; **15**: 27-9, 144, 163-4; **16**: 320, 418; **17**: 543-4, 559-60; **18**: 602; plans to stay in France after TJ leaves, **14**: 215, 617, 623; **15**: 143-4; interest in architecture, **14**: 311-2, 452; and macaroni mold, **14**: 540; **15**: 29, 324, 372, 409; Monroe hopes will return to America, **14**: 559; and askos from Nîmes, **15**: xxvii, xxx, 67, 125n; introduced to Bondfield, **15**: 43; buys prints and books in Rome, **15**: 78; Va. law concerning family, **15**: 78; handles TJ's bills in Paris, **15**: 536, 546; **17**: 316-7, 392, 411,

SHORT, WILLIAM (*cont.*)

632; recommends school for Peter Carr, **15**: 612; and TJ's household furnishings, **16**: xxxiii, 229-30, 320-4, 500-1, 583, 590; **17**: 11, 28-9, 212, 258, 282, 315, 392, 394-5, 402n, 410-2, 436n, 506, 547, 559; **18**: xxxiii, 30-2, 33n-9n, 307; Tatham's regard for, **16**: 9; packet for, **16**: 91; shares estate and slaves with brother, **16**: 107-8; robbed by Nomeny, **16**: 203, 263, 271-2, 417, 444; **18**: 448; La Luzerne's dislike of, **16**: 361n; Horry introduced to, **16**: 377; value of estate reduced, **16**: 419; sends news of TJ to Mme Ethis de Corny, **17**: 260, 261; converses with Mme d'Enville, **17**: 286; relations with Donald, **17**: 566, 626-7; **18**: 71-2, 74-5; sends TJ's account from Paris, **18**: 30-2, 33n-9n, 450; Rutledge sends message to, **18**: 53; returns TJ's Paris residence to owner, **18**: 357-8, 447; remembers countrymen, **18**: 445-6; on titles of honor, **18**: 451; portrait by Rembrandt Peale, **20**: xxxi, 384 (illus.); friendship with Pio, **20**: 662; sister. *See* Edmunds, Mrs. Thomas

Secretary to TJ

willingness to become legation secretary, **6**: 266-7, 271; discussed, **7**: 253-4; **8**: 445, 454, 547, 593; and appeal by Chevallié, **8**: 34, 35; and U.S.-Prussian treaty, **8**: 266, 301, 310, 313, 315-7, 323-4, 375-6, 424, 606; recommended to Thulemeier, **8**: 324; **10**: 140; recommended to Hogendorp, **8**: 325; suggested as emissary to Barbary States, **8**: 400; buys books for TJ, **8**: 461-2; salary, **8**: 546; **12**: 55, 674; **13**: 168-70; **14**: 581; praised by Thulemeier, **8**: 625; and crew of *William and Catherine*, **9**: 314, 315, 317, 394, 439, 537; accuracy as copyist, **9**: 489n-90n; inquires on Dutch constitution, **10**: 190; corrects Lamb's letters, **10**: 218n; represents TJ at presentation of bust of Lafayette, **10**: 408, 414, 415, 416n; **11**: 171n; translation of Calonne's letter by proposed, **10**: 486; forwards mail to TJ, **11**: 127; acts in TJ's absence, **11**: 142, 144,

SHORT, WILLIAM (*cont.*)

157, 158, 182, 184, 246, 253; **12**: 640, 641, 661, 670, 693; time spent at St. Germain, **11**: 258; refusal to commit TJ signature to petitions, **11**: 315-6; account against U.S., **11**: 609; requested to forward letter, **13**: 535; and Consular Convention, **14**: 90; recommended by TJ as secretary of legation in Paris, **14**: 216

Virginia Council of State

recommended by TJ as delegate to Congress, **6**: 548; **7**: 119, 149; successor to on, **6**: 549; **7**: 597; seat on, **7**: 257; and Chevallié affair, **7**: 550, 554; retirement from, **7**: 597

Shoula Springs, Va.: postal service, **20**: 711

shovels: for army, **4**: 378

Shower, Sir Bartholomew: cited on kidnapping, **2**: 497n

Shrewsbury, N.J.: landing of French troops at, **2**: 208

shrubs: to be sent TJ from S.C., **9**: 441; offer to ship to France, **12**: 428; duty on in France, **12**: 469, 480

Shudi & Broadwood, **7**: 534, 535

Shuker, Thomas: in *Dover* case, **20**: 206n-7n

Shuldam, Commodore Molyneux, **1**: 247

Shuter's Hill, Va.: Shippen visits, **17**: 465

Shylock: French & Co. compared to, **11**: 670

Siam: embassy to France, **16**: 572

Siberia: archaeological discovery in, **7**: 123, 227; bones of prehistoric animals found in, **7**: 312; tobacco culture, **7**: 371; Ledyard's attempted journey across, **11**: 638; Washington's reputation in, **19**: 47

Sicily: attitude toward U.S., **7**: 390; treaty of amity and commerce, **7**: 424; trade with, **8**: 308; attitude toward plan for concert of power against Barbary States, **10**: 562n, 565n; ambassador of. *See* Circello

Sickle, Mr.: inn rated by TJ, **20**: 471

Siddons, Sarah: acting in London, **9**: 278, 283

Sidi Muhammad ibn Abd Allah, Dey of Algiers: U.S. relations with, **8**: 46-7; **9**: 168; **10**: 76-7; tribute from Dutch,

8: 321; and crew of *Betsy,* 8: 376, 401, 460; attitude toward U.S., 8: 418; 13: 200; Carmichael's negotiations with, 8: 465; letter to drafted, 8: 521; and Barclay, 8: 542, 613-6; 9: 14; 10: 71, 141, 359-61; 11: 77; commission of American ministers to treat with, 8: 611-3; presents to, 8: 614; 11: 584n; TJ's "heads for a letter" to, 8: 617-9; letter to, from the American Commissioners, 8: 619-21; letter from, to European consuls, cited, 8: 665; character, 9: 96; asks King of Spain to negotiate peace with U.S., 9: 352; protects U.S. shipping, 9: 473; attitude toward Portugal, 9: 547; attitude toward Britain, 9: 547, 566; 10: 142; attitude toward Spain, 9: 547; 10: 357; letter from quoted, 10: 265; supports existing treaties, 10: 344; 17: 19; extent of dominions, 10: 359; harem, 10: 360; letters from, to Congress, cited, 10: 418; 13: 527n; 14: 46; correspondence with king of Spain, 10: 418, 510, 535; letter to, from Jay, cited, 11: 619; medal presented to, 12: 106n; 16: 65n; grants favors to Americans, 12: 644; Dutch ambassador sent to, 13: 134, 527; 14: 577; correspondence handled by Chiappe, 13: 526-7; 15: 341, 342n; letters from, to Beys of Tunis and Tripoli, cited, 13: 527n; 14: 46; releases American captive, 15: 342, 405, 418; death of, 16: 440, 441n; 17: 320; 18: 402; proposal to present *Alliance* to, 18: 387; mentioned, 8: 47, 119, 140, 607; 9: 187; 14: 288; 15: 628

Sidney (Sydney), Algernon, 6: 111n; 20: 662

Sidney, Sir Philip: TJ asks for copy of portrait of, 14: 467; bust of, 14: 525

Sidon Hill, Conn.: visited by TJ and Madison, 20: 459

Sieur Adams, Le (ship), 15: 109n

Siéyès, Emmanuel Joseph, Abbé: draft declaration of rights, 15: 390-1; in National Assembly, 16: 508n; letter from, to Washington, cited, 17: 214n; and Franklin's death, 19: 81, 82, 84, 86n, 90-1, 109-10; letter to cited, 19: 425; opposes Lafayette, 20: 351; speech on religious freedom, 20: 384; supports French monarchy, 20: 610; reply to

Paine, 20: 645

Sigaud de la Fond, Joseph Aignan: work on chemistry, 8: 559; *Essai sur différentes especes d'air fixe,* 11: 318, 327

signals: for Va. and Md. armed vessels, 3: 591; lack of criticized, 6: 107; agreed upon by Moroccan and American vessels, 10: 418, 421

Sigougne, Chevalier de: inquires about brother, 14: 185-6

Silbey, Thomas: letter from, 11: 98

Silesia: desire of Austria to annex, 12: 311

S'il est permis de faire arrêter un ambassadeur, 12: 688; 14: 491, 707n

silk: possible American production of, 2: 211; TJ asked to purchase for Mrs. Hopkinson, 7: 286; import by U.S., 8: 309; 10: 147; import by S.C. desirable, 12: 301; cultivation in Piedmont, 14: 43

Sillery, Mme de, 12: 701

silver: and currency, 7: 163-5, 170-1, 172, 180-1, 183, 190-1, 194-6, 199; 8: 90; 15: 25-6; 17: 535-40; 18: 455-6; price of, 7: 167, 182, 183, 200; imported, 7: 191; 9: 21; 10: 147; regulation in France, 9: 137; gold-silver ratio, 18: 455-6

silver lace: U.S. import of, 10: 147

silver plate: Lafayette purchases for Washington, 7: 47; TJ orders, 11: 518, 563, 608

silverware: manufactured in Conn., 7: 336; TJ requests permission to bring from England to France, 9: 313; at Monticello, 16: 196n

Simcoe, John Graves: raids in Va., 3: 147n; 4: 11n; 5: 557n; 6: 78n, 98, 625n, 626n, 634, 636, 637; quoted, 4: 623n; 5: 485n-6n; cavalry corps, 5: 526; on battle of Petersburg, 5: 559n

Simiane, Charles François, Comte de: suicide of, 11: 211, 247, 282

Simitière, Pierre Eugène du. *See* Du Simitière

Simkins, Arthur: Presidential elector from S.C., 14: 666; 15: 51

Simmons, Capt. (master of the *William and Henry*), 9: 392

Simmons, Mr.: and bill establishing ferries, 2: 460

Simmons, Anthony: makes silver askos for TJ, 15: xxxi, xxxii

Skinner, Howard, **5**: 294n

Skinner, John: marshal of N.C., **16**: 478n

Skinner, Robert: cited on kidnapping, **2**: 497n

Skinner, William: jailed as loyalist, **6**: 330n

Skinner's landing: ferry at, **2**: 456

skins. *See* hides

Skipwith, Mr.: catalogues sent by, **10**: 234; mentioned, **13**: 412

Skipwith, Anne Wayles (Mrs. Henry Skipwith): letter to, **7**: 229; birth of daughter, **6**: 473; Mary Jefferson writes to, **14**: 355; health of, **15**: 627; **17**: 239, 332; **19**: 295; **20**: 162, 166; marriage of, **15**: 658; visits Monticello, **20**: 167, 376; mentioned, **7**: 500; **9**: 92, 159; **10**: 594; **11**: 634, 636, 637; **13**: 348; **15**: 625; **16**: 16, 52, 91; **17**: 582

Skipwith, Fulwar: letters to, **14**: 354, 605; **16**: 560-1; **17**: 423-5; **20**: 401-3, 570, 708-9; letters from, **14**: 11-2, 337-8, 517; **15**: 529; **16**: 90; **17**: 510-1, 585-90; **19**: 268-9, 297-8; **20**: 342, 655, 718; economic success in London, **8**: 358; letters from cited, **9**: 367; **11**: 209; **17**: 598n; **19**: 604; letter sent by, **9**: 395; settles in London, **9**: 398; letters from quoted, **9**: 400n; **16**: 561n; packet sent by, **9**: 435; letter to quoted, **10**: 635n; tobacco trade with England, **10**: 635n; losses in Richmond fire, **11**: 209; letter from, to Limozin, cited, **13**: 301; asks TJ's help in obtaining consulship, **15**: 529; **16**: 90; gives information of TJ's plans, **16**: 16; U.S. consul at Martinique, **16**: 560-1; **17**: 246, 253n, 280, 510; **20**: 254, 342, 367, 570, 655, 708-9; describes disorders in Martinique, **17**: 510-1, 585-90; **20**: 342; letter from, to Short, cited, **19**: 540; returns to U.S., **20**: 568; mentioned, **9**: 400, 465; **10**: 615; **11**: 281; **15**: 632

Skipwith, Fulwar, & Co.: sends holly berries and cones, **11**: 256

Skipwith, Gray: in England, **9**: 465

Skipwith, Col. Henry: letters to, **6**: 423; **7**: 114, 230; **9**: 464-5; **11**: 635-7; **16**: 16, 51-2; **20**: 166-8, 373-6; letters from, **5**: 475; **6**: 472-4; **9**: 250; and sale of Wayles' lands, **1**: 100, 103; supports American state papers series,

1: 146; land purchase, **3**: 18; commands Cumberland co. militia, **5**: 82; TJ visits, **5**: 636n, 657; **6**: 5; **16**: 28; certifies TJ's statement of losses, **6**: 225; receives presents from TJ, **7**: 364, 501; **16**: 91; Le Maire visits, **8**: 122; and Wayles estate debt, **9**: 396; **13**: 327-8; **14**: 357, 362; **15**: 132, 161, 626, 645-7, 660, 674, 676; and Col. Cary's estate, **11**: 329; letter to cited, **11**: 654; copy of *Notes on Virginia* sent to, **12**: 133; letter to, from Randolph, cited, **16**: 30; letter from, to Short, cited, **16**: 228, 419; **17**: 566; **20**: 352, 545, 644; Tatham's map sent to, **17**: 659; sells land, **20**: 151; mentioned, **8**: 540; **9**: 92, 159; **10**: 594; **11**: 246, 634; **14**: 355, 358; **15**: 625; **16**: 48, 107; **17**: 582

Skipwith, Martha: birth of, **6**: 473; health of, **20**: 162

Skipwith, Nancy. *See* Skipwith, Anne Wayles

Skipwith, Sir Peyton: health of, **9**: 465; marriage of, **14**: 530, 608

Skipwith, Robert: letter to, **1**: 76-81; letters from, **1**: 74, 83-4; marries Tabitha Wayles, **1**: 75n; TJ lists books for, **6**: 128n; admitted to share in Nash's land scheme, **6**: 245; mentioned, **1**: 185; **6**: 220, 253

Skipwith, Tabitha (Tibby) Wayles (Mrs. Robert Skipwith): marries, **1**: 75n; mentioned, **1**: 78, 84, 185; **6**: 220, 253, 360

Skipwith family, **9**: 396

skunks: weight of, **6**: 343

slate: importation from France suggested, **8**: 368; use in Genovese houses, **11**: 440

Slater, Jonathan: land purchased for capital, **20**: 82

Slate river: ferry across, **2**: 459

Slaughter, Ens.: commission sent for, **3**: 121; member of court-martial, **3**: 350

Slaughter, Arthur (?), **4**: 20

Slaughter, Francis: signs Virginia Association, **1**: 108

Slaughter, George: letters from, **4**: 188, 332, 355-6, 375, 375-6, 391-2, 410-1, 429-30; **5**: 439, 452, 493-4; **6**: 55; letter sent by, **3**: 70; commands troops, **3**: 161, 258, 274; **4**: 31, 234; TJ asks to aid expedition against hostile Indi-

Slaughter, George (*cont.*)
ans, **3**: 357; aids G. R. Clark, **3**: 560;
money for, **3**: 613; supplies for, **4**:
199; **5**: 467; recommended for surveying, **4**: 200; condition of recruits under, **5**: 16-7; criticized by Clark, **5**:
252-3; letter to, from George, quoted,
5: 494n; mentioned, **4**: 653; **5**: 154,
320n
Slaughter, James: letter to, **5**: 408; letter
from, **5**: 407-8
Slaughter, John: in Regiment of Guards
for Convention troops, **3**: 156
Slaughter, Ruben(?), **4**: 20
Slaughter, Thomas: made speaker of
Transylvania convention, **2**: 108
Slaughter, William: in Regiment of
Guards for Convention troops, **3**: 121,
156; **4**: 541
slavery: TJ comments on, **1**: 129-30; **8**:
160, 184, 185, 229, 245; **9**: 441; **10**:
58; **12**: 578; **14**: 492; **20**: 160; in TJ's
draft Va. Constitution, **1**: 353, 363;
and issue of treason, **5**: 641; in TJ's
proposed revision of Va. Constitution,
6: 298; proposed abolition in new
states, **6**: 588n, 604, 608, 612n; **7**:
118, 205; Hogendorp's notes on, **7**:
216-8; inferior to free labor, **7**: 217;
10: 35; social effects in U.S., **7**: 217;
Mass., **7**: 339; N.H., **7**: 343; Lafayette
opposes, **7**: 446; proposed abolition of,
8: 258-9, 356-7, 667-8; **9**: 9; **10**: 18,
62-3; **13**: 285, 607; American opinion
on, **8**: 667-8; article on in *Encyclopédie
Méthodique*, **10**: 64n; Emperor of Morocco opposed to, **10**: 343-4; Martha
Jefferson opposes, **11**: 334; compromise on in Constitutional Convention,
13: 205; TJ's notes from Condorcet's
work on, **14**: 494-8; S.C. reaction to
TJ's criticism of, **15**: 72
slaves: and Va. nonimportation agreements, **1**: 30, 44; runaway, **1**: 33; **2**:
23; **4**: 436, 521; on TJ's estate, **1**: 40-
1; **13**: 340-1, 343, 363-4; **14**: 362; **16**:
167n-8n; **17**: 657; **18**: 29; devise of, **1**:
96; sale of, **1**: 96; **4**: 153-4; and Va.
Convention of 1774, **1**: 138; and Association of 1774, **1**: 150; Dunmore
emancipates, **1**: 261n, 265, 266, 267;
10: 372, 376n; debate on in Congress,
1: 320-3; costs of, **1**: 322; property
laws on, **1**: 560-2; Va. legislation on,
2: 22-4, 470-3, 475-6, 616-7; **15**: 78;
taxed in Va., **2**: 186-7, 218, 220; **7**:

362; inheritance in Va., **2**: 398, 405n;
6: 153; hire of, **2**: 403; **10**: 615; **11**:
640-1, 653; **20**: 717; emancipation of,
2: 470-1, 473n; **6**: 281n; **8**: 401; **9**:
199; **12**: 538; transportation as punishment of, **2**: 504; in execution of
judgment, **2**: 642; public use of, **3**:
214, 221, 229, 313, 344; **4**: 133, 438,
474-5, 518, 519, 583, 584, 592-3,
596-7, 621, 626; **5**: 127, 627; prices
of, **3**: 313; from S.C. and Ga., **3**: 492;
deserted by British, **4**: 127, 128; title
to, **4**: 154n; restitution to owners, **4**:
447, 681n, 691; **5**: 31; taken by British, **5**: 143, 445, 678n; **6**: 144, 224,
429, 533-4, 564-5; **7**: 47-8, 269, 381,
394, 458, 497, 522, 523, 524n, 532;
9: 111, 184, 297, 388, 389,
404, 501; **10**: 20; **13**: 363-4; **18**: 285-
6, 289-90; **20**: 478-9; as Congressional
messengers, **6**: 565; trials of, **6**: 644-5;
marriage of, **7**: 284; N.Y., **7**: 327; proportion to free inhabitants, **7**: 332 (in
Conn.), 337 (in R.I.); Conn. export of,
7: 334; R.I. export of, **7**: 338; imported by S.C., **8**: 199-200; **11**: 470;
Mayo's emancipation of, **8**: 342-3,
346n; **14**: 492; insurrections of, **8**:
343; in Algiers, **9**: 553; **17**: 30-3; population of, **10**: 56; proportion of TJ's
income consumed by, **11**: 640; power
of Congress over import, **12**: 279;
Spanish government holds fugitives
from Ga. and Fla., **12**: 284; **16**: 330n,
451n; **17**: 341n, 472n-3n, 638-9, 645;
18: 491-2; **19**: 518; **20**: 98n; textiles
for clothing, **13**: 392-3; **14**: 253; **15**:
662; **17**: 482; experiments with freed
and hired, **13**: 607; **14**: 492; Quakers
settle as tenants, **14**: 492; homicide
committed by, **15**: 636-7; in Wayles
estate debt, **15**: 644, 647, 650-7; importation into Va., **15**: 654-5; and
Short's estate, **16**: 107-8; in marriage
settlement of Martha Jefferson Randolph, **16**: 154, 155n, 189-90; **18**: 12;
McGillivray receives in Creek territory, **17**: 341n-2n; TJ's study of labor,
17: 346; Eppes sells, **18**: 579n
slave trade: TJ opposes, **1**: 129-30; **2**:
24n; **6**: 298; and Declaration of Independence, **1**: 314, 317-8; abolition of,
6: 281n, 298; **15**: 146; Va., **7**: 232;
10: 38; statistics, **7**: 349; reduction in,
8: 199-200; S.C., **8**: 199, 204, 258-9,
581; **11**: 589; U.S. import of, **10**: 147;

French attitude toward, **10**: 296; **12**: 577-8; **16**: 201; and Cary's slaves, **11**: 650-1; British attitude toward, **12**: 602; **13**: 338; **14**: 569; **15**: 103, 146, 193; Farrell & Jones in, **15**: 650-7; in West Indies, **16**: 80, 220; **20**: 367

Sleepy Hole, Va.: ferry at, **2**: 457; British encampment near, **4**: 422

Sligo, Ireland: and U.S. commercial policy, **19**: 134

slippers: TJ orders, **9**: 152; **10**: 479, 518

Sloan, James: favors moving capital to Philadelphia, **19**: 20n

Sloan, Philip: captured by Algerians, **14**: 395; **17**: 32; **20**: 625; on crew of *Dauphin*, **19**: 333

Sloane, Mr.: inn rated by TJ, **20**: 471

Sloane, Alexander: recommended as consul, **17**: 253n

Sloane, John: bill for riding express, **5**: 252n

Slodtz, Michael Angelo: statues of Diana and Endymion, **11**: 226, 232, 254, 420

Sluyter & Co.: bankruptcy of, **7**: 393

Small, Alexander, **9**: 487

Small, Thomas: settles near Fort Pitt, **2**: 101

Small, William: letter to, **1**: 165-7; death of, **1**: 166n; mentioned, **1**: 17, 32; **9**: 401n; **17**: 347

Smallman, Thomas: and Henderson land claims, **2**: 98; mentioned, **3**: 362

smallpox: reported in Williamsburg, **1**: 8; TJ inoculated against, **1**: 18n, 20; in Canadian campaign, **1**: 412, 435, 437, 444, 448, 449; **10**: 373, 377n; in Continental army, **1**: 458, 474, 483; Va. bills concerning, **2**: 122-4, 522-3; Walker family recovers from, **3**: 441, 455; measures to counteract, **5**: 96; outbreak of, **5**: 169; in Revolution, **13**: 363-4; **15**: 575, 577

Smallwood, Gen. William: letter to, **9**: 599-600; letter from, **3**: 636-7; fights British in south, **3**: 596; **4**: 5, 32, 80, 206, 207, 318, 326, 399, 492; letter from, to Gates, cited, **4**: 87, 103; Md. delegate in Congress, **7**: 572; mentioned, **4**: 6

Smeaton, John: failure of bridges at Hexham, **13**: 589; *Narrative of the building of the Edystone Lighthouse*, **20**: 391, 392n

Smilie (Smiley), John: articles attributed to, **12**: 231n; candidate for Congress

from Pa., **14**: 473; favors Potomac capital site, **20**: 5n

Smith, Capt.: commander of the *Fanny*, **8**: 94; **9**: 212; master of the *Ruby*, **12**: 231n

Smith, Col. (of Baltimore): orders flour, **3**: 171

Smith, Ens.: refusal of captaincy to, **4**: 179

Smith, Mr. (Eng.): theory of need for British trade, **9**: 4; unreliability as to facts about the U.S., **10**: 262-3; cited, **11**: 662

Smith, Mr. (U.S.): asks warrant on Treasury, **5**: 17-8; Mrs. Trist dislikes, **6**: 375, 382

Smith, Abigail Adams (Mrs. William Stephens Smith): letter to, **11**: 618; letters from, **10**: 572-3; **11**: 580-1; quoted, **8**: 44n; describes trousseau of Spanish Infanta, **8**: 66n-7n; describes crowds in Paris streets, **8**: 68n; marries W. S. Smith, **8**: 250n; **9**: 635; shoes for, **9**: 278; tour to Portsmouth, **10**: 68; purchases for, **10**: 154, 393; **12**: 148, 559, 619; TJ comments on, **10**: 479; letters from cited, **10**: 578; letters to cited, **10**: 620; children of, **11**: 515, 552; **13**: 458; **14**: 560; notifies TJ of Sullivan's draft, **12**: 72; returns to America, **13**: 458; correspondence with J. Q. Adams, **14**: xxxviii; **15**: 279n; **18**: 245n-7n; and husband's mission to England, **18**: 245n-6n; mentioned, **8**: 180, 241, 595, 602; **9**: 48, 126, 128, 260, 337, 646; **10**: 65, 363, 399, 400, 417, 518; **11**: 169, 502, 515, 531, 592, 598; **12**: 66, 357, 392; **15**: 116; **18**: 262, 273n

Smith, Adam: *The Wealth of Nations*, **8**: 59n, 111, 216; **16**: 449, 481; attacks mercantilism, **18**: 224; mentioned, **14**: 221

Smith, Augustine: in Albemarle co. militia, **1**: 668n

Smith, Bright & Gray: present bill to Adams, **11**: 580

Smith, Daniel: letters to, **3**: 278-9; **20**: 390; letter from, **19**: 354; and case of Thomas Johnson, **2**: 42n; court meets at house of, **2**: 115; appointed boundary commissioner, **3**: 13-4; letter to cited, **3**: 273; secretary of Southwest Territory, **16**: 478, 562; **17**: 293n

Smith, Devereux: settles near Fort Pitt, **2**: 101

Smith, Reuben: TJ buys land from, **16**: 94n

Smith, Richard: signs Continental Association, **1**: 153; signs Congress' second petition, **1**: 222; signs agreement of secrecy, **1**: 253

Smith, Robert (Eng.): in *Rachel* case, **20**: 508n

Smith, Robert (Pa.): promotes candidacy of Telles, **19**: 310; petition quoted, **19**: 311

Smith, Robert (Va.): appointed to receive recruits, **5**: 508

Smith, Samuel (Md.): letter to, **5**: 452; sword presented to, **16**: 55n; as congressman, **16**: 455n; mentioned, **3**: 279-80; **5**: 441

Smith, Samuel (N.J.): *History of the Colony of Nova Caesaria, or New Jersey*, **6**: 489; **12**: 18

Smith, Samuel A., **6**: 405n

Smith, Samuel & John: send letter, **16**: 116

Smith, Samuel Harrison: in controversy over *Rights of Man*, **20**: 271-4; biographical note, **20**: 271n; mentioned, **18**: 457n

Smith, Samuel Stanhope: letters from, **2**: 246-9, 252-5; biographical note, **2**: 249n; travels of, **20**: 335

Smith, Thomas (impostor): petition, with TJ's comments, **10**: 653-4

Smith, Thomas (London): Sir Walter Raleigh assigns rights in Va. to, **1**: 281

Smith, Thomas (Pa.): letter to, **17**: 288; appointed to confer with Va. delegates, **1**: 466n; letter to cited, **17**: 286; letter from cited, **17**: 644

Smith, Thomas (S.C.): letter from, **10**: 115; recommended to TJ, **10**: 524; passport issued by TJ, **15**: 485

Smith, Thomas (Va.): letter from, **3**: 111-2; in Albemarle co. militia, **1**: 666, 667; votes for bill for religious freedom, **2**: 549n; invoices for merchandise, **3**: 90, 92; as agent in Europe, **3**: 101, 111-2, 123, 358; **6**: 115; capture of, **3**: 201-2; purchase of slaves for public works, **3**: 313; exemption from militia duty, **4**: 632; ammunition for, **5**: 232; elected to Va. ratifying convention, **12**: 651; mentioned, **3**: 310; **4**: 283; **5**: 81; **6**: 197, 200, 322n

Smith, Thoroughgood: proposes exchange of corn for Bermuda salt, **3**: 326

Smith, William (Md.): letters to, **20**: 323, 636-7; letter from, **16**: 547-8; signs agreement of secrecy, **1**: 253; letter to, from Stephen Wilson, quoted, **16**: 548n; letter to cited, **20**: 121n; auditorship of treasury, **20**: 230n-1n, 636-7

Smith, William (Va.): letter to, **4**: 397

Smith, Dr. William: map of, **3**: 664; **5**: 325; **6**: 169

Smith, Dr. William (tavern keeper), **3**: 308; **5**: 331n; **8**: 118

Smith, Rev. William: letter to, **19**: 112-4; and eulogy of Franklin, **19**: 98, 99-101; characterized by Benjamin Rush, **19**: 99n

Smith, William, Jr.: *History of the Province of New-York*, **6**: 381, 489, 537, 544; **11**: 666; **12**: 18; son visits New York, **20**: 337

Smith, William Loughton: criticizes TJ, **4**: 273n; marries Charlotte Izard, **10**: 84; congressman from S.C., **14**: 394, 666; **15**: 51; **16**: 455n, 517; **18**: 229; on bankruptcy law, **15**: 264n; miniature by Trumbull, **17**: xxxii, 395 (illus.); in residence bill controversy, **17**: 172, 173, 176-83; identified as "Junius Americanus," **17**: 178, 180, 183, 191n-2n; biographical note, **17**: 178-9; *The Politicks and Views of a Certain Party, Displayed*, **17**: 180, 192n; **19**: 281n; on President's power of removal, **17**: 205n; associated with British interests, **18**: 227n; amendment defeated, **18**: 230n; and compromise of 1790, **19**: 4n; and motion to reply to French, **19**: 84, 84n; and the fisheries, **19**: 160; comments on national bank and capital site, **19**: 281n; shown capital plan by L'Enfant, **20**: 25; tours Conn., **20**: 444

Smith, William Stephens: letters to, **8**: 249-50; **9**: 447-8, 545, 605-6, 655; **10**: 115-7, 211-6, 362-3, 400, 478-9, 620; **11**: 45, 46-7, 168-9, 380; **12**: 71-3, 192-3, 355-7, 484-5, 557-9; **13**: 458-9; **19**: 363-4; letters from, **8**: 541-2; **9**: 118-9, 281-3, 437-8, 554-7, 557-8, 634-5; **10**: 92, 152-5, 291, 315-6, 393, 398, 417-8, 431, 518-9, 553, 578-9; **11**: 90-1, 365-7, 511-3; **12**: 145-8, 148, 204-6, 220, 243, 289-90, 390-2, 401, 501-4, 517-8, 618-9, 620-

Soria, Antonio (*cont.*)
298; TJ's introduction to, **11**: 266, 463n
Sorrer, Samuel: signs petition, **6**: 290
Sorrow, John: in Albemarle co. militia, **1**: 666
Sorrow, William: signs Va. oath of allegiance, **2**: 129
Sospello, Italy: TJ describes, **11**: 432
Soubeinan, Mme de: vineyard of, **11**: 445; Frontignan wine produced by, **11**: 621
Soubise, Charles de Rohan, Prince de: Gargaz' brochure given to, **9**: 100
Souche, M. (called Blondin): letters from, **15**: 124-5, 187; copies askos, **15**: xxviii, xxx-ii, 124, 187; letter from cited, **15**: xxxi; letter to cited, **15**: xxxi; letter to missing, **15**: 309
Soulès, François: letters to, **10**: 363; **11**: 56, 110; **14**: 691; letters from, **10**: 352-3; **14**: 684; *Histoire des troubles de l'Amérique Anglaise*, **10**: 166, 201; **11**: 43, 666; **12**: 42, 130, 588; TJ's comments on, **10**: 364-83; relations with TJ, **10**: 365n, 367n-8n; criticizes U.S., **10**: 368n; *Le Vade-mecum parlementaire*, **14**: 684n; *Statuts, ordre et reglements du Parlement d'Angleterre*, **14**: 684n; criticism of, **20**: 431
Soulanges, M. de: letters from cited, **8**: 334, 409; commandant at Toulon, **18**: 382n
Soulavie, Jean Louis, Abbé: letter to, **11**: 111-2
Sousa, Pinto de. *See* Pinto de Sousa Coutinho, Luis
Sousa de Coutinho, Francisco Inocêncio, Conde de: letter to, **10**: 559; letters to, from American Commissioners, **7**: 419-20, 551; letters from, to American Commissioners, **7**: 428, 580; fails to return TJ's visit, **8**: 173; TJ's opinion of, **8**: 174n, 603, 607; **9**: 61, 64n, 137
Southall, Henry: votes for bill for religious freedom, **2**: 549n; on committee to inquire into conduct of Executive, **6**: 134; introduces miliary relief bill, **6**: 140n
Southall (Southal), Col. James: letters to, **5**: 166, 292, 295, 412; letter to cited, **4**: 626; revaluation of horses by, **5**: 286, 287; mentioned, **1**: 470; **5**: 545, 549
Southall, James Barrett: dance at home of, **1**: 7, 9n, 237

Southall, Philip: marriage of, **14**: 530
Southall, Stephen: letter to, **4**: 642-3; letters from, **4**: 632, 643; payment to, **3**: 486, 494, 495; as commissioner of army provisions, **4**: 89, 97, 342, 531; warrants to, **4**: 444; as Continental deputy quartermaster, **4**: 445n, 474n; letter from, to William Davies, quoted, **6**: 49n; mentioned, **5**: 83n, 288n, 577, 667n, 703; **6**: 22, 48-9
Southall, Turner: letter to, **4**: 621; letter from, **4**: 632; director for public buildings, **3**: 19n; **4**: 434-5; **8**: 343; recommended to secure slaves for work at Hoods, **4**: 597; death of, **20**: 293, 405; mentioned, **3**: 43, 144, 174, 175, 182, 270n; **4**: 435n
South Amboy, N.J.: visited by TJ and Madison, **20**: 460
South America: paleontology, **6**: 545; revolt in, **9**: 218, 555; population of, **10**: 56-7; maps of, **10**: 212-3, 214n-6n, 216-7, 620; **12**: 178n, 558; **20**: 582, 592-3, 602; lack of news concerning, **12**: 357; Spanish policy toward, **12**: 673; rumors of British interference in, **13**: 209, 231; Spanish fleet said to be in, **13**: 209, 231
Southampton co., Va.: letters to county lieutenant of, **5**: 32, 416; appoints infantry officers, **1**: 581; place of court of assize, **1**: 629; militia, **2**: 131; **3**: 601; **4**: 62, 63, 295n, 297, 352, 371; **5**: 29, 35, 47, 181, 311, 665; **6**: 83; senatorial district, **2**: 336; levies of soldiers, **3**: 8; tobacco loan office certificates, **3**: 515; appointment of cattle commissioner for, **3**: 612; collections under provision law, **4**: 7; supply post for, **4**: 286; commissioner for, **5**: 274; mentioned, **5**: 175
South Carolina: letters to delegates in Congress, **12**: 148, 509; letter to governor, **12**: 204; letter from delegates in Congress, **13**: 107, 368; population of, **1**: 182; **10**: 34, 35, 39, 54-6; Revolution in, **1**: 252, 313, 468, 471; **3**: 558; **4**: 132; **5**: 149; attitude on slavery, **1**: 314; **7**: 118; **8**: 581, 667; **10**: 18; **11**: 470, 589; **12**: 279; **15**: 72; votes on independence, **1**: 314; votes for Chase's taxation plan, **1**: 323; and aid from Va., **2**: 234-5; **3**: 225, 299, 301-2, 307; British campaigns in, **2**: 236; **3**: 343, 399-401, 650; **4**: 80, 82; **5**: 421, 541; **6**: 118, 126; European atti-

tude toward, **3**: 93; and Cherokees, **3**: 175, 179-80; loses credit in France, **3**: 202; military supplies in, **3**: 426; **4**: 323; military situation, **4**: 150, 369; Greene moves toward, **5**: 361; votes on permanent seat for Congress, **6**: 366; demands extradition of George Hancock, **6**: 513-5; **7**: 38; votes on Va. land cession, **6**: 575n; **7**: 4-5; cession of western territory, **6**: 594n; **7**: 21; boundary with proposed northwest colonies, **6**: 602; founding of, **6**: 658; financial quota to national treasury, **7**: 5, 55, 70-1, 233; **10**: 34, 35, 54-6; unrepresented in Congress, **7**: 21, 31; attitude toward Society of the Cincinnati, **7**: 110n; **10**: 50; approves 1783 impost, **7**: 130; divisiveness in, **7**: 130; Indian agencies, **7**: 280; TJ offers services abroad, **7**: 283; votes on R.I. delegates, **7**: 291; debts, **7**: 348; land south of the Ohio, **8**: 124; agriculture of, **8**: 158-9; commerce of, **8**: 195-204, 581; **10**: 39; **19**: 136-8; David Ramsay's history of, **8**: 210-1, 293, 359-61, 457; TJ thanks Izard for notes on commerce, **8**: 552; article on in *Encyclopédie Méthodique*, **9**: 155; **10**: 39; law concerning foreign debts, **9**: 504-5; evacuation of loyalists from, **10**: 14; climate, **10**: 84; emits paper money, **10**: 231; attitude toward Annapolis convention, **10**: 233; rice, **10**: 463-4; **11**: 339; **12**: 295; **13**: 372; **14**: 331, 708; **15**: 372; **16**: 332; Agricultural Society founded (1785), **10**: 464; laws favorable to debtors, **10**: 513; **11**: 279; TJ receives Jay's instructions on, **11**: 100; delegates to Federal Convention, **11**: 154, 219, 401; claim against Spain, **11**: 236-7; **12**: 51, 99-100, 148, 151, 173, 204; copy of laws sent TJ, **11**: 265; effects of Revolution on, **11**: 265; evades injunctions of Congress, **11**: 308; attitude on Mississippi navigation, **11**: 309; possibility of growing olives, **11**: 648-9; attitude toward Constitution, **12**: 254, 281; claims against, **12**: 267; Dutch in, **12**: 299; **14**: 15-6; exports to France, **12**: 386; ratification of Constitution, **12**: 609, 655, 676; **13**: 101, 156, 160, 205, 209, 232, 244, 248, 283, 292, 315-6, 318, 331, 348, 359, 370, 413; debt to Lamarque & Fabre, **12**: 633; vote on location of Congress, **13**: 498,

540; figs, raisins, etc., ordered for, **13**: 508; **14**: 183; Cutting negotiates with, **13**: 608; **14**: 15-6; **15**: 218-20, 257, 450, 452, 463, 464n; TJ's correspondence for carried by Trumbull, **13**: 610; elections (1788), **14**: 394, 415, 666; **15**: 51; cotton, **14**: 546; **15**: 452; representatives in Congress (1789), **14**: 666; ordinance on funding of foreign debt, **15**: 31-2, 32n-3n; bonds, **15**: 218, 257-8, 277, 348-9, 450, 452, 463, 464n, 469; **16**: 324-5, 390; **17**: 487, 577; debt to Streckensen, **15**: 218-20, 264, 463, 464n; elections (1790), **18**: 52; ratifies constitutional amendments, **18**: 595; and need to appoint Commissioners on a sectional basis, **19**: 59; Cathalan's relations with, **19**: 74. *See also* olive culture in S.C.

South Carolina (ship): assistance to Spain in reduction of Bahamas, **10**: 559; owned by king of France, **10**: 592; payment of expenses incurred by, **11**: 133; claim of crew of *L'Indien* against, **11**: 300-1; new name for *L'Indien*, **11**: 301n; Coram's service on, **19**: 409; mentioned, **11**: 164. *See also Indien, L'* (ship)

South Carolina, Agricultural Society of. *See* Agricultural Society of South Carolina

South Carolina, Council of, **3**: 397

South Carolina, Governor of. *See* Pinckney, Charles

South Carolina campaign. *See* Carolina campaign; Charleston, S.C.

South Carolina Gazette: publishes letter from TJ, **11**: 279

South Carolina Yazoo Company: actions of agent, **19**: 273n

Southerland, John, **3**: 542n

southern army: insurrection among Tories, **3**: 317, 325-6, 340; reinforcements for, **3**: 530, 539, 574, 584-5, 588, 589, 592, 593, 601-4; **4**: 83, 175-7, 301, 613-5, 622, 624; supplies for, **3**: 606, 610-2, 641, 668; **4**: 131, 183, 196, 206-7, 210, 212, 219-20, 323, 547, 580, 667, 696-7; **5**: 16, 47-8, 77-8, 101, 175, 215, 245, 258, 264, 269, 290, 291-2, 318-9, 325, 338, 340, 342, 429, 575, 578n, 620; Gates weighs position of, **3**: 621; volunteers, **3**: 653, 654; **4**: 85; transportation, **3**: 660; **4**: 184; **5**: 225-6, 240-

southern army (*cont.*)
1; cavalry, **4**: 6; **5**: 103, 360; Gen.
Greene commands, **4**: 60-1, 130, 133-4; Va. aids, **4**: 109, 212-4; officers, **4**: 125; physical requirements for, **4**: 131; and Steuben's organization, **4**: 152; joined by Lafayette, **4**: 190; artificers for, **4**: 250; lack of money, **4**: 251; positions, **4**: 253; horses for, **4**: 478; disparity against British, **4**: 495; need of greater support by north, **4**: 575; quota of troops for, **4**: 667; skirmishes, **5**: 23, 102-3; strength of, **5**: 44; means of supporting, **5**: 66; light infantry, **5**: 111, 115; T. S. Lee desires news of, **5**: 169; casualties, **5**: 183; lead shortage, **5**: 232; situation of, **5**: 269; deputy quartermaster general, **5**: 574. *See also* Greene, Nathanael
southern states: Washington promises relief to, **5**: 663; relations wih Congress, **6**: 334; **7**: 248; interest in trade treaties, **7**: 48, 293; paper currency, **7**: 212; culture, **7**: 218; economy compared to that of north, **8**: 217; attitude toward power of Congress over trade, **8**: 413; characteristics of inhabitants, **8**: 468; Indian tribes in, **9**: 641-2; tendency toward aristocracy in, **10**: 533; climate compared with southern France, **11**: 646; attitude toward Constitution, **12**: 411; confederacy proposed by Henry, **13**: 359; British devastations in Revolution, **13**: 364
South Mountain, **2**: 113
Southold, N.Y.: visited by TJ and Madison, **20**: 459
South Quay: naval officer for, **2**: 375; post service from, **2**: 389; cannon at, **4**: 356, 358; **5**: 279, 280, 299, 359; **6**: 107; as port for Va. supplies, **4**: 502; **5**: 607; trunk seized at, **5**: 4; removal of goods to Point of Fork, **5**: 660
Southwest Territory: recommendations for federal offices, **16**: 476-8; act establishing government of, **17**: 292n-3n; Anderson appointed judge of, **19**: 381-408 (editorial note and documents
Southwick, Solomon: supports American state papers series, **1**: 145
Souza, Pinto de. *See* Pinto de Sousa Coutinho
Souza de Coutinho, Francisco. *See* Sousa de Coutinho, Francisco
sovereignty: between Britain and colonies, **1**, 117, 119, 121-35, 141-3, 170-4, 193-222, 225-33, 241-2, 290-1, 417-32; right to reject act of plenipotentiary, **7**: 32; position in feudal system, **12**: 275; S. Adams comments on, **19**: 106n. *See also* Congress, Continental: Authority; Constitution of the United States
spades: for army, **3**: 645; **4**: 9, 378
Spafford, Horatio Gates: letter to quoted, **14**: 221
Spaight, Richard Dobbs: member of committee on letters of commissioners in Europe, **6**: 401n; **7**: 207n; member committee on Va. land cession, **6**: 575n; motion on Ordinance of 1784, **6**: 612n; motion on report on state claims defeated, **6**: 617n; delegate to Congress from N.C., **7**: 7n, 119, 273n; member of committee on treaties, **7**: 204n; borrows books from TJ, **7**: 240n-1n; member Committee of the States (1784), **7**: 299; dispute with Hugh Williamson, **7**: 461; delegate to Federal Convention, **11**: 401
Spain: relations with U.S., **1**: 310, 313; **3**: 116, 117-8; **6**: 265, 393; **7**: 403-7, 548-9, 566-7, 570, 572, 593; **8**: 64, 77, 93, 95, 114, 130-1, 150, 251, 322n, 401, 464-5; **9**: 246-7, 552; **10**: 84; **11**: 566; **12**: 240, 673; **14**: 288; **16**: 288n, 301; **17**: 5, 614-5; **18**: 241-2, 292, 293, 299; **19**: 429-531; **20**: 96-7, 364-5, 674; position in American Revolution, **2**: 217; **3**: 76, 167, 202, 470, 474; **6**: 61, 62, 149; relations with Britain, **2**: 236; **3**: 63-4, 82, 88, 106, 117, 306; **6**: 170; **8**: 252-3, 341; **9**: 653; **10**: 179, 606; **11**: 222, 237; **12**: 51, 673; **13**: 92, 94-5, 134, 590; **16**: 253-4; **17**: 398; **18**: 10-2, 24-5, 48-9, 64, 85, 111, 362; **20**: 235, 653, 694; and navigation of Mississippi, **3**: 88, 343, 521; **4**: 137, 203; **7**: 403-7, 416-7, 422, 433, 569-70; **8**: 130-1; **9**: 653; **10**: 233, 274-6, 293, 310, 330, 456-7, 575; **11**: 93-4, 202, 309, 314, 481; **12**: 173; **13**: 494, 540, 624, 626n; loan to U.S., **3**: 159, 555; **7**: 65; **8**: 630; **10**: 24; activities in Fla., **3**: 260; British capture merchantmen of, **3**: 285; navy, **3**: 374; **4**: 105; **10**: 428; **12**: 324, 673; **13**: 114, 143, 173, 174, 191, 193, 209, 239, 231, 465, 579; **20**: 674; captures by rumored, **4**: 28; at New Orleans, **4**: 199; alliance with Va., **4**: 203; takes Pensa-

cola bay, **5**: 551; attitude toward offer of mediation, **6**: 65, 96; claims territory east of Mississippi, **6**: 213; and Definitive Peace Treaty, **6**: 338; U.S. treaty of amity and commerce, **7**: 48, 263, 267, 423-4, 425-6, 455-6, 510, 638; **8**: 137, 605, 608; **9**: 42; **10**: 286, 606; **12**: 363-4; U.S. trade with, **7**: 90, 231, 380, 571; **9**: 611; **13**: 93, 609; **20**: 710; coinage, **7**: 194; **8**: 90; rate of exchange with, **7**: 201; **18**: 455-6; trade with Mass., **7**: 339; trade with N.H., **7**: 344, 346; trade with Va., **7**: 370; rivers, **7**: 405; settlement on west shore of Mississippi, **7**: 406, 642; purchase of land from proposed by Madison, **7**: 407; relations with France, **7**: 416-7, 422; **10**: 537; **11**: 130; **12**: 240, 362; **13**: 125, 405; **17**: 437-8; **18**: 296, 343; **20**: 364, 609, 694; at Natchez, **7**: 454; **8**: 483; relations with Barbary States, **7**: 511; **8**: 253, 321, 401, 624, 665; **10**: 138, 310; Congress' indifference toward, **7**: 548; **10**: 537; death of princes, **7**: 550; postal service to U.S., **7**: 564; relations with Algiers, **8**: 4, 65-6, 69, 321, 376, 399, 401, 419, 444, 455, 460, 567; **9**: 233, 244-9, 376, 377-8, 525, 529, 531, 539, 568, 590, 595, 619; **10**: 137, 150, 266, 329, 412; **11**: 566-7; **12**: 100, 182, 183, 565; **14**: 502; **15**: 284; foreign relations, **8**: 70; relations with Morocco, **8**: 83; **9**: 547; **10**: 357, 389; **17**: 615, 629, 641; **18**: 50, 402-3; **19**: 256; **20**: 679, 684; trade with S.C., **8**: 201; effect of possible European war on, **8**: 252; climate, **8**: 253; intercedes for crew of the *Betsy*, **8**: 460, 464, 512; succession to crown, **8**: 466; aid to U.S. in negotiations with Barbary States, **8**: 657-8, 670; **9**: 352, 550, 551, 648; **10**: 178-9, 248, 251, 265, 294, 302, 624, 649; **11**: 102; **12**: 240; weaknesses advantageous to U.S., **9**: 218; relations with Indians, **9**: 297; **10**: 110, 314; probable part in French-Dutch treaty, **9**: 366; relations with Naples, **9**: 366, 470, 527, 546, 648-9; **10**: 179, 330, 413, 428, 537, 605, 606-7, 613, 624, 650; **11**: 42; relations with Portugal, **9**: 527; opposition to rule in South America, **9**: 555; relations with Turkey, **9**: 568; colonies, **9**: 631-2; **11**: 567; relations with Russia, **9**: 648-9; **12**: 673; **13**: 114n, 134,

216, 217n, 458; orders destruction of map of South America, **10**: 212, 214n; Jay favors good terms with, **10**: 275; cavalry reduction, **10**: 537; financial affairs, **10**: 537; **12**: 100; relations with Netherlands, **10**: 607; **13**: 239n; possibility of war against by inhabitants of west, **11**: 94; new council of state established, **12**: 50-1; claim of S.C. against, **12**: 204; alliance with Austria and Russia, **12**: 484; travel in recommended, **13**: 358, 375, 531; Ky. intrigues with reported, **13**: 540-1; **14**: 387n-8n; politics and government, **13**: 576-9; **14**: 499-502; **18**: 504-5, 599; exports foreign cloth to South America, **13**: 579; wines, **13**: 664; relations with Tunis, **14**: 46; grants land on Mississippi to Col. Morgan, **14**: 530, 608; **15**: 7, 106; Rutledge plans to visit, **14**: 538, 613-4, 666, 705; **15**: 66, 72-3, 77; revolutionary sentiments rumored, **15**: 338; American medals sent to, **16**: 67; suppresses French books, **16**: 123; U.S. ships forbidden to use Spanish ports, **16**: 329-30; war with Britain, **16**: 413-4, 415n, 417-8, 425-6, 427, 430-1, 439, 541, 541n, 554, 562, 575, 577, 580, 598, 599, 601; **17**: 18, 25, 26, 27, 209, 257-8, 263, 266, 269, 270, 275-6, 311-2, 415, 438, 473, 474, 480, 481, 488-9, 495, 498n, 500, 502, 522, 525, 557, 567, 593-4, 603-5, 605, 614-5, 618-9, 627, 629, 648-51, 658, 671-2; **18**: 111, 293, 294; Humphreys' mission to, **17**: 86-9, 94, 103-5, 120-1, 125-7; **18**: 472-5, 497-8; peace with Britain (Madrid convention, 1790), **18**: 10-2, 24-5, 48-9, 64, 85, 353, 483-4, 579; **19**: 290; in Russo-Turkish peace negotiations, **18**: 606; **20**: 658; and the fisheries, **19**: 175n, 178, 185, 186; counter-revolutionary activity against France, **19**: 636-7; finances, **20**: 364; minister to U.S., **20**: 538; regulates imported wheat, **20**: 563; unrest in, **20**: 654, 656; army, **20**: 674; population, **20**: 674. *See also* Jay, John: Secretary of Foreign Affairs, negotiations with Gardoqui

Spain, King of. *See* Charles III; Charles IV

Spain, Queen of. *See* Maria Luisa

Spallanzani, Lazzaro: works on digestion and generation, **14**: 698, 699n

541; correspondence with George Muter, **4**: 408-10; resignation as commissary of military stores, **4**: 410; pay for services, **4**: 418

Spilly, Count. *See* Expilly

spinet: quilling of, **7**: 286-7; jacks for, **16**: 490; **17**: 389-90; sent from Monticello to Philadelphia, **18**: 41-2, 69

Spinola, Cristoforo, Marquis de: letter from, **8**: 336; letter from, to Franklin, quoted, **7**: 420n

Spinola, Marquise de: letter from, **8**: 336

Spire. *See* Speyer

spirit level: TJ seeks, **2**: 175

Spittall, George, **3**: 542n

Spoleto, Italy: aqueduct at, **14**: 381

Spooner, George Wilson: and bill establishing ferries, **2**: 454

spoons: manufactured in Conn., **7**: 336

Spotswood, Gen. Alexander: letter to, **4**: 490; letters from, **4**: 158-9; **5**: 331-2; TJ buys horse from, **2**: 39; tents for, **4**: 531; proposes legionary corps for Va., **5**: 34; swords for, **5**: 285, 296-7; appointed brigadier general, **5**: 332n, 636n; letter to, from Weedon, quoted, **5**: 564n; mentioned, **5**: 372, 630; **9**: 487

Spotswood, John: prisoner of war, **3**: 390

Spotsylvania, Va., **13**: 363

Spotsylvania co., Va.: letters to county lieutenant of, **5**: 128, 616; **6**: 34; militia, **1**: 160; **2**: 132; **3**: 599; **4**: 63, 304, 377; **5**: 128, 141, 181, 224, 271, 273, 309n, 311, 329n, 332-3, 411n, 561, 616-7, 646; **6**: 84, 93; sulphur mine found, **1**: 289; appoints infantry officers, **1**: 581; place of court of assize, **1**: 629; grand jury in, **1**: 638-9; senatorial district, **2**: 336; levies of soldiers, **3**: 7; tobacco loan office certificates, **3**: 516; taxes, **6**: 565

Spotsylvania Court House, Va.: time of holding court of assize, **1**: 628-9; proposed meeting of school overseers at, **2**: 530

Spradling, John: in Albemarle co. militia, **1**: 665

Sprigg (Sprig), Sophia: courtship by Arthur Lee, **6**: 546; marries John Mercer, **8**: 79, 134

Sprightly Nancy (ship), **15**: 664, 666, 667

Spring block: used for sailing, **10**: 625; Hopkinson's invention, **11**: 289

Spring Forest, **1**: 98n

springs, medicinal: in Va., **3**: 60

Springstone, William: deposition of, **4**: 408n

Sproat, David: on deaths of prisoners, **10**: 269

Sprowle, Mr. (son of Andrew Sprowle): commission in British army, **8**: 329

Sprowle, Andrew: signs nonimportation resolutions (1770), **1**: 46; accused of dealing with British, **8**: 243-4, 244n; confiscation of property in Va., **8**: 259, 329-30, 364

Sprowle, Mrs. Andrew. *See* Douglas, Katherine Sprowle

Spy (ship): disbursements for, **11**: 602

Squire, Capt. Matthew: at battle of Hampton, **1**: 257

Squires, Capt. (master of *Julius Caesar*), **16**: 562-4

Squirrel (ship), **20**: 243n

Squirrel Bridge, Va., **5**: 664

Stabb, Capt. Augustine, **4**: 539

Stabler, Thomas, **1**: 54

Stadnitski (Stadnitzky), Pieter: loan for payment of Fizeaux debt, **12**: 566, 574; speculates in U.S. debts, **13**: 323n; **16**: 135; **18**: 592; and Society for Establishing Manufactures, **19**: 454n; loan to U.S., **20**: 619

Stadtholder. *See* William V

Staël de Holstein, Anne Louise Germaine Necker, Baronne de: TJ meets with, **8**: 242n; marriage of, **9**: 466, 470

Staël de Holstein, Eric Magnus, Baron de: letters to, **9**: 631-4; **10**: 472; **12**: 4; letter from, **8**: 336; letter to, from American Commissioners, **7**: 428-9; letter from, American Commissioners, **7**: 434-5; marries Germaine Necker, **9**: 466, 470; asks TJ's advice, **9**: 646; package from, **11**: 234, 253; discusses subject of American representative at Stockholm, **16**: 107

Stafford, Robert: recommended to TJ, **19**: 627

Stafford co., Va.: letters to county lieutenant of, **5**: 255; **6**: 34-5; militia, **1**: 160, 481; **2**: 132; **3**: 600; **4**: 63, 377; **5**: 255, 309n, 311, 329n, 404-5, 451; appoints infantry officers, **1**: 581; place of court of assize, **1**: 629; senatorial district, **2**: 336; levies of soldiers, **3**: 7; tobacco loan office certificates, **3**: 516; supply post for, **4**: 286

439. *See also* Willink & Van Staphorst
Staphorst, Nicholas van: letters to, **12**:
421-2; **13**: 213, 559; **14**: 614; letters
from, **12**: 669; **14**: 5-6; pays Dumas
for *Gazette de Leide*, **13**: 279n, 558,
559; declines position as U.S. consul,
18: 510-1
Staples, Mr.: land surveyor, **20**: 163
Stark, Gen. John: attacks Col. Baum's
troops, **2**: 29
Starke (Stark), Bolling: letter from, **5**:
579-80; signs nonimportation resolutions, **1**: 30, 46; and bill to abolish entail, **1**: 561n; and bill to revise Va.
laws, **1**: 563n; asked to prepare bill to
prevent importation of slaves, **2**: 24n;
appointed auditor of Va., **4**: 302n; **5**:
35; elected to Va. Executive Council,
10: 577; resigns, **13**: 621; mentioned,
9: 183
Starke, Col. John: recommended to secure slaves for work at Hoods, **4**: 597;
mentioned, **3**: 85; **5**: 358; **6**: 22
Starke, Richard: signs nonimportation
resolutions (1769), **1**: 31; as witness,
1: 67
stars: variations of light in, **7**: 602; **9**:
355; double discovered by Herschel, **7**:
602; **8**: 575; Caille's catalogue of fixed,
8: 298; positions of, **8**: 299; periodical
variation of fixed, **12**: 30
state debts: payment, **3**: 584; **5**: 626; assumption by U.S., **6**: 262-4, 266; **16**:
213, 278, 351, 386, 449-50, 493,
540-1, 553, 574-5, 577, 596-7, 598,
601; N.Y., **7**: 327; Conn., **7**: 331;
R.I., **7**: 337; Mass., **7**: 339; N.H., **7**:
343; Va., **9**: 183; Monroe on, **17**: 231-
2; TJ on, **17**: 266-7, 269-71, 276; **18**:
82; Harvie on, **17**: 296; Va. Assembly
resolves on, **18**: 131n; mentioned, **3**:
402. *See also* assumption bill
State Department. *See* Department of
State, U.S.
State Gazette of North-Carolina, **17**: 509n
State Gazette of South-Carolina, **17**: 509n
Staten Island, N.Y.: military action
around, **1**: 473, 483, 488; **2**: 207;
Congressional committee meets with
Lord Howe at, **1**: 520
state papers, American: Hazard's edition
of, **1**: 164, 176; **5**: 562-3; **19**: xxxv-vi,
284-5, 287-9n, 348 (illus.); Hazard's
list of for Va., **1**: 176; **3**: 196; preservation of by Congress, **3**: 252
states: sovereignty of in Articles of Con-

federation, **1**: 177; division of western
territories into, **3**: 629; and trade, **5**:
474; **7**: 102; **8**: 483-4; **9**: 198, 204;
10: 15; conflicts between, **6**: 475n,
505-7; **10**: 19; Morris' statement on
arrears and payments of, **6**: 558-64; financial quotas, **7**: 54-5, 66-72, 123,
213, 233; **10**: 14, 298; **11**: 672; **12**:
342; relation to federal authority, **8**:
89, 215-6, 579-80; **10**: 603; **11**: 220,
480-1; **12**: 271-2, 274-5; boundaries
of, **8**: 519; lack of unity among, **9**:
334-5; **10**: 11n, 187; emit paper
money, **10**: 25-7; political conduct of,
11: 408; constitutions of, **11**: 631; and
proposed federal veto power over laws
of, **12**: 273-9; representation in Congress, **12**: 440; proposed amendment
forbidding personal suits against, **13**:
608; interests of, **15**: 114; communications to Congress through President,
16: 286, 287, 288n; bill for settlement
of claims, **16**: 597; civil rights in constitutions of, **18**: 132-3. *See also*
United States: Secretary of State, state
laws collected by
states, new: republicanism of, **4**: 387; **6**:
582n, 604, 608, 614; admission of, **6**:
587n, 604, 608-9, 612n, 614, 615;
10: 14, 27-8, 143; boundaries of, **6**:
603, 613-4; government of, **6**: 603-4,
608; **8**: 217; **9**: 510-1; **10**: 144; **12**:
256; Monroe's opinions on, **8**: 442;
proposal before Congress on, **8**: 684;
and slavery question, **10**: 58; cession of
land, **10**: 59; division of, **10**: 112-3,
603; immigration to, **11**: 360; north of
the Ohio, **12**: 173; mentioned, **8**: 482-
3; **9**: 257
States General, Dutch. *See* Netherlands
States General, French *See* France: Estates General
states rights: Jones comments on, **5**: 470;
TJ comments on, **6**: 248; **12**: 28, 34,
36, 128; R.I. on, **6**: 263n-5; and
peacetime requisition of troops, **7**: 412;
Carrington comments on, **12**: 255
Statham, Charles: in Albemarle co. militia, **1**: 665
Statham, David: in Albemarle co. militia,
1: 665; as guard for British prisoners,
2: 33
Statham, William: in Albemarle co. militia, **1**: 665; as guard for British prisoners, **2**: 33; signs Va. oath of allegiance, **2**: 129

Stephens, Capt. William W. (master of *Cato*), **14**: 352
Stephenson, Capt., **6**: 637
Stephenson, Aaron: letter from, **12**: 372-3
Stephenson, Maj. David, **3**: 652
Stephenson (Stevenson), James: recommended for ordination, **1**: 48-51; signs petition, **5**: 349; **6**: 294; certificate quoted, **14**: 259
Steptoe, James: letter from, **6**: 55; as witness, **1**: 67; as agent for TJ, **1**: 73, 92; **6**: 204, 208; appointed commissioner for Ky., **3**: 17
stereotype printing, **10**: 322n
Sterett, David: letter sent by, **20**: 594
Steriby, David: passport issued by TJ, **15**: 486
Sterling, Capt. Walter, **5**: 677n
Sterne, Laurence: TJ comments on, **1**: 77; **12**: 15; cited, **6**: 161; *Tristram Shandy*, **6**: 196-7; **13**: 104n; **15**: 176; *Sentimental Journey*, **9**: 542n; **15**: 163, 176; *Works* ordered by TJ, **11**: 85; **15**: 163, 176; *Slawkenbergius' Tale*, **13**: 104n; *Sermons*, **15**: 176; mentioned, **1**: 75; **14**: 350, 608; **15**: 278, 279n
Stettin, Prussia: free port at proposed, **7**: 566, 611, 649; **8**: 14
Steuart, Sir James: *Plan for Uniform System of Weights and Measures*, **16**: 604n; *Principles of Political Economy*, **18**: 455
Steuben, Friedrich Wilhelm, Baron von: letters to, **3**: 107-8; **4**: 152, 156, 159, 175-6, 176-7, 178-9, 185, 188-9, 219-20, 229, 233, 250, 254-5, 298, 308, 316-7, 318, 326-7, 332-3, 338-9, 344-5, 351-3, 356-7, 398, 411-2, 477, 507-8, 555, 555-6, 583, 592-4, 603, 603-4, 621-2, 623, 632-3, 633, 643, 644, 644-5, 660, 661-2, 668-70, 679-80, 682, 688, 700-1; **5**: 8, 28, 65-6, 89, 98, 117-9, 119-20, 332-3, 366, 366-7, 400-1, 452-4, 500-1, 511-2, 525, 525-6, 536-7, 549-50, 559, 560, 560-1, 565; **15**: 599-600; letters from, **4**: 163, 175, 176, 189-90, 193-5, 195-6, 209, 210, 212-4, 214, 216, 219, 244-5, 250-1, 251-2, 291-2, 298-9, 312, 317-8, 327-8, 337-8, 345-6, 383-4, 392, 393, 422-3, 483, 584-5, 622-3, 624, 645, 652, 662, 680-2, 695-6, 701-2; **5**: 9, 66-70, 90, 98-9, 106-8, 121, 250, 316, 349-50, 459, 479-81, 502, 526-7, 543-4, 601; **6**: 30-2; book

of military regulations, **3**: 108, 110; ordered to serve in southern department, **4**: 85n; commands Continental troops, **4**: 132, 604; organization of Va. troops, **4**: 152, 159, 654-5; **5**: 181; relations with Muter, **4**: 161; **5**: 45-6, 133-4; Senf's report to, **4**: 169; requisitions for army, **4**: 214, 581; **5**: 665-8; relations with TJ, **4**: 259, 508, 677; **5**: 73, 173; **6**: 619n; **15**: 599-600; and militia, **4**: 260, 263, 308, 314, 371, 372, 429n, 450, 570; **5**: 5, 36, 92, 101-2, 122, 483, 500-1, 520, 532, 533, 623, 662; **6**: 619n, 623n; efforts to check British, **4**: 260, 399; plan for preventing desertion, **4**: 278-9; supplies for, **4**: 284, 305, 328, 357-8, 383, 453, 532; **5**: 70n, 319; **6**: 12, 13; orders as to arms issue, **4**: 288; copy of letter to retired officers sent to, **4**: 290-1; arms for, **4**: 306, 696; **5**: 42; **6**: 27, 49, 50; relations with Claiborne, **4**: 315; **5**: 195n; **6**: 10n-1n; ammunition for, **4**: 319; reinforcements for, **4**: 332, 385; praised by TJ, **4**: 335; correspondence with Davies, **4**: 337; **5**: 176n, 368n, 419n, 480n-1n, 544-5, 581n, 667n-8n; **6**: 38n, 631-2; letters from cited, **4**: 339; **5**: 230n; **6**: 15; artillery for, **4**: 344; approves Maj. Claiborne as deputy quartermaster, **4**: 374, 511; **5**: 60n, 578n; desire to raise regulars, **4**: 379-80; unfamiliarity with Va., **4**: 400; orders to Gen. Nelson, **4**: 427; gives Lawson command of advanced posts, **4**: 459, 630; plan for defending Hoods, **4**: 475-6, 584, 609; opinion on raising of volunteer cavalry, **4**: 485; orders to Gen. Muhlenberg, **4**: 488; promises to remedy complaints, **4**: 494n; orders court-martial, **4**: 499; asks for surgeons and medicine, **4**: 504; orders Capt. Irish to N.C., **4**: 518; election to American Philosophical Society, **4**: 545n; relations with Davies, **4**: 557; **5**: 205n; permits Gibson to join Gen. Clark, **4**: 596, 597, 598, 653; correspondence with Greene, **4**: 615, 616n; **5**: 8, 215n, 262n-3n, 440, 551, 667n; **6**: 31n, 638; need for boats, **4**: 626; plans for fortifying Yorktown, **4**: 631; attitude toward Va. government, **4**: 652n; **5**: 106n-8; **6**: 38n, 619n-20n; discontent with in Va., **4**: 661n-2n; correspondence with Gen. Nelson, **4**: 678n; **5**:

Stevens, Daniel: letter to, **19**: 363-4

Stevens, Edward: letters to, **3**: 497-8, 500, 528-30, 593, 640-1, 649; **4**: 59, 111-2, 129, 159; letters from, **3**: 558-9, 563-4, 576-7; **4**: 65-6, 76, 81-2, 112-3, 125-6, 153, 216-7, 322-4, 359, 440-1, 561-4; number of militia under, **3**: 433; **4**: 103, 152; **5**: 103; efforts to discipline militia, **3**: 492, 519-20; **5**: 63; payment to, **3**: 494; loss of command feared, **3**: 525; complaints of, **3**: 526; letter to, from Dudley Digges, **3**: 553-4; marches with Va. militia to Guilford Court House, **3**: 574; at battle of Camden, **3**: 593, 594-6, 597n; reinforcements for, **3**: 598, 603; command reduced by desertion, **3**: 621; return of arms, **4**: 40; aid requested by Gates, **4**: 50; ordered to return to Va., **4**: 58, 59, 60, 61; advice to Gates, **4**: 86; letter from cited, **4**: 127; relations with Gen. Greene, **4**: 455; **5**: 44, 156, 258, 301; discharge of militia under, **4**: 588; stores arms in Va., **4**: 648; brigade, **5**: 7; at Guilford Court House, **5**: 156, 199; appointed brigadier general, **5**: 636n; quoted on effect of titles on public opinion, **19**: 51n

Stevens, Isaac. *See* Stephens, Isaac

Stevens, Thomas: signs petition, **6**: 290

Stevenson, Mr.: agent for *Clermont*, **15**: 516; unacceptable as U.S. consul in St. Eustatius, **20**: 582

Stevenson, Mrs.: Paradise's debt to, **13**: 600

Stevenson, James. *See* Stephenson, James

Stevenson, Lieut. William: describes British campaign of 1780, **15**: 596

Steward, James: and bill establishing ferries, **2**: 460

Steward, Thomas: and bill establishing ferries, **2**: 460

stewards: for grammar schools, **2**: 532

Stewart, Mr.: introduction to TJ, **12**: 204-5; passport issued by TJ, **15**: 485

Stewart, Sgt., **6**: 464n

Stewart, Alexander: offers to supply gunpowder, **3**: 195; reports on books of Col. Aylett, **5**: 628

Stewart, Archibald. *See* Stuart, Archibald

Stewart, Dugald: letter to, **15**: 204-5; letter from, **14**: 648; introduced to TJ, **13**: 241-2; goes to Paris, **15**: 91; letters to cited, **15**: 148n; **18**: 71n;

teaches moral philosophy, **15**: 205n; mentioned, **15**: 103, 133, 182, 425

Stewart, John: signs nonimportation resolutions (1770), **1**: 47; court of Greenbrier co. at house of, **2**: 115; warrants issued to, **5**: 142n, 164n; clerk of Va. HD, **16**: 11n

Stewart, Maj. John: medal of, **16**: xxxvii, 52 (illus.), 54n, 59n, 71, 73n-5n

Stewart, Peter: paid by Department of State, **17**: 369

Stewart, Col. Walter, **4**: 325

sticcado-pastrole, **8**: 263

Stiles, Ezra: letters to, **7**: 304-5; **8**: 298-301; **10**: 316-8, 629; letters from, **7**: 312-7, 364-5; **9**: 476-8; **10**: 385-7, 584-6; **13**: 118; **17**: 442-4; and Bradshaw's epitaph, **1**: 679; councillor of American Philosophical Society, **4**: 545; extract from diary, **7**: 302-4; relations with TJ, **7**: 312n; **17**: 443-4; letter to, from Parsons, **9**: 477-8; quoted on white Indian, **10**: 643; letters from cited, **12**: 303, 304; **16**: 616n; letter to cited, **13**: 37n-8n; letter to published, **13**: 37n-8n, 118; introduces Barlow to TJ, **13**: 118; on TJ's authorship of Declaration of Independence, **15**: 241n; Report on Weights and Measures sent to, **16**: 616; **17**: 442; sends plan of Indian site on Muskingum river, **17**: xxxi; on Roman imperial debt, **17**: 442-3; and new system of penmanship, **19**: 120n

Stillwater, N.Y.: visited by TJ and Madison, **20**: 453-6, 458, 465, 466

Stimpson, James. *See* Simpson, James

Stirling (Sterling), Lord (William Alexander): Continental regiments under, **3**: 204; mentioned, **1**: 275; **3**: 437; **11**: 493n

Stirling, John: edition of Florus, **11**: 523; edition of Ovid's *Tristia*, **11**: 523; edition of Phaedrus, **11**: 523; edition of Pomey's *Pantheon*, **11**: 523; edits Terence's works, **15**: 406

Stith, Col.: announces raids, **5**: 406

Stith, Griffin: votes for bill for religious freedom, **2**: 549n

Stith, P., **1**: 19

Stith, Polly: in Williamsburg, **16**: 27

Stith, Richard: letter to, **17**: 600-1; imports slaves, **15**: 654; letter from missing, **17**: 601n

Stith, Thomas: signs nonimportation resolutions (1770), **1**: 46

ward U.S., **8**: 57n-8n; visits New England, **8**: 58n; obtains lodging for A. Adams, **8**: 178; mail sent by, **8**: 499; correspondence with Adams, **17**: 349n

stores, public. *See* public stores

Storey, Capt. (master of the *Betsy*), **9**: 644

stork, **13**: 17

Stormont, David Murray, Viscount: French minister replies to, **2**: 30

Stotesbury, Capt. Arthur (master of *Nancy*), **15**: 420, 421n, 428, 429, 494

Stovall, George: and bill establishing ferries, **2**: 459

Stoval's creek: land on, as lottery prize, **1**: 22

stoves: TJ's drawing of, **13**: 25; fuel for in Netherlands and Germany, **13**: 26; TJ orders from Cologne, **13**: 43-4, 107, 148, 172, 185, 186, 255

"Stowe House": garden at described by TJ, **9**: 371

Strabo: *Rerum Geographicarum*, **12**: 678; **14**: 491

Strachan, T., **1**: 63

Strachan, William, **9**: 487

Strackeiser, J. G. *See* Streckensen, J. G.

Strada, Famianus: *De Bello Belgico*, **12**: 688; **13**: 290; *Histoire de la guerre de Flandre*, **15**: 406

Strahan, Mr.: letter from, to Auldjo, cited, **15**: 469n, 504

Strait of Magellan, **10**: 529

Stranford, Mr.: inn rated by TJ, **20**: 471

Strange, James: letter to, **20**: 390

Strange, Sir John: *Reports of Adjudged Cases in the Courts of Chancery, King's Bench, Common Pleas and Exchequer*, **11**: 548; **16**: 277, 481

Stranton, Mr.: and Hessian fly, **20**: 459

Strasbourg, France: TJ's lodgings in, **13**: xxvii-viii, 17 (illus.); TJ's notes on, **13**: 26, 33n-5n, 48, 104n, 267; **17**: 466n; Shippen visits, **13**: 312; and reestablishment of nobility and clergy, **19**: 117; disturbances in, **19**: 257, 324; **20**: 379; bishop elected in, **19**: 532

Stratford, Va.: British landing at, **5**: 529

Stratford-upon-Avon: Adams describes, **9**: 374n

Stratton, Capt. Henry (master of *Thomas*), **20**: 214, 381, 387, 412, 414, 417, 478, 618, 671

strawberries: French and American com-

pared, **8**: 683; Alpine, **10**: 228; **16**: 492; **17**: 333

stray animals. *See* estrays

Streckensen (Strackeiser), J. G.: letter to, **15**: 219-20; S.C. debt to, **15**: 218-20, 264, 463, 464n

Street, John: letters to, **17**: 423-5; **20**: 401-2; vice consul at Fayal, **17**: 247, 251, 256, 319; candidate for consul in Azores, **19**: 312n

street lighting: use of whale oil for, **8**: 144n-5n; **9**: 117

Stretch, Joseph: administrator of the estate of Joseph Wright, **17**: xxxiii

Strettell, Amos: estate of, **9**: 485

Strettell, John: executor of Amos Strettell's estate, **9**: 485

Stricker, John: signs petition, **6**: 290

Stringer, Dr. Samuel, **1**: 392

Stringfellow, Mr., **9**: 485

Strode, John: letter to cited, **16**: 371n

Strong, Capt., **18**: 52

Strong, Mr.: inn rated by TJ, **20**: 471

Strong, Caleb: TJ consults on Mass. commerce, **7**: 324n; Mass. delegate to Federal Convention, **11**: 219, 400; senator from Mass., **14**: 339, 394, 519, 529, 560, 615; federalism of, **14**: 394, 529; **18**: 410; King's effort to influence, **17**: 169; and diplomatic establishment, **17**: 218; and Northwest Territory, **18**: 167; and tonnage act, **18**: 546; and arrearages in soldier's pay, **18**: 617n; and the fisheries, **19**: 155, 167n; gives advice on candidates for Vt., **19**: 379

Strong, Jedediah: nominated as congressman from Conn., **14**: 525

Strother, French: letter from, **5**: 272; and land office bill, **2**: 136n; votes for bill for religious freedom, **2**: 549n; on Va. HD committee to welcome TJ, **16**: 11n; mentioned, **5**: 251, 252, 278

Strozzi: translations by, **6**: 173

Stuard, Mr.: copy of *Notes on Virginia* sent to, **12**: 133

Stuart, Maj. Alexander: captured at Guilford Court House, **5**: 508

Stuart (Stewart), Archibald: letters to, **6**: 374; **9**: 217-9; letter from, **8**: 644-7; votes for bill for religious freedom, **2**: 549n; letters from quoted, **6**: 85n; **12**: 444; attitude on cession of western territory, **6**: 266; proposes reforms in Va. HD, **7**: 360; TJ requests natural history specimen from, **9**: 240; **11**: 328;

Stuart (Stewart), Archibald (*cont.*)
letter to cited, **10**: 108; letter from
cited, **12**: 284; supports Constitution,
13: 98; mentioned, **6**: 105n, 387n
Stuart, David: votes for bill for religious
freedom, **2**: 549n; visits Mount Vernon, **10**: 535n; **11**: 390n; correspondence with Washington, **11**: 390n; **18**:
524; **19**: 53; supports Constitution,
13: 98; Presidential elector from Va.,
15: 5; federalism of, **15**: 5; **19**: 438; as
Federal District Commissioner, **20**: 9,
28, 45
Stuart, Dugald. *See* Stewart, Dugald
Stuart, Gilbert: portrait of William S.
Smith, **18**: xxxv, 268 (illus.)
Stuart, John: letter to, quoted, **14**: xxx,
xxxi
Stuart (Stewart), John: superintendent of
Indian affairs in the south, **2**: 75, 77,
78, 79, 80, 81, 91, 93, 96; and Cherokee archives, **6**: 141n; map of Vandalia, **6**: 602
Stuart, Stephen, **5**: 336
Stuart, Thomas: signs Virginia Association, **1**: 109
Sturges (Sturgis), Jonathan: nominated
as congressman from Conn., **14**: 525
sub-clothier: role of discussed, **4**: 493,
500, 514, 558; **5**: 200-1
Sublime Porte. *See* Turkey
submarine: Bushnell's *Connecticut Turtle*,
7: 643; **8**: 299, 301, 557; **9**: 150; **12**:
303-5
"Subscriber, A": possible TJ pseudonym, **18**: 457n
Sudermania. *See* Södermanland, Karl,
Duke of
Suetonius Tranquillus, Gaius: TJ seeks
best Italian translation, **11**: 159; TJ
recommends to Peter Carr, **12**: 18;
Opera omnia quae extant, **12**: 689; **13**:
420; TJ orders Delphin edition of, **15**:
406
Suffolk, Va.: British forces at, **4**: 92; defense of, **4**: 423; rendezvous of recruits,
5: 40; provisions for troops at, **5**: 46;
Lafayette at, **5**: 188; Muhlenberg at, **5**:
188; cannon at, **5**: 279; TJ criticized
for not sending militia to, **6**: 107; place
of court of assize, **7**: 588
suffrage: in TJ's draft constitution for Va.
(1776), **1**: 341, 348, 358; in George
Mason's plans of government for Va.,
1: 366, 370; in Va. constitution, **1**:

380; TJ's and Pendleton's views on, **1**:
504-5; in Kentucky, Washington, and
Montgomery counties, **1**: 574; Va. law
on, **2**: 337; solicitation of votes, **6**:
287; and Albemarle co. instructions, **6**:
292; in TJ's proposed Va. constitution
(1783), **6**: 296; Pa. test law, **7**: 20
Suffren (Suffrein, Souffrein) de Saint-
Tropez, Pierre André: letter from, **9**:
322; naval command of, **12**: 216, 224,
309; death of, **14**: 432; praised, **14**:
180
sugar: price of brown, **2**: 379; purchase
for Va. troops, **3**: 209, 238; Va. unable
to provide, **3**: 607; lack of, **4**: 9; Conn.
import of, **7**: 334, 335; West Indian
trade in, **7**: 350, 352; **9**: 29-31; **10**:
148; S.C. import of, **8**: 199; export
from Brazil, **9**: 20, 62; U.S. import of,
10: 146, 148; shipped from Boston to
Le Havre, **11**: 116; maple as substitute
for cane, **16**: 579, 580n; **20**: 332-3,
341, 343-4, 442, 605, 616, 640-1,
645; prices, **20**: 616
sugar cane: TJ corrects Démeunier's article on, **10**: 17-8, 59
sugar tree: seeds desired by TJ, **9**: 520
suicide: Va. laws regarding, **2**: 325,
496n; **6**: 152-3; Martha Jefferson on,
11: 282
sulla. *See* sainfoin, Spanish
Sullevan, Lity.: signs Va. oath of allegiance, **2**: 129
Sullivan, Capt. (master of the *Etorion*), **9**:
392
Sullivan, Fort: seige of, **1**: 461
Sullivan, James: letter to, **20**: 709; letter
from, **20**: 376; draft on, **11**: 296; recommends Samuel Cooper Johonnot,
20: 376; *Observations upon the Government of the United States of America,*
20: 709
Sullivan, Capt. James: delivered as hostage to British, **1**: 399; bills drawn in
favor of, **4**: 375; accused of cheating
Va., **4**: 391-2; mentioned, **4**: 365; **5**:
252, 466
Sullivan, Gen. John: letters to, **7**: 132; **9**:
160; **12**: 41-2, 208-9, 307; letters
from, **6**: 447-52; **7**: 21-4, 62, 317-20;
9: 314; **11**: 68, 68-9, 295-7, 298, 320,
321, 326, 359, 384; signs Continental
Association, **1**: 153; in Canadian campaign, **1**: 293, 294; **17**: 575; retires to
Île-aux-Noix, **1**: 412; at Chambly, **1**:

Sussex co., Va. (*cont.*)
levies of soldiers, **3**: 8; tobacco loan office certificates, **3**: 515; collections under provision law, **4**: 7; supply post for, **4**: 286

Sussex Court House, Va.: time of holding court of assize, **1**: 628; proposed meeting of school overseers at, **2**: 529

Sutton, John, Jr.: in Albemarle co. militia, **1**: 668n

Svishtov (Szistow): conference at, **19**: 336; **20**: 168, 169, 586, 611, 656, 683

Swaine, John. *See* Childs, Francis

Swallow (schooner): sent to Saint-Domingue, **5**: 209

swallows: seen in Piedmont, **11**: 435

swamp maple. *See* maple, swamp

swamps: right of preemption by owner of contiguous land, **2**: 152n-3n

Swan, Mr.: ordered to keep mouth of Swina River closed, **10**: 556n

Swan, James: letters to, **12**: 576; **13**: 278; **14**: 691-2; **15**: 99; letters from, **12**: 541-2, 636-7; **13**: 242-4, 313; **15**: 261-3, 361-2, 381-2; **17**: 560-4; **19**: 575; **20**: 523-4; *Causes qui se sont opposées aux progrès du commerce, entre la France, et les Etats-Unis de l'Amérique*, **12**: 541n; **14**: 692n; **17**: 564n; *National Arithmetick: or, Observations on the finances of the Commonwealth of Massachusetts*, **12**: 541n; biographical note, **12**: 541n-2n; letter from quoted, **12**: 542n; proposes supplying beef and flour to French government, **13**: 243, 244n, 278, 313, 383-6 (text), 387n, 659; **15**: 245-7, 249, 361-2, 483n; Limozin asks TJ's advice on contract, **13**: 425; letter from, to Limozin, quoted, **13**: 425n-6n; relations with TJ, **13**: 437, 438n; **14**: 691-2; advice on ships from Bordeaux to America, **13**: 478-9; letter to cited, **13**: 616; letter from missing, **13**: 658-9; on whale fishery, **14**: 227; signs Fourth of July tribute to TJ, **15**: 240; proposes supplying timber to French navy, **15**: 261-3; **17**: 560-1; **18**: 505-6; **20**: 523-4; speculates in U.S. debt, **15**: 381-2; **20**: 177, 178n, 183n, 188-91, 196, 201n, 523; passport issued by TJ, **15**: 487; signs Bastille Day address, **17**: 214n; proposals for supplying salted provisions to French troops in West

Indies, **17**: 504-5, 529, 557, 561-4; **18**: 22-3; and Short's negotiations for loan, **18**: 22; proposals to Spain on salted provisions, **18**: 505-6; meets with Raymond on U.S. trade, **19**: 345; supplies French army, **20**: 186n

Swan, Mrs. James, **12**: 576, 636

Swan, John: passport issued by TJ, **15**: 486

Swan's creek, Va.: ferry at, **2**: 459

Swan's Point, Va.: ferry at, **2**: 457

Swanwick, John: letter from, **18**: 156-8; notes drawn on, **7**: 214, 284; in Telles affair, **19**: 309; prosecutes Barclay, **20**: 239

Swartz, Mr.: inn rated by TJ, **20**: 471

Swearingen (Van Swearingen), Josiah: letters to, **15**: 588, 594; county lieutenant of Berkeley, **4**: 451, 575n

Swearingen, Thomas: and bill establishing ferries, **2**: 455

Swearingham, Mr.: and bill establishing ferries, **2**: 455

Sweden: protests British seizure of Dutch vessels, **3**: 412; minister to U.S., **6**: 276; U.S. treaty of amity and commerce, **6**: 319, 334, 396; **7**: 269, 305, 308-9, 428-9, 434-5, 466n, 475-6, 494, 638, 644; **8**: 382, 605; **9**: 497; **10**: 286; import of iron from, **7**: 344; exports from Pa. to, **7**: 347; tobacco import from Va., **7**: 370; rivers, **7**: 405; relations with Barbary States, **8**: 69, 72; **10**: 358, 562n, 565n; **11**: 626-7; ships in Charleston harbor, **8**: 201; free port at St. Barthélemy, **8**: 608; **9**: 631-4, 646; U.S. trade with, **9**: 631; **10**: 100; preparations for war, **13**: 173, 174, 191, 193, 215-6, 295, 298, 316, 344, 360, 365, 373, 378-9, 404-5; **16**: 120; in Russo-Turkish war, **13**: 436-8, 455, 456, 458, 465, 471, 475, 483, 489, 491, 496-7, 501, 503, 506, 510, 531, 538, 579, 633, 650; **14**: 212, 597; **15**: 357, 513n; **17**: 209, 313-4; attacks Finland, **13**: 472, 482, 491; TJ's comments on politics and government of, **13**: 491, 579; **14**: 659; British papers distort news from, **13**: 572; army officers refuse to serve in offensive war, **13**: 591, 633; alliance with Britain, Prussia, and Netherlands, **14**: 46, 47, 328; peace with Russia and Denmark, **14**: 54, 186, 287, 333, 362-3, 672; **15**: 110, 116; war with Denmark and Sweden, **14:** 645, 653, 661; conflict between king and nobles, **14:** 658-9, 672, 702; **15:** 121; American medals sent to, **16:** 67; proposed American representative in, **16:** 107; in alliance against Russia and Austria, **16:** 538, 541; peace with Russia, **17:** 500, 501n, 503, 526, 542, 593, 628; **18:** 64, 296; **20:** 695; Russian naval victory over, **17:** 522; and U.S. commercial policy, **19:** 130; and the fisheries, **19:** 177-8, 180; claims of cruelty against naval captain, **19:** 272-3; relations with Turkey, **20:** 169; foreign trade, **20:** 589-90; relations with Britain, **20:** 700

Sweden, King of. *See* Gustavus III

Swedish minister to Britain. *See* Nolken, Gustaf Adam

Swedish minister to France. *See* Staël de Holstein, Eric Magnus

Sweedland Hill, **2:** 113

sweet bay. *See Magnolia glauca*

sweet gum: TJ requests seeds and plants, **9:** 255; **11:** 121; **12:** 135

Sweet Hall, Va.: ferry at, **2:** 456

Sweet Springs, **2:** 114; **5:** 446

Swift (British ship): ordered up Chickahominy river, **5:** 682n, 696; mentioned, **5:** 64, 344n, 674n, 677n, 687

Swift, Rev. Job, **20:** 444

Swift, Jonathan, **8:** 407

Swimmer, Mr.: clerk to St. Marie, **19:** 522-3, 525

Swina river: mouth ordered closed, **10:** 558n

Swinburne, Henry: *Treatise of Testaments and Last Wills*, **11:** 548

swine. *See* hogs

Switzerland: attitude toward America, **3:** 382; government of, **8:** 636; **12:** 274; Rutledge praises, **13:** 552; Short in, **14:** 25-8; American medals sent to, **16:** 67; unrest in, **16:** 443

swivel: for defense of Chantilly, **5:** 435

swords: patterns specified in contract with Penet, Windel & Co., **3:** 132; prices, **3:** 135; for cavalry, **5:** 274, 285, 296-7, 412; **6:** 25, 41; ordered from Amsterdam for U.S., **8:** 157; made in France, **11:** 144; ordered from France, **11:** 169; money for, **11:** 199; presentation, **16:** 54n, 55n, 56n-9n, 62n-4n

Sycamore Shoals, Treaty of: depositions

concerning, **2:** 68-110; Robertson considers fair and open, **2:** 104

Sydney, Lord. *See* Townshend, Thomas, first Viscount

Sydnor, Fortunatus: lands of, **3:** 174-5, 182, 439

Sydnor, Mrs. Fortunatus, **3:** 175

Sylva, or the Wood, **11:** 522

"Sylvania" (TJ's name for new state), **6:** 604

Syme, John: letters to, **4:** 491, 508; **5:** 18, 527-8; letters from, **4:** 412-3, 458-9, 498, 670; **5:** 14, 126, 209-10, 512, 528-9; signs Virginia Association, **1:** 108; awaits orders, **4:** 315; quoted, **4:** 459n; removes public stores, **4:** 526; **5:** 140; seeks repair of arms, **5:** 17; letter from, to Davies, quoted, **5:** 528n-9n; mentioned, **5:** 91, 178

Symmachus, Quintus Aurelius: *Epistolarum ad diversos libri X*, **12:** 678; **13:** 290

Symmes, John Cleves: on origin of Mexican Indians, **11:** 324; land company, **12:** 256, 283

Symonds, Capt., **5:** 693

Symonds, Mr.: letters sent by, **12:** 552; **13:** 142-4, 176-7, 215; cipher for Carmichael sent by, **13:** 398; passport issued by TJ, **15:** 485

Symonds (Symmonds), Commodore Thomas: captures American prisoners, **4:** 311; commander of *Charon*, **4:** 399; quarrel with Gen. Arnold, **5:** 73; letter to intercepted, **5:** 343n; orders to Hare, **5:** 689

Syon, M. de, **1:** 677

Sysson, George. *See* Sisson, Capt. George

Szistow. *See* Svishtov

T——, Mrs. *See* Townsend, Mme

Tabb, John: signs nonimportation resolutions (1770), **1:** 47; and Mazzei's agricultural co., **1:** 158; signs TJ's commission, **1:** 246; declines to run for office, **1:** 476; offers to buy land, **15:** 653; mentioned, **1:** 254, 267

Tableau de Paris: TJ seeks copy of, **11:** 663, 666

table linen: TJ asks Mrs. Adams to purchase, **8:** 549, 594

tables: sent to TJ, **18:** 591-2

Tacitus, Cornelius: *Opera quae existant*,

Tacitus, Cornelius (*cont.*)
11: 523; *Works* edited by Gordon, 11: 523, 577; Bible compared with works of, 12: 15-6; *Agricola*, 12: 18; *Germania*, 12: 18; birthplace, 14: 381; *Opera supplementis*, 16: 321; mentioned, 15: 406; 20: 381, 417, 634n

Tackberry, Robert: prisoner of war, 5: 432

Tadlock, Joshua: in Albemarle co. militia, 1: 666, 667

Tadlock, Thomas: signs petition, 6: 293

Taffe, Peter: reputed murderer of Le-Brun, 10: 470n

taffia: as medium of exchange, 5: 171n

Tafilet, Kingdom of, 10: 359

Tagliaferri, Francesco di Giuseppe, 10: 155

Tagliaferri, Giovanni, 10: 155

Tagliaferro, Tuscany, 10: 155

Tagliaferro family. *See* Taliaferro family

Tagnerette, Dubu de La. *See* La Tagnerette

Taher Fennish. *See* Fennish

Taillepied, M.: letter from, to Chalon, 16: 18-20

tailors, army: needed at Chesterfield, 4: 300, 493, 500, 557; pay, 4: 447, 453

Tains, France: TJ's comments on, 11: 420; 13: 273; wine of, 11: 421

Taitbout, Cul-de-sac. *See* Cul-de-sac Taitbout

Taitt, David: and Cherokee archives, 6: 141n

Talbe Houdrani: errors in drawing Moroccan treaty, 10: 141, 390, 391

Talbot, Capt. (master of *Neptune*), 15: 263

Talbot, Mr.: and county courts bill, 1: 593n

Talbot, Charles, Baron: *Cases in Equity*, 11: 548

Talbot, Cyrus: in French navy, 14: 275

Talbot, George Washington: in French navy, 14: 275

Talbot, John: signs nonimportation resolutions, 1: 31, 46; signs Virginia Association, 1: 109; mentioned, 6: 3n, 136n

Talbot, Mark: sued by Va. for breach of contract, 3: 223-4

Talbot, Silas: letter from, 14: 275; sons in French navy, 14: 275, 595-6, 623-4, 654-5; 15: 65, 69; letter from cited, 14: 624

Taliaferro, Col.: neighbor of Paradise in

Va., 11: 355-6; death of, 16: 25; mentioned, 10: 245

Taliaferro, Mr., 6: 125

Taliaferro, Becca: death of, 16: 25

Taliaferro, Francis: signs Va. oath of allegiance, 2: 130

Taliaferro, Jenny, 1: 12, 16

Taliaferro, Laurence, 10: 592

Taliaferro, Mary: marries brother of Gen. Nelson, 9: 66

Taliaferro, Richard: coat of arms engraved for, 9: 165, 276; mentioned, 1: 38, 65, 298; 10: 245

Taliaferro, Samuel: pledges to support clergyman, 2: 7; signs Va. oath of allegiance, 2: 128

Taliaferro, T.: petition from, 5: 349

Taliaferro, Walker, 6: 646

Taliaferro (Tagliaferro) family: coat of arms of, 9: 165, 276, 572, 10: 243; 11: 240, 280; Fabbroni's account of, 10: 155, 156, 243; Wythe's efforts to trace in Va., 10: 592; documents on, 12: 127

Taliaferro's landing: ferry at, 2: 456

Talleyrand-Périgord, Charles Maurice de (Bishop of Autun): plan for paying national debt with church property, 15: 534; proposes uniform system of weights and measures, 16: 279, 281n, 418, 510, 512, 542, 543, 569, 611, 614, 623, 652n, 668n-70n, 672n; 17: 281; 18: 457n; 19: 636; 20: 346, 354n, 364; Report on Weights and Measures sent to, 17: 281, 528; Vaughan's memorandum sent to, 18: 115; *Opinion . . . sur la fabrication des petites monnoies*, 18: 358-9; opposes Lafayette, 20: 351; excommunication of, 20: 384; report on religious freedom, 20: 384

Tallon, M.: discusses commerce with Sardinia, 11: 352, 353

Tamage, Mrs., 8: 438

Tamerlinson, William: signs petition, 1: 588

Tandy, Mr. (father of Moses Tandy): character of, 8: 582

Tandy, John: signs Va. oath of allegiance, 2: 129

Tandy, Moses: applies to Dumas for aid, 8: 561; madness of, 8: 582; aided by Robeson, 9: 107

Tandy, Roger: in Albemarle co. militia, 1: 667

Tandy, Smith: loss of money transmitted

by, **3**: 442, 443; mentioned, **3**: 386

Tandy, William: in Albemarle co. militia, **1**: 667; pledges to support clergyman, **2**: 7

Tandy, William, Sr.: signs Va. oath of allegiance, **2**: 128

Taney, Francis Lewis: recommended for consular appointment, **16**: 429n

Tangier island, Chesapeake Bay: inhabitants aid British, **3**: 671; mentioned, **5**: 305

Tangiers, Morocco: destroyed by British (1684), **10**: 340-1; harbor, **10**: 340-1; Dutch gifts sent to, **13**: 527

Tankersley, Mr.: and bill establishing ferries, **2**: 455

Tankerville, Earl of: and bill establishing ferries, **2**: 454

Tannehill, Josiah: sent to Richmond from Fort Pitt, **6**: 40; mentioned, **6**: 69

Tanner, John: and form of address to President, **19**: 87n

tanneries, **5**: 170, 476

Tantalus: reference to, **11**: 3

tape measure: ordered by TJ, **11**: 46, 91

Tapon, Jean, **11**: 465n

Tappahannock, Va.: ferry across, **2**: 455; port of entry, **7**: 360, 562

Tapscott, James, **5**: 373n

tar: Va. bill concerning, **2**: 444-7; U.S. export of, **8**: 201, 202, 203, 309, 372; Portugal's desire to import, **9**: 19; import at L'Orient, **11**: 429; French duty on, **11**: 516, 541; **12**: 163, 165, 167, 172, 469, 480-1

Tarbé, M.: letter to, **11**: 139; letters from, **10**: 548; **11**: 62; relations with Ethis de Corny, **13**: 659; **15**: 246, 247n; Le Couteulx' proposals to, **15**: 247n; mentioned, **11**: 67; **15**: 247

Tardieu, Antoine François: map of Paris by, **10**: xxviii, 211 (illus.)

Tardiveau, Barthélemi: agent to Congress, **5**: 600n; Moustier recommends for consular appointment, **14**: 65n-6n

tares: cultivation of, **8**: 197

Target, Guy Jean Baptiste: praise of, **7**: 414; motion in Estates General, **15**: 196; *Les états-généraux convoqués par Louis XVI*, **15**: 197n; mentioned, **15**: 266

tariff. *See* duties

Tarleton, Banastre: forces left in S.C., **3**: 465; and Carolina campaign, **3**: 597n, 620; **4**: 276, 277, 437, 440-1; **5**: 43, 62, 115, 162, 183, 507; ordered to

surprise legislature and TJ, **4**: 261, 264, 265; and Va. campaign, **4**: 278n; **6**: 19, 41, 53n, 78n, 85n, 98, 627n, 634, 636, 637; damages TJ's property, **12**: 101; **13**: 105, 363

Tarquin (horse), **16**: 223n; **17**: 241-2, 242n-3n

Tarragon, Jean Rémy, Chevalier de, **3**: 211

Tarrasson (Tarascon?): TJ describes, **11**: 425

Tartar (ship): transferred to Board of Trade, **3**: 331; offered for sale, **3**: 530; prepares to aid French fleet, **4**: 640; mentioned, **3**: 246, 315; **5**: 344

Tartars: resemblance to American Indians, **11**: 638

Täscher, Philippe Athanaze: Mazzei's comments on, **7**: 387, 388; receives copy of Mazzei's notes on trade between U.S. and French West Indies, **7**: 389; TJ referred to, **15**: 614

Tassel (Indian). *See* Corn Tassel

Tate, Mr.: payment to refused, **1**: 289; meat bought from, **3**: 554, 562, 648, 661; procures lead, **4**: 408; on Cherokees, **18**: 6-7

Tatem, Samuel: signs nonimportation resolutions, **1**: 31

Tatham, Howel: recommended for federal office in Southwest Territory, **16**: 477, 478

Tatham (Tatum), William: letters from, **16**: 9-10, 185-7; **17**: 659-60; TJ introduces to Gen. Greene, **4**: 240; defends TJ, **4**: 273-7, 314; letter from, to William Armistead Burwell, **4**: 273-7; letter from, to Short, **13**: 621-2; denies betraying secrets of Va., **13**: 622; **16**: 9-10; letter from missing, **13**: 659; map of southern states, **16**: 185-6; **17**: 659-60; plans for a topographical analysis of Va., **16**: 185-7; map of counties, **19**: 265n

Taubenheim, Joanne Louise de Stendt, Mme de: letter from cited, **11**: 503; death of, **20**: 670; mentioned, **11**: 204, 252, 381

taverns: rates, **2**: 447; Va. bill for licensing and regulating, **2**: 447-8; forbidden to permit gambling, **2**: 560

Tawa Indians: enemy of the Cherokee, **2**: 74, 90

tax assessors: Va., **2**: 219-20

taxes: colonial resentment of, **1**: 171, 200; **2**: 55; **10**: 353; in Declaration of

taxes (*cont.*)
Causes, **1**: 207, 214; and Lord North's Proposal, **1**: 225-7, 231-2; debate in Congress on, **1**: 320-3; payment of, **2**: 121; **5**: 346-9, 409-10; **6**: 386; **9**: 335; on slaves, **2**: 186-7; collectors of, **2**: 187, 645; **6**: 562; **7**: 558; Va., **2**: 217-8, 288; **5**: 11; **8**: 509; **9**: 75; **11**: 153; military exemption from, **2**: 378; Va. bill for amending act on, **2**: 418; payment of, in grain, **3**: 250, 402, 464, 566-7, 575, 656; state quotas, **3**: 379-80, 402, 507, 509-10, 583; **4**: 366-8; specific tax, **3**: 606; **4**: 43; in Northampton co., **5**: 153; in Frederick co., **5**: 219; in Culpeper co., **5**: 278, 323; in Prince William co., **5**: 323; Great Britain, **5**: 378-9; for Greenbrier co. militia, **5**: 445; in Ky. area, **5**: 462; in Hampshire co., **5**: 513; in Accomac co., **5**: 651-5; exemptions from, **6**: 369; **8**: 682; table of payments and arrears for states, **6**: 563-4; within new states, **6**: 611n, 612n, 615; coin of payment, **7**: 168; N.Y., **7**: 327; Conn., **7**: 331-2; R.I., **7**: 337; Mass., **7**: 339; N.H., **7**: 343; TJ comments on, **7**: 557-8; **14**: 328; and agricultural surplus, **7**: 558; land transfers, **7**: 558; **8**: 112; U.S., **10**: 13; **12**: 326, 446; in Morocco, **10**: 345; in Constitution, **13**: 208, 210n, 624; **14**: 385. *See also* county rates; France; Finances; impost
tax commissioners (Va.): letter to, **5**: 268; accountability of, **2**: 219-20
taxidermy: preparation of animals for, **9**: 158, 160, 161; method described by TJ, **9**: 218
Tayloe, John: and Mazzei's agricultural co., **1**: 158; votes for bill for religious freedom, **2**: 549n; executors of, **11**: 329
Tayloe, Col. John: slave of, **5**: 640-3; mentioned, **5**: 393
Taylor, Capt. (officer of Alexandria artillery co.), **5**: 336
Taylor, Mr.: in Tucker case, **1**: 53, 59, 69, 73, 83, 84, 85; and bill establishing ferries, **2**: 457, 460; letter to quoted, **16**: 92n
Taylor, Mrs. (sister to Mr. Trist), **10**: 169
Taylor, Brook. *See* Fournier, Daniel
Taylor, Rev. Edward: and account of giant, **7**: 313-4; biographical note, **7**: 317n
Taylor, Col. Francis: letters to, **3**: 121,

339, 374; **4**: 299, 308, 604-5; **5**: 147, 322-3, 408-9; letters from, **4**: 252-3, 565; **5**: 100-1, 333-4, 426-8, 607-8, 661-2; **6**: 21-2, 66-7; commands Regiment of Guards for Convention troops, **3**: 154, 155, 192, 204, 365, 378; **4**: 73, 93, 210, 249, 471, 472, 556, 574, 603, 622, 672; **5**: 64, 71, 259, 332, 341, 403; irregularities of regimental paymaster, **5**: 245, 269; correspondence with Davies quoted, **5**: 608n; **6**: 67n
Taylor, George (Pa.): signs Declaration of Independence, **1**: 432
Taylor, George (Va.): in Albemarle co. militia, **1**: 668n
Taylor, George, Jr.: quoted, **4**: 116n; alters Consular Convention text, **14**: 90; employed in Dept. of State, **17**: 353n, 356n-8n, 375, 387n, 519; paid for sundries, **17**: 363; supervises move from N.Y. to Philadelphia, **17**: 596-7; applies for translator's position, **20**: 728n; dismissed, **20**: 729n
Taylor, Henry: signs nonimportation resolutions, **1**: 30, 46; signs Virginia Association, **1**: 108
Taylor, James: letter from, **1**: 102; in Albemarle co. militia, **1**: 667; one of managers of conference on Johnson case, **2**: 43n; passport issued to, **15**: 484; signs address to TJ, **15**: 556
Taylor, James, Jr.: signs Virginia Association, **1**: 109
Taylor, Jesse: sells suit of colors, **3**: 324
Taylor, John (of Caroline): letters from, **4**: 180-1; **5**: 461; and land office bill, **2**: 136n, 138n; and revisal of Va. laws, **2**: 324n; and proposed remonstrance against Congress, **5**: 76n; member of committee on parole, **5**: 294n; attitude on cession of western territory, **6**: 266; against payment of British debts, **7**: 260; opposes Constitution, **12**: 284; letter to cited, **18**: 685n; angers Va. governor and council, **19**: 53n
Taylor, Lieut. John: letter from, **4**: 556n; officer in Regiment of Guards for Convention troops, **3**: 121, 156; member of court-martial, **3**: 350
Taylor, Maud Trist, **10**: 169
Taylor, Michael: enlistment, **5**: 430
Taylor, Miles: letter sent by, **15**: 574
Taylor, Robert (shipowner): signs address to TJ, **15**: 556; mentioned, **15**: 380, 411
Taylor, William: receipt, **20**: 243n; men-

Tench, Watkin (*cont.*)
dition to Botany-Bay, **15**: 182, 183n
Tende, Italy: TJ describes, **11**: 432-3
Tenerife, Canary Islands: imports from
S.C., **8**: 203; American consulate at,
19: 315n; **20**: 628-9
Tenières, David, **11**: 367
Tennessee: census of, **20**: 639
Tennessee river: Cherokee lands on, **2**:
73, 77, 81, 85, 87, 88, 91, 105, 150n;
defense of, **4**: 362, 500; floods in, **6**:
536; bounty land to soldiers on, **6**:
572n, 574n; Chickasaw land on, **7**: 45;
mentioned, **1**: 572; **3**: 89n
tennis rackets (battledores): sent to TJ,
16: 13, 29, 81
tents: cloth for, **3**: 492, 501, 646, 658; **4**:
471, 554, 591, 674; **5**: 670; military
need for, **3**: 496, 513, 526, 529, 550,
606, 621, 643, 647, 651, 660; **4**: 9,
27, 38, 41, 216, 234, 328, 346, 357,
378, 471, 473, 496, 527, 558, 617; **5**:
67, 666; poles needed for, **4**: 516, 524;
list of, **4**: 531-2
tenure of office: TJ's views on, **12**: 356
Terence (Publius Terentius Afer): TJ
seeks information on best Italian translation, **11**: 159; Stirling's edition of
works, **15**: 406; mentioned, **8**: 407;
20: 635n
Terence (servant of Short): death of, **16**:
25
Ternant, Jean Baptiste, Chevalier de: biographical note, **6**: 161n-2n; payment
to, **8**: 87; reaction of British royalty to,
12: 621n; return to Paris, **12**: 676; as
minister to U.S., **14**: 521, 522n; **15**:
120; **17**: 528, 558, 606, 616; **18**: 253,
536, 543, 554n; **19**: 259; **20**: 251; negotiates with German princes, **17**:
526; confers with Hamilton, **18**: 277-
8, 280; letters from, to Montmorin,
quoted, **18**: 278n-9n; and U.S.-French
trade, **19**: 345-6; **20**: 366, 529, 533,
548, 642; and U.S. debt to France,
20: 179; arrival in U.S., **20**: 262; recommended to TJ, **20**: 524, 540; letter
sent by, **20**: 546, 548; letter from, to
Washington, cited, **20**: 558; mentioned, **15**: 190; **16**: 161
Ternay, Charles Louis d'Arsac de, Chevalier: fleet sails from Brest, **3**: 374;
squadron blocked up at R.I., **3**: 549;
reinforcements for, **4**: 146; asked to
send arms from *Le Comité* to Va., **4**:
567

Terni, Italy, **14**: 381
Terracina (formerly Anxur), Italy, **14**:
541, 542
Terrason, Amy: letter from, to John Jay,
10: 184
Terrasson, Antoine: letter to, **13**: 140;
letters from, **13**: 117, 475-6; on canal
in S.C., **13**: 117, 475; and rice con-
tract, **13**: 476n; letters sent by, **14**: 55;
20: 528, 529, 541; departs from Phila-
delphia, **19**: 529
Terrick, Richard, Bishop of London, **1**:
38, 50, 67-8
Terrière, Col. de la: with Brissot de
Warville, **15**: 64n
Terrière, Mme de La: plans to go to
America, **15**: 64
Terril, Chiles: in Albemarle co. militia,
1: 666
Terril, Joseph: signs Va. oath of allegiance, **2**: 129
Terry, Mr.: and Hessian fly, **20**: 460,
471
Terry, Dominique & Cie., **15**: 539
Terry, John: signs nonimportation reso-
lutions (1769), **1**: 31
Terry, Nathaniel: signs nonimportation
resolutions, **1**: 30, 46; signs Virginia
Association, **1**: 108; and county courts
bill, **1**: 593n; and General Court bill,
2: 228n; and bill establishing ferries,
2: 460
Terry's run: post service on, **2**: 389
Tertre, Marguerite Louis François Duport du, **18**: 114
Tessanier, Jacob: captured by Algerians,
14: 397n; **20**: 625
Tessé, René Mans, Comte de: health of,
11: 60, 65; described, **14**: 629; recalled from Queen's household, **16**: 47;
mentioned, **11**: 259, 273, 368; **12**:
246; **13**: 110; **16**: 228, 378
Tessé, Adrienne Catherine de Noailles,
Comtesse de: letters to, **11**: 187, 226-
8; **12**: 245-6; **13**: 108-9; **15**: 363-4;
16: 226-8, 378; letters from, **10**: 157-
60, 413-4; **11**: 60-1, 65, 206-7, 257-
60; **12**: 247; **13**: 110, 187-8, 476-7;
14: 629; **15**: 371; **17**: 8-9; plants and
seeds for, **9**: 228, 230n, 238, 505; **10**:
514n; **11**: 187, 233, 253, 268, 349,
362, 373; **12**: 697; **13**: 110, 138, 187,
188n, 476-7, 483, 484, 485n; **14**:
629; **16**: 222, 223n, 227, 237, 308n;
relations with Short, **9**: 354; **11**: 269;
14: 406; **15**: 87; portrait being painted

by Mme de Tott, **10:** xxvii, 178 (illus.); biographical note, **10:** 158n-9n; relations with Mme de Tott, **10:** 158n-9n; urged to invite Trumbull to Chaville, **10:** 312; applauds Va. act for religious freedom, **10:** 413-4; health of, **11:** 60; **17:** 9, 12; letter from cited, **11:** 208; love of Roman remains, **11:** 226-7; visit to TJ's house, **11:** 239, 268; pamphlets sent to TJ, **11:** 269; gardens of, **13:** xxx, 480 (illus.); correspondence with Short, **14:** 406n, 575n, 667; **15:** 78; G. Morris comments on, **14:** 704n; republicanism of, **14:** 704n; and opening of Estates General, **15:** 87n-8n; letter from, to Bernis, cited, **15:** 309; pedestal presented to TJ, **15:** 363, 363n-4n, 506; **17:** 378n; **18:** xxxiii-iv, 35n, 37n, 268 (illus.), 306, 307n; compliment to TJ, **15:** 371; fear of Revolution, **15:** 535; in Switzerland, **16:** 47, 107, 474; letters to cited, **16:** 230, 502; **17:** 378n; Horry introduced to, **16:** 378; mentioned, **10:** 154, 309, 554n; **11:** 215, 232, 273, 368; **14:** 528n; **15:** 371, 630; **17:** 546

Tessier (Teissier), Louis: letter of credit for, **10:** 217-8; TJ's accounts with, **10:** 362-3, 398, 400; **13:** 179, 280, 281n, 293-4, 300, 304-5, 345, 393; **15:** 638; bill of exchange on, **12:** 66, 72; refuses to pay bill, **12:** 112; Grand & Cie. bill on, **12:** 202, 206; **15:** 327, 328, 339; **16:** 109, 213n; letter to, from John Adams, cited, **13:** 281n; mentioned, **10:** 417

Test Act: revised in Pa., **9:** 320-1

Teste, M., **8:** 529

Tetuan, Morocco: harbor, **10:** 541

Teutoburger Wald: battle of, **13:** 13

Tevernal, M. de: Short recommends, **17:** 410

Texel (ship), **10:** 88

Texier, Felix, **7:** 555

textbooks: for use in Va. public schools, **2:** 528

textile manufacture: Lavallée's scheme for establishing in U.S., **8:** 377, 511; France, **13:** 392-3; **15:** 100; U.S.-French trade in, **14:** 253-4, 284, 292; woolen, in Va., **18:** 120-1, 121n-4n; cotton. *See* cotton manufacture

textiles: French and English compared, **9:** 485; import from Sardinia desired, **11:** 353

Thackara, James: engraves map of Federal City, **20:** 62n, 68-9

Thames (British ship), **4:** 399

thanksgiving and prayer: days of, in Va., **2:** 556; **3:** 177-9; established by Congress, **3:** 109; **4:** 50; **6:** 59

Tharman, Guttredge: signs petition, **6:** 293

Tharman, John: signs petition, **6:** 293

Thau, pond of, **11:** 449-50

Thaubenen, Mme. *See* Taubenheim, Joanne Louise de Stendt, Mme de

theatre: in Provence, **11:** 254; Quesnay's plan for, **12:** 499

theft. *See* stolen goods

Thellusson fils & Cie., **14:** 663; **15:** 214

Theocritus, **8:** 407; **12:** 18

Theoctistus of Caesarea, **1:** 552

theodolite: TJ obtains, **2:** 202; ball and screw sent to Zane, **6:** 348

Theophrastus: *Historia Plantarum*, **15:** 83, 96

thermometer: Fahrenheit's, **2:** 195; TJ sends to Isaac Zane, **6:** 347; **7:** 41; Rev. James Madison describes, **6:** 507; TJ keeps records of, **6:** 545; Madison lacks, **7:** 122; difficulty in seeing mercury in, **11:** 75-6; Vaughan sends to TJ, **13:** 37; TJ orders, **14:** 346, 347, 411; mentioned, **6:** 420

The Three Friends (merchant ship), **6:** 398

Thetis (ship): cannon for, **4:** 354, 426; outfitting, **5:** 30, 170-1, 209; defense of, **5:** 186, 190; rumored burned, **5:** 546; mentioned, **3:** 491, 642; **5:** 344

Thévenard, Antoine Jean Marie: letters to, **9:** 173-4, 294, 455-6; letters from, **9:** 276, 302-3, 545-6; **10:** 435-6; and portrait of Washington, **8:** 168, 177, 256-7, 281, 574; **9:** 122, 170, 173-4, 276, 545; **10:** 304, 310, 331, 435-6; and packet boats, **8:** 272n; and Wuibert's claim, **9:** 378, 563, 564; **11:** 40; dismissal of late prize money claims, **9:** 157; esteem for Barclay, **10:** 254; friendliness to U.S., **10:** 304; in *Alliance* case, **14:** 316, 319, 320; interest in American timber, **15:** 539

Thewait, Thomas: prisoner of war, **3:** 390

Thibaud, M. Archevesque. *See* Larchevesque-Thibaud

Thibault, Capt. Adrien: commands *Louise*, **11:** 509n

Thiebault, M., **8:** 60

323-4, 403; and Congress' agreement of secrecy, **1**: 253-4n; and Declaration of Independence, **1**: 306n, 417n; and Cedars report, **1**: 404n; responsibility for U.S. seal, **1**: 497n; councillor of American Philosophical Society, **4**: 545; letter delivered by, **6**: 234; correspondence with Washington, **6**: 408n; **17**: 349n; quoted, **6**: 522n; **7**: 147n, 307n-8n; witnesses cession, **6**: 580; notes on committee report, **7**: 33; and TJ's Notes on Coinage, **7**: 157n-8n, 186n; counsel on western posts useful, **7**: 280; letters from, to American Commissioners, **7**: 308-9, 377-8, 394; letter to, from Joseph Wharton, **7**: 454-5; remarks on animal magnetism, **8**: 15-6, 17n, 379; and *Notes on Virginia*, **8**: 229; **11**: 37; **12**: 136; box sent to, **8**: 598; cylinder lamp sent to, **9**: 398, 400; Ramsay sends part of new book to, **10**: 513; opinion on Marbois-Longchamps affair, **11**: 496n; TJ pays money to, **12**: 138, 412; letters to cited, **12**: 169; **13**: 207; TJ introduces Saint Trys to, **13**: 122-3; TJ introduces Brissot de Warville to, **13**: 122; copies Randolph's report, **13**: 132, 541n; letter from cited, **14**: 68n; payment to, **14**: 341; as possible secretary of foreign affairs, **15**: 336; bust of J. P. Jones sent to, **15**: 438; resigns as secretary of Continental Congress, **17**: 348n-9n; letter to, from Franklin, quoted, **18**: 95n; letter to, from Jones, cited, **19**: 588; and Hessian fly, **20**: 245n, 446; mentioned, **5**: 42n; **6**: 95, 142, 149, 178, 202n, 215, 240, 259, 400n, 406n, 445, 452n, 464n, 481n, 483n, 504, 519n, 572n, 585n, 615; **7**: 57, 246, 263, 266, 271, 295, 572; **10**: 563n; **11**: 88; **14**: 462

Thomson, George: votes for bill for religious freedom, **2**: 549n

Thomson, Hannah Harrison (Mrs. Charles Thomson), **6**: 445; **7**: 57, 246, 262, 282, 306, 433; **9**: 380; **10**: 105, 609

Thomson, James: Adams comments on garden of, **9**: 375n

Thomson, John, **3**: 542n

Thomson, Thomas: freight sent, **17**: 362

Thomson, William, **8**: 662

Thorn: Prussia demands from Poland, **17**: 542, 558; **18**: 294; **20**: 583

Thornbury, Mr., **4**: 500, 557

Thornton, Lieut., **5**: 275

Thornton, Mr., **4**: 437

Thornton, Col. Anthony: letter from, **4**: 384

Thornton, Francis: and bill establishing ferries, **2**: 456

Thornton, John: Baptist enlisted in army, **1**: 662

Thornton, Matthew: signs agreement of secrecy, **1**: 253; signs Declaration of Independence, **1**: 432

Thornton, Presley: granted full citizenship, **6**: 332n

Thornton, William: votes against bill for religious freedom, **2**: 549n; *Cadmus*, **8**: 506n

Thornton, Col. William, **5**: 123

Thoroughgood, Col. John, **4**: 617

Thorpe, Thomas: signs Va. oath of allegiance, **2**: 128

Thou, Jacques Auguste de: *Histoire Universelle*, **7**: 506; **11**: 666; works of, **8**: 111

"Thoughts on English Prosody": possible date of, **10**: 498n-9n

Thouin, André: letters to, **12**: 246, 596-7; letter from, **12**: 305

Thouret, Jacques Guillaume: plan for reform of clergy, **16**: 573

Thrasymene, Lake, **14**: 381

thread: lacking in southern army, **5**: 199

Three Brothers (ship): parcels for TJ on, **19**: 581n

Three Friends (ship): taken as prize, **7**: 269, 496

Three Sisters (ship): whale oil sent in, **13**: 119

Threlkeld, Elizah: petition from, **5**: 405; reply to, **5**: 405n

Threlkeld, John: signs petition, **17**: 471

Thrift, George: signs nonimportation resolutions (1770), **1**: 47

Throop, Daniel: in *Dover* case, **20**: 207n

Thruston, Charles Mynn: votes for bill for religious freedom, **2**: 549n; meets Morgan at Winchester, **6**: 71n; attitude on cession of western territory, **6**: 266; letter to, from Washington, cited, **6**: 648n; opposes Va. Revised Code, **9**: 195; opposes federal control of commerce, **9**: 198, 199

Thucydides: *History of the Peloponnesian War*, **8**: 323; recommended to Peter Carr, **8**: 407, 408; **12**: 18; TJ comments on, **10**: 72; **11**: 159; Martha Jefferson studies, **11**: 238; works of,

539-40; **19**: 183; cod-liver oil for preserving, **16**: xliii, 579-80; quality of
unseasoned, **18**: 506

Timberlake, Benjamin: officer in Regiment of Guards for Convention troops,
3: 155

time: Va. bill for regulating computation
of, **2**: 638-40; Hopkinson's device for
measuring, **11**: 562; TJ's observations
of, **15**: 237-8

Timmons, John: petition from, **5**: 349

Timoni, Antoine: Carmichael advised to
consult on Turkish treaty, **9**: 540n

Timor: Capt. Bligh brings rice from, **16**:
274, 276n, 492, 495, 496n, 578; **17**:
564-5; **18**: 97

Timothy, Ann: paid by Department of
State, **17**: 366, 369; publishes *State
Gazette of South-Carolina*, **17**: 509; let-
ter to, from Remsen, quoted, **18**: 66n

Timothy, B. F.: paid by Department of
State, **17**: 371

Timothy, Epistle to: quoted by TJ, **1**:
551-2

Timothy, Peter: supports American state
papers series, **1**: 145

Timotlee (Tomolley, Cherokee town), **4**:
360

tin: scarcity of, **4**: 201, 202; sale of, **4**:
571; U.S. import of, **10**: 147

Tinker, Capt., **11**: 323

Tinsley, Mr., **15**: 671n

tin ware: manufacture in Conn., **7**: 336

Tipoo Sahib (Tipú Sultán): biographical
note, **13**: xxx-xxxi; French relations
with, **13**: 175, 191; ambassadors of arrive in France, **13**: 250, 255, 256,
359, 464-5, 479, 481 (illus.), 492,
497; Cornwallis opposes, **17**: 515,
629; rebellion against British, **17**: 629;
18: 10, 300, 354; **19**: 259, 270; **20**:
166, 343

Tipton, Maj.: destroys Cherokee town,
4: 360-1

Tirionear, Jacob: on crew of *Dauphin*,
19: 333

titles, hereditary: proposed prohibition in
new states, **6**: 588n, 604, 608

titles of honor: TJ comments on, **15**:
336-7, 367; Short comments on, **18**:
451. *See also* United States: President,
titles of honor proposed

titles of nobility: in France, **16**: 571; **17**:
18, 521-2; U.S. action on, **17**: 521

titles to land: Va. bill on, **2**: 520-1; and
Conn.-Pa. dispute, **6**: 495; and west-

ern territory, **7**: 144-5; TJ discusses
working of, **14**: 360-1

titles to unappropriated land: G. Mason's
bill for settling, **2**: 250

titles to unpatented land: bill for settling,
2: 155-67

Titt, Samuel: makes tables for TJ, **18**:
591, 592n

Titus, Emperor: baths of, **14**: 449

Titus, Epistle to: quoted by TJ, **1**: 552

"T. L." (pseud. used by Hamilton), **20**:
719

tobacco: free trade in by colonies prohibited, **1**: 124; and nonexportation agreement, **1**: 139-40; sale by TJ, **2**: 4n;
southern Europe as market for, **2**: 210;
taxes on in Va., **2**: 221, 540; **11**: 154;
as medium of exchange, **2**: 232, 273,
274-5; **3**: 14, 211, 272, 275, 298,
307, 323, 326, 337, 342, 345, 357,
366, 372, 481, 492, 517, 525-6, 575;
4: 51, 224, 373, 380, 434, 449, 512,
518, 524, 585-6, 590, 642, 657; **5**:
15, 27-8, 33, 38-9, 52, 141, 146, 166,
177, 209, 220, 265, 278, 304, 311,
316-7, 322, 323, 324, 372, 388n,
391, 493, 670; **6**: 130, 135n, 138,
188, 195, 200n, 270, 321n; **8**: 35, 36;
10: 231, 576; **11**: 11-2, 16-7; damaged, **2**: 233-4; prices, **2**: 263; **4**: 481;
6: 415-6; **7**: 99, 366, 371, 402, 522,
592, 604; **8**: 94, 115, 303, 344, 358,
393, 413, 415, 642, 659; **9**: 75, 76,
202, 297, 335, 386-7, 391, 519, 660;
10: 108, 195, 198, 274, 577, 588,
614-5, 623, 628, 630; **11**: 193, 353,
507-8; **12**: 83, 85-6, 88-93, 207, 211-
2, 226, 373, 465, 467, 511, 535, 653,
667; **14**: 276; **16**: 29-30, 116, 188,
384, 492; **18**: 69; **19**: 259; **20**: 99,
102, 153, 154, 214, 405, 598, 600,
614, 632, 658; quantity on hand in
Va., **3**: 19; quantity to be purchased
by Va. Board of Trade, **3**: 23, 24, 32,
35, 108-9; Va. crops, **3**: 85; **7**: 209-
12, 365-72, 403, 592; **8**: 415, 509,
642, 660; **9**: 184; **10**: 388, 577, 588;
19: 262; Prussia or Holland as market
for, **3**: 92; use as payment for salt, **3**:
200-1; **4**: 376; taxes payable in, **3**:
250, 511; transportation, **3**: 315; **12**:
88; as medium of exchange in Tuscany, **3**: 366; for American prisoners of
war, **3**: 481, 570-1, 594, 639; **4**: 33,
481, 482; **5**: 243, 307, 363, 400-1,
435, 460, 509-10, 559, 588-92; **6**: 20-

tobacco (*cont.*)

1, 27; act to amend law on, **3**: 492; as pay for militia, **4**: 18; plans for inspection of, **4**: 227-8; purchase for army, **4**: 375; exportation to Bermuda, **4**: 466; warehouses for, **4**: 582; taken by British, **5**: 406, 424, 435; burned by British at Petersburg, **5**: 623; Fairfax co., **6**: 34; TJ's destroyed by British, **6**: 195; use as medium of exchange, **6**: 200n; Oroonoko, **7**: 209; sweet scented, **7**: 209; insect pests, **7**: 211; French regulations on import, **7**: 291; **9**: 597-601, 605, 624-5, 627, 628, 644, 645; **12**: 373; freight costs, **7**: 348; U.S. export of, **7**: 353, 406; **8**: 40, 308, 309; **10**: 147; cultivation in Europe, **7**: 371; **10**: 385; brokers of, in London, **7**: 525-7; S.C., **8**: 197, 198, 200; duty on, in Britain, **8**: 310, 311; smuggling of, **8**: 311; **9**: 35-6; **12**: 648; **20**: 632; consumption in France, **8**: 385; duty on, in France, **8**: 385-93; **9**: 139-40, 308, 337, 4; **12**: 314; sale through England, **8**: 504; **9**: 43-4, 601; sale in Britain, **8**: 634; **12**: 288; sorting, **9**: 3, 43; Portuguese production, **9**: 19; weights, **9**: 34n; Tripolitan compared with American, **9**: 285; debts of planters of, to British creditors, **10**: 27; cultivated in south only, **10**: 37; consular convention on, **10**: 99; owned by Paradise, **10**: 175, 198; indebtedness of merchants trading in, **10**: 304-5; shipped from Va. by Maury, **10**: 558; TJ pays debts in, **11**: 11-2, 16-7, 639-40, 652-3; **16**: 211, 350; **17**: 266, 582, 584, 631, 657; losses of cargoes during Revolution, **11**: 14-5; tax on, **11**: 154; shipped on the *Minerva*, **11**: 358; Barclay's delivered in Ireland, **11**: 504; speculation in, **12**: 211; sold for John Page, **12**: 652; sent to TJ, **13**: 288, 298; in Wayles estate debt, **13**: 327-8; **15**: 644, 647, 649-53, 656, 658-9, 661-75; as rent for land, **13**: 339-40; Va. production affected by price of wheat, **15**: 353; Donald's advice on sale of, **16**: 29-30; **17**: 482; TJ owes to Marsden, **16**: 82; Paradise pays debt in, **16**: 84-5; cultivation decreased, **16**: 599; cultivation in Alsace, **17**: 395; cultivation in France proposed, **17**: 414, 439-41, 527; **20**: 172; pamphlet on, **20**: 528-9

tobacco, public: sale of, **3**: 423, 542, 543, 638; protection from enemy, **5**: 451

tobacco canoes. *See* canoes

tobacco inspectors: exemption from militia duty, **2**: 350

tobacco loan office certificates: list sent to county lieutenants, **3**: 515-6; mentioned, **3**: 503; **4**: 512

tobacco notes: punishment for theft of, **2**: 501; sent by commissioners of specific tax of Essex co., **3**: 606; **4**: 43; as payment for militia, **15**: 603-4; mentioned, **5**: 268, 654

tobacco trade: with France, **3**: 14, 168, 274, 384, 551; **7**: 380, 563; **8**: 213-4, 220-4, 244, 291-2, 303, 386-9, 390n-1n, 394, 429-30, 641, 642, 644, 646, 650-1, 660, 666-7; **9**: 3, 31, 112, 113n, 135n, 139-40, 142, 144, 214, 291-2, 297, 338-44, 386-7, 390-3, 442, 445, 457-61, 471, 472, 473-4, 501-3, 538, 570n, 583-5, 597-8, 599-600, 601, 602, 613-4, 650-1; **10**: 87, 101, 106, 125, 173, 192, 195, 197, 198, 274, 277, 314, 327, 328, 399, 474, 484-5, 590, 595, 602, 612; **11**: 30, 41, 110, 169, 193-4, 370-1, 507, 508, 513, 516, 594, 599, 600, 605, 607, 614-8, 632-3; **12**: 46-7, 57, 76-93 (editorial note and documents), 106-7, 117-8, 121, 131-2, 133, 209, 211-2, 222, 226, 235-6, 248-9, 320-1, 347, 354-5, 373, 385, 437, 443, 464, 465, 467, 481, 511, 514-5, 534-5, 552, 561-2, 571, 593, 648, 653, 684, 691; **13**: 52-91 (editorial note and documents), 485; **14**: 185, 252, 331, 336-7, 424-5, 428, 444-5, 550-1, 585; **15**: 45, 135, 323, 378, 402; **16**: 270, 271n, 375, 505-6; **17**: 395-6, 401, 439-41, 480, 493, 526-7, 556, 566, 646; **18**: 17-20, 76, 352-3, 478, 507, 586, 604; **19**: 289-90, 335-6, 347-50, 361-3, 533, 538, 576-8, 597; **20**: 171-2, 251, 303, 365-6, 405, 533, 548, 567, 582, 601-2, 632, 674, 681-2, 687-8, 710; proposed with Sweden, **7**: 347; **9**: 633; with Britain, **7**: 525-7; **13**: 76, 82; **18**: 18-9; with Naples, **7**: 613; with Sardinia desirable, **11**: 353; TJ's observations on letter from Calonne, suppressed article in, **13**: 56; consuls needed in France for, **13**: 641; Irish and Scottish vessels seized at L'Orient, **14**: 392n-3n; value of, **18**:

371; Delamotte describes, **19**: 260-1.
See also Berni, order of; farmers-general
Tobago: taken by Marquis de Bouillé, **6**: 110; lumber shipped to, **8**: 541
Todd, Mr.: TJ interprets will of, **6**: 145-6
Todd, John, Jr.: letters to, **3**: 271-2, 319-21; letters from, **3**: 70-2, 415-7, 440; **4**: 169-70, 441-3, 498; **5**: 461-2, 462-3; signs petition from Hanover co., **1**: 589n; appointment as county lieutenant of Illinois, **2**: 259; order to purchase horses, **3**: 154; recommends Pollack, **3**: 158; to train militia as protection against Indians, **3**: 317; notifies Va. of lack of credit, **3**: 319-20; TJ regrets his desire to resign office in Illinois, **3**: 320; asks indemnification for losses in Ohio, **3**: 440, 444; instructions to Dodge, **3**: 520; bills drawn by, **6**: 320; statement in Nathan case, **6**: 323n; mentioned, **3**: 69, 159, 316, 329; **4**: 283, 355
Todd, Rev. John: letter from, **3**: 68-9
Todd, Robert: expedition against Indians, **20**: 481; mentioned, **5**: 439n
Tolentino, Italy, **14**: 380
Tollot père et fils, **11**: 464n
Tolozan, Jean François de: gift to, **16**: 362n, 501, 584-5; **17**: 544; **18**: 357, 601, 602n; **20**: 346, 544; note to, missing, **16**: 387, 388n; meets with Short, **17**: 11-2; letter from, to Short, cited, **17**: 213; payment to, **20**: 645n
Tom (slave), **4**: 436, 521
tomahawks: supplied to Gen. Gates' army, **3**: 526, 528; Turkish weapon resembling, **14**: 379; mentioned, **4**: 402
Tom Johnson (ship), **4**: 310
Tomlinson, William: Baptist enlisted in army, **1**: 662; in Albemarle co. militia, **1**: 664
Tompkins, William: in Albemarle co. militia, **1**: 664
Toms, Joso.: in Albemarle co. militia, **1**: 666
Tomson, James: signs petition, **1**: 588
Tomson, John: signs petition, **1**: 588
Tomson, William: signs petition, **1**: 588
tonnage. *See* shipping
tonnage acts, U.S.: passage of, **16**: 450, 517, 520: **19**: 89; representation by France against, **18**: 221, 230, 516-77 (editorial note and documents); **19**:

162; TJ corresponds with Otto about, **18**: 558-9, 560-2, 571-7; **19**: 82, 109n; TJ to Hamilton on, **18**: 563-4
Tonnelier, M. (land agent): sells Oneida land, **18**: 31
Tooke, John Horne: *Diversions of Purley*, **14**: 512; persecuted in Britain, **20**: 270
tools: not subject to execution, **2**: 649; held for arrears of rent, **2**: 652; lack of, **5**: 638; requisitioned by Steuben, **5**: 666; TJ asks permission to bring from England to France, **9**: 313
toothbrushes: TJ orders, **9**: 152
tooth drawers: Rumsey investigates, **15**: 145, 172, 404
toothpick case: TJ orders, **9**: 152
toothpicks: ordered from London, **11**: 531
Topham, Ross & Newman, **12**: 564
Toppan, Richard: signs petition, **11**: 336
Toquo (Toque, Cherokee Indian town), **4**: 362
Tories. *See* Loyalists
Torquemada, Juan de: *La Monarquia Indiana*, **11**: 554
Torremanianal, Marquis de: replaced by Ricardos, **13**: 578
Torriano, Charles (?): pass for, **4**: 280-1
Tortona, **11**: 440
Toscan, Jean: and claim of Mme Grégoire, **10**: 239; French vice consul in Portsmouth, N.H., **14**: 64n-5n
Totness: residence of Hore Browse Trist's relatives, **10**: 610
Tott, François, Baron de, **9**: 595; **10**: 159n
Tott, Sophie Ernestine, Mme de: letters to, **10**: 553-4; **11**: 187-8, 270-3; letters from, **10**: 160, 554, 652; **11**: 117, 198-9, 367-8; painting portrait of Mme de Tessé, **10**: xxvii, 178 (illus.); biographical note, **10**: 158n-9n; friendship with Mme de Tessé, **10**: 158n-9n; TJ sends edition of Homer to, **10**: 553-4; health of, **11**: 60, 65, 117; letters from cited, **11**: 207, 208, 374; invited to visit TJ's house, **11**: 239; opinion of Drouais' painting, **11**: 259, 414; fears Revolution, **15**: 535; in Switzerland, **16**: 107; mentioned, **10**: 309, 414; **11**: 215, 227, 232, 350; **12**: 246, 247, 697; **13**: 110, 187; **16**: 228, 378; **17**: 9
Toul, France, **13**: 28
Toulon, France: TJ describes, **11**: 429-

Toulon, France (*cont.*)
30; **13**: 274; summer heat at, **11**: 430; caper cultivation at, **11**: 647; signs of peace or war in port of, **13**: 507; consular agent recommended for, **14**: 61; dockyard and arsenal at, **14**: 592, 608, 649, 667, 705; **15**: 29; riots in, **15**: 24, 29; **16**: 42

Toulouse, Archbishop of. *See* Loménie de Brienne

Toulouse, France: TJ's arrival at, **11**: 370; TJ comments on, **11**: 370, 449, 454-5; **13**: 275; Parlement of, **13**: 192

Toulouse-Lautrec, Pierre Joseph, Comte de: vineyard of, **11**: 456; wine recommended by TJ, **20**: 405

Toulson, Capt. (master of *Union*), **19**: 537

Touraine, France: wine exported from, **11**: 460

tourists: cheating of, **11**: 350

Tourneri, M., **11**: 463n

Tournillon, M.: hospitality to TJ, **11**: 287

Tournillon ainé, M., **11**: 463n

Tournus, France: TJ describes, **11**: 418

Tourny, Jacques: reported to have commanded U.S. frigate, **11**: 604; unknown to TJ, **12**: 3

Tours, France: Chastellux comments on, **11**: 262, 325; TJ describes, **11**: 460-1; **13**: 275

Tourtille Sangrain, Pierre. *See* Sangrain

Tourton & Ravel: bill of exchange on, **17**: 497n; mentioned, **10**: 301; **12**: 27, 191, 192

Tourves, France: TJ describes, **11**: 443

Toutant, Bourgard: makes claim on Va., **9**: 513

Tow, Edward: British war prisoner, **2**: 32

Towanoganda (Seneca Chief): replies to Lafayette's speech, **7**: 450n

Towles, Capt., **20**: 154

Towles, Henry: letter from, **5**: 394; signs voucher, **5**: 373n

Towles, Col. Oliver: letter to, **5**: 454; letters from, **4**: 33-4; **5**: 513; prisoner of war, **3**: 389, 390, 665; **4**: 68; letters from, to Steuben, quoted, **5**: 312n-3n, 448n; defends Fredericksburg, **5**: 447-8

town major: to be appointed at War Office, **5**: 244-5, 269

town meetings, **6**: 386

Townsend, Mme ("Mme T"): letters to, **12**: 243-4, 329-30; letters from, **12**:

327-8, 330-1, 357; J. P. Jones comments on, **12**: 96-7; correspondence with J. P. Jones, **12**: 97n, 269; requests money, **12**: 331, 357; J. P. Jones inquires for, **13**: 581, 582n

Townsend, Charles, **9**: 488

Townsend, Lord John: in election of 1788, **13**: 434, 462-3

Townshend, Mr. (British war prisoner), **2**: 32

Townshend, George, Earl of Leicester, Marquis, **9**: 487

Townshend, Thomas, first Viscount: comments on U.S. trade, **7**: 523-4; McClenachan case taken up with, **7**: 524; correspondence with Martin, **7**: 524, 529-30, 530-3; letter to, from crown law officers, **7**: 531; letter to, from Emperor of Morocco, refused, **10**: 142; converses with Beckwith, **17**: 43; mentioned, **6**: 251

townships: settlement on unappropriated land, **2**: 157, 163n-4n

toys: U.S. import of, **10**: 147

tractofages (word): Stiles uses, **10**: 586n

Tracy, Mr.: and U.S. commercial policy, **19**: 130

Tracy, Mary Lee (Mrs. Nathaniel Tracy), **8**: 399

Tracy, Nathaniel: letters to, **7**: 395; **8**: 45, 398-9, 554-5; letters from, **9**: 352, 380; owner of *Ceres*, **7**: 311, 321, 363n; consulted by TJ on U.S. commerce, **7**: 324n, 339-43; TJ sails with, **7**: 358, 382; TJ's payment for passage, **7**: 362; recommended to Hogendorp, **7**: 383; opinion on French and English manufactures, **7**: 511; mentioned, **7**: 413, 429, 430, 576; **8**: 17; **15**: 381

Tracy & Co., **3**: 656

trade: restrained by Parliament, **1**: 172; mentioned in Declaration of Causes, **1**: 215; and Lord North's Proposal, **1**: 228; privateers interfere with, **3**: 5; resolves of Congress against inland restrictions on, **3**: 87; between New Orleans and Va., **3**: 168; with British forces criticized, **4**: 141; laws prohibiting, with British ports, **6**: 263; British regulations resented in Va., **6**: 354, 372; condition after Revolution, **6**: 377; with European territorial possessions in America, **6**: 394. *See also* balance of trade; commerce; treaties of amity and commerce; and individual countries trade, public: in private vessels, **2**: 209; **5**: 169-71

Trade, Virginia Board of. *See* Virginia: Board of Trade

trade cards: power of Congress to make, **8**: 484-5. *See also* treaties of amity and commerce

trading with the enemy. *See* commerce with the enemy

train oil: prices of, **7**: 346

Traité de Morale, **7**: 507

Trajan, Emperor, **14**: 380

transit instruments, **5**: 478

transportation: of army supplies, **3**: 392, 394, 408, 409, 410n, 476; **4**: 27, 132, 150-1, 292, 464; of provisions, **3**: 641, 658; **4**: 8; **5**: 16, 77-8, 241; of troops, **4**: 184; costs of, **4**: 458; vessels for Cornwallis' expedition, **7**: 127; Paris to Va., **7**: 504; of criminals, **10**: 8n, 30; **11**: 74

Transylvania colony: pressures Va. Convention, **1**: 384n; as 14th colony, **1**: 564-5n; land purchases for, **2**: 64-111; boundaries of, **2**: 72, 73, 74, 78, 81, 85-6, 87-8, 95-6, 105, 106, 108; land claimed by Callaway in, **2**: 82-3; convention on, **2**: 83, 93-4, 108-9; government, **2**: 94

Trappist monks: Shippen describes, **13**: 445

Traubenheim, Mme de. *See* Taubenheim, Joanne Louise de Stendt, Mme de

Trauttmansdorff, Ferdinand, Count von, **12**: 386

Travis, Col. Champion: signs nonimportation resolutions (1769), **1**: 30; signs Virginia Association, **1**: 109; commissioner for the Va. navy, **3**: 223; contract with E. H. Moseley, **3**: 223

Travis (Travers), Capt. Edward: letters to, **5**: 223, 401; letter from, **5**: 171-2; commands *Tempest*, **4**: 640; ordered to take the *Swift* up the Chickahominy, **5**: 682n, 696; mentioned, **5**: 456, 689n; **6**: 19

Treadway, Moses, **4**: 275

Treadwell, Jacob: petition of, **6**: 448-52

Treadwell, John: nominated as congressman from Conn., **14**: 525

treason: defined by British statute, **1**: 143; TJ comments on, **1**: 505; Va. legislation on, **1**: 597; **2**: 510-1, 612-6; **3**: 534; **4**: 692n; **5**: 31; punishment for, **2**: 325, 493-4; **5**: 593; **6**: 311; trial

of slaves for, **2**: 616-7; **5**: 640-3; trial of leaders of western Va. Tory conspiracy for, **3**: 519-20, 523, 533-4

treason, petty: punishment for, **2**: 325, 494-5; confiscation of property, **2**: 495

treasurer, state (Va.). *See* Virginia: Treasurer

treasurer of Va. HB. *See* Nicholas, Robert Carter

Treasury, Commissioners of. *See* Commissioners of the Treasury, U.S.

treasury certificates, **2**: 146; **9**: 164, 171

Treasury Department. *See* Department of the Treasury, U.S.

treasury notes: Va. bills concerning, **2**: 184-6, 507-10; redemption, **2**: 185

treaties: discussed in Congress, **1**: 477; **7**: 90, 95; power of Congress to enter into, **2**: 120; **8**: 484-5; **10**: 14-5; to be made only by federation of states, **6**: 394; ratification of, **6**: 424; **7**: 32-4; excluded from powers of Committee of the States, **6**: 523-4; reform of language used by, **7**: 463n-5n, 476-7; rights of aliens under, **9**: 259

treaties of amity and commerce: European overtures for, **6**: 389; and Continental Congress, **6**: 393-6; **7**: 123, 203-5, 226, 228, 231, 248-9, 265-71, 275, 493-500; **8**: 217, 266-7, 382; terms of, **6**: 396; Monroe comments on, **6**: 539; **8**: 76-7; **9**: 188-90; with Great Britain, **7**: 48, 422, 456-9, 494-5, 509-10, 547, 560-1, 563, 573-4; **8**: 55-9, 88, 143, 238, 267, 273-5, 297, 310, 332-3, 354-5, 382-3, 608; **9**: 42, 281-2, 375, 398, 402, 406, 446, 449, 465, 469, 647; **16**: 544-5; with Barbary States, **7**: 263, 269, 496; **8**: 19, 46, 347-54; TJ's work on, **7**: 323n, 463-90; **14**: 72; with Portugal, **7**: 419-20, 428, 454-5, 551, 573-4, 580, 646; **8**: 603, 607-8; **9**: 11, 18-22, 42, 61-5, 128, 137, 182, 295, 325, 402, 407, 408-33, 448-9, 462, 468, 469, 500, 515, 595, 647; **10**: 61, 87, 106, 135, 137, 140, 179, 241, 285, 488, 597, 607; **11**: 118, 513n; **12**: 146; with Prussia, **7**: 421, 436-7, 466n, 490-2, 494, 565-6, 574, 611-2, 616-28, 646, 649-50; **8**: 8-10, 14-5, 26-33, 37, 134-5, 141, 143, 165, 173, 234, 265-6, 267n-8n, 301-2, 305-6, 310, 312-20, 323-4, 375, 431-6, 459, 478-9, 505-6, 515, 544, 566, 585, 603, 606, 608, 625, 639, 664; **9**: 136, 349, 462, 466,

treaties of amity and commerce (*cont.*)
511, 666; **10**: 61, 106, 176, 196, 285,
313, 317, 348, 403, 473, 479, 556;
12: 359; **14**: 72, 76-7; with Spain, **7**:
423-4, 425-6, 455-6, 510; **8**: 137,
608; **9**: 42; **10**: 606; with Sicily, **7**:
424; with Saxony, **7**: 424, 424n; with
Russia, **7**: 424n; with Sardinia, **7**:
424n, 425, 632-3; with Venice, **7**:
424n, 427; with Tuscany, **7**: 424n,
430, 437-8, 533, 561-2, 573-4, 649;
8: 104-10, 140-1, 152, 173, 187-95,
205, 608; **9**: 26, 45, 46n-7n; **15**: 616-
7; with the Vatican, **7**: 424n, 575;
with Sweden, **7**: 428, 434-5, 466n,
475-6, 494, 644; **8**: 382; terms of, **7**:
463n, 479, 486; **8**: 459; with Denmark, **7**: 466n, 467n, 469n, 476-8,
494, 631-2, 633, 644, 646-7; **8**: 608;
9: 514-5, 649; with France, **7**: 471-3,
494; **8**: 266, 497-8, 608, 625-6; **9**: 42,
188; **17**: 431-2; **20**: 529, 547, 642-3,
651; with Netherlands, **7**: 473-5, 495-
6; **8**: 521, 608; **9**: 188; with Genoa, **7**:
494; with Austria, **7**: 494; **8**: 479,
608; **9**: 166-7, 234-5, 238, 501, 507-
8, 515, 564-5; **10**: 405; **12**: 359; with
Hamburg, **7**: 495-6; with Turkey, **7**:
496; **9**: 407; with Naples, **7**: 612-4,
647; **8**: 608; difficulties in negotiating,
7: 638; **9**: 168; with Algiers, **8**: 19;
with Morocco, **8**: 19; **10**: 76, 419-27;
12: 121-2, 150-1, 175, 186, 324, 644;
14: 46, 72; with Tripoli, **8**: 19; **9**:
285-8, 325, 358; with Tunis, **8**: 19; **9**:
325, 358; power of Congress to make,
8: 230-2; relative importance of European states, **8**: 605; value of, to U.S.,
9: 235; need for, **10**: 15-6; status
(Aug. 1786), **10**: 286; delay in ratification, **11**: 30, 35, 65-6, 78; Jay's desire for continuance of negotiations,
11: 130; with Austrian Netherlands,
12: 258, 376, 383, 388-9, 394, 435;
changes in plan of, **12**: 407; draft of
Model Treaty of 1784, **18**: 384n
Treaty of Breda (1667), **6**: 489
Treaty of Hopewell: Cherokee violations
of, **20**: 481
Treaty of Newtown, **20**: 129-30
Treaty of Paris (1783). *See* Peace
Treaty, Definitive
Treaty of Westminster (1673), **6**: 489
Trebell, William, **5**: 317
"tree of liberty": refreshed with blood of
patriots and tyrants, **12**: 356
trees: Ky., **8**: 125-6; transplanting of, **11**:

229; transportation of, **12**: 408-9; TJ's
interest in, **12**: 443, 630, 684, 687;
13: 47, 417; **15**: 376-7, 621, 632; **20**:
453-6, 463-4, 465; French import of,
12: 469, 480; **13**: 69; sent to Mme de
Tessé, **13**: 187, 476-7 (list); **14**: 629;
Paine's problem on, with drawings,
13: 225-6; experiments with grafting,
16: 370; TJ sends seed to Randolph,
18: 308. *See also* fruit trees; olive culture
Tremoulet, M.: vineyard of, **11**: 444
trench tools: for Senf, **5**: 87, 248; to be
made at Fredericksburg, **5**: 270
Trent, Alexander: signs nonimportation
resolutions, **1**: 30, 46; manages lottery,
1: 22
Trent, Alexander, Jr.: testimonial in favor of Philip Turpin, **6**: 331n, 332n
Trent, Henry: and bill establishing ferries, **2**: 459
Trent, Peterfield: testimonial in favor of
Philip Turpin, **6**: 331n, 332n; mentioned, **1**: 22
Trent, William: appointed captain of
company to treat with Indians, **2**: 98;
and western land, **6**: 654n, 655n
Trent & Co.: payment to, **16**: 211
Trenton, N.J.: battle of, **2**: 3; considered
as seat for Congress, **6**: 345, 349, 352,
362, 366, 371, 547; **7**: 35, 535; **8**: 78,
99; **13**: 625; **19**: 7, 8; meeting of Congress at, **6**: 363; **7**: 118, 248, 306,
310, 572; comparative table of distance
from various states, **6**: 366-7; meeting
of Court of Commissioners at, **6**: 478n,
481n, 482n, 501, 504
Tresca, A.: sale of tobacco, **12**: 222
Tresilian, Sir Robert: articles of impeachment against, **1**: 131
trespass: actions for in common law
courts, **2**: 604
Tretheway, John: land grant to, **6**: 658
Treuttel, Jean Georges: painting by, **13**:
xxviii, 17 (illus.)
Trèves. *See* Trier
Trèves, Archbishop of. *See* Clemens
Wenceslaus
Trevett *v.* Weeden, **16**: 453n-4n
trials, criminal. *See* criminal trials
Trier (Triers), **13**: 15, 265
Trieste: trade with U.S., **9**: 123; men-
tioned, **13**: 146
Trigg, Daniel: votes for bill on religious
freedom, **2**: 549n
Trigg, John: votes for bill on religious
freedom, **2**: 549n

private secretary, **15**: 144, 152, 164, 176, 179; sketch of Yorktown, **15**: 157-8; painting of American history, **15**: 176-7; prints and engravings, **15**: 177-9; need of patronage, **15**: 178-9; Paine's financial transactions with, **15**: 274; brother of, **15**: 297; candlesticks for TJ, **15**: 335 (sketch), 400, 453-4, 504; goes to Paris, **15**: 339, 384-5; returns to America, **15**: 427, 441, 468-9, 501, 504, 515-6, 524n, 525, 526, 527, 530, 553, 560n, 561; and TJ's voyage to America, **15**: 467-8, 471, 499-500, 504, 516, 517-8; passport issued by TJ, **15**: 485, 487; letter from, to Pitt, **15**: 517-8; reports to Washington, **16**: 8; plans painting of standards captured at Yorktown, **16**: 58n; in Philadelphia, **16**: 549-50; portrait of Washington, **17**: xxix; portraits of Creek Indian chiefs, **17**: xxix-xxx, 218 (illus.); portrait of Arthur St. Clair, **17**: xxxii, 395 (illus.); portrait of William Loughton Smith, **17**: xxxii, 395 (illus.); Beckwith obtains information from, **17**: 55; portrait of Oliver Wolcott, Jr., **18**: xxxvii, 268 (illus.); portrait of William Temple Franklin, **18**: xxxviii-ix, 269 (illus.); miniature portrait of John Brown, **19**: xxxiv, 348 (illus.); TJ advises to see Natural Bridge, **19**: 298-301; TJ recommends, **19**: 298n, 330; letter from, to Adams, quoted, **19**: 462n; relations with Thomas Digges, **20**: 317n; criticizes Madison, **20**: 445; mentioned, **8**: 78; **9**: 364n, 545, 557; **10**: 162; **11**: 3, 503; **12**: 394, 403, 417, 517, 554, 624, 631; **13**: 284, 288, 317, 423, 461, 639, 650-1; **14**: 345, 418, 445, 454, 474, 647; **15**: 130, 275, 328, 351, 414, 434, 469, 476, 479, 513, 521; **16**: 313, 446

Trumbull, Jonathan, Jr.: congressman from Conn., **14**: 525; **15**: 216; votes for capital bill, **19**: 36n

Trumbull, Jonathan, Sr.: and Conn.-Pa. boundary dispute, **6**: 476n, 478n, 481n, 482n, 486n, 501, 502n, 503n; proclamation of, **7**: 134; TJ's relations with, **7**: 312n; recommends Bushnell, **8**: 557; TJ meets son of, **9**: 456

trunk: TJ orders, **15**: 38-9, 84

Trusdale, Capt. (master of *Carolina Planter*), **15**: 538, 543; **16**: 95

Trusler, John: *London Adviser and Guide*, **11**: 522

trustees: legal opinion on, **6**: 180-2

trusts, **2**: 408

"Truth" (pseud.): on residence bill, **17**: 180-1, 203-5

Truxton (Truxen), Capt. Thomas: commands ship on which Franklin sails, **8**: 281, 302, 306, 585; commander of *Canton*, **13**: 4n; arrives in Philadelphia, **20**: 343

Tryon, Gov. William: and British strategy, **1**: 247; commands British troops on Long Island Sound, **3**: 31; visits Williamsburg, **10**: 247n

Tryon co., N.Y.: Schuyler to march against Tories in, **1**: 438; militia, **2**: 29

Tual, Jacques, **10**: 94

Tubbs, Jasper: settlement near Fort Pitt, **2**: 101

Tuckahoe (home of Thomas Mann Randolph): TJ sends family to, **4**: 259; quarry at, **8**: 368; mentioned, **4**: 263, 276; **5**: 517n; **8**: 342; **10**: 107

Tuckahoe, Va.: postal service at, **20**: 618

Tucker, Charles: signs Va. oath of allegiance, **2**: 129

Tucker, Henry: suit against estate of, **1**: 52-9, 69-70, 73-4, 84-5

Tucker, Mrs. Henry: suit against, **1**: 53, 59

Tucker, Henry, Sr. (1713-1787): proposal concerning Bermuda, **1**: 169n, 239-40

Tucker, St. George: letters to, **1**: 170; **3**: 12-3; letters from, **1**: 167-9, 239-40; quoted on Josiah Philips' case, **2**: 191n; revises Va. laws, **2**: 324n; **20**: 303, 304; commissioner for Va. on federal control of commerce, **9**: 197, 199, 206n; *Reflections on Encouraging the Commerce of the United States*, **9**: 296; opposes Constitution, **12**: 284; appointed to Va. General Court, **12**: 609; **13**: 49; death of wife, **12**: 654; pamphlet on federal government attributed to, **13**: 337; urges low tonnage rates, **18**: 521; remarriage, **20**: 405; mentioned, **6**: 343

Tucker, Thomas Tudor: letter from, **13**: 107; and admission of Ky., **13**: 248n; as S.C. representative in Congress, **14**: 666; **15**: 51; correspondence with Mitchell, **16**: 335n, 338n, 339n, 342-5; opposes establishment of mint, **16**: 341n; and response to Washington's address, **18**: 229n; supports Smith

Tucker, Thomas Tudor (*cont.*)
amendment, **18**: 230n; recommended as commissioner of Federal District, **19**: 59; mentioned, **6**: 207n

Tucker, Travis: in Albemarle co. militia, **1**: 664

Tucker, William: lawsuit of, **1**: 86

Tuckers Point: British ship off, **5**: 74

Tuffin, Armand Charles, Marquis de La Rouërie. *See* La Rouërie, Charles Armand Tuffin, Marquis de

Tufton, Lady Caroline: impending marriage of, **17**: 402

Tugaloo river: S.C. cedes territory west of, **7**: 21

Tuggle, John: signs petition, **6**: 293

tuition: at grammar schools, **2**: 532

Tuley, William: signs petition, **6**: 290

tulip bulbs: TJ sends to Cary, **10**: 228

tulip tree: Malesherbes comments on, **9**: 453; TJ seeks plants and seeds of, **11**: 46, 90, 121; **13**: 187

Tull, Jethro, **12**: 18

tuna, **11**: 442

Tuningius, Gerardus: *Apophthegmata* ordered by TJ, **15**: 223

Tunis (Tanis): U.S. treaty of amity and commerce, **6**: 396; **7**: 263, 269, 496; **8**: 19, 46; **9**: 325, 358; naval weakness of, **7**: 639; U.S. relations with, **8**: 61-2; **9**: 469; **10**: 71, 241, 396; relations with Venice, **8**: 69; tribute, **8**: 71, 72, 419; **10**: 207; relations with Turkey, **9**: 531; effect of blockade of Algiers on, **10**: 177; hostility of, **10**: 246, 248; relations with Morocco, **10**: 359; relations with Spain, **14**: 46

Tunis, Bey of. *See* Hammuda Bey

Tunkins, John, **3**: 542n

Turberville, Betty Tayloe Corbin (Mrs. George Lee Turberville), **5**: 678n

Turberville, George (father of Maj. Turberville), **5**: 410

Turberville, Maj. George Lee: letters to, **4**: 605; **5**: 121, 250-1; letters from, **4**: 594-5, 624-5; **5**: 201-2; votes against bill for religious freedom, **2**: 549n; and Westover Affair, **4**: 668, 669, 680, 690; **5**: 48-9, 98-9, 180, 250-1, 261, 674n, 675n-80n, 682n, 683n, 684n-5n, 688, 690, 693, 694, 695, 696; biographical note, **5**: 678n; retires to Westmoreland, **5**: 685n; letters from, to Steuben, **5**: 698-9, 699-700, 700-1, 702; list of charges against, **5**: 701-2; letter from, to Madison, cited, **14**: 4; mentioned, **5**: 410

Turberville, Martha Lee (Mrs. George Turberville): robbed by British soldiers, **5**: 121n; son of, **5**: 678n

Turckheim, Jean de: payment to, **13**: 147, 149n, 167, 301

turf: as fuel, **13**: 26

Turgot, Anne Robert Jacques: Mazzei comments on, **7**: 390; letter from, to Price, cited, **8**: 54; material by in *Encyclopédie Méthodique*, **10**: 8n; biography by Condorcet sent to TJ, **10**: 354, 397, 404; Adams replies to, **11**: 239; **12**: 56, 291; biography by P. S. Dupont, **12**: 213; criticism of America, **12**: 579; epigram on Franklin, **13**: 326, 327n; friendship with Dupont, **14**: 40; writings on economics, **16**: 449; mentioned, **14**: 437; **15**: 384

Turin, Italy: regulations on rice export, **11**: 339; tobacco trade, **11**: 353; TJ comments on, **11**: 435, 586; **13**: 272; proposed import of whale oil by, **11**: 516; Short describes, **14**: 27; refugees at, **18**: 502

Turin Royal Academy of Sciences: *Mémoires* asked for Franklin and American Philosophical Society, **11**: 468

Turk, Mr.: and bill establishing ferries, **2**: 456

Turkey: as market for American rice, **2**: 210; **15**: 13, 22, 37-8, 372, 408-9, 444, 450, 451; Russo-Austrian alliance against, **6**: 389, 437; U.S. treaty of amity and commerce, **6**: 393; **7**: 48, 263, 267, 496; **9**: 407; war against predicted, **6**: 433; relations with Russia, **6**: 469, 471, 540, 567, 568; **7**: 3, 5, 16, 31, 41; **10**: 330, 405, 605, 613, 624, 629, 634, 650; **11**: 476, 490; **12**: 108, 109, 110, 111, 113, 128, 132, 134, 145, 152, 157, 160-1, 166, 167, 174, 292, 307, 320, 361, 446, 448, 490, 564; relations with Austria, **6**: 540, 567, 568; **7**: 501; **8**: 4, 149, 226, 228, 236, 237-8, 245, 261, 287, 300, 373, 399, 418, 457, 460, 553, 592; **9**: 151; **10**: 330; **12**: 464, 482, 483, 564; **15**: 622; **16**: 201; **20**: 311, 535, 586, 656, 677; freedom of trade on rivers, **7**: 405; part in possible European war, **7**: 506, 509, 514, 515-6, 517, 518, 566, 577; TJ's comments on, **8**: 287, 300; relations with Barbary States, **8**: 622; and U.S. minister to, **9**: 376, 407; relations with U.S., **9**: 442, 539-40, 590; **10**: 329, 396, 405, 536; **14**: 288; relations with Algiers, **9**: 527,

531, 550, 553; **12**: 182; **17**: 15; relations with Tripoli, **9**: 531; relations with Tunis, **9**: 531; mediation among Algiers, Austria and Russia, **9**: 532; Barclay offers to undertake mission to, **9**: 566; utility of U.S. treaty with, **9**: 567-8, 595, 611, 612; **10**: 71; relations with Spain, **9**: 568; relations with France, **9**: 649; **12**: 309, 482; foreign relations, **10**: 224, 240, 247; **12**: 446, 447; relations with Morocco, **10**: 359; letters from Emperor of Morocco recommending U.S., **10**: 391; relations with Venice, **10**: 405; relations with Britain, **10**: 405; **14**: 665; war with Austria and Russia, **11**: 334; **12**: 616, 672-3, 682; **14**: 211-2, 328, 333, 375, 387, 531, 597; **16**: 538, 541; withdrawal from Europe predicted, **12**: 190; war with Russia, **12**: 209; **13**: 103, 124-6, 134, 139, 145, 212, 215-6, 388, 404-5, 438, 455, 456, 458, 465, 475, 510, 531, 538, 565, 572; **14**: 186, 212, 305, 366, 370, 429, 443, 444-5, 448, 482, 506, 516; **18**: 86, 354, 452-3, 477-9, 504, 593, 606-7; **19**: 418, 552; **20**: 169, 303, 327, 369, 410, 535, 658; desire of Austria to annex, **12**: 311; interest of Britain and France in, **12**: 327; insurrections in, **12**: 442; tribute to Morocco, **12**: 462; ambassador to Spain, **13**: 92; Black Sea naval action, **13**: 126, 134, 404, 427-8, 436-8, 454-6, 458-9, 461, 465, 471, 483, 488-9, 491, 497, 503, 529, 580, 632-3, 650; **17**: 593, 627-8; peace with Russia and Austria, **13**: 263; **14**: 645, 652-3, 661, 672; **15**: 110, 187, 195; **16**: 254-5; **18**: 452-3, 606-7; **20**: 582-3, 704, 712; war with Austria, **14**: 414-5; relations with Prussia, **16**: 304-5; **20**: 649, 658, 673; treaty with Poland, **19**: 270; relations with Denmark, **20**: 169; relations with Sweden, **20**: 169; relations with Hungary, **20**: 561
Turkey Island: list of vessels at, **5**: 152n; vessels and supplies ordered to, **5**: 173, 177, 184; militia ordered to, **5**: 544n, 545, 549
turkeys: in Germany, **13**: 17
Turkheim & Peuchen: payments to, **15**: 88
Turnbull, Andrew: Edward Rutledge describes, **15**: 11-2; encourages rice trade with Turkey, **15**: 13, 22; on Carthaginian settlements in America,

15: 14-5, 451; biographical note on, **15**: 16n; advises force in dealing with Algerians, **16**: 390, 600
Turnbull, John: introduced to TJ, **12**: 643; delivers meteorological observation to TJ, **12**: 691; **13**: 95; letter from, to Cathalan, cited, **13**: 180
Turnbull, Marmie & Company: bill paid, **7**: 56; draft on, **7**: 111
Turnbull, Robert: marriage of, **16**: 300
Turnbull & Co., **4**: 118
Turner, Capt. (captain of the *Garrick*), **7**: 429
Turner, Mr.: and Hessian fly, **20**: 460
Turner, Francis: quills purchased from, **17**: 360
Turner, George: petition of, **6**: 448-52
Turner, John, **4**: 542
Turner, Thomas: criticizes TJ, **4**: 266, 267n-8n
Turner, Zephaniah, **7**: 6
turnips: French and American compared, **10**: 641
turnpikes: in Alexandria, Va., **14**: 304, 529-30
turnspit: Short describes, **14**: 43, 382
turpentine: Va. bill on, **2**: 444-7; U.S. export of, **7**: 372; **8**: 201, 202, 203; **10**: 147; Portugal's desire to import, **9**: 19; French duty on, **10**: 602; **11**: 516, 541; **12**: 163, 165, 167, 172, 469, 480-1; **13**: 72, 74
Turpin, Baron de: takes measurements of Natural Bridge, **19**: 300n
Turpin, Horatio, **4**: 224
Turpin, Mary Jefferson (Mrs. Thomas Turpin), **4**: 224; **7**: 137
Turpin, Philip: letters to, **6**: 324-33; **7**: 134-7; TJ on legal training of, **1**: 24; letter to cited, **7**: 116; copy of *Notes on Virginia* sent to, **12**: 133; in England, **19**: 543n
Turpin, Thomas: letter to, **1**: 23-5; letters from, **4**: 224-5, 253; **6**: 194-5; TJ rents house of, **6**: 195, 200; letter to cited, **6**: 330n; TJ purchases lot from, **7**: 601, 606; Richmond property of, **8**: 344; mentioned, **7**: 137
Turtle creek: settlement on, **2**: 101
turtle shells: U.S. import of, **10**: 148
Turton, Dr. John: treats George III, **14**: 50
Tuscany: and U.S. treaty with, **6**: 393; **7**: 48, 263, 267, 424n, 430, 437-8, 533, 561-2, 573-4, 649; **8**: 104-10, 140-1, 152, 173, 187-95, 205, 608; **9**: 26, 45, 46n-7n; **10**: 286; **15**: 616-7;

UNITED STATES (*cont.*)

499; manners described by Moustier, **12**: 589-90; Moustier complains of formality, **12**: 662; Capital. *See* Residence Act; seat of U.S. government on Potomac

Agents in France

letters to, **12**: 209-10, 475

Army

drafting of men in peacetime, **7**: 412; **8**: 77; report to Congress on, **7**: 651; disbandment of, **9**: 608-9; **10**: 18; pay, **10**: 490n; for use against Indians, **10**: 578, 633-4. *See also* Continental army

Boundaries

defined in Definitive Peace Treaty, **6**: 457-8; with Spain, **7**: 433; **8**: 138n; Passamaquoddy Bay and St. Croix river, **16**: xxxiv-v, 52 (map), 283, 284n, 326

Commerce

R. H. Lee's views on, **2**: 210-1; with southern Europe urged by Mazzei, **7**: 63; restrictions on, **7**: 231, 523-4; **8**: 209, 354-5; of northern states, **7**: 323-55 (editorial note and documents); restrictions on with Canada recommended by Monroe, **7**: 460; decline of, **8**: 382, 545; Adams' opinions on, **8**: 477; European opinions on, **8**: 479; Hogendorp's opinions on, **8**: 503-4; *entrepôts*, **8**: 515; state duties on foreign goods, **8**: 580-1; TJ's opinions on, **8**: 633; Mediterranean countries, **9**: 75, 500; **18**: 369-445 (editorial note and documents); disadvantages of state regulation, **9**: 333-5; lack of credit a detriment to, **9**: 504; area free from Algerian interference, **9**: 616; lack of commodities for export, **10**: 247; Brissot de Warville's writings on, **10**: 262; Coxe's book on, **11**: 661; objections to constitutional provisions on, **12**: 254-5; compared with European, **12**: 649; "Further Documents Concerning American Trade," **13**: 59-91 (editorial note and documents); Washington on, **13**: 557; "Documents on American Commercial Policy," **16**: 513-30 (editorial note and documents); "Commercial and Diplomatic Rela-

UNITED STATES (*cont.*)

tions with Great Britain,"**18**: 220-306 (editorial note and documents); "Memoranda and Statistics on American Commerce," **19**: 121-39. *See also* individual countries, products, and states

Congress

pays TJ's expenses as minister, **14**: 17, 290; organizes national government, **14**: 17; **15**: 6-7, 418; and consular convention, **14**: 67-90; **19**: 304-8; elections of 1788-1789, **14**: 339-40, 352, 394-5, 529, 615, 619; **15**: 5-8; counts electoral votes (1789), **14**: 628; **15**: 6; difficulty of convening, **14**: 628; **15**: 6, 17; resolution on duties, **15**: 114-5, 175, 225; debates commercial policy, **15**: 148, 153-4, 225-7; Madison praises, **15**: 154; Madison on difficulties of proceedings, **15**: 224-5; establishes executive departments, **15**: 227-9; salaries of members, **15**: 264n; TJ on proceedings of, **15**: 336-7; praised in London, **15**: 414; and foreign debt, **16**: 316, 317n; TJ on right of adjournment, **17**: 195-7; Short's account with, **17**: 262; **18**: 447-50; collection of acts sent to members, **17**: 474, 475n; elections of 1790, **18**: 82-3; receives Northwest Territory documents, **18**: 166-8, 177, 192, 216; and navigation bill, **18**: 229-30, 232, 234-5, 237-9; **19**: 571; and TJ's reports on commerce, **18**: 230-1; receives Washington's messages on Morris' mission to Britain, **18**: 232-3, 304-6; and TJ's reports on Mediterranean, **18**: 409-10, 412; and Algerian captives, **18**: 409-10, 412, 414n, 429n, 444-5; and tonnage acts, **18**: 521-4, 546-8; and residence bill, **19**: 3-73 (editorial note); receives translation of Siéyès' letter, **19**: 85; letter to, from M. Benière, **19**: 107; and the fisheries, **19**: 144, 153, 155, 158n, 159; and N.C. land cession, **19**: 605-6; and desalination of sea water, **19**: 610-1; recesses, **19**: 642; place of meeting, **20**: 30-1; proposal for cooling meeting place, **20**: 596-7. *See also* United States: House of Representatives, Senate

UNITED STATES (*cont.*)

3, 415; authorized in Constitution, **18**: 397; TJ's Proposal to Use Force against the Barbary States, **18**: 416-22; Barry's views on construction of vessels for, **19**: 271-2

Population

by states, **10**: 34-5, 54; growth rate, **10**: 56; **11**: 617. *See also* census

President

election methods, **12**: 102, 272; office of discussed in Federal Convention, **12**: 272; tenure of office, **12**: 272, 351, 356, 396, 416, 425, 440-1, 558, 571; **13**: 128, 208, 232, 378, 443, 490, 502, 619; **14**: 370, 650-1, 678-9, 688; power of appointment, **12**: 273; relation to states, **12**: 275; W. S. Smith fears powers of, **12**: 391; veto power, **12**: 440; Lafayette on powers of, **12**: 460; J. P. Jones fears temptation of power, **13**: 581, 583-4; election (1789), **13**: 620; **14**: 385; **15**: 6, 92; titles of honor for proposed, **15**: 115, 147-8, 315, 336-7, 418; power to remove officers, **15**: 217, 227-8; salary, **15**: 263n, 277, 418. *See also* cabinet, U.S.; Washington, George

Public Finance

in Revolution, **2**: 30; **3**: 321-2, 335-6, 369-70, 379-80, 402, 405, 424, 506; **4**: 366-9; **5**: 415, 520; **6**: 14, 469, 510, 531-3, 558-64; TJ recommends establishment of banks in Europe, **2**: 224; decline of credit abroad, **2**: 267; requisitions on states, **3**: 105; **7**: 5, 6, 8, 359, 592; **8**: 218, 286-7, 325, 334, 369; **9**: 176-7, 185, 334, 480, 612, 666; **10**: 14, 225, 251, 277, 298; **12**: 342, 444; domestic debt, **5**: 520, 669; **6**: 14, 531-3, 558-64; **8**: 331, 674-5, 684; **10**: 24; **13**: 467; pamphlet on debts issued by Congress, **6**: 269; military expenses, **6**: 530; assumption of state debts discussed, **6**: 539; partial payment of debts by new states proposed, **6**: 604, 608, 614; reduction of expenditures, **7**: 12-5; Grand Committee of Congress on, **7**: 53, 65-80, 90; circular letter from Washington to the states on, **7**: 54-5; non-payment of debts, **7**: 65-80; **9**: 217-8, 479-81; **10**: 135-6; **12**:

UNITED STATES (*cont.*)

696; payment of debts, **7**: 71-2, 94, 114, 123, 145, 226, 232, 497; **8**: 154; **10**: 17, 311; **12**: 583, 623-4; and land sales, **7**: 145; **8**: 482-3; **11**: 470, 481; **12**: 103, 426, 439, 446; TJ's account of, **7**: 212-5; Hogendorp's queries on, **7**: 298; taxation, **7**: 542; **10**: 12-3; **12**: 326; power of Congress over, **7**: 573; foreign debts, **8**: 87, 196, 218, 331, 402, 541, 630, 655, 674-5, 684; **10**: 12-3, 23-4, 44, 366; **11**: 19; **12**: 397, 417-8, 420-1, 421-2, 429, 432, 566, 573-4; private loan, **8**: 311-3; securities, **8**: 312, 331, 531, 630; **9**: 123-4; Vergennes' inquiry concerning, **8**: 374; salaries of ministers and foreign agents, **8**: 561, 582, 583, 664; **12**: 147, 341, 695; credit, **8**: 588-9, 633; **10**: 406; **11**: 6-9, 62-5; **12**: 418, 432, 456-7, 472-3, 485, 496, 506-7, 508, 543-9, 566, 573-4, 581-2, 623, 672; bills drawn by foreign agents, **8**: 589-91; disbursement practices in Europe, **9**: 225; money in Paris to meet bills, **9**: 243; depletion of treasury, **9**: 608; **10**: 598; TJ's comments on article in *Encyclopédie Méthodique*, **10**: 7n; possible bankruptcy of, **10**: 17; emission of paper money, **10**: 54; account with Grand, **10**: 194; **11**: 607-8, 609; revenues, **10**: 298; **11**: 160-1; resolution of Congress authorizing loan, **10**: 490n; TJ's unsuccessful efforts to obtain loan in France, **10**: 605; Brissot de Warville's queries on debt and credit, **11**: 7-8; TJ's comments on eventual solvency, **11**: 128; settlement of accounts, **11**: 308-9; payment of salaries, **11**: 382, 383; funds at Amsterdam, **12**: 171, 172, 189; disbursement of funds by Treasury delayed, **12**: 542-3; Ast's account, **12**: 625; summary of funding operation executed by Adams and TJ in Amsterdam, **12**: 674; sale of domestic debts to foreigners, **12**: 700; transfer of foreign debt to Netherlands proposed, **13**: 127, 130-1, 556; **14**: 194; **15**: 472n-3n, 474-5; **17**: 425; credit in Europe, **13**: 127-31; proposed funding of foreign debt, **14**: 190-209 (editorial note

UNITED STATES (*cont.*)

and documents); abstract of G. Morris' plan, **15:** 123-4; Cutting suggests loan to France, **15:** 440-1; plans for revenue, **16:** 125-6; TJ's opinion on, **17:** 425-30; proposed purchase of debt to France, **20:** 175-203 (editorial note and documents). *See also* coinage; foreign debt; impost; France: Loan to U.S.; Netherlands: loan to U.S.; Willink, Van Staphorst & Hubbard

Secretary of State

clerks and assistants, **16:** 181n, 182, 353, 385, 485-6, 548; **17:** 349n-50n, 351n-3n, 356n-9n; **18:** 73; office established, **16:** 181n; state laws collected by, **17:** 338, 340n, 484-5, 530-3, 607-8, 625-6, 647; **18:** 73n, 125-30, 137-9, 151, 346, 360-1, 461-71, 595; **19:** 632; **20:** 89, 90, 91, 92, 155-6, 326, 388, 565, 681; salary account, **17:** 358-9, 596, 598n; recording of letters and papers, **17:** 381-7; summary of letters received (Sep.-Oct. 1790), **17:** 644-5. *See also* Department of State, U.S.; Jefferson, Thomas: Secretary of State

Senate

letter to, **19:** 238-9; method of election, **12:** 102, 273; representation of states in, **12:** 275; authority over foreign agents,, **12:** 696; eligibility for re-election in, **13:** 208, 232, 378, 443, 490; consular convention ratified by, **14:** 88-90; election (1788), **14:** 394-5, 415, 529, 560, 615; federalists in, **14:** 529; address to Washington (May 7, 1789), **15:** 147, 148n, 214-6 (text); resolution on TJ's leave and Short's appointment, **15:** 202, 203n; salaries of senators, **15:** 264n; TJ's opinion on powers respecting diplomatic appointments, **16:** 378-82; motion to move to Philadelphia, **16:** 444, 445, 449, 474; letters to, from Washington, **18:** 192, 216, 571; **19:** 292-4; pro-British sentiment in, **18:** 269-72; **19:** 88, 89; and Algerian captives, **18:** 409-10, 412, 444; resolution on coinage, **18:** 456-7; and Franklin's death, **19:** 78-106; letter to, from Tobias Lear, quoted, **19:**

UNITED STATES (*cont.*)

83; attitude toward France, **19:** 85n, 89, 93; and protocol toward foreign communications, **19:** 87; attitude toward Saint-Domingue, **19:** 89; and tonnage duties, **19:** 89; anti-republican attitudes, **19:** 103; and the fisheries, **19:** 148, 151n, 152, 153n, 160, 165n; approves appointments of Anderson and Murry, **19:** 404; funds money for negotiations with Morocco, **19:** 535; rejects bill for federal buildings, **20:** 88. *See also* United States: Congress; individual states

Vice President

choice of, **13:** 502; **14:** 4, 17-8, 275-6, 302, 344, 385; election (1789), summary, **15:** 92; titles of honor for rejected, **15:** 115; salary of, **15:** 263n-4n, 277, 418. *See also* Adams, John; cabinet, U.S.

United States Chronicle: Howell encloses, **16:** 452; publishes laws, **17:** 477

Universal Magazine of Knowledge and Pleasure, **6:** 538

Unquachog Indians: TJ's vocabulary of language, **20:** xxxii, 384 (illus.), 449-52, 467-70 (text)

Updike & Earl: owners of *Nancy*, **17:** 420, 421n; letter to quoted, **17:** 421n

upholstery: U.S. import of, **10:** 147

Upshaw, Thomas: letter from, **17:** 291

Upshur, Arthur: report on petition of, **1:** 652-3

Upton, Mr. (cabinet maker): boxes for medals, **16:** 65n, 77, 78, 203-4, 271; **17:** 632; **18:** 450; money for payment stolen, **16:** 203

Upton, Clotworthy (afterwards Lord Templeton): land grant, **8:** 85

Upton, Clotworthy, Jr.: land claim of, **8:** 85-6

Upton, Francis: land claim of, **8:** 85-6, 482, 587

Upton, Joseph: signs petition, **6:** 290

Upton, Sophia: land claim of, **8:** 85-6

Upton, Thomas: in Albemarle co. militia, **1:** 666; signs petition, **6:** 290

Uranus: called Georgium Sidus by English, **8:** 117; described by Mayer, **8:** 299, 419; and calculation of *Connaissance de temps*, **8:** 575; **9:** 355; satellites, **11:** 162; **12:** 30

Urbanna, Va.: ferry at, **2:** 455

Vanet, M. (*cont.*)
581; leaves for Va., **13**: 574; correspondence with missing, **13**: 604n; mentioned, **14**: 182, 369

Vanhorn, Col.: in British service, **1**: 659

Van Horne, Mr.: mail contract, **20**: 666

Vanhorne, Catherine: engaged to Jacob Read, **8**: 79

vaninium, **9**: 453

Van Meersen. *See* Meersch, Gen. van der

Van Meter, Garret: letter to, **5**: 565-6; letters from, **4**: 688-9; **5**: 409-10, 455, 513-5; letter from, to auditors, **5**: 515; letter from quoted, **6**: 67n

Vanmeter, Solomon: recommended as cavalry officer, **5**: 514

Vanmiter, Isaac: votes for bill for religious freedom, **2**: 549n

Van Moorsel, Theodore, & Co.: in *Rachel* case, **20**: 508n

Vann, John (Joseph): interprets for Cherokees, **2**: 71, 72, 93; and sale of Indian lands, **2**: 88, 89; dispute with Henderson, **2**: 96, 97, 108

Van Rensselaer (Ransaleer), Jacob: in Albany riot, **13**: 549

Van Rensselaer, James: appointed deputy muster master general, **1**: 439, 440

Van Rensselaer, Jeremiah: letter to, **20**: 619; and Osmont's land claim, **20**: 617-8, 619

Van Schaack, Peter: compiles N.Y. state laws, **17**: 484-5

Van Staphorst. *See* Staphorst, van

Van Wart, Isaac: and capture of André, **4**: 487; **16**: 54n

Vanwart, William: supplies purchased from, **17**: 360

Varick (Varrick), Col. Richard: elected to N.Y. Assembly, **10**: 154

Varick and Jones: publish N.Y. state laws, **17**: 484

Varicourt, Rouph de, Chevalier: killed at Versailles, **16**: 278

Varina (Va. estate): given to T. M. Randolph, Jr., **16**: 135, 155n, 189; Randolph's interest in, **16**: 385, 441, 474, 475n; **17**: 274; sale of, **17**: 275; **18**: 43; TJ inquires about, **20**: 161

Varina, Va.: ferry at, **2**: 458

Varnum, Gen. James Mitchell: R.I. delegate to Congress, **4**: 606; **6**: 111n; letter to, from Greene, quoted, **5**: 570n; letter from cited, **12**: 105; appointed

temporary judge of western territory, **12**: 256; in committee on medals, **16**: 57n; pamphlet on Trevett *v.* Weeden, **16**: 453n-4n

Varus, Publius Quintilius: encampment of, **13**: 13, 264

Vasari, Giorgio: *Vite de' piu Eccellenti Pittori*, **12**: 245

Vassal, M., **9**: 303

Vatican: treaty of amity and commerce with, **7**: 263, 267, 424n, 575; Short describes, **14**: 381, 405-6, 449. *See also* Pamphili, Prince Doria (papal nuncio)

Vattel, Emmerich de: *Law of Nations* (*Droit des gens*), **1**: 406; **16**: 481; cited on right to booty, **4**: 571-3; cited in Conn.-Pa. dispute, **6**: 490; cited on extradition, **6**: 513; **7**: 593; cited in support of privilege of foreign minister, **11**: 495n; Jay cites, **17**: 135; Hamilton cites, **17**: 144, 145, 147

Vaucheres (Vaucheret), Jean Baptiste: sent to TJ from Vincennes, **4**: 479

Vaucluse, France: fountain at, **11**: xxxiii, 358, 369, 414 (illus.), 443; TJ describes, **11**: 443; Petrarch's chateau at, **13**: 23, 104, 267, 273

Vaudreuil (Veaudreuil), Louis Philippe de Rigaud, Marquis de: letters to, **12**: 116; **13**: 182-3; letter from, **12**: 20; captain of *Le Fendant*, **3**: 210n, 247; consulted on defense of York, **3**: 247-8; promises French division, **6**: 236, 242; Breck as protegé of, **11**: 317; interest in Monset case, **12**: 143-4; leaves Versailles, **15**: 261, 289, 300

Vaughan, Mr., **9**: 554

Vaughan, Benjamin: letters to, **10**: 646-8; **11**: 532-3; **13**: 394-8; **14**: 640-1; **15**: 133-4, 425-6; **16**: 578-80; **20**: 391-2, 420; letters from, **11**: 69-70, 162, 195; **13**: 36-8, 112, 241-2, 346, 459-61; **14**: 351-2, 673-4, 707-8; **15**: 102-3, 146-7, 182-3; **16**: 274-6; **17**: 514-6, 619-20; **18**: 10, 115-7, 479; Rush introduces to TJ, **6**: 223; sympathy with America, **9**: 399n; invites Adams and TJ to visit steam mill, **9**: 401n; letter from quoted, **9**: 488n; letters to cited, **11**: 47; **16**: xliii, 276n; and hygrometers, **13**: 37, 395, 459-60; *The Repository*, **13**: 37n, 367, 376, 395; **15**: 182, 204, 425; introduces Baillie to TJ, **13**: 112; introduces

Stewart to TJ, **13**: 241-2; on Rumsey's scientific investigations, **13**: 346, 459; **15**: 145, 172, 404; on air pump, **13**: 460; on climate, **13**: 460; on odometer, **13**: 460; introduces Cleghorne to TJ, **14**: 351-2; on dry culture of rice, **14**: 673-4, 707-8; sends rice seed to TJ, **14**: 707-8; **15**: 133, 425; **16**: 274, 276n, 492, 495, 496n, 578; **17**: 564-5; **18**: 97; letters from cited, **15**: 80n; **16**: 496n, 616n; TJ sends information on cod liver oil, **16**: xliii; letter to quoted, **16**: 242n; sends mutiny on the *Bounty* account to TJ, **16**: 274-6, 578; letter to, sent to Nepean, **16**: 580n; correspondence with Anderson, **17**: 514, 516n; on British politics and government, **17**: 619-20; suggests prizes for arts and sciences, **17**: 620; Report on Weights and Measures sent to, **17**: 620; Franklin sends autobiography ms. to, **18**: 91n, 94n; on universal standard of weights and measures, **18**: 116-7; letter to, from John Vaughan, quoted, **18**: 238n; conveys news of Franklin's death, **19**: 79-80; concerned about U.S. maple sugar production, **20**: 344n; mentioned, **3**: 149; **9**: 363n; **11**: 277; **13**: 623; **15**: 430

Vaughan, John: letter to, **19**: 114; and book on megatherium, **14**: xxx; house bought by, **17**: 237, 238; letter from, to Benjamin Vaughan, quoted, **18**: 238n; sends paper to Coxe, **18**: 461; and Franklin's death, **19**: 98, 100; mentioned, **4**: 540; **11**: 363, 402; **18**: 458

Vaughan, Gen. John: embarkation of British troops under, **2**: 265

Vaughan, Sir John: *Reports and Arguments*, **11**: 548; **16**: 277, 481; **20**: 330-1; TJ's opinion of, **20**: 378

Vaughan, Samuel: judges harpsichord experiment, **8**: 50

Vaughan, Samuel, Jr.: letter to, **18**: 97-8; letter from, **17**: 564-5; power of attorney for Ingenhousz, **13**: 488n; Ingenhousz' work on vegetables sent to, **15**: 119; on mountain rice culture, **17**: 564-5; letter from cited, **17**: 565n; rice seed sent to TJ, **18**: 97

Vaughan, William: *New and Old Principles of Trade Compared*, **13**: 242n; **15**: 102-3, 133, 426; suggests introduction

of bamboo in America, **17**: 515; mentioned, **9**: 363n; **15**: 103

Vaughn, Mr.: trip up Hudson with Monroe, **7**: 392

Vaughter, William, **4**: 541

Vaugondy, Robert de: *Partie de l'Amérique Septentrionale*, **6**: 598n

Vauguyon, Duc de la. See La Vauguyon

Vaune. See Vosne

Vaune river. See Huveaune

Vause (Vance, Voss), Capt. William: recommended as cavalry officer, **5**: 514

Vautelet, Jean: letter to, **12**: 188; letter from, **12**: 196; bill on, **12**: 209; letter from cited, **12**: 307

Vautelet, Jean Baptiste: settles in N.H., **12**: 188

Vaux, Noël, Comte et Maréchal de: death of, **13**: 492

Vavaseur, Capt. (master of *Neptune*), **11**: 192n

Veaune. See Vosne

Veaux, Jacques de: as creditor of Langeac, **10**: 456

Veillant, M. de: *Travels of M. de Veillant in Africa from 1780 to 1785*, **16**: 47-8

Vella, Joseph, Abbé: translation of Livy from Arabic (hoax), **13**: 382, 383n

Velleius Paterculus, Marcus: TJ seeks works by, **20**: 634n

Venable, Abraham Bedford: candidate for Congress, **16**: 130n; portrait of, **18**: xxxvii, 268 (illus.); in Reynolds case, **18**: xxxviii, 634-5, 639-40, 642, 644n, 645-50, 659-65, 669n, 671, 679, 682; correspondence with Hamilton cited, **18**: 661-2, 663-4

Vendangeur (ship): wines shipped in, **11**: 396n; bears letter for TJ, **19**: 261

Vendres, bay of, **11**: 450

Venegas, Miguel: *Noticia de la California*, **11**: 554

Venetian blinds: TJ describes, **11**: 440; orders, **16**: 350

Venice: U.S. treaty of amity and commerce, **6**: 393; **7**: 48, 263, 267, 424n, 427; freedom of trade on rivers of, **7**: 405; relations with Barbary States, **7**: 511; **8**: 37, 69, 72; **9**: 527, 528, 619; **10**: 358, 486, 562n, 563n, 565n; alliance with Russia, **8**: 373, 418; relations with Turkey, **10**: 247, 405; **11**: 334; foreign relations, **10**: 251; Paradise family in, **13**: 315; Rutledge visits, **13**: 318; Short visits, **14**: 273,

Venice (*cont.*)
312, 377, 383; American medals sent
to, **16**: 67; Durfort appointed French
ambassador to, **19**: 637
Venice, ambassador to France. *See* Dolfin, Daniele
Ventimiglia: TJ describes, **11**: 441, 442
Ventura Caro, Gen.: introduced to TJ
by Carmichael, **14**: 642, 643n
Venus (goddess), **8**: 548
Venus (planet): transit of, **2**: 210
Venus (ship), **20**: 361n
Venus' flytrap. *See dionaea muscipula*
Vérac, Charles Olivier de Saint-Georges,
Marquis de: minister to Netherlands,
9: 138; **10**: 354; **12**: 167n; recommends Dumas to TJ, **9**: 180-1; son's
tutor, **9**: 279; correspondence with
Vergennes, **9**: 303; **12**: 675-6; minister
to Switzerland, **12**: 68, 153; mentioned, **9**: 301
Vercelli, Italy: TJ describes, **11**: 435;
13: 272; rice from, **11**: 587, 646
Ver Cnocke, Francis James: U.S. vice
consul for Portugal, **20**: 262
Verdier, Lieut. Baptiste: taken prisoner
by British, **6**: 634
Vergennes (ship), **8**: 472
Vergennes, Charles Gravier, Comte de:
letters to, **8**: 315, 385-93, 631, 656-7;
9: 31-8, 50-1, 76-7, 119, 192, 307,
442-3, 601; **10**: 261, 467, 472-3; **11**:
140; letters from, **8**: 164-5, 458, 680,
685-6; **9**: 72-3, 180-1, 590-1, 597-8;
10: 497, 507-8, 531, 551; correspondence with La Luzerne, **6**: 114, 419;
advice rejected by Adams, **6**: 128; reportedly recommends minister to U.S.,
6: 276; instructions to Franklin regarding, **6**: 398; propositions from, **7**:
269; and Longchamps-Marbois affair,
7: 308n; **8**: 374; esteem for Täscher,
7: 387; relations with Mazzei, **7**: 388,
389, 390; **15**: 614; Lafayette asked to
write to, **7**: 417, 422; sent papers respecting Iroquois, **7**: 440, 448n; negotiations with, **7**: 494, 496; relations
with TJ, **8**: 33n, 226, 361, 372; **9**:
107-15, 137, 139-46, 312-3, 501,
503; **11**: 280; and treaty with Netherlands, **8**: 44n; and Barbary States, **8**:
46-7, 82, 474; **10**: 265n, 562n, 565n;
correspondence with American Commissioners, **8**: 61-3, 120, 625-7; **18**:
376, 377n; letter to, from Le Maire,
cited, **8**: 132n; correspondence with

Barbé de Marbois, **8**: 139n, 384n; letters to cited, **8**: 150, 523, 542; **10**:
114, 474, 484, 631; **11**: 596; **12**: 76n;
16: 271n, 375; passports received
from, **8**: 172; **10**: 590, 619; **15**: 49;
application to, for newspapers, **8**: 297;
on Ramsay's history, **8**: 361n; removal
to Fontainebleau, **8**: 362; conference
with British chargé d'affaires, **8**: 372;
enquiry concerning U.S. finances, **8**:
374; complains of U.S. navigation acts,
9: 43; and case of *William and Catherine*, **9**: 52, 99; **10**: 100; and whale oil
duties, **9**: 88; and Mezières case, **9**:
113n, 127, 181-2, 259; recommendation of Dumas, **9**: 180-1, 235, 243,
562; petitioned for safe conduct, **9**:
293; correspondence with Vérac, **9**:
303; informed of TJ's visit to London,
9: 325; letters from cited, **9**: 367; **10**:
554; **12**: 211-2, 674, 675-6; correspondence with Calonne, **9**: 368n,
443n; and U.S.-French tobacco trade,
9: 387, 583-5; **11**: 599, 615-6; **17**:
414; correspondence with Otto, **9**:
451n; **10**: 278n, 492n; **11**: 130n-2n,
147n, 196n, 411n; **14**: 78-9; **18**:
390n, 517n; attitude toward U.S.-
French trade, **9**: 502; and U.S. treaty
with Turkey, **9**: 567-8, 590, 595, 611,
612; Gross case papers sent to, **10**: 70,
71; J. P. Jones requests letter to
French ambassador to Denmark, **10**:
209-10; letter of recommendation for
Mme Grégoire, **10**: 239; letter to,
from La Houze, cited, **10**: 281; Jay
urges TJ to discuss case of *South Carolina* with, **10**: 592; letter from
quoted, **10**: 640n; and publication of
TJ's confidential letter to Jay, **11**: 30;
illness of, **11**: 48, 95, 101, 118, 126,
127; attitude toward U.S., **11**: 95-6;
death of, **11**: 132n, 143, 144, 145,
163, 164, 180, 191, 217, 306n, 313,
482; **12**: 315; efforts to enlist influence
in Spanish negotiations, **11**: 222,
224n; successor of, **11**: 490; **12**: 502n;
and LaVayse and Puchelberg claim,
11: 593; Jay opposed to, **13**: 410n-1n;
and 1784 Consular Convention, **14**:
70-1, 77-8; **16**: 87n; and Lafayette's
plan to stop Algerian piracy, **18**: 378,
398; Jay's conversation with reported,
18: 380; and U.S. right to navigate
Mississippi, **20**: 652; mentioned, **7**:
438; **8**: 121, 140, 167, 222, 578; **9**:

24, 230, 237, 625, 643; **10**: 270, 295, 640; **11**: 96, 494n; **12**: 119, 154n; **13**: 53n, 409n; **14**: 76, 387n; **15**: 613; **16**: 505; **18**: 373, 410, 538n, 543

Vermanton, Château de, **11**: xxxiii, 414 (illus.)

Verme, Francesco, Count: letters to, **12**: 42-3; **13**: 356, 605; letter from, **12**: 587-9; and pendulum odometer, **11**: 437; aids TJ at Milan, **12**: 38-9, 42; Adams recommends, **12**: 43n; books sent to, **12**: 555; Shippen and Rutledge introduced to, by TJ, **13**: 356, 605; **14**: 41; Constitution sent to, **13**: 605; Short introduced to, **13**: 605; **14**: 41; mentioned, **12**: 198; **13**: 277

Verme, Francesco, Count (son): acquaintance with TJ at Milan, **11**: 586

Vermond, Matthieu Jacques, Abbé de: leaves Versailles, **15**: 289, 300

Vermont: admission to union, **6**: 164, 213, 506n; **10**: 13-4, 596; **11**: 221, 223; **13**: 494, 620; **15**: 154, 337, 418, 421; **18**: 83, 596; **19**: 364-81; **20**: 703; doctrine on dissolution of laws with change of government, **6**: 247-8; federal court to decide claims on, **6**: 505; dispute with N.Y., **7**: 120, 261-2, 630; **8**: 483, 684; **9**: 186; **11**: 286, 314, 383; papers relating to, **7**: 282; immigrants from Conn., **7**: 332; TJ comments on, **8**: 287; **19**: 376-77; dispute with Canada, **20**: 466-7; federal appointments in, **20**: 627-8

Vermont, Abbé de. *See* Vermond, Matthieu Jacques, Abbé de

Vermont Gazette: quoted, **18**: 266n; **20**: 441; TJ subscribes to, **20**: 443-4

Verner, Col., **4**: 323

Vernes, Jacob: letter to, **14**: 457; letters from, **11**: 513-4; **12**: 359, 607; **13**: 50-1; **14**: 391-3; **15**: 57-8, 129, 134-5, 150-1, 158-9, 313, 538-43, 545; **16**: 94-7, 116, 188; notes on rice, **11**: 592n; assists Bérard, **12**: 76n, 77n; *Mémoire pour des négocians de l'Orient, intéressés au commerce des Etats-Unis, contre la ferme générale*, **13**: 51, 52n, 54n-6n, 75-91 (text); as U.S. consul in L'Orient, **14**: 60; **15**: 374; letter to cited, **15**: 43n; relations with TJ, **15**: 135, 150; introduces Sabatier to TJ, **15**: 313; and rice trade, **15**: 448n, 544; correspondence with Brailsford & Morris, **15**: 538, 543-4; on timber, **15**: 539-40; consulship at Bordeaux, **15**:

540; **16**: 95; recommendations on consuls, **15**: 541-2; letters from cited, **16**: 97n; letter to, from Short, quoted, **16**: 97n; mentioned, **15**: 191n; **17**: 255n

Vernes & Cie.: letter from cited, **16**: 97n

Vernet, Mr.: asked to serve in British army, **1**: 473; attached to American cause, **1**: 474

Vernon, Mr.: sells horse, **17**: 418n

Vernon, M. de: letters to, **10**: 300; **13**: 506-7; letters from, **13**: 478; **14**: 409; claim against Mark, **9**: 219, 457; **10**: 519; **13**: 478, 507, 602; **14**: 409, 592-3; **16**: 22, 23; interest due, **11**: 351; letter from missing, **13**: 602n; leaves for America, **19**: 292; mentioned, **18**: 450

Vernon, France: riot over wheat storage at, **15**: 534

Vernon, George William: *Reports of Cases Argued and Adjudged in the Court of King's Bench*, **11**: 548

Vernon, Lieut. N., **5**: 40, 41

Vernon, Samuel: in Franklin's autobiography, **9**: 486

Vernon, Thomas: chancery reports cited, **1**: 57; **16**: 481

Vernon, William: letter to, **19**: 247; Bondfield asks TJ's aid for, **14**: 445, 621-2; Grand pays, **14**: 621; returns to America, **17**: 483-4, 631-2, 655, 656n

Vernon, William, Sr.: letter from, **17**: 483-4; son of, **17**: 631-2, 655

Vernon & Dangerard, **11**: 351

Verona, Italy: Short in, **14**: 311

Verplanck, N.Y.: British post at, **3**: 30; **4**: 29

Versailles, France: navy and foreign affairs building, **7**: xxviii, 453 (illus.); balloon trial at, **7**: 136; collection of paintings at, **10**: 250; proposed for assembly of powers against Barbary States, **10**: 570; Shippen describes court at, **12**: 502n-4n; *lit de justice* at, **13**: 189, 193n; disorder at, **15**: 208, 267, 289, 511, 531, 533; **16**: 4n; **17**: 9; Louis XVI and family at, **15**: 222; fountains at, **15**: 630

versification, English: compared to Latin and Greek, **10**: 498

Vert-galant, France, **13**: 32

Vertot, René Aubert de: TJ orders histories by sent to Peter Carr, **8**: 411

Vesey (Weasy), Capt.: and prisoners of war, **3**: 307, 327; contracts to supply salt, **3**: 326n, 327n

Vesey, Francis: cited, **1**: 596; *Reports of Cases Argued and Determined in the High Court of Chancery*, **6**: 489; **16**: 481

Vesoul, France: explosion at, **15**: 314-5

Vespucci, Amerigo: TJ seeks copy of portrait of, **12**: 245, 558; **14**: 440, 467-8; **15**: xxxv-vi, 152, 157, 425 (illus.)

vessels, American: TJ promises to d'Anmours, **3**: 618; TJ orders destruction of, **5**: 190, 614; and British clearance practices, **5**: 668; **9**: 407; and French trade, **9**: 391-2; **10**: 474, 493; **11**: 487-8, 602; **12**: 52, 191, 469, 480-1, 582; insurance rates on, **9**: 601-2; and Morocco, **10**: 347, 423, 425; **12**: 644; regulation in Île-de-France, **11**: 589; advantages of neutrality to, **12**: 210; Blackden inquires about foreign regulations on, **12**: 554-5; sale of, in French ports prohibited, **20**: 533

vessels, armed. *See* armed vessels

vessels, British: Va. imposes additional tonnage on, **9**: 201; use of American flag by, **12**: 234, 237, 351, 368

vessels, French: refuse to salute British flag, **8**: 456, 457

vessels, neutral: captured by British, **4**: 689-90

vessels, private: impressment of, **5**: 51, 55, 57, 125, 181, 186; on public service, **5**: 169-71; valuation of, **5**: 176; and trade treaty stipulations, **7**: 478. *See also* armed vessels, private

vessels, recaptured: convention on, **6**: 227n

vessels, sailing. *See* sailing vessels

vessels, unarmed: wartime protection advocated by TJ, **7**: 492

Vessey, Reidan, **3**: 542n

vestrymen: authority to execute contracts made by, **2**: 554

Vesuvius, Italy: Short describes, **14**: 573-4

veto power: in TJ's draft Va. Constitution, **1**: 342, 350, 360; not vested in Va. governor, **6**: 281n; in TJ's proposed revision of Va. Constitution (1783), **6**: 302-3; and federal government, **11**: 220, 409; of Congress over state legislatures, **12**: 273-4; history of, **12**: 274; in Constitution, **12**: 440

Vettori, Piero: *Trattato di Piero Vettori delle lodi e della coltivazione degli ulivi*, **12**: 527n

Veuve Samuel Joly aîné et fils: Barclay's debt to, **10**: 163, 164n; **11**: 495n

Veytard, M., **11**: 171n

Via, Micajah: signs petition, **1**: 588

Vialli, Marquis de: cited on Morocco tribute, **9**: 566-7

Viar, José (Joseph) Ignacio de: letters to, **16**: 472-3, 638-9; letters from, **17**: 572; **18**: 367; proposed letters to cited, **17**: 644; Spanish agent in U.S., **19**: 270; **20**: 558; mentioned, **17**: 340n

vibrating rod. *See* rod

Viburnum acerifolium: sample to be sent to France, **10**: 227

Viburnum nudum: sample to be sent to France, **10**: 227

vice consuls, American: lack of salary, **7**: 587; and trade treaty stipulations, **7**: 623; **9**: 420; functions of, **14**: 58-9; **17**: 423-4. *See also* consuls, American

Vicenza, Italy: Short admires architecture in, **14**: 311

Vicomte de Roth (ship), **8**: 377

Victoire (Victoria), Princess Louise Marie Thérèse (daughter of Louis XV), **9**: 487; **12**: 502n

Victor, Mr., **2**: 206

Victor Amédée Marie, king of Sardinia: American medals sent to, **16**: 67; orders French subjects to leave, **16**: 123

Victor, Frederick: letter to, **4**: 689

Victoria, Queen: TJ's letter to his daughter given to, **6**: 361n

Victory (ship): at Gosport, **16**: 427

Vidauban, France: TJ describes, **11**: 431

Vidourle river, **11**: 450

Viel, M.: letter from, **12**: 9; letter to, from Derieux, cited, **11**: 394

Vienna, Austria: Rutledge and Shippen plan to visit, **13**: 146, 318, 551

Vienne, France: Praetorian Palace, **11**: 226, 423; TJ comments on, **11**: 226, 420, 423; **13**: 273

Vierne & Veillon: bankruptcy of, **14**: 401

Vieuzac, M. de, **18**: 353

"View of C-o-n-ss on the Road to Philadelphia" (cartoon), **17**: xxxvi, 427 (illus.)

Vieyra, Antonio (Anthony): letters to, **11**: 85-6; **12**: 116-7; letters from, **12**: 43-4, 104-5; *Brevis, clara, facilis ac jocunda non solum Arabicam Linguam sed etiam hodiernam Persicam*, **11**: 85-6

Vigée-Lebrun, Marie Anne Elisabeth: portrait of Marie Antoinette and her three children, **12**: xxxiv; portraits at Salon praised, **12**: 69; TJ dislikes "fan colouring" of, **16**: 318

Vigan, Le, France: James Laurens makes bequests to indigent Protestants of, **11**: 582

Vigarous, Barthélemi, **10**: 427

Vigilant (ship), **8**: 530

villages: settlement on unappropriated land, **2**: 157, 163n-4n

Ville (Deville), Capt. Antony de: Asquith sends to Paris, **8**: 493, 494, 495, 496, 501, 518, 528; and crew of the *William and Catherine*, **9**: 98

Villebrune. *See* La Villebrune

Villedeuil, Pierre Charles Laurent de: letters to, **11**: 550; **14**: 536-7, 575; letters from, **11**: 533-4; **14**: 584; report to, **10**: 591; on free port status of Honfleur, **10**: 601; as comptroller general, **11**: 346, 356, 490; **12**: 153; **13**: 573; **15**: 279; and duty on fish oils, **11**: 488-9; **12**: 106; letter from cited, **11**: 578-9; memorial to, from Bordeaux merchants, cited, **12**: 57; appointed to Council of Finance, **12**: 70, 72; attitude toward tobacco monopoly, **12**: 78n; lack of will, **13**: 441; in ministry, **13**: 441, 455, 464, 492; **15**: 280, 286, 299; and Nesbitt's case, **14**: 527, 536-7, 575, 577, 584, 637; mentioned, **12**: 76n, 162, 163; **15**: 80

Villefranche, France: Short and Paradise family in, **13**: 634, 636

Villeneuf, France: Short in, **13**: 635

Villeneuve-Bargemont, Barthélemy Joseph, Comte de: in Estates General, **15**: 45

Vincennes, Château de: attacked by mob, **20**: 168

Vincennes, France: TJ visits, **14**: 498n

Vincennes (Auposte), Ill.: expedition against, **2**: 246, 256-8, 298; **3**: 5, 6, 26; crop failures at, **3**: 89; Le Gras' plea for inhabitants of, **3**: 328-9; garrison at, **3**: 416; **4**: 355, 479; **5**: 320; Va. asks reimbursement for reducing British post at, **4**: 387, 390n; **6**: 578; British prisoners taken at, **5**: 365; discontent at, **5**: 574; French settlement at, **6**: 61; protection of rights of citizens of, **6**: 579; Sargent reports on, **18**: 166, 179-86; land claims of citizens, **18**: 167; TJ's report on lands, **18**: 186-7

Vincent, Alexandre de: letter from, **5**: 430

vinegar: supplies for southern army, **3**: 645; **4**: 9; as medicine, **4**: 26; TJ sends to Hopkinson, **11**: 563; **13**: 144-5, 173, 185; **14**: xxxv, 33, 52, 54-5, 182, 324, 369, 371, 650; **15**: 16, 46; Maille's price list, **14**: xxxv, 55n, 73 (fac.); letters soaked with in quarantine, **14**: 184

vineyards: Ky., **8**: 126; Monticello, **9**: 253, 623; Burgundy, **11**: 416; Piedmont, **11**: 434; Lombardy, **11**: 437; Bordeaux, **11**: 455; Va., **12**: 127; Germany, **13**: 14-6, 19-21, 447, 448; France, with TJ's map, **13**: 28-32; Italy, **14**: 43

viniculture. *See* viticulture

Vining, John: letter from, **19**: 354-5; proposes department of domestic affairs, **15**: 217; **17**: 348n; and residence bill, **17**: 166n; on permanent seat of government, **17**: 453; **19**: 8-9; and motion to reply to French, **19**: 84n; carries letter declining appointment, **19**: 384; friendly to Anderson candidacy, **19**: 387; letter from, to Anderson, **19**: 404-5

Vinnard, Thomas: signs nonimportation resolutions (1770), **1**: 47

violin: TJ's agreement with John Randolph concerning, **1**: 66-7, 240-4

Vioménil, Antoine Charles du Houx, Baron de: commands French ships sent to Va., **4**: 631n; portrait in Trumbull's "Surrender of Cornwallis at Yorktown," **12**: xxxv, 60, 67 (illus.); mentioned, **5**: 262n

Virgil: translations of, **6**: 173; *Opera*, **12**: 678; **13**: 420; tomb of, **13**: 621; **14**: 572; mentioned, **8**: 407; **14**: 311

VIRGINIA: population of, **1**: 182; **7**: 303; **10**: 34, 35, 38, 54-6; designated as commonwealth, **1**: 368, 372, 382; European attitude toward, **3**: 93; French subjects in, **3**: 162-6; TJ desires French consul in, **3**: 197; seizure of vessels in, **10**: 388; commissioner of trade, **3**: 491; commissioner of war, **3**: 491; building of frigates for Spain, **4**: 12; commercial agents, **4**: 506-7; commissary of hides, **5**: 223; article on, in *Encyclopédie Méthodique*, **10**: 4n, 9n, 11n, 38-9; and capital site. *See* seat of U.S. government on Potomac

VIRGINIA (*cont.*)

Convention, **11:** 401; attitude toward, **12:** 254, 281, 284, 335-6, 345, 410, 423, 425, 444, 490, 583, 609, 616-7; proposal for amendments to, **12:** 409; **13:** 619; **14:** 385; popular support of, **12:** 411; ratification of, **12:** 490; **13:** 39, 50, 99-101, 103, 156-7, 160, 205, 209, 215, 232, 244, 248, 254, 277, 292, 315-6, 330n, 351-5, 359, 370, 392, 393n, 402-3, 412, 417, 434, 436n, 438, 440, 477, 480-1, 482, 495, 506, 511, 512n, 513, 514, 531, 539-40, 541-2, 549, 550, 571, 594, 619, 620; **14:** 458; and declaration of rights, **13:** 619; resolution on second Convention, **14:** xxxviii-xl, 329 (fac.), 558, 615; TJ on, **18:** 132-3

Convention

nature of anticipated, **1:** 118; and Declaration of Rights, **1:** 119, 526n; resolutions and association, **1:** 137-41; instructions to delegates to Congress, **1:** 141-4; drafts resolution on N.Y. support of Association, **1:** 159-60; plan for militia, **1:** 160-2; drafts resolution respecting land grants, **1:** 162-3; TJ asked to communicate important occurrences to, **1:** 268; letters to, from Va. delegates in Congress, **1:** 223-4, 294-5; authorizes Treasury notes, **1:** 254-5; resolutions calling for independence, **1:** 290-1, 330n; resolution on purchase of lands from Indians, **1:** 565n; appoints commissioners on land claims, **2:** 65n; fails to adopt Constitution, **2:** 305n

Council of State

letter from, **3:** 183-4; and TJ's draft Constitutions (1776), **1:** 342, 350, 360; and Mason's plan of government, **1:** 367-8, 370-1; and Va. Constitution, **1:** 381-2; bill indemnifying for handling of suspected persons, **2:** 119n; bill establishing clerkship of foreign correspondence, **2:** 181-2; and removal of Convention troops from Albemarle barracks, **2:** 237-44; order placing Henry Hamilton and others in irons, **2:** 292-5; bill empowering a member to act as lieutenant governor, **2:** 347-8; bill empowering governor to lay embar-

VIRGINIA (*cont.*)

goes with advice of, **2:** 348-9; bill giving war powers to, **2:** 363-4; bill for appointment of clerks to, **2:** 377-8; salaries of members, **2:** 425; oath of office, **2:** 589; actions against members, **2:** 600; advice concerning prisoners of war, **3:** 103-4; advises Governor to act during recesses, **3:** 183-4; letters from, to Board of Trade, **3:** 309, 310; moves to Richmond, **3:** 333-4; notes on proceedings, **3:** 339-40; and purchase of horses, **3:** 419-20; and western defense, **3:** 420-1; order for security of Convention prisoners, **3:** 423-4, 453; orders to George Muter, **3:** 439-40; advice concerning money collected by Sampson Mathews, **3:** 442-3; act to give further powers to, **3:** 492; TJ calls meeting of, **3:** 564; advice on embodying militia of three western counties, **4:** 82-4; advice respecting consolidation of state regiments, **4:** 536-7; advice respecting purchase of gunpowder, **4:** 585-6; advice on reforming state regiments, **5:** 35; not responsible for executing orders, **5:** 120; advice on clothier's department, **5:** 200; discontinues impressment of horses, **5:** 286n; Tyler's resignation from, **5:** 316; opinion on prisoner exchanges, **5:** 352n; Prentis' resignation from, **5:** 383; advice on Hayes' newspaper, **5:** 386; resolution on flags, **5:** 445; meetings, **5:** 449n; TJ's absence from, **5:** 468; resolution on Albemarle co., **5:** 469; recommends withdrawal of state commissions for negotiators with Cherokees, **5:** 477; delay in meeting, **5:** 613n-4n; and destruction of public records, **5:** 631-2; order concerning copying of public records, **5:** 631-2; TJ calls meeting at Charlottesville, **5:** 640; criticism of, **6:** 89n; given wider powers by GA, **6:** 96; and TJ's draft Constitution (1783), **6:** 281n, 299-300; president of, **6:** 300; Madison's comments on TJ's proposals for, **6:** 312; TJ recommends Gates for, **6:** 549; Madison's opinions on, **7:** 35; letter to, from J. F. Mercer, **7:** 94-5; Short retains seat in, **7:** 257; change in membership, **12:** 445

VIRGINIA (*cont.*)

County Courts

letters to first magistrates of, **4**: 414-5; **5**: 242-3; in TJ's draft Constitutions (1776), **1**: 343-5, 351-2, 361-2; in Kentucky, Washington, and Montgomery counties, **1**: 572-3; in Pittsylvania and Henry counties, **1**: 592-4; delay in reorganizing, **1**: 606n-7n; bills concerning, **1**: 650-2; **2**: 336-7, 418-9, 578-82; **3**: 492; clerks of, **2**: 145, 160-1; **3**: 272; practice in, **2**: 235; and jurisdiction over seizures, **6**: 428; act for reforming, **9**: 197. *See also* under names of counties

Court of Admiralty

establishment of, **1**: 606n, 645-9; bill constituting, **2**: 572-5; denied criminal jurisdiction, **3**: 249; judges, **6**: 300; cases before, **6**: 428

Court of Appeals

in TJ's draft Constitutions (1776), **1**: 342, 343, 351, 361; delay in establishment of, **1**: 606n; bill for establishing, **1**: 607-10; **2**: 575-7; judges of, **6**: 301, 313; limitations on the Court of Chancery, **9**: 69-70; proceedings of sent to TJ, **13**: 337, 338n

Courts of Assize
See Virginia: District Courts

Currency

value of pound, **7**: 178; value of dollar, **7**: 184, 200. *See also* currency; depreciation of currency; money

Declaration of Rights

drafted by TJ, **1**: 119-20; praised by Hanover Presbytery, **1**: 526n; omitted from Revisal, **2**: 315n, 657n; and TJ's 1783 draft constitution, **6**: 281n; praised by inhabitants of Albemarle co., **6**: 285-6

Defenses

for protection against British invasion, **3**: 190-1, 193-4, 238-40, 241; **4**: 197; TJ explains use of arms for, **3**: 224-7; of eastern frontier, **3**: 491, 518; after battle of Camden, **3**: 564; Steuben's plan for, **5**: 66-70, 76-7; Congress recommends removal of public stores from Eastern Shore, **5**: 392; asked to aid in protecting Delaware bay, **5**: 551; arms to be repaired and sent to, **5**: 567; Gen.

VIRGINIA (*cont.*)

Morgan's plan for, **6**: 71n-2n; Congress promises arms and troops, **6**: 73-4; expenditures for, **6**: 557; purchase of military stores abroad, **8**: 67-8; **9**: 213; **10**: 472, 497, 523; purchases arms in France, **8**: 213, 507; **9**: 174n-5n, 381, 523, 524, 536-7, 540-1, 581, 593, 629; **10**: 66-7, 81-2, 136, 161, 189, 191-2, 196, 198, 203, 228-9, 261, 290-1, 292, 309-10, 331, 399, 461, 497, 503, 542, 551, 589-91, 619; **11**: 25, 36, 62, 83, 255, 261, 355; **12**: 3, 131

Delegates in Continental Congress

letters to, **3**: 579-80, 656-7; **4**: 76-7, 118, 122-4, 376, 398-400, 456-7, 556-7, 689-90; **5**: 101, 152-3, 251, 367-8, 395, 440, 632-4, 634-5, 650-1; **8**: 289-90; **15**: 598-9; letters from, **5**: 193, 266, 334-5, 550-2, 566-7; draft of instructions to (*A Summary View*), **1**: 121-37, 669-76; instructions for the Convention of 1774, **1**: 141; letters from, to the Va. Convention, **1**: 224, 294-5; introduce resolution of independence, **1**: 298-9, 309, 413-4; vote for independence, **1**: 314; vote for Chase's taxation plan, **1**: 323; representation in Congress, **1**: 326; appointment, **1**: 371, 381; **2**: 15-8; **6**: 277, 303-4; **9**: 241-2; letters from, to Va. Executive, **1**: 460-1; **4**: 96, 196, 203-4, 292-3, 436-7, 483-4, 605-6, 606-7, 670-1; **5**: 81, 481-3, 556-7, 586-7, 608-9, 620-1; **6**: 9-10, 39, 76-7, 510, 552-5; **7**: 44-5, 248-50; letter from, to Speaker of Pa. Convention, **1**: 465-6; number reduced to five, **1**: 475; delay in sending credentials, **1**: 486; payment of, **1**: 503; **2**: 16, 264, 265n, 267, 371; **3**: 112n; **4**: 96, 118; **6**: 565; length of term of, **2**: 16-7; bill for annual appointment of, **2**: 367-70; oath not to engage in trade, **3**: 28; financial straits, **4**: 121; **6**: 72-3, 100, 549; G. R. Clark complains of treatment by, **4**: 394; TJ asked to write to, **5**: 458; letter to, from R. H. Lee, **6**: 90-3; letters to, from Gov. Harrison, **6**: 345-7, 347, 354, 372-3, 421-2, 551; **7**: 293-4; vote on permanent seat for Con-

VIRGINIA (*cont.*)

gress, **6**: 352, 366; correspondence with Oliver Pollock, **6**: 356-7, 511; and proposed union with Md. for erecting buildings for Congress, **6**: 362n, 367-8; reports to governor by, **6**: 390, 420; **7**: 4; TJ vacates seat, **7**: 244; divisiveness, **7**: 251-2; vote on R.I. delegates, **7**: 291; death of Hardy, **9**: 191; composition, **9**: 241-2; vote on British commerce, **9**: 259; attitude toward land cession by Conn., **9**: 653, 654n; Maury praises, **10**: 387; instructions on Mississippi question, **11**: 221; interview with Otto, **11**: 222; letter from, to Randolph, cited, **14**: 83, 84n

District Courts

bills establishing, **2**: 612n; **8**: 415, 659; **9**: 197, 297; **11**: 123; **12**: 609; objections to act establishing, **7**: 588; favored by Madison, **10**: 576; Monroe on, **13**: 49-50, 353; mentioned, **8**: 113, 646

Economic Conditions

extravagance, **8**: 641, 642, 645, 667; **11**: 318-9, 328-9, 636; debts of tobacco planters, **10**: 27; scarcity of money, **11**: 413; textile manufacture, **13**: 153-4, 183-4, 260-1; **18**: 120-1, 121n-4n. *See also* Virginia: Agriculture, Commerce

Elections

qualifications for voting, **1**: 314, 348, 358, 366, 369, 379; **6**: 297, 309-11; law setting time of, **2**: 337; penalty for failure to vote, **2**: 338; methods of taking poll, **2**: 339-40; provision in bill for investigating complaints, **2**: 340-2; mayors certify election of delegates to GA, **2**: 342; postponement of, **6**: 288; conduct of, **6**: 305; Adams' aversion to, **12**: 396; election districts, **14**: 3, 529, 531n, 558; Congress (1788-1789), **14**: 281, 302, 339-40, 352, 394-5, 458, 529, 607; **15**: 5-8, 92; Presidential electors, **14**: 559; **15**: 5; electoral votes (1789), **15**: 92

Executive Council

See Virginia: Council of State

General Assembly

letters to, **3**: 417-8; **4**: 433-4; letter to clerks of, **5**: 502-3; and TJ's draft

VIRGINIA (*cont.*)

Constitutions (1776), **1**: 340-1, 348-9, 358-9; and Mason's plan of government, **1**: 366, 369; in Constitution, **1**: 379; methods of election discussed by Pendleton, **1**: 476; and disestablishment of the Church of England, **1**: 525-58; list of acts on religion, **1**: 539-44; election of TJ and John Harvie as delegates to, from Albemarle co., **2**: 10-1; bill for regulating appointment of delegates to Continental Congress, **2**: 15-8; election of delegates to, from Fluvanna co., **2**: 24-5; payment to Cherokees for cession of land, **2**: 79; ratification of Articles of Confederation, **2**: 111-2, 120-1; representation of western counties in, **2**: 118n; bill to enforce attendance of members, **2**: 188-9; bill for giving members an adequate allowance, **2**: 231-2; bill proposed for the relief of landlords, **2**: 263; bill amending act for fixing allowance of members, **2**: 273-4; balloting for TJ as governor, **2**: 278n; approval of treaty with France sent to Gérard, **2**: 289-90; bill concerning election of members of, **2**: 337-47; privilege of members, **2**: 344; absences of members, **2**: 345; payment of members, **2**: 371; bill concerning licenses, **2**: 511-2; bill for repealing certain acts of, **2**: 656-7; TJ's notes on acts of, **2**: 661-3; **3**: 486-7; ratifies treaty with France, **3**: 10, 11-2, 16; dealings with John Ballendine, **3**: 126-30; public opinion of, **3**: 231; levies taxes payable in grain, **3**: 250; resolution appointing TJ governor, **3**: 410; text of oath of allegiance, **3**: 482n; agrees to financial scheme of Congress, **3**: 483; and western land, **3**: 630-2; **4**: 386-91, 483; **6**: 189; acts of sent to other states, **3**: 669; **4**: 185; action on British invasions, **4**: 264, 289n; convening of, **4**: 407, 427, 432, 522-3; **5**: 33; members must leave military commands for legislative service, **4**: 699; Recruiting Act, **5**: 33, 91n, 153, 173, 178, 212n-3; Treason Act, **5**: 49n; Salary Act, **5**: 78-80; resolution on McIntosh family, **5**: 218; resolution on parole, **5**: 227; resolutions on impressment of

VIRGINIA (*cont.*)

pure drink, **2**: 521-2; printing of revised laws, **2**: 548n; **6**: 537, 544; **7**: 597; bill concerning distresses, **2**: 650-4; bill concerning detaining, **2**: 655-6; bill declaring when laws shall be in force, **2**: 658; TJ's notes on English statutes, **2**: 658-61; TJ's memorandum on bills to be drafted, **2**: 664-5; sent to other states, **4**: 241; Council of Revision proposed by TJ, **6**: 302-3; Madison's comments on Council of Revision, **6**: 315; discovery as claim to possession, **6**: 496, 656; international offenses, **7**: 307n; extradition of criminals, **8**: 93; debts to British subjects, **9**: 111-2; general diffusion of knowledge, **9**: 151; **10**: 244-5; **11**: 152; acts not included in revisal, **9**: 196-201; failure to pass revised bill on crimes and punishments, **11**: 152. *See also* Virginia: Committee of Revisors

Lieutenant Governor

bill establishing office, **2**: 347-8

Militia

committee report on plans for, **1**: 160-2; mobilization of, **1**: 237; pay of, **1**: 255; **2**: 360; **4**: 45, 634; **5**: 339, 513; in Mason's plan for Va. government, **1**: 367, 370; in Constitution, **1**: 381; cowardly behavior on Potomac, **1**: 480; returns of, **2**: 130-2; **3**: 254 (illus.); **4**: 216-7, 677, 686; **5**: 29; **6**: 35; exemption from, **2**: 350; **4**: 632; **5**: 442; officers, **2**: 350, 352-3, 358-9; **4**: 125; **5**: 657; **6**: 5, 292-3; bill for regulating and disciplining, **2**: 350-6; division into ten parts in each county, **2**: 356-8; called to meet invasion of Va., **2**: 357; **3**: 238, 241; **4**: 57, 269, 270, 302, 303, 333, 334, 352, 400-3; **5**: 204, 271, 520-1, 533, 546; **6**: 50; punishments for neglect of duty, **2**: 360; provisioning, **2**: 361; **4**: 41, 65, 94, 347-8; bill allowing governor to send to aid of neighboring states, **2**: 363; needed for Western District, **3**: 42, 623-4; officers' commissions, **3**: 254-5; **5**: 465-6, 476; **6**: 642; sent against Indians, **3**: 356; for S.C., **3**: 401, 487; quota for Continental army, **3**: 409-10; for support of

VIRGINIA (*cont.*)

southern army, **3**: 433, 457, 463, 468, 472, 593-4; **4**: 163, 662; **5**: 291; bill for drafting in Va., **3**: 485; under martial law, **3**: 492, 497; delinquency among, **3**: 519-20; **5**: 415-6, 531; return of arms at discharge, **3**: 529; **4**: 95, 156; **5**: 615; behavior at the battle of Camden, **3**: 559, 563, 592, 595-6; **4**: 20; clothing, **3**: 563-4; **4**: 445-6, 453; desertions, **3**: 577, 621, 640; **4**: 81-2; **5**: 183, 185; morale, **3**: 590; reinforcements for, **3**: 597-8, 601-4; estimate of strength, **3**: 599-601; shortage of arms, **3**: 647; battalion under Col. Crockett, **3**: 667; recruitment, **4**: 18; from western counties to join Col. Morgan, **4**: 40; used to guard Convention troops, **4**: 73; arms for, **4**: 94-5, 364; dismissal of Gen. Lawson's corps, **4**: 178-9; called to defend Richmond, **4**: 258; **6**: 107; put under Steuben's command, **4**: 308, 345; rendezvous at Richmond, **4**: 339; discharge of, **4**: 356, 371-2, 379, 398, 554, 558, 564, 699, 700; **5**: 37, 61-2, 73, 163-4, 233, 244, 301, 337, 560-1; **6**: 18, 106; lack of ammunition, **4**: 385; reorganization, **4**: 427, 654-5; behavior at Cowpens, **4**: 441; terms of enlistment, **4**: 455; in service, **4**: 472; discharge of married men, **4**: 564; not used on public works, **4**: 578; criticized by Campbell, **4**: 587; use for other than military duty, **4**: 593; **5**: 114, 120; relief for, **4**: 602, 698; **5**: 308-9, 312, 316, 332-3, 349-50, 352, 358, 369, 441-2, 444, 464, 484; called out to meet Cornwallis' invasion, **4**: 613-5, 621-2, 624, 645-7; Greene advises putting under Continental officers, **4**: 615; supply shortages, **4**: 617; Continental command over, **4**: 661; destitution of men at Williamsburg, **4**: 675; county quotas, **4**: 686; disaffection of, **4**: 699, 700; **5**: 15, 101, 102, 105, 109, 116, 122, 295-6, 583, 584; courts-martial, **5**: 10, 284, 371; **6**: 35; for use in Portsmouth expedition, **5**: 50, 75; discipline, **5**: 63; Steuben's views on, **5**: 68-9, 76n, 101, 181, 275n-7, 308n; laws concerning, **5**: 82, 134n; **9**: 200; **10**: 371, 376n; varying numbers in ac-

VIRGINIA (*cont.*)

tion, **5**: 112; at Guilford Court House, **5**: 156, 162; Lafayette requests copy of laws on, **5**: 167, 180; act for ascertaining number, **5**: 243; discharges hamper Greene, **5**: 258; militia board, **5**: 267; bounty, **5**: 278; praised by Carrington, **5**: 298; recapitulation of tours of duty, **5**: 310-1; under Gen. Muhlenberg, **5**: 328-9; delay in summoning, **5**: 366; prisoners of, **5**: 402; work at Hoods as substitute for tour of service, **5**: 487, 510, 536; report on number in the field, **5**: 500-1; used to guard prisoners of war, **5**: 530; Lafayette advises against general engagement, **5**: 554; TJ hopes to keep within Va., **5**: 598; delay in answering calls, **5**: 644; **6**: 28; countermanding of orders to join Greene, **6**: 101, 102; TJ criticized for not calling more, **6**: 108; affidavits respecting TJ's orders for, **6**: 118-20; under direction of governor in TJ's draft of Va. Constitution (1783), **6**: 281n

Navy

letter to officers of, **5**: 146; letter to commissioner of, **5**: 502-3; bill for appointing officers, **2**: 375-7; bill for enlistment of, **2**: 378-81; bill concerning seamen, **2**: 382-8; salaries of commissioners, **2**: 425; officers' fees, **2**: 433; and wrecked vessels, **2**: 439; counterfeit bill of health for ships clearing port of Norfolk, **3**: 254 (illus.); sale of state vessels, **3**: 314, 331-2; appointment of commissioner of, **3**: 491; provisioning, **3**: 348; **5**: 176; Barron made commodore of, **3**: 485; TJ's memorandum on, **3**: 491; Maxwell appointed commissioner of, **3**: 498; form for list of seamen, **4**: 3; TJ's report on, **4**: 119; desertions, **4**: 221-2; preparations to meet British, **4**: 290; instructions to, **4**: 530; neglect of ships, **4**: 599-600, 607-8, 662-3; supports French fleet, **4**: 630, 640-1; operations in Hampton Roads, **5**: 64; preparations for Portsmouth expedition, **5**: 132, 135; officers, **5**: 146; pay of officers, **5**: 146, 171-2; commissary needed, **5**: 151; pay and clothing for, **5**: 171-2, 223; weakness of, **5**: 474n; list of armed

VIRGINIA (*cont.*)

vessels, **5**: 557-8; lack of supplies, **6**: 6; within powers of Committee of the States, **6**: 523-4

Public Finance

bill to establish auditors of public accounts, **1**: 654-5; sale of unappropriated lands to create sinking fund, **2**: 135n; bill providing revenue for public exigencies, **2**: 184-6; bills to amend act for raising supply of money, **2**: 186-8, 217-24; currency depreciation, **2**: 259; **4**: 501; financial quota to national treasury, **2**: 290; **3**: 109, 425, 471, 494-5, 507, 509-10; **4**: 122-3; **7**: 5, 43, 55, 71, 114, 232-3, 592; **8**: 325; **9**: 201, 334; **10**: 34, 35, 44, 54-6; **11**: 470; **12**: 444; bill establishing Board of Auditors, **2**: 370-4; bill declaring bills of credit legal tender, **2**: 434; measures for improving, **3**: 10-1, 34; efforts to borrow money in Europe, **3**: 36, 90-3, 381, 470; **4**: 51; **5**: 376; **6**: 115, 162; account with Congress, **3**: 199, 261; **7**: 250; credit of, **3**: 202, 299-301, 320; **4**: 199, 511; **5**: 209, 265, 607; **8**: 645; limits warrants issued, **3**: 264; bills of exchange for indebtedness, **3**: 270; lack of hard money, **3**: 272, 274-5; debts of, **3**: 274; **4**: 433; **5**: 669; **6**: 137; **7**: 94-5; **8**: 508, 659; **9**: 183; **10**: 12, 45; **12**: 346; **13**: 544; use of escheated property, **3**: 282-3; inability to repay loans, **3**: 295; **4**: 4, 611-2; **5**: 346-9; lack of money to buy pork for troops, **3**: 299; orders to Board of Trade, **3**: 322-3; and calling in of Continental currency, **3**: 322n, 473, 493, 506; Penet as agent in France, **3**: 357-9; money collected from individuals, **3**: 386; paper money, **3**: 492; **4**: 383; **5**: 33; **7**: 213; **9**: 199; **10**: 26, 128, 133, 232; **11**: 402; proclamation concerning redemption of Continental money, **3**: 565-6; necessity of waiting for GA to convene, **3**: 592; bills drawn by Gen. Gates, **3**: 604-5; payment of bills delayed, **3**: 637; Congress appoints commissioners to endorse bills of credit issued by, **4**: 25; drafts on the state, **4**: 37, 39; account owed to Simon Nathan, **4**:

VIRGINIA (cont.)
282-4; **6**: 197, 200-1, 319-24; payment for timber rejected, **4**: 332; warrant for Robertson, **4**: 351; unpaid warrants, **4**: 463; Elliott needs money to pay creditors, **4**: 484; St. Laurence asks payment for transporting supplies, **4**: 543; payment for supplies and services, **4**: 634; Clay's accounts against state, **5**: 390-1; delay in paying delegates in Congress, **6**: 549; collection of taxes by sheriffs, **7**: 117; confusion in revenue, **7**: 362; act to remit half of 1785 tax, **7**: 592; bill for liquidating depreciated payments into Treasury, **7**: 596; claims against, **8**: 34-6; bill for general assessment of taxes, **8**: 113; payment of Mazzei's expenses, **8**: 475, 510, 538; consideration of taxes in GA, **9**: 75; bill for postponing tax collection, **9**: 199-200; account with Grand, **10**: 194; **11**: 607-8, 609; TJ's statement of account, **10**: 229; payment of taxes in tobacco, **10**: 576-7; export duties, **11**: 304; lack of funds for paying agents, **11**: 365, 377, 382; account with Barclay, **11**: 626, 669; complaints against taxes, **12**: 103; fund in France, **13**: 169, 170, 192; debt assumed by federal government, **17**: 266-7, 269-71, 276; assumption of debt opposed, **18**: 82

Quartermaster's Department
duties and compensation in Va., **3**: 284-5, 292; Board of War asks housing for, **3**: 330; duties, **3**: 537; **5**: 4-5, 10-1; Pickering asks appointment of quartermaster general, **3**: 559; deputy of, **4**: 48, 374, 521-2; offices, **4**: 173; organization criticized, **4**: 250, 340; plan of Carrington and Claiborne for, **4**: 285-8, 340-2, 464; **5**: 575; character of personnel, **4**: 299, 305-6; lack of, **4**: 317; reorganization, **4**: 510-4; assistant deputy's pay, **4**: 548; exemption from draft queried, **4**: 627, 635; western quartermasters discontinued, **5**: 38; Claiborne's resignation, **5**: 340; amount needed for, **5**: 582

Representatives in Congress
political alignment of, **14**: 340; **15**: 5-6; election (1788-1789), **14**: 458, 558, 607; **15**: 5-6

VIRGINIA (cont.)
Seal
Page asks TJ to have made in Philadelphia, **1**: 468, 482; motto, **1**: 482, 484n; George Wythe's comments on, **1**: 604; payment for, by Arthur Lee, **3**: 83

Senate
letters to Speaker of, **6**: 391-2; **7**: 8, 40, 245; according to Constitution, **1**: 379, 476; proposed method of election to, **1**: 503-4; and right to amend money bills, **2**: 40-62 (editorial note and documents); bill to arrange counties into senatorial districts, **2**: 336-7; salary of Speaker, **2**: 425; on Spotswood, **5**: 332n; letter from Steuben to Speaker of, **6**: 75-6; institution questioned, **6**: 287; election of delegates, **6**: 296; Madison's observations on, **6**: 308-9; accepts terms of Congress on western lands, **6**: 428; election, **7**: 293; absence of members, **7**: 596; address of welcome to TJ, **16**: 11-3; antifederalism in, **16**: 13n, 26; opposition to national government, **19**: 51-2

Senators, U.S.
election (1788-1789), **14**: 281, 302, 339, 394, 458, 525, 529, 607

Treasurer
letter to, **5**: 502-3; in TJ's draft Va. Constitutions (1776), **1**: 342, 350, 360; in Mason's plan of government, **1**: 368, 372; in Constitution, **1**: 383; rights to wastelands, **2**: 140-1, 142, 149n, 155, 156; accounts to be audited, **2**: 373; bill concerning, **2**: 374-5; salary, **2**: 425; appointment by GA, **6**: 298

Troops
cavalry, **1**: 386; **2**: 184, 194; **3**: 330, 645; **4**: 353-4; **5**: 67, 350; **6**: 18; companies of riflemen to be regimented, **1**: 390; TJ on plan to enlist Indians, **1**: 500; bounty, **2**: 140; **3**: 156-7; **4**: 189; **6**: 572n-4n, 579; for garrison duty, **2**: 179-81; bill for enlistment of, **2**: 378-81; half pay for retired officers, **2**: 379; supplies for, **3**: 79, 240, 279-80, 299, 309, 324, 326, 345, 346-8, 384, 438, 496, 503, 529, 569-70, 657; **4**: 89, 136, 324, 326, 337-8, 342-3, 351-2, 378, 415, 416, 419, 426, 433, 509, 666;

randa quoted, **18**: 621-3; owns *Belvedere*, **18**: 643n; letter to, from J. Beckley, cited, **18**: 659n; mentioned, **18**: 686

Vulture (sloop): Arnold's escape on, **4**: 13, 29

Vulture, H.M.S.: destroys *Mentor*, **18**: 347n-8n

Vuy, Mlle: recommended to Short and TJ, **7**: 388, 389

Waal river, Netherlands, **13**: 12

Wabash Company: list of members cited, **6**: 655n

Wabash (Ouabache) Indians, **5**: 320

Wabash river: Clark's projected excursion up, **2**: 246, 257; **3**: 89; plans for defense of, **3**: 55; floods in, **6**: 536; boundary of proposed northwest colony, **6**: 600; east boundary of proposed colony E, **6**: 602; west boundary of proposed colony C, **6**: 602; west boundary of proposed colony D, **6**: 602; Le Maire's account of, **8**: 123; settlements on, **11**: 308; rich in furs, **11**: 386; mentioned, **2**: 85; **3**: 666; **4**: 234

Wadden, Mr., **1**: 453

Waddey, Ens.: deserter, **5**: 214

Waddington, Mr.: TJ visits in London, **9**: 363n

Wade, Mr.: and bill establishing ferries, **2**: 455, 460

Wade, Ferrall: deposition of cited, **3**: 32

Wadsworth, Col. James: opposes resolution of Wyoming residents, **6**: 483n; House asks commissions from, **7**: 393-4; replaced in Congress, **7**: 572; letter from, to E. Trist, cited, **8**: 25

Wadsworth, Jeremiah: letter to, **20**: 392-3; letters from, **19**: 377-8; **20**: 245-6; and business activities, **8**: 516; **9**: 168n; aid solicited by Washington, **12**: 325n; political activities, **14**: 301; nominated congressman from Conn., **14**: 525; on establishment of Treasury Department, **15**: 217; bust of J. P. Jones sent to, **15**: 438; Greene's medal sent to, **16**: 63n; introduces appropriation bill, **16**: 455; on commercial policy, **16**: 518; visited by Smith, **17**: 183n; and soldiers' arrearages, **18**: 624n; involvement with J. Reynolds, **18**: 626, 627, 628; in Reynolds case, **18**: 629, 635-7, 643, 645, 647n, 649,

674-5, 676n; in Glaubeck case, **18**: 687n; land speculation, **19**: 10n; **20**: 126, 128, 595; votes for capital bill, **19**: 36n; and the whale fisheries, **19**: 145; recommends Chipman, **19**: 378; and speculation in U.S. foreign debt, **20**: 177n; supports Wolcott, Jr., for treasury appointment, **20**: 221; confers with Beckwith, **20**: 435; entertains W. L. Smith, **20**: 444; and Hessian fly, **20**: 446, 447-8; mentioned, **3**: 584; **14**: 619; **18**: 686

Wagener (Waggoner), Peter: letter to, **4**: 523; letter from, **5**: 335-6; actions of, **5**: 72; letter from cited, **5**: 420; mentioned, **4**: 493

wages: workmen at small arms factory, **4**: 119; in Va. quartermaster's department, **4**: 465, 548; inflation of, **5**: 355; Hogendorp's queries on, in U.S., **7**: 297; N.Y., **7**: 327; Conn., **7**: 332-3; R.I., **7**: 338-9; Mass., **7**: 342; N.H., **7**: 343; Pa., **7**: 348; France, **11**: 419, 422, 425, 427, 455. *See also* workmen: wages; and individual occupations

Waggoner, Andrew: signs petition, **3**: 652

Waggoner, Peter. *See* Wagener

Wagner, Mr., **9**: 130

Wagon Act (Va.), **4**: 478; **5**: 298, 340

wagon conductors: pay, **4**: 548, 552

wagon drivers: exemption from military service recommended, **2**: 292; pay, **4**: 547, 548, 552, 553; issue of liquor to, **5**: 12; impressment, **5**: 592; requisitioned by Lafayette, **5**: 666

wagonmasters: pay of, **3**: 583; need of, **4**: 412

wagons: care of assigned to quartermasters, **3**: 284; shortage of, **3**: 476, 526, 550, 553, 592, 641, 658, 660; **4**: 66, 92, 111; **5**: 225, 278-80, 389, 417, 429, 516, 537; impressment of, **3**: 487; **4**: 42, 62, 73, 172, 313, 330, 405-6, 477, 592, 643; **5**: 465, 523; **6**: 10; for Continental army, **3**: 513; **4**: 185; **5**: 34, 373; TJ asks for return of, **3**: 530; requisitions for, **3**: 536; for southern army, **3**: 583; **4**: 23-4, 50, 133, 220, 500; **5**: 240-1; loss at battle of Camden, **3**: 593, 596; purchase of, **3**: 598, 643; manufacture of, **4**: 8, 9; **5**: 391; for transporting supplies, **4**: 286-7, 581, 582, 583; to accompany recruits, **4**: 402; Va. act for supplying

Watts, Thomas: judged guilty of high treason, **6**: 55

Watts, William: and establishment of Va. courts, **1**: 606n; in Albemarle co. militia, **1**: 665; petition from, **5**: 349

Wautauga co., Va: Tatham's map of, **19**: 265n

wax: likenesses in, by Patience Wright, of signers of peace treaty, **8**: 380; duty on, in France, **12**: 451

wax chandlery: Hopkinson's plans for, **13**: 40

Waxhaw, N.C.: Tarleton at, **3**: 620

Wayles, Elizabeth. *See* Eppes, Elizabeth Wayles

Wayles, John: letter from, **1**: 95; signs nonimportation resolutions (1770), **1**: 46; death of, **1**: 96n, 100; **15**: 657; sale of lands, **1**: 100, 103; involvement in litigation, **6**: 198; estate of, **6**: 416, 470; illness of, **15**: 571; letter from, to J. Thompson, **15**: 649; correspondence with Farrell & Jones, **15**: 649-51 653-4; letter from, to Bivins, **15**: 655; will of, **15**: 657-8; marriage of daughters, **15**: 658; tobacco warehouse tickets, **15**: 670-1; Bryan as clerk to, **16**: 84n; Elk Island and Elk Hill property, **16**: 94n; **17**: 571n; Hanbury's account with, **17**: 581, 592. *See also* Wayles estate debt

Wayles, Martha. *See* Jefferson, Martha Wayles Skelton

Wayles, Tabitha. *See* Skipwith, Tabitha Wayles

Wayles & Randolph: letters to, from Farrell & Jones, **15**: 651-2, 656-7, 667

Wayles estate debt: settlement of account with Wakelin Welch, **7**: 384, 423; exchange endorsed by T. M. Randolph, **11**: 651-2; payments to McCaul, **13**: 328, 340, 349, 512-3; **15**: 212-3, 327, 328, 339, 647; TJ's settlement of, **14**: 357-8; **15**: 131, 161-2, 647-8; **16**: 154, 171, 212n-3n, 387; **17**: 657; **19**: 246; **20**: 103, 153-4, 166-8, 313, 373-6, 379, 388-9, 597-8; Eppes as executor for, **15**: 626; **19**: 542; editorial note and documents, **15**: 642-77; TJ as executor of, **15**: 645-7, 657-62, 670-1, 674-7; sale of Elk Hill as payment for, **17**: 512-3, 581, 657; funds advanced to Dobson, **19**: 554; mentioned **9**: 395-6; **10**: 483; **11**: 10-1, 14, 17; **13**: 251-2, 324-8, 349

Wayne, Anthony: captures Stony Point,

3: 57, 342; quells mutiny of Pa. line, **4**: 325; **11**: 493n; election to American Philosophical Society, **4**: 545n; joins Lafayette, **5**: 86; **6**: 19, 52, 85, 97, 98, 629n, 635, 639; to go south, **5**: 351, 415; **6**: 90, 92; needed in Va., **5**: 624; **6**: 76; expected to leave York, **6**: 26; objections to serving under Lafayette rumored, **6**: 92; medal, **16**: xxxvii, 52 (illus.), 54n, 55n-6n, 59n, 60n, 64n-6n, 70-1, 73n-6n, 289n; correspondence with Knox quoted, **16**: 408n-9n; letter to, from Lafayette, cited, **18**: 495; electoral contest with James Jackson, **20**: 361n

wealth: dependence of commerce on, **7**: 350; inequalities in division of, in France, **8**: 681-2; distribution of, in U.S., **10**: 399; TJ's views on acquisition of, **12**: 38

Weare, Meshech: letter from, **4**: 185; and Barbé de Marbois' queries on Va., **4**: 167n; and case of the brig *Lusanna*, **6**: 452n, 454n

weasel: comparison with ermine, **9**: 661-5

Weastcoat, Capt. Wright. *See* Westcott, Capt. Wright

Weasy, Capt. *See* Vesey

weather: observations of Bernard, **12**: 634-5, 643, 691; Marseilles observations, **13**: 95, 501, 508; France, **14**: 305, 343, 358-9, 363, 371, 377, 409, 429, 444, 446, 464, 483, 653, 656; **15**: 43; **16**: 48, 133; Italy, **14**: 382-3, 405; Rittenhouse's observations on, **20**: 383. *See also* Virginia: Climate

Weaver, David: signs petition, **6**: 290

weavers: wages in N.Y., **7**: 327; wages in Conn., **7**: 333; wages in N.H., **7**: 343

Webb, Capt., **4**: 152

Webb, Armiger: prisoner of war, **5**: 294n

Webb, Bernard: clerk in Dept. of State, **17**: 357n; **18**: 648n-9, 658n

Webb, Cutbut: signs petition, **6**: 290

Webb, Foster (Forster): letter from, **5**: 428; invoices for paper and printing materials, **3**: 90, 92; commissioner to endorse bills emitted by Va., **3**: 471; **4**: 25n; Sansum obtains authority from, **4**: 694; financial affairs, **5**: 435; **20**: 713; Mazzei's relationship with, **9**: 154; **11**: 85, 354; **13**: 166, 499; mentioned, **4**: 311

Webb, Foster, Jr., **6**: 65n

Webb, George: in Franklin's autobiography, **9**: 486

Webb, George (Va.): and sale of Moore estate, **1**: 60, 64-5; and bill establishing ferries, **2**: 457; member Va. Executive Council, **3**: 35n, 349n; **5**: 449n, 558n, 614n; **16**: 89n; letter to, from Scott, quoted, **4**: 36n; opinion of Steuben, **6**: 97; debts, **15**: 644; letter from cited, **16**: 94n; letter to cited, **16**: 94n

Webb, Col. John, **5**: 21

Webber, Capt. Philip: proposal to raise troop of cavalry, **5**: 534n

Webster, Daniel: medals purchased by, **16**: xxxv

Webster, Noah: letter to, **18**: 131-5; letters from, **17**: 598-9; **18**: 153-4; **19**: 120; *Grammatical Institute*, **17**: 598; **18**: 131, 133n; *Essays*, **17**: 598-9; **18**: 131-2, 134n, 153; controversy with TJ on constitutional government, **18**: 132-3, 134n, 153-4; *American Magazine* articles, **18**: 134n; *Little Readers Assistant*, **18**: 154; "A Pendulum without a Bob," **18**: 480-2; Callender on, **18**: 659, 660; *Minerva*, **18**: 659; on Hamilton, **18**: 659; and new system of penmanship, **19**: 120; authorship of letter conjectured, **20**: 22n

Webster, Noah, Jr.: and new system of penmanship, **19**: 120n

Webster-Hayne Debate, **6**: 612n

Wedderburn, Alexander, Earl of Cosslyn, Baron Loughborough: tenant of estate at Woburn, **9**: 370; political prospects, **14**: 482

Wederstrandt, Conrad Theodore: recommends son for consular appointment, **20**: 593; biographical note, **20**: 593n

Wedge, William, **18**: 657n

Wedgwood, Josiah: urged to establish factories in Paris, **11**: 32; ceramics, **18**: 52

Weeb, Jules: signs petition, **6**: 294

Weecaunsee creek, **3**: 611

Weedon, Gen. George: letters to, **4**: 61, 91, 94-5, 97, 100, 335-6, 339-40, 346, 384, 423, 491; **5**: 70-1, 122, 141, 203, 308-9, 337, 351-3, 401-2, 456, 483-4, 545-6; letters from, **4**: 94, 347, 376-7; **5**: 28-9, 54-5, 108-10, 122-3, 185-6, 203, 267, 273-4, 283-4, 297, 317-8, 324, 338, 383-5, 410-1, 456-8, 529-30, 555-7; **15**: 602, 607-8; army commission, **1**: 500; ordered to

south, **3**: 457n; requested to certify arms used, **3**: 514n; called to command troops on Va. coast, **4**: 58, 60, 61, 78, 81n; position of forces under, **4**: 111; asked to protect Fredericksburg munitions works, **4**: 330, 332, 338, 339-40, 343, 344, 351, 364, 448; ordered to Williamsburg, **4**: 384, 680, 687; forces under, **4**: 398, 412; directed to remain at Fredericksburg, **4**: 423; relations with Steuben, **4**: 661n; **5**: 205n, 275n-7, 366, 556n; **6**: 573n, 574n, 619n; ordered to march to Hanover Court House, **4**: 701; **5**: 65; and authority to summon militia, **5**: 252; **6**: 26, 50; correspondence with Callis, **5**: 258n; on Va. military board, **5**: 267n; orders up Culpeper co. militia, **5**: 272; British inquiries on, **5**: 317; and Curle, **5**: 331n; orders to Va. navy, **5**: 344; views on British plans, **5**: 350; correspondence with Gen. Phillips, **5**: 364-5, 457n, 590n-2n; views on exchanges, **5**: 384n-5n; orders to Col. Slaughter, **5**: 407, 408; criticizes TJ, **5**: 457n; letter to, from Spotswood, quoted, **5**: 564n; letter from, to R. H. Lee, cited, **5**: 629; letter from, to Langborn, cited, **5**: 637; letter to, from Davies, quoted, **5**: 647n; letter to, from Jenifer, quoted, **6**: 28n; letters to, from Continental Board of War, quoted, **6**: 28n; letter from, to Lafayette, quoted, **6**: 42n; junction with Lafayette, **6**: 52; mentioned, **4**: 357, 501; **5**: 217; **6**: 13n, 96

Weeks, Capt. *See* Wickes (Wicks), Capt. Benjamin

Weeks, Capt. Lambert. *See* Wickes, Capt. Lambert

Weenix, Jan: paintings, **13**: 446, 449n

weights and measures: and Committee of the States, **6**: 523-4, 626n; decimal system conceived by TJ, **7**: 155n-6n; uniformity in, **7**: 160-1; TJ's notes on, for Hogendorp, **7**: 221; in Morocco, **10**: 348; Talleyrand proposes uniform system of, **16**: 279, 281n, 418, 510, 512, 542, 543, 569, 611, 614, 623, 652n, 668n-70n, 672n; **20**: 346; Sir John Riggs Miller's proposals for, **16**: 542, 543, 611, 614n, 623, 668n, 672n; Madison urges regulation of, **16**: 602-3, 610; Bonne's work on, **17**: 636-8; Vaughan's opinion of universal system of, **18**: 116-7; Rotheram's observations on, **18**: 366, 367n; coinage related to, **18**: 455-8; British experiments on, **18**: 569-70; Cooke on, **19**: 626; Academy of Sciences report on, **20**: 346; uniform system proposed by Keith, **20**: 592; pamphlet on sent to TJ, **20**: 617; unit of measure adopted by National Assembly, **20**: 689

Weights and Measures, Report on: TJ consults Kemp on, **16**: xxxii, 580-1, 607, 614; rough draft of, **16**: 483, 484, 509, 511, 614, 668n; TJ consults Rittenhouse on, **16**: 484-5, 509-10, 542-3, 545-7, 567-70, 574, 587-8, 594-6, 607-8, 643n, 645n, 668n, 669n, 672n; T. Coxe on, **16**: 576, 604-5, 618-9; editorial note and documents on, **16**: 602-75; and Waring's plan, **16**: 604, 605, 619-23; Madison as collaborator on, **16**: 607-14, 643n, 646n, 649-50; Schuyler's corrections of, **16**: 616; **17**: 403-10; sent to Stiles, **16**: 616; **17**: 442; sent to Wythe, **16**: 616; **17**: 478; sent to House of Representatives, **16**: 623-4; first state of, **16**: 624-8; second state of, **16**: 628-50; final state of, **16**: 650-74; postscript to, **16**: 674-5; sent to Senate, **16**: 674; sent to Condorcet, **17**: 281, 528; sent to Talleyrand, **17**: 281, 528; sent to Rittenhouse, **17**: 295; sent to Randolph, **17**: 298-9; sent to Carmichael, **17**: 320; sent to Livingston, **17**: 325, 553; sent to Short, **17**: 528; **19**: 425; sent to Vaughan, **17**: 620

Weisiger, Daniel, & Co.: imports slaves, **15**: 654

Welch, Richard, **3**: 542n

Welch, Wakelin, Jr.: letter from, **6**: 273

Welch, Wakelin, Sr.: letters to, **7**: 384, 587; letters from, **6**: 272-3; **7**: 386, 422-3, 568; letter from cited, **6**: 470; claims on Wayles estate, **7**: 384, 423; **9**: 396; TJ visits in London, **9**: 364n, 465; debt to Washington, **20**: 698

Welcker, Dietrich: marriage of, **8**: 339

Welcker, Sara Pierson (Mrs. Dietrich Welcker): marriage of, **8**: 339

Weld, Isaac: *Travels*, **20**: 473n

Weldon, Daniel: and bill establishing ferries, **2**: 458

Well, Col.: advises TJ on W.I. trade, **7**: 338

Wells, Mr.: court-martial, **5**: 104, 136

Wells, Col. John S.: gives private notes to buy pork for troops, **3**: 299

Wells, William Hill: recommended as consul, **17**: 250

Welsh, Mr.: seeks consulship, **17**: 250, 254n, 255n

Welsh, Capt. Nathaniel, **4**: 539

Wentworth, Benning, **7**: 318

Wentworth, Joshua: letter to, **19**: 363-4; petition of, **6**: 448-52

Wentworth, Thomas: *The Office and Duty of Executors*, **11**: 523

Werff, Adriaen van der: paintings, **13**: 14, 103, 199

Wernecke (Warneck, Warnecke), Frederick Christian: letter to, **12**: 360-1; letter from, **12**: 298; drunkenness of, **4**: 474; parole, **4**: 480; exchange, **4**: 622n, 644; biographical note, **4**: 644n; captured by British, **5**: 627; claim against Va., **10**: 544, 545; services in Revolution, **11**: 406; claims inheritance in Va., **12**: 360-1; mentioned, **4**: 581, 582; **12**: 10

Wernecke, Wilhelm Ludwig: letter to, **10**: 545; wounded in French service, **11**: 406

Werner, Dr. *See* Warner

Wertemburg, Duke of. *See* Württemburg, Karl Eugen, Duke of

Wescot, Lord: owner of "Hagley," **9**: 372

Wesley, John: reportedly critical of Junius' letters, **1**: 557

West, Capt. (master of *Minerva*), **18**: 5

West, Mr.: on N.C. Constitutional Convention, **13**: 644

West, Benjamin: letter from cited, **8**: 45; Adams comments on, **8**: 160; advice on equestrian statue of Washington, **10**: 186; **12**: 36; Duché as student of, **13**: 141n; letter to, from Rumsey, quoted, **15**: 81n; designs seal for Va. court, **18**: 487; **19**: 556-7; mentioned, **12**: 630; **13**: 241; **15**: 144

West, Elizabeth Shewell (Mrs. Benjamin West), **12**: 630

West, Hugh: and bill establishing ferries, **2**: 454

West, John: signs Virginia Association, **1**: 108

West, John, Jr.: land grant for military service, **6**: 645

West, Joseph: master of the *Adventure*, **12**: 462; departure for Martinique, **12**: 626

7: 218-21; purchase of land from Indians, **7**: 250; **8**: 482-3; trading posts in, **7**: 280; troops raised for defense of, **7**: 393; **8**: 77; **10**: 490n, 586, 620; attitude of Spain toward, **7**: 404, 642; importance of Mississippi navigation to, **7**: 405-6; **11**: 221; immigration, **7**: 409n-10n; **8**: 328; **11**: 314; access to, **7**: 459; communications with, **8**: 3-4; **12**: 36; land sales in, **8**: 124, 154, 220n, 229, 317, 401-2, 445, 633-4, 684; **10**: 385; **11**: 308, 481; **12**: 27, 113, 283, 426, 439, 446, 563, 583; **19**: 601, 626; Monroe's unfavorable opinion of, **9**: 189-90; character of people, **9**: 441; discontent of troops in, **9**: 608-9; Rittenhouse's observations on, **10**: 73; effect of proposed treaty with Spain, **10**: 233-4, 575; archaeology in, **10**: 316; climate of, **10**: 527; interests considered at variance with those of east, **10**: 596; government, **11**: 308, 314, 619; **12**: 256; fur trade, **11**: 386; union with U.S., **11**: 481; land prices, **11**: 519; lease of land to foreigners, **12**: 6; paleontology in, **12**: 159; threat of disunion in, **19**: 429-531 (editorial note and documents). *See also* Northwest Territory; Virginia: Boundaries, dispute with Pa.; Virginia: Cession of Western Territory; Virginia: Claim to Western Land

West Fincastle, Va.: petition to make separate county of, **1**: 565n-6n

West Florida. *See* Florida, West

Westham, Va.: power of state to survey in, **3**: 142; magazine at, **3**: 491; records and public stores ordered moved to, **4**: 258, 259; British at, **4**: 270; **5**: 36; removal of military stores from, **4**: 271, 381; rendezvous of recruits, **4**: 303; salvage of public papers at, **4**: 312; care of arms at, **4**: 314, 357; **5**: 280; defense of, **4**: 356; **5**: 516; buildings damaged by British, **4**: 373; Senf asked to plan shops and magazines for, **4**: 375; temporary shop for military stores, **4**: 609; works at, **5**: 169; plans for buildings at, **5**: 249; workers needed at, **5**: 417; removal of boats to, **5**: 580

Westham foundry: Ballendine's account of, cited, **3**: 43, 126-8; destruction of, **3**: 147n; **4**: 263, 334, 336; proposal for operation by state, **3**: 187-90, 214,

221, 270; advantages of its situation, **3**: 188; removal of manager, **4**: 201, 202; inventory of military stores at, **5**: 140n

West Indies: Raleigh's expeditions, **1**: 279; danger from continued warfare, **2**: 215; possibility of withdrawal of British troops to, **2**: 264; U.S. trade with, **3**: 260-1; **6**: 268, 421-2; **7**: 389-90, 640; **8**: 232, 515-6; **9**: 472; **10**: 146, 148; **11**: 101, 265; **14**: 331; **15**: 502; **18**: 279; **19**: 127-31; naval operations in, **3**: 411, 419, 474; **6**: 74, 177; Americans in, **5**: 669; rumors of peace settlement from, **6**: 231; Britain's desire for carriage of trade in, **6**: 338; Norfolk trade with, **7**: 216; whale fishing, **7**: 328, 329; **19**: 196; Conn. trade with, **7**: 334, 335; Mass. trade with, **7**: 339-40; market for fish, **7**: 340; N.H. trade with, **7**: 344, 346; Pa. trade with, **7**: 347; commerce, **7**: 350-5, 401, 641, 644; sugar exports, **7**: 352; flour imports, **7**: 352, 459; **15**: 64; tobacco exports, **7**: 369, 370; tobacco consumption, **7**: 370; Va. trade with, **7**: 402; lumber imports, **7**: 459; S.C. trade with, **8**: 201-3; admission of U.S. vessels to, **9**: 4; humidity, **11**: 72; duty on stock fish, **11**: 317; attacks on by Britain feared, **12**: 205; situation in case of European war, **12**: 424; linen imports, **12**: 532; liberation of slaves discussed, **13**: 607; **15**: 360; rice culture, **14**: 673-4, 707-8; **17**: 565n; wheat imports, **15**: 256; consular appointments for recommended, **17**: 252; spermaceti candle imports, **19**: 129; U.S. trade with, **19**: 135, 137, 138n, 139. *See also* Antigua; Bahama islands; Barbados; Bermuda; Grenada; Jamaica; St. Lucia

West Indies, British: restrictions on U.S. trade, **7**: 123, 203, 350-1, 523, 638; **8**: 40, 201; **10**: 83; U.S. trade with, **7**: 231; **8**: 545; Va. trade with, **8**: 509; British troops sent to, **13**: 173, 175; fortification of, **13**: 462; and the fisheries, **19**: 150, 174

West Indies, Danish, **7**: 478

West Indies, Dutch: importation of supplies from urged, **1**: 591; British attack, **5**: 176, 177

West Indies, French: favorable to Americans, **1**: 498, 505; U.S. trade with, **1**:

West Indies, French (*cont.*)
591; **5**: 171n; exports to, **2**: 221; U.S.
trade with, **8**: 44, 228, 341, 361; **9**:
42-3, 50, 95, 139, 143, 145; **10**: 541;
11: 336, 345; **12**: 153-4; trade restrictions, **8**: 94; commerce, **8**: 142-3, 145;
12: 649; emancipation in proposed,
15: 360; reported plan for selling to
Britain, **15**: 360; relations with National Assembly, **16**: 80, 104, 109,
220, 280, 450; **20**: 366-7, 369-70,
385, 704; slave trade, **16**: 80, 220; **20**:
367; disorders in, **16**: 201, 234, 598;
18: 353, 452; **19**: 271, 602; **20**: 367;
Americans settled in, **17**: 283; and the
fisheries, **19**: 150, 158, 168, 174; U.S.
right to appoint consuls in, **19**: 297-8;
20: 324-5, 342, 367, 403n, 588, 655;
racial relations, **20**: 367. *See also* Martinique; Saint-Domingue
Westley, Mr. *See* Wesley, John
Westminster, Treaty of, **6**: 177
Westmoreland co., Pa.: incorporation by
Conn., **6**: 499
Westmoreland co., Va.: letter to county
lieutenant of, **6**: 34-5; resolutions
against Boston Port Act, **1**: 118n; appoints infantry officers, **1**: 581; place of
court of assize, **1**: 629; militia, **2**: 132;
3: 600; **4**: 63, 376-7; **5**: 311; senatorial
district, **2**: 336; levies of soldiers, **3**: 7;
delay in raising troops, **3**: 106; and
Va.-Pa. boundary dispute, **3**: 206,
207; tobacco loan office certificates, **3**:
516; small quantity of grain in, **3**: 566;
supply post for, **4**: 286
Westmorland (Westmoreland), John
Fane, tenth Earl of: reported appointment as British minister to Holland,
15: 175
Westover, Va.: ferry at, **2**: 458; British
at, **4**: 258, 259, 262, 263, 269, 270,
303, 304, 307, 321-2, 326, 330, 333,
334, 335, 336, 399; **5**: 549, 686n; **6**:
19, 32, 101; return of British to rumored, **4**: 315; British depart, **4**: 339;
horses left by British at, **4**: 344; map,
5: 672n; Turberville's raid on, **5**:
680n-2n, 690, 693; advertised for sale,
5: 685n
Westover affair, **4**: 625n, 650-1, 668,
669, 676, 680, 687, 688, 690-2, 701;
5: 9, 31-2, 98-9, 117-9, 121, 180-1,
201-2, 250-1, 261, 294n, 331n, 671n-
705n (editorial note and documents)

Westover Library. *See* Byrd, Col. William III: library of
Westphal, Nicholas Ferdinand: TJ's report on petition of, **19**: 326-8
West Point, N.Y.: Arnold's scheme to
deliver to British, **4**: 12, 29; troops retained at, **7**: 412
West Point, Va.: ferry at, **2**: 456; proposed defense of, **3**: 194; Lafayette's
detachment from, **5**: 160; Braxton protests posting soldiers at, **5**: 656-7
West Springfield, Mass.: visited by TJ
and Madison, **20**: 459
"Westsylvania" scheme, **1**: 465n
Westwood, Worlich: signs Virginia Association, **1**: 109; votes against bill for
religious freedom, **2**: 549n
Wetherburn, Henry, **1**: 9n
Wetherhead, John: correspondence with
Williamos, **8**: 271n, 272n
Wethersfield, Conn.: Washington confers
with French officers at, **5**: 663n; **6**:
83n
Wetmore, Hezekiah: circulates letter, **18**:
520n; mentioned, **18**: 627n
Wetstein, Johann Rudolf: *Pro Graeca et
genuina Linguae Graecae pronuncia-
tione*, **15**: 223
Wetzel (Whitsyl, Wistill), Martin: captured by Shawnee, **4**: 410, 429, 442;
land grant, **6**: 646
Wetzell's (Whitesyls) mill: skirmish at, **5**:
111
Wetzlaer, Imperial chamber of, **16**: 120-
1; **18**: 453, 607-9
Wexford, Ireland: and U.S. commercial
policy, **19**: 134
Weymouth, Thomas Thynne, third Viscount of: recommends Kinloch, **15**: 72
whalebone: trade statistics, **7**: 349;
French duties on, **13**: 72, 74; British
duties on, **16**: 397-9
whale fisheries: locations, **7**: 328, 329;
U.S., **7**: 328, 329, 340, 342-3, 344; **8**:
333; **9**: 73; **12**: 328; **13**: 291, 450; **14**:
220-5, 226-8, 236-7; **19**: 228, 230,
231, 597; Dalton's comments on, **7**:
468n; Portugal, **9**: 20; France, **9**: 45n;
14: 229-31, 247-9; **18**: 142-3; **19**:
141, 142, 146, 147, 150, 151n, 158n,
162, 163, 165, 167, 168, 173n, 174,
178, 182-7; Brazil, **11**: 341; TJ's *Observations on the Whale-Fishery*, **13**:
52n, 53n; **14**: 217-9, 224, 225, 242-
56 (text), 269-72, 292, 304, 305n,

332, 334-5; **17**: 58; **19**: 162, 167; French reports on, **13**: 54n-5n, 66-8, 72, 74; **14**: 256-67; **20**: 528; Britain, **13**: 66, 450-2, 663; **14**: 13-5, 213-4, 220-5, 228-9, 236-7, 248-9, 442, 447, 478; **15**: 455, 481; **19**: 141, 142-3, 146, 147, 150, 151n, 155, 158n, 163, 168, 174, 176, 177, 178, 179, 180, 182-9, 191, 193, 194, 196; British southern whale fishery bill, **13**: 291-2, 450, 452n; TJ sends Jay documents on, **14**: 213, 214, 216n-7n, 219, 225, 254n-6n, 304, 305n, 447, 478; TJ's negotiations on, **14**: 214, 217-68 (editorial note and documents), 284, 286, 297, 334-5, 375-6, 386, 442-3, 485-6; arrêt of Sep. 28, 1788, **14**: 216n-7n, 218-20, 254, 260, 263; Lafayette and, **14**: 225-6, 234-42; TJ's memoranda on, **14**: 226-34; arrêt of Dec. 29, 1787, **14**: 251, 260; arrêt of Dec. 7, 1788, **14**: 268-9, 435-6, 441-2, 447, 457, 465-6, 478, 483, 485, 486, 490; J. C. Jones reports on, **16**: 397-9; Barrett sends information on, **17**: 285; Rotch's company and, **17**: 295-6; TJ's Report on the American Fisheries, **17**: 419-20; **19**: xxxii-iii, 140-237 (editorial note and documents); Netherlands, **19**: 228. *See also* fisheries; Nantucket whalers; whale oil

whale fishermen: compensation of, **12**: 398, 404

whale oil: prices, **7**: 346; **12**: 388; **14**: 227-34, 255n; **16**: 188; French trade with U.S., **8**: 143, 516, 663; **9**: 15, 72-5, 82-3, 112, 116-7, 127, 140, 142, 160, 161-2, 183, 359, 471; **10**: 579, 631, 633; **13**: 188, 195n-7n; **14**: 284, 286, 331, 338, 349-50, 352, 353, 368, 390-1, 643; **15**: 99; **18**: 20-1, 142-3, 587; **19**: 532, 537; used for street lighting, **8**: 144n-5n; **9**: 15; English and French compared with American, **8**: 477; duty on, in France, **9**: 29, 82-3, 88-9, 117, 124, 127, 140, 142, 152, 160, 168, 173, 262, 602; **10**: 100, 106, 195-6, 294, 403, 474-5; **11**: 540, 579, 596; **12**: 314, 355, 398-9, 404-5, 418-9, 449, 468, 480, 604, 687; **13**: 72, 74, 119, 192, 250, 299, 433, 450-2; **14**: 34; **17**: 617; **19**: 532; **20**: 172, 251, 257, 262, 303, 349, 533, 548-9, 632, 674, 701; American compared with Dutch and English,

10: 349; export from U.S. lessened, **10**: 631, 633; Honfleur as port for, **11**: 41, 169; TJ proposes export to northern Italy, **11**: 516; French compared with English markets, **12**: 398-9; duty on, in Britain, **12**: 403-5; **16**: 397-9; import at Marseilles, **12**: 437; French declaration removing favors granted on, **13**: 180; British trade in, **13**: 450-2; **14**: 334; France prohibits importation of, **14**: 34-5, 36-7, 46, 48, 53, 184, 185, 213-4, 334, 416; **19**: 229; France agrees to except U.S. from embargo, **14**: 214, 268-9, 335, 376, 386, 435-6, 441-2, 447, 457, 465-6, 478, 483, 485, 486, 490; French consumption of, **14**: 229-30, 246-7, 261; TJ's memoranda on, **14**: 231-4; TJ's *Observations* on, **14**: 249-54; complaint from Bayonne against arrêt of Sep. 28, 1788, **14**: 297-8; Parker's plan for refinery of, **14**: 308n; Brac de la Perrière's circulars to farmers-general, **14**: 391n; France orders ports to receive oil before final decision, **14**: 391n, 397-8; reduction in Nantucket production, **19**: 173n. *See also* spermaceti

whales: teeth, **7**: 317; TJ describes, **14**: 233-4, 250-1

Wharton, James (master of *Laurel*), **20**: 361n

Wharton, John: signs petition, **1**: 588

Wharton, Joseph: letter from, to Charles Thomson, **7**: 454-5

Wharton, Samuel: *Plain Facts*, **5**: 585n; **6**: 667; efforts to obtain royal grant south of the Ohio, **6**: 647n, 655; member committee of Congress on coinage, **7**: 153n; accusation against, **8**: 23, 24n, 55; debt to Guillibaud & Cie., **8**: 102, 162; represents Ingenhousz, **13**: 488n

Whately, Thomas: *Observations on Modern Gardening*, **1**: 294n; **9**: 369, 370, 371, 372; **13**: xxx; **15**: 272, 273n, 278n

Wheary, John: in Albemarle co. militia, **1**: 664

wheat: southern Europe as market for, **2**: 210; bill empowering governor of Va. to prohibit exportation of, **2**: 348; crops in Va., **3**: 93-4; **7**: 402; **8**: 509, 642; **9**: 660-1; **10**: 108, 230; **11**: 601; permission of Congress for exporting from Md. to Va., **3**: 100; taxes payable

wheat (*cont.*)
in, **3**: 250, 402; for Albemarle barracks, **3**: 573; improvement of, **4**: 227; collection for flour, **5**: 562; export from Conn., **7**: 336-7; export from N.H., **7**: 345; trade statistics, **7**: 349; export from Va., **7**: 372; prices, **8**: 115; **9**: 202; **11**: 424, 425, 426, 437; **12**: 373, 691; **14**: 460; **15**: 353, 409; **16**: 126, 183, 600; **17**: 26, 324, 474; **18**: 64-5, 111, 142, 308, 309n, 483, 488, 489, 579, 587; **20**: 103, 405, 600, 606, 717; pests, **8**: 344, 509, 660; **9**: 61, 427; **13**: 414, 662-3; **14**: 13, 567; **15**: 103, 130, 134, 146n-7n, 182, 425-6; U.S. export of, **10**: 147; export from Morocco, **10**: 336, 338; duty on, in France, **12**: 469, 480; French importation of, **13**: 250, 331; **14**: 185, 187n, 304, 305n-6n, 315, 327, 343-4, 369, 386, 409-10, 425-6, 446, 460, 465, 551, 597; **15**: 77, 85, 104, 147, 250-1, 255-6, 323, 401, 402, 432-3, 464-5; seed sent to Bernard, **13**: 502, 508; in France, **13**: 524; **14**: 186, 187n, 216, 304, 306n, 343, 409, 425, 460, 465, 653, 654; **15**: 64, 104, 135, 203, 243-7, 316, 336, 383, 410, 534; **17**: 479, 567; **18**: 587; Swan and Blackden proposals for supplying to Paris, **13**: 659; **15**: 245-7, 249; British importation of prohibited, **14**: 12-3; **15**: 133-4; **18**: 52; Hanover said to forbid importation of, **14**: 13; Spanish importation of, **14**: 185; **15**: 256; **20**: 563; preservation of, **15**: 130-1; West Indian trade in, **15**: 256; British imports of, **15**: 303; **17**: 658, 664; **20**: 100-1, 145, 445-6; TJ urges increase in production, **16**: 599-600; **17**: 26, 474; Washington's choice, sent to Monticello, **18**: 44-5; exports to Portugal, **20**: 539. *See also* flour; Hessian fly
Wheatcroft, Mr.: TJ's baggage attended by, **15**: 518-9; mentioned, **7**: 395
Wheatcroft family: in Nathaniel Cutting's diary, **15**: 491-2, 494-6, 498-9
wheelbarrow: TJ orders, **4**: 524; Dutch, with TJ's drawing, **13**: 10; geometric, **15**: 194, 266
Wheeler, Capt.: in Albemarle co. militia, **1**: 666
Wheeler, Mr.: TJ rates inn of, **20**: 471
Wheeler, Adam: interview with Gen. Putnam, **11**: 241

Wheeler, Benjamin Dod: signs Va. oath of allegiance, **2**: 129
Wheeler, Bennett: publishes laws in *United States Chronicle*, **17**: 477; letter from quoted, **17**: 477n
Wheeler, John: in Albemarle co. militia, **1**: 667
Wheeler, Luke: introduced to TJ, **7**: 17
Wheeler, Micajah, Jr.: in Albemarle co. militia, **1**: 667
Wheeler, Samuel: engaged to make rollers for mint, **7**: 154n
Wheeling, Mr., **5**: 398
Wheeling, Fort, **8**: 128
Wheeling, W. Va., **4**: 442; **6**: 40
wheels: single-piece circumference, **11**: 43-4; invention for relieving friction in axis, **11**: 195
wheelwrights: needed to repair damage at Richmond and Westham, **4**: 373
Wherry, John: signs petition, **1**: 588; on Albemarle co. militia roll, **1**: 668
Wherry, Thomas: signs petition, **1**: 587; in Albemarle co. militia, **1**: 665
Whipple, Capt. Abraham: charges against, **15**: 581n
Whipple, David: in Albemarle co. militia, **1**: 667
Whipple, William: letters to, **7**: 132; **9**: 161-2; letter from, **7**: 28-30; signs agreement of secrecy, **1**: 253; signs Declaration of Independence, **1**: 432; appointed commissioner in Conn.-Pa. dispute, **6**: 477n, 478n; effort to procure moose skeleton, **7**: 22, 29, 318; information on moose, **7**: 28-30
whippoorwills, **16**: 492; **17**: 333
whiskey: price for soldiers and sailors, **2**: 379; supplied to army, **3**: 543, 609; **4**: 375; **5**: 342; dishonest transactions in, **4**: 391-2; David Watson's consumption of, **6**: 129n
White, Capt.: in Charlotte co. militia, **5**: 371, 571; proposal to raise troop of cavalry, **5**: 534n; carries hams for TJ, **16**: 566
White, Col., **6**: 18
White, Mr. (surgeon): hygrometer sent to, **1**: 74
White, Alexander: letter to, **1**: 25-6; letter from, **5**: 18; in Albemarle co. militia, **1**: 666; votes for bill for religious freedom, **2**: 549n; attitude on cession of western territory, **6**: 266; Va. judge, **13**: 49; supports Constitution, **13**: 98;

widows (*cont.*)
cerning dower and jointures of, **2**: 414-6

Wiggins, Dr.: and Madison's accounts, **8**: 536

Wilberforce, William: and abolition of slave trade, **14**: 569

Wilbleduf, George: in Albemarle co. militia, **1**: 665, 667

Wilbur, Mr.: translation of life of Alfred the Great, **13**: 652

Wilcocks, John, Jr.: promotes candidacy of Telles, **19**: 310-1; introduced to Humphreys, **20**: 345, 592

Wild, Henry. *See* Wyld

wild rice: discovery in S.C., **11**: 375

Wilfelshieme & Co.: referred to TJ by Maury, **10**: 588

Wilhelmsbad (Williamsbath), Germany: Landgrave's palace, **13**: 17-8, 266

Wilkens, Capt. Daniel: and Cedars affair, **1**: 451

Wilkerson, Lieut.: deserter, **5**: 214

Wilkes (Va. state brigantine), **5**: 150, 151, 182, 557, 658

Wilkes, John (Eng.), **9**: 486

Wilkes, John (notary), **20**: 515

Wilkie, James: letter to, **8**: 568; letter from, **8**: 525; Cathalan recommends Ledyard to, **14**: 185

Wilkins, David: cited on counterfeiting, **2**: 498n; cited on larceny, **2**: 501n

Wilkins, James: imports slaves, **15**: 654

Wilkinson, Mr.: mentioned, **1**: 65

Wilkinson, Mr. (Paradise's steward): TJ confers with, **16**: 84-5; mentioned, **14**: 513n; **15**: 10, 34

Wilkinson, Edward: and Cherokee archives, **6**: 141n

Wilkinson, Jacob: in *Rachel* case, **20**: 496, 508n

Wilkinson, James: Spanish agent in U.S., **14**: 388n, 499-500; expedition against Indians, **19**: 467; **20**: 481; "Desultory Reflections" quoted, **19**: 515; and settlement of Ky., **20**: 553n

Wilkinson, John (Eng.): Paine's intent to correspond with, **13**: 588

Wilkinson, John (Va.): signs Va. oath of allegiance, **2**: 129

Wilkinson, Nathaniel: votes for bill for religious freedom, **2**: 549n; mentioned, **3**: 144

Wilkinson, William, Jr.: letter to, from Paradise, quoted, **15**: 270n

Willard, Dr.: and Hessian fly, **20**: 458; inn rated by TJ, **20**: 471

Willard, Joseph: letters to, **14**: 697-9; **16**: 289; **20**: 432-3; letters from, **13**: 637-8; **16**: 111-2; presents LLD from Harvard to TJ, **13**: 637-8; **14**: 697; asks about scientific publications, **13**: 638; introduces Read to TJ, **16**: 111, 289n; notifies TJ of election to American Academy of Arts and Sciences, **16**: 111-2

Willcocks (Wilcocks), Mr.: bill on, **7**: 206, 245

Willett, Marinus: at Fort Stanwix, **2**: 29; victory at Johnstown, N.Y., **6**: 132; sword presented to, **16**: 55n; Washington sends to McGillivray, **17**: 290n

Willett, Samuel (volunteer of British Legion), **5**: 41

William III, king of England, **3**: 48; **10**: 572

William V, Prince of Orange: power of, **6**: 432, 433, 438; **12**: 274; influence in Netherlands, **7**: 610; relations with France, **9**: 436n-7n; **10**: 645n; **12**: 675-6; duties, **10**: 572; Frederick William's interest in, **10**: 605, 613, 624, 629, 634; **11**: 42; aid to, **11**: 470; support by Britain, **11**: 476, 490; **12**: 33, 37, 293, 312; support by Prussia, **11**: 476, 490; **12**: 33, 37; triumph of party, **11**: 510n, 581, 672; **12**: xxxviii; Frederick II's attitude toward, **11**: 696; birthday celebration, **12**: xxxvii, 515 (illus.), 617, 659; **15**: 443n; restored in Netherlands, **12**: 189, 307; hostility to France and Spain, **12**: 339; TJ comments on, **12**: 356; Shippen describes, **13**: 219-20

William, John M.: signs petition, **6**: 294

William and Catherine (ship): prosecution by farmers-general, **8**: 492-8, 500-1, 517-8, 527-9, 639-40; **9**: 31-8, 72, 77; **10**: 99-100; imprisonment of crew, **8**: 530, 578, 661-2; **9**: 12-3, 66, 177; log of voyage, **8**: 551; **9**: 33-4; Picrel's deceitfulness to crew of, **8**: 560, 578; Father Mehegan intercedes for crew, **8**: 597; TJ's efforts in behalf of crew, **8**: 627-8, 647; **9**: 31-8, 52-3, 55, 56, 162, 169-71, 307; names of crew, **8**: 662; sentence of crew, **9**: 98-9, 119, 124-5, 136, 162; **10**: 100; ill-treatment of crew, **9**: 135; damage to, **9**: 290; allowance for crew, **9**: 313; release of

Williamson, Joseph: loyalist, **7**: 116

Williamson, Capt. William (master of *Liberty*), **15**: 67-8

Williamsport, Md.: as possible capital site, **19**: xxxii, 22, 348 (illus.), 23

William the Conqueror: church at Rouen, **8**: 437

Willigen, F. von: Bavarian chargé d'affaires at The Hague, **13**: 548n; **16**: 282n

Willing, Capt., **2**: 258

Willing, Miss: marriage, **14**: 584

Willing, Ann Shippen (Mrs. Charles Willing), **5**: 671n, 677

Willing, Charles: daughter of, **5**: 671n, 677n; Monroe visits, **18**: 81

Willing, James: as prisoner of war, **3**: 99, 103

Willing, Mary. *See* Byrd, Mary Willing

Willing, Morris & Swanwick: ship tobacco to France, **11**: 358; **12**: 121; and Barclay's debt to Cathalan, **15**: 323, 409; **17**: 480; **18**: 584; **20**: 239; congratulate Cathalan, **17**: 517; promote candidacy of Telles, **19**: 309, 311

Willing, Thomas: signs agreement of secrecy, **1**: 253; manages Paine's funds, **15**: 274-5; president of national bank, **20**: 705; mentioned, **1**: 261; **5**: 677

Willing & Morris: buy TJ's tobacco, **2**: 4n

Willing Lass (Va. state brigantine), **5**: 150, 151, 182, 557

Willink (ship): departs for Baltimore, **18**: 453

Willink, Mr.: and purchase of swords and medals, **8**: 157; and French naval purchases, **18**: 506; mentioned, **13**: 318

Willink, Van Staphorst & Hubbard: letters to, **15**: 40-2, 89, 331-2, 347, 352, 407, 438-9, 479-80, 523, 527; **17**: 318; **19**: 586-7; **20**: 393, 393-4, 407, 626-7; letters from, **15**: 19-20, 58, 91-2, 313-4, 342-4, 439, 471-5; **17**: 547; payment to French officers in U.S., **15**: 19-20, 40-1, 313, 321, 331-2, 343, 347, 356-7; payment for medals, **15**: 40-1, 58, 91, 113, 313, 332, 343, 357; bills sent by, **15**: 58, 89, 342-3; payment of Carmichael's salary, **15**: 105; letters from cited, **15**: 321, 347n, 357, 360n, 537n; bonds handled by, **15**: 343-4; letters to cited, **15**: 344n; **17**: 21n; **19**: 573; **20**: 680n; payment for Algerian captives, **15**: 356-7; com-

petitor of seeks to obtain business of U.S. government, **15**: 357, 360n-1n; account of, **15**: 407, 439, 475, 526-7; **16**: 387-8; Short's transactions with, **15**: 471-2, 472n-3n, 501-2; **16**: 205n; **17**: 411; **20**: 393; praise TJ, **15**: 472; and U.S. debt to France, **15**: 472n-3n, 474-5; **20**: 179, 181; letter from, to Commissioners of the Treasury, **15**: 474-5; loan to U.S., **16**: 134-5, 161-2, 259; **17**: 126n, 425-30, 433-4; **18**: 22-3, 115n, 592-3; Humphreys' account with, **17**: 89n; **20**: 407, 592, 626-7; correspondence with Hamilton cited, **17**: 126n, 427n; relations with Hamilton, **20**: 173n; TJ's account with, **20**: 393, 407; G. Morris' account with, **20**: 680; mentioned, **15**: 88, 126, 134n, 470n; **16**: 230, 320. *See also* Staphorst & Hubbard; Willink & Van Staphorst

Willink, Wilhelm & Jan: letter from cited, **8**: 531; letter forwarded by, **8**: 615; **13**: 311; Shippen resides with, **13**: 220; draft on, **13**: 230; and Society for Establishing Useful Manufactures, **19**: 454n; mentioned, **6**: 212n; **8**: 655; **14**: 433n

Willink & Van Staphorst: letters to, **12**: 123-4, 196, 387, 422, 473, 510, 701; **13**: 170-1, 257, 552, 657; **14**: 49, 586-8, 641-2, 702-3; letters from, **12**: 172, 457-8, 485, 506, 543-9, 623-4; **13**: 149, 188, 294, 600; **14**: 12, 56, 570-1, 609-11, 681-3; drafts on, **8**: 561, 583; **11**: 185; **12**: 194; **13**: 329; letters from cited, **8**: 600; **12**: 471, 573; letters to cited, **11**: 161; **12**: 463; **13**: 575-6; **14**: 593, 644, 647n, 657; letter of credit on, **11**: 169; payment to Carmichael, **11**: 560; **12**: 341; **13**: 414, 419, 470-1, 509, 533, 552, 568, 661; **14**: 52, 54-5, 182; **15**: xxxviii, 457 (illus.); loan to U.S., **12**: 420-2, 429, 432; payment of Fizeaux loan, **12**: 472, 474, 495, 496, 506-7, 508-9, 566; correspondence with Commissioners of Treasury, **12**: 545-8; **14**: 586, 593, 609, 683; **15**: 41-2; speculation in foreign debt, **12**: 581; **14**: 191-2; funds supplied by, **13**: 148, 149, 159, 294; payment to Ast, **13**: 257; **14**: 279; letter to, from Dumas, cited, **14**: 7n; and loan from Netherlands to U.S., **14**: 12, 433n; statement of account with U.S., **14**: 49, 570; and

Willink & Van Staphorst (*cont.*)
funding of foreign debt, **14**: 191; **15**: 33n, 472n-3n; payments for captives in Algiers, **14**: 587, 593, 644-5; **15**: 112; refuse to accept requisitions on U.S. account, **14**: 609-11, 644-5, 656-7, 681-3, 702; **15**: 19-20; payment of salaries of U.S. ministers, **14**: 610, 641-2, 644-5, 656, 681-3; payment for medals, **14**: 642; payment to French officers in U.S., **14**: 702-3; **15**: 19-20; mentioned, **8**: 511, 541, 543, 573, 623, 664; **11**: 189, 575; **12**: 55, 350, 459, 507, 637, 659, 666; **13**: 630; **14**: 5; **15**: 470

Willis, Dr. Thomas: physician to George III, **14**: 567

Willis, Francis: letters to, **1**: 21; **16**: 352-3; letters from, **16**: 165-6; **17**: 546-7; wager with TJ, **1**: 8; leaves Williamsburg, **1**: 16; mentioned, **9**: 446; **12**: 654

Willis, John: in Albemarle co. militia, **1**: 667; prisoner of war, **3**: 390

Willis, Maj. John, **5**: 373

Willis, John Whittaker: votes for bill for religious freedom, **2**: 549n

Willis, Mary: marriage to Dangerfield, **1**: 8

Willis, Col. Robert Carter: letter from, **4**: 452

Willis creek: ferry at, **2**: 458; mentioned, **6**: 634

Willock, Alexander: draft on, protested, **13**: 419, 422

willow oak: sample to be sent to France, **10**: 227

wills: Va. bill concerning, **2**: 394-405; witnesses for, **2**: 395; contested, **2**: 395-6, 397; probate of, **2**: 400-1; **7**: 360

Wills, Elias: votes against bill for religious freedom, **2**: 549n

Wills, Emanuel: petition of, **5**: 148-9

Wills, Frederick W.: petition from, **5**: 349

Wills, Henry: publishes *State Gazette of North Carolina* with Abraham Hodge, **17**: 509n

Wills, James: petition of, **5**: 148-9

Wills, John Scarsbrook: letter to, **5**: 625

Wills, Richard: arrest for desertion ordered, **4**: 526-7

Wills' creek, **7**: 50; **8**: 3

Willy, A.: Va. debt to, **4**: 462

Wilmer, Mr.: passport issued by TJ, **15**: 486

Wilmington, Del.: as possible location of Congress, **6**: 352, 366; **13**: 498, 620, 625

Wilmington, N.C.: British attack on foreseen, **1**: 296, 621; tent cloth at, **3**: 501; British capture of, **4**: 610; Cornwallis near, **5**: 361, 403; tobacco received from, **11**: 507; and trade with Ireland, **19**: 134

Wilson, Capt.: letter from cited, **3**: 224; master of the *Catherine*, **9**: 392

Wilson, Mr.: purchases cattle for Fort Pitt, **3**: 353; **5**: 264, 492; letters to, from Donald, cited, **16**: 222; payment to Dobson, **20**: 103, 572

Wilson, Arthur: *The History of Great Britain, being the Life and Reign of King James I*, **12**: 18

Wilson, Dr. Goodwin: superintendent of Continental medical department in Va., **6**: 53

Wilson, James (Jamaica): lawsuit of, **1**: 72, 85

Wilson, James (Pa.): letter from, **17**: 354; signs Congress' second petition, **1**: 222; and Va.-Pa. boundary dispute, **1**: 234, 245n; appointed Indian commissioner, **1**: 245n; signs agreement of secrecy, **1**: 253; argues against resolution of independence, **1**: 309; debates taxation of slaves in Congress, **1**: 322; debates Congressional representation, **1**: 326; signs Declaration of Independence, **1**: 432; Pendleton's warning against, **1**: 464; and foreign mercenaries, **1**: 510n; vice president of American Philosophical Society, **4**: 544; consulted by Mr. Nathan, **5**: 152; motion to acquire library for Congress defeated, **6**: 216n; and Conn.-Pa. dispute, **6**: 476n, 477n, 479n, 484n, 488n-92; Pa. delegate to Federal Convention, **11**: 400, 626; **12**: 231n; supports Constitution, **12**: 423, 425; **13**: 6n-8n; argues against bill of rights, **12**: 440; **14**: 18; Paine criticizes, **13**: 5; speech at 1788 Independence Day celebration, **13**: 371n; suggested as minister to London, **13**: 621; member of Society for Political Enquiries, **14**: 50n; suggested as attorney general, **15**: 336; justice of Supreme Court, **15**: 530; **16**: 27; TJ introduces to Nicho-

las Lewis, **16**: 411; Gilmer dines with, **16**: 433; contrasted with TJ, **17**: 354n; letters to cited, **17**: 354n, 378n; opinion of T. Coxe, **19**: 126; mentioned, **6**: 240; **16**: 478, 492
Wilson, James (Va.): in Albemarle co. militia, **1**: 666
Wilson, John: signs nonimportation resolutions, **1**: 30, 46
Wilson, Col. John: comments on Princess Anne militia, **2**: 192n
Wilson, Nathaniel: does not seek election to Va. GA, **10**: 109
Wilson, Philip: letter from, **20**: 637-9; recommended as consul at Dublin, **17**: 251, 254n; papers on ship *Mentor*, **18**: 347n-8n; **20**: 638n; loss of *Mentor*, **20**: 637-9; letters from cited, **20**: 638n
Wilson, Rachel Bird (Mrs. James Wilson): death of, **10**: 169, 282, 288, 314
Wilson, Samuel: deposition concerning Henderson's land claims, **2**: 96-7
Wilson, Stephen: letter from, to William Smith of Md., quoted, **16**: 548n
Wilt, Delmestre & Co.: letters to, **9**: 512-3; **10**: 589; **11**: 534, 589-90; **12**: 523; letters from, **9**: 390-3; **10**: 579; **11**: 377, 474, 571; **12**: 20, 513-4; bankruptcy, **12**: 513, 523; **14**: 60
Wilton, Va.: Lafayette's camp at, **5**: 664
Winchester, Capt., **4**: 47
Winchester, Va.: construction of barracks at, **2**: 300; post service to, **2**: 389; as place for rendezvous of recruits, **3**: 181, 283, 360; **4**: 401, 686; **5**: 322; British prisoners of war at, **3**: 605, 614, 624; **4**: 98, 104, 119-20, 210; **5**: 19, 84, 131; **6**: 51; supply post at, **4**: 285; Convention troops at, **4**: 672, 685, 702; **5**: 71, 100, 240, 333, 432-3, 510, 542, 595; quartermaster at, **5**: 37; TJ asks to have natural history specimens sent to, **6**: 219; retail prices at, **7**: 402; place of court of assize, **7**: 589
windmill: described by TJ, **7**: 517; sawmills, with TJ's drawings, **13**: 9; mentioned, **7**: 508; **11**: 429
Windsor, England: visited by the Adams family, **10**: 68
Windward islands: ports, **7**: 348
wine: possible American production of, **2**: 211; used as medicine, **4**: 26; ordered by TJ, **6**: 270; **7**: 110; **8**: 93-4, 158, 549; **9**: 25, 210-1, 455, 581; **10**:

129, 193, 197, 199, 248, 465, 473, 547 637; **11**: 139, 211-2, 243, 465, 472-3, 484-5, 501, 506, 552-3, 607, 608, 654; **12**: 227, 431, 455-6, 465-6, 500, 514, 516, 541, 560, 612, 618, 642, 658, 661; **13**: 96, 171, 297; **14**: 45, 336, 353, 445, 480-1, 570, 589, 638, 679-80; **15**: 66, 67n, 592; **17**: 321-2, 493-4, 496-7, 653; **19**: 630; **20**: 210, 334-5, 346, 372, 420, 555, 569, 622, 691; French duty on, **8**: 94n; **10**: 193, 194, 476; sent to Eppes, **8**: 141; **9**: 212; **11**: 378-9, 396, 650; British duty on, **8**: 166, 172; ordered by John Adams, **8**: 175, 177, 183-4, 241, 264, 297, 317, 354, 368; import by S.C., **8**: 199, 200, 201; **12**: 301; import by U.S., **8**: 309; **10**: 147; French, **8**: 683; **10**: 637; **11**: 617, 646-7, 672; **12**: 385, 434; **13**: 26, 29-32, 635-6; Portuguese, **9**: 19-20, 62; **10**: 85, 242; Walker's idea for producing, **9**: 252; U.S. regulations on importation of, **10**: 15; Bordeaux, **10**: 62; **11**: 67, 379, 396, 455-7; Graves, **10**: 197; **11**: 456, 457; passport for, **10**: 467, 507; **12**: 616; Greek, **11**: 47; Cahusac, **11**: 67-8; Va. duty on, **11**: 146, 147n, 153, 222, 241; Beaune, **11**: 212; Chambertin, **11**: 212; Pommard, **11**: 212; Romanie, **11**: 212; Veaune, **11**: 212; Vougeau, **11**: 212; Volnay, **11**: 212, 472-3, 654; Monrachet, **11**: 212, 243, 417, 418; Nuys, **11**: 212, 417; Meursault, **11**: 212, 472-3, 484, 654; import from Sardinia desirable, **11**: 353; Burgundy, **11**: 417; Romanée, **11**: 417; prices, **11**: 417, 443; **13**: 20, 30-2; Rhône, **11**: 421; Hermitage, **11**: 421-2; Nice, **11**: 432; Gatina, **11**: 435; Montferrat, **11**: 435; Nebiule, **11**: 435; Piedmont, **11**: 435; Salusola, **11**: 435; Avignon, **11**: 443; Muscat de Lunel, **11**: 443-4; Muscat de Frontignan, **11**: 445; Muscat, **11**: 445, 465, 584, 596n; **13**: 274; Sauterne, **11**: 454, 456-7; Arboete, **11**: 456; Calons, **11**: 456; Candale, **11**: 456; Château de Lafite, **11**: 456; Château Margaux, **11**: 456; Dabbadie, **11**: 456; de Carbonius, **11**: 456; Durfort, **11**: 456; Gassie, **11**: 456; Guirouen, **11**: 456; Haut-Brion, **11**: 456; La Rose, **11**: 456; La Tour de Ségur, **11**: 456; Mouton, **11**: 456; Pontette, **11**: 456; Rozan, **11**: 456; St.

funds for College of New Jersey, **7**: 399n; letter sent by, **8**: 259; on vacation, **20**: 335; mentioned, **4**: 167n; **6**: 432; **8**: 243

witnesses: allowed in criminal prosecutions, **2**: 504; rules concerning, **2**: 607-8; subpoenas to in criminal cases, **2**: 615 .

Witt, M. de: claims American funds are above par, **16**: 161

Woburn, England: garden, **9**: 370; **13**: 270; pisé building, **15**: 185n

Wodrow, Andrew. *See* Woodrow

Woedtke, Friedrich Wilhelm, Baron: characteristics as officer, **1**: 446; confines priest, **1**: 453; death of, **1**: 500

Woerden, Holland: capitulation, **12**: 166, 167

Wokokon (Wococon). *See* Ocoa Bay, W.I.

Wolcott, Erastus: nominated as congressman from Conn., **14**: 525

Wolcott, Oliver, Jr.: criticizes TJ, **4**: 273n; letters from, to Hamilton, quoted, **16**: 472n-3n; **18**: 647n, 662; plan for weights and measures, **16**: 616, 616n-7n; in Reynolds case, **18**: xxxvi, 624n, 630, 632-5, 641-6, 647n, 648n, 649-50, 652-7, 659n, 661n, 668, 670, 674, 677n, 681-2, 687n; portrait by Trumbull, **18**: xxxvii, 268 (illus.); and Commonwealth *v.* Reynolds and Clingman, **18**: 655-6; recommended as commissioner of Federal District, **19**: 59; auditor of treasury, **20**: 221-2; comptroller of treasury, **20**: 223-30, 232, 667-8

Wolcott, Oliver, Sr.: signs agreement of secrecy, **1**: 253; signs Declaration of Independence, **1**: 432; and Congress' instructions to TJ, **6**: 240; Indian commissioner, **7**: 8, 11, 396, 444; **8**: 79; approves Lafayette's speech to Indians, **7**: 445

Wolfe (Wolf, Woulfe), John: and ransom of captives in Algeria, **9**: 527n, 532-3, 539-40; **18**: 425-6, 429n; proposed as consul at Algiers, **9**: 552, 619; **12**: 180, 182; **18**: 374-5; and expenses of captives in Algiers, **9**: 621; account of mission of Lamb and Randall, **12**: 181; characterization of, **12**: 550; mentioned, **9**: 550, 620; **11**: 322

Wolff (Wolfius), Christian, Baron von: works, **7**: 37, 288

Wolfhills: and Transylvania land claims, **2**: 65n

Wolfius. *See* Wolff, Christian, Baron von

Wollaston, John: portrait of John Page as boy, **1**: lvii, 119 (illus.)

Wollecer, Mr.: in Henderson's account, **5**: 446

Wollops Island: attacked by British privateer, **3**: 81; fort on, **6**: 46

Wolsey, Cornet: serves under Simcoe, **6**: 637

wolves: weight, **6**: 342

women: miscegenation among, **2**: 471; plan to collect funds for soldiers' clothing, **3**: 441, 532n-3n; work at Westham foundry, **4**: 439; fashions for, **6**: 350; **12**: 66; TJ's views on courtesy toward, **6**: 380; alienage of, **6**: 435; protection in enemy countries, **7**: 486, 622; **9**: 419, 426; life in Paris and in America contrasted, **11**: 122-3; labor of, in France, **11**: 214-5, 415, 428, 430, 435, 440, 445, 446-7, 458; **13**: 27; life in America, **11**: 251; character of, in France, **11**: 392-3; **13**: 151-2, 623; **14**: 330, 677, 704n; **15**: 284n, 511, 531, 533; **16**: 4n; wages, **11**: 415, 419, 422, 425, 427, 455; labor of in Germany, **13**: 18, 27; as companions and objects of pleasures, **13**: 27-8

Woneycott, Capt. Edward: depositions concerning, **5**: 588-92

wood: for exterior cornice of Va. Capitol, **8**: 367; Swan's proposal for supplying to French navy, **15**: 261-3; **17**: 560-1; quality of, in America and Europe, **15**: 539-40. *See also* timber

Wood, Capt. (master of *Minerva*), **20**: 676n

Wood (Woods), Capt. Archibald: performs rescue, **5**: 256

Wood, David: and Albemarle co. militia, **1**: 668n

Wood, Henry: signs petition, **1**: 588; in Albemarle co. militia, **1**: 666

Wood, James: in lawsuit, **1**: 25-6; signs Virginia Association, **1**: 108; and nonimportation agreements, **1**: 110; signs letter to Va. HB, **1**: 112

Wood, James (Albemarle co.): signs petition, **1**: 588

Wood, Gen. James: letters to, **3**: 308-9, 322, 377-8, 428-9, 436-7, 453-4, 486, 506, 562, 572-3, 648-9, 661-2; **4**: 14-6, 23, 34-5, 46-7, 64-5, 72-5, 79, 87-

495-6; **19**: 556-7; letters from, **1**: 38, 163-4, 476-7, 585, 597-8, 603-4; **5**: 110-1; **6**: 144-5; **9**: 165; **10**: 592-3, 622-3; **11**: 99; **13**: 329-30; **16**: 368; **17**: 478; **18**: 486-7; witnesses TJ's agreement with J. Randolph, **1**: 67; and Tucker case, **1**: 74, 83; law practice, **1**: 91; signs Fast-Day Resolution, **1**: 106; and royal land grants, **1**: 163; signs agreement of secrecy, **1**: 253; drafts letter from Va. delegates, **1**: 295n; argues for resolution of independence in Congress, **1**: 311; and Va. Constitution, **1**: 333n, 334n, 354n-5n, 364n-5n, 377n, 384n, 385n, 507n; and Indiana Company, **1**: 386n; **2**: 250; rough draft of Declaration of Independence sent to, **1**: 415n; signs Declaration of Independence, **1**: 432; and Va. seal, **1**: 468, 484n; and foreign mercenaries, **1**: 509n; and report on coinage, **1**: 518n; **7**: 152n; and revisal of Va. laws, **1**: 563n; **2**: 266, 305n, 308n, 311n-2n, 313n, 320n, 323n, 328, 334n, 663n; **10**: 4n, 576; and Transylvania Company, **1**: 565n; and instructions to commissioners to France, **1**: 577n; lends house in Williamsburg to TJ, **1**: 585, 604; calls for election in Fluvanna co., **2**: 24n; introduces Shore, **2**: 27n; correspondence with Dr. Redman, **2**: 39; and Kaskaskia expedition, **2**: 133n; payment of British debts by, **2**: 171n; letter from, to Benjamin Harrison, **2**: 301-2; and bill concerning elections, **2**: 345n; and bill concerning bank notes, **2**: 435n; and TJ's bill on crimes, **2**: 504n; and bill to prevent forestalling, regrating, and engrossing, **2**: 564n; prepares Admiralty bill, **2**: 575n; and TJ's memo on bills to be drafted, **2**: 665; Mazzei's affection for, **3**: 469; teaches law at William and Mary College, **3**: 507; **7**: 112, 303n; **8**: 635, 636, 668; **12**: 21-2; shoots at British, **4**: 274; opinion on Nathan case, **5**: 152; **6**: 320, 323n; opinion on powers of Congress requested, **5**: 471n-2n; certifies Short as attorney, **6**: 122n; signs honorary degree for TJ, **6**: 222; on Commonwealth *v.* Caton, **6**: 279n; tutors Banister's son, **7**: 98; examiner at Maury's school, **7**: 112, 408; **8**: 115; pays money for Mazzei, **7**: 274; anti-slavery views, **8**: 357; **10**: 63; books sent to,

8: 575; **12**: 29, 129, 136, 570n; **13**: 329, 416; **14**: 533; and *Notes on Virginia*, **9**: 38, 194; **11**: 186; **12**: 130; supervises Peter Carr's education, **10**: 549, 648; **11**: 402, 623; **12**: 14, 677; **13**: 329, 470; **15**: 156; member committee to amend unpassed Va. bills, **11**: 153; and Federal Convention, **11**: 154, 219, 310, 312, 331, 352, 363; **12**: 279; letters from cited, **11**: 240, 280, 351; **13**: 338n; **16**: 616n; **17**: 509n; illness of wife, **11**: 250, 401; ability as teacher, **11**: 299; religious unbelief, **11**: 299; T. M. Randolph, Jr. recommended to study under, **11**: 557; TJ's admiration for, **12**: 14; **13**: 372; **14**: 659; **20**: 165; failure to return to Congress, **12**: 104; Izard desires to have son study with, **12**: 339; supports Constitution, **12**: 410; **13**: 98; letters to cited, **12**: 634; **16**: 35, 36n, 276n, 279n; **17**: 164n; sends Va. resolution on Constitution to TJ, **13**: 329, 330n; in Va. Constitutional Convention, **13**: 351-2, 620; judge of High Court of Chancery, **15**: 52, 434; Bolling *v.* Bolling, **15**: 586, 587n; leaves William and Mary College, **16**: 25; TJ as student of, **16**: 113, 115; Report on Weights and Measures sent to, **16**: 616; **17**: 478; Webster's opinion of, **18**: 134n; John Brown studies with, **19**: xxxiv; letter to, from Adams, cited, **20**: 581; mentioned, **1**: 250, 261, 297, 406, 456, 471, 480, 483; **2**: 176n, 216, 217, 262-3, 271; **6**: 266, 508; **8**: 576; **9**: 66, 357; **12**: 19, 30, 414, 453, 650; **13**: 40n; **16**: 308

Wythe co., Va.: postal service to, **20**: 664, 711

Xenophon: *Expeditio Cyri*, **8**: 323; **10**: 72; *Graecorum Res Gestae et Agesilaus*, **8**: 323, 407, 408; *Memorabilia*, **8**: 323, 407, 408; *Anabasis*, **8**: 407, 408; **12**: 18; studied by Peter Carr, **9**: 38, 201; *Hellenica*, **10**: 72; *Memoirs of Socrates*, **10**: 72; TJ seeks information on best Italian translation, **11**: 159; works, **13**: 317; *Lacedaemoniorum respublica*, **13**: 656

Xenophon of Ephesus: *De Amoribus Anthiae et Abrocomae*, **15**: 130

Xiphilinus, Joannes: TJ recommends works of, **8**: 411

Zix, Benjamin: engraving by, **13**: xxvii, 17 (illus.)

zizanie: definition, **14**: 483n

Zonaras, Joannes: cited by TJ, **1**: 554; TJ recommends works of, **8**: 411

Zosimus: TJ recommends works of, **8**: 411

Zyl, Johannis van: *Theatrum Machinarum Universale, of Groot Algemeen Moolen-Boek*, **13**: 9, 34n